The Unheard Voice of Law in Bartolomé De La Casas's Brevísima Relación De La Destruición De Las Indias

The Unheard Voice of Law in Bartolomé De La Casas's Brevísima Relación De La Destruición De Las Indias reinterprets Las Casas's controversial treatise as a legal document, whose legal character is linked to civil and ecclesial genres of the Early Modern and late Renaissance juridical tradition.

Bartolomé de las Casas proclaimed: "I have labored to inquire about, study, and discern the law; I have plumbed the depths and have reached the headwaters." *The Unheard Voice* also plumbs the depths of Las Casas's voice of law in his widely read and highly controversial *Brevísima relación*—a legal document published and debated since the 16th century. This original reinterpretation of his *Very Brief Account* uncovers the juridical approach voiced in his defense of the Indigenous peoples of the Americas. *The Unheard Voice* innovatively asserts that the *Brevísima relación*'s legal character is intimately linked to civil and ecclesial genres of the late Renaissance juridical tradition. This paradigm-shifting book contextualizes the formation of Las Casas's juridical voice in canon law and theology—initially as a secular cleric, subsequently as a Dominican friar, and finally as a diocesan bishop—and demonstrates how his experienced juridical voice fought for justice in trans-Atlantic debates about Indigenous peoples' level of humanity, religious freedom, enslavement, and conquest. Reaching the headwaters of Las Casas's hitherto unheard juridical voice of law in the *Brevísima relación* provides readers with a previously unheard interpretation—an appealing voice for readers and students of this powerful Early Modern text that still resonates today.

The Unheard Voice of Law is a valuable companion text for many in the disciplines of literature, history, theology, law, and philosophy who read Bartolomé de las Casas's *Very Brief Account* and study his life, labor, and legacy.

David T. Orique is an Associate Professor of Colonial and Modern Latin America, as well as the Iberian Atlantic World, and the Director of Latin American and Latinx Studies, at Providence College.

Routledge Studies in the History of the Americas

14 **Hearing Enslaved Voices**
African and Indian Slave Testimony in British and French America, 1700–1848
Edited by Sophie White and Trevor Burnard

15 **Kinship and Incestuous Crime in Colonial Guatemala**
Sarah N. Saffa

16 **Education in Revolutionary Struggles**
Iván Illich, Paulo Freire, Ernesto Guevara and Latin American Thought
Andrés Donoso Romo

17 **Cartographic Expeditions and Visual Culture in the Nineteenth-Century Americas**
Edited by Ernesto Capello and Julia B. Rosenbaum

18 **The Johnson Administration's Cuba Policy**
From "Dirty War" to Passive Containment
Håkan Karlsson and Tomás Diez Acosta

19 **The Unheard Voice of Law in Bartolomé De La Casas's Brevísima Relación De La Destruición De Las Indias**
David T. Orique

20 **The Nixon Administration and Cuba**
Continuity and Rupture
Håkan Karlsson and Tomás Diez Acosta

For more information about this series, please visit: https://www.routledge.com/Routledge-Studies-in-the-History-of-the-Americas/book-series/RSHAM

The Unheard Voice of Law in Bartolomé De La Casas's Brevísima Relación De La Destruición De Las Indias

David T. Orique

Routledge
Taylor & Francis Group
NEW YORK AND LONDON

First published 2021
by Routledge
52 Vanderbilt Avenue, New York, NY 10017

and by Routledge
2 Park Square, Milton Park, Abingdon, Oxon, OX14 4RN

Routledge is an imprint of the Taylor & Francis Group, an informa business

Library of Congress Cataloging-in-Publication Data
Names: Orique, David Thomas, O.P., 1959– author.
Title: The Unheard Voice of Law in Bartolomé De La Casas's Brevísima Relación De La Destruición De Las Indias / David T. Orique.
Description: Milton Park, Abingdon, Oxon; New York, NY : Routledge, 2021. |
Series: Routledge studies in the history of the Americas |
Includes bibliographical references and index.
Identifiers: LCCN 2020049284 (print) | LCCN 2020049285 (ebook) | ISBN 9780367898045 (hardback) | ISBN 9781003021247 (ebook)
Subjects: LCSH: Indians—Legal status, laws, etc.—Latin America—History. | Indians, Treatment of—Latin America—History. | Casas, Bartolomé de las, 1484–1566. Brevísima relación de la destrucción de las Indias. | Spain—Colonies—America.
Classification: LCC KG480.O75 2021 (print) | LCC KG480 (ebook) | DDC 342.808/72—dc23
LC record available at https://lccn.loc.gov/2020049284
LC ebook record available at https://lccn.loc.gov/2020049285

ISBN: 978-0-367-89804-5 (hbk)
ISBN: 978-0-367-74449-6 (pbk)
ISBN: 978-1-003-02124-7 (ebk)

Typeset in Times New Roman
by codeMantra

I dedicate this effort to all those who suffered and suffer from conquests, then and now.

Contents

Figures

Preface

Figure 0.1 Bartolomé de las Casas. Published by the Real Imprenta of Madrid, 1791.

Source: Wikipedia

This book uncovers Bartolomé de las Casas's consistent juridical approach that he voiced in defense of the Indigenous people in the Americas in his *Brevísima relación*. My interest in Las Casas—a frequently misunderstood and highly sophisticated Dominican friar—began during my novitiate year in the Order of Friars Preachers. Since then, I have studied in-depth his life, labor, and legacy in the Iberian Atlantic world. My unfolding examination of the impact and implications of Las Casas's *Brevísima relación*—as well as of his larger corpus of writings on history, theology, philosophy, and law—convinced me that his works in general and in particular his famous and infamous *Very Brief Account* were much more than being the most widely read treatise from Colonial Latin America—with tremendous staying power in world literature: it is in fact a legal document. This discovery changes our understanding of this treatise—and arguably of the rest of his writings—in significant ways, as we listen to his persistent juridical approach in addressing the evils and harm done to the Indigenous peoples during the complex and conflictual history of the contact, conquest, and colonization of the American hemisphere—first by Spaniards and then by many others. These sixteenth-century issues, such as human dignity, equality, liberty, and justice—confronted and contested by Las Casas in his lifetime—continue to challenge and confound people in the twenty-first century. This uncovering of Las Casas's juridical voice is significant not only for those examining the *Brevísima relación* in its particular historical context, but also for the critiques contained within, which still resonate today. This is why the treatise has remained in print and continues to be read by countless individuals in numerous languages.

As with so many of life's efforts, debts to those who have supported us are incurred. Gratitude is the currency to acknowledge this support. As such, I humbly recognize the many who have inspired and sustained my academic ministry. I thank the numerous members of the Dominican community, at the eternal, interprovincial, provincial, and local levels—most proximately the daily contact with friars at Thomas Aquinas Priory at Providence College, who provide a home that affords a fruitful place and time to think, study, write, and pray. I thank many other amazing colleagues: at the University of Oregon, in History, Professors Robert Haskett, Carlos Aguirre, Stephanie Wood, David Luebke, and from the Department of Religious Studies, Stephen Shoemaker; at Providence College, the students, staff, and faculty—especially in the History Department—who offered resources and inspiration to complete this book and who provide motivation and collegiality to produce future projects. Importantly, I thank my family, especially my parents and siblings, grandparents, and godparents, who initiated and lovingly nurtured my intercultural understanding. Special thanks to Dominican Sister Dodi Poelzer, MM, PhD, and to Anne Marie Le Chevallier for carefully reading and thoughtfully commenting on the final manuscript, as well as to Max Novick at Routledge for all his help. Also, a heartfelt thanks to the following individuals: Leonard Ramírez—a *compadre* and confidant; Matthew Restall, Amara Solari, and their priceless Catalina for their friendship and inspiration; Rady Roldán-Figueroa from Boston University, and Ramón Valdivia Giménz from Sevilla—amazing colleagues, brothers, and friends; Kristian Fabian—once my student, increasingly my teacher. I thank all of you, and many others, who in countless ways supported, modeled, and encouraged me as a scholar. Finally, I thank God, who with my parents gave me the gift of life and called me to a meaningful life of service.

1 Argumento

In 1564, Bartolomé de las Casas said that

> during the last fifty years, from the year fourteen when I became a cleric, and then later as a friar, and then as bishop for another thirteen years, in which I have seen what happened, I have not ceased tirelessly to inquire how, according to God and natural reason, divine and human justice, we should relate to those people ...[1]

Many voices in history can be heard through the pens and speeches of prominent individuals. Few voices of history have generated as much scorn and praise as that of Bartolomé de las Casas (1484–1566).[2] Of his countless writings, the most infamous and famous was the *Brevísima Relación de la Destruición de la Indias*, in which Las Casas narrated events, condemned atrocities, and labored to halt the devastation and depopulation of the Indies. This controversial *Very Brief Account of the Destruction of the Indies* has been read and commented on by countless generations.[3] Since publication in 1552, this short work has been either derided as a polemical tract of burden or extolled as an exemplary text of liberation. Most readers have heard his voice either as a "promoter" of the Black Legend of exceptional Spanish colonial cruelty or as a "writer" of Golden Age literature.[4] Through these portrayals, the *Brevísima relación* has been alternately condemned and ignored for its supposed exaggerations, or published and defended for its purported veracity.[5] These types of polemical examinations of and approaches to the *Brevísima relación* have dominated Lascasian scholarship about this *Very Brief Account*.

However, such rhetorical and literary interpretations are important to comprehend how Las Casas's tract has been explicated academically and employed historically. For example, the *Brevísima relación* has played a pivotal role in the debates over the centuries about Spanish colonization and, by extension, any colonial enterprise. Indeed, this tract has been linked even with contemporary struggles of the oppressed against neo-colonialism.[6] Yet, such examinations and uses of this famous work have tended to discourage further probing for an alternative understanding of the *Brevísima relación*. Since this text has been—and will continue to be—widely discussed, studied, and debated, new interpretations of this frequently quoted work are important.[7] As historian John Fiske stated concerning Las Casas,

> [f]or the thoughts, words, and deeds of such a man, there is no death. The sphere of their influence goes on widening forever. They bud, they blossom, they bear fruit, from age to age.[8]

Argument and Rationale

This book listens again to Las Casas's voice and offers a new interpretation that elucidates the juridical approach taken by Las Casas in the *Very Brief Account*. This study argues that the *Brevísima relación de la destruición de las Indias* belongs predominantly to genres of inquiry in the juridical tradition, both civil and ecclesial. To develop this argument, this investigation explicates in detail both indirect contextual support—derived from evidence about Las Casas's exposures to, training in, and proclivity for the juridical—and direct textual support derived from an examination of the legal character and content of the text of the published *tratado*.

Indirect contextual support for this argument is discernible in four ways. First, Las Casas had direct exposure to the juridical because he lived in an era of titanic Atlantic world transition as Spain encountered, conquered, and colonized a "New World," and as legal thinking and structures adapted to the reality of an emerging and expanding Spanish empire. Second, Las Casas received formal education in Latin, canon law and the corresponding sphere of civil law, as well as in philosophical-theological-canonistic-Thomistic scholasticism, which he enhanced by lifelong autodidactic study. Third, Las Casas utilized a juridical approach in his responses to the anthropo-status, religious, economic, and political debates about the Indies and its inhabitants.[9] Fourth, the specific context of the genesis, writing, and eventual publication of the *Brevísima relación* (which spanned the decade from 1542 to 1552) possesses a discernible juridical character.

Direct textual support for this analysis derives from an examination of the character and content of the published *tratado*. From an assessment of its legal character, this study will demonstrate that the discernible triple function of the *Brevísima relación*—to inform, to denounce, and to petition—corresponds most appropriately to the genres of *relaciones* (official reports), *denuncias* (accusatory condemnations), and *peticiones* (remedial requests) that are found in the civil juridical tradition. This investigation will also demonstrate that the content of the treatise employs forms of discourse from the ecclesial juridical tradition, namely, genres of canon law, of the scholastic tripartite scheme of law, and of biblical juridical scripture.

Historical Significance

This book places the *Brevísima relación* in its proper genre as a piece of legal writing in the canon of colonial Latin American texts and, as such, moves scholarship away from the polemical and atemporal to the juridical and historical. Moreover, this research contributes to the small but growing body of Lascasian scholarship by systematically demonstrating that, since 1515, Las Casas was primarily a jurist in his training and perspectives rather than predominantly a controversial polemicist, a pragmatic activist, and/or a Thomistic theologian, and that he functioned as a jurist in his labors, writings, and responses to the issues and debates of his time.[10] This book corrects some of the, perhaps, overly encomiastic or anachronistic descriptions of Las Casas as, for example, a virtuous figure, the father of Liberation Theology, a father of the Latin American Church, an early modern historian, a proto-anthropologist, and a Renaissance man. At the same time, this specific focus on Las Casas's lifelong juridical approach links the context and content of the *Brevísima relación* more appropriately to the events of the time, to contemporaneous intellectual history, as well as to juridical dimensions of other writings by Las Casas. By addressing these kinds of issues and topics, this examination adds to historical knowledge by demythologizing the *tratado,* which has grown over time into a "larger-than-life" text—far beyond the original intention of Las Casas.

This book counteracts such aggrandizement by reestablishing the *Very Brief Account* within its own contemporaneous context and by seeking to understand the tract on its own terms, such that the modern reader might approximate the perspective of the originally intended reader. One of the ways to accomplish this is to indicate what is and is not included in the text. The *Brevísima relación* is about the actions and agency of certain Spaniards (and Germans), namely, of tyrannical conquistadors, captains, encomenderos, and royal officials. This purposely one-sided *Very Brief Account* challenges twenty-first-century readers who find the *tratado,* for the most part, "silent" about the particular actions and differentiating characteristics of Indigenous peoples. Las Casas excluded dissimilarities in their specific pre-Contact political, economic, and social organization. One of the challenges for twenty-first-century readers is this deliberately one-sided *Very Brief Account.* However, Las Casas's strident legal critique of the abusers, and his juridical defense of the abused, arose at the very beginning of the modern human rights movement. As such, his past critique is clearly echoed in contemporary calls for responses to ongoing rampant injustices. Both the *Brevísima relación* and Las Casas's opus of writings serve as juridical inspiration for legal and economic assessments as well as amelioration of the deplorable situations confronting vulnerable populations in the Americas and around the globe.

Methodology

In general, the methodology utilized in this study is both contextual and textual. Exegetical analysis of the text is also employed to elucidate the presence of juridical genres, which—for heuristic purposes—are categorized as two analytically distinguishable branches of the juridical tradition: civil and ecclesial. By explication of the legal character of the text and its corresponding function(s) (a social feature of genres) and by analysis of its narrative content (a structural feature of genres), the presence of genres of the civil juridical tradition (*relaciones*, *denuncias*, and *peticiones*) as well as of the ecclesial juridical tradition (Thomistic, canonistic, and scriptural) is discernible.[11]

To situate these identified genres of the text in their contemporaneous contexts, several kinds of lateral contextualization are employed. The first type compares the *Brevísima relación* with texts of similar genres. This method of analysis addresses questions such as "how typical or atypical are the civil juridical genres of the *Brevísima relación* in comparison to other contemporaneous juridical treatises?" With respect to genres of the ecclesial tradition, "how typical or atypical is the use of these genres in contemporaneous writings?"

A second kind of lateral contextualization situates the *Brevísima relación* in relevant institutional matrices of the Indies, Spain, and the Church. This method aids in binding this analysis more closely to institutional contexts, for example, to broader contexts such as the papal donation, Hispano-Indiano law (from Burgos to the New Laws), and its institutions such as the encomienda, the *Requerimiento*, the Protectorate, and the *Consejo de las Indias.* This method also helps to better understand the specific juridical circumstances attendant to the original writing of the *Brevísima relación* in 1542 until its publication in 1552.

A third kind of lateral contextualization elucidates the trajectories of development in the anthropo-status, religious, economic, and political debates that began with the encounter with the Indies and that continued throughout the conquest and early colonial period. By contextualizing the discourses about the different issues within their historical and contemporary scenarios, distinctive factors shaping the discourse as well as those ideas reflected in the *Brevísima relación* may be uncovered.

An important textual approach of this book employs the traditional genetic mode of historiography. For example, where appropriate in a content analysis of the treatise, the criteria of Las Casas's condemnatory judgments of the Spaniards' behavior as violations of divine, natural, and human laws are traced backward in time to their respective points of origin in Thomistic thought. Similarly, Las Casas's references to canonistic principles are traced back to their original articulation. Because this traditional genetic approach implies a temporal dimension—that of a return to the source as well as an inclusion of any thematic progression of this thought over time—this method is appropriate to understand both the origins and the developments of concepts such as tyranny, blasphemy, and heresy that Las Casas brought into his discourse.

Literature Review

Focusing on Las Casas's juridical approach is consistent with Lascasian scholarship that, since the early 1900s, has referred to his juridical abilities. For example, Abigail Mejía de Fernández (1934) and Pedro Henríquez Ureña (1949), Spanish historians, identified Las Casas as an *abogado* (attorney) for the Indigenous peoples; John Leddy Phelan (1956), colonial Latin American historian, specifically described Las Casas's approach as generally that of a canon lawyer, and particularly so in the *Brevísima relación*.[12]

Manuel María Martínez (1958), Dominican scholar from the juridical-theological tradition of Salamanca, contended that it was "in the juridical terrain that Las Casas excell[ed] in an extraordinary manner among all sixteenth-century authors."[13] Manuel Giménez Fernández (1966), Spanish canonist and Lascasian historian, recognized Las Casas as an adroit *fiscal* (prosecuting attorney) whose juridical insights were "incisive" and whose canonical censures of the evils and harm done in the Indies "struck like lightning."[14] Manuel Ballesteros Gaibrois (1977), Spanish historian and anthropologist, contended that Las Casas's role as an "*abogado de la causa de los indios*" (a lawyer for the Indians' cause) was the basis for all "his diverse activities that varied according to the needs of the time."[15] André Saint-Lu (1977), French Lascasian scholar, pointed out that Las Casas's "mode of seeing" was "fundamentally juridical."[16] In recent decades, Kenneth Pennington (1993), a scholar of medieval ecclesiastical and legal history, also identified Las Casas as "essentially a jurist" and demonstrated that the content and sources of several significant Lascasian ideas "were based on medieval juridical theory … [that Las Casas] developed … in original and interesting ways."[17] Paolo Carozzo (2003), Harvard legal scholar, pointed out that Las Casas's "arguments were strewn with juridical sources and language," and that such juridical aspects were present "in a manner more overt and persistent" than his contemporaries.[18] J. Scott Davidson (1994), New Zealand Law professor, who also called Las Casas a jurist, contended that the Dominican's underlying juridical approach was present even in writings that were highly polemical and characterized by moral outrage and that these features often overshadowed detection of Las Casas's legal orientation, which seems to be the case with the *Brevísima relación*.[19] In accord with scholars' persistent portrayal of Las Casas as a legal advocate, Rolena Adorno (2008), perhaps the foremost expert in colonial Latin American literature, authoritatively and forcefully contended that "Las Casas followed juridical tradition and augmented it with theological sources, [although] theology was not his primary expertise," and specifically stated that "Las Casas's juridical perspective is essential to understanding … his *Brevísima relación*."[20] As such, this book's reassessment of the *Brevísima relación* builds on and adds to these scholars' common identification of Las Casas as a jurist and of the predominance of a juridical perspective in his lifelong defense of Indigenous people by revisiting the text and demonstrating its legal character and juridical content.

Introductions to nine contemporary editions of the *Brevísima relación* (five in Spanish, three in English, and one in French) show that this type of juridical recasting of Las Casas's life is the exception rather than the rule. Most of the scholarly introductions to the treatise include a broad chronological or a partial episodic biography that offers valuable insights about different aspects of Las Casas's life. However, only Dominican historian-philosopher-theologian, Isacio Pérez Fernández (1992), and political-scientist-historian, Anthony Pagden (1992), as well as Saint-Lu (1991) present Las Casas's biography in terms of the developing legal climate that unfolded on both sides of the Atlantic, the ensuing debates, and the Crown's various juridical initiatives. Most academics simply indicate without elaboration, as did historian Franklin Knight (2003), that Las Casas "helped shape the jurisprudential nature of the Spanish American colonial world."[21]

No study has systematically addressed how Las Casas functioned as a *fiscal* throughout his life, nor how the character and content of the *Brevísima relación* might belong to genres of the juridical traditions. Surprisingly, even Pérez Fernández in his monumental critical edition of the *Brevísima relación* in 2000 did not assess the legal character of the treatise; he simply states that Las Casas's ethical-juridical judgments are one of its major components.[22]

There has been little consensus among scholars about the genre(s) of the *Brevísima relación* although all the editors of the modern editions, except Bill Donovan (1992), have addressed this dimension in one way or another. Some, such as Consuelo Varela (1999), Spanish historian of colonial Latin America, position Las Casas's widely known and frequently read tract as both an example of Golden Age literature and a source of the Black Legend, but do not offer any juridical interpretation. Roberto Fernández Retamar (1980), Cuban essayist and literary critic, discusses the treatise predominantly for its contribution to the Black Legend. In his discussion of the formal literary genres of the treatise, José Miguel Martínez Torrejón (2006), professor of Spanish and Portuguese literature, argues that the treatise is "a powerful rhetorical machine" in keeping with the parameters of the classical tradition and thus may be characterized as juridical or forensic discourse in the *tratadística* (the corpus of treatise writing). For Torrejón, this mixture of rhetorical genres—both juridical and persuasive—lends a clear depositional and narrative quality to the text.[23]

Some editors and other scholars point to the presence of both literary and juridical genres in the *Brevísima relación*. For example, Pagden (1992) acknowledges that the treatise employed literary and rhetorical strategies, but insists that it is principally a legal tract, and specifically both a *relación* and a *petición*.[24] Luís Veres (1998), linguist and communication theorist, regards the *Brevísima relación* as a historical chronicle that informs and narrates, but does not consider whether these functions might be characteristic of a *relación*; he does, however, contend that the "superior functionality" of the treatise is that of a *denuncia*.[25] Pérez Fernández (1992) also recognizes a denunciatory quality in the text and sees this as a genre of legal writing. He contends that Las Casas employs "shocking language" to speak directly in an expository manner to the problem of the conquest, rather than employing words as "a professional literary writer would."[26] These scholars contend that the juridical dominated over the literary, a position also taken in this study.

Other scholars have focused solely on one or another genre of the civil juridical tradition. For example, Saint-Lu (1998) argues that "the only theme that occupies all of [Las Casas's] texts" is denunciation, and that Las Casas's writings are essentially *memoriales de agravios* (memoranda of grievances), thus implying that the *Brevísima relación* is at best a *denuncia*.[27] Alberto Moreiras (2000), Professor of Hispanic Studies and Cultural Theory, classifies the *Brevísima relación* as a request (*petición*) to Philip II "to end the savage extraction of capital from the Indies" and "to preserve the integrity of the imperial *dominium*."[28] Manuel Ballesteros Gaibrios (1977), Spanish anthropologist and historian, does not regard the *Brevísima relación* as "a public denunciation, but what would be called today a report to a superior," but he did not explicitly denominate the treatise as a *relación*.[29] However, Torrejón argues against designating the treatise as a *relación* in the "Introduction" to his 2006 critical edition of the text. He believes that historically the genre of *relación* functioned as an official and testimonial document about events that happened in time and space. Texts of this type tended to be written by someone who had the obligation to inform the emperor of what he had seen. Because Las Casas's treatise includes information that was compiled from sources other than his own eyewitness testimony, Torrejón concludes that the treatise lacked what constituted legal evidence and therefore could not belong to the legal genre of a *relación*.[30] This position is refuted by scholarship on what constitutes legal evidence.[31] Most *relaciones* from this time period were not based solely on eyewitness observations by the author but by works and accounts of others as well.

In addition to this scholarship about genres of the civil juridical tradition, some of the "Introductions" and other scholarship have pinpointed the ecclesial juridical tradition found in the *Brevísima relación*: the Thomistic genre of the tripartite scheme of divine, natural, and human laws. For example, Saint-Lu (1991) holds that the treatise constitutes a "very clearly formulated juridical refutation" of the Spaniards' violation of natural and divine laws.[32] José María Reyes Cano (1994), scholar of Spanish Literature, maintains that the way in which divine law was understood by Thomists is the core of the treatise's legal reflection; however, he does not identify the Thomistic tripartite scheme of law as a juridical genre. Indeed, Reyes Cano's only reference to any legal genre is in the context of the 1542 New Laws, asserting that the *Brevísima relación* is "no more than an *alegato informativo* (informative accusation) of a quasi-juridical character."[33] In contrast, Marta Inés Waldegaray, Argentinian Professor of Spanish Literature, characterized the treatise as both a "*petition*" for justice and a "*dénonciation*" (accusatory condemnation) of the violations of divine, natural, and human laws.[34] She did not, however, develop this. In this study, an analysis of the analytic framework underlying the content of the *Brevísima relación* explicates this Thomistic genre of the ecclesial juridical tradition.

While no other genres of the ecclesial juridical tradition, namely, canonistic and scriptural, were addressed by these scholars, other recent studies do. For example, José Cárdenas Bunsen, Professor of Spanish Literature, who studied the *tratados* published by Las Casas in 1552, demonstrates the canonistic approach in the Dominican's use of two juridical concepts—tyranny and fraud—in the *Brevísima relación*.[35] With respect to the presence of biblical juridical genres in the *Brevísima relación*, Francisco Rodríguez's 1995 doctoral dissertation drew on the Pentateuch (the first five books of the Hebrew Bible called by Christians the Old Testament) to structure Las Casas's assessment of the Spaniards' deeds in terms of selected normative dimensions of Exodus and Deuteronomy, for example, in terms of the rules pertaining to the Israelites' encounter with an alien people.[36]

Given this recent scholarship as well as the fact that scholars have not understood nor systematically explicated the nature of the *Brevísima relación* as belonging to the genres of the two branches (civil and ecclesial) of the juridical tradition, this study endeavors to break needed new ground in the understanding of this text as one replete with genres of legal discourse.

Sources

All these works have been consulted in some way in the preparation of this present study. In addition to secondary scholarship, editions of the

Brevísima relación are both "primary" and "secondary" in nature. Additional valuable primary and secondary sources were acquired from archival research at the Library of Congress, Yale University Beinecke Library, and the University of Florida, as well as from the *Archivo General de las Indias* in Seville, Spain, and the *Archivos Generales de los Dominicos de la Provincia de Santiago de México*, Querétaro, Mexico.[37] Secondary textual sources, such as those discussed above, were complemented by interviews and discussions with leading Lascasian and other scholars at the 2006 *International Quincentenary Congress*, "De Ávila a La Española: Una mirada desde la otra orilla" in Ávila, Spain; at the 2007 *Encuentro internacional*: *Presencia de fray Bartolomé de las Casas*, in Havana, Cuba; at the 2009 *Fifty-third International Congress of Americanists*, "The People of the Americas: Continuity and Change" in Mexico City, Mexico; and at the 2010 *Ninth International Congress of Dominican Historians*, in Oaxaca, Mexico.[38]

However, with respect to primary sources available for this study, there remain some significant limitations. In general, these sources are constricted by time, language, culture, and methodology. Temporally, these texts were produced nearly five hundred years ago. Linguistically, sixteenth-century Spanish sources tend to be archaic in style, limited in availability, and one-sided in perspective. Culturally, these texts represent an only partially known Hispano-Indiano worldview long past. Methodologically, the texts were generated at the beginning of the early modern period, prior to the development of modern historiographic conventions. As such, these primary texts must be considered on their own terms and examined carefully. Furthermore, with respect to the *Brevísima relación*, Las Casas's "working papers" are not available. As such, the various editions of the text cannot be compared to *borradores* (draft copies) such as the *Larguísima relación* from which the shorter summary was distilled. Nevertheless, the bibliography of this study represents a solid quarry of primary and secondary sources related to the particular focus of this study.

Organization

This book consists of three major parts. The first part (Chapters 1–3) presents the formation of Las Casas's juridical voice by contextualizing his life within the broader milieu of his native land that shaped his worldview, facilitated his early education and subsequent academic studies, and immersed him in the affairs of the Indies. Accordingly, Chapter 2 first offers a general historical overview beginning with intellectual and cultural developments attendant to the ascendancy of the Renaissance, and extending to Iberia's social history with its *letrados* and litigations, its politics and religion, that eventually culminated in the encounter of

Castilian and Indigenous people as well as generated the *Brevísima relación* fifty years later. Chapter 3 then presents the specific development of academic disciplines within Castile's distinctive matrix from which Las Casas benefited—first in canon law, later in theology. These two disciplines along with reforms in the Dominican Order converged in Las Casas's life, when he became a friar, and resulted in the distinctive canonistic-Thomistic accent of his juridical voice.

The second part (Chapters 4 and 5) addresses the articulation of Las Casas's juridical voice by examining his participation in and contributions to four kinds of major debates that took place during the first half of the sixteenth century. Accordingly, Chapter 4 considers the debates about the level of humanity of Indigenous peoples, and about their evangelization and eternal salvation. Chapter 5 focuses on issues related to the institutions of encomienda and slavery, as well as to the legitimacy of *dominium* (dominion) and its exercise by wars of conquest. These chapters demonstrate that Las Casas applied his doctrine of natural rights, as well as his knowledge of divine, natural, and human (including canon and civil) laws, to these debates.

The third part (Chapters 6 and 7) delineates the focus of Las Casas's juridical voice in the *Brevísima relación* by addressing the specific context, character, and content of the *Very Brief Account.* Chapter 6 presents the particular juridical circumstances that accompanied the genesis, revision, and publication of the text, and then examines the legal character of the treatise as a piece of juristic writing belonging to the civil juridical genres of *relaciones*, *denuncias*, and *peticiones.* Chapter 7 examines the content of the treatise to elucidate its juridical structural components, epistemological rationale, and analytic framework to demonstrate that Las Casas also employed genres from the ecclesial juridical tradition. Using these genres, this study then explicates how the juridical figure of tyranny in its political, moral, and theological spheres was discernible in the content of the treatise, and how justice was the basis of his ethical-juridical judgments pertaining to these spheres. The final chapter summarizes the argument of this study, and offers additional interpretations related to the *Brevísima relación* that await future scholarship, followed by a brief discussion of voices of conscience, including the multifaceted tenor of Las Casas's juridical voice, that were raised on behalf of the Indigenous people (Figures 1.1 and 1.2).

Figure 1.1 Bartolomé de las Casas. Published by the Real Imprenta of Madrid, 1791.

P V

Breuiſſima rela
cion de la deſtruycion de las In-
dias: colegida por el Obiſpo dõ
fray Bartolome de las Caſas / o
Caſaus de la orden de Sãcto Do
mingo.

Año. 1552.

Figure 1.2 Cover of the *Brevisima relación de la destrucción de las Indias*. Published in 1552 in Seville.

Notes

1 Bartolomé de las Casas, *Doce dudas* in *Obras Completas* (Madrid: Alianza, 1998), 11.2:16.

2 For a brief summary of Las Casas's critics, see Bartolomé de las Casas, *Brevísima relación de la destruicion de las Indias*, ed. Isacio Pérez Fernández, vol. 3 (Bayamon, Puerto Rico: Centro de Estudios de los Dominicos del Caribe and Universidad Central de Bayamón, 1999), 3:917–38 (hereafter cited as Pérez Fernández, *Brevísima*). Scholars who praised Las Casas include the following: Manuel Giménez Fernández, Lewis Hanke, Manuel M. Martínez, Vicente D. Carro, Marcel Bataillon, André Saint-Lu, Helen Rand Parish, Isacio Pérez Fernández, Gustavo Gutiérrez, among others. Perhaps the most famous derision of Las Casas was written by Ramón Menéndez Pidal in his *El Padre Las Casas: Su doble personalidad* (Madrid: Espasa-Calpe, 1963); his scorn for Las Casas was echoed in Julián Marías, *Understanding Spain*, trans. Frances M. López-Morilla (Ann Arbor: Univ. of Michigan Press, 1990), 211–12.

3 Juan Comas succinctly synthesized the scholarly debates about Las Casas's writings in his "Historical Reality and the Detractors of Father Las Casas," in *Bartolomé de Las Casas in History: Toward an Understanding of the Man and His Work*, eds. Juan Friede and Benjamin Keen (DeKalb: Northern Illinois Univ. Press, 1971), 487–537 (hereafter cited as *Las Casas in History*). Benjamin Keen traced the main currents of international opinion about Las Casas's writings in his "Introduction: Approaches to Las Casas, 1537–1970," in *Las Casas in History*, 3–63. André Saint-Lu stated, "All too often Las Casas is identified solely with the *Brevísima*–or the focus is on libel ... [thus treating] this work in isolation from his other efforts and writings." "Introducción," in Bartolomé de las Casas, *Brevísima relación de la destruición de las Indias*, ed. André Saint-Lu (Cátedra: Quinta Ediciones, 1991), 11 (hereafter cited as "Introducción" and *Brevísima relación*).

4 In André Saint-Lu's critical examination of how the *Brevísima* was used, he elucidated its function for both sixteenth-century anti-Spanish propagandists and for nineteenth-century Latin American revolutionaries to foment independence movements. "Introducción," 46–50. After its publication in Seville in 1552, this famous text was translated over time into a number of other modern languages—many in the tongues of Spain's enemies. These translated editions generated anti-Spanish propaganda. The translations of the *Brevísima relación* were read publicly (and visualized with woodcuts) especially for the benefit of the illiterate; as such, Las Casas's text was turned again into an oral report—a report that took on legendary proportions in the Black Legend. Fernando Domínguez Reboiras, "'Y hasta agora no es poderoso el rey'. Sobre monarquía y elites de poder en los orígenes de la Brevíssima," in *Talleres de la memoria—Reivindicaciones y autoridad en la historiografía de los siglos XVI y XVII*, eds. Robert Folger and Wulf Oesterreicher (Münster: LIT, Druck, 2005), 47–54. For an analysis of the Black Legend, see the Hanke-Keen debate in Lewis Hanke, "A Modest Proposal for a Moratorium on Grand Generalizations: Some Thoughts on the Black Legend," *Hispanic American Historical Review* 51, no. 1 (1971): 112–27. Also see Benjamin Keen, "The Black Legend Revisited: Assumptions and Realities," *Hispanic American Historical Review* 49, no. 4 (1969), 703–19. For an assessment of the literary heritage of Las Casas, see V. Afanasiev, "The Literary Heritage of Bartolomé de las Casas," in *Las Casas in History*, 539–78; and Raymond Marcus, "Las Casas in Literature," in *Las Casas in History*, 581–600.

5 Decades after Las Casas wrote his *Brevísima relación*, Bernal Díaz questioned the veracity of the Dominican friar's version of the events at Cholula. See Bernal Díaz del Castillo, *The Conquest of New Spain*, trans. and intro. by J. M. Cohen (London: Penguin Books, 1963), 203. In 1596, Fray Agustín Dávila Padilla ardently defended the veracity of Las Casas's *Very Brief Account* in his *Historia de la fundación y discurso de la provincial de Santiago de México, de la Orden de Predicadores* (Mexico: Editorial Academia Literaria, 1955), 303–30, 341. For a contemporary defense of Las Casas's *Brevísima relación*, see, among others, Manuel María Martínez, *Fray Bartolomé de las Casas: El gran calumniado* (Madrid: La Rafa, 1955), and Saint-Lu, "Introducción," 46–57.

6 Benjamin Keen, "Introduction: Approaches to Las Casas," in *Las Casas in History*, 55.

7 The *Brevísima relación*'s broad use in academia is demonstrated using an internet search. The results show how frequently this tract is included in course syllabi. Study of the *Brevísima relación* has also increasingly extended into the fields of the Humanities. Examples of literary examinations of the tract include Camacho's analysis of the *Brevísima relación* as a discourse of resistance as well as Benitez-Rojo's delineation of the role of the tract in delaying the publication of Las Casas's *Historia*. See Jorge Luis Camacho, "Meta-Historia y ficción en la Brevísima relación de la destrucción de las Indias de Fray Bartolomé de las Casas," *Hispanófila* 134 (2002): 37–47; and Antonio Benítez-Rojo, "Bartolomé de Las Casas: Entre el infierno y la ficción," *Modern Language Notes* 103, no. 2 Hispanic Issue (1988): 259–88.

8 John Fiske, *The Discovery of America with Some Account of Ancient America and the Spanish Conquest* (Boston, MA: Houghton and Mifflin, 1892), 2:440–41, 476, 482.

9 The neologism, anthropo-status, uses the hyphenated Greek-Latin word "anthropo-status" meaning "human-status" to avoid anachronistic confusion with the focus of the modern discipline of anthropology as the study of human culture. The rationale for this neologism will be further explicated in Chapter 4.

10 Kenneth Pennington, *Popes, Canonists and Texts, 1150–1550* (Aldershot: Variorum, 1993), XIII, 3. A jurist is a legal expert, practitioner, and writer. Enrique Alcaraz Varó y Brian Hughes, *Diccionario de Términos Jurídicos* (Inglés-Español; Spanish-English), 7th ed. (Madrid: Ariel, 2003), 307.

11 Structural features of genres include: (1) channel (how the text is transmitted: spoken, written, signed), (2) content (what the text is about: its meanings and concepts), (3) macro-structure (its parts and how they are arranged), and (4) micro-structure (particular configurations within). Social features of genres include: (1) name (culturally recognized or individually agreed-upon), (2) transmission (explicitly conforms to a template), (3) function (the purpose of text, and what social role(s) it plays), and (4) participants (who produces it, who reads it, and the relationship of their roles). "Narrative and Genre," Department of Linguistics, University of California, Santa Barbara, class notes, *Linguistics* 124, January 17, 2001, accessed October 1, 2010, from http://www.linguistics.ucsb.edu/.

12 Abigail Mejía de Fernández, *Historia de la literatura castellana: estudio histórico crítico que comprende la literatura hispanoamericana* (Barcelona: Araluce, 1934), 276; Pedro Henríquez Ureña, *Las corrientes literarias en la América hispánica* (Mexico: Fondo de Cultura Económica, 1949), 23, 5; John Leddy Phelan, *The Millennial Kingdom of the Franciscans in the New World: A Study of the Writings of Gerónimo de Mendieta (1525–1604)* (Berkeley: Univ. of California Press, 1956), 6, 142–43n16.

13 Manuel María Martínez, *Fray Bartolomé de las Casas "Padre de América,"* estudio biográfico-crítico (Madrid: La RAFA, S. L. Abato, 1958), 3.
14 Manuel Giménez Fernández, "Actualidad de Las Téses Lascasianas," *Estudios Lascasianos* (Estudios Hispano-Americanos, 1966), 6. Manuel Giménez Fernández, *Bartolomé de las Casas: delegado de Cisneros para la reformación de las Indias 1516–1517* (Madrid: Consejo Superior de Investigaciones Científicas, 1984), 1: xix; Manuel Giménez Fernández, *Bartolomé de las Casas: capellán de S.M. Carlos I, poblador de Cumaná 1517–1523* (Madrid: Consejo Superior de Investigaciones Científicas, 1984), 2:1224.
15 Bartolomé de las Casas, *Brevísima relación de la Destrucción de Indias*, intro. Manuel Ballesteros Gaibrois (Madrid: Alcalá, 1977), viii (hereafter Gaibrois, *Brevísima relación*).
16 André Saint-Lu, *Las Casas indigéniste. Etudes sur la vie et l'oeuvre du défenseur des Indiens* (Paris: L'Harmattan, 1982), 56.
17 Pennington, "Bartolomé de Las Casas and the Tradition of Medieval Law," in *Popes, Canonists and Texts*, 151.
18 Paolo Carozzo, "From Conquest to Constitutions: The Latin American Tradition of the Idea of Human Rights," *Human Rights Quarterly* 25, no. 2 (2003): 292.
19 J. S. Davidson, "The Rights of Indigenous Peoples in Early International Law," *The Canterbury Law Review* 5 (1994): 393, 411.
20 Rolena Adorno, "The Intellectual Life of Bartolomé de Las Casas: Framing the Literature Classroom," in *Approaches to Teaching the Writings of Bartolomé de Las Casas*, eds. Santa Arias and Eyda Merediz (New York: Modern Language Association of America, 2008), 27.
21 Bartolomé de las Casas, *A Short Account of the Destruction of the Indies*, ed. and trans. Nigel Griffin; intro. Anthony Pagden (London: Penguin Books, 1992); Pérez Fernández, *Brevísima*; Saint-Lu, *Brevísima relación*; Bartolomé de las Casas, *An Account, Much Abbreviated, of the Destruction of the Indies*, trans. Andrew Hurley, intro. and ed. Franklin W. Knight (Indianapolis: Hackett, 2003), xiii (hereafter Knight, *An Account*).
22 Pérez Fernández, *Brevísima*, 326–33. This 1,056-page critical edition greatly enhanced my understanding of the content of the *Brevísima relación*. Bartolomé de las Casas, *Brevísima relación de la destruición de las Indias*, ed. and intro. José Miguel Martínez Torrejón (Alicante: Universidad de Alicante, 2006), 44 (hereafter cited as Torrejón, *Brevísima relación*).
23 Bartolomé de las Casas, *The Devastation of the Indies: A Brief Account*, intro. Bill M. Donovan; trans. Herman Briffault (Baltimore, MD: Johns Hopkins Univ. Press, 1992); Bartolomé de las Casas, *Brevísima relación de la destruición de las Indias*, intro. Consuelo Varela (Madrid: Castalia, 1999), 42; Bartolomé de las Casas, *Très Brève Relation de la Destruction des Indes*, intro. Roberto Fernández Retamar, trans. Fanchita González Batlle (Paris: Maspero, 1980); Bartolomé de las Casas, *Brevísima relación de la destruición de las Indias*, ed. and intro. José Miguel Martínez Torrejón (Alicante: Universidad de Alicante, 2006), 44 (hereafter cited as Torrejón, *Brevísima relación*).
24 Pagden, "Introduction" in Bartolomé de las Casas, *An Account, Much Abbreviated, of the Destruction of the Indies*, ed. and trans. Nigel Griffin, intro. Anthony Pagden (London: Penguin Books, 1992). xxx–xxxi.
25 Luís Veres, "El marco de la ficción en la 'Brevísima relación de la destrucción de las Indias' de Fray Bartolomé de las Casas," *Revista de Estudios Literarios* 9 (1998): 4.
26 Bartolomé de las Casas, *Brevísima relación de la destruición de las Indias*, ed. and intro. Isacio Pérez Fernández (Madrid: Tecnos, 1992), xiv–xvii.

27 André Saint-Lu, "Bartolomé de Las Casas en sus escritos," España y América en una perspectiva humanista, ed. Joseph Pérez (Madrid: Casa de Velázquez, 1998), 112.
28 Alberto Moreiras, "Ten Notes on Primitive Imperial Accumulation: Ginés de Sepúlveda, Las Casas, Fernández de Oviedo," *Interventions* 2, no. 3 (2000): 343–63.
29 Gaibrois, *Brevísima relación*, xviii.
30 Torrejón, *Brevísima relación*, 46–47.
31 Walter D. Mignolo, "Cartas, crónicas y relaciones del descubrimiento y la conquista," in *Historia de la literatura hispanoamericana, época colonial*, coord., Luis Iñigo Madrigal (Madrid: Cátedra, 1982), 71.
32 Saint-Lu, *Brevísima relación*, 30.
33 Bartolomé de las Casas, *Brevísima relación de la destrucción de las Indias*, ed. and intro. J. M. Reyes Cano (Barcelona: Planeta, 1994), xxx–xxxi, xlii, xlv.
34 Marta Inés Waldegaray, "Discours et relations de sociabilité dans La Brevísima Relación de las Indias de Bartolomé de Las Casas," *Caravelle*: *Cahiers du Monde Hispanique et Luso-Bresilen* 82 (2004): 19, 24, 37.
35 José Alejandro Cárdenas Bunsen, "Escritura y derecho canónico en la obra de fray Bartolomé de las Casas" (Ph.D. diss., Yale University, 2008), 122–40.
36 Francisco Rodríguez, "La Brevísima Relación del Padre Las Casas: Texto y Subtexto" (Ph.D. diss., University of California, Davis, 1995), 199–216.
37 Part of these research activities were funded by a Kislak Short Term Fellowship, in addition to two Summer Research Grants and the Maxwell Angus Award from the University of Oregon Department of History. Other investigative research was facilitated by the University of Oregon Knight Library holdings and Interlibrary Loan collections.
38 Remote preparation for this book consisted of research-related travel to eleven Latin American countries to investigate broad thematic issues about Latin America in general and Las Casas in particular. Additionally, this study benefited from the writing of two master's theses, one in theology and one in history, which focused on Las Casas's *Confesionario* and *Brevísima relación*, respectively.

2 The Formation of Las Casas's Juridical Voice

Historical Matrix

For some, a popular refrain is "In fourteen-hundred-ninety-two, Columbus sailed the ocean blue" (Figure 2.1).

So chanted the voices of past generations of school children about Christopher Columbus's (1451–1506) mythical expedition into the Atlantic.[1] However, the scholarly value of this facile mnemonic device about the Genoese mariner's westward departure from Europe ends there. The poem fails miserably to surface the complexities that followed in the wake of Columbus's initial contact between "two worlds, both already old"—complexities generated by the consequent mutual encounters of Europeans and different peoples on different lands, and by the subsequent Spanish invasions, conquests, and colonization of this so-called

Figure 2.1 Landing of Columbus (October 12, 1492). Painting by John Vanderlyn, 1847.
Source: Wikipedia.

"New World."[2] Fifty years after Columbus's initial encounter with and identification of these people as "Indians," the voice of Bartolomé de las Casas (1484–1566) thundered forth in his *Brevísima relación de la destruición de las Indias* to condemn the initial forty-nine years of devastation and depopulation of the Indies—a treatise first written in 1542 and subsequently published in 1552.

Eight years before Columbus's first contact with the Indigenous inhabitants and their lands, Las Casas was born on November 11 in the Andalusian city of Seville in a Castilian "Spain" ripe for expansion and eager to support the personal ambition of the Genoese mariner to sail westward into the *mar Océano*.[3] Las Casas was raised in a Spain characterized by certain Renaissance intellectual and cultural developments that was also marked during the 1400s and early 1500s by distinctive socio-economic and politico-religious patterns.[4]

In broad historiographical strokes, this chapter presents the general historical matrix of Spain in order to elucidate the particular character of Las Casas's native land and, where appropriate, to contextualize his early life experiences, and some of the initial future developments of the Spanish colonial system in the Indies. The first section contextualizes the general historical matrix of Spain by a brief overview of the developments in Renaissance intellectual and cultural history. This intellectual milieu of the European Renaissance—its philosophical, legal, and theological developments—as well as its artistic and linguistic aspects, greatly influenced the development of fifteenth-century Spain. Consequently, the second section addresses the intellectual and cultural continuity and change that characterized Renaissance Spain, and that influenced Las Casas's early formation. Then, the third section presents a survey of Spain's social history, namely, two particular demographic characteristics of Spain, the economic development of the Crowns of Castile and Aragon, as well as their relevance to certain aspects of Las Casas's life and of the future colonization in the Indies. The fourth section focuses on the political power and ideology of Isabel and Ferdinand as they unified and consolidated the Crowns of Castile and Aragon, and it shows how their centralized hierarchical system of governance was replicated in the Indies.[5] The fifth section considers the Catholic Monarchs' strategies for reforming the national *ecclesia* (church), their methods for converting the *patria* (country), and their vision for Christianizing the *orbis* (world). The last section offers a contrast between Columbus's juridical possession of Indigenous lands and peoples, and Las Casas's juridical condemnation in the *Brevísima relación* of the destruction of the Indies.

Ascendancy of the Renaissance

The broader European Renaissance was a complex period of intellectual and cultural developments generally bridging three centuries

(1300/1350–1550/1600).[6] While this movement of rebirth varied regionally and socially, its general features significantly contoured the historical matrix of fifteenth-century Spain. These common features included the return to ancient classical literature, the enrichment of medieval thought through innovative scholarship, and the emergence of new and diverging intellectual traditions, in addition to the development of various artistic and linguistic expressions.

The renewed interest of the Renaissance in classical literature constituted a return *ad fontes* (to the sources)—to authoritative texts—to that font of powerful knowledge that educated persons pursued in the writings of antiquity: the Bible, the Church Fathers, in addition to the philosophical, legal, theological, historical, literary, and oratorical works of the Greeks and Romans.[7] Renaissance thinkers and writers especially celebrated the Romans and extolled the Greeks of the ancient world. Indeed, with the thirteenth-century rediscovery of Aristotle (384–322 BCE), scholars of various disciplines "neither read commentaries nor paraphrases but the works of Aristotle themselves in order to drink his thought 'directly from the springs.'"[8] The fall of Constantinople in 1453 further elevated the importance of ancient writings by bringing intellectuals from the Greek East to the Latin West who, in turn, disseminated new translations of and circulated additional commentaries on texts of the Greco-Roman intellectual tradition. About this same time, some elite intellectuals searched for an even more remote past than that of Rome and Greece—for the very ancient cultures of "deep time" and of esoteric knowledge as found, for example, in Egyptian and Chaldean antiquity. Implicit in this revolutionary sense of time and the pursuit of "the pristine source of truth and original source of knowledge" was belief in "a golden past" and in the subsequent gradual degeneration of humankind.[9] Knowledge gleaned from the Renaissance return to Greco-Roman and more remote pasts would influence the intellectual exploration of the encountered "New World." The ancient texts and the differing interpretations—one deductive, another inductive—would later serve both as tools and as obstacles for understanding the Indigenous peoples, their cultures, and their lands.[10]

In the Renaissance philosophical refocus on the past, three dominant strains—classical, scholastic, and humanist—permeated the thought of the period.[11] In classical thought, the revival of Aristotelianism, Platonism, Epicureanism, and Stoicism generated ancient models for humans' ethical formation as well as for the polity.[12] In scholastic philosophy, the various medieval schools—Averroism, Albertism, Thomism, Scotism, Ockhamism—focused on resolving textual contradictions in their study of the ancient sources.[13] Although fueled by new ideas from the East, scholastics continued their adherence to the speculative pursuit of "the true" in their utilization of the method of logical dialectical reasoning and metaphysical abstraction—whether focusing on theoretical disciplines such as theology and philosophy, or on practical disciplines such as law and medicine. In humanist discourse, an emerging intellectual movement traditionally thought to have been initiated by Francesco Petrarch (1304–1374), who discovered historical discontinuities in copies of the ancient texts, scholars increasingly utilized the philological and historical method of Lorenzo Valla (c. 1406–1454) to study classical literature and languages as quarries of valuable knowledge and civilized standards; they placed their focus on the practical application of learning in social and political life, which method and application challenged the abstract academic approach of the scholastic method.[14] As such, in the *quattrocento* (1400s), humanist scholarship, which was first intended for a select cultured social stratum and particularly for those who ruled society and Church, addressed itself to the lay public—to all literate citizens—in an effort to shape their education, culture, and lives according to the models of the ancient texts. In contrast to the scholastic emphasis on metaphysical philosophy and the primacy of the intellect in the speculative pursuit of "the true," humanists championed moral philosophy because of its usefulness in daily human life, and the need to persuade the will in the practical pursuit of "the good." Because of humanism's goal of changing the heart, Petrarch argued that humanist philosophy was superior to scholasticism.[15]

In law, the return *ad fontes* began with twelfth-century codifications of both Roman and canon laws. The recovery and recomposition of the texts of the Justinian Code (529–565 CE)—also called the *Corpus Iuris Civilis* (Body of Civil Law)—took place at the newly established *studium generale* or "university" of Bologna (1088), principally through the efforts of Irnerius (c. 1050–1125) who founded the school of glossators, taught Roman law, and initiated the study of Roman jurisprudence as a science.[16] Shortly thereafter, the scientific integrity of canon law was established by the work of Gratian, a learned Bolognese jurist who, in about 1140, evaluated and compiled the entire tradition, methods, and underlying philosophy of ecclesiastical law in his encyclopedic *Concordia Discordantium Canonum* (Concordance of Discordant Canons). This work—generally referred to as the *Decretum*—became the first component of what would become the *Corpus Iuris Canonici* (Body of Canon Law) four centuries later.[17]

In their study of the universal law of venerable antiquity, jurists at Bologna initially embarked upon a thorough glossing of the Justinian texts using scholastic reasoning and strictly dialectical methods, and culminating in time with a compendium of all extant interpretations of the Justinian texts in the *Glossa Ordinaria* (The Ordinary Gloss) compiled in about 1230 by Franciscus Accursius (1182–1260).[18] Unable to proceed further in abstract glossing, and as conflicts arose between local and customary laws as well as in inter-city commerce, jurists at universities other than Bologna shifted their attention to writing *commentaria* that reworked a particular aspect of the law and reconciled the differences of interpretation. Similarly, in their study of classical canon law (1140–1378), legal scholars, aided by the rediscovery of Aristotle in the West, developed and utilized the analytical approach to authoritative texts that was associated with scholasticism and its dialectical method of organizing texts and resolving inconsistencies.[19] The methods of both the civil and ecclesial disciplines of law did not include the philological and historical kinds of analysis proffered by humanists.[20] Even during the postclassical period (1378 onward), the scholastic method (and Aristotelian logic) continued to undergird the extensive commentaries on canon law.[21]

Roman law sought two systems of universal law—one, a system of legal thought elucidating principles, concepts, and modes of argument; the other, a system of positive law as a standard for *ius proprium* (particular law—whether royal, city, or local) about what is rational and just. Significantly, the Justinian Code of Roman law received inspiration from "a Christian spirit" based on equity and *humanitas*, and also included directives about the clergy and the Church.[22] Canon law, whose *Decretum Gratiani* coincided with the rise of the papacy as the main form of governance in the Church, was greatly influenced by Roman law during the Early Middle Ages and by civil laws that worked their way into canonical collections, such that "much of Roman law was 'canonized.'"[23] Both Roman and canon law studies sought to generate principles of universal jurisprudence that were applicable to contemporary life.[24] Because many jurists were trained in both civil and ecclesiastical laws, common jurisprudential principles were more readily identified and merged.[25]

Together, Roman and canon laws formed the so-called *ius commune* (common law) of the Christian world.[26] The most influential of the commentators on both the *ius commune* and the *ius proprium* was Bartolus de Saxoferrato (1314–1354), an eminent professor, scholar, and legal advocate in public life. His commentary on the whole of Roman law rather than solely on particular aspects of the Justinian Code was regarded as "a work of authority" and an exemplar of how to apply the wisdom of ancient jurisprudence directly to contemporaneous legal situations. Extraordinary originality characterized Bartolus's work, especially in his understanding of the unity of the law, and in his explication of the centrality of the authority of *ius commune* in all interpretations of *ius proprium*.[27] This theoretical practice, referred to as *mos italicus* (the Italian method) and adopted by most jurists and legal practitioners throughout Western Europe, had consequences for the historical method of teaching and applying Roman law. First, universal principles exemplified in the law were clarified and applied to contemporaneous situations; second, efforts were made to incorporate the histories and legal systems of polities of the same time into one universal history. Students of Bartolus, such as the famous "Spanish Bartolus," Baldus de Ubaldis (c. 1319–1400), continued the Bartolian theoretical and methodological approach, which remained dominant in the *quattrocento* and beyond.[28] In Spain and Portugal, Bartolus's professional stature was such that the Catholic Monarchs decreed that, in cases where there were divergent opinions, the *opino Bartolo* should receive priority.[29]

Many *quattrocento* humanists, such as Valla, denounced the Bartolian traditional scholastic approach to law although, during the early growth of humanism, there was fundamental affinity in the value both jurists and humanists placed on public service.[30] Valla and other fifteenth-century humanists (and later in the sixteenth century those who espoused the *mos gallicus* (the French method) of teaching Roman law) insisted that the proper object of legal study was the history and development of "the laws and customs of one's own country" and not the ancient Roman Code, which was "an artifact of an alien culture."[31] That is, for them, law was specific to a given society, changed over time, and was not universal. Other disparagers of *quattrocento* jurisprudence included the famous humanist grammarian, Antonio de Nebrija (1441–1522), who omitted the legal connotations of the word *letrados* in his Castilian-Latin dictionary and defined the term simply as "learned men"![32]

In theology, the return to the past also broke new ground in the West. In addition to the taken-for-granted authority of scripture and tradition, scholastic theology went beyond the patristic theology of the Roman Empire to draw on Aristotelianism and Platonism from the legacy of antiquity. As such, Augustinian pessimism about the "City of Man" eroded with the recognition of the value of nature and the world as components in the "City of God." Additionally, given the Christian tenet that "faith seeks understanding" (*fides quaerens intellectum*), rational knowledge received deliberate emphasis as theologians sought to develop the "science of theology" and an accompanying conceptual synthesis during this "Age of the *Summae*" that explicated doctrine, soteriology, eschatology, and ecclesiology (which constituted canon law).

For example, the theological writings of Thomas Aquinas (1225–1274), philosopher and theologian in the scholastic tradition, constituted a dialogical exegesis of the whole of theology much more comprehensive than the pre-scholastic compilation of biblical texts and patristic passages in the *Libro de Sentencias* of Peter Lombard (1095–1160).[33] Aquinas's most extensive works, the *Summa Theologiae*, the *Summa contra Gentiles*, and the *Scriptum super Sententias*, synthesized the known Christian tradition (scripture, patristics, and canon law) with ancient sacred and secular thinkers (including Aristotle, and the famous Jewish and Muslim commentators, Moses Maimonides and Ibn Rushd Averroës). Aquinas's *Summa Theologica* was written at a critical juncture of Western thought with the rediscovery of Aristotle and the reopening of the question about the relationship between faith and reason. His *Summa Theologica* was gradually used because of its comprehensive doctrinal basis, its usefulness for preaching to Jews and Muslims, and its applicability in confronting new societal issues, including those in the Indies.[34]

While during the Middle Ages, the hegemony of orthodox theology was challenged by groups such as the Albigensians who questioned the theological sources of certain propositions that Christendom regarded as axiomatic, humanism did not threaten the foundation of the theological edifice. Indeed, theologian Paul Cortese (1475–1520) encouraged the use of humanist learning in philosophical and theological work.[35] Petrarch appreciated how the Church Fathers had reconciled classical and Christian philosophies about human life and morals.[36] Humanists—especially Valla—also aided biblical scholarship by contributing the philological method for assessing the reliability of the translations of the Vulgate Bible when compared with earlier Greek and Hebrew texts; the philological method was also used in the compilation of the Polyglot Bible at Spain's University of Alcalá.[37]

Other new intellectual endeavors were pursued during the Renaissance that also implicitly challenged the hegemony of the scholastic method and of certain medieval theological tenets. Natural philosophy emerged as a heterogeneous area of study on various aspects of nature and how nature could be usefully transformed in the interests of humankind.[38] Fifteenth-century scholarship ranged from studies of the heavens (including the cosmology of Marsilio Ficino) and studies of the earth (including agriculture, navigation, botany, biology, and mining), in addition to studies of the human body (such as physiology and medicine). Scientific ideas, garnered from new empirical methods, cast doubt on traditional models.[39] For example, the heliocentric discoveries of Nicolaus Copernicus (1473–1543) challenged the Ptolemaic system of geocentrism.[40] Dissident religious beliefs, such as those of John Wyclif (c. 1320–1384) and John Hus (1372–1415), questioned certain interpretations of traditional Christendom, and they contributed to the eventual emergence of the reformers and their emphasis on a return to the Bible and the Church Fathers.

Finally, in the spheres of learning, the *studia humanitatis* of *quattrocento* humanism became "the middle ground" between—and a preparation for—the theoretical disciplines (e.g. philosophy, theology) and practical disciplines (e.g. law, medicine) of learning.[41] In this educational program, which consisted of grammar, rhetoric, poetry, history, and moral philosophy, rhetoric was central. For humanists, the ability to use spoken and written languages—and use it well—resulted in eloquence, which when paired with wisdom both developed the human person and maintained civilization.[42] Rhetoric was also closely related to other subjects of study. For example, the study of grammar taught how to create meaningful speech and use appropriate language—including how to learn proper Latin through imitation of classical authors. There were three principal ancient sources for *studia humanitatis* and particularly for the cultivation of rhetoric. Marcus Tullius Cicero (106–43 BCE), allegedly the greatest orator and politician in ancient Rome, exemplified that the "ideal orator" must also master both philosophy and jurisprudence. Marcus Fabius

Quintilianus (c. 35–100 CE), rhetorician and literary critic of ancient *Hispania*, developed a model curriculum for a classical educational program and also embodied Cicero's ideal of the broadly educated, literary, and philosophical orator, as well as developed a model curriculum for a classical educational program. Aristotle, the Greek philosopher and student of Plato, developed the foundational concept of rhetoric, namely, that "evidence and proof are the definitive ingredients in all rhetorical discourse," and that "purely persuasive or politically expedient discourses" were "only tenuously connected to the notion of truth."[43]

As teachers in general schools and universities or as writers of letters and official documents as well as of poems and historical works, humanists produced a vast array of literary works in their study, interpretation, and imitation of writers from ancient antiquity. For example, their return to classical writings recovered the literary genres of ancient epic poems such as Homer's *Iliad* and *Odyssey* from Greece, and Virgil's *Aeneid* from Rome, in addition to ancient templates of letters and prose compositions, of orations and dialogues such as those of Aristotle whose literary style Cicero described as "a river of gold." These kinds of literary and rhetorical accomplishments heralded the coming dawn of the golden age of literature.[44]

The dissemination of philosophical, legal, theological, historical, literary, and oratorical developments catapulted around 1440 with the invention of moveable type in the West—the single greatest technological achievement of the period.[45] However, the widespread use of printing had consequences for the humanists' lofty goal of returning to the ancient form of discourse: classical Latin. Although medieval Latin was commonly used in intellectual discourse and spoken in the universities, humanists decried this medieval barbarization of the classical language of the ancient texts. Further impeding their efforts to resurrect classical Latin as the tongue of the citizenry was the spread of the vernacular.[46] The proliferation of printed materials in the vernacular fed an increasingly literate population and prompted an ever-increasing "democratization" of knowledge.[47] Given that scholastic literature since the Middle Ages was directed toward specialists and that Renaissance humanist literature demanded some level of cultural sophistication, vernacular literature served both to meet the needs of the common populace and to satiate the appetites of the intellectually curious who might not have had specialized scholastic and humanistic training.[48]

For example, the very important early account in 1501 of the so-called *De orbe novo* by the Milanese humanist and tutor at the Castilian court, Peter Martyr (1457–1526), was written in Latin and consequently less accessible to a wide audience, whereas Las Casas's *Brevísima relación* was written in the vernacular—albeit forty-one years later, and became, as Bartosik-Vélez concluded, "a page-turning international bestseller."[49]

The Renaissance promotion of glorious ancient models for personal and societal formation in its pursuit of the good also spawned diverse artistic developments, for example, in painting, sculpture, and architecture. One of the distinguishing features of Renaissance artistic expression was the development of the linear perspective. In painting and sculpture, this perspective achieved the effect of realistic space and lifelike dimensions; in architecture, the perspective gave depth to flat surfaces through, for example, the vaulted windows, ornate façades, arches, and domes of its constructions. With the return to classical styles, ancient media, and material culture of Greco-Roman civilizations, the period produced—for example, in Italy—great painters such as Raphael (1483–1520) and Michelangelo (1483–1546), great sculptors such as Niccolò Donatello (c. 1386–1466) and Andrea del Verrocchio (1436–1488), and great architects such as Leon Battista Alberti (1404–1472) and Filippo Brunelleschi (1377–1446). In their creations, Renaissance artists and builders also sought to improve upon the artistic expressions of classical antiquity.[50]

Continuity and Change in Fifteenth-Century Spain

During this era of rebirth, Spain experienced little rupture with its medieval intellectual and cultural past—perhaps because of its situation "in many senses on the periphery of the continent of Europe."[51] In continuity with its intellectual past (due in part to the contrails of the long history of Christendom), Spain retained scholasticism—albeit weakly.[52] Eventually, under the influence of Pierre Crockaert (c. 1465–1514), the Thomistic variant of scholasticism was revived, which would contribute substantially to philosophical-juridical-theological debates about the "discovered" Indigenous peoples and their lands.[53]

In jurisprudence, the Iberian peninsula—beginning with *Castilla y León*—had a history of seeking to establish its own *ius commune*, first with the Visigoth-law-based *Fuero Juzgo* (1241) of Fernando III, then the *Siete Partidas* (1251–1265) of Alfonso X (1221–1284), followed by the *Ordenamiento de Alcalá* (1348, 1351) of Alfonso XI, and the *Ordenanzas Real de Castilla* (1485) of Isabel and Ferdinand.[54] The general legislative text of the *Siete Partidas* included passages from ancient philosophy and medieval theology in addition to extracts from Roman and canon laws. The *Ordenamiento* established the order of precedence for applying existing legislation: first, the *Ordenamiento* or royal law, and then proven customary or municipal law, with the *Siete Partidas* as a last resort.[55] However, revisionist historiography shows that this hierarchy of *ius proprium* did not replace the *ius commune*. During the *quattrocento* as Spain became an increasingly litigious society, copies of the *Corpus Iuris Civilis* and of the canon law collections increased "by the tens of thousands"; student bodies expanded in the universities' faculties of law; academicians proliferated *commentaria* and other discourses on *ius commune*, and graduates in jurisprudence used *ius commune* as an indispensable tool in their legal practices.[56] Research on *consilia*—for example, the records of courtroom procedures—gives evidence of a "massive and constant use" of *ius commune* because "only in the *ius commune* must one, and therefore could one, find the arguments … needed for trials."[57] In the last quarter of the *quattrocento*, these reflections on "ancient sources" (as humanists did) also became the bases of interpretations that were sought by the Catholic Monarchs from the *letrados*—from the civil jurists, canonists, and theologians alike. However, in the sixteenth century, the validity and role of the *ius commune* would be reappraised with the critiques of juridical humanism, of the Spanish School, and of the natural law theories of philosophy, theology, and jurisprudence.[58]

In the realm of rhetoric, Spain developed "a tolerably fair herd of humanist rhetoricians," beginning at the end of the *quattrocento* with Nebrija and flourishing in the sixteenth century.[59] Spain's intellectual and cultural concern for the eloquence of speech and writing in addition to the pursuit of "the true" and "the good" was present in the fields of politics and law, and also in the activities of preaching and converting.

For the most part, humanism in Spain by the beginning of the 1400s relied heavily on foreign influences and expertise, in addition to Spanish ambassadors, prelates, scholars, public officials, and merchants who brought back and disseminated Renaissance ideas.[60] Yet, humanism had its own adherents and innovators in the Iberian peninsula.[61] For example, just as intellectually inclined scholar-writers were regulars in the Castilian court of Alfonso X, *El Sabio*, so too Juan II of Castile (1406–1454) surrounded himself with a proto-Renaissance literary court, which included Jews and Jewish converts, in his attempt to embrace the movement through a profound interest in literature.[62] His daughter, Isabel of Castile, who became the only sovereign queen with her own authority in all of fifteenth-century Europe, was also both a beneficiary and a patron of Renaissance erudition. Perhaps influenced by important humanist-trained women writers, she insisted that her court be a place of learning.[63] Isabel also insisted on educating her four daughters—Isabel, Juana, María, and Catalina—in languages, poetry, music, dance, literature, Latin, Greek, philosophy, canon law, and the sciences (Figure 2.2).[64]

This inland port on the Guadalquivir River in Bartolomé de Las Casas's birthplace of Seville became the gateway to the West Indies. Alonso Sánchez Coello. Vista de Sevilla, late 16th century.

Las Casas also received a solid early education in Seville from 1490 or 1492 to 1498 at the cathedral school of San Miguel, which had been established during the reign of Alfonso X.[65] During these years of study at San Miguel, Bartolomé benefited from the vigilant tutoring of a distant

Figure 2.2 Alonso Sánchez Coello. Vista de Sevilla, late sixteenth century.
Source: Wikipedia.

relative, cathedral Prebendary Luis de Peñalosa.[66] San Miguel's curriculum followed the medieval tradition of the *trivium* (grammar, rhetoric, and logic) and the *quadrivium* (arithmetic, astronomy, geometry, and music), as well as taught logic and philosophy.[67] These liberal arts areas of study were considered foundational for any future specialization in theology or law, and for future employment in Crown and/or ecclesial administration. In addition, the curriculum of cathedral schools included nonprofessional study of both canon law and theology because so many of their students were preparing to become *curas* (priests).[68] San Miguel, as one of the most accomplished cathedral schools in Spain, would have offered such studies in canon law and theology, and these would have been part of Las Casas's program of learning.[69]

The imprint of Renaissance humanism at San Miguel was also evident. First, Spain's most famous humanist, Nebrija, lectured at San Miguel from 1488 to 1491.[70] Las Casas would have been influenced by humanism because, as José Alcina Franch contended, Nebrija taught Las Casas.[71] Second, research on library holdings of cathedral schools from the eleventh to the fifteenth century demonstrates that the humanist ethical dimension of *studia humanitatis* learning was an integral part of *trivium* studies in the *quattrocento*.[72] In the first *trivium* subject, *gramática*, students not only learned to write, speak, memorize, and copy examples of good Renaissance Latin but also studied what the Latin texts and their commentaries taught about moral behavior and civic virtue. Data also show that Latin grammar textbooks used in Castilian cathedral schools by the late fifteenth century included those of humanist Guarino da Verona (1374–1460), who showed the continuity of humanist Latin with elementary Latin, and of Nebrija whose 1481 *Introductione latinae* was followed by his 1492 Latin-Spanish dictionary and his 1494 Spanish-Latin dictionary.[73] In the second *trivium* subject, *retórica*, studies extended beyond the techniques of writing and speaking in the arts of letter-writing (*ars dictaminis* and *epistolar*), of poetic compositions (*ars poetriae*), and of forensic speech and preaching (*ars arengandi* and *praedicandi*) to learning how to evaluate works from the perspective of moral philosophy. Toward this end and in addition to the basic texts—Cicero's *De inventione* and *De oratore*, Aristotle's *Rhetoricorum*, and Quintilian's *Institutio oratoria*, and works by Catón, Seneca, Virgil, and Josephus—students studied Petrarch's rhetoric and other treatises on the education of princes in addition to the exemplary lives of the saints. In the third *trivium* subject, *lógica*, which focused on Aristotle and the commentaries by Boethius, study shifted emphasis away from the medieval effort of building syllogistic edifices of logic to the Renaissance project of applying reason to historical experience, and also away from the separation of *trivium* subjects to the integration of *gramática* and *retórica* with *ars histórica* and its innovative philological and incipient empirical method. Las Casas's broad exposure to and adroit learning from the program of studies—especially in the *trivium*—is demonstrated in the extensive bibliographies accompanying his writings, wherein he refers, among many others, to Aristotle, Cicero, Quintilian, Catón, Virgil, Boethius, Isidore of Seville, and Petrarch.[74]

The *Brevisíma relación* also reflected Las Casas's early studies. In this *Very Brief Account*, he used Aristotle's poetic form of writing when narrating the conquests insofar as he described general principles or universal aspects rather than particular events of that history and, in accord with ancient historiography, his narrative included fictitious speeches.[75] In this treatise, he also subscribed to Josephus's reasons for writing history; this first-century Jew witnessed and recorded the fall of Jerusalem in 70 CE in order to articulate the truth about the misunderstood Jewish nation, just as Las Casas articulated the truth about the derided and devastated Indigenous peoples and lands.[76] In this, Las Casas went beyond humanists' predominant emphasis on "the good," to which he was exposed during his cathedral school days, to emphasize what he regarded as "the true," an intellectual approach surely honed by his later Thomistic scholastic studies.

Spain's continuity with the past was also evident in the retention of certain artistic traditions.[77] The medieval Spanish ballad survived predominantly through oral tradition, and its courtly aspects served as a forerunner to the romances of chivalry—a literary genre from medieval times that was disseminated by the advent of printing in the 1470s and that later inspired Hernando Cortés's men at Tenochtitlan in the 1520s.[78] Spanish sculpture, which was predominantly the work of foreigners or of Spanish sculptors trained in foreign lands (such as Castilian Sebastián de Almonacid (1460–1526)), developed an opulent decorative Isabelline style rich in composition and in abundant detail. In addition, artistic expression in Renaissance Spain, and especially in the south, reflected the centuries of Moorish influence.[79] Gothic architecture, which was asymmetrical and complex as compared to highly symmetrical and carefully proportioned Renaissance architecture, dominated structural designs, for example, of the cathedrals in Toledo, Burgos, León, and Seville, and continued as an art form in Spain until the reign of Ferdinand of Aragon and Isabel of Castile.[80]

Las Casas's youth was steeped in the Gothic architectural tradition, expressed particularly in the grand edifices of the exceptionally enormous cathedral—the location of his early education in his natal Seville, as well as of the highly venerated University of Salamanca—the place where in 1498 he most likely began and subsequently completed his studies for the secular priesthood. Under construction for most of the fifteenth century and also during Las Casas's youth, Seville's *Catedral de Santa María de la Sede* with its five spectacular Gothic naves would supplant the Hagia Sophia to become the largest cathedral in the world.[81] The University of Salamanca was also famous for its unique plateresque architectural style and, during the renovations in the early 1400s, for its mixture of this flamboyant Gothic style with Renaissance and *Mudéjar* elements.[82] These two edifices would stand as monumental structural symbols of the young Las Casas's future spiritual and intellectual growth. Significantly, Las Casas's apparent *alma mater* rose to academic prominence during the fifteenth and sixteenth centuries as a result of the encounter with the Indies and the growth of the Spanish empire. Cortés could also claim this most prestigious university as his *alma mater* insofar as he pursued studies for two years seemingly in Latin at Salamanca in preparation for a career in law before dropping out; in contrast, Las Casas apparently completed his program of studies at Salamanca and, throughout his life, maintained dialogue with Salamancan theologians and jurists.[83]

The culture of Castile was also distinctive by its promotion of the vernacular. In the thirteenth century, Alfonso X first gave primacy to the vernacular by his decree that Castilian was the official language of his realm, rather than any of the regional dialects of, for example, Catalonia, Aragon, Galicia, Navarra, and Andalusía.[84] By the end of the fifteenth century, Castilian had progressed from simply being a Latin-derived dialect to becoming the legal and administrative language of the most powerful kingdom of Iberia. In 1492, Nebrija published his *Gramática de la lengua Castellana* in the same "Old Castile" variant of the Castilian language. With this, the grammarian helped catalyze cultural change by reducing the multiplicity of oral traditions of Castile into a standardized mother-tongue taught in schools.[85] Las Casas, who as an Andalusian spoke the regional Castilian variant with its distinctive accent, was both fluent and proficient in the dominant peninsular language of *Castellano*—a language that he had heard and spoken from birth and formally studied in his early years.[86]

Nebrija's Spanish grammar also served a political function: the text, which was published in the same year as Spain's reconquest of the last of Muslim-controlled Iberian lands, was based on the grammarian's conviction that "language is the instrument of empire."[87] For Nebrija, the codification of a kingdom's language constituted a necessary step in the development of any great power because, in addition to teaching vocabulary and syntax, grammar imposed a culture upon the kingdom's peoples.[88] This first grammar of *Castellano* (that was also the first grammar of any modern European language) gave Spaniards linguistic tools to better serve as civil and ecclesial functionaries. Indeed, at the close of the *quattrocento*, Nebrija's philological achievement helped to propel Spain to the forefront of Western European culture and, in the territory of Spain, to solidify the hegemony and the transfer of Castilian culture—the *translatio studii* that accompanied the fifteenth-century transfer of political power—the *translatio imperii*—of the Catholic Monarchs.[89] That is, in addition to its cultural achievements, Spain attained renown under Isabel and Ferdinand because of the significant social, economic, political, and religious accomplishments realized by the 1474 union of the Crowns of Castile and Aragon—of the kingdoms of Castilla, Toledo, León, Sevilla, Córdoba, Jaén, Murcia, and Galicia, the principality of Asturias and the lordship of Vizcaya, with the Levantine kingdoms of Aragon, Catalonia, and Valencia.[90]

Demographic and Economic Developments in Spain

Spain's diverse intellectual and cultural contours and its patterns of socio-economic and politico-religious developments during the reign of the Catholic Monarchs were shaped in part by its initial population pluralism and its ongoing population fluctuations. The Iberian demography in the fifteenth century was distinctive in the historical character of its population and in its sparse population density.

The historical character of Spain's population was altered over time by multiple invasions. Spain's most significant early autochthonous population, the Celtic-Iberian populace, endured a series of demographic influxes: first, the sparse and episodic entrances of the Phoenicians and Greeks between 500 and 300 BCE; then, in 218 BCE, the substantive and sustained presence of the Romans lasted for over six hundred years—during which time Jews came to Iberia, and then, in 409 CE, the brief and transitory influx of the Germanic Suevi and Vandals, together with the Sarmatian Alans, who were quickly displaced by the Visigoths in 410. While these remote waves of invaders and colonizers shaped the initial demographic character of the peninsula's population, the initiation in

711 CE of the decisive Muslim conquest of three-quarters of the Iberian peninsula radically changed the population in ways previously unseen.[91] The Moors's incursion into and occupation of the Iberian peninsula was the most consequential for the continuing tripartite social pluralism of the Spanish population, as well as the most proximate to the eve of the encounter.

Throughout the nearly eight hundred years of oscillation between conflict and peace, as well as territorial expansion and contraction from 711 to 1492, Spain's Christians gradually reconquered its former territory from the Moors. During this period, Jews, Muslims, and Christians—all proto-Spaniards—developed a complex *convivencia*—albeit with the eventual erection of separate quarters in urban centers for these distinctive population cohorts.[92] Their coexistence and interaction created a distinctive hybridization of culture, a unique mixture of ethnicities, and a calibrated toleration of religious minorities that reached its apogee in the thirteenth century under Alfonso X. However, rather than being a solid blissful marriage, this *convivencia* increasingly became a fluid arrangement of coexistence punctuated by periodic bouts of intolerance and persecution.[93] A fifteenth-century notorious nadir of prejudice occurred with the anti-Semitic Toledo riots of 1449 and provoked the first decree of *limpieza de sangre*, which prohibited *conversos* of Jewish ancestry from holding municipal offices in Toledo.[94] While the Catholic Monarchs were initially tolerant of religious minorities, relations deteriorated among Old Christians, New Christians (namely, *Marranos* or converted Jews, and *Moriscos* or converted Muslims/Moors), and the unconverted Jews and Muslims. Ironically, many prominent Spaniards were of Jewish ancestry, such as Ferdinand of Aragon, Hernando de Talavera, and, presumably, Las Casas.[95] The Castilian Inquisition, established in 1478, would contribute to the draconian expulsion of non-Christians—of Jews in 1492 and of Moors in 1502. These events initially reduced Spain's population and then changed its character as foreign immigrants—Flemings, Germans, Genoese—many from regions influenced by Spanish political interests, subsequently arrived from diverse parts of the Habsburg realms to assume many of the positions vacated with the expulsions.[96]

Spain's sparse population density initially improved as Christian settlers, such as the Asturian and Cantabrian mountaineers of old Hispanic ancestry, repopulated territories that were gradually recaptured from the Moors.[97] Yet, demographic recovery was selective.[98] For example, most of this population gravitated to Castile where servile labor had been abolished in the twelfth century—unlike in Valencia where Muslims remained on the land as servile laborers.[99] According to revisionist historiography, universal population recovery did not take place even after the Black Death (1347–1350) and the War of the Two Pedros (1356–1375)—generally regarded as part of the Hundred Years War (1337–1453).[100] Data from 1300 and 1480 show that, within this almost two-century period, the population in Aragon and Valencia increased modestly, in Castile-León not at all, and in Catalonia, the population decreased by almost fifty percent.[101] Even so, by the late fifteenth century, eighty percent of the population and two-thirds of the territory of the Iberian peninsula belonged to the Crown of Castile.[102] Within Castile, the demographic density varied in accord with different population movements. For example, many villages were abandoned as peasants moved from the countryside to urban areas—just as later many from the metropolitan areas would migrate to the Spanish colonies developed in the Indies.[103]

Such population movements and the resultant variegated population density were consequential for the kinds of economic development and underdevelopment that were occurring in Spain on the eve of the "discovery." As in other parts of Europe, Spain's generally attenuated population had more resources to exploit for economic benefit. Different population cohorts generated different kinds of development.

Peasant farmers had greater access to fertile lands for cultivating crops, and consequently more opportunity for raising livestock and frequent fallowing after ever-increasing harvests.[104] In Castile's predominantly pastoral economy, many peasants migrated cyclically with their flocks and herds, while others lived mainly a sedentary life, such as the unassuming *Mudéjar* peasants who tilled and irrigated the soil on Andalusian estates of Castilian noblemen.[105] Others, such as those in the north, owned or rented land.[106] Still, others migrated to urban centers as seasonal or day workers, or toiled in rural areas from sun-up to sun-down on collective agrarian enterprises, made possible in part by the gradual demise of the semi-feudal seignorial regimes of "*protección y pan*" in exchange for "labor and loyalty."[107] Changes in these medieval systems of communal agrarian ownership included public and village ownership of *ejidos* (communal property), the expedient revival of *hermandades* (brotherhoods), and the steady adaptation of military orders to new conditions and to secular economic attitudes.[108] For example, Castile's three major military orders—Santiago, Calatrava, and Alcántara—changed "from [military] conquest to [territorial] defense, from a monastic [spirituality] to a secular ethos, from a predatory war economy to one based on the encomienda system."[109] Later, with repartimientos of Indigenous laborers in both Hispaniola and Cuba, Las Casas would oversee a "New World" adaptation of the Spanish encomienda and the pre-Contact tribute systems; in New Spain, the *ejido* would combine with pre-Contact forms of economic organization.[110]

The economic basis of the few large urban centers in late fifteenth-century Castile and the towns and villages reflected the surrounding countryside and the consequent diversity of occupations. For example, Castile's largest city, Seville, had a growing population of thirty-one thousand—not counting foreigners, slaves, criminals, and the destitute. It was situated on the banks of the river Guadalquivir, which was navigable for oceangoing ships as far as Seville. Urban population cohorts of this important mercantile center, which would acquire monopoly of Atlantic trade after 1492, ranged from well-to-do merchants, bankers, and navigators to working-class seafarers and builders, metal and leather tradesmen, weavers and other artisans, local shopkeepers and pub-tenders, domestic servants and royal or municipal employees, as well as agricultural and livestock laborers.[111] In this thriving *quattrocento* urban landscape, Las Casas's merchant-father and baker-mother earned a livelihood. The young Las Casas worked in both trades, learning mercantile and artisan skills firsthand, as well as about nautical life from his experiences in this bustling seaport.[112]

Economic strength in the Crown of Aragon coalesced during the early *quattrocento* in its coastal cities, and particularly in the dominant urban centers of Barcelona—the capital of Catalonia, and Valencia—an urban jewel. However, Barcelona's population decreased as its laborers and professionals moved south, and its economic power declined because hoped-for Mediterranean markets of cloth and spice did not materialize. Valencia remained a vibrant mercantile center in active relationship with its agricultural hinterland. Typical of port conurbations, its occupations included mariners and builders, tradesmen and artisans, domestic and public employees.[113]

Of particular note in the urban populations of Spain were the growing entrepreneurial classes who benefited from technological and commercial skills originating during the High Middle Ages. By the mid-*quattrocento*, new techniques for mining and metallurgy had been developed; later, these skills would also be utilized in and combined with existing silver mining techniques in the Indies.[114] Such technological and commercial skills contributed to manufacturing and trade in Castile and Aragon.

Castile's manufacturing industries were silk production in the south, cloth weaving in the center, and iron extraction in the north. However, capital and skilled-labor shortages, geographic distances, and inadequate communication infrastructures diminished these industries' competitive edge and militated against their economic progress.[115] Nevertheless, Isabel encouraged textile industries and artisanships for local markets and for the production of luxury goods. She significantly expanded the medieval merino wool trade of Castile by promoting sheep-raising as the most important sector of Castile's rural economy.[116] In addition, by Castile's promotion of shipbuilding, its lively internal trade extended externally to Africa and Central Europe.

Aragon's manufacturing industries included glass, leather, and metal wares in addition to silk, wool, and other textile production. The region's mercantile economy was intermeshed through networks of "settlement cores" or villages and, particularly in Catalonia, of merchant colonies.[117] In this manner, the Crown of Aragon focused on promoting the merchant class—albeit unsuccessfully—rather than the peasantry, as in

Castile. Additionally, Ferdinand inaugurated agrarian development in Catalonia after the pirating of Catalan ships further impaired Aragon's maritime-based economy, whereas Castile considered agriculture too labor-intensive as compared with herding. In general, the economies of the principal kingdoms of Aragon concentrated on fleet expansion, textile export, and trade development with the Mediterranean rather than with Africa and Central Europe. In the Crowns of both Castile and Aragon, navigation and trade were regulated by a *Consulado*, which consisted of a merchant guild and a mercantile court.[118] This "House of Trade," along with adaptations from the Portuguese *Casa de Guiné, Mina e Índia*, would provide the blueprint for the future *Casa de la Contratación de las Indias*, which would govern all commercial, scientific, and legal aspects of trade with the Indies, and with which Las Casas would have many dealings in his ten crossings of the *mar Océano* during the course of his periods of residence in the Indies from 1502 to 1547.[119]

For all intents and purposes, the Crowns of Castile and of Aragon had different economic systems. The only hint of similarity in their economic systems was in two monetary aspects. First, the principal coins of Valencia, Catalonia, and Castile were of equal worth; the Spanish colonial system in the Indies would also adopt the Castilian *maravedí* as its principal coin.[120] Second, the payment of the tribute—of a head tax usually paid in cash by wealthy Jews or in labor by poorer Muslims—was economically significant in both Castile and Aragon; this system of tributes in fungible commodities and in obligatory labor was also adapted in Spain's colonial system by Columbus and other early governors.[121]

Political Power of Isabel and Ferdinand

While there was little economic unification between Aragon and Castile, much consolidation did take place in Spain's political and religious spheres under the reign of Isabel and Ferdinand (Figure 2.3). The political unification of the Crowns of Castile and Aragon began on October 19, 1469, with the marriage of Isabel, heiress of Castile, and Ferdinand, King of Sicily and heir to the throne of Aragon.[122] During the public sacred ceremony in which Padre Pedro López de Alcalá gave the nuptial blessings, the future Catholic Monarchs united in religious bond and political ambition.[123] Both approval and disapproval surrounded this marital union of two branches of the Trastámaran dynasty. Ferdinand's father, John II of Aragon (1458–1479), approved, as did Castile's papal legate, the Aragonese at the Castilian court headed by the Archbishop of Toledo, and Jewish *letrados*. Isabel's half-brother, Henry IV of Castile (1454–1474), disapproved, as did nobles of high rank, including *grandees*, and Louis XI of France.[124] The source of approval was the anticipated strengthening of the Castilian throne by this union with the heir of the Aragon throne. The source of the disapproval centered on concerns

Figure 2.3 Ferdinand and Isabella with their subjects, Unknown author.
Source: Wikipedia.

about potential loss of power by Castilian nobles and about the union's threat to French power.

After Isabel and Ferndinand's marriage, ten years of struggle ensued about who was the rightful heir to the Castilian throne: Juana la Beltraneja, the presumed daughter of Henry IV, or Isabel, Henry's half-sister. When King Henry died in 1474, Isabel became the Queen of Castile. Apparently—and interestingly, Isabel's ascension to the throne even troubled Ferdinand, perhaps because a fifth-century Salic law in effect in his father's kingdom prohibited women from wielding direct rule. According to Castilian law, though, a woman had the right to become the ruling monarch.[125] Not only did Isabel—a Renaissance woman—make her own decision in January of 1469 to marry Ferdinand rather than one of the other two proposed candidates, but she also refused to renegotiate the prenuptial agreement, which her future husband signed on March 5, 1469, and which Ferdinand and his advisors later sought unsuccessfully to change.[126] The strength and clarity of resolve, which typified Isabel's decisions, would be recognized by Las Casas in his repeated recourse to her firm and clear instructions about the treatment and conversion of the inhabitants of the Indies.[127]

In time, the intrepid Isabel and her supporters—with the help of Ferdinand's resources—did win the War of Castilian Succession that broke out in 1475 and ended with the 1479 defeat of the Portuguese military invasion that had supported the succession of Henry's presumed daughter Juana. However, Isabel's initial victories over her rivals did not insure the consolidation of the Crown of Castile or the solidification of its union with Aragon.[128] The continuing divisiveness reflected the earlier factors and the deeper factions that characterized the first seventy-five years of fifteenth-century Spain, especially under the largely ineffectual rule of Henry IV, during which time political infighting and corruption had weakened the Castilian monarchy.[129] Moreover, shifting political alliances, conspiracies, and betrayals had generated waves of rebellion and warfare in the constituent (and often petty) kingdoms of Castile and Aragon. Additionally, the strong mutual antipathy of Castilians and Aragonese had deep roots; for example, Aragon invaded Castile in 1429, and Castile forcefully removed the Aragonese branch of the Trastáraman dynasty in 1432.[130] These complex historical realities required rectification to congeal and strengthen the precarious realities of the political landscape.[131] Isabel and Ferdinand's neutralization and control of these factors and factions during their reign would contribute significantly to the birth of modern Spain.[132]

Isabel and Ferdinand faced the challenge of redressing their heritage of weakened monarchical rule, which included the degree of their royal power in relation to the different ruling classes. According to a medieval principle that Las Casas also espoused in his assessment of the sovereign rule of the Spanish monarch over Indigenous peoples, the rule of a monarch required the consent of the governed. In effect, though, the resultant "representative assemblies were not very representative."[133] During the early *quattrocento*, this medieval tradition was "forcefully reasserted" within the Crown of Aragon—albeit to the monarch's detriment; however, in the Crown of Castile, the resolution of the issue of royal power and the crafting of new monarchical rule was still in process.[134] In the Crown of Aragon, the monarchy was checked by the power of the representative *Cortes* in each of its component kingdoms and by the muscle of its ruling classes: the high nobility and the strong guilds—merchant and town. In the Crown of Castile, unlike Aragon, the *Cortes* did not have legislating power nor did the members meet regularly; however, Castile's independent aristocracy and its mosaic of competing jurisdictions did challenge monarchical power.[135]

Consequently, in the 1480 *Cortes de Toledo*, Isabel and Ferdinand increased royal power by a series of reforms that created a centralized collegiate hierarchy of political power for administrative and judicial functions. To this end—and to base royal prerogatives on ancient Justinian law rather than on local and feudal jurisdictional traditions, the new *Consejo Real y Supremo de Castilla* consisted primarily of university-trained *letrados*.[136] Nobles and clergy had representation on this council, but other strata of the ruling classes did not. For example, those excluded were *grandees*—whose titles of upper nobility conferred aristocratic dignity and royal privilege, and also the lesser (and often impoverished) nobility or *hidalgos*—whose aspirations to upward mobility were also the ambitions of many of the future conquistadores of the Indies. Others excluded were the military orders—whose masterships in the three great orders would be taken over by the monarch, and the *mesta*—whose powerful sheep-farming guild controlled the large north-south migrations to grazing lands.[137] The interests of these strata were addressed at the provincial level. Here, in adherence to the Castilian-Aragonese political system of regional self-governance, Isabel and Ferdinand created new legal tribunals to represent and safeguard royal interests; similarly, in local governments, they gave royal authority to *corregidores* who were mostly *letrados*.[138]

Other administrative strategies to balance power included the resolution of mixed jurisdictional conflicts between the Crown and the Church by lay judges.[139] In like manner, because the Council of Castile included the archbishops of Toledo and Santiago, this *Consejo Real* served as the Crown's nexus in matters of secular and ecclesiastical jurisdictions.[140] In addition, the continuous travel of their court throughout their realms enabled Isabel and Ferdinand to quell incipient revolts, to protect the rights of the common people, and to undercut any resistance from the nobility by judiciously and personally bestowing rewards and titles on them.[141] Indeed, according to Pérez Fernández, the presence of the peripatetic court in Seville in 1490 afforded the six-year-old Las Casas his first distant encounter with the Spanish monarchy—an initial glance that would be followed by a lifetime of face-to-face encounters and ongoing relationships with Spanish royalty.[142]

The centralized system of government of the Catholic Monarchs would also be adapted gradually in what was called the Indies. The initial colonial system consisted of administrative and judicial governorship over the encountered islands. The first governor, Francisco de Bobadilla, was appointed in 1499 to replace the beleaguered Columbus; in accord with Isabel's mandate, Bobadilla also brought back to the Indies in 1500 those surviving Indigenous persons whom the admiral had taken to Spain in 1493, 1496, 1498, and 1499. The second governor, Nicolás de Ovando, a commander-major turned tyrant-major of the Order of Alcántara, arrived in Hispaniola in 1502—on the same ship on which Las Casas sailed when he went to spend his first five years in the Indies, and on which Pedro de Las Casas, Bartolomé's father, returned to Hispaniola to spend the rest of his life there.[143] The third governor, Columbus's son Diego Colón, arrived in 1510—and would become a confidant of the young secular priest Las Casas, who returned to the Antilles in 1508.

The next institution for colonial administration was the *Casa de Contratación*, which House of Trade was erected in 1503, followed by the 1511 establishment of the *Audiencia de Santo Domingo* (high court) to oversee and adjudicate issues of colonial governance. In accord with Castilian law, these three institutions of royal authority in the Indies also came under the jurisdiction of the Council of Castile and were the specific charge of one of its members—Bishop Juan Rodríquez de Fonseca. In 1524, the Crown established a parallel institution in the Indies—the *Consejo Real y Supremo de las Indias*—to address all colonial administrative, judicial, and legislative matters, and with Fonseca in its membership.[144]

In the political philosophy underlying their administrative hierarchy, the Catholic Monarchs reflected the dominant Renaissance ideology of the era: "princely humanism."[145] Proliferated through *quattrocento* writings in the "mirror for princes" genre, this political thought continued Petrarch's 1373 recourse to ancient Roman discourses such as Cicero's about the art of princely rule.[146] In humanist advice books and other works of political thinkers that taught the prince how to govern virtuously and successfully, one of the tenets of princely humanism stipulated that the monarch, who was chosen by and responsible to God—acted as the steward of his people—ruled by the grace of God, and was expected to take advice from the wisest and most honest people of the realm.[147] In Castile, this was done through the *Consejo Real de Castilla* and, in Aragon, through the *Cortes* system—which institutions also helped mitigate tensions and contradictions between republican ideals of representative government and classical absolutist principles of centralized bureaucracy.[148] This *Consejo* and *Cortes* type of rule was also coupled with the medieval understanding of law-giving and justice-rendering as the primary function of the monarchy.[149] Later, in the *Brevísima relación*, Las Casas would also remind the monarch that he, as "the lover and cultivator of justice," made the 1542 New Laws "after many gatherings of persons of great authority, letters, and conscience … and also [after] debates and conferences … and finally with the agreement and consent of all others."[150]

The establishment of a well-ordered, peaceful, and "godly" government so desired by the Catholic Monarchs was also motivated by the developing national myth of *translatio imperii* (transfer of empire), which regarded Spain as "the legitimate heir to the Western empire."[151] The long-sought-after goal of a reunified Hispania—the Hispania of the Roman Empire—was made more possible by the consolidation of the medieval Christian kingdoms of Castile and Aragon that was initiated by the 1469 union of Isabel and Ferdinand.[152] The Catholic Monarchs yearning to return to the glorious Roman past of a reunified Hispania were poignantly epitomized in the symbolic religious-political architecture of the façade on the chapel of the Dominican Priory of Santo Tomas in Ávila.[153] The monarchs ordered that the structural design of the main exterior portal of the central chapel be conspicuously shaped as an "H" symbolizing "Hispania," and that the cloister's interior arches be opulently decorated with carvings of pomegranates (*granadas*). This architectural propaganda in the bold letter and the subtle fruit both heralded and celebrated the ongoing reconquest and the future reestablishment of a Christian enclave—both constituent components of the reunified Hispania of old. The full recovery and reestablishment of this historical vision of greater peninsular unity would be accomplished on the cusp of the fifteenth and sixteenth centuries: geopolitical reunification was definitively accomplished by the 1492 reconquest of Granada; after the expulsions of the last non-Christians in 1492 and 1502, Spain would be homogeneously (at least nominally) Catholic.[154] However, prior to that, Isabel and Ferdinand had a lot of housekeeping to do in the Church.

Religious Purview of the Catholic Monarchs

To transform Spain into a truly and solely Christian territory and a faithful and militant instrument of God's Will in the world, the Catholic Monarchs' religious zeal and political ambitions extended to three religion-related levels of purposive endeavor: the *ecclesia*, the *patria*, and the *orbis*. First, the powerful Spanish Church needed to be brought under royal control by judicious reforms; second, extensive and effective methods of conversion needed to be utilized to fulfill Spain's historic obligation to make Spain Catholic; and, third, Spain's messianic vision of Christianizing the world needed to be encouraged and pursued.

From 1475 onward, Isabel dedicated herself to Church reform. At issue was the credibility and moral leadership of the Church. Systemic corruption in the hierarchy resulted from the "Babylonian Captivity" of the Papacy in France (1305–1378), the consequent Great Schism (1378–1417), and the periodic reigns of anti-popes until 1450. Church leaders failed to provide adequate moral guidance in the face of warfare, disease, and religious divisiveness, which prompted many Renaissance humanists to seek desired ethical inspiration from the "better" times of the classical age. At the level of the episcopate and secular clergy, Isabel first enforced ecclesiastical discipline and improved clerical education; she tightened Crown control of the Church and strengthened it at the expense of regional, episcopal, papal, and the nobility's power.[155] For example, she promoted pious priests of humble origins rather than those of noble ancestry.[156]

In 1480 with the authorization of Pope Sixtus IV (1414–1484), Isabel established the Spanish Inquisition, which disciplinary measure against heretics and crypto-Jewish *conversos* (called *marranos*) purged Church membership and generated fratricidal conflicts, jealousy, and rivalry within the Jewish population.[157] Thirty-six years later, in his 1516 *Memorial de remedios*, the young cleric, Padre Las Casas, would "implore" the Crown to send the *Santa Inquisición* to the Indies because "heretics" (*morisco* and *marrano* emigrants) had gone there and might be contaminating the new Indigenous converts. Accordingly, the first tribunal was held in 1519 in Puerto Rico. These earlier informal tribunals were replaced in 1569 by a more formal bureaucratic inquisitorial office.[158]

Isabel also initiated the reform of religious orders at the urging and with the guidance of Hernando de Talavera (1428–1507), her Hieronymite confessor. Although long-standing internal "schisms" were already being addressed in some religious orders—such as the Dominicans, Augustinians, Mercedarians, and Franciscans—Isabel's promotion of the reform of religious orders as a specific royal policy extended to both monks and nuns, to contemplative and apostolic orders, to ordained and lay religious alike.[159] She focused on raising the moral and intellectual standards of the orders and "regularizing" their lifestyles, which included the prohibition of concubinage. Some religious resisted reform: for example, certain religious women successfully defended their historic rights to their communal estates and family patrimony (and resented the male agents of reform); some four hundred Andalusian friars fled to Africa with their wives and converted to Islam.[160] In 1491, with the authorization of Alexander VI (1431–1503), Isabel focused more on monastic reform, and, later, under the direction of the austere Francisco (later Cardinal) Jiménez de Cisneros, OFM (1436–1517), she reformed and reorganized the Franciscans. As part of her reform efforts, she also promoted humanist learning and new opportunities for preaching and evangelizing.[161]

In addition to these widespread reform measures, conversion efforts continued as, for example, in defeated Granada where the recently appointed *converso* archbishop, Talavera, utilized the same method of evangelization as Las Casas would advocate—that of convincing the intellect through cogent explanation and persuading the will through good example. Because Cisneros did not consider this rational and peaceful method very successful for convincing and attracting the Muslims to Christianity, he convinced the Crown to abandon Talavera's conversion policy and, beginning in 1499 with militant fervor, used force and bribes in Granada to conduct baptisms en masse and without adequate instruction.[162] According to canonical norms shaped by centuries of compulsory conversions of the Moors and Jews, these forced or induced baptisms were considered valid as long as the proper liturgical actions and words were used. Baptism in this manner was simply a perfunctory ritual, which was also later utilized by Cisneros's Franciscan millenarian-motivated confreres in the Indies, and had little to do with the intention of the baptized or with their understanding of the reality of the sacrament.[163] In effect, in these circumstances, baptism constituted a politicized religious action in Spain that symbolized the acceptance of Castilian political hegemony and served to promote the goal of Hispania as solidly Christian.[164]

As storm clouds of Protestantism gathered on the horizon of Catholicism at the end of the fifteenth century, a powerful messianic atmosphere continued to permeate the Spanish Church.[165] A strong sense of mission pervaded the thought world of Hispania: "God favored their cause …"[166] Continuing the tradition about messianic Spanish kings, Isidore of Seville (c. 560–636 CE), the last of the ancient Christian philosophers and the Latin Church Fathers, had supposedly predicted that at the end of time a "hidden" Spanish monarch would defeat the Muslims, conquer Jerusalem, and give the world and its kingdoms back to God. Gripped with a "messianic fervor," Ferdinand, the court, and Spanish Christians believed that they would indeed capture Jerusalem, convert the remaining Jews, and thereby bring Christianity to the whole world during these last days of humankind.[167] Drawing on ancient texts—including the extra-canonical Book of 4-Esdras—and the Church Fathers, Columbus mirrored this official messianic vision of conquering Jerusalem, as well as cherished the dream of finding a shorter westward route to the Indies.[168] His desire to recover the *santa casa* of Jerusalem as part of his "glimmering project of planetary struggle against Islam" found partial realization in the 1492 acquisition of one of the crown jewels of Islam: the great city of Granada.[169] His dream to reach Cathay by a westward route was for the purpose of converting the Great Khan, the "King of Kings" and Emperor of China, to Christianity and then securing this ruler's support in the "planetary struggle" to defeat Islam.[170] So intense was Columbus's desire to convert the known world to Christianity that he elicited a promise from Queen Isabel that she would allocate any wealth garnered from discovered lands to the worldwide crusade against Islam.[171]

Possession and Destruction of the Indies

Columbus's 1492 journey led to the "discovery" of a world that was not part of the then-known *orbis terrarum*—Europe, Asia, and Africa—although the admiral thought that he had encountered the gateway to what was generically referred to as "the Indies"—that is, to all lands east of the Indus River, those of the Himalayas and present-day Kashmir and Pakistan, and down to the Arabian Sea. As Columbus's son Fernando later explained, his father believed that he had encountered "the eastern part of India, beyond the Ganges, to which no geographer had set bounds on the east."[172] Accordingly, in a letter to the Catholic Monarchs in which Columbus announced his "discovery" and which he posted after anchoring near the Portuguese town of Cascais, the admiral wrote, "I have come from the Indies," and the Western Hemisphere henceforth became known as "*Las Indias.*"[173]

Columbus took juridical "possession" of the Indies in accord with instructions from the Catholic Monarchs to "acquire" any discovered lands—a directive based on medieval Castilian law and, in turn, on Justinian Roman and Visigoth law, which declared that discovering new lands bestowed the right to possess them.[174] The procedure for such acquisition in the Roman legal tradition involved both physical presence on the land, as well as declaration through ceremony and words of the intent to remain on the land.[175] Employing this civil judicial procedure, Columbus disembarked on an island and unfurled the royal banner, while a pair of captains held the two flags of the Green Cross—one with the letter "F" above a crown, the other with the letter "I" above the monarchical symbols.[176] Having no official formula or text and using Spanish vernacular speech, he "took possession in Your Royal Highnesses' name … by a royal crier."[177] He further contended that he did not have to perform this ritual of possession at every island, because given his "will … not to pass any island without taking possession … [by] taking one, one is able to say all [were taken]."[178]

In the "most appropriate" island sites, the admiral planted the cross of Christianity, which, historian Patricia Seed maintains, constituted a political message to other Europeans rather than a religious proclamation. Columbus followed the medieval legal tradition of having recourse to Christianity for authority to expand.[179] He then proceeded to "name" (in effect, to rename) "the very many islands" that were inhabited by "innumerable people" whom he proclaimed would be vassals of the Crown; he called them "Indians."[180] In effect, Columbus's juridical possession of the Indies was the moment that Castilian law began to function in the Indies.[181] By early 1493, the explorer had visited and expropriated various islands, and his flagship, the Santa María, had run aground. Columbus left thirty-nine men on Hispaniola seemingly "in possession of the village of Navidad" who would "suffice to subjugate the entire island," and sailed to Spain with a group of Taínos—whom he wished to school in "our speech."[182] Seven Taínos survived the voyage that lasted from January 2 to March 15.[183] Once in Spain, the seven were allegedly instructed in the faith and baptized in accord with ecclesial juridical procedure and orders from the Catholic Monarchs.[184]

Because Columbus displayed the Taínos in Spain's major urban centers, Las Casas first glimpsed the "Indians" at the age of nine when he, with "wonder and awe," watched the seven Indigenous persons being paraded through the streets of Seville during Holy Week.[185] Five years later, he had a face-to-face experience of Indigenous people when his father brought Juanico, a Taíno teenager, back to Spain to be his son's companion for apparently two years.[186]

Meanwhile in the Indies—and beginning in 1493 with Columbus's seizing of Indigenous persons to take to Spain—bellicose actions toward and hostile encounters with the Indigenous inhabitants became the norm. During Las Casas's first sojourn in the Indies (1502–1506), when he worked as a *doctrinero* (catechist) and assisted his father in provisioning the Spaniards, Bartolomé was blind to the atrocities taking place. During his second stay in Hispaniola and Cuba (1508–1515), Las Casas, now a secular cleric, underwent a change of heart and perspective, and set about "searching for the total remedy" for the Indigenous peoples who were "doomed to destruction."[187]

For his subsequent lifelong struggle for justice for Indigenous people, Las Casas arguably benefited from the Renaissance intellectual and cultural developments that distinctively shaped opportunity in his native land. His narrations drew *ad fontes* from Roman, Greek, and Judeo-Christian sources. His arguments, which applied universal legal principles from canon and civil jurisprudence, reflected the Bartolian juridical approach. His assessments combined ancient philosophy with medieval scholastic methods and teachings of Thomistic theology. His writings in Latin and in the vernacular were as florid and fluid as Salamantine plateresque architecture, and as sound and summoning as Sevillian Gothic cathedral art. His exposure to population pluralism in Spain's demographic history seemingly sensitized him to cultural diversity in the Indies. His awareness of Spain's economic emergence and expansion apparently shaped his initial commercial undertakings. His experience of the greater union of Church and Crown—of the ecclesial and the civil—likely contoured his intercessory role as cleric, friar, and bishop. In any case—whether narrating or writing, arguing or assessing, or whether by exposure, experience, or awareness, Las Casas employed a preeminently juridical approach in his battle for justice. For example, he denounced the *destruición de las Indias* by encomenderos, conquistadores, and corrupt crown officials on the basis of law.[188] He even reproached Columbus for what he considered illegal expropriation of Indigenous lands and his enslavement of its peoples. He charged that the admiral had sown the seeds of the destruction of the Indies—the seeds of the consequent incremental conquests of the Indies and its peoples.[189]

In the *Brevísima relación*, Las Casas presented a textual mapping of the trajectory of the conquests that had taken place during the forty-nine years of the Spaniards' misdeeds. Territory by territory, the *Brevísima relación* chronicled the Spaniards' *entradas*: first, the Antilles Islands (Hispaniola, San Juan, Jamaica, Cuba, and the Lucayos), then the Central Continental Region (Nicaragua and Tierra Firme, i.e. Castilla del Oro), then the Northern Continental Region (New Spain, Naco, Honduras, Guatemala, Pánuco, Michoacán, Jalisco, and Yucatán), then the Southern Continental Region (Santa Marta, Cartagena, Costa de las Perlas, Paria, Trinidad, Río Yuyaparí, and Venezuela), then the Extreme Continental Region (Florida in the north and Río de la Plata in the south), and lastly the regions of Perú and Nueva Granada.

In this official account, Las Casas stridently condemned the conquests and consequent enslavement of Indigenous people on the basis of both civil and ecclesial juridical traditions—of "divine, natural, and human law." Las Casas was qualified to make these allegations in the *Brevísima relación* because his formation on both sides of the Atlantic in canon law, philosophy, and theology equipped him well to utilize a juridical approach.

Notes

1 Thomas Benjamin, *The Atlantic World: Europeans, Africans, Indians, and Their Shared History, 1490–1900* (Cambridge: Cambridge Univ. Press, 2009), 3.

2 J. H. Parry, *The Spanish Seaborne Empire* (Berkeley: Univ. of California Press, 1966), 65.

3 Even today, the denotation "Spain" carries various connotations. In this book, Spain signifies the regions of the Iberian peninsula that would later be directly or indirectly under the control of Castile and Aragon. This "control" began with the union of the Crowns of Ferdinand and Isabel in 1474. The phrase *mar Océanus* seemingly derives from Seneca's legend of the Medea, which in the mythology of the Hellenistic era redefined Okeanos as the God of the newly accessible Atlantic and Indian oceans. Benjamin, *The Atlantic World*, 1–2. John Crow, *Spain: The Root and the Flower*, 3rd ed. (Berkeley: Univ. of California Press, 1985), 7. Concerning the dating of Las Casas's birth, see Helen Rand Parish and Harold Weidman, "The Correct Birthdate of Bartolomé de las Casas," *Hispanic American Historical Review* 56, no. 3 (1976): 385–403.

4 As John H. Elliot noted in his *Imperial Spain*, and as argued by Teofilio Ruiz, Spain's history is best presented not as a movement from one discrete historical period (the late medieval times) to another (early modern times), but rather as a period of historical transformation characterized by both continuity and change. J. H. Elliot, *Imperial Spain 1496–1716* (New York: St. Martin's Press, 1963), 13–14; Teofilio Ruiz, *Spanish Society, 1400–1600*, A Social History of Europe Series (Harlow: Pearson Education Limited, 2001), 1.

5 Castile was the central Iberian kingdom that played the dominant role in the conquest and colonization of the Indies following Columbus's initial encounter.

6 Paul Oskar Kristeller, *Renaissance Thought and Its Sources* (New York: Columbia Univ. Press, 1979), 18.

7 Anthony Grafton, April Shelford and Nancy Siraisi, *New Worlds, Ancient Texts: The Power of Tradition and the Shock of Discovery* (Cambridge, MA: The Belknap Press of Harvard Univ. Press, 1992), 6–7.

8 Luca Bianchi, "Continuity and Change in Aristotelian Tradition," in *The Cambridge Companion to Renaissance Philosophy*, ed. James Hankins (New York: Cambridge Univ. Press, 2007), 57.

9 Their consciousness of time led to new types of history, and "the older the better." Robin W. Winks and Teofilo F. Ruiz, *Medieval Europe and the World: From Late Antiquity to Modernity, 400–1500* (New York: Oxford Univ. Press, 2005), 258–60 (hereafter *Medieval Europe and the World*).

10 Grafton, *New World, Ancient Texts*, 6.

11 In his *Renaissance Thought: The Classic, Scholastic, and Humanist Strains* (New York: Harper, 1961), Paul Oskar Kristeller contended that these three major early Renaissance intellectual currents shared concern about the purpose of human life and about standards for individual behavior, human relationships, and societal solidarity.

12 Aristotelianism refers to the philosophical tradition drawn from the writings of Aristotle (384 BCE–322 BCE). Later, Jewish, Christian, and Muslim scholars employed aspects of his thinking. Platonism refers to the philosophical understanding inspired by the thought of Plato (428/27 BCE–347/48 BCE). Along with Aristotle, his thinking greatly shaped the development of Western thinking concerning epistemology, ethics, and politics. Epicureanism refers to the philosophical system founded upon the ideas of Epicurus (341 BCE–270 BCE). In contrast to Aristotle and Plato, Epicurus was a materialist and a determinist, and, as such, his thought appealed to "pure" empiricists. Stoicism refers to the philosophical school founded by Zeno of Citium (334 BCE–262 BCE). Central to Zeno's thinking was the goal of

living a life of virtue in accord with nature; as such, he sought a balance between collective cosmic determinism and individual human freedom.

13 Averroism refers to the name given by Western scholars to the philosophical and theological thought of the Muslim scholar Averroës or Ibn Rushd (1126 CE–1198 CE), especially his understandings of Aristotle. Averroës's thought was first brought into the West in the thirteenth century. Albertism refers to the philosophical and theological school of thought inspired by Albert of Cologne, OP (1193/1206–1280). Albert was especially noted for his promotion of the coexistence of science and religion. Thomism refers to the philosophical and theological school of thought inspired by the work of Thomas Aquinas, OP. Aquinas followed and exceeded his teacher Albert in using non-Christian thinkers such as Aristotle and Plato. Scotism refers to the philosophical and theological system of thinking inspired by John Duns Scotus, OFM (1265–1308). As did many other medieval philosophers and theologians, Scotus freely employed the thinking of non-Judeo-Christian sources to the delight of some and to the consternation of others. Ockhamism refers to the philosophical and theological method of scholasticism promoted by William of Ockham, OFM (1288–1348). Considered one of the most important medieval thinkers, Ockham was especially known for his nominalist views that contrasted with Aquinas's moderate realist positions.

14 Charles G. Nauert, Jr., *Humanism and the Culture of Renaissance Europe* (Cambridge: Cambridge Univ. Press, 1995), 36–40; Lodi Nauta, "Lorenzo Valla and the Rise of Humanist Dialectic," in *The Cambridge Companion to Renaissance Philosophy*, 193; Charles Lohr, "Renaissance Latin translators of the Greek commentators on Aristotle," in *Humanism and Early Modern Philosophy*, eds. Jill Kraye and M.W.F. Stone (London: Routledge, 2000), 25; Quentin Skinner, *The Foundations of Modern Political Thought: Vol. 1 The Renaissance*; *Vol. 2 The Age of Reformation* (Cambridge: Cambridge Univ. Press, 1978), 1:105–07 (hereafter cited as *The Foundations of Modern Political Thought*); James Hankins, "Humanism, scholasticism, and Renaissance philosophy," in *The Cambridge Companion to Renaissance Philosophy*, 39.

15 James Hankins, "The Significance of Renaissance Philosophy," in *The Cambridge Companion to Renaissance Philosophy*, 342–43; James Hankins, "Humanism, scholasticism, and Renaissance philosophy," in *The Cambridge Companion to Renaissance Philosophy*, 43, 45.

16 Justinian's works include the *Institutiones*, *Digestum*, *Codex*, and *Novellae*. In addition to this collection, another main body of knowledge about Roman law is contained in the sixth-century "barbarian codes" applicable to Roman subjects of the Gothic and Burgundian kings. P.G. Stein, "Roman Law," in *The Cambridge History of Medieval Political Thought c. 350–c.1450*, ed., J. H. Burns (New York: Cambridge Univ. Press, 1988), 37–47; Manlio Bellomo, *The Common Legal Past of Europe, 1000–1800*, vol. 4, trans. of 2nd ed., Lydia G. Cochrane (Washington, DC: Catholic Univ. of America Press, 1995), 38–39 (hereafter cited as *The Common Legal Past*). This development of Roman and canon law ended the era denominated as the "Age without Jurists" (c. 500–1140). Wolfgang P. Muller, "Medieval Church Law as a Field of Historical Inquiry," in *Medieval Church Law and the Origins of the Western Legal Tradition*, ed. Wolfgang P. Muller and Mary E. Sommar (Washington, DC: Catholic Univ. of America Press, 2006), 10. For a detailed history of canon law, see Kenneth Pennington, "A Short History of Canon Law from Apostolic Times to 1917," accessed April 3, 2010, http://legalhistorysources.com/Canon%20Law/PenningtonShortHistoryCanonLaw.pdf (hereafter cited as "A Short History."

17 Gratian is regarded as the "Father of the Canon Law." His *Decretum*, which is believed to be the product of classroom presentations and discussions, remained a foundational handbook of canon law until 1917. In 1500, the French jurist, Jean Chappuis, began the compilation of all canon law collections into one body. In 1582, Gregory XIII (1572–1585) promulgated the finished product as the *Corpus Iuris Canonici*. In addition to the *Decretum Gratiani*, this corpus contained the *Liber Extra* or *Decretals* of Gregory IX (1227–1241), the *Liber Sextus* of Boniface VIII (1294–1303), the Clementinae of Clement V (1305–1314 Avignon), the *Extravagantes* of John XXII (1316–1334 Avignon), and the *Extravagantes Communes* of Sixtus IV (1471–1484). Katherine Christensen, "Introduction," in Gratian, *The Treatise on Laws* (Decretum DD. 1–20) with the *Ordinary Gloss, Studies in Medieval and Early Modern Canon Law*, vol. 2, intro. Katherine Christensen; trans. Augustine Thompson and James Gordley (Washington, DC: Catholic Univ. of America Press, 1993), xiii; Pennington, "A Short History," 10–11; Muller, "Medieval Church," 17–94; Bellomo, *The Common Legal Past*, 71–74, 145; James A. Brundage, "The Teaching and Study of Canon Law in the Law Schools," in *The History of Medieval Canon Law in the Classical Period, 1140–1234: From Gratian to the Decretals of Pope Gregory IX*, eds., Wilfried Hartmann and Kenneth Pennington (Washington, DC: Catholic Univ. of America Press, 2008), 99 (hereafter cited as *History of Medieval Canon Law*); Kenneth Pennington, "Decretal Collections 1190–1234," in *History of Medieval Canon Law*, 293–318.

18 George Mousourakis, *The Historical and Institutional Context of Roman Law* (Burlington, VT: Ashgate, 2003); Bellomo, *The Common Legal Past*, 147–48.

19 R. H. Helmholtz, *The Spirit of Classical Canon Law* (Athens: Univ. of Georgia Press, 1996), 4–5.

20 Bellomo, *The Common Legal Past*, 64–65.

21 Constant Van De Wiel, *History of Canon Law* (Louvain: Peeters Press, 1991), 133.

22 Van De Wiel, *History of Canon Law*, 129.

23 Helmholtz, *The Spirit of Classical Canon Law*, 17. According to Pennington, Christian communities did not initially have a body of written law. For more than five centuries, early Christian communities were governed by custom based on scripture and oral tradition. In the third century, some communities produced "handbooks" of guidelines for Church functionaries and for the sacraments. In the fourth century, bishops administered local churches. Subsequently, under Constantine, ecclesial Councils began to govern all of the Christian communities; the canons of these assemblies became the established pattern of Church governance until the late ninth century. Over time, canon law also adopted from Roman law what related to obligations, contracts, judiciary actions,@@@@nts were preparing to become and, to a great extent, civil procedures. Meanwhile, in the late ninth century, clerical compilers of canonical collections produced the Pseudo-Isidorian Forgeries. Such falsifications were not an unusual occurrence in the Early Middle Ages. While the clerics' initial purpose was to protect the rights and property of clerics and bishops from lay control and judicial authority, the permanent contributions of these canons were related to matters of papal power, authority, and monarchical government. These canons remained an uncontested part of canon law until the sixteenth century. Pennington, "A Short History," 1–8; Manuel Giménez Fernández, *Instituciones jurídicas en la iglesia Católica*, 2 vols. (Madrid: Sociedad Anónima Española de

Traductores y Autores, 1940), 1:111–17; James A. Brundage, *Medieval Canon Law* (London: Longman, 1995), 5–17, 112.

24 Unlike Roman law that consisted of an already completed body of law in the form of the Code of Justinian, the actual corpus of canon law developed over four centuries beginning with the *Decretum Gratiani*, followed by the conscious creation of canon law in authoritative commentaries, conciliar decrees, and papal decretals. The new collections were regularly communicated to canon law faculties, which enabled canonists to respond to new problems with the latest legal precedents. Helmholtz, *The Spirit of Classical Canon Law*, 6.

25 Indeed, canon law students needed substantial grounding in civil law, just as civil law scholars and practitioners needed study in canon law. Brundage, "The Teaching and Study of Canon Law," in *History of Medieval Canon Law*, 99–100.

26 The *ius commune*, in its historical meaning, is commonly thought of as a combination of canon law and Roman law which formed the basis of common legal thought in Western Europe after the rediscovery and reception of Justinian's Digest in the twelfth and thirteenth centuries, and served as the prototype and paradigm of legal ordinances. Antonio García y García, *Derecho común en España: los juristas y sus obras* (Murcia: Secretariado de la Universidad de Murcia, 1991), 13–15.

27 Bellomo offers a clarifying metaphor by likening the *ius commune* to the sun, and *ius proprium* to the planets of one solar system. *The Common Legal Past*, 192–92. See also Mousourakis, *The Historical and Institutional Context of Roman Law*, 429; Francesco Maiolo, *Medieval Sovereignty: Marsilius of Padua and Bartolus of Saxoferrato* (Delft: Eburon Academic Publishers, 2007), 225; Skinner, *The Foundations of Modern Political Thought*, 1:105–6, 2:269.

28 Van De Wiel, *History of Canon Law*, 131.

29 Maiolo, *Medieval Sovereignty*, 226.

30 Katherine Elliot Van Liere, "Humanism and Scholasticism in Sixteenth-Century Academe: Five Student Orations from the University of Salamanca," *Renaissance Quarterly* 53, no. 1 (Spring 2000): 75.

31 Their assessments did encourage the eventual development of a genuinely historical jurisprudence. Skinner, *The Foundations of Modern Political Thought*, 1:105–6, 2:270.

32 As a juridical term, "*letrado*" is defined as lawyer, counselor, attorney, advocate, and barrister. See Alcaraz Varó y Hughes, *Diccionario de Términos Jurídicos*, 811. Although Nebrija taught at Salamanca from 1488 to 1492, he did not enjoy a large audience there—perhaps because he was so often remiss in meeting his classes! Antonio García y García, "Consolidaciones del Siglo XV," in *La Universidad de Salamanca*, 3 vols., dir., Manuel Fernández Álvarez (Salamanca: Europa Artes Gráficas, S. A., 1989), 1:51–52; Katherine Elliot Van Liere, "Humanism and Scholasticism in Sixteenth-Century Academe: Five Student Orations from the University of Salamanca," *Renaissance Quarterly* 53, no. 1 (Spring 2000): 82.

33 Thomas Aquinas (1225–1274) was a former Benedictine oblate who became a Dominican friar, a student of Albert the Great, OP, and a professor of theology in Paris and at the Papal Curia. His theological writings constituted a significant landmark in the history of theology. Isacio Pérez Fernández, "La doctrina de Santo Tomás en la mente y en la acción del Padre Las Casas," *Communio* 27 (1987): 283. Edward J. Gratsch, *Aquinas's Summa: An Introduction and Interpretation* (New York: Alba House, 1985); Gregorio

Celada Luengo, *Tomás de Aquino, testigo y maestro de la fe* (San Esteban Editorial San Esteban, 1999). Peter Lombard was a celebrated scholastic theologian who taught at the cathedral school of Notre Dame in Paris and was appointed the bishop of Paris the year before he died. His four books of *Sentencias* constituted the required official text for the study of theology from the thirteenth to the mid-sixteenth centuries. For a translation of his first book, see Peter Lombard, *The Sentences, Book 1: The Mystery of the Trinity*, trans., Giulio Silano (Toronto: Pontifical Institute of Medieval Studies, 2007). Also see Ford Lewis Battles, *Study Outline Number 15: Peter Lombard* (Pittsburgh: Pittsburgh Theological Union, 1973).

34 The Council of Trent was held during three periods for a total of twenty-five sessions between 1545 and 1563; the Council declared Thomism as the most authentic expression of doctrine in the Church at that time.

35 For example, he wrote his commentary on *The Sentences* in classical Latin style as an example of such learning. See Paul Cortese, "Introduction to the First Books of the 'Sentences'," in *Renaissance Philosophy*, ed. Leonard A. Kennedy (The Hague: Mouton, 1973), 29–40.

36 Alastair Hamilton, "Humanism and the Bible," in *The Cambridge Companion to Renaissance Humanism*, ed. Jill Kraye (Cambridge: Cambridge Univ. Press, 1996), 100.

37 Skinner, *The Foundations of Modern Political Thought*, 1:210–11.

38 Robert Black, "The philosopher and Renaissance culture," in *The Cambridge Companion to Renaissance Philosophy*, 13–29.

39 For example, Marsilio Ficino spearheaded the revival of Platonism and challenged the Aristotelian representation of the universe. Miguel A. Granada, "New Visions of the Cosmos," in *The Cambridge Companion to Renaissance Philosophy*, 270.

40 William A. Wallace, "Traditional Natural Philosophy," in *The Cambridge History of Renaissance Philosophy*, eds. Charles B. Schmitt, Quentin Skinner, Erkhard Kessler, and Jill Kraye (Cambridge: Cambridge Univ. Press, 1988), 206–7.

41 Pierpaolo Vergerio (c. 1369–1444) coined the term *studia humanitatis* for the course of studies on the classical texts to teach students to read, write, and speak well in Latin, that is, as a program for social and civic transformation. See also Ann M. Blair, "Organizations of Knowledge," in *The Cambridge Companion to Renaissance Philosophy*, 299; James Hankins, "Humanism, Scholasticism, and Renaissance Philosophy," in *The Cambridge Companion to Renaissance Philosophy*, 32.

42 Skinner contends that the first to embark upon a "revival of letters" were early *quattrocento* jurists and students of law who studied the classics for their literary value in order to enrich and strengthen existing genres of political writing. Skinner, *The Foundations of Modern Political Thought*, 1:37–39.

43 Sarah H. Beckjord, *Territories of History: Humanism, Rhetoric, and the Historical Imagination in the* Early Chronicles of Spanish America (University Park: Pennsylvania State Univ. Press, 2007), 11. Rapp contends that Aristotle's general theory of the persuasive contained many concepts and arguments from his logical, ethical, and philosophical writings. Christ of Rapp, "Aristotle's Rhetoric," Stanford Encyclopedia of Philosophy, modified February 1, 2010; accessed April 15, 2010, https://plato.stanford.edu/entries/aristotle-rhetoric/#4.5. See also Paul Oskar Kristeller, *Medieval Aspects of Renaissance Learning: Three Essays*, ed. and trans. Edward P. Mahoney (Durham, NC: Duke Univ. Press, 1974).

44 The coming of the Spanish Golden Age was a transitional period for literature in which two significant genres were present: humanistic works characterizing a rebirth and movement "from the dark into the light," and books of chivalry symbolizing the medieval tradition. Guillermo Díaz-Plaja, *Historia general de las literaturas hispánicas*, 3 vols (Barcelona: Editorial Barna, S.A., 1953), 75; Nicholson B. Adams and John E. Keller, *Spanish Literature: A Brief Survey* (Paterson, NJ: Littlefield, Adams & Co., 1960), 78–80.

45 Black, "The Philosopher and Renaissance Culture," 26. In Spain, foreign entrepreneurs from Germany, France, and Italy dominated the entire printing industry during the *quattrocento.* Henry Kamen, *Empire: How Spain Became a World Power 1492–1763* (New York: Harper Collins, 2003), 4; see also John F. D'Amico, "Manuscripts," in *The Cambridge History of Renaissance Philosophy*, 11–24; Paul F. Grendler, "Printing and Censorship," in *The Cambridge History of Renaissance Philosophy*, 25–53.

46 Teofilio Ruiz, *Spain's Centuries of Crisis: 1300–1474* (Malden, MA: Blackwell Publishing, 2007), 16.

47 Black, "The Philosopher and Renaissance Culture," 26. In Castile, the popularity of reading initially increased between 1407 and 1458 as book collecting became fashionable among elites. However, even before the advent of the printing press, literacy levels among Castilian non-elites increased during the second half of the fifteenth century; as a result, by the mid-sixteenth century, sixty-nine percent of Madrileños could sign their names. See Sara T. Nalle, "Literacy and Culture in Early Modern Castile," *Past and Present* 125 (November 1989): 65–69.

48 Paul Oskar Kristeller, *Medieval Aspects of Renaissance Learning*, 16, 24–25.

49 Elise Bartosik-Vélez, "Translatio Imperii: Virgil and Peter Martyr's Columbus," *Comparative Literature Studies* 46, no. 4 (2009): 584–85. V. Afanasiev, "The Literary Heritage of Bartolomé de Las Casas," in *Bartolomé de las Casas in History: Toward an Understanding of the Man and His Work*, 555–69, eds. Juan Friede and Benjamin Keen (DeKalb: Northern Illinois Univ., 1971) (hereafter *Bartolomé de las Casas in History*).

50 Charles Hope and Elizabeth McGrath, "Artists and Humanists," in *The Cambridge Companion to Renaissance Humanism*, ed., Jill Kraye (Cambridge: Cambridge Univ. Press, 1988), 161–88.

51 Crow, *Spain: The Root and the Flower*, 132–33; Kamen, *Empire*, 5.

52 James Hankins, "Introduction," in *The Cambridge Companion to Renaissance Philosophy*, 2.

53 See Chapter 5 on the revival of Thomism, in Skinner, *The Foundations of Modern Political Thought*, 2:135ff.

54 A debate currently exists about when the *Siete Partidas* were promulgated. Some contend that Alfonso X redacted and promulgated them during his reign. Others claim that he redacted them because he thought he would become the emperor of the *Sacro Imperio Romano Germánico*, which he did not, and so did not promulgate the *Siete Partidas*, and that his código was promulgated in 1348 by Alfonso XI in the Ordenamiento de Alcalá. See Leonel Leal Salinas, "Resumen Historia del Derecho Profesor Óscar Dávila," accessed July 15, 2020, https://www.scribd.com/document/184977607/141345043-HISTORIA-DEL-DERECHO-I-Profesor-Oscar-Davila-Campusano-docx-pdf. Iberia included the territory of all the kingdoms of Castilla, Toledo, León, Sevilla, Córdoba, Jaén, Murcia, and Galicia, the principality of Asturias and the lordship of Vizcaya, with the Levantine kingdoms of Aragón, Catalonia, and Valencia, as well as Portugal.

55 This same order of Castilian law was one element contributing to the formation of new Hispano-Indiano law. Javier Barrientos Grandón, *La Cultura Jurídica en la Nueva España* (Sobre la recepción de la tradición jurídica europea en el virreinato) (Mexico, DF: Univ. Nacional Autónoma de México, 1993), 29 (hereafter *La Cultura Jurídica*).

56 Bellomo, *The Common Legal Past*, 82; Richard L. Kagan, *Lawsuits and Litigants in Castille, 1500–1700* (Chapel Hill: Univ. of North Carolina Press, 1981).

57 Bellomo, *The Common Legal Past*, 81, 147–48, 154–55, 211–15; Barrientos Grandon further contended that *ius commune* penetrated the Indies through the *Siete Partidas*. *La Cultura Jurídica*, 11–12.

58 Bellomo, *The Common Legal Past*, 101.

59 Jerrold E. Siegel, *Rhetoric and Philosophy in Renaissance Humanism: The Union of Eloquence and Wisdom, Petrarch to Valla* (Princeton, NJ: Princeton Univ. Press, 1968), 5.

60 Richard L. Kagan, *Students and Society in Early Modern Spain* (Baltimore, MD: Johns Hopkins Univ. Press, 1974), 33.

61 Julián Marías, *Understanding Spain*, trans. Frances M. López-Morilla (Ann Arbor: Univ. Michigan Press, 1990), 146.

62 Peggy K. Liss, *Isabel the Queen: Life and Times*, rev. ed. (Philadelphia: Univ. of Pennsylvania Press, 2004), 98; Crow, *Spain: The Root and the Flower*, 97–102, 132–33.

63 Humanists' discussion of the relative merits of men and women began with Boccaccio's *De claris mulieribus* (1361; About Famous Women), a compilation of short biographies of one hundred and six historical and mythological women who were renowned for any sort of notable deed, either good or bad. The first woman to respond directly to misogynistic treatises of the time was Christine de Pizan (1364–c. 1430) who used Boccaccio's portraits of mostly classical women in 1405 to "construct" her allegorical "city of ladies" (*Le livre de la cité des dames*; The Book of the City of Ladies), in which each of the famous women represented a building block for the walls and houses of "the city," as well as for women's rights. Among the dozen or so women humanists in fifteenth-century Italy who addressed the importance of women's active contributions to society were Isotta Nogarola (1418–1466), who advocated the equality of women and men in the realm of education and who modeled actual dialogue across genders, and defended Eve in a dialogue with Venetian humanist, Ludovico Foscarini, on the relative responsibility of Adam and Eve for the Fall. Also of importance is Laura Cereta (1469–1499), who addressed the oppression of married women and championed women's rights in education. Prudence Allen, *The Concept of Women. Vol 2: The Early Humanist Reformation 1250–1500* (Grand Rapids Michigan: W. B. Eerdmans Publishing Company, 2002); Margaret L. King, "The Religious Retreat of Isotta Nogarola (1418–1466): Sexism and Its Consequences in the Fifteenth Century," *Signs* 3, no. 4 (Summer 1978), 807–22.

64 Vicente María Márquez de la Plata y Fernández, *Mujeres Renacentistas en la corte de Isabel la Católica* (Madrid: Castalia, 2005), 12; Liss, *Isabel the Queen*, 285–86. Isabel and Ferdinand sought to prepare their daughters well to enter into the Renaissance courts, which they did through marriage. Isabel (1470–1498) became Queen of Portugal; Juana (1479–1555), Queen of Castile; María (1482–1517), Queen of Portugal; and Catalina (1485–1536), Queen of England. However, some were not successful: Juana became known as "Juana la loca," and Catalina was "discarded" by Henry VII in favor of Ann Boleyn. In addition to their four daughters, the Catholic Monarchs had two sons: Juan (1478–1497), who was Prince of Asturias, and Pedro (1488–1490).

65 Isacio Pérez Fernández, *Cronología documentada de los viajes, estancias y actuaciones de Fray Bartolomé de las Casas*, vol. 2 (Bayamón, P.R.: Centro de Estudios de los Dominicos del Caribe, 1984), 98–108 (hereafter cited as *Cronología*).

66 Bartolomé de las Casas, *The Only Way*, ed. Helen Rand Parish, trans. Francis Patrick Sullivan (New York: Paulist Press, 1992), 12 (hereafter cited as Las Casas, *The Only Way*).

67 José Sánchez Herrero, "El estudio de San Miguel de Sevilla durante el siglo XV," *Historia, Instituciones y Documentos* 10 (1983): 297–333; Susana Guijarro González, "Las escuelas y la formación del clero de las catedrales en las diócesis castellanos-leonesas (siglos XI al XV)," in *La enseñanza en la edad media: X Semana de Estudios Medievales*, Nájera 1999, coord., José Ignacio de la Iglesia Duarte (Logroño: Instituto de Estudios Riojanos, 2000), 68–69.

68 Brundage, "The Teaching and Study of Canon Law," in *History of Medieval Canon Law*, 115.

69 Daniel Sánchez Sánchez, "Catedral y universidad en sus origins," in *La Universidad de Salamanca*, 1:329; Juan Gutiérrez Cuadrado, "Christian Universities," in *Medieval Iberia: An Encyclopedia*, eds. E. Michael Gerli, Samuel G. Armistead, et al. (New York: Routledge, 2003), 817.

70 Manuel Giménez Fernández, "La juventud en Sevilla de Bartolomé de las Casas," *Miscelánea de Estudios dedicados al Fernando Ortiz* (Havana: Sociedad Económica de Amigos del País, 1956), 2:670–717.

71 This lends credence to the suggestion of some scholars that Las Casas began his studies at the age of six in 1490. José Alcina Franch, "Introducción," in Bartolomé de las Casas, *Obra indigenista*, ed. and intro. by José Alcina Franch (Madrid: Alianza, 1985), 13.

72 Guijarro González reconstructed the study programs from her extensive research on library holdings of Castilian and Leonese cathedral schools. See her "Las escuelas y la formación del clero de las catedrales en las diócesis castellanos-leonesas (siglos XI al XV)" (Logroño: Instituto de Estudios Riojanos, 2000), 61–96.

73 John Edwards, *The Spain of the Catholic Monarchs: 1474–1520* (Oxford: Blackwell, 2000), 267; Katherine Elliot Van Liere, "After Nebrija: Academic Reformers and the Teaching of Latin in Sixteenth-Century Salamanca," *The Sixteenth Century Journal* 34, no. 4 (2003): 1067.

74 Jesús-Ángel Barreda, "Bibliografía Lascasiana de la Apologética Historia," in Bartolomé de las Casas, *Obras Completas* (Madrid: Alianza, 1998), 6:221–33 [hereafter cited as *O.C.*].

75 Stephanie Merrim, "The Counter-Discourse of Bartolomé de Las Casas," in *Early Images of the Americas: Transfer and Invention*, eds., Jerry M. Williams and Robert E. Lewis (Tucson: Univ. of Arizona Press, 1993), 152; Kristeller, *Renaissance Thought and its Sources*, 250.

76 Lawrence Clayton, "Teaching Las Casas Through the Lens of a Historian," in *Approaches to Teaching the Writings of Bartolomé de las Casas*, eds. Santa Arias and Eyda M. Merediz (New York: Modern Language Association of America, 2008), 34.

77 Marías, *Understanding Spain*, 162; Díaz-Plaja, *Historia general de las literaturas hispánicas*, 75.

78 Bernal Díaz del Castillo wrote that "we were amazed and said that it was like the enchantments they tell of in the legend of Amadis." *The History of the Conquest of New Spain*, ed. and trans. Davíd Carrasco (Albuquerque: Univ. of New Mexico Press, 2008), 156. John Elliot contends that Amadis of Gaul was read or heard by vast bodies of Spaniards. *Imperial Spain*, 63.

Indeed, Las Casas refers to the legend in his 1563 letter to his Dominican confreres.

79 Crow, *Spain: The Root and the Flower*, 104.

80 Ibid., 103–04.

81 Hugh Thomas, *Rivers of Gold: The Rise of Spanish Empire, from Columbus to Magellan* (New York: Random House, 2003), 525–26; Crow, *Spain: The Root and the Flower*, 104–05.

82 Mudéjars were Moors living under Christian rule.

83 Vittorio Salvadorini, "Las 'Relaciones' de Hernán Cortés," accessed November 11, 2010, http://cvc. cervantes.es/lengua/thesaurus/pdf/18/TH_18_001_085_0.pdf. Bartolomé de las Casas, *Historia de las Indias*, ed., André Saint-Lu (Caracas: Biblioteca Ayacucho, 1986), 3: chap. 27 [hereafter cited as *Historia* (Ayacucho)]; J. H. Elliot, *Spain and its World 1500–1700* (New Haven, CT: Yale Univ. Press, 1989), 29.

84 The Castilian language had three variants—Old Castilian or Toledean, Andalusían, and Aragonese. Crow, *Spain: The Root and the Flower*, 99, 151; Marías, *Understanding Spain*, 146; Henry Kamen, *Golden Age of Spain*, 2nd ed. Studies in European History Series (New York: Palgrave MacMillian, 2005), 2.

85 Ruiz, *Spain's Centuries*, 167.

86 Isacio Pérez Fernández, interview by David Orique, October 15, 1999, tape recording, Madrid, Spain.

87 Kamen, *Empire*, 3–4.

88 In the prologue of his Castilian Grammar, Nebrija wrote "When Your Highness has subjected many barbarous peoples and nations of foreign tongues … they will have to accept the laws which the conqueror imposes on the conquered, and with them our language," that is, all would learn Castellano. Antonio de Nebrija, *Gramática de la lengua Castellano* (1492), ed. I. González-Llubera (New York: Oxford Univ. Press, 1926), 39.

89 Bartosik-Vélez, "Translatio Imperii," 561. Another towering linguistic achievement that lent prestige to Spain was the publication of the polyglot Bible of Alcalá. Crow, *Spain: The Root and the Flower*, 150.

90 Elliot, *Imperial Spain*, 125; Crow, *Spain: The Root and the Flower*, 150–52.

91 Kamen, *Empire*, 6.

92 Roberto Fernández Retamar, "Introducción," in Bartolomé de las Casas, *Très Brève Relation de la Destruction des Indes*, trans. Fanchita Gonzalez Batlle (Paris: François Maspero, 1980), 24ff.

93 Ruiz, *Spain's Centuries*, 143ff.

94 Elliot, *Imperial Spain*, 104.

95 Ferdinand's mother was a member of the Jewish Enríquez family who converted to Christianity. A new Christian family that prospered in this era of popular suspicion of conversos was the Santángels from Aragon, whose members included lawyers, treasurers, judges, royal tax collectors, financiers, and even a bishop. In 1492, Luís de Santángel convinced Isabel and Ferdinand to endorse Columbus by securing the necessary loans for the voyage. Las Casas's mother belonged to a Sevillian family of converso heritage. Manuel Giménez Fernández, "Bartolomé de las Casas en su IV centenario de su muerte," *Arbor* 62, no. 252 (Diciembre 1968): 273.

96 Elliot, *Imperial Spain*, 108.

97 Crow, *Spain: The Root and the Flower*, 79.

98 Ruiz, *Spain's Centuries*, 32–33.

99 Ibid., 16.

100 Ibid., 32–33; Carla Rhan Philips, "Time and Duration: A Model for the Economy of Early Modern Spain," *The American Historical Review* 92, no. 3 (June 1987): 538–39; Dennis O. Flynn, "Fiscal Crisis and the Decline of Spain (Castile)," *Economic History* 42, no. 1 (March 1982): 140.
101 J. A. García de Cortázar, *Historia de España Alfaguara II: La época medieval* (Madrid: Alianza, 1973), 391.
102 Kamen, *Empire*, 7.
103 Ruiz, *Spain's Centuries*, 32–24.
104 Flynn, "Fiscal Crisis and the Decline of Spain," 140.
105 Parry, *The Spanish Seaborne Empire*, 31–33.
106 Ruiz, *Spanish Society*, 40–41.
107 Elliot contends that feudalism was never deeply rooted in Spain. *Imperial Spain*, 120.
108 In medieval Spain, in particular Castile, *hermandades* acted as armed peacekeepers. Elliot, *Imperial Spain*, 84–86, 140; Crow, *Spain: The Root and the Flower*, 122–123.
109 Crow, *Spain: The Root and the Flower*, 88; Francisco J. Hernandez, review of *Église et pouvoir dans la Péninsule Ibérique. Les ordres militaires dans le royaume de Castille (1252–1369)*, by Philippe Josserand, *The Catholic Historical Review* 93, no. 2 (April 2007): 389–90.
110 David M. Traboulay, *Columbus and Las Casas: The Conquest and Christianization of America, 1492–1566* (New York: Univ. Press of America, 1994), 55–7; Gustavo Gutiérrez, *Las Casas: In Search of the Poor of Jesus Christ* (Maryknoll, NY: Orbis Press, 1995), 24; also see Lynne Guitar, "No More Negotiation: Slavery and the Destabilization of Colonial Hispaniola's Encomienda System," accessed April 15, 2007, http://cai.sg.inter.edu/revistaciscla/volume29/guitar.pdf.
111 Ruiz, *Spanish Society*, 56–59.
112 Pérez Fernández, *Cronología*, 66–77, 105, 197, 109.
113 Ruiz, *Spanish Society*, 61–65; Jocelyn Hunt, *Spain 1474–1598* (London, Routledge, 2001), 12. Castile's powerful sheep-raising guild opposed Aragon's desire to market its cloth and spice in Castile and to share in the export of wool; furthermore, trade with the Genoese was more lucrative for Castile. John Lynch, *Spain, 1516–1598* (Oxford: Blackwell, 1991), 25.
114 Flynn, "Fiscal Crisis and the Decline of Spain," 140.
115 Elliot, *Imperial Spain*, 120; Lynch, *Spain*, 23.
116 Kagan, *Lawsuits and Litigants in Castile 1500–1700*, 116; Elliot, *Imperial Spain*, 116–17.
117 Parry, *The Spanish Seaborne Empire*, 33.
118 Elliot, *Imperial Spain*, 118.
119 Bailey W. Diffie and George D. Winius, *Foundations of the Portuguese Empire, 1415–1580*, Europe and the world in the Age of Expansion, v. 1. (Minneapolis: Univ. of Minnesota Press, 1977), 317; Thomas, *Rivers of Gold*, 229; Alberto E. Ariza S, "Acotaciones sobre Fr. Bartolomé de Las Casas," *Boletín de Historia y Antigüedades* 44, no. 718 (Julio-Septiembre, 1977): 511.
120 Elliot, *Imperial Spain*, 122. The maravedí was named after the Moor word "almoravids," which denominated the twelfth-century rulers of Muslim Spain.
121 With the discovery of gold in 1494, Columbus sent both enslaved Indigenous people and *repartido* Indigenous persons to the mines; in 1497, Isabel approved *repartimientos* of land but not of Indigenous people. Isacio Pérez Fernández, *El Derecho Hispano-Indiano: dinámica social de su proceso*

histórico constituyente (Salamanca: San Esteban, 2001), 30–31. Luis N. Rivera Pagán, *A Violent Evangelization: The Political and Religious Conquest of the Americas* (Louisville: Westminster/John Knox Press, 1992), 93–98; Troy S. Floyd, *The Columbus Dynasty in the Caribbean, 1492–1526* (Albuquerque: Univ. of New Mexico Press, 1973), 29.

122 Although Teofilio Ruiz points out that "[i]n 1412, Castile and Aragon came to be ruled by closely related members of one family, the Trastámaras." Ruiz, *Spain's Centuries*, 86. Hence, he is pointing toward unification as a process rather than the result of one event, such as in this case, the marriage of Isabel and Ferdinand.

123 Liss, *Isabel the Queen*, 67.

124 Although historians have raised many questions about Juana's alleged paternity, no clear documentation of her legitimacy or illegitimacy exists; consequently, this is still a question of historiographic speculation and debate. Liss, *Isabel the Queen*, 422n49; also see Ruiz, *Spain's Centuries*, 99–100; 196–99.

125 Edwards, *The Spain of the Catholic Monarch*, 22; Winks and Ruiz, *Medieval Europe and the World*, 126.

126 Ruiz, *Spain's Centuries*, 100.

127 Lynch, *Spain*, 1; Las Casas, *Historia* (Ayacucho), 2: chaps. 17, 31, 32, 74; about the "Cláusula del testamento de la Reina," see Bartolomé de las Casas, *Carta al Consejo de Indias 1531*, in *O.C.*, 13:74ff; also see Bartolomé de las Casas, *An Account, Much Abbreviated, of the Destruction of the Indies*, trans. Andrew Hurley, intro. and ed. Franklin W. Knight (Indianapolis: Hackett, 2003), 17 (hereafter, Knight, *An Account*). Isabel's accomplishments were also lauded in a 1485 statement by Fernando de Pulgar wherein he wrote: "Evil was so deep rooted that the cure was beyond all human thought, when God … gave the people their Queen and shepherd Doña Isabel … By her diligence and government in a very short time, all injustice was changed to justice, all pride to meekness, all wars and divisions … to peace and quiet, so that the whole Kingdom enjoyed security. It was certainly a marvelous thing that what many men and great lords could not agree to effect in many years, one lone woman carried out in a little time." Hunt, *Spain*, 29.

128 Ruiz, *Spain's Centuries*, 91. In keeping with their royal motto, *Tanto monta, monta tanto, Isabel como Fernando* ("it comes to the same thing, Isabel is the same as Fernando"), any reference to Isabel alone in this book also implies the involvement of Ferdinand. Crow, *Spain: The Root and the Flower*, 141.

129 Ruiz, *Spain's Centuries*, 94–101.

130 Ibid., 89–93.

131 Ibid., 48–50.

132 Marías, *Understanding Spain*, 153; Crow, *Spain: The Root and the Flower*, 141–42.

133 Teofilo F. Ruiz, "Oligarchy and Royal Power: The Castilian Cortes and the Castilian crisis 1248–1350," *Parliaments, Estates and Representation* 2, no. 2 (December 1982): 97; Ruiz, *Spain's Centuries*, 93.

134 Ruiz, *Spain's Centuries*, 93.

135 Lynch, *Spain*, 10–12.

136 Kagan, *Lawsuits and Litigants in Castile 1500–1700*, 70–71.

137 Lynch, *Spain*, 6–8; Hunt, *Spain*, 24; Parry, *The Spanish Seaborne Empire*, 236.

138 Kagan, *Lawsuits and Litigants in Castile 1500–1700*, 70–71. Urban oligarchies initially collaborated with this local government, but as municipalities increasingly refused to accept the *corregidores* as agents of the central

government, aristocratic power regained dominance in most towns by the end of the fifteenth century.

139 Jurisdiction in ecclesiastical courts was also made subject to oversight by royal courts. Helmholtz, *The Spirit of Classical Canon Law*, 140.

140 Lynch, *Spain*, 6–8.

141 Thomas, *Rivers of Gold*, 27–28. Grandees were also encouraged to attend to the royal couple and to spend a great deal of time with the peripatetic court—a policy that later became standard with royal states.

142 Pérez Fernández, *Cronología*, 98.

143 Manuel Giménez Fernández, "Fray Bartolomé de Las Casas: A Biographical Sketch," in *Bartolomé de Las Casas in History*, 69.

144 Pérez Fernández, *El Derecho Hispano-Indiano*, 26, 27, 40, 134.

145 Eric Nelson, "The Problem of the Prince," in *The Cambridge Companion to Renaissance Philosophy*, 319–37; Black, "The Philosopher and Renaissance Culture," 27.

146 This political thought in the *quattrocento* assumed the superiority of princely rule, stressed the correspondence of sound princely education with sound princely governance, and viewed the promotion of virtue as the essence of Christianity, and the key to political wisdom as an understanding of the past. Political thinkers contributed to the ongoing conversation in the 1500s and extended the discourse into the sixteenth century in works such as Niccolo Machiavelli's *The Prince* and Thomas More's *Utopia*.

147 Winks and Ruiz, *Medieval Europe and the World*, 185; Skinner, *The Foundations of Modern Political Thought*, 1:34–35, 117–18.

148 While Juan II may have had pretensions to "absolute power," the Catholic Monarchs had no such aspirations, as discernible, according to Kamen, by the position of the crown relative to the law of the land—such as, the need for consent in order to legislate, the limits to crown power, and the relative infrequency of actual law-making. Kamen, *Golden Age of Spain*, 6–8. See also Liss, *Isabel the Queen*, 106; J. M. Reyes Cano, "Introduccíon," in *Brevísima relación de la destruición de las Indias*, ed. and intro. Reyes Cano (Barcelona: Planeta, 1994), xi; Helen Nader, *Liberty in Absolutist Spain: The Habsburg Sale of Towns, 1516–1700* (Baltimore, MD: Johns Hopkins Univ. Press, 1990), 71–98.

149 Kagan, *Lawsuits and Litigants in Castile 1500–1700*, 71.

150 Knight, *An Account*, 87.

151 Bartosik-Vélez, "Translatio Imperii," 560–61.

152 Marías, *Understanding Spain*, 141. By the time of Contact, the denomination Hispania reflected the ideological imagining of both a glorified past of peninsular unification under the Roman Empire and the aspiration of a hoped-for reunification under the new and expanding "Roman" empire—*Translatio imperii*—led by Spanish monarchs.

153 In testimony of their high regard for the Dominican mendicants, the sovereigns helped to fund the extensive edifice's ongoing construction from 1482 to 1493. They so highly valued the structure that it functioned as their summer home and would become the final resting place of their deceased only son—Juan (1478–1497).

154 While the 1491 "Surrender Treaty of the Kingdom of Granada" stipulated that all Jews born in Granada and the surrounding area who had not converted must leave for the Berber lands by December 8, 1494, this directive was dramatically changed by the 1492 "Edicto de los Reyes Católicos (31 Marzo 1492) desterrando de sus estados a todos los judíos," which gave them four months to leave or face death. Jon Cowans, ed., *Early Modern*

Spain: A Documentary History (Philadelphia: Univ. of Pennsylvania Press, 2003), 15–27.

155 Liss, *Isabel the Queen*, 206–210.

156 Ruiz, *Spanish Society*, 83–85.

157 Norman F Cantor, "The Idea of a Christian commonwealth," *Commonweal*, November 6, 1992, 12. Although from the beginning of Christianity there were methods of regulating dissenters from the faith, the Inquisition as an institution was not established as a special court until 1233 to deal with Albigensianism; the Spanish Inquisition was set up in Seville in 1480 to investigate and judge the sincerity of the Jewish conversos—also known as marranos, or "swine"—as well as to punish the errant. Lynch, *Spain*, 26–38; Crow, *Spain: The Root and the Flower*, 142; Liss, *Isabel the Queen*, 191–96.

158 Bartolomé de las Casas," Memorial de remedios para las Indias (1516)," in *Obras Escogidas: Opúsculos, cartas, y memoriales*, ed. Juan Pérez de Tudela Bueso (Madrid: Biblioteca de autores españoles, 1958), 5:15a (hereafter cited as *O.E.*). Mark Burkholder and Lyman L. Johnson, *Colonial Latin America*, 6th ed. (New York: Oxford Univ. Press, 2008), 116.

159 The Dominicans were divided over the obligation of study; the Augustinians and Mercedarians, over leadership positions; the Franciscans, over poverty.

160 Elizabeth A. Lehfeldt, *Religious Women in Golden Age Spain: The Permeable Cloister* (Aldershot: Ashgate, 2005), passim; Elliot, *Imperial Spain*, 102.

161 Elliot, *Imperial Spain*, 101–106; Ruiz, *Spanish Society*, 82–85.

162 Parry, *Spanish Seaborne Empire*, 36–37; Liss, *Isabel the Queen*, 372–77.

163 Osvaldo F. Pardo, *The Origins of Mexican Catholicism: Nahua Rituals and Christian Sacraments in Sixteenth-Century Mexico* (Ann Arbor: Univ. of Michigan Press, 2006), 39.

164 Rivera Pagán, *A Violent Evangelization*, 229–34.

165 For example, Luther (1483–1546), Zwingli (1484–1531), Calvin (1509–1564). See Cantor, "The Idea of a Christian Commonwealth," 12, 14; D. A. Brading, *The First America: The Spanish Monarchy, Creole Patriotism, and the Liberal State 1492–1867* (New York: Cambridge Univ. Press, 1991), 13–14.

166 Anthony Pagden, *Lords of all the World: Ideologies of Empire in Spain, Britain and France, c. 1500—c. 1800* (New Haven, CT: Yale Univ. Press, 1995), 15, 68–74.

167 David Abulafia, *The Discovery of Mankind: Atlantic Encounters in the Age of Columbus* (New Haven, CT: Yale Univ. Press, 2008), 10–14; Brading, *The First America*, 13–14.

168 "Et tertio die imperasti aquis congregari in septima parte terrae, sex vero partes siccasti et conservasti, ut ex his sint coram te ministrantia seminata adeo et culta." Ezrae 6:42 (Vulgate IV). Luis Madureira, "The Accident of America: Marginal Notes on the European Conquest of the World," *The New Centennial Review* 2, no. 1 (2002): 121–25. Winks and Ruiz, *Medieval Europe and the World*, 260–61.

169 Alain Milhou, "Apocalypticism in Central and South American Colonialism," in *Continuum History of Apocalypticism*, eds. Bernard McGinn, John J. Collins, Stephen J. Stein (New York: Continuum Publishing Group, 2003), 418; Abulafia, *The Discovery of Mankind*, 176.

170 Las Casas, in *O.C.*, 14:41; Liss, *Isabel the Queen*, 316. Abbas Hamdani, "Columbus and the Recovery of Jerusalem," *Journal of the American Oriental Society* 99, no. 1 (January–March 1979): 39–40.

171 Las Casas's rendition of the diary of Columbus records that the admiral exacted a promise from Isabel that the wealth accrued by the discovery would

be used to win back the land and the *casa santa*. Las Casas, *Historia* (Ayacucho), 1:23–28, chap. 2.

172 Fernando Colón, *Historia del Almirante (year 1571)*, 4 vols, ed. Luis Arranz Marquez (Madrid: Historia 16, 2000), 4:40.

173 Margarita Zamora, "Christopher Columbus's 'Letter to the Sovereigns': Announcing the Discovery," in *World Encounters*, ed. Stephen Greenblatt (Berkeley: Univ. of California Press, 1993), 1, 3.

174 Las Casas, *Historia* (Ayacucho), 1:206, chap. 40. These instructions were part of the agreement between the monarchs and Columbus, as articulated in the *Capitulaciones de Santa Fe* (17 Abril 1492) and in the Stipulations bestowing titles (April 30, 1492); see Pérez Fernández, *El Derecho Hispano-Indiano*, 22; Bartolomé de las Casas, *Las Casas on Columbus: Background and the Second and Fourth Voyages*, Repertorium Columbianum vol. VII, ed. and trans. Nigel Griffin, intro. Anthony Pagden (Turnhout: Brepols Publishers, 1999), 7:63.

175 *Digest of Justinian*, 4 vols, trans. Alan Watson (Philadelphia: Univ. Pennsylvania Press, 1985), 4:1, 2, 3.

176 Las Casas, in *O.C.*, 14:56; Las Casas, in *O.C.*, 3:552, chap. 40.

177 Zamora, "Christopher Columbus's 'Letter'," 3; Pérez Fernández, *El Derecho Hispano-Indiano*, 22–23.

178 Recorded in Columbus's diary on October 15, 1492. Las Casas, in *O.C.*, 14:59. In subsequent voyages and in like manner, Columbus claimed other new territories that he discovered for Castile.

179 Patricia Seed, "Taking Possession and Reading Texts: Establishing the Authority of Overseas Empires," in *Early Images of the Americas*, eds., Jerry M. Williams and Robert E. Lewis (Tucson: Univ. of Arizona Press, 1993), 130; Griffen, *Las Casas on Columbus: Background*, 7:75; Las Casas, in *O.C.*, 3:552–53; Zamora, "Christopher Columbus's 'Letter'," 4; Las Casas, in *O.C.*, 14:57.

180 Zamora, "Christopher Columbus's 'Letter'," 3–4. That Columbus made a juridical claim on the islands is not unusual, given that he was influenced by the notarial and documentary culture of the time. Theodore J. Cachey, Jr. "Italy and the Invention of America," *The New Centennial Review* 2, no. 1 (Spring 2002): 22.

181 Pérez Fernández, *El Derecho Hispano-Indiano*, 23.

182 Zamora, "Christopher Columbus's 'Letter'," 6; Las Casas, *Historia* (Ayacucho), 1:361–62, chap. 82. Columbus's desire to take Indigenous people back to Spain was recorded in his diary entrance for October 12, 1492, where he states, "if it please Our Lord, at the moment of my departure, I shall take from this place six of them so that they may learn our speech." *Bartolomé de Las Casas: Diario*, in *O.C.*, 14:57. Apparently, with the beaching of the Santa María, there was not enough room and provisions for all the crewmembers to return to Spain on the remaining two ships. Therefore, Columbus ordered his men to construct a fort or settlement out of timbers of the scuttled ship. Although Columbus claimed that he could subdue the island with fifty men, ironically, upon returning in November of 1493, he found the charred remains of the Spanish settlement; these burnt remains portended the future conflagration of the conquest of colonization. David T. Orique, "Christmas in Latin America: From Collision to Inculturation" in *Oxford Handbook of Christmas*, ed., Timothy Larsen (Oxford: Oxford University Press, 2021), 552–36.

183 Las Casas, *Historia* (Ayacucho), 1:346, chap. 78.

184 As Columbus wrote on October 12, 1492, his ideal was "to convert without force." Las Casas, in *O.C.*, 14:56; Las Casas, *Historia* (Ayacucho), 1:358, chap. 81.

185 Griffen, *Las Casas on Columbus: Background*, 7:70–71; Las Casas, *The Only Way*, 11–12.

186 Ibid., 12–13; Las Casas, *Historia* (Ayacucho), 1:702, chap. 176.

187 Las Casas, *Historia* (Ayacucho), 3:282–88, chap. 79. Jesús H. Alvarez, "Fray Bartolomé de las Casas," *Cuadernos Dominicanos Ensayo* 8 (1984): 17; Marcel Bataillon, "The Clérigo Casas, Colonist and Colonial Reformer," in *Bartolomé de Las Casas in History*, 360, 421n30; Manuel Giménez Fernández, *Bartolomé de las Casas: delegado de Cisneros para la reformación de las Indias 1516–1517*, vol. 1, 1953 reprint (Madrid: Consejo Superior de Investigaciones Científicas, 1984), 1:45–54.

188 The writings of the royal scribe, Alonzo de Santa Cruz, included comments about the Spanish encomenderos, conquistadores, and other officials who perpetrated evils and harm in the Indies. Bartolomé de las Casas, *Brevísima relación de la destruicion de las Indias*, ed. Isacio Pérez Fernández, vol. 3 (Bayamon, Puerto Rico: Centro de Estudios de los Dominicos del Caribe and Universidad Central de Bayamón, 2000), 60–62; Henry Raup Wagner and Helen Rand Parish, *The Life and Writings of Bartolomé de Las Casas* (Albuquerque: Univ. of New Mexico Press, 1967), 109.

189 Las Casas, *Historia* (Ayacucho), 1:210–14, chap. 41; 1:701–04, chap. 176; Griffen, *Las Casas on Columbus*: *Background*, 7:11, 116, 154; "Memorial de Fray Bartolomé de Las Casas y Fray Rodrígo de Andrada al Rey (1543)," in *O.E.*, 5:202ab; Las Casas, *Historia* (Alianza), 3:560–62, chap. 41; Rivera Pagán, *A Violent Evangelization*, 10, 231.

3 The Formation of Las Casas's Juridical Voice

Disciplines of and Studies in Canon Law and Theology

In 1517, Friar Pedro de Córdoba (c. 1460–1525), along with other reform Dominicans and Picard Franciscans, attested to Las Casas's "zeal for God's Law."[1]

In 1544, chronicler (*cronista*) Pedro Gutiérrez de Santa Clara (1521–1603) stated that, when Pedro de las Casas took his eighteen-year-old son to Hispaniola in 1502, Bartolomé "was already a man well-formed and very studious."[2]

In 1552, humanist Juan Ginés de Sepúlveda (1489–1573) described Las Casas's erudition as "most subtle, most vigilant, and most fluent, compared with whom Homer's Ulysses was inert and stammering."[3]

These three contemporaries of Las Casas—the first, an ardent supporter; the second, an ambivalent observer; the third, a strident detractor—offer some indication of the resources that Las Casas brought to his battle for justice. This fight was initiated after his first spiritual conversion and was strengthened by his innate intellectual aptitude and diverse acquired skills, which he developed during his early education in liberal arts at the cathedral school of San Miguel. This chapter demonstrates that Las Casas's adroit juridical approach resulted from his studies in the higher disciplines of canon law and theology, in addition to other formative experiences as a secular priest and Dominican friar. Accordingly, to contextualize the young Las Casas's choice to study canon law, the following section presents the origins of the discipline of canon law, its development and programs in two prestigious universities (that Las Casas presumedly attended) and their relationship to the Catholic Monarchs' employment of *letrados* (learned men) in governance.[4]

Discipline of Canon Law

Since the thirteenth-century founding of *studia generalia*, Castilian Christian education in the higher disciplines was generally organized in the Faculties of Arts, Theology, Medicine, and Law—with separate faculties, as recognized in the *Siete Partidas*, for the study of canon law and of civil (Roman) law.[5] In the evolving university system, canon law became the largest and most popular discipline—first, as another avenue of clerical formation in addition to studies and training offered by convent, monastic, and cathedral schools (including San Miguel in Seville where Las Casas studied), and then, as a springboard for Churchmen to secure positions in papal, royal, diocesan, or cathedral chapter enclaves.[6] Subsequently, in the course of the fifteenth (and sixteenth) century, because legal practice was based on *ius commune* and thus relied greatly on Christendom's canonical jurisprudence as its model, lay would-be civil servants also pursued canonistic training to equip themselves for royal, regional, municipal, or local administrative-judicial service.[7] Indeed, canon law became the highest paid academic discipline (along with civil law), the most sought-after profession, and the subject greatest in demand within the student body.[8]

In Spain, the development of canon law as a distinctive academic discipline, and its dominance over other fields of higher education, began and continued in its oldest universities: Salamanca (in the old kingdom of León), and Valladolid (in the old kingdom of Castile). As will be shown, Las Casas most likely studied at Salamanca and Valladolid. Salamanca was erected in 1218 by Alfonso IX and was endowed since its foundation with more *cátedras* (chairs or professorships) in canon law than in civil law.[9] Valladolid was established about 1264 as a *studium particulare* by Alfonso X el Sabio, and as a *studium generale* in 1293 by Sancho IV el Bravo.[10] As at Salamanca, *cátedras* in canon law at Valladolid outnumbered those in civil law.[11]

Programs of study in canon law were text-based, rigorous, long, and costly. Students studied Gratian's *Decretum* and Gregory's *Decretales* to which gradually were added subsequent papal decrees.[12] The academic year traversed twelve months, with at least six to eight months of course work required each year. A *bachiller* in canon law usually required five to six years of study.[13] The six daily classes—always in Latin—began with early morning *lecciones* (lectures), one before breakfast or at 9 a.m. taught by *prima cátedras* (morning professors), followed by *repeticiones* (review sessions) and *disputaciones* (debates about and application of the laws learned and memorized for ready recall). Classes taught by the *vísperas cátedras* (afternoon professors) proceeded in the same manner.[14] To cope with the expenses of higher education, two avenues were available to students. Some had recourse to residential colleges that were established around or near the university with the initial purpose of providing scholarships and other assistance to poor students.[15] Other students reportedly worked as copyists, servants, and tutors to help pay for food, lodging, books, copy materials, class fees, and the costly graduation ceremony.[16] Las Casas's merchant father had earned sufficient money in the Indies to send his son to Salamanca in 1498.[17]

In addition to these considerations, the advancement of canon law study at Salamanca and Valladolid benefited greatly during the last half of the *quattrocento* when the Catholic Monarchs wrestled control of the universities from the hands of the papacy with the aim of raising educational standards in general, and of producing a more cultivated clergy.[18] Because Isabel and Ferdinand endeavored to rule with "the counsel of the learned" and less with the aid of "the noble," their royal ordinances sought to promote quality education in order to ensure that ecclesial and civil functionaries were highly trained.[19] For example, at the 1478 National Council of Clergy, and with the encouragement of the assembled Spanish Church leaders, the Catholic Monarchs announced their resolve to appoint university-degreed *letrados* to the bishoprics and other senior clerical positions.[20] This implicit move toward *Patronato Real*, which in the Indies became a reality in 1508, was quickly followed by proclamations from the Cortes of Toledo, most of whose members were *letrados*. In 1480, the Cortes announced that only degrees granted by Salamanca and Valladolid would be recognized, and that anyone who graduated from other universities or *escuelas generales* after 1464 must "certify the legitimacy of their academic titles."[21] This policy may also have been the reason why Las Casas was sent to study canon law at Salamanca. In any case, the universities of Salamanca and Valladolid became virtual quarries of *letrados*.[22]

Las Casas understood and identified with this professional cohort. In the twelfth remedy of his 1516 *Memorial de remedios*, he asked the Regents not to send any clergy to the Indies to be a *cura* for the Spanish Christians unless he be a *letrado*. In reference to his conversation with a member of the Royal Council in 1517, Las Casas wrote in his *Historia* that he had "responded *como letrado*."[23] Additionally, when writing about Las Casas's 1514 conversion experience, Gutiérrez de Santa Clara spoke of the young cleric as a "*gran letrado*."[24]

Las Casas's Canon Law Studies

That Las Casas studied canon law is confirmed in sixteenth- and early seventeenth-century documents. Although he did not specify having studied canon law, Las Casas himself referred to his having studied law both in his 1552 publication on *Treinta proposiciones muy jurídicas* and in his 1564 letter to his Dominican confreres.[25] Later, in 1596, Las Casas's confrere—Fray Agustín Dávila Padilla (1562–1604)—stated in his history of the Dominican Province of Mexico that Las Casas studied law "with great care" and benefit.[26] Later in 1629, Juan de Solórzano y Pereira (1575–1655), jurist and member of the Council of Castile as well as a severe critic of Las Casas, alleged that before Las Casas was ordained, he dedicated himself to "*sacrorum canonum studium*" (the study of sacred canons).[27] While current historiography does not question that Las Casas studied canon law and that he did so in preparation for the priesthood, questions remain in current Lascasian scholarship about his juridical formation: Where did he study? How did he earn degrees in *cánones*?

For the most part, there is consensus among Lascasian scholars today as well as indications in colonial chronicles that Las Casas studied in Salamanca from 1498 to 1502. Dominican Friar Antonio de Remesal (1570–1639) wrote in 1619 that when Las Casas's father returned to Hispaniola in 1498, Bartolomé *estudiaba derechos en Salamanca.*[28] In 1595, Gutiérrez de Santa Clara, creole chronicler of the conquest of Peru, wrote that Las Casas was "taken from his studies in Salamanca" when, in 1502, he accompanied his father to Hispaniola.[29] While these chronicles state that Las Casas studied in Salamanca, the source of this information is unknown.

That Las Casas also earned the degree of *bachillerato* is attested in two royal documents. In 1516, a royal *cédula* from the Regents of Castile in Madrid, dated September 16th, ordered the officials of the *Casa de Contratación* in Seville to pay the "Procurador de los Indios, Bachiller Bartolomé de las Casas" the cost of his journey to the Indies.[30] In 1517, a certificate of payment, dated April 6th in Seville, from the treasurer of the House of Trade, Doctor Sancho de Matienzo, stated that Juan Fernández was paid 10,000 *maravedis* for the passage and cargo of "*Bachiller* Bartolomé de las Casas."[31] However, neither of these sources specifically mention Salamanca. In 1953, Giménez Fernández questioned the validity of the title of *bachiller* and suggested that it was merely honorific or, as some suggest, that it was simply used to designate secular clergy.[32] However, writing in 1994, James Lockhart asserted that such "degree titles had great significance as marks of social prestige," and that, as such, they were not used capriciously, especially by well-known persons and in highly public ways.[33]

If Las Casas earned the degree of *bachillerato,* when would he have completed the required five or six years for the *bachillerato* in canon law at Salamanca?[34] Four of the required years of law study could have been completed during his reported residence at Salamanca from 1498 to 1502 before he left for the Indies. After that, Las Casas was back in Europe only from November or December of 1506 until September or November of 1507—during which time he was ordained a deacon in Seville in December 1506—and he was in Rome from January 1507 to April 1507 where he was ordained a secular priest on March 3, 1507.[35] That is, the length of time that he would have had to complete his studies in residence at Salamanca at this time was at best this "window" of six months, since he left for the Indies in late 1507. He returned to Spain in 1515, and in September of 1516, he was first addressed as *bachiller.*[36] Given these data, it seems that Las Casas could not have met the requirements for graduation as a *bachiller*. However, scholarship about the University of Salamanca draws attention to the university's Constitutions promulgated by Benedict XIII in 1381, and reiterated by Martin V in 1413 and 1422, in which authorization was given to reduce the required years of study by taking courses during the summer. That is, after completing the required months of coursework in residence, students could advance their standing by taking courses during the remaining months of the twelve-month academic year, which courses accrued to the following year's work. In this manner, five, and possibly six, years of study could be reduced to three and a half or four years.[37] Moreover, the 1422 Constitutions that Martin V promulgated for the University of Salamanca (and of Valladolid) were modified in 1497, and the dispensations, given particularly for clerics, were in effect when (and if) Las Casas was at Salamanca; indeed, clergy could petition a reduction of one year in the total number of years required.[38] These relaxations of requirements during the *quattrocento* were seemingly due to the rapidly growing student enrollment in programs of civil and canon laws, and to the significantly increasing complexity in the assignment of *cátedras* and student-teachers, as well as to the fact that Spain needed practitioners of jurisprudence to attend to the increasing litigations.[39]

Assuming that Las Casas took advantage of the academic alternatives, his period of study at Salamanca—beginning in May or September 1498 and ending in January 1502—could have constituted reducing five years of coursework to three and a half or four years—depending on precisely when he began his studies in 1498. Moreover, since "with dispensations," the number of years for the study of canon (and civil) law could have been reduced from, for example, six to five, Las Casas could have expeditiously finished all of the requirements for a five-year program for the *bachillerato* by February 1502 when he left for Hispaniola. Additionally, Las Casas's studies may have been accelerated if the accomplished cathedral school of San Miguel included preliminary canon law studies.

Credence is lent to this suggestion by the astounding trajectory of studies undertaken by Diego de Covarrubias (1510–1577). Covarrubias completed the study of humanities by the age of ten, classical literature and "all kinds of juridical works," including the Latin and Greek Fathers (of whose works he had seventy-five) by the age of sixteen, and then became a student in the Faculty of Canon Law. He obtained his *bachillerato* in civil and canon laws at the age of twenty-two, then completed his juridical and humanist formation with theological study, graduated with a *licenciatura* in canon law at age twenty-six, and a doctorate at age twenty-seven.[40]

Supporting these conjectures about Las Casas is the long-held contention of Helen Rand Parish, reiterated in an interview with Paul Vickery, that "by 1502, Las Casas had completed his canonical studies, but was unable to afford the fee traditionally presented to the faculty to actually receive his final [*bachillerato*] degree."[41] Moreover, Parish's assertion would help to explain why Las Casas committed himself to work five years in the Indies. As one fluent in Latin, ordained in minor orders, and schooled in canon law—degree in hand or not, he could secure salaried employment in the Indies as a *doctrinero*—which he did, in addition to helping his father in the provisioner business that was faring poorly. When Las Casas returned to Spain in 1506, he was probably financially able to pay the fees associated with the *bachillerato* degree and graduation ceremonies.

That Las Casas also earned the degree of *licenciatura* (licentiate) is indicated in three royal documents.[42] The first is a record of a discourse in December of 1519 by "*Licenciado* Bartolomé de Las Casas" with Emperor Charles V at Molíns de Rey in reply to the position of Fray Juan de Cabedo, bishop of Darien, that Indigenous people were slaves by nature.[43] The second is a *pregón* (proclamation), dated November 19, 1520, about the privileges given by the king to those who were accompanying "*Licenciado* Bartolomé de Las Casas" to Tierra Firme.[44] The third is a *relación* by Miguel de Castellanos narrating the trip he took in 1521 with "*Licenciado* Bartolomé de Las Casas" to the coast of Paría.[45] Other writings of the colonial period also referred to Las Casas as a *licenciado*. Historian and chronicler Gonzalo Fernández de Oviedo y Valdés (1478–1557), who knew Las Casas at court in 1519, referred to him as *licenciado*.[46] Gutiérrez de Santa Clara—whose father was in Cuba at the same time as Las Casas and whose portrayal of selected aspects of Las Casas's life was accurately sequenced—referred repeatedly to Las Casas as *licenciado* in his narration of the reform project that Las Casas initiated in 1521 in Cumaná.[47] Writing in the third person, Las Casas also retrospectively referred to himself as "*licenciado* Las Casas" when he wrote in his *Historia* about being assigned to Narvaez's expeditions in Cuba.[48] In 1571, *Licenciado* Juan Polo de Ondegardo, a major opponent of Las Casas's position on Inca sovereignty, had commented—albeit derisively—that before Las Casas joined the Dominicans, he "was a cleric licensed in law."[49] Finally, Remesal, who lived at Salamanca, wrote in 1619 that Las Casas *graduó de licenciado* from Salamanca, which raises the question of where Las Casas might have earned the licentiate (Figure 3.1).[50]

The answer to this question is perhaps related to opportunity. First, after Las Casas spent from December 1515 to August 1517 in Spain and in Hispaniola seeking and promoting "a total remedy" for the evils and harm done to the Indigenous people, he stayed at the Dominican convent of San Pablo in Valladolid. While there—from September 11, 1517 to March 22, 1518—he frequented the nearby College of San Gregorio, which was affiliated with the University of Valladolid; there, he could consult with the theologians, philosophers, and jurists of the college who were part of the discussions leading up to the 1512–1513 legislation of the Laws of Burgos in the Indies; he could use the college library, and also assist in the *lecciones* that were given.[51] Seemingly, this was the period—indeed, an important milestone in his study of jurisprudence—to which Las Casas referred when in 1552 he stated at the end of his *Treinta proposiciones muy jurídicas* that it had been "thirty four years since he [I] studied law."[52] Second, he would have been aware of the differences in the degree programs of the Universities of Valladolid and of Salamanca. Valladolid required four years of study for the *bachillerato* in canon law and passing an examination to earn the licentiate. Salamanca, which complained about the brevity of Valladolid's programs, required six years for the *bachillerato*, and five years of teaching as a *bachiller formado* plus

Figure 3.1 Conventual Church of San Pablo, Valladolid.
Source: Image provided by Alexis González de León, OP and Sixto Castro, OP.

an examination to graduate as *licenciado*.[53] Third, since Las Casas had the *bachillerato*, all that he would need to do to earn a licentiate from the University of Valladolid would be to prepare for and take an examination, which he could have done during his seven months at San Gregorio and/or by his study and consultation from March 1518 onward with the royal preachers as he and they accompanied the peripatetic court of the monarch.[54] That he may have earned this advanced degree is indicated by the transition in denomination of his title from *bachiller* to *licenciado*: in the April 1517 certificate of payment, he was addressed as *bachiller*; in the court record of December 1519, he was addressed as *licenciado* (Figure 3.2).

Figure 3.2 Colegio de San Gregorio, Valladolid.
Source: Image provided by Alexis González de León, OP and Sixto Castro, OP.

Finally, further support that Las Casas obtained a licentiate from the University of Valladolid comes from the significant decades-long scholarship of Helen Rand Parish.[55] In addition to having ascertained Las Casas's correct birth date as well as the date and location of his ordination by meticulous archival research at the Vatican Library and the *Archivo General de las Indias* (among others), she repeatedly asserted in print and oral interviews that Las Casas had earned the *bachillerato* in canon law at Salamanca as well as the *licenciatura* in canon law at Valladolid.

In addition to his studies in canon law, Las Casas's second area of expertise was theology. To contextualize his formation in Dominican life and the sacred science of theology, the next section will present the development of the discipline of theology, the Dominican reform movement, and the revival of Thomism, which coalesced in Las Casas's time with the prominence of two Dominican schools—San Esteban and San Gregorio, and of the *Escuela Española.* These developments and institutions both shaped the tenor of Las Casas's voice as a Dominican friar, and anchored the vocal range of his resources as a Thomist.

Discipline of Theology and Dominican Reforms

The study of the higher discipline of theology was initially not an official part of the twelfth-century *studia generalia* of Spain's oldest institutions of higher learning. Instead, Salamanca and Valladolid relied on nearby mendicant convents of the Dominican Order of Preachers and of the Franciscan Friars Minor for the teaching of theology.[56] In the Jewish city of Salamanca, the Spanish Province of the Dominican friars established the convent of San Esteban in 1222—one year after the death of Dominic of Guzmán (1170–1221) who founded the Order of Preachers to reform Christian life, evangelize the Jews and Muslims, and refute heresy.[57] In time, San Esteban became famous within the Order of Preachers for its high-quality instruction and theological formation of its friars.[58] Indeed, by 1270, San Esteban's resources for study included an extensive library acquired through bequests and donations, as well as through benefices and privileges for the purchase and/or copying of written works from Alfonso X, and later from Sancho IV.[59] In 1289, the Spanish Dominican Province assigned more students and professors to San Esteban and, in 1299, elevated San Esteban to the rank of *studium generale.* As such, San Esteban could receive student friars from the entire order as well as grant them teaching certificates.[60] In 1305, the Dominican General Chapter initiated uniformity in the theology program of its *studia generalia*, which by 1328 consisted of preparatory studies in Latin and the *humanidades,* followed by three sequential levels of specialization in logic, philosophy, and theology.[61]

Later, in 1416, Pope Benedict XIII (1394–1417) took advantage of the Dominican (and Franciscan) programs in theology to form the basis for an eventual Faculty of Theology at Salamanca. The pontiff also endowed the *studium generale* of Salamanca with three chairs in theology: *prima, vísperas,* and *biblia.*[62] In the same year, Benedict endowed the *Colegio de San Esteban* (as an *escuela menor* of Salamanca) with five chairs of theology, including a minor chair in Thomism.[63] In 1418, Pope Martin V (1417–1431) established a Faculty of Theology at both Salamanca and San Esteban. The two chairs of theology were occupied by Dominicans—indeed, with few exceptions, an almost uninterrupted chain of Dominicans in one or both of these two *cátedras* would continue until 1606.[64]

At that same time, Martin V established a Faculty of Theology at the University of Valladolid and at its *escuela menor*—San Pablo; Fray Luis de Valladolid, an alumnus of San Pablo, became Dean of the Valladolid Faculty.[65] The institutional relationship between San Pablo and Valladolid with respect to the teaching of theology subsequently developed in the same collaborative way as did San Esteban and Salamanca.[66]

Martin V also structured theological formation at Salamanca, San Esteban, Valladolid, and San Pablo in accord with the twelfth-century model of *lectio* (lectures), *disputatio* (discussions), and *praedicatio* (preaching).[67] Specialization in the science of theology required five years of study at Salamanca, and four years at Valladolid; the two *escuelas menores*—San Esteban and San Pablo—required preparatory study of grammar and *humanidades* (often taught by humanists), three years of Aristotelian logic along with natural and moral philosophy, and then five more years of text-based study of scripture and the *Sentencias.*[68]

These four early *quattrocento* centers of higher learning and their constitutional parameters for the study of theology constituted the principal avenues for theological formation until the construction and subsequent 1499 inauguration of the *Colegio de San Gregorio* at Valladolid by the Dominican bishop of Palencia, Alonso de Burgos. Like San Esteban and San Pablo, this *escuela mayor* closely collaborated with the University of Valladolid's Faculty of Theology.[69] Moreover, like older schools, San Esteban also offered studies in arts, languages, sciences, and mathematics, which probably explains why Columbus spent time there. However, San Gregorio constituted the first Spanish Dominican school dedicated principally to the study of theology.[70]

This steady development of the academic study of theology in Dominican centers of learning was accompanied by a centuries-long struggle within the Order of Preachers about education as an integral component of their mendicant vocation. Dominic insisted on study and, for that reason, located his friars' convents near principal university centers. He exemplified the absolute necessity of study in the search for doctrinal truth, and especially in preparation for preaching the Christian message with knowledge and accuracy, by his ten years at Palencia, where he himself pursued education in liberal arts, philosophy, and theology. However, already in the thirteenth century, some friars, known as *claustra* (cloister), argued that academic study and teaching were detrimental to religious life and sacerdotal ministry, and consequently rejected this dimension of Dominican mendicant life. Other friars insisted on the indispensability of study for effective preaching and of university teaching for ensuring doctrinal orthodoxy. These study-oriented friars, known as observants, called for radical reform in the sense of a return to the roots (*radix*) or origins of their order, and to the four fundamental elements of Dominican mendicant life: assiduous study, doctrinal preaching, contemplative prayer, and communal life.[71]

The changing Iberian world also influenced the Dominican friars' internal affairs: scholasticism gradually declined with the ascendancy of Renaissance philosophies; population numbers decreased with wars, famine, and natural disasters such as the Black Plague (1348–1349). Vocations were fewer, and many who entered the order were less than desirable candidates; strict mendicant poverty became more difficult to live; some friars began living outside of their convents; others lived a more relaxed way of life within, and many were generally negligent about study. To stem this tide of deterioration, the order mandated in 1390 that every province must have at least one convent of observants.[72] During the Western schism, the mounting decadence within the order with respect to doctrinal study further fueled the struggle between the growing group of *claustra* friars and the diminishing minority of radical reformers.[73]

During the *quattrocento*, many prominent Dominicans, in particular, those who taught or studied at San Esteban, Salamanca, San Pablo, or Valladolid, contributed to the eventual triumph of the reform movement in the next century. For example, through the efforts of jurist, theologian, writer, and future cardinal, Juan de Torquemada (1388–1468), the priory of San Pablo accepted reform in 1460.[74] The presence of Fray Diego de Deza (1433–1523) at Salamanca and San Esteban, in addition to the certitude that study would remain an essential component of Dominican life, contributed to San Esteban also becoming part of the Congregation of priories of radical reform in 1486.[75] Deza also accomplished the observant reform of San Gregorio in 1499 and, in keeping with the emphasis on study, augmented the number of students at this center of theological studies from sixteen to thirty student friars, and extended the length of study from seven to eight years. A key figure in fostering radical reform at the beginning of the sixteenth century was Friar Juan Hurtado de Mendoza (1456?–1525) who greatly elevated the atmosphere of study and observance in the order during his tenure at San Esteban.[76] His consistent and zealous commitment to reform would bear fruit, particularly in the Dominicans who were assigned to the Indies.

In addition to the reform movement and its revival of study as an arm of the Dominican apostolate, another discernible change was taking place: Thomism began to be added to and/or replaced the *Sentencias* in the study of theology at Dominican centers of learning.[77] Instead of writing commentaries on the *Sentencias* using Aquinas's *Summa theologiae*, friars wrote commentaries directly on the *Summa*. Eventually, the *Summa* became the basic text in theology in Dominican Houses of Study.[78]

In Spain, the progressive advance of the Thomist philosophical-theological perspective in academia, and the consequent revitalization of scholasticism, began in the mid-*quattrocento*. Torquemada, who held the *prima cátedra* of theology at Valladolid and who was known as one of the most erudite and illustrious of Spanish Dominican Thomists, used Aquinas in his 1453 *Summa de Ecclesia*. Friar Alonso Fernández de Madrigal (c. 1410–1455), an alumnus of the *escuela mayor* of San Bartolomé, who taught at Salamanca in the *prima cátedra* of moral philosophy, the *biblia cátedra* (using three languages), and the *vísperas cátedra* of theology, published biblical commentaries based on Aquinas. Madrigal's disciple, theologian Pedro Martinez de Osma (1420–1480), who was regarded by his pupil, Nebrija, as "the wisest Spaniard since [Madrigal]," and who first taught philosophy and then theology in the *prima cátedra* at Salamanca from 1444 to 1478, introduced Thomistic Aristotelianism in all of his courses at Salamanca in 1475.[79] Friar Diego de Deza—Osma's student who occupied the chair vacated by Osma's dismissal and death—taught Aquinas's theology in that *prima cátedra* of theology at Salamanca from 1480 to 1486, and is credited with influencing San Esteban to accept Thomism. Indeed, as Andrés commented, the friars at the reformed San Esteban "*hizo gala*" (gloried in) Thomism.[80] Outside of this *quattrocento* Spanish Dominican enclave of the adoption of Thomism, the Catholic Monarchs, who had much association with Deza and who generally "favored" the Dominican mendicant friars, welcomed Thomism as a vehicle for the defense and expansion of the Catholic faith, which they regarded as one of the new functions of higher education in the formation of Church and Crown officials. Outside of Spain, Friar Girolamo Savonarola (1452–1498), known for his zeal for religious, ecclesial, and political reforms, his condemnatory apocalyptic sermons, and his austere religious lifestyle, also drew on Aquinas and Aristotle.[81]

At the turn of the century, Thomism was promoted even more widely in academia and in Dominican formation and scholarship. Deza's 1499 reform of San Gregorio included the study of Aquinas's philosophical-theological scholarship in its curriculum of theology. The 1505 General Chapter of the Order of Preachers mandated that the doctrine of Aquinas must be studied in all Dominican convents as an important aspect of the friars' initial and ongoing formation.[82] Cardinal Tomás de Vio Cajetan (1469–1536), Master General of the Order of Preachers from 1508 to 1512, became one of the foremost sixteenth-century defenders and exponents of Thomism. Las Casas would study and employ Cajetan's *Commentaries* on Aquinas's writings in his defense of Indigenous peoples.[83] Equally influential and productive through his many commentaries on the *Summa* was the Dominican Spanish theologian, Matías de Paz (c. 1468–1519), who taught Thomistic theology at San Gregorio from 1497 to 1511 and *Biblia* at Salamanca from 1513 to 1519, and who, as noted by Las Casas, also expeditiously wrote a Latin treatise in defense of Indigenous people within the span of a fortnight.[84]

These curricular, scholarly, and reform components of Dominican life coalesced in the Spanish Province's two great centers of learning: San Esteban and San Gregorio. While both institutions were models of observant life and communal prayer, of the apostolate of study and preaching, as well as strongholds of Thomism, they differed. San Esteban was a first-rate academic center of medieval Thomism for the Spanish Dominican province and applied this variant of scholasticism to issues related to the Indies. San Gregorio was the center and wellspring of theological innovations and was open to European scholastic trends such as nominalism, to cultural trends such as Christian humanism and traditional asceticism, as well as to mystical spiritual currents such as those of Savonarola and the *illuminati*.[85]

Upon this Thomistic foundation of speculative and applied theology, a new approach to scholastics' pursuit of truth and a new school or movement—the *Escuela Española*—gradually took shape during the first half of the sixteenth century.[86] Spearheaded in the work of the Dominican theologian, Francisco de Vitoria, this more or less loose association of scholars—from San Esteban and Salamanca, from San Gregorio and Valladolid, from Dominican as well as other religious orders, from regular as well as secular clergy, and even some from Portugal—represented a new type of theology that, while solidly Thomistic, was more flexible and less rigid, more open to multiple *Maestros* (teachers or experts) and sources, and more independent in thinking than the traditional medieval approach to Thomistic thought. While Aquinas remained the best theologian and the best guide for the theological task of the pursuit of truth, scholars in the *Escuela Española* felt free to adapt, change, or even dissent from Aquinas's position as they sought to integrate theological, philosophical, economic, and political knowledge in their responses to the issues of their era.[87]

Such was the sea of historical context surrounding the archipelago of informal and formal opportunities for Las Casas's theological and Dominican formation. These included the influence of the early Dominicans, his profound conversions, and subsequent training in the novitiate and *studentate* of the *studia generalia* in Santo Domingo on the island of Hispaniola.

Las Casas's Dominican Formation

In September of 1510, the arrival of the first Friars Preachers to Hispaniola initiated Las Casas's informal introduction to his future life as a Dominican friar. The first community of Dominicans, composed of three priests (Pedro de Córdoba, Antón de Montesinos, and Bernardo de Santo Domingo) as well as one lay brother (Domingo de Villamayor), quickly made their presence felt in the Indies. In December of 1511, during the Mass of the Fourth Sunday of Advent, Friar Antón Montesinos delivered a community-formulated denunciatory homily directed at the Spaniards' injustices committed against the Taínos on the island.[88] Although Las Casas was not present to listen to this fiery Sunday homily or to the following Sunday's accusatory reiteration, which he heard from others and recorded in his *Historia* about the controversy initiated by these reform Dominicans, the Spaniards were horrendously unjust to the Indigenous people.[89] The friars' public presence and their prophetic message challenged all—including the young Padre Bartolomé de Las Casas.

These first Dominicans in the Indies—followed by many others—were Salamanca-trained and religiously observant. For example, Córdoba took the habit at the reformed *Colegio de San Esteban* in Salamanca where, as Las Casas commented, he studied "to great benefit the arts and philosophy and theology."[90] Indeed, all of the friars assigned to Hispaniola had studied and lived at San Esteban. Their academic training in the philosophical and theological tradition of Thomism at this prestigious *Colegio* was part of the first collective expression of the scholastic revival that eventually became known as the School of Salamanca and that would later greatly influence Las Casas's legislative efforts as well.[91]

In addition to the first Dominicans' dedication to preaching and study, their religious life was marked by austerity and strict observance. Before coming to Hispaniola, all of the friars had also lived at the convent of Santo Tomás de Ávila. Life in this most austere of all the priories in Spain was guided by the priorship of Juan de Hurtado de Mendoza, as well as propelled by the climate of Isabelline reforms of religious orders and by the atmosphere of Savanarola's criticisms of Church decadence in Italy.[92] In Hispaniola, these friars, with Córdoba as their vicar, espoused an austere lifestyle of absolute poverty as noted by Las Casas in his *Historia*—one even more austere than that advocated by Girolamo Savanarola.[93] Through their life of strict observance, coupled with communal prayer, and the apostolate of study and preaching, the friars desired to be a Christian model for societal transformation. Accordingly, they and other contemporaneous reformed religious sought to live like the early Christian apostolic community as narrated in scripture that exemplified unanimity in faith, simplicity of lifestyle, communal living, and unity of apostolate.[94]

Furthermore, in their zeal for the proclamation of the gospel and the salvation of souls, they identified, challenged, and condemned the injustices committed by the Spanish conquest and colonization of the Indies. In addition to their incendiary pulpit denunciations, intellectual penchant, and radical lifestyle, the friars utilized the Sacrament of Confession as another instrument in their fight against the injustices: they denied absolution to those holding Indigenous people in encomienda. Although Las Casas considered himself a "good" encomendero and a man of peace, in the eyes of these Dominican friars, he was just like the rest.[95] As such, sometime between the end of 1511 and the beginning of 1512, when Las Casas went to one of the Dominicans (probably Córdoba) to confess his sins, he, too, was refused absolution because he held an encomienda.[96] The powerful example of the Dominicans' bold use of the Sacrament of Confession, prophetic preaching, austere lifestyle, and learned approach to justice issues shaped and provoked Las Casas's conscience. This bold example, coupled with his traumatic witness of the tragic massacre of Arawaks in Caonao (Cuba) in October 1513, as recorded in his *Historia*, led to what scholars refer to as his "first conversion" in 1514.[97]

Las Casas's conversion from a secular cleric and gentleman-encomendero to a strident reformer and adroit *fiscal* was neither an instantaneous episode nor without preparation—proximate and remote, but rather the fruit of a long process culminating in 1514 when his life took a radical turn: he gave up material pursuits, freed the Indigenous persons he had in *encomienda*, and began to seek "a total remedy" for the evils and harm done by the Spaniards to the Indigenous peoples.[98] Consequently, in 1515 on the recommendation of Córdoba, Las Casas returned to Spain with Montesinos to enlist Crown and Church backing for three successive reform projects that he proposed over the next seven years. Throughout this period, Las Casas received ongoing fraternal support from Dominicans on both sides of the Atlantic. In the Indies, Córdoba was his "spiritual godfather"; the Dominicans and Picard Franciscan friars supported him. In Spain, Juan Quevedo, OFM, bishop of Darien, corroborated Las Casas's narration at a royal audience about the mistreatment of Indigenous people. Diego de Deza, OP, then archbishop of Seville, wrote letters recommending Las Casas to the king and the court. Tomás de Matienzo, OP, a royal confessor, advised Las Casas to consult with Bishop Fonseca and Secretary Conchillos of the Council of Castile. Reginaldo Montesinos, OP, Antón's brother in Valladolid, informed Juan Hurtado, OP, the Prior of San Esteban, who, in turn, solicited advice from thirteen university professors at Salamanca. Hierónimo Peñafiel, prior of San Pablo, notified the Dominican Master General, Cardinal Cajetan, about the oppression of the Indigenous people.[99] The Dominicans' own *Memoriales* to the Crown, as well as the 1517 *Memorial* written jointly by the Hispaniola Dominicans and the Picard Franciscans, lauded Las Casas's tenacious endeavors, which included *denuncias, peticiones*, and other genres of the civil-juridical tradition, as well as corroborated the urgent need for reform.[100] So similar were their descriptions and assessments that the 1519 *Memorial* written by the Dominicans to Monsieur de Xévres, the chief chamberlain of Charles V, could have been a template for the content of Las Casas's *Brevísima relación* that he produced twenty-three years later.[101] During the period of project proposals, Las Casas also received support and advice from jurist-theologians at Salamanca and at Valladolid for his "great providential mission."[102] That is, in assessing and addressing the consequences of the conquest and colonization that impeded the rational and peaceful proclamation of the gospel, Las Casas was neither alone, nor was he "an isolated figure." Rather, he was part of the apostolic tradition of prayer, study, and action that an active minority used to battle for justice; in time, Las Casas would become the center of this tradition.[103]

Las Casas's immersion into this tradition resulted from a "second conversion."[104] The trajectory that brought him to this change encompassed a number of years. Initially, he was discouraged by the failure of his 1516 utopian plans for a "total remedy" on the islands of Hispaniola, Cuba, and Jamaica. Subsequently, his 1518 "Peasant Plan," which proposed bringing farmers to the Indies as peaceful settlers, was sabotaged. The project was stonewalled by corrupt royal officials—particularly by Bishop Fonseca, as well as opposed by large Spanish landowners, and denied the financial support of the Council of Castile.[105] Finally, Las Casas's ambitious 1521–1522 Cumaná project (Venezuela), which was his first experiment in peaceful evangelization solely by friars accompanied by would-be farmers, disastrously ended when, due to slave raids, the enraged Indigenous people massacred the handful of friars and other Spaniards at the settlement. Having avoided this brush with death, Las Casas abandoned the life of an active diocesan cleric and embraced the life of a mendicant friar in the studious Order of Preachers in Santo Domingo.[106] All that had gone before this radical decision was "a prelude to a new stage of his life, [which would develop into a] very distinctive … [and] long career."[107]

Las Casas's initial formal training as a Dominican friar at the Santo Domingo *studium generale* consisted of a one-year novitiate from 1522 to 1523 and a three-year *studentate* from 1523 to 1526.[108] Las Casas began this period of formation at the age of thirty-eight and was, as is said in Spanish, *un hombre hecho* (a mature man); for him, there was no wasting of time or opportunity for distractions—especially since he had entered a community where the tension and the intensity of the reforming spirit brought from Spain by Pedro de Córdoba and the other friars was in full force.[109]

At the beginning of his novitiate, Las Casas apparently received the habit from Tomás de Berlanga, the Prior of Santo Domingo.[110] His novice master was most likely Domingo Betanzos.[111] Ironically, the 1506 Provincial Chapter of the Dominicans of Spain had issued a statute ordering that no one of Jewish descent was to receive the habit.[112] Las Casas, presumably of Jewish ancestry, was in good company—he, Talavera, Vitoria, and other prominent Spaniards shared this sanguinal "impurity."[113]

During his novitiate, Las Casas became schooled in the fundamentals of Dominican life: observant community life, prayer, the apostolate of study, preaching, teaching, and sacerdotal ministries. Under the guidance of Betanzos, Berlanga, and other friars, Las Casas was systematically immersed into the rhythm and rigor of communal life, with its regularly scheduled communal prayer, community meetings, and penitential practices—which asceticism he continued throughout his life. As part of their observant-cloistered community life, the Hispaniola friars observed silence throughout the day, fasted six months annually, abstained from meat, kept vigil in prayer at night, and walked to their destinations rather than be transported.[114] According to Pérez Fernández's erudite knowledge of the historical development of Dominican life, Las Casas adhered "from the first day to all the rules and regulations of the community in order to learn what he needed to do" as a Dominican friar.[115]

With respect to liturgical prayer, Las Casas needed to familiarize himself with the Dominican variance of this worship. Although already a priest, he needed to learn to celebrate Mass according to the Dominican Rite.[116] As a neophyte friar, he also needed to learn the Dominican variant of the Divine Office—of the Liturgy of the Hours. Since the order's foundation in 1216, all Dominicans were required to pray the full Divine Office—*Matins*, *Lauds*, *Prime*, *Terce*, *Sext*, *None*, *Vespers*, and *Compline* (ending with the singing of the *Salve*).[117] Las Casas would have been exposed to liturgical prayer at the cathedral school in Seville as well as prayed the canonical Hours as a diocesan priest.[118] That Las Casas was faithful to liturgical prayer and its daily rhythm is implied by his comments in the *Apologética historia sumaria* about his recourse to the light of fireflies when praying early morning *Matins*. He wrote that "the fireflies are so large that, with one alive in the hand—and better with two, *Matins* can be prayed from a small print breviary, and so I have prayed them as though [I had] two small candles."[119]

With respect to the apostolic dimension of the Dominican life, the focus in the novitiate was primarily on study related to the order, the Bible, Church history, patristics, and spirituality. Accordingly, as Pérez Fernández pointed out, Las Casas studied the history and the Constitutions of the order, as well as memorized the Rule of St. Augustine and the Epistles of St. Paul. Furthermore, the novitiate was a time to deepen one's knowledge of sacred scripture, to study more ecclesial tradition and ecclesiastical history, as well as the Church Fathers and biographies of the saints, to read various spiritual writers, and, in particular, to learn Dominican spirituality.[120]

Although, as all novices, Las Casas most likely did not engage in any public preaching, he did spend time periodically after meals teaching Christian doctrine to local Taínos. In this interaction with the first peoples of Hispaniola, he also developed additional understanding of their three principal languages, but his level of linguistic skill is unknown.[121] Finally, in preparation for his future labors, Las Casas also devoted at least part of his free time to drafting his first book—a missionary tract on the method of rational and peaceful evangelization, which would be commonly known as *De unico vocationis modo omnium gentium ad veram religionem* (The Only Way to Call all People to a Living Faith).[122]

After finishing his novitiate year and with the vote of the community, Las Casas professed the solemn vows of poverty, chastity, and obedience to Berlanga, as prior of the community.[123] These vows would have canonically sealed his total commitment, without reservation, to the order. From this moment on, he began his life as a student friar.[124]

Las Casas then spent three years in the *studentate* at the priory of Santo Domingo. Previously, in 1518, Santo Domingo had become part of the new Spanish Province of Andalusia (or Bética), and was designated the *studium generale* of the order in the Indies.[125] The designation of this convent of thirty-six friars as a *studium generale* meant that a contingent of friar-professors was among those assigned to Santo Domingo. These friars alternated in teaching required courses and, according to their Franciscan students, excelled in lecturing.[126] The ideal for the full course of studies consisted of Latin and three consecutive levels of learning: arts (grammar, rhetoric, logic); Aristotelian philosophy (natural and moral, and also physics, metaphysics, and ethics); and theology (beginning with scripture study, followed by systematic, dogmatic, moral, and practical theologies).[127] However, since Las Casas had studied Latin and liberal arts at the cathedral school of San Miguel, it is also possible that he had earned a *bachillerato* in canon law at Salamanca, as well as had exposure to at least some introductory theological and moral study in his preparation for the secular priesthood—not to mention the licentiate in canon law that he likely earned at Valladolid. The range of studies at the theological level that Las Casas might have taken may be partially inferred from Córdoba's formation (1501–1509) at San Esteban, which in accord with the mandated Dominican *ratio studiorum* included courses in systematic theology (Lombard's *Sentencias* and Aquinas's *Summa theologiae*), in dogmatic and moral theologies, as well as in scripture and the Psalter.[128] Pérez Fernández contended that Las Casas's training at Santo Domingo was theological, philosophical, and canonistic; he and others also maintain that his theological studies extended beyond the study of Aquinas's *Summa contra Gentiles*, *Scriptum super Sententias*, and *Summa theologiae* to include the recently published commentaries of Dominican Cardinal Cajetan on *Secunda secundae* of the *Summa theologiae*.[129] This contention is credible when comparing his pre-and-post-Dominican-formation writings, as well as evidenced in his copious citations and references to these sources.

In addition to this *tomista-cayetanista* formation, Las Casas probably also studied Aristotelian philosophy and logic, and, as Pérez Fernández stated, updated himself on the law that was in force at the time.[130]

According to her archival study of sixteenth-century Dominican preachers in the Indies, Pita Moreda stated that the *studentate* studies also included "anything else that could be useful to the study of theology and to the illumination of truth."[131] To this end, Las Casas's surely studied Córdoba's *Doctrina cristiana para instrucción de los Indios*, which drew from Spanish catechisms of Talavera, Cisneros, and Deza.[132] In any case, student friars were encouraged to read, write, and privately pray in their cells, and could stay up an extra hour to study after *Compline*.[133] This fostering of "attentive and meditative" study was also balanced by domestic chores and some public apostolic activities.[134]

The designation of Santo Domingo as a *studium generale* of the order also meant that an adequate library would have been available at the priory. Since the twelfth century, Dominican General and Provincial Chapters have stressed the need and the right of individual friars, as well as the obligation of convents and Dominican *studia generalia*, to acquire needed useful and valuable books.[135] Each friar must receive a stipend from the province or priory to buy books for his personal library and may keep any books he received. Each convent had to have books for general use, for specific disciplinary study, and for reference (which books were chained down). Accordingly, Dominicans were "prepared to go to great lengths to insure a constant supply of the right type of books for the use of all members of the Order."[136]

By the end of the *quattrocento*, the usual holdings in Dominican libraries were biblical commentaries and exegesis, theological works, including the *Summas* and *Sentencias*, in addition to commentaries, extensive philosophical works, books on canon law, some on civil law, and a good variety of contemporary writers; the libraries held few books in arts, except for those related to grammar and music. Assuming a similar development in the holdings of the *studium generale* of Santo Domingo, access to books may help explain how Las Casas was able to begin drafting his first missionary tract in 1522. The presence of an adequate supply of written and printed works at Santo Domingo would also have offered an opportunity for Las Casas to pursue autodidactic study—as some Lascasian scholars note.[137]

Finally, the combination of rich sources for learning during the *studentate* in the acknowledged expertise of friar-teachers and in the mandated range of library holdings at Santo Domingo could have resulted, as Pérez Fernández contended, in Las Casas's studies at Santo Domingo being the equivalent to a *licenciatura* in theology, and that his *De unico vocationis modo*, the first missiological tract of the modern era, was a kind of licentiate thesis.[138] This is plausible and important to help sort out the opportunities available to him to engage in additional studies, which assists in arguing that he earned this advanced degree.

Be this as it may, Las Casas's post-formation writings, in the form of more than three hundred *cartas*, *memoriales*, *informes*, and *obras*—beginning with his first known exigent text, the 1531 *Carta* to the Council of the Indies—do demonstrate a significant change in the level of theological, philosophical, juridical, and historical sophistication when compared with those written before 1522.[139] His citations from canon and Roman laws became impressively extensive and detailed, as well as dialectically interwoven with Thomistic philosophical-theological arguments—even in his historical works: the *Historia de las Indias* and the *Apologética historia sumaria*. His dialogues engaged jurists as well as theologians and philosophers and, in particular, the multifaceted perspectives of the emerging *Escuela Español* in the writings, for example, of Vitoria, de Soto, Cano, and Carranza. His persistent juridical approach—enriched with Thomistic thought—mirrored the confluences of canon law and theology that were standard as jurists, theologians, and philosophers addressed the issues associated with the historical presence of the Spaniards in the Indies.[140] What Las Casas had learned, knew, and wrote was manifested in certain general features of this discernible confluence.

Convergence of Canon Law and Theology

While the progressive development and institutionalization of human knowledge in *studia generalia* created separate faculties as well as academically independent disciplines, the spheres of canon law and theology overlapped and intermingled.[141] Many features of these two sciences were not separate. This section presents four common features as points of confluence in these two disciplines to show the propitiousness of Las Casas's study of theology and canon law. This section also presents the distinctiveness of Las Casas's juridical approach.

The first common feature—indeed, the basic vital unity—of the disciplines of canon law and theology consisted in their fundamental focus on the Christian life. Both disciplines were sacred sciences because they addressed the spiritual order and those aspects of the temporal order that pertained to eternal salvation. Theology studied and explained revealed truths about God and about humans' relationship to God and one another, while canon law governed the life of the Church and those aspects of secular society that pertained to eternal salvation and, additionally, those behaviors that threatened to affect the good order of society.[142] In the *Brevisima relación*, Las Casas repeatedly affirmed the primacy of the spiritual end of the *salus animarum* (salvation of souls), and forcefully condemned behavior in the temporal order that was not in accord with the Christian life.[143]

A second common feature of both canon law and theology was that they addressed many of the same topics. For example, both canonistic prescriptions and dogmatic teachings addressed salvation-oriented matters such as heresy, blasphemy, and apostasy—areas on which Las Casas also specifically focused in the *Brevísima relación*.[144] In addition to all aspects of the spiritual order and to the Church's exclusive jurisdiction over anyone of clerical status—from student to pope, canon law and theology also claimed jurisdiction over most aspects of Christians' conduct from cradle to grave.[145] While the jurisdictional boundaries between ecclesial and secular orders were not always clearly defined, an example of an unambiguous area of jurisdiction was with respect to the *miserabiles personae*. Both canonists and theologians viewed special solicitude for the poor and powerless as a permanent part of God's plan; unlike all other persons, the *miserabiles personae* were not required to exhaust all temporal remedies before seeking assistance from the Church.[146] How this solicitude for the *miserabiles personae* was operationalized differed: accordingly, for the most wretched of their respective societies, Augustine called for *aid* in fourth-century Roman Africa; Ubaldis advocated *protection* in fourteenth-century Italy; and Las Casas demanded *justice* in sixteenth-century "America" in his *Very Brief Account*.[147]

A third common feature of canon law and theology was that both disciplines utilized, among others, the same theological and canonistic sources. Theologically, much of canon law was shaped indirectly by scripture: biblical passages substantiated decrees and decretals; biblical examples served to justify a canonical rule or decision; biblical principles guided or corroborated conclusions.[148] While the text of the *Brevísima relación*, which summarized an extremely lengthy official report, did include direct biblical references to both the Old and New Testaments, Las Casas's use of sources from his "immense fund of classical and medieval learning" is better exemplified in his *El unico vocationis modo* (The Only Way).[149] In this missionary treatise, he copiously cited the Vulgate Bible, especially the Gospels of Matthew and Luke, the Epistle of Paul to the Thessalonians, and the Letter to Timothy.[150] As with the development of Christian doctrine, the writings of the Church Fathers and of theologians also informed the articulation and application of canon law.[151] In *El unico vocationis modo*, Las Casas cited the first Apostolic Fathers in addition to Latin and Greek patriarchs. Theologians that he used as sources included a third-century pope, French and English scholars, as well as Franciscan and Dominican intellectuals.[152]

Las Casas also drew from other sciences considered auxiliary to canon law, such as philosophy, logic, Roman and civil laws, as well as sacred, ecclesiastical, and secular history.[153] For example, in *The Only Way*, he referred to philosophers and jurists of antiquity and of the medieval period.[154] He quoted copiously from the juridical collections of the *Corpus Juris Canonici* and the *Corpus Juris Civilis*.[155] In the *Brevísima relación*, Las Casas also referenced ancient writers, philosophers, jurists, and legal sources, as well as utilized Aquinas's theology for his epistemological rationale and juridical analysis of the destruction of the Indies.

In like manner, theology utilized auxiliary sciences. For example, in his theological works, Aquinas made extensive use of Gratian's *Decretum*, as well as of sources from philosophy, logic, and [other] secular sciences.[156] Similarly, in the Spanish School, scholarship routinely combined systematic elements of Aquinas's *Summa theologiae* with philosophic and canonistic perspectives. Indeed, deliberations and writings of this early modern period, including those of Las Casas, were remarkably multi-disciplinary in their skillful intertwining of theology, philosophy, canon (and civil) law, patristics, classical works, as well as of past and contemporary history.[157]

The fourth common feature of the convergence of canon law and theology was substantive and consisted of confronting the complex moral issues surrounding the encounter, conquest, and colonization of the Indies. Emerging during the first half of the sixteenth century, this convergence applied both canon law and Thomism to this reality. The applicability of canonistic and theological approaches to contemporaneous situations was derived from canon law's character as a practical theology. Simply put, theology was the study of revelation, and canon law was the application of theology. For example, the revealed scriptural mandate to "go teach all nations" was expressed in part by papal privileges—in the form of *cánones*—that were granted to the mendicant orders to carry out this mission. Similarly, canonical directives concerning the instruction of would-be Christians prior to their baptism were an application of the revealed mandate to "baptize … in the name of the Father, and of the Son, and of the Holy Spirit." In the *Brevísima relación*, Las Casas included both the canonical duty to preach the gospel and the canonical right to hear the gospel preached.[158]

As a form of practical theology, canon law was similar to and yet different from moral theology. Both canon law and moral theology prescribed and proscribed human conduct: *cánones* by external law related to proximate ends; moral theology in terms of humans' "last end." Canon law related to the external good order of Christian society, whereas moral theology focused on internal Christian formation and conscience.[159] In the *Brevísima relación*, Las Casas both condemned "the hell that is the Indies," that is, the lack of good order on the part of the Spaniards, and called on the conscience of the king to take the right moral action by reforming laws about conquests, encomiendas, and slavery—that is, by establishing new laws.[160]

Distinctiveness of Las Casas's Juridical Voice

These four major features of the intermingling of canon law and theology doubly anchored Las Casas in the basic vital unity of the two disciplines, in specific topics, in common sources, and in the underlying applicability of canonistic-theological study. The distinguishing aspect of his approach to the pressing problems of his day was related to the progressive nature of canon law. This aspect of *cánones* derived from the fact that, unlike Roman law and—to some extent—theology, canon law was not a closed system of texts. For example, in medieval times, the law was moved forward and beyond the original juristic texts by commentaries and subsequently *summas*—such as Hostiensis's *Aurea* (from which Las Casas also drew on his works).[161] Indeed, canon law was a "living law" that was open to further development, and was practiced daily in Spanish ecclesiastical and civil courts, as well as applied to innumerable cases that today would be regarded as the proper jurisdiction of secular authorities.[162] The extensiveness of ecclesiastical jurisdiction as well as this discipline's ability to create new laws by new enactments and/or by reinterpretation of old texts demonstrated the capacity and advantage of a canonistic juridical approach to respond directly to new issues such as those pertaining to the Indies. Las Casas clearly relied on this progressive attribute of canon law in his efforts to establish the ecclesiastical arm of jurisdiction and protection of the Indigenous peoples, and to create new laws for the governance of the Spaniards' presence in the Indies—efforts which Las Casas brought to his audience's attention in the *Brevísima relación*—this reliance was his *forte*.

Las Casas's penchant for a practical juridical approach was further honed by his espousal of the legal scholarship of Bartolus de Saxoferrato, and in particular of two methodological tenets that characterized Bartolus's thinking, writing, and jurisprudential practice. For Las Casas to adopt Bartolist scholasticism was in keeping with the unbroken continuity of the *mos italicus* tradition and with the Crown's preference for the *opino Bartolo* during the reigns of the Catholic Monarchs and of Charles V. The *Escuela Española* also championed this brand of legal scholarship in their speculative attempts to reconcile both human and natural laws with Catholic theology.[163]

The first of Bartolus's methodological tenets to which Las Casas had repeated recourse was in accordance with this *mos italicus* tradition, which stipulated that the known time-honored legal "rules and principles of law" must be employed in the application of law.[164] Examples of principles derived from Roman law and institutionalized in canon law included natural justice (objective "right order" or *naturalis aequitas*), reinstatement of unjust losses (*restitutio in integrum*), and the rule that "what touches all must be approved by all" (*quod omnes tangit ab omnibus approbari debet*).[165] In his *Brevísima relación*, Las Casas supported his judgments with such legal principles and drew attention to the relevant "rule" in several instances.[166]

The second tenet that Las Casas adopted from Bartolist methodology stipulated that law is formed and reformed out of a true account (*relación*) of the facts (*los hechos*).[167] The inductive reasoning from the facts that this method required was a recognized form of legal judgment.[168] In precisely the area of facts, Las Casas surpassed other Spanish jurist-theologians by his years of firsthand experience beginning in 1502 among the Indigenous peoples and by his *relaciones* (official accounts) of facts based on eyewitnesses, corroborative reports, and notarized testimony. In the *Brevísima relación*, Las Casas inducted from the facts of his own experiences and those of others to articulate the "outward scaffolding" of the history of the destruction, which narration was akin to the poetic approach of Aristotle not only in its focus on universals but also in its foretelling of calamities that might befall the Indigenous people, the monarch, and Spain.[169] His narration drew from the particular aspects of the facts—and went beyond the *species facti*—to the general universal factual reality, which Las Casas defined as a question of justice based on principles of law and for which he demanded new legislation.[170]

These considerations about *why* Las Casas may have taken a juridical approach can contribute to Lascasian scholarship about whether or not Las Casas *did* take such an approach. Some scholars, such as Venancio Carro, held that Las Casas's approach was predominantly Thomistic.[171] While Las Casas's thought was certainly rich with the canonistic-philosophic-theological thought of Aquinas, he used that thought to augment or substantiate his juridical arguments, and he drew out the juridical dimensions of that thought as well. Indeed, as will be shown in a later chapter, the epistemological rationale as well as the analytic framework of the *Brevísima relación* utilized the Thomistic understanding of the hierarchy of law and corresponded to components of the ecclesial juridical tradition. Pennington also suggested why Las Casas did not take a primarily theological approach: he pointed out that the theological tradition in the sixteenth century was "more mixed" than that of canon law, and that "legal sources ... carried more weight" than theological speculations.[172] Adorno also contended that "theology was not [Las Casas's] primary expertise," and supported her contention by recourse in part to the level of his formal studies in the discipline of canon law.[173] While Pérez Fernández speculated that Las Casas's theological studies may have been the equivalent of a licentiate, Vidal Abril Castelló pointed out that Las Casas's theology did not have the "technical rigor, ... critical-scientific level, ... [and] analytic punctiliousness" as found in the works of theologians such as Vitoria and De Soto.[174] Pennington, Adorno, and other Lascasian scholars also cited Las Casas's persistent use of ideas from the tradition of medieval legal theory as evidence that Las Casas was "essentially a jurist."[175] Certainly, his sources for texts and authorities in the field of *derecho* were encyclopedic, as Castelló opined after his thorough study of Las Casas's *Apologética história sumaria*. And, as also attested by Castelló, Las Casas was an able practitioner of the law.[176] Finally, Las Casas's own words attest to the primacy of law in his approach: in his 1564 letter to his Dominican confreres, he wrote "for forty eight years, I have labored to inquire about, study, and discern the law, and, I believe, if I am not deceived, that I have plumbed the depths ... and have reached the headwaters."[177]

This study contends that Las Casas employed the logic and substance of the medieval juridical tradition; he capitalized on the progressive nature of canon law in his search for a "total remedy" for the harm done to Indigenous peoples and their world. He brought this juridical approach to the debates taking place on both sides of the Atlantic—debates that will be the focus of the next two chapters.

Notes

1 "Carta Latina de Dominicos y Franciscanos de las Indias a los regentes de España (27 Mayo 1517)," in Miguel Angel Medina, *Una Comunidad al servicio del Indio: la obra de Fr. Pedro de Córdoba, O.P. (1482–1521)* (Madrid: Instituto Pontificio de Teología, 1983), 261 (hereafter cited as *Una Comunidad al servicio*); Gustavo Gutiérrez, *Las Casas: In Search of the Poor of Jesus Christ* (Maryknoll, NY: Orbis Press, 1995), 481n87.

2 … un hombre bien entendido y estudioso … Pedro Gutiérrez de Santa Clara, *Quinquenarios o Historia de las guerras civiles del Perú (1544–1548) y de otros sucesos de Las Indias* (Madrid: Atlas, 1963), chap. 2, 149a (hereafter cited as *Quinquenarios o Historia*). It is believed that Gutiérrez de Santa Clara utilized information from the Dominican chronicler, Juan de la Cruz.

3 Cited in Francis Augustus MacNutt, *Bartholomew De Las Casas: His Life, His Apostolate and His Writings* (Cleveland, OH: Arthur H. Clark, 1909), 6. MacNutt quoted from *Sepulvedae Opera*, tom. 3, lib. 5, pg 241.

4 The term *letrado* was used from the twelfth century onward to denote men trained in civil or canon law. Katherine Elliot Van Liere, "Humanism and Scholasticism in Sixteenth-Century Academe: Five Student Orations from the University of Salamanca," *Renaissance Quarterly* 53, no. 1 (Spring 2000): 75, 82.

5 According to García y García, the term "university" was not used in medieval times, and first appeared in the fifteenth century, for example, in documents related to Salamanca. However, in this book, the term will at times be used to designate pre-*quattrocento studia generalia* of higher learning. Studia generalia (*studium generale*, sing.) was the designation given to an international university of quality by the Holy Roman Empire. These *studia generalia* or "universities" provided opportunity, after the required initial basic academic preparation, to specialize in these higher disciplines, and to obtain graduate degrees at the level of *bachiller, licenciado*, and *doctorado*. The basic academic preparation in Latin, the *trivium*, and the *quadrivium* did not require enrolling in the Faculty of Arts. By the end of the thirteenth century, *studia generalia* also sought the papal privilege of *ius ubique docendi* (the right to teach anywhere), which gave their graduates license to teach in most institutions throughout Christendom without further examination. See Antonio García y García, "Génesis de la universidad, Siglos XIII–XIV," in *Historia de la Universidad de Salamanca:Trayectoria histórica e instituciones vinculadas*, coord., Luis E. Rodríguez-San Pedro Bezares (Salamanca: Ediciones Universidad de Salamanca, 2002), 1:22, 1:50 (hereafter cited as *Historia de la Universidad de Salamanca*); García y García, "Consolidaciones del Siglo XV," in *Historia de la Universidad de Salamanca*, 1:50.

6 In addition to these reasons for clergy rather than laity to pursue canon law study, clerics were able to obtain more exemptions even in the number of years of study, as well as had access to major benefices that were not

available to lay students. Furthermore, in 1219, Honorius III forbade secular and regular clergy to study civil law. Mariano Peset and Pilar García Trobat, "Poderes y modelos universitarios, siglos XV–XVI," in *Historia de la Universidad de Salamanca*, 2:39.

7 A gradual shift in the purpose of learning also became evident as the humanists' goal of learning as a preparation for *la vida activa y civil* in service to the prince, the nation, and God was replaced with the pursuit of desirable credentials by higher studies in those specialized disciplines from which a living could be earned, or in which there were opportunities for advancement, prestige, or new careers in royal and ecclesial hierarchies. James A. Brundage, "The Teaching and Study of Canon Law in the Law Schools," in *The History of Medieval Canon Law in the Classical Period, 1140–1234: From Gratian to the Decretals of Pope Gregory IX*, eds., Wilfried Hartmann and Kenneth Pennington (Washington, DC: Catholic Univ. of America Press, 2008), 99 (hereafter cited as *History of Medieval Canon Law*), 60–61; Juan Gutiérrez Cuadrado, "Christian Universities," in *Medieval Iberia: An Encyclopedia*, eds. E. Michael Gerli, Samuel G. Armistead, et al. (New York: Routledge, 2003), 820.

8 For example, by the late thirteenth century, 194 of Salamanca's students were studying canon law as compared with 50 in Roman law, and 52 of Valladolid's students were enrolled in *cánones* as compared with 13 in civil law. In 1381, of Salamanca's 331 students, 166 or 50.1% studied canon law as compared with 20 or 6% who studied civil law. This is even more significant when taking into account that three-fourths of Castilian students were attending Salamanca in 1400. Susana Guijarro González, "Las escuelas y la formación del clero de las catedrales en las diócesis castellanos-leonesas (siglos XI al XV)," in *La enseñanza en la edad media: X Semana de Estudios Medievales, Nájera 1999*, coord., José Ignacio de la Iglesia Duarte (Logroño: Instituto de Estudios Riojanos, 2000), 90. Antonio García y García, "Consolidaciones del Siglo XV," in *Historia de la Universidad de Salamanca*, 1:56; Richard L. Kagan, *Students and Society in Early Modern Spain* (Baltimore, MD: Johns Hopkins Univ. Press, 1974), xvii–xxv, 231, 214–15.

9 Salamanca received its foundational statutes in 1254 from Alfonso X el Sabio, who subsequently endowed its faculties of canon law, civil law, medicine, and liberal arts with twelve *cátedras* (chairs or professorships): three in canon law (one in *Decretum* and two in *Decretales*), two in civil law (one *prima*—taught by a doctor of law, and one *vísperas*—taught by a *bachiller* in canon law), and two each in grammar, logic, and medicine. In 1393, Clement VII granted Salamanca six more professorships in canon law (two in *Decretum* and four in *Decretales*) and two professorships in civil law. Papal approval to grant academic degrees, as well as the papal *licentia ubique docendi*, was given to Salamanca in 1255 and to Valladolid in 1346. García y García, "Génesis de la universidad, Siglos XIII–XIV," in *Historia de la Universidad de Salamanca*, 1:28.

10 Scholarship indicates that Valladolid has its roots in the *studium generale* of Palencia, which was founded between 1175 and 1180 by Alfonso VII, and that upon its closure in about 1264—or perhaps as early as 1237—this oldest "university" in Spain was transferred to Valladolid as a *studium particulare*, which lacked the full complement of faculties and the right to grant academic degrees. See Calixto Valverde, "Introducción, in *Historia de la Universidad de Valladolid*, trans. del Libro de Bezerro (1757) por Vicente Velázquez de Figueroa (Valladolid: Imprenta Castellana, 1918), 1:x–xvi; Luis Enrique Rodríguez-San Pedro Bezares, "La universidad Hispana del

Renacimiento: Salamanca," in *El Siglo de Frai Luis de León: Salamanca y el Renacimiento*, coords. Mercedes Aznar López and Luz de Gaztelu y Quijano (Salamanca: Junta de Castilla y León, 1991), 52 (hereafter cited as *El Siglo de Frai Luis de León*).

11 In 1346, Pope Clement VI instructed Valladolid to teach all faculties (except theology, in which discipline Paris exercised monopoly); in 1404, Henry III endowed Valladolid with seven *cátedras*: three in canon law (one in *Decretum* and two in *Decretales*), two in Roman law, and one each in logic and grammar. Constitutions for both Valladolid and Salamanca were authorized first in 1381 by Pedro de Luna (the future schismatic Pope Benedict XIII, 1394–1417) and then in 1411, and consolidated by Pope Martin V in the 1422 pontifical constitutions. Julian Álvarez Villar, *La Universidad de Salamanca: arte y tradiciones*, 4th ed. (Madrid: Europa Artes Gráficas, S.A., 1990), 3:13–19.

12 Brundage, *History of Medieval Canon Law*, 51–56.

13 Scholars note that the length of study for a degree varied from one center of higher education to another. Valladolid generally required fewer years of study than did Salamanca. Moreover, with respect to Salamanca, Peset and González González contend that Salamanca's yearly required period of residence was eight months, while Rodríquez Cruz contends that only six months of residence were required. See Mariano Peset and Enrique González González, "Las facultades de leyes y cánones" in *La Universidad de Salamanca*, 2:31–39; Águeda Rodríguez Cruz, "Régimen docente," *La Universidad de Salamanca*, 2:470; García y García, "Consolidaciones del Siglo XV," in *Historia de la Universidad de Salamanca*, 1:59.

14 The adjectives, *prima* and *vísperas*, which specify the kinds of *cátedras*, indicate academic rank; *prima cátedra* was the principal chair taught by scholars with a doctoral degree, and *vísperas cátedra* was a "cursatoria" or chair of lower rank taught, as in civil law at Salamanca, by a bachelor of canon law. The two terms also drew from the Liturgy of the Hours of Prayer: "Prime" was prayed at nine o'clock in the morning—or earlier after "Lauds"; hence, *prima cátedras* were taught in the morning; "Vespers" was prayed in the late afternoon—indeed, in the evening, so *vísperas cátedras* were taught in the afternoon. Laureano Robles describes the *horarium* (schedule) in detail in his "El Pensamiento filosófico de España," *Filosofía iberoamericana en la época del Encuentro*, ed. Laureano Robles (Madrid: Editorial Trotta, S.A., 1992), 17–18 (hereafter *Filosofía iberoamericana*). See also Luis Enrique Rodríguez San Pedro Bezares, "Vida estudiantil en la Salamanca del Quinientos," *El Siglo de Frai Luis de León*, 59–68.

15 Many of the residential colleges were *escuelas menores* of a religious nature such as those established by monastic orders, mendicant orders, regular clergy, religious congregations, canons regular, and military orders; others were oriented toward the secular priesthood, such as Salamanca's (1386) *Pan y Carbón* college for poor students to study *cánones* "for God's service and the conservation of the Catholic faith." See Francisco Martín Hernández, "Los colegios menores," *La Universidad de Salamanca*, 1:357–68. *Escuelas mayores* with substantially reduced graduation fees were established by bishops for poor "mature" students who were pursuing graduate studies after having earned a *bachiller*. These institutions offered substantially reduced graduation fees to the less advantaged student for a variety of reasons: for "the help of his soul and of his family" such as Salamanca's (1401) San Bartolomé, and/or for "the common good of all and especially for those studiously pursuing *letras* ... and to obtain eternal glory" such as

Valladolid's (1484) Santa Cruz. Luis Sala Balust, *Constituciones, estatutos y ceremonias de los antiguos colegios seculares de la Universidad de Salamanca* (Madrid: CSIC, 1974), 3:13; María de los Ángeles Sobaler, *Los colegiales mayores de Santa Cruz (1484–1670): una elite de poder* (Salamanca: Junta de Castilla y León, 1987), 16–17. *Escuelas mayores* also enjoyed greater patronage and endowments than did the *escuelas menores.* In time, however, these institutions tended to become simply residences of the privileged—of both the nobility and second-born children—and of *limpieza de sangre.* Elliott maintained that these colegios mayores "virtually acquired the status of independent republics within the university." *Imperial Spain*, 312. See also Baltasar Cuart Moner, "Un grupo singular y privilegiado: los colegios mayores," in *Historia de la Universidad de Salamanca*, 1:503–36. Kagan points out that, much to the chagrin of *escuelas menores* such as those of the military orders, gaining entrance to the *escuelas mayores* became increasingly characterized by nepotism and bribery. Richard L. Kagan, "Universities in Castile 1500–1700," *Past & Present* 49 (November, 1970): 44–71.

16 Luis Enrique Rodríguez-San Pedro Bezares, Juan Luis Polo Rodríguez, and Francisco Javier Alejo Montes, "Matrículas y grados, siglos XVI–XVII," in *Historia de la Universidad de Salamanca*, 2:617; Bénédicte Pons, "Fiestas y protocolo, los siglos XVI y XVII," *La Universidad de Salamanca*, 2:540–42.

17 Gutiérrez de Santa Clara, *Quinquenarios o Historia*, chap. 2, 149a; Bartolomé de las Casas, *The Only Way*, ed. Helen Rand Parish, trans. Francis Patrick Sullivan (New York: Paulist Press, 1992), 13 (hereafter cited as Las Casas, *The Only Way*).

18 Due in part to the wars of the fourteenth and early fifteenth centuries, universities under Crown-sponsorship led an uncertain existence; consequently, higher education became increasingly controlled by the papacy until the Catholic Monarchs, beginning with opposition to certain episcopal appointments, consolidated control over institutions of higher learning. Mariano Peset and Pilar García Trobat, "Poderes y modelos universitarios, siglos XV–XVI," in *Historia de la Universidad de Salamanca*, 2:48–57; Manuel Fernández Álvarez, "Etapa renacentista," *La Universidad de Salamanca*, 1:62–65.

19 André Azevedo Alves and José Manuel Moreira, *The Salamanca School* (New York: The Continuum International Publishing Group, 2010), 6–8.

20 John Edwards, *The Spain of the Catholic Monarchs: 1474–1520* (Oxford: Blackwell, 2000), 207.

21 Later, in 1493, the Catholic Monarchs also decreed that no *letrado* would be hired unless he could produce a notarized statement that he had studied canon or civil law for at least ten years in Spain or abroad. Kagan, *Students and Society*, 72; Edwards, *The Spain of the Catholic Monarchs*, 269. Moreover, all graduates of Salamanca and Valladolid were also given tax exemptions—a privilege that was upheld some fifty years later in a 1534 royal edict. Van Liere, "Humanism and Scholasticism," 73. Interventions by the monarchs through the *Consejo real* coupled with periodic visitations resulted in reforms and modifications of many university statutes. Rodríguez-San Pedro Bezares, "La universidad Hispana del Renacimiento: Salamanca," 45–58.

22 Manuel Fernández Álvarez, "Etapa Renacentista 1475–1555," in *Historia de la Universidad de Salamanca*, 1:68; Kagan, *Students and Society*, 72, 214–15.

23 Bartolomé de las Casas, "Memorial de remedios para Las Indias" (1516) in *Obras Completas* (Madrid: Alianza, 1998), 13:23–48 (hereafter cited as *O.C.*), Bartolomé de las Casas, *Historia de las Indias*, ed., André Saint-Lu

(Caracas: Biblioteca Ayacucho, 1986), 3:360, chap. 99 [hereafter cited as *Historia* (Ayacucho)].

24 Gutiérrez de Santa Clara, *Quinquenarios o Historia*, 149b.

25 Bartolomé de las Casas, "Aquí se contienen treinta proposiciones muy jurídicas," in *O.C.*, 10:214; Bartolomé de las Casas, "Carta a los Dominicos de Chiapa y Guatemala (1564)," in *O.C.*, 13:353–63.

26 "Tenía inclinación a la virtud y letras, y determinando seguir la Iglesia, estudió cánones con mucho cuidad y salió con buen aprovechamiento," Fray Agustín Dávila Padilla, *Historia de la fundación y discurso de la provincial de Santiago de México, de la Orden de Predicadores*, 3rd ed., prologue by Agustín Millares Carlo (México, DF: Academia Literaria, 1955), 303–04.

27 Juan de Solórzano y Pereira, *Disputationum de Indiarum Jure*, 2 vols. (Madrid, 1629–1639), 1:170b.

28 Fray Antonio de Remesal, *Historia General de las Indias occidentales y particular de la gobernación de Chiapa y Guatemala*, ed. Carmelo Sáenz de Santa Maria, (Madrid: Atlas, 1964–66), 2: chap. 9. For a biographical sketch of Las Casas's life that is gleaned from Remesal's *Historia*, see Antonio de Remesal, *Bartolomé de las Casas (1474–1566) in the Pages of Father Antonio de Remesal*, trans., Felix Jay (Lewiston, NY: Edwin Mellen Press, 2002), 10.

29 ... a la vuelta que [Pedro de las Casas] hizo truxo consigo a su hijo Bartolomé de las Casas, sacándolo de los estudios de Salamanca ... Gutiérrez de Santa Clara, *Quinquenarios o Historia*, chap. 2, 149a. For the cronista's biography, see Robert B. Knox, "Notes on the Identity of Pedro Gutiérrez de Santa Clara and some Members of his Family," *Revista de Historia de América* 45 (June 1958): 93–105.

30 "Real cédula. de los Gobernadores [Adrian y Cisneros] a los Oficiales de la Casa de Contratación en Sevilla, mandándoles pagar el pasaje al Procurador de los Indios, Bachiller Bartolomé de las Casas, u a cuatro criados suyos: y el flete de su librería y ropas. Madrid, 16 de septiembre, 1516." See Manuel Giménez Fernández, *Bartolomé de las Casas: delegado de Cisneros para la reformación de las Indias 1516–1517* (Madrid: Consejo Superior de Investigaciones Científicas, 1984), 486 (hereafter *Las Casas: Delegado*); Lewis Hanke and Manuel Giménez Fernández, *Bartolomé de las Casas 1474–1566: Bibliografía crítica y cuerpo de materiales para el estudio de su vida, actuación y polémica que suscitaron durante cuatro siglos* (Santiago de Chile: Fondo Histórico, 1954), 4 (hereafter cited as *Bibliografía crítica*).

31 "Certificación del pago por el Tesorero Dr. Sancho de Matienzo de 10.00 mrs. a Juan Fernández por el pasaje y flete de Bachiller Bartolomé de las Casas. Seville, 6 de avril, 1517" in Giménez Fernández, *Las Casas: Delegado*, 571.

32 Giménez Fernández, *Las Casas: Delegado*, 486; "Compilation of Colonial Spanish Terms and Documents Related Phrases," accessed April 28, 2010, http://www.somosprimos.com/spanishterms /spanishterms.htm.

33 James Lockhart, *Spanish Peru, 1532–1560: A Social History*, 2nd ed. (Madison: Univ. of Wisconsin Press, 1994), 68–69.

34 Salamanca required five years of coursework and one year of lecturing, which could be in locales other than the University.

35 Las Casas, *The Only Way*, 15; Isacio Pérez Fernández, *Cronología documentada de los viajes, estancias y actuaciones de Fray Bartolomé de las Casas*, vol. 2 (Bayamón, P.R.: Centro de Estudios de los Dominicos del Caribe, 1984) 2:183–86 (hereafter cited as *Cronología*).

36 Dates and information referring to Las Casas's whereabouts are taken from Pérez Fernández, *Cronología*, 2:163–92.

37 Mariano Peset and Enrique González González, "Las facultades de leyes y cánones," *La Universidad de Salamanca*, 2:39.

38 García y García, "Consolidaciones del Siglo XV," in *Historia de la Universidad de Salamanca*, 1:62; Vicente Beltrán de Heredia, *Bulario de la Universidad de Salamanca 1219–1549*, 3 vols. Acta Salamanticensia. Historia de la Universidad 12, 13, 14 (Salamanca: Universidad de Salamanca, 1967), 2:177, 3:201.

39 For adjustments in teaching obligations and coursework because of increased enrollment, see García y Garcia, "Consolidaciones del Siglo XV," *La Universidad de Salamanca*, 1:47–49. By the sixteenth century, litigation was habitual for peasants and nobles and merchants alike because of the proliferation of advocates, attorneys, and judges, as well as the emergence of strong monarchical government, literacy, and economic development. See Richard Kagan, *Lawsuits and Litigants in Castile 1500–1700* (Chapel Hill: Univ. of North Carolina Press, 1981); Richard L. Kagan, "Pleitos y poder real: La chancillería de Valladolid, 1500–1700," *Cuadernos de investigación histórica* 2 (1978): 291–316; Julián Caballero, "Los Reyes Católicos y los procuradores," *Procuradores* (Octubre 2004): 57–62, accessed August 14, 2020, https://silo.tips/download/h-istoria-y-derecho-los-reyes-catolicos-y-los-procuradores.

40 Luciano Pereña Vicente, *Misión de España en América 1540–1560* (Madrid: Gráficas Benzal, 1956), 151–53.

41 Telephone interview by Paul Vickery with Helen Rand Parish, October 13, 1998. Paul S. Vickery, *Bartolomé de Las Casas: Great Prophet of the Americas* (Mahwah, NJ: Paulist Press, 2006), 33. Rand-Parish's discoveries and the supporting documents were to be published as *The Untold Story*. Lascasian scholar José Alejandro Cárdenas Bunsen suspects that Helen Rand Parish obtained her information from Fray Juan de la Cruz, OP, who wrote the *Crónica de la Orden de Predicadores*—an unpublished history of the Dominican Order in Mexico. This *Crónica*, dated 1567 includes information about Las Casas and was written while Las Casas was living. There are two rare originals, one in Germany (in Spanish) and the other in Canada (in Portuguese). Moreover, apparently, there is a copy in the Vatican Library. Given that Parish spent significant time in Rome and other archives and refers to this *Crónica* in her *Las Casas en México: Historia y obra desconocidas*, as well as in her article, coauthored with Harold E. Weidman, entitled "The Correct Birthdate of Bartolomé de Las Casas," she seems to have located the "smoking gun" or "smoking manuscript," if you like. After her death, the unfinished manuscript of *The Untold Story* and her substantial collection of working papers from her life's work were sent to the Bancroft Library at U.C. Berkeley. These materials need to be accessed to confirm the purported important findings related to Las Casas's academic degrees. Unfortunately, at present, her collection remains uncatalogued. Regrettably, my several requests to see these items have been unfruitful. Bancroft librarians said they will not be available for study for the foreseeable future.

42 *Licentiate* is an advanced academic degree between a *bachillerato* and *doctorado*. *Licentiate* comes from the Latin meaning *licentia docendi* (license to teach). As will be presented later, while Salamanca and Valladolid differed in study requirements, the core of the *licentiate* for both institutions was an examination in the form of a scrutinized lengthy lecture.

43 Hanke and Giménez Fernández, *Bibliografía crítica*, 27. For a narration of what took place, see chaps. 147–51 of Las Casas's *Historia* (Ayacucho), 3:539–54.

44 Hanke and Giménez Fernández, *Bibliografía crítica*, 37. The details of this public announcement can be found in ch. 132 of Las Casas's *Historia* (Ayacucho), 3:481–86.

45 Manuel José Quintana, *Fray Bartolomé de las Casas* (Buenos Aires: Editorial Poseidon, 1943), 179–81.
46 Gonzalo Fernández de Oviedo y Valdés, *Historia general y natural de Las Indias, Islas y tierra-Firme del Mar Océano (1535)*, ed. José Amador de los Ríos (Madrid: R. Academia de la historia, 1851–1855), bk. 19, chaps. 4, 5, 6. Las Casas quotes Oviedo's references to him as *licenciado* in vol. 3, chap. 160, pg. 587 of his *Historia* (Ayacucho).
47 Gutiérrez de Santa Clara, *Quinquenarios o Historia*, 150b, 151ab.
48 In this narration, Las Casas was referring to what happened in 1510 and he wrote about it in the third person. See chapter 28 of his *Historia* (Ayacucho), 3:109. Given the time periods that Las Casas was in Spain and in the Indies, he could not have earned a licentiate by 1510.
49 Rolena Adorno, *The Polemics of Possession in Spanish American Narrative* (New Haven, CT: Yale Univ. Press, 2007), 70–71, 337n21.
50 Remesal, *Historia General*, 2: chap. 9; Remesal, *Bartolomé de las Casas*, 10.
51 Mónico Mélida y González-Monteagudo, "El Padre Las Casas y Valladolid," in *Estudios sobre Política Indigenista Española en América: Iniciación, pugna de ocupación, demografía, linguistica, sedentarización, condición jurídica del Indio*, 4 vols. (Valladolid: Universidad de Valladolid, 1975), 1:9–27.
52 *Y treinta y cuatro [años] que estudió el derecho*. Fray Bartolomé de las Casas, "Aquí se contienen treinta proposiciones muy jurídicas," in *O.C.*, 10:214. As a result of his stay in Valladolid, Las Casas also established important connections with prominent men of the city and the region who collaborated with him in plans for his reform projects. Mélida y González-Monteagudo, "El Padre Las Casas y Valladolid," 16–19.
53 García y García, "Consolidaciones del Siglo XV," in *Historia de la Universidad de Salamanca*, 1:55.
54 Royal Preachers issued fraternal corrections to the king, the council, and the people by defending truth on the basis of faith and the love of one's neighbor, and by pointing out prejudicial aspects of unjust laws. Manuel Giménez Fernández, *Bartolomé de las Casas: capellán de S.M. Carlos I, poblador de Cumaná 1517–1523*, vol. 2. 1960 Reprint (Madrid: Consejo Superior de Investigaciones Científicas, 1984), 649.
55 Helen Rand Parish and Harold E. Weidman, *Las Casas en México: Historia y obra desconocidas* (México DF: Fondo de Cultura Económica, 1992), 134.
56 Because the development of the convent (and later *Colegio*) of San Francisco, which was established in 1222 in the environs of Salamanca, is not relevant to the focus of this book (Las Casas and his *Brevísima relación*), suffice it to say that its academic trajectory from the thirteenth to the early fifteenth centuries was similar to that of San Esteban. However, in 1435, the Franciscans retired from teaching in secular academia; they did continue studies in such institutions but chose not to receive the degrees associated with their academic work. See Isaac Vásquez Janeiro, "El convento y estudio de San Francisco," in *Historia de la Universidad de Salamanca*, 1:611–33; García y Garcia, "Consolidaciones del Siglo XV," in *Historia de la Universidad de Salamanca*, 1:51–57.
57 When Dominic requested official recognition of his order in 1216, the first Preachers numbered sixteen; fifty years later, the number of friars in the order totaled 13,000. During the course of the thirteenth century, friars assigned to San Esteban diligently pursued studies within the priory, regularly engaged in public debates with local rabbis and mullahs, and gradually established institutional relations with the nearby *studium generale* of Salamanca by interactions with students and teachers. Ramón Hernández Martín, "El convento y estudio de San Esteban," in *Historia de la Universidad de Salamanca*, 1:590–91.

58 José Luis Espinel, *San Esteban de Salamanca: Historia y guía (Siglos XIII–XX)*, 2nd ed. (Salamanca: Editorial San Esteban, 1995), 17–26 (hereafter cited as *San Esteban*); Hernández Martín, "El convento y estudio de San Esteban," in *Historia de la Universidad de Salamanca*, 2002, 1:590.

59 Melquiades Andrés Martín, *La teología española en el siglo XVI* (Madrid: La Editorial Católica, 1976), 1:124; Martín, "El convento y estudio de San Esteban," in *Historia de la Universidad de Salamanca*, 1:592.

60 In 1304, the Dominican Order set up *studia generalia* in all their Provinces, except in those in the Holy Land, Greece, and Dacia. Additionally, in keeping with the policy that all centers for the study of theology such as monastic, mendicant, and cathedral schools were open to the public, students who were enrolled at Salamanca and who wished to specialize in theology could also attend classes at San Esteban. Ramón Hernández, "El convento y estudio de San Esteban," in *Historia de la Universidad de Salamanca*, 1:370–72; Andrés Martín, *La teología española*, 1:123.

61 Andrés Martín, *La teología española*, 1:120.

62 The pope also granted one *cátedra* each to the Dominicans and the Franciscans, under the condition that the two chairs given to the two mendicant orders would be integrated into Salamanca's curriculum as part of their offerings. García y García, "Génesis de la universidad, Siglos XIII–XIV," in *Historia de la Universidad de Salamanca*, 1:5.

63 The pope also endowed the San Esteban with three more *cátedras* in Hebrew, Aramaic, and Arabic as part of the study of theology, along with the right to grant degrees. Juan Belda Plans, *La Escuela de Salamanca y la renovación de la teología en el siglo XVI* (Madrid: Biblioteca de Autores Cristianos, 2000), 63n163; Espinel, *San Esteban*, 26.

64 The study of theology at the two autonomous institutions was further integrated in the sense that courses taken at—and degrees conferred by—either institution were recognized by the other. Ramón Hernández, "El convento y estudio de San Esteban," *La Universidad de Salamanca*, 1:374; García y García, "Consolidaciones del Siglo XV," in *Historia de la Universidad de Salamanca*, 1:51.

65 The convent of San Pablo, erected in 1276, was the headquarters for the friars' Spanish province and an important *studium* of the order. After being granted a cátedra in theology by Enrique III (1379–1406) in 1404, and being endowed with its own Faculty of Theology, San Pablo steadily developed as a *studium generale*. Sixtus IV granted San Pablo the right to grant degrees in 1481. Belda Plans, *La Escuela de Salamanca*, 137.

66 Andrés Martín, *La teología española*, 124–27.

67 Lectures focused on both books of the Bible and on the four books of *Sentencias*; later, with the advent of printing, the way of teaching and note-taking changed somewhat since students had their own copies of the texts. Disputations consisted of exercises in debate and in arriving at conclusions through logical argumentation; students were expected to participate in ten major and twelve minor *disputatio* each year. Preaching was required every Sunday in nearby churches and other venues, with a final sermon before graduation at the cathedral. See Andrés Martín, "Organización de las facultades de teología," *La teología española*, 52; García y García, "El mundo del derecho en el siglo de oro de Salamanca," *El Siglo de Frai Luis de León*, 74 (hereafter "El mundo del derecho").

68 Hernández Martín, "El convento y estudio de San Esteban," in *Historia de la Universidad de Salamanca*, 1:593.

69 In 1501, San Gregorio was granted the right to confer academic degrees by Alexander VI. In 1502, San Gregorio was accepted as an

intra-and-inter-provincial School of theology by the Spanish Dominican province, and in 1505 was approved by the order.

70 Columbus went to San Esteban to persuade the monarchs of Castile of his plans and to communicate his reasons to the masters of astrology and cosmology; he received a favorable hearing from the Dominicans, who, especially, Diego de Deza, advocated for his plans before court. Furthermore, during Domingo de Soto's formal and ongoing study of Aristotelian logic and physics there, this notable friar discovered the laws of falling bodies eighty years before Galileo Galilei did. William A. Wallace, "Domingo de Soto and the Iberian Roots of Galileo's Science," *Hispanic Philosophy in the Age of Discovery*, ed. Kevin White (Washington, DC: Catholic Univ. of America Press, 1997), 113–29; Espinel, *San Esteban*, 49–52; Andrés Martín, *La teología española*, 130–31; Juan José Pérez Camacho and Ignacio Solis Lucía, "Domingo de Soto en el origen de la ciencia moderna," *Revista de Filosofía* 3 época, vol. VII (1994), num. 12, accessed August 14, 2020, https://revistas.ucm.es/index.php/RESF/article/view/RESF9494220455A.

71 The Dominican Provincial Chapter of 1241 upheld the position of the radical reformers when they warned all Dominican Priors not to impede academic studies for those friars who are apt and diligent. Moreover, the order's first constitutions mandated "intellectual work, day and night, at home and during travels," and almost all of the Provincial chapters in Spain during the thirteenth century stipulated norms about study and/or students, including the perspective that "books are arms, and without books nothing can be explained for certain in preaching or in hearing confessions." Developing from the primitive rule and building on early Constitutions, the Constitutions of 1241 reaffirmed implicitly the four essential means of the Dominican life: solemn vows, monastic life, choral office, and study. As such, uniquely built into the Dominican charism was the essential pillar of study. James A. Weisheipl, OP, "The Place of Study in the Ideal of St. Dominic," accessed December 17, 2010, http://www.domcentral.org/study/opstudy.htm. Pedro Fernández Rodríguez, *Los Dominicos en el contexto de la primera evangelización de México, 1526–1550*, Monumenta Histórica Iberoamericana de la Orden de Predicadores, vol. III (Salamanca: Editorial San Esteban, 1994), 29; K. W. Humphreys, *The Book Provisions of the Medieval Friars 1215–1400* (Amsterdam: Erasmus Booksellers, 1964), 18; Andres, *La teología española*, 119.

72 This mandate was under the leadership of Master Raymond of Capua. See P. Mandonnet, "Order of Preachers," *The Catholic Encyclopedia: An international work of reference on the constitution, doctrine, discipline, and history of the Catholic Church*, eds. Charles Herbermann; Edward A. Pace; Condé Bénoist Pallen; Thomas J. Shahan; John J. Wynne, et al. (New York: Encyclopedia Press, 1913 and 1950): 12:359.

73 However, radical reform had taken hold in Lombardy through the efforts of Master General Raymond of Capua (1330–99) with the encouragement and insights of the cloistered Dominican, Catherine of Siena (1347–80). Such reform did not reach Iberia until initiated in 1423 by Álvaro de Córdoba (c. 1360–1430) who, as the Dominican professor in the Salamanca *cátedra* of theology, promoted intellectual life as an essential reform measure. Subsequently, in 1427, Martin V organized the Dominican reformed priories as a semi-autonomous Congregation within the Order of Preachers and appointed Córdoba as the Congregation's vicar general.

74 Belda Plans, *La Escuela de Salamanca*, 137. Juan de Torquemada, who was made a cardinal in 1439, was the uncle of the inquisitor Tomás de Torquemada, OP (1420–1498).

75 Fray Deza was a student at Salamanca in 1473, was named Provincial of the Spanish Dominicans in 1476, and Prior of San Esteban in 1477. He taught at Salamanca from 1480 to 1486. Subsequently, he served as the bishop of Zamora (1487–1494), of Salamanca (1494–1498), of Jaén (1498–1500), of Palencia (February 1500–4), and then as the Archbishop of Seville (1505–1523). He was also named Grand Inquisitor for Castile, León, and Granada in 1498.

76 At San Esteban, Hurtado de Mendoza was professor of Arts and of Theology (1495–1502), master of students (1506–1509), and Prior (1517–1519, 1522–1525). In the interim years (1504–1506, 1509–1511), he was the Prior at the convent of Santo Tomás in Avila. Belda Plans, *La Escuela de Salamanca*, 70, 137; Fernández Rodríguez, *Los Dominicos en el contexto*, 27–28.

77 During the first fifty years after Aquinas's death that were characterized by polemics and *apologías* between Thomism and Scotism, Dominican General Chapters consistently recommended Aquinas's writings to their membership. After his canonization in 1323, the order mandated that his works and doctrine were to be studied in their convents' theology courses in addition to the classic text of Lombard's *The Four Books of Sentences* (*Libri Quattuor Sententiarum*).

78 Belda Plans, *La Escuela de Salamanca*, 59–60.

79 *Apologia earum rerum quae illi obijciuntur* (Granada, Sancho de Nebrija, 1535). Cited in Isabella Iannuzzi, "La condena a Pedro Martínez de Osma: 'ensayo general' del control ideológico inquisitorial," accessed July 23, 2020, https://dialnet.unirioja.es/servlet/articulo?codigo=2361355.

80 Belda Plans, *La Escuela de Salamanca*, 63–68; Andrés Martín, *La teología española*, 128.

81 Luis Enrique Rodríguez-San Pedro Bezares, "La Universidad hispana del Renacimiento. Salamanca," *El Siglo de Frai Luis de León*, 49.

82 Concomitantly, Crockaert's decision in 1509 to use Aquinas's *Summa Theologiae* as the handbook for theological studies at the University of Paris precipitated a flood of commentaries on the *Summa*, including those of Cajetan. Belda Plans, *La Escuela de Salamanca*, 60.

83 Among his one hundred and fifteen works, Cajetan is best known for his ten-volume commentaries on the Secunda Secundae of Aquinas's *Summa Theologiae*, which Cajetan began to write in 1507, partially published in 1517 and finished in 1522. In addition to being a philosopher, theologian, and exegete, Cajetan was skilled in letters and commerce. Accordingly, he ably engaged in a variety of secular and ecclesiastical negotiations and transactions at the behest of Louis XII, Leo X, Julius II, Charles V, Adrian VI, and Clement VII. He was also recognized as an ardent indofile. Parish and Weidman, *Las Casas en México*, appendix 17, 322–325; Paulino Castañeda Delgado, "Los métodos misionales en América ¿Evangelización pura coacción?" in *Estudios sobre Fray Bartolomé de las Casas*, Filosofía y Letras 24 (Seville: Universidad de Sevilla, 1974), 124–25.

84 Belda Plans, *La Escuela de Salamanca*, 69; Las Casas, *Historia* (Ayacucho), 3:31.

85 Both centers produced scholars (theologians and jurists) who applied the systematic and juridical elements of Aquinas's works as well as natural law and canon law to contemporary practical problems of a moral, economic, political, and jurisprudential character. In this endeavor, scholars from both centers adhered to Aquinas's understanding of law as "an ordinance of reason promulgated by the one who had care for the community"; as such, law must be adapted to the needs of the time. Thomas Aquinas, *Summa*

Theologica (New York: Benziger Brothers, Inc, 1947), la–2ae, q. 90., a. 1, 4., q. 91., a. 1. Andrés Martín, *La teología española*, 132–37; Belda Plans, *La Escuela de Salamanca*, 70.

86 The *Escuela Española* is historically known as the "School of Salamanca"; however, many scholars were part of this revival of Thomism and of engagement in the issues attendant to the Indies who had neither attended nor taught at Salamanca. This loose association of scholars has also been referred to as the "School of San Esteban," but, again, this designation restricts participants to students or teachers or friars at this Dominican center of study. Finally, some erroneously refer to this movement as the "Second Scholasticism," which designation does not stipulate the kind of scholasticism, namely, Thomism that was revived. See discussions about naming this school in García y García, "El Mundo del derecho," 72–73; Alves Azevedo and Moreira, *The School of Salamanca*, 1–3.

87 Belda Plans, *La Escuela de Salamanca*, 209–13, 222–29; Alves Azevedo and Moreira, *The School of Salamanca*, 3–5.

88 Las Casas, *Historia* (Ayacucho), 3:3–6; Carlos A. Azpiroz, "A message for Christmas and the New Year 2010 Towards the 8th centenary of the confirmation of the Order: 2010; How can people preach unless they are sent?" accessed July 20, 2020, http://www2.dominicos.org/kit_upload/file/especial-montesino/Fichas-del-V-centenario-ingles.pdf; Espinel, *San Esteban*, 59–62; Fernández Rodríguez, *Los Dominicos en el contexto*, 26–30; Maria Teresa Pita Moreda, *Los Predicadores Novohispanos del Siglo XVI*, Los Dominicos y América, vol. 9 (Salamanca: San Esteban, 1992), 70 (hereafter *Los Predicadores*); Javier Atienza y Jesús Espeja, eds., *Predicadores de la gracia: Los Dominicos en la República Dominicana* (Salamanca: San Esteban, 1992), 25–27; Fernando Romero y Mauricio Beuchot, *Los Derechos Humanos y Los Dominicos* (México, DF: Cuadernos "Oasis," 1998), 47–49; Raymond Marcus, "El primer decenio de Las Casas en el Nuevo Mundo," *Ibero-Amerikanisches Archiv* 3, no. 2 (1977): 114.

89 Las Casas, *Historia* (Ayacucho), 3:13–16. Eduardo Frades Gaspar, *El uso de la Biblia en los escritos de Fray Bartolomé de Las Casas* (Caracas: Instituto Universitario Seminario Interdiocesano Santa Rosa de Lima, 1997), 21.

90 Las Casas, *Historia* (Ayacucho), 2:54; Marcus, "El primer decenio de Las Casas," 113; Miquel Ángel Medina, "Introducción general," in *Doctrina Cristiana para instrucción de los Indios: redactada por fr. Pedro de Córdoba, O.P. y otros religiosos doctos de la misma Orden*, originally published in México in 1544 and 1548 (Salamanca: Editorial San Esteban, 1987), 15 (hereafter "Introducción general").

91 Ana Cairo and Amavari Gutiérrez, eds., *El Padre Las Casas y Los Cubanos* (Puerto Rico: Universidad Central de Bayamón, 2007), 173; Isabel Monal, *Ensayos Americanos* (Havana: Editorial de Ciencias Sociales, 2007), 17, 40–41; 1:14–5. Quentin Skinner, *The Foundations of Modern Political Thought: Vol. 1 The Renaissance*; *Vol. 2 The Age of Reformation* (Cambridge: Cambridge Univ. Press, 1978), 2:135–36.

92 Marcus, "El primer decenio de Las Casas," 113; Medina, "Introducción general," 18–23.

93 Las Casas, *Historia* (Ayacucho), 2:196, chap. 54.

94 Atienza and Espeja, eds., *Predicadores de la gracia*, 43.

95 Frades Gaspar, *El uso de la Biblia*, 21.

96 Ibid.

97 This massacre of Arawak men, women, and children was carried out one evening in Caonao near Camagüey by Pánfilo de Narváez and his soldiers

in 1513. Apparently, the Arawaks had prepared food for the Spaniards and were seated awaiting their arrival. Upon arrival, one of the soldiers suddenly drew his sword and began slaying the waiting Indigenous people. The other soldiers immediately joined in. Las Casas, who witnessed the tragedy, was unable to stop the indiscriminate killing. Las Casas, *Historia* (Ayacucho), 3:113–15, chaps. 29–30; Bartolomé de las Casas, *An Account, Much Abbreviated, of the Destruction of the Indies*, trans. Andrew Hurley, intro. and ed. Franklin W. Knight (Indianapolis: Hackett, 2003), 20–21 (hereafter, Knight, *An Account*). Marcus, "El primer decenio de Las Casas," 113–14.

98 Frades Gaspar, *El uso de la Biblia*, 17, 23.

99 Henry Raup Wagner and Helen Rand Parish, *The Life and Writings of Bartolomé de Las Casas* (Albuquerque: Univ. of New Mexico Press, 1967), v, 17, 36, 36n3, 51.

100 "Carta Latina de Dominicos y Franciscanos de las Indias a los regentes de España (27 Mayo 1517)," Medina, *Una Comunidad al servicio*, 258–62. Rodríguez, "La 'Brevísima relación' del Padre Las Casas," 14–66; Juan Durán Luzio, *Bartolomé de las Casas ante la conquista de América: las voces del historiador* (Heredia, C.R: EUNA, 1992), 113–73.

101 "Carta que escribieron varios Padres de las Órdenes de Santo Domingo y San Francisco, residentes en la isla Española, a Mr. de Xèvres (presumably on 4 Dec. 1519)," Medina, *Una Comunidad al servicio*, 269–87.

102 Andre Saint-Lu, "Fray Bartolomé de Las Casas," in *Historia de la literatura hispanoamericana, época colonial*, coord. Luis Iñigo Madrigal (Madrid: Catedra, 1982): 1:117.

103 J.M Chacón y Calvo, "La experiencia del indio ¿Un antecedente a las doctrinas de Vitoria?," *Anuario de la Asociación Francisco de Vitoria* (Madrid) 5 (1933): 203–25.

104 For a discussion on the first two conversions, as well as a third, see Armando Lampe, "Las Casas and African Slavery in the Caribbean: A Third Conversion," in *Bartolomé de las Casas, OP: History, Philosophy, and Theology in the Age of European Expansion*, eds. David Thomas Orique and Rady Roldán-Figueroa (Leiden: Brill, 2018).

105 This Peasant Immigration Plan was not, however, a total disaster because the statute privileges granted to farmers who immigrated to the Indies remained permanent. Giménez Fernández, *Las Casas: Capellán*, 648; Wagner and Parish, *The Life and Writings*, 35–45.

106 In his *Historia*, Las Casas wrote about how his entrance into the Order of Preachers gave joy to the tyrants, and how Gonzalo Hernández de Oviedo said that "Licentiate Las Casas" was attempting to make up by prayer and sacrifice for the deaths and harm that took place at Cumaná. *Historia* (Ayacucho), 3:590–91, chap. 160.

107 Saint-Lu, "Fray Bartolomé de Las Casas," 117–18.

108 Although this community of Dominicans did not officially accept novices until 1518, in 1511 these friars did receive and give the habit to Juan Garcés. This encomendero had killed his *cacica* wife in a jealous rage, fled to the mountains, and then sought out the mendicants under cover of night to request admission to the order as a lay brother for the purpose of doing penance and serving justice. Ironically, Garcés was killed by Taínos in 1516 at his first mission post in Piritu, Venezuela. Nevertheless, because of his narrations of the atrocities and the horrors committed by the Spanish colonists against the Indigenous people, he indirectly precipitated Montesinos's denunciatory homily in December of 1511. See Atienza and Espeja, *Predicadores de la gracia*, 34–6; Espinel, *San Esteban*, 63.

109 Isacio Pérez Fernández, *Bartolomé de Las Casas viajero por dos mundos: su figura, su biografía, su personalidad*, Archivos de Historia Andina 30 (Cuzco, Perú: Centro de Estudios Regionales Andinos Bartolomé de Las Casas, 1998), 64.

110 Espinel, *San Esteban*, 69; Remesal, *Historia general*, lib. II, chap. xxiii.

111 Pérez Fernández, *Bartolomé de Las Casas viajero por dos mundos*, 64.

112 "... aliquem ad habitum nostrae religionis assumant, nec quem a genere judaeorum invenerit..." See "Estatuto ordenando por el Capítulo provincial dominicano de Burgos mandando que no se reciban el hábito a descendientes de raza judía—Burgos 16 de septiembre 1506," *Cartulario de la universidad de Salamanca*, edición patrocinada y sufragada por la fundación (Calouste Gulbenkian de Lisboa, 262. Salamanca, España, 1972), 262.

113 Talavera, the Archbishop of Granada, who opposed Cisneros's method of forced conversion of the Muslims of Granada, suffered the indignity of his family being investigated on the grounds of heretical associations relating to their Jewish ancestry.

114 Medina, *Una Comunidad al servicio*, 69, 72–73; A. Fernández, "Los dominicos en América. Documentos inéditos," *Santísimo Rosario* 18 (1903): 342; Isacio Pérez Fernández, *Fray Bartolomé de Las Casas: brevísima relación de su vida, diseño de su personalidad, síntesis de su doctrina* (Caleruega: Editorial OPE, 1984), 29.

115 Pérez Fernández, *Bartolomé de Las Casas viajero por dos mundos*, 64.

116 For more information on the Dominican Office and the Dominican Rite, see William A. Bonniwell, *A History of the Dominican Liturgy, 1215–1945*, 2nd ed. (New York: Joseph P. Wagner, 1945); Pérez Fernández, *Bartolomé de Las Casas viajero por dos mundos*, 64–66.

117 Throughout the centuries, the Divine Office changed and developed to meet the needs of the clergy dwelling and working beyond the centralized and large locations of monasteries and cathedrals, where monks and canons chanted liturgical prayer antiphonally in choir. As clergy became more dispersed and mobile because of the demands of their apostolates, the requirement to recite the Office was simplified and privatized. As a result, diocesan priests and mendicant friars had access to portable breviaries from which to pray, either privately or collectively. By the time of Las Casas, diocesan clergy prayed the Breviary of the Roman Curia, while the Franciscans and the Dominicans each had breviaries adapted to the particular needs and spirituality of their respective orders. In general, the Hours of the Office would have been prayed as follows: *Vigils* (later called *Matins*) in early morning hours; *Lauds* at sunrise; *Prime* at 6 a.m.; *Terce* at 9 a.m.; *Sext* at 12 p.m.; *None* at 3 p.m.; *Vespers* at sunset; *Compline* after sunset and before bed. Concerning the simplification of the Office and the formation of the breviary, see Pierre Batiffol, *History of the Roman Breviary*, trans. Atwell M. Y. Baylay (London: Longmans, Green and Company, 1912), 120–21, 155–57, 174–5; also, see Dom Baudot, *The Breviary, its History and Contents*, trans. Benedictines of Stanbrook, Catholic Library of Religious IV (St. Louis, MO: Sands and Company, 1929), 38–47. Regarding the Dominican breviary, see Bonniwell, *A History of the Dominican Liturgy*, 38–45, 61–97. The Dominican breviary was standardized about 1244 and was revised again in 1535. See Bonniwell, *A History of the Dominican Liturgy*, 74–76, 271–72.

118 For information on the life of a diocesan priest, see G. W. Addleshaw, "The Early Parochial System and the Divine Office." Alcuin Club Prayer Book Revision Pamphlets, XV (London: A. R. Mowbray & Co. Limited, 1957), 11–18.

119 "Las luciérnagas ... son tan grandes que con uno vivo en la mano, y mejor si con dos, se pueden rezar maitines en un breviario de letra menuda, e yo los he rezado según creo como con dos candelitas ..." Las Casas, in *O.C.*, 6:293.
120 Pérez Fernández, *Bartolomé de Las Casas viajero por dos mundos*, 64–65; Luis Ortega Iglesias, *Bartolomé de Las Casas: Cuarenta y cuatro años infinitos* (Seville: Fundación José Lara, 2007), 319–20.
121 Las Casas, in *O.C.*, 8:1281; Álvaro Huerga, Las Casas, in *O.C.*, 1:187. For a discussion on these pre-Contact languages, see Julian Granberry, Gary Vescelius, *Languages of the Pre-Columbian Antilles* (Tuscaloosa: University of Alabama Press, 2004).
122 The tract is published in Latin and Spanish in Bartolomé de Las Casas, *De unico vocationis modo omnium gentium ad veram religionem*, in *O.C.*, 2:13–557. The English version of the tract is published in *The Only Way*, 59–182.
123 The definitive form of the rite of profession of the Order of Preachers was established in 1267 and continues to the present day. Pierre-Marie Gy. "On the Consecratory Nature of the Very Act of Solemn Vows in the Theology of Saint Thomas Aquinas," *Analecta O.P.* 106 (1998): 408–10; Pérez Fernández, *Bartolomé de Las Casas viajero por dos mundos*, 65.
124 Pérez Fernández, *Bartolomé de Las Casas viajero por dos mundos*, 65.
125 Espinel, *San Esteban*, 69. The *studium generale* of Santo Domingo would constitute the base on which the first European-styled university was established in the Indies in 1538. See Fernando Aporta García, *Fray Bartolomé de las Casas y su vinculación a Sevilla* (Málaga, Spain: Gráficas Anarol, 2002), 83, 86; Vicente Muñoz Delgado, "El pensamiento lógico," in *Filosofía iberoamericana*, 358–59 (hereafter "El pensamiento lógico").
126 Medina, *Una Comunidad al servicio*, 65; Pita Moreda, *Los Predicadores*, 142–44; Muñoz Delgado, "El pensamiento lógico," 359.
127 Pita Moreda, *Los Predicadores*, 142; Muñoz Delgado, "El pensamiento lógico," 359.
128 Medina, *Una Comunidad al servicio*, 32–3.
129 Las Casas, *The Only Way*, 29.
130 Isacio Pérez Fernández, "La doctrina de Santo Tomás en la mente y en la acción del Padre Las Casas," *Communio* 27 (1987): 283–4; Pérez Fernández, *Brevísima relación de su vida*, 29–30.
131 Pita Moreda, *Los Predicadores*, 142.
132 Medina, "Introducción general," 63–67.
133 Pita Moreda, *Los Predicadores*, 141.
134 Aporta García, *Fray Bartolomé de las Casas y su vinculación*, 86; Luis Iglesias Ortega, *Bartolomé de las Casas: Cuarenta y cuatro años infinitos* (Sevilla: Fundación José Lara, 2007), 326.
135 Humphreys, *The Book Provisions*, 18–45; Muñoz Delgado, "El pensamiento lógico," 358–59.
136 Humphreys, *The Book Provisions*, 90–98.
137 Pérez Fernández, *Bartolomé de Las Casas viajero por dos mundos*, 66.
138 Ibid., 66.
139 Ibid., 66.
140 Venancio D. Carro, "The Spanish Theological-Juridical Renaissance and the Ideology of Bartolomé de Las Casas," in *Bartolomé de Las Casas in History: Toward an Understanding of the Man and His Work*, eds. Juan Friede and Benjamin Keen (DeKalb: Northern Illinois Univ. Press, 1971), 248.
141 R.H. Helmholtz, *The Spirit of Classical Canon Law* (Athens: Univ. of Georgia Press, 1996), 10, 19.
142 Because of its regulatory function for the spiritual and temporal orders, in the hierarchy of sciences, canon law as both a juridical and a sacred science

was considered second to theology—the discipline that was at the time considered the "queen of the sciences." See Kagan, "Universities in Castile 1500–1700," 58.

143 Knight, *An Account*, 17, 22, 68, 84, 86.

144 Ibid., 9, 52, 66, 68.

145 Brundage, *History of Medieval Canon Law*, 71.

146 Maiolo, *Medieval Sovereignty*, 128–44.

147 Brundage, *History of Medieval Canon Law*, 84–85; Helmholtz, *The Spirit of Classical Canon Law*, 128–44.

148 Helmholtz, *The Spirit of Classical Canon Law*, 21.

149 Benjamin Keen, "The Legacy of Las Casas," *Ibero-Americana Pragensia* 11 (1977): 57–58.

150 All bibliographic data for *El unico vocationis modo* has been gleaned from the text of the treatise in Parish's *The Only Way*, as well as from the work of Ortega, *Bartolomé de las Casas*, 326–27.

151 Because theology and both kinds of laws formed a trilogy of knowledge about spiritual and temporal society, the *Siete Partidas* of Alfonso X el Sabio, as well as other civil legal texts, also incorporated many theological elements. Antonio García y García, "Miscelánea: la penetración del derecho clásico medieval en España," in *Anuario de historia del derecho Español* 36 (1966): 588–89.

152 The Apostolic Fathers cited by Las Casas were Polycarp, Clement, Sylvester, and Cyprian; the Latin and Greek patriarchs cited were Jerome, Anastasia, Cyril of Alexandria, John Damascene, Gregory of Nazianzus, Gregory the Great, Ambrose, Isidore of Seville, the Venerable Bede, Bernard of Clairvaux, John Chrysostom, and Augustine of Hippo. The citations for theologians included Pope Dionysius of Alexandria, French theologian Pedro de Palude, OP, English philosopher-theologian Roberto Grosseteste, and Jean Gerson (who tried to convince Benedict XIII to resign), as well as John Duns Scotus, Thomas Aquinas, OP, Vicente de Beauvais, OP, Alonso de Espina, OFM, and Nicholas of Lyra, OFM.

153 Manuel Giménez Fernández, *Instituciones jurídicas en la iglesia Católica*, 2 vols. (Madrid: Sociedad Anónima Española de Traductores y Autores, 1940), 1:4–5.

154 Las Casas referred eleven times to Aristotle's *Politics and Ethics*, three times to the works of Seneca and Marcus Tulio Cicero, twice to different works of Marcus Valerius Maximus Lactuca, Valerio Maximo, Plutarch, and Boecio, as well as once to Lactancio (Stoic), Crates of Thebes, Marco Aurelio Severino, and Averroes. He referred to the following jurists: Ciceron, Albericus de Rosate, Baldus de Ubaldis, Bartolus de Saxoferrato, Hostiensis (Henry of Susa), Pope Hadrian I, Pope Nicholas V the Great, and Vicente Arias de Balboa.

155 From canon law, he cited Gratian's *Decretum*, Gregory's *Decretales*, the Sexto and Clementines *Decretales*, and the *Extravagantes*, and specifically referred to "the rules for understanding the Law" in a *decretal* chapter on *Propterea.* He minutely cited his source from *De verborum significatione caus.* 22, q.2,c. *Is autem, de las Decretales.* From civil law, he cited the *Digesto, Mutationes, Código, Novelas*, and *Auténtica.*

156 Brian Tierney, *The Idea of Natural Rights: Studies on Natural Rights, Natural Law and Church Law 1150–1625*, Emory University Studies in Law and Religion 5 (Atlanta: Scholars Press, 1997), 286.

157 Because of this intellectual ambidexterity, their participants and scholars were often referred to as canonist-theologians or theologian-canonists. García y García, "El mundo del derecho," 72–73.

158 Knight, *An Account*, 6, 22–23, 47.
159 In these functions, canon (and Roman) law also provided moral theologians with necessary juridical categories, technical vocabulary, and procedural rules to address moral reality.
160 Knight, *An Account*, 56, 86.
161 Helmholtz, *The Spirit of Classical Canon Law*, 23–24.
162 Brian Tierney, "The Canonists and the Medieval State," *The Review of Politics* 15, no. 3 (July 1953), 379; Helmholtz, *The Spirit of Classical Canon Law*, 6.
163 Kagan, *Lawsuits and Litigants in Castile 1500–1700*, 141; Paul Oskar Kristeller, *Renaissance Thought: The Classic, Scholastic, and Humanistic Strains* (New York: Harper Torchbooks, 1961), 119.
164 George Mousourakis, *The Historical and Institutional Context of Roman Law* (Burlington, VT: Ashgate, 2003), 181, 289, 305.
165 Ibid., 188, 219; Tierney, *The Idea of Natural Rights*, 283–84.
166 Knight, *An Account*, 17, 29, 84.
167 The crucial significance of this relationship of fact (*hecho*) and law (*derecho*) was evident in Bartolus's most notable achievement in theoretical jurisprudence: his *de jure* justification for the *de facto* political independence of certain Italian communes from imperial authority. Maiolo, *Medieval Sovereignty*, 231. Las Casas referred to this tenet in the *Prólogo* of his *Historia* (Ayacucho), 1:16. Also see Anthony Pagden, "Ius et Factum: Text and Experience in the Writings of Bartolomé de Las Casas," *Representations* 33 (Winter 1991): 153.
168 Donald R. Kelley, "Jurisconsultus Perfectus: The Lawyer as Renaissance Man," *Journal of the Warburg and Courtauld Institutes* 51 (1988): 98–99.
169 Stephanie Merrim, "The First Fifty Years of Hispanic New World Historiography: The Caribbean, Mexico and Central America," *The Cambridge History of Latin American Literature*, vol. I., eds. Roberto González Echevarría and Enrique Pupo-Walker (Cambridge: Cambridge University Press, 1996): 94, 96.
170 Mousourakis, *The Historical and Institutional Context of Roman Law*, 305; Stephanie Merrim, "The Counter-Discourse of Bartolomé de Las Casas," in *Early Images of the Americas: Transfer and Invention*, eds., Jerry M. Williams and Robert E. Lewis (Tucson: Univ. of Arizona Press, 1993), 152; Amélie Oksenberg Rorty, *Essays on Aristotle's Poetics* (Princeton, NJ: Princeton Univ. Press, 1992), 23.
171 Venancio Diego Carro, *La teología y los teólogos-juristas españoles ante la conquista de América*, 2 vols. (Madrid: Talleres Gráficos Mariega, 1944), 2:314.
172 Kenneth Pennington, *Popes, Canonists and Texts, 1150–1550* (Aldershot: Variorum, 1993), XIII, 9. However, Brundage pointed out that Las Casas's Dominican formation would have enhanced his position for some because practitioners of law tended to be looked down on due to their lack of "sound theology." See his James A. Brundage, *Medieval Canon Law* (London: Longman, 1995), 186.
173 Rolena Adorno, "The Intellectual Life of Bartolomé de Las Casas: Framing the Literature Classroom," in *Approaches to Teaching the Writings of Bartolomé de Las Casas*, eds. Santa Arias and Eyda Merediz (New York: Modern Language Association of America, 2008), 26–27.
174 Vidal Abril Castelló, "Estudio preliminar," in *O.C.*, 6:163.
175 Pennington, *Popes, Canonists and Texts*, XIII, 3; Adorno, "The Intellectual Life," 26–27. See also Juan Pérez Tudela y Bueso, "Letra y espíritu de la

ley in Padre Las Casas," in *España y América en una perspectiva humanista: homenaje a Marcel Bataillon*, ed. Joseph Pérez (Madrid: Casas de Velázquez, 1998), 98–99; Ramón Jesús Queraltó Moreno, *El pensamiento filosófico-político de Bartolomé de las Casas* (Seville: Escuela de Estudios Hispano-Americanos de Sevilla, 1976), 5–57; Jesús Antonio de la Torre Rangel, *El uso alternativo del Derecho por Bartolomé de las Casas* (México, DF: Universidad Autónoma de Aguascalientes, 1996), 8–149.

176 Vidal Abril Castelló, "Estudio preliminar," in *O.C.*, 6:163.

177 "Carta a los dominicos de Chiapa y Guatemala," in *O.C.*, 13:354.

4 The Articulation of Las Casas's Juridical Voice

Debates about Level of Humanity and Religious Capacity

In the years before the Spaniards arrived, according to the *Florentine Codex*, a Mexíca daughter was counseled that she was "a noblewoman," and encouraged "to esteem thyself as a precious person … even though thou art a woman"; in 1498, hermit-friar Ramón Pané recorded that the Indigenous people and Spaniards were "not all of the same nature."[1]

In 1542, Cabeza de Vaca championed "good treatment [as] the path most certain and no other" to evangelize the Indigenous people; in 1555, Augustinian friar Alonso de la Vera Cruz, OSA, admonished the emperor "to govern [the Indigenous people] to the best of his ability either personally or through his agents so that they attain their supernatural end."[2]

These narrative snippets allude to two of the four kinds of major debates that ensued with Spain's "discovery," "conquest," and colonization of the Indies. Study of these four major debates will demonstrate that Las Casas's approach to the issues of the time was consistently juridical, and that the *Brevísima relación* reflected his legal thought. In this chapter, the first section presents the anthropo-status debate about the level of humanity of the Indigenous people.[3] Various initial and ongoing European assessments of the Indigenous peoples' level of humanity will be explicated, as well as juxtaposed with Las Casas's appraisal of and contribution to these evaluations as a young cleric, and then as a friar and bishop.[4] The second section discusses the religious challenges associated with the presence of the Spaniards in the Indies and, in particular, with its principal goal of evangelization and the consequent hoped-for salvation of the Indigenous peoples.

Anthropo-status Debate

Assessment of Initial Appraisals

Initial European observations and writings about the level of humanity of Indigenous people reflected the Renaissance exaltation of nature in addition to an idealization of them as "natural people" as compared with "civilized people."[5] Both Columbus and Amerigo Vespucci described encountering idyllic scenes of flora and fauna akin to an "earthly paradise"—a depiction that Las Casas also used when writing about the Yucatán in his *Brevísima relación*.[6] The two explorers also framed their perceptions of this pristine state of nature with theological interpretations; for example, Columbus surmised that this yet-to-be-located earthly paradise also generated the Orinoco River—one of four great rivers that according to scripture flows from the Garden of Eden.[7]

Initial observers and writers not only identified the Indigenous people as living with nature but also as part of the pristine state of nature—before humans were corrupted by the distractions, ambitions, envy, and other accoutrements of the "civilized" world—as what the eighteenth-century Swiss philosopher Jean-Jacques Rousseau would later call "the noble savage." For Rousseau, "the natural man," as compared with "the civilized man," was the image of happiness and goodness. The first detailed portrayal and exaltation of Indigenous people living in such idyllic freedom is found in Martyr's 1504 *De Orbe Novo*, and it is regarded by some scholars as the origin of the utopian elaboration of "the noble savage."[8]

Contemporary studies, such as Hilaire Kallendorf's interdisciplinary research on the Taínos, challenge "the noble savage" concept for its Eurocentric approach.[9] While José Rabasa draws on Old World understandings to point out that "the noble savage" is a contradiction in terms, he argues that, insofar as *limpieza de sangre* (and religious orthodoxy) were conditions of "nobility." The "noble" were Old Christians; the "non-noble" were New Christians.[10] Accordingly, in the Indies, the Indigenous people (or "savages")—as the recently converted or to-be-converted—are thus "non-noble."

While scholarship debates whether Las Casas contributed to a romanticized elaboration of "the noble savage," part of his descriptions in the *Brevísima relación* about the Indigenous people (most probably those in the Antilles) do suggest that he believed they were indeed living in a pristine state of nature.[11] For example, he wrote that these "most unoccupied" people "possess and desire to possess the fewest temporal goods"; they sleep "upon a piece of matt or in a *hamaca*"; their diet is "frugal," and "their dress is generally nakedness itself."[12] However, he prefaced this description with "God created" them "to be" so. After his description, he asserted their aptitude to receive the Christian message. By doing this, he interpreted these "noble savages" within the Christian ideational framework, as he would demonstrate in the *Apología* that he wrote, like the *Brevísima relación*, more than fifty years after the "discovery."

Martyr had also connected his depiction of the people of the Caribbean and the Antilles islands with another framework: the classical account of the Golden Age of Saturnalia where people live in complete happiness. Three decades later, Juan Vasco de Quiroga (c. 1477–1565), who was an *oidor* of New Spain's second *Audiencia* and subsequently the bishop of Michoacán, also associated the Indigenous people of his diocese with the Age of Saturnalia.[13] Indeed, in spite of differences in the social organization of the natives in the Caribbean as compared with those in the central highlands, the notion of the "natural" state of Indigenous life continued, as well as was extended to another framework: the primitive Church. Those who regarded "the natural state of the Indigenous people" as representative of the first age of Christianity included Quiroga, the first Franciscans in New Spain, and Las Casas. In addition to this theological interpretation, all of them also hailed the Indigenous peoples as a welcomed "new lineage" or as "the greatest part of the entire human lineage."[14]

Initial descriptions of the Indigenous peoples also ranged from physical appearances—such as "handsome," "lean," and "good stature," to social behaviors—such as their hospitality and ritual of food-giving before gift-giving, to personal attributes—such as their "contentment," "generosity," and "innocence."[15] The trait of innocence was most consistently mentioned and also constituted an important dimension of Las Casas's portrayal of Indigenous people in his *Brevísima relación.*[16] Las Casas's perennial contention that the inhabitants of the Indies were innocent seems to be part of a literary trope and scriptural metaphor that he utilized in the *Brevísima relación* to contrast the goodness of Indigenous people and the evilness of certain Spanish people—and in which he, as others before him, depicted the former as "innocent lambs and sheep," and the latter as "ravenous wolves."[17] For example, in 1519, the Hispaniola Dominicans and Franciscans employed this metaphor to describe how some "Christians ... were like ravenous wolves among docile sheep"; centuries before, Alfonso X el Sabio also used this trope and scriptural metaphor to describe the marauding Muslim army who were "more cruel and harmful [in pursuing innocent Christian lambs] than is the wolf in the flock of sheep at night."[18]

In the *Brevísima relación*, Las Casas did not, however, cite ignoble aspects of Indigenous peoples' lives, which was unlike some early observers and writers. For example, while initially Columbus regarded the Taínos favorably, he later referred to them as "cowards" after the Spaniards that he had left at Navidad on the island of Hispaniola were massacred.[19] Subsequently, on Columbus's fourth voyage when he was ill and seemingly near death, he used the stereotype of *salvaje* to describe how he was surrounded by "*salvajes llenos de crueldad y enemigos nuestros*" (savages full of cruelty and our enemies).[20] In their chronicles, Oviedo and Gómara portrayed the native peoples as "vicious and lazy"; Oviedo also associated their generally negative traits with a physical feature: their "thick" skulls.[21]

Other chroniclers also noted achievements of Indigenous people that connoted the opposite of living "naturally" in the lush natural environment in some regions where the Indigenous inhabitants had state-level societies. That is, the type of culture encountered influenced the way Spaniards interpreted and described Indigenous people.[22] For example,

Francisco López de Jerez and Pedro Cieza de León lauded the Inca cities and urban achievements as "something so great," just as did Cortés and Díaz del Castillo with respect to New Spain.[23] Although also recognizing this, Cortés nevertheless described the people he encountered as both brutal and generous. Vespucci also reported less savory aspects of Indigenous life, such as cannibalism. Similarly, Díaz del Castillo recalled the Indigenous practice of offering human sacrifices to their gods. Later, Sepúlveda would also demonize these behaviors by associating them with the devil, which added a Judeo-Christian theological consideration to these religion-based appraisals of Indigenous life.[24]

These charges of ignobility, as well as the assessments that romanticized, mythologized, idealized, and/or denigrated the Indigenous peoples are akin to paintings on a canvas that depict the artists' perception of the Indigenous people's physical appearances, personal behaviors, and cultural expressions; on this canvas, the brush strokes are dictated by epistemological sources with which the Spaniards were familiar. As the Spaniards recognized and learned that the Indigenous inhabitants and their lands were not part of their scriptural and ancient textual epistemological sources, the canvas became too small for expressing the new Other—the new reality encountered. Their options were threefold: to expand the canvas by augmenting their European epistemological sources; to create a new canvas by acquiring linguistic skills and utilizing Indigenous sources; or to force the new reality onto the canvas, for example, by developing sophisticated biblical genealogical trees, as the first New Spain Franciscans did in order to fill the scriptural and epistemological gap in their pursuit of some tribal biblical roots for this "new lineage" of people.[25]

Initiation of Public Debate

The canvas was expanded by public debate about the Indigenous peoples' level of humanity, which moved the discourse from descriptive considerations of external factors to polemical argumentations about ontological dimensions. This public debate drew in varying degrees on the ancient Greco-Roman classical tradition and on European medieval philosophical, juridical, and/or theological teachings to support several assessments of the Indigenous peoples: were they fully human, or were they not?[26] If they were fully human, were they the Spaniards' equals or inferiors (… or the Spaniards' superiors)?

In 1511, Montesinos's sermon brought the issue directly into the public forum in both Spain and the "New World." Through him, the Hispaniola Dominicans pronounced their convictions: Are they not human? Do they not have rational souls? Are you not to love them as you love yourselves?[27] Their questions couched the debate in terms of philosophical, theological, and canonistic teachings of medieval Thomistic thought about the nature of human beings, humans' dignity as created in the image and likeness of God, and humans' embeddedness in an objective normative moral order.[28] According to philosophical reasoning, humans were rational, free, and social by nature. According to Christian theological revelation, God created humans in the divine image and likeness; moreover, through the redemptive action of God-made-flesh in Jesus Christ, all humans were potential participants in salvation and the beatific vision, and all were sisters and brothers.[29] According to canonistic principles incorporated into Thomism, humans' first obligation by natural law was "to do good and avoid evil." This was because humans were also the natural objects of reason-based natural and human laws, participants (as all creation) in eternal divine law, and, as members of human communities, the objective bearers of obligations and rights in accord with justice and equity.[30] These medieval Christian perspectives about the human person were espoused and supported by the emerging *Escuela Española*, as Dominicans, as well as other *catedráticos* and academics, sought to address the epistemological "problem" produced by the "discovery" of the Indies.[31]

The first person in Europe to address this "problem" was the Scottish logician and theologian John Major in his 1508 lectures.[32] In his academic assessment about the level of humanity of the inhabitants of the Antilles, Major drew on Aristotle's teaching in his *Politics* that some people were slaves by nature—that "on grounds both of reason and fact … from the hour of birth, some are marked out for subjection, others for rule." Major also had recourse to Aristotle's categories of barbarians, a term which initially meant those who were not Greeks and referred to (1) those who were generally cruel, inhumane, savage, and pitiless, (2) those who knew no Greek, or spoke it poorly, or, more generally, those who spoke another language, and (3) those who were uncultured and uncivilized. Major opined that Indigenous people belonged to Aristotle's third category of barbarians, and accordingly were at best subhuman, although Major did insist that empirical evidence must be garnered to prove that they were indeed *bárbaros*.[33]

Subsequently, Aristotle's theory of natural slavery became part of the discussions of seven jurists and four theologians at the 1512 junta in Burgos that was precipitated by the Dominicans' outcry. Although the junta discussed the need for evangelization and the welfare of Indigenous people, particularly in encomiendas, the underlying ontological issue was the Indigenous peoples' level of humanity and, most overtly, was about the human attributes of freedom (liberty) and rationality.

At one extreme of the assessments offered, two royal preachers and both clerics—Dominican theologian Bernardo de Mesa and *Licenciado* jurist Gil Gregorio—espoused the Aristotelian theory of natural slavery. Accordingly, the Dominican friar described the Indigenous inhabitants of the Indies as "brute and irrational" because of their "lack of understanding and of capabilities." Gregorio referred to them as being "like animals that speak," and opined that giving them "total liberty" would do them harm because of their "lack of judgment and reasoning" as well as their state of "natural servitude."[34] At the other extreme, Matías de Paz, a Dominican theologian at Valladolid (and later at Salamanca), quickly composed a treatise in 1512 entitled *De Dominio Regnum Hispaniae super Indos* (Concerning the Rule of the King of Spain over the Indies) in which he based his perspective on humanity's creation and place in salvation history in order to repudiate the application of Aristotle's theory to Indigenous people; he asserted their freedom as a matter of principle based on revealed doctrine and the dictates of reason.[35] Why two friars educated in Thomism, and who would have been aware of Aquinas's repudiation of Aristotle's doctrine of natural inequality, would adopt contrary positions is perhaps explained by Las Casas's allegation in his 1516 *Memorial de remedios* that some of the junta members (and definitely Gregorio) had taken counsel from and championed the personal interests of those who held Indigenous persons in encomienda rather than legislate for the common good.[36] In any case, jurist Palacios Rubios assumed a middle position at the junta: the Indigenous people were rational and free creatures, and their "absolute liberty" must not be restricted. However, as he wrote in his 1512 *De las islas del mar Océano*, although they were not born into a state of natural servitude, they could be forced into legal servitude by justly waged war if they resisted peaceful evangelization or payment of tributes owed the Spanish monarch.[37]

On the pro-Indigenous side of the debate, the junta generated the 1512 Laws of Burgos (and the subsequent 1513 additional laws). As the first of all Hispano-Indiano legislation, these ordinances acknowledged and confirmed both freedom and rationality as attributes of the human nature of Indigenous people, as well as legislated that these people were free.[38] The Laws of Burgos reflected the medieval understanding of natural law as that fundamental principle or universally applicable law that was dictated by reason and woven into the fabric of human nature.[39] In this tradition, which informed the epistemologies of sixteenth-century jurists and theologians, natural law consisted of an objective moral order that constrains humans' social behaviors and bestows obligations with respect to their behavior in accord with its first principle—to do good and avoid evil.[40] As Pérez Fernández argued, the Laws of Burgos centered on the "good" treatment that the Spaniards were obliged to give the Indigenous people, because the authorities, as well as the agents and the executors of such treatment, were those same Spaniards. Accordingly, when the Laws of Burgos legislated that the natives were to be given time for rest and food, their own lodging, and a salary for their work, these ordinances were not considered subjective "rights" given to Indigenous people but rather were "obligations" that Spaniards had with respect to them.[41] Nevertheless, the laws did constitute an attempt at a juridical solution to the problems attendant to the Spaniards' presence in the Indies.

Response of Las Casas, the Young Cleric

In Las Casas's response to the legislation and to the continuing plight of the Indigenous, he had recourse to a genre of juridical literature known as the *memorial.* This form of juristic writing, which was widely used during the first half of the sixteenth century, combined a description of the facts (*los hechos*) with an exposition of the juridical (*el derecho*) on which foundation some *merced* (favor or action) was solicited from the authority addressed.[42] Accordingly, in Las Casas's 1516 *Memorial de remedios* to the two Castilian regents, Cisneros and Adrian, he offered a juridical perspective that took into account natural rights, natural and canon laws, and the Laws of Burgos. He documented the need for a "total remedy" to halt the continuing depopulation and devastation of the island territories and Tierra Firme.

In this *Memorial*, Las Casas presented fourteen remedies and two community plans. He incorporated the notion of subjective natural rights into this text. Canon law had long since set a precedent for subjective natural rights when it stipulated that the *miserabiles personae* could take from the rich what was needed for life's basic necessities.[43] Rights language saturated medieval society and typified medieval jurisprudential discourse, for example, about property, marriage, infidels, due process, and self-defense, as well as about consent to government.[44] Using canonistic precedents, Las Casas began to attach "natural rights" that were derivable from the very nature of human beings as free, rational, and social creatures to the "natural duties" obligated by the objective moral order of natural law.[45]

Toward this end, Las Casas addressed what he regarded as the three attributes of human nature in this 1516 *Memorial.* With respect to the attribute of freedom and its corresponding right to natural liberty, he reiterated the legislation of the Laws of Burgos that "these Indian men [and women] are free, and should be treated like free men [and women]," and he pointed out the option to "leave them totally free as they were before."[46] In the *Brevísima relación,* he also stated categorically that the Indigenous peoples "all were once free men [and women]," and demanded their right to be "truly free as I."[47]

As was done in the Laws of Burgos, Las Casas also upheld the rationality of Indigenous people. He recognized their rational capability and natural right to "live by themselves and govern themselves," but until they were able to recover from the disastrous situation that resulted from some Spaniards' activities, he advocated clerical guardianship and supervision of the Indigenous.[48] Nevertheless, Las Casas acknowledged the Indigenous peoples' rights to their own cultures and to learn about (and reject) the Christian culture, as well as to have a say in legislative matters.[49] More than thirty years later, in the *Brevísima relación*, he continued to insist that they were "reasonable creatures... [and] reasonable people," and to advocate on their behalf for their natural rights as rational human beings.[50]

Unlike the Burgos legislation, Las Casas's remedies also implied needs and rights, such as the right of association, which corresponds to the human attribute of sociability, and which enables humans to live in harmony.[51] His subsequent proposals for Indigenous pueblos in Hispaniola and for farmer communities in Terra Firme sought to address rights derived from humans' social nature. In the *Brevísima relación*, he acknowledged the capability of the Indigenous people's sociability in his description of how they lived as a "beehive" of "well-ordered" and "loyal" people, who were "notable in prudence and policy."[52] In addition to these considerations about natural rights related to the three attributes of human nature, Giménez Fernández suggested that Las Casas's fourth remedy also contained certain inalienable natural rights for Indigenous people: namely, the right to life and bodily integrity (*no ser maltratados*), the right to personal security (*vivir en todo sosiego*), and the right to dignity (*no ser agraviados*).[53]

Besides highlighting natural rights, Las Casas also retained the medieval scholastic understanding of natural law as the objective moral ordering of human life, and in accord with canon law's foundation in scripture, he equated natural law with divine law.[54] In this, he drew directly from the first of two definitions of natural law in Gratian's Decretum: "natural law is what is contained in the Law and the Gospel in virtue of which each is commanded to do to others what he wants done to himself..."[55] Accordingly, for Las Casas, the objective moral standard for the treatment of Indigenous people, as well as for any legislation with respect to them, must be in keeping with natural law's first principle, namely, "do good and avoid evil."

In the ninth remedy of his 1516 *Memorial*, Las Casas elaborated his conception of human law, and again directly applied the *cánones* in his appraisals of and reforms for the Laws of Burgos. Drawing his criteria for human laws from the *Decretum*, Las Casas insisted that those laws must be "useful" (not "useless," as a glossator wrote), "just" (for "it is only a law when it is just"), and "holy" (meaning "in accord with nature"). Other characteristics of human law from the *Decretum* included in Las Casas's Memorial were that human laws must be

> in accord with the custom of the country, suitable to the place and time, necessary, varying according to necessity, clear, [with] no hidden deception, [and] composed for the common utility of the citizens ... not accommodated to some private individuals.[56]

Las Casas concluded the fourteen remedies of his 1516 Memorial by overtly aligning himself with the Burgos pro-Indigenous forces: he advocated that the works of Paz, a *catedrático* at Valladolid, and Palacios Rubios, a member of the Consejo Real, be "printed, published, and sent to the Indies."[57]

During this time, Las Casas's contributions to the debate were also supplemented by the pro-Indigenous discourse that was clearly articulated in the many *cartas* written to the Crown by the Hispaniola Dominicans and Picard Franciscans. Among these *cartas*, which often served in juridical literature as an alternative for the *memorial*, was the 1517 letter from the Hispaniola Dominicans to their religious confreres. This document (of which Las Casas had a copy) contained the Thomistic distinction between divine and natural laws, as well as assessed the situation in the Indies using the tripartite scheme of divine, natural, and human laws.[58] After Las Casas's Thomistic training as a friar in the *studentate*, his predominantly canonistic approach constantly reflected these juridical distinctions of Thomistic theology in his subsequent writings. In the *Brevísima relación*, he consistently condemned the evils and harm done to Indigenous people by certain Spaniards as violations, as the Hispaniola Dominicans first asserted, of *toda ley divina, natural, y humana*.[59]

These Thomistic understandings from the ecclesial juridical tradition, the Burgos legislations out of the civil juridical tradition, and Las Casas's grafting of natural rights to natural law all reflected aspects that he believed needed to be taken into account in the establishment and functioning of a just society for the treatment of Indigenous people as fully human persons.[60] By suggesting that Indigenous people, by virtue of their humanity, have subjective natural rights, Las Casas highlighted the juridical character of such rights in a just society, and sought legal expression of these rights by building on the value that was attached to liberty (freedom) by earlier medieval natural law theorists.[61] Indeed, one phrase could encapsulate Las Casas's singular contribution at this time to the debate: the right to natural liberty. In his next contribution to the debate, he would draw on another jurisprudential teaching: equality.

In 1519, the anti-Indigenous pole of the anthropo-status debate became the source of a "terrible combat" at the royal court between Las Casas and Juan de Quevedo, bishop of Darien in Tierra Firme. According to Las Casas, the bishop had come to tell the monarch "secret things" about Indigenous people, namely, that "those people are slaves by nature." In his reply to the bishop, Las Casas utilized an ontological premise found in Greco-Roman antiquity and in canon law tradition: that all humans and all nations are equal.[62] From the latter tradition, he drew on Gratian's second definition of natural law: that "natural law is common to all nations because it exists everywhere through natural instinct, not because of any enactment."[63] Las Casas also pointed out that "our Christian religion is equal and adapts itself to all nations of the world, receives all equally, takes from none their liberty nor sovereignty, nor places them in servitude."[64] He further cautioned against the use of Aristotle by Quevedo and his ilk. The young cleric argued that Aristotle must be used only insofar as his teachings were in keeping with "our holy Faith and the customs of our Christian Faith," which he claimed rightly that Aristotle did not know. For a Christian to do otherwise, as did Quevedo, created a conceptual gap that Las Casas asserted was as big as between "heaven and earth."[65]

Polarized Discourse in Church, Academia, and Court

Nevertheless, the anthropo-status debate continued to rage, as a great number of authors, theologians, and even missionaries insisted on the human inferiority of the Indigenous people—not because the Europeans thought Indigenous people *were* beasts but rather that they were *like* beasts. The one exception, according to historian Patricia Seed, was Lucas Vásquez de Ayllón, who in his 1517 *Parecer* (opinion) judged that it was "better that [the Indigenous people] be enslaved men than free beasts" and that they "will always be beasts condemned to hell."[66] Nevertheless, as Las Casas charged in the *Brevísima relación*, the result of this attitude was that respect for the Indigenous was "less than [for] the dung heaps of the town."[67] The polarized discourse about the humanity of Indigenous people became more aggressive among church functionaries on both sides of the Atlantic just prior to and after the passage of the 1530 anti-slavery law. This legislation resulted from the pro-Indigenous position of Juan de Tavera, OP, who was president of the *Consejo real* and archbishop of Toledo, and had presided over the 1529 junta that was held to curb the maltreatment of Indigenous inhabitants of the Indies. At this time, the Dominican Provincial in Mexico, Domingo de Betanzos, took advantage of his trip to Rome to convince Clement VII (and, en route, Cardinal Juan García de Loaysa, OP, then President of the Council of the Indies) that the Indigenous people were subhuman by reason of their irrationality. Betanzos informed the pope and prelate, as well as the monarch and the *Consejo real*, that because of their sins, the bestial Indigenous people were condemned to extermination by God.[68] Loaysa aligned himself with Betanzos in the belief that the Indigenous people were "without true minds and hence incapable of syllogizing accurately," a position of the cardinal that greatly influenced the subsequent revocation in 1534 of the anti-slavery law.[69]

Such declarations and actions received fierce opposition from Bishop Sebastián Ramírez de Fuenleal, President of the Second *Audiencia* of New Spain and its councilors (*oidores*), in addition to opposition from Jacobo de Tastera, OFM (c. 1473–1543) and many other friars of the mendicant orders.[70] Pro-Indigenous clerical forces also appealed to the highest level of the Church: Bernardino de Minaya, OP (c. 1484–1566) journeyed to Rome twice to solicit the support of the papacy; Julian Garcés (1457–1547), Dominican bishop of Tlaxcala, wrote Pope Paul III to make clear that he regarded Indigenous people as fully rational beings, and to express his opinion that the attitude of some Spaniards toward Indigenous culture was what was *bárbaro*.[71]

In 1535 and 1536, ecclesiastical conferences, which upheld the full humanity of Indigenous people, took place among the New Spain hierarchy and among the friars. The episcopal junta produced three *Actae*: the third *Acta* consisted of Las Casas's *De unico vocationis modo*, which served significantly as the blueprint for the landmark papal bull *Sublimis Deus*, which Pope Paul III promulgated on June 2, 1537.[72] This decree proclaimed that Indigenous people were fully human and capable of receiving the faith and, as such, were not to be deprived of their liberty or property, even though they may be outside of the faith.

During this time, academics in Spain were also addressing the anthropo-status question. For example, Vitoria, who held the *catedrático de prima* in theology at the University of Salamanca, opposed the Aristotelian philosophical concept of the natural slave. In his lectures, which were published as *De Indis* (On the Indians), he reminded his students and the other professors that Indigenous people were "fellow" human beings, their sisters and brothers. He argued that all humans were one because all were created by God and, in accord with the redemptive salvific plan, all were potential or actual children of God.

Vitoria also rejected the position that Indigenous people were of unsound minds by recourse to the ample evidence of rationality that was present in their orderly polities, their systems of laws, exchange, authority, and marriage, all of which, including their religion, called for the use of reason. Thus, the Indigenous people's achievements were evidence of their rationality. As for those Indigenous individuals who seemed to be lacking in intelligence, Vitoria attributed their supposed "stupidity" to a "bad and barbarous upbringing" and a lack of education. He likened such individuals to Spain's own peasants whose behavior he claimed "differ[ed] little from brutes." With respect to the "perverse practices" of Indigenous people, Vitoria reminded his hearers that they were "a pagan people, unenlightened by Christianity," whose intellects were "clouded by original sin," and whose sins of cannibalism and human sacrifice violated natural law.[73]

In addition to these assessments from the halls of learning, the Crown addressed the issue of the Indigenous people's level of humanity at the 1550–1551 junta in Valladolid. The monarch called this assembly to assess the legitimacy of Spain's rights and the ethical basis of Spain's actions in the Indies. Sepúlveda and Las Casas famously presented their opposing views of the Indigenous peoples' humanity as part of their response to the monarch's query (Figure 4.1).[74]

During the mid-1550s, Juan Ginés de Sepúlveda, a devotee of Aristotle, was the most articulate exponent of the opinion that Indigenous people

Figure 4.1 Juan Ginés de Sepúlveda. "Retratos de Españoles ilustres." Published by the Real Imprenta of Madrid, 1979.

Source: Wikipedia.

were slaves by nature, a position espoused a half-century earlier by his mentor, John Major.[75] Sepúlveda also placed them in Aristotle's third category of barbarians, which he justified by citing their bestial inclinations, undeveloped talents, and perverse customs.[76] The sources for his assessment were primarily Oviedo's *Historia general*, which Sepúlveda regarded as "facts," and the opinions that he garnered, for example, from Vasco de Quiroga who had described how cruel, barbaric, and fierce Indigenous inhabitants of Michoacán were to one another.[77] Sepúlveda also drew on Aquinas's understanding of barbarians as those lacking the use of reason—those generally "incapable" and mentally deficient—to support his assessment that "they do not live in conformity with natural reason."[78] He linked this aspect of their savagery to the rough and unsophisticated level of their skills, except, he acknowledged, in manual activities. As "obviously barbarian," he regarded them as inferior to the Spaniards just as "brute animals [were] to men, women to men, and children to adults."[79] As natural slaves, they were destined by natural law to obey those who had more developed aptitudes. Accordingly, Sepúlveda contended that the Indigenous peoples were a naturally inferior race, and that their very nations were barbaric.[80] He also viewed their idolatry as "evil and blasphemous ritual," and their cannibalism and human sacrifices, for example, "in Nueva España, of more than twenty million persons each year," as crimes against nature.[81]

Sepúlveda's assessments are understandable within emerging conceptualizations of race on both sides of the Atlantic. European social constructions of race as culturally defined differences among population cohorts, such as between Moors, Jews, French, Castilians, and so forth, tended to reflect the attitude that the "West" defines the "rest."[82] Along with other European countries, Castile also made and acted in accord with invidious distinctions among people on a variety of attributes, real or imagined, as well as on past and present events, and thought. For example, Moors were deemed a menace to Spanish physical security, and Jews a threat to both economic well-being and Spanish Christian orthodoxy. Key to these distinctions was the sense that the "West" was the "best," the superior, the culturally advantaged. Such hierarchical evaluations, bolstered by hierarchical organization, defined the inferior person, such as the serf or servant, the slave, the non-urban dweller, the uncivilized, the barbarian or "savage."[83] Sepúlveda's assessment of the Indigenous peoples reflected these notions of inferiority and barbarism based on differences.

Sepúlveda also based his invidious distinctions on cultural considerations of a religious nature, and specifically on religious practices. The decades that Peter Martyr considered in his *De Orbe Novo* offer some insight with respect to how religious practices shifted from being indicators of civilized culture to being markers of depraved culture. Consider that the first three decades of Martyr's writings focused on Indigenous inhabitants of the Caribbean as "the natural man," and that he hints at the end of his 1504 publication that the Indigenous inhabitants of Tierra Firme may be more representative of "the civilized man." His subsequent study of the people of the Yucatán (published in 1521) told of their "well-constructed cities with stone houses and grand temples," of "paved roads and marketplaces," of "structured governments and judicial bodies," as well as of marriage, religion, and books.[84] Of these Aristotelian categories for the assessment of culture, Martyr focused on the religious practices of the Maya as an important indicator of their high civilization. However, subsequent sixteenth-century ethnographic discourse shifted away from Martyr's descriptive and more neutral discussions of these practices to value-laden assessments in glosses and *marginalia* made on his manuscript. When published posthumously in 1530, the text included the notations that were added about the alleged "uncivilized state" of the Maya due to their religious practices, and the words "Indians" and "inhabitants" were replaced with the word "barbarians."[85] Sepúlveda's recourse to the barbaric inferiority of Indigenous people could be a reflection of this conceptual shift. In accord with this development in interpretation of "non-Western" religious practices, Sepúlveda seemingly focused on behavior and culture to argue for the Indigenous peoples' inferior ontology. As will be shown, Las Casas studied the same cultural practices to arrive at a different interpretation and to argue for their equality as humans and nations.

Response of Las Casas, the Friar and Bishop

In his response to Sepúlveda's philosophical argument, Las Casas first demonstrated that the humanist had erred with respect to the law *(el derecho)*.[86] Citing the jurisprudential teaching that all nations and all human beings are equal, Las Casas argued that a whole lineage of the human race could not be barbarians for two fundamental reasons.[87] First, a whole nation of physically abnormal, generally incapable, and mentally deficient people implied "a frustration of natural law," which was not possible, since nature "always does what is best for that which is possible."[88] Second, the creation of a whole lineage of such "freaks of nature" would imply that God's plan for humankind was less than good, wise, and just, or that God had "failed," which was an impossibility.[89] Furthermore, Las Casas argued that while some individuals might belong in Aristotle's third category and resemble Aquinas's definition of barbarians, these kinds of "freaks of rational nature" were "in a strict sense" the only barbarians.[90] Las Casas then reiterated his employment of a fourth category to supplement Aristotle's three categories of barbarians and Cajetan's categories of infidels: those who had never embraced—or heard about—the faith of Christ, and who were not Christian subjects.[91]

Given Las Casas's position that no nation consists of slaves by nature and that all people are genetically equal, he then used the right to liberty to refute Sepúlveda's charges about the Indigenous peoples' idolatry and their crimes against nature. Insisting—as did the first Dominicans on Hispaniola—on the absolute freedom of Indigenous people, he contended that those who had never had the opportunity to know Christ could not be forced to change their practices and ceremonies.[92] Citing the *Digest* of the *Corpus Iuris Civilis*, Las Casas maintained that an injustice was done by forcing even ignorant barbarians to yield their liberty, because "no free person—much less a free people—was bound to submit to another."[93] He further declared that the Spaniards could not judge or punish Indigenous people for their idolatry or "perverse practices" (no matter how atrocious the crimes such as cannibalism and human sacrifices might seem), because only God could judge and/or punish them. In this, he drew from the *Decretum* and *Decretales* of canon law as well as from the *Codex* of civil law, wherein it was stipulated that when a superior judge summons a case, a lower judge cannot make any judgment on it.[94] Indeed, even though both he and Sepúlveda held that these crimes "were against natural law," Las Casas further argued that human sacrifice was not always evil. He recalled that the "common ancient practice of human sacrifice" was found "among so many different people" and became "established as law." Then citing Roman law that "one does not err when obeying a public law," he contended that the Indigenous peoples did not err in offering human sacrifice. Las Casas also seemed to recognize this practice as an integral part of certain Indigenous peoples' religion, by his recourse to Gratian's dictum that "every person, no matter how innocent, owed God more than one's life," because "all men and women are obliged to give their blood and their life whenever God's honor demands it."[95] He also inferred the right to religious freedom in his explanation of idolatry as the fruit of common knowledge of God that was naturally implanted in the mind, and of humans' natural inclination to worship God.[96] As such, the idolatry of ancient nations, which Las Casas described at great length in his *Apologética história sumaria*, simply manifested the fact, according to his understanding of natural law, that "nature itself teaches that every race must worship God."[97]

To further counter Sepúlveda's assessment of Indigenous people as irrational and to demonstrate his errors with respect to the facts (*los hechos*), Las Casas first attacked his sources. He refuted Major's "mistaken opinion," and questioned the reliability of Oviedo's account. He rejected Major's teachings as "contrary to natural reason and divine law … [including] to the Christian Faith," and alleged that Major knew "neither the law or the facts."[98] He exposed Oviedo as a "liar and slanderer" who "as he himself testified … [was] a despotic master who kept unfortunate Indians oppressed by slavery like cattle … [and was] one of the looters" who along with Governor Pedrarias Dávila "laid waste to Tierra Firme" with "inhumane savagery."[99]

Then, Las Casas presented a portrayal of the Indigenous people that was the exact antithesis of Sepúlveda's. Claiming that they were fully rational rather than "dull-witted or stupid," he argued that "in the liberal arts that they have been taught up to now ... they are easy to teach and very talented"; he noted how "adept" they were in "grammar and logic, ... in song and with all musical instruments," as well as how their reading and writing were "skillful" and "elegant." [100] In his 1532 letter to the emperor, Fray Pedro de Gante, OFM, also lauded the ability of Indigenous people as "very good scribes and preachers or speakers... and singers."[101] In sharp contrast to Sepúlveda's assessment, Las Casas extolled their skills "in every mechanical art ... [the level of which was] far beyond all nations of the known world" and reflected "habits of the intellect" such as "inventiveness, ingenuity, industry, and right reason."[102] Even the conquistador Bernal Díaz had praised the "beautiful stonework" and woodwork in their "spacious and well built" lodgings.[103] As Vitoria had taught in his lectures almost twenty years earlier, Las Casas also pointed out the rational capacities evident in their religious organization, which consisted of "their own priests, their own theologians, their own prophets," and in their public authority, which included "kings, lords, magistrates, and laws."[104] Harkening back to "long before they heard the word 'Spaniard'," he likened the Indigenous civilizations of "properly organized kingdoms [which were] wisely ordered by excellent laws, religion, and customs" to those of the Egyptians, Greeks, and Romans.[105]

To reconcile this portrayal of the Indigenous peoples' rational achievements with the variations in their lifestyles, such as those first sedentary (Taínos) and semi-sedentary (Caribs) cultures he had witnessed in Hispaniola and Cuba with the empire-level cultures encountered in the Mesoamerican and Andean worlds, as well as to retain his central thesis of the equality of all peoples as rational, free, and social beings by nature, Las Casas elaborated a rudimentary theory of cultural evolution.[106] In doing so, he rejected Sepúlveda's deterministic theory of racial inferiority that condemned the Indigenous peoples "to wander the world in search of wise men of other nations."[107] Accordingly, Las Casas observed what he believed was a rational progressive development of Indigenous cultures; he believed that their waning cultures could be redeveloped or recaptured to the extent that there was an opportunity to do so. According to Las Casas, all people experienced cultural progression and, in its early stages of development, Spain itself was "barbarian and wild" as compared with the Romans.[108]

Pointing to Indigenous *ciudades*—by which he simply meant "groupings"—as evidence of greater (or lesser) cultural complexity, Las Casas held that Indigenous cultures (as those of all humankind) had developed—and would continue to develop—through the exercise of reason, the guidance of God's Providence, and the occasional intervention of great leaders or teachers.[109] He recognized the existence of a plurality—not a hierarchy—of cultural forms. This understanding of cultural development was in keeping with humanist teachings of the time that humans could progressively improve themselves. Indeed, Las Casas suggested that the Spaniards ought to look closely at the organization of Indigenous societies and possibly "with good reason, we might be able to learn [something] to improve our own."[110]

However, Las Casas was not a moral relativist; he believed in an objective and knowable moral order and contended that the Christian message furthered and perfected cultural change. According to his perspective, only a Roman Catholic republic could arrive at perfection. By his evolutionary (and substantive pro-Christian and innovative semi-secular) theory, Las Casas adhered to the Christian tradition about the inherent goodness of human beings—including those who are "the greatest part of the human lineage," and he also posited that the "natural human" was an entity in transition.[111] In his *Apologética historia sumaria*, Las Casas systematically recorded and copiously documented his theory with extensive contemporaneous "ethnographic" data in which he demonstrated his knowledge and appreciation of the Indigenous peoples and also his conviction that they had met Aristotle's requirements for "the good life": they were not an inferior race.[112]

Finally, to put in writing his defense of Indigenous people during his debate with Sepúlveda, Las Casas created the *Apología*. This treatise represents another genre of juridical literature: the *controversiae*.[113] In this form of juristic writing, Las Casas presented his comprehensive rebuttal of Sepúlveda's position by using a syllogistic method of reasoning that had emerged in Roman jurisprudence and later became part of university study.

Several decades previously, the Dominicans had asked, "Are they not our brothers [and sisters]?" At the end of Las Casas's *Apología* in which he argued for the Indigenous peoples' full humanity, Las Casas answered that query: "The Indigenous people are our brothers [and sisters]—and Christ has given His life for them."[114] That response—backed by Las Casas's forty-six years of law-based discourse and juridical writings—encapsulated the four major premises in the *Brevísima relación* about the full humanity of Indigenous peoples: namely, as good and innocent people; as rational, free, and social human beings according to natural law; as persons created by God and redeemed by Christ, and as equal therefore in personhood and nationhood to the Spaniards. However, the disregard of the rights of Indigenous peoples attendant to their full humanity, inherent dignity, and equality was compounded by issues related to the primary justification of the Spaniards' presence in the Indies:

the Christianization of the Indigenous peoples through peaceful evangelization and their hoped-for eternal salvation.

Religious Debate

Primary Goal of Evangelization

Religious issues attendant to the "discovery" of the Indies emerged from the Christian purview of Isabel and Ferdinand. In 1492, the Catholic Monarchs, flush with messianism after their final push to eliminate the last Muslim Iberian enclave in Granada and bursting with confidence after the expulsion of the Jews, welcomed Columbus's intent to make contact and unite with the so-called Great Khan of Cathay (China) in order to enhance Christendom's struggle against Islam.[115] The initial goal of Columbus's journey was to establish increased trade, political cooperation, and military alliances, in addition to better realizing the Christian vision to recapture Jerusalem.[116] However, according to the 1493 papal bull, *Inter Caetera II*, the primary goal for Spanish presence in the Indies was the Christianization of its inhabitants.[117]

The *Brevísima relación* manifested three underlying premises pertaining to the Spanish presence in the Indies: the evangelization of the Indigenous people; the method of peaceful evangelization of them; and the ultimate goal of their salvation.[118] This section focuses on issues pertaining to evangelization and salvation. With respect to preaching the gospel in the Indies, three important considerations that complicated this missiological task are presented: first, that the Indigenous inhabitants and the Spaniards had no prior knowledge of each other or of their respective religions; second, that the primary goal of the Christianization of the Indigenous people became subordinate to secondary goals related to economic and political interests; and third, that certain methods of evangelization militated against the peaceful, rational, and persuasive "only way" of converting the Indigenous people that Las Casas and others espoused. This discussion of the task of evangelization along with its underlying premises concludes with an explication of the ultimate aim of the enterprise of evangelization—the salvation of the Indigenous people, and with Las Casas's soteriological perspectives about their salvation.

Missiological Challenges of Ignorance

The primary task of evangelizing the Indigenous implied three serious challenges. The first challenge was ignorance: the Indigenous non-Christians were unknown to the Spaniards, and the Indigenous people knew nothing about Spanish Christians. Spaniards had some experience with and knowledge of the non-Christians who were part of the historical reality of Europe or who lived on its periphery, such as Jewish communities in Europe, Muslim enclaves in Spain and the Holy Land, and the Turkish domains in the Mediterranean. Indeed, contact with known classes of non-Christians was a regular feature of the religious terrain in the *Orbis Christianus* of Europe. Spaniards also had experience of varieties of Christianity, from Eastern Christianity to various sects and movements that were frequently dubbed heretical.[119]

As the Atlantic world opened up for Europeans, Spaniards (and even more the Portuguese) also encountered sub-Saharan Africans who were not people of The Book.[120] Unlike the Spanish and Indigenous people of the late fifteenth and early sixteenth centuries, these Christians and non-Christians knew something about each other and their respective religions. While Indigenous people were indeed *neoinfideles* to Europeans, the Spaniards were at least partially equipped to deal with complicated realities as a result of their experiences with the people of the Canary Islands—although the religions of the vast new hitherto-unknown non-Christian hemisphere were arguably more complex.[121]

How different from Christianity were the religions of the Indigenous people? The complex cosmologies of Christianity and of Indigenous non-Christians religions were distinctive in their understanding of the origins of life, the transition to death, and the hereafter, as well as of divinity and order out of chaos. Yet, these Christian and Indigenous cosmologies were similar in several respects. First, they attempted to make sense out of fundamental existential questions. In each cosmology, there was a search for the satisfaction of common universal human longings and for answers to the perennial human questions: What can be known? How should one live individually? What is the way to coexist communally?[122] Second, both kinds of religious worlds drew *ad fontes* from their respective human traditions and experiences. For Europeans, classical Greek and Roman ideational narratives both reinforced and redefined the Judeo-Christian message, which was equally reinvigorated and recalibrated with the humanistic trends of Renaissance rebirth and early modern discoveries.[123] For the inhabitants of the Indies, Mesoamerican ideological perspectives drew from and built upon earlier complex Olmec and Toltec cultural archetypes, from sophisticated historical narratives, and also from the classical Mayan high cultures. The equally complex and divergent Andean ideological perspectives were also built upon the cultural achievements and originating self-understandings of previous groups.[124]

An example of cosmological differences was manifested in conceptions of time and creation. For Christian Europeans, time was linear and progressive; time moved providentially from creation *ex nihilo* by God at a moment in time toward the Christian eschaton, when the summation of human history would be weighed on the scales of divine justice, and the history of salvation would be completed. For many Indigenous peoples, especially in Mesoamerica, time was circular and linear, repeating and progressing simultaneously in a cosmogonic exchange between the eternal and the temporal, the divine and the human, the sacred and the profane. For example, Mesoamericans believed that creation occurred in a moment in time and enjoyed plentitude from the moment of its origin.[125]

For Indigenous people and Spaniards alike, an understanding of these complex and different religious cosmologies was seriously hampered by language and other communication barriers as well as by distance and geography. Consequently, religious dialogue (let alone conversion) was acutely, if not impossibly, limited. However, certain Indigenous persons learned Spanish, and some Spaniards learned a number of Indigenous languages. Moreover, learning Indigenous languages was a gigantic and persistent pursuit of the friars. Only with those kinds of development was some understanding of the diverse and complex religions of the Indigenous peoples obtained, such as revealed in Bernardino Sahagún's *Florentine Codex*.[126] A process was also underway at the grassroots level to establish the use of one universal Indigenous tongue (Nahuatl). This process may have predated the Spaniards' arrival. Additionally, by the mid-sixteenth century, Philip II had mandated the use of a common language for greater ease in conversion activities and administrative matters. However, because this royal ordinance proved linguistically and logistically unwieldy, Philip III reversed his father's policy, and the friars returned to learning a variety of languages to facilitate evangelization and their knowledge of Indigenous culture.[127]

Missiological Challenge of Goals

The second challenge derived from the failure to retain evangelization as the primary reason for the Spanish presence in the Indies. In *Inter Caetera II*, Alexander VI had stipulated a crucial condition to the papal donation to the Spanish monarchs of the "discovered and yet-to-be discovered" lands and peoples: that "the residents and inhabitants" of the Indies be brought "to the worship of our Redeemer and the profession of the Catholic faith."[128] In the *Brevísima relación*, Las Casas reminded the prince of this mandate to "convert [the Indigenous people] to belief in Christ and the Holy Catholic Church."[129] Furthermore, Isabel reiterated this primary goal in her Last Testament wherein she affirmed: "our principal intention was, at the time of our request to Pope Alexander VI [to grant us concessions to these lands] … to induce and bring these people to our Holy Catholic Faith."[130] In the *Very Brief Account*, Las Casas reminded his readers that the Queen "took exceeding great care and admirable zeal for the salvation … of those peoples and those nations."[131]

This primary papal mandate of integrating the Indigenous peoples by evangelization into the ecclesial community—from being "sheep of Christ's flock" to being "sheep of Christ's Church"—was encumbered by the task of incorporating them into the Crown as loyal vassals, as well as of developing Spanish colonies and economic enterprises to yield needed (and coveted) revenue from trade, material, and mineral resources as well as from Indigenous labor. As countless Indigenous people became part of the developing Spanish imperial system of cross and Crown (after all, the Papal Bull *Eximiae Devotionis I* had mandated "the spread of Christian government"), as stated earlier, the primary goal of evangelization became subordinate to the secondary goals of political and economic pursuits.[132] Although the ostensible motivating factor was the conversion of Indigenous people to Christianity and its spiritual riches, Spain's embryonic empire in the colonies emerged from and was fueled by an insatiable desire for material wealth and earthly power.[133] Clearly, the two goals stipulated in the papal pronouncements were inverted in their order of priority (Figure 4.2).[134]

With respect to material wealth, this inversion of goals began with the initial greedy behavior of the conquerors and ambitious colonizers. Even, Hatüey, a "high cacique and lord" in Cuba, recognized these particular Spaniards' covetousness for wealth. This incident was reported by the Hispaniola mendicant friars in 1517 and by Las Casas in the *Brevísima*

Figure 4.2 Theodor de Bry's 1664 engraving of narrated Spanish atrocities committed in the conquest of Cuba in Las Casas's *Brevísima relación de la destruición de las Indias.*

relación, as well as something similar in Book 12 of the *Florentine Codex*. Apparently, Hatüey proclaimed to his people that "gold and gems" were "the god of the Christians ... a god that [the Spaniards] worship and love much."[135] While seemingly many Spaniards continued this inversion of goals by their greedy pursuit of wealth, decades later the king himself reversed the order of priority of evangelization and wealth. Judging from Philip II's refusal to stop the forced labor and consequent deaths that continued to take place in the lucrative pearl fisheries in Cabo de la Vela (Venezuela), Lascasian scholarship opines that the king "never renounced his posture that the principal goal of the colonization of America was the exploitation of its riches [and] of the labor of human beings in order to finance his European imperial ambitions."[136] In this example, Philip II clearly subordinated the conversion of the Indigenous people to the goal of revenue. He was not alone in this; the majority of Spaniards also exploited the riches of the Indies and the labor of its inhabitants.

With respect to earthly power, the enterprise of evangelization was always politically important as the legal basis of Spain's overseas colonies; yet, the markedly confessional character of governance made church activities subordinate to the Crown. Additionally, flowing from the *reconquista* and its policy of *repoblación*, militant Christianity was an integral part of the Spaniards' worldview in the late fifteenth and early sixteenth centuries. Symptoms of the mutual alliance of the conquests of the sword and of the cross in the Indies included practices such as clergy accompanying expeditions, in addition to convents and monasteries serving as fortresses (if needed) or as places of refuge for Spaniards during Indigenous rebellions. Yet in expeditions linking sword and cross, Spanish tactics (such as capturing the cacique, employing terrorizing techniques, and exploiting micro-patriotism to divide Indigenous groups) and their technology (such as firearms, crossbows, steel weapons, horses, and war dogs), as well as disease epidemics determined the outcome, and did not extend the *imperium fidei*. Instead, as repeatedly charged in the *Brevísima relación*, the Indigenous people "perish without faith and without sacraments."[137] Consequently, political and military conquests accompanied the beginning of the subsequent "spiritual conquest."[138]

Missiological Challenge of Methods

The third challenge pertained to the diversity of methods of evangelization. The first phase of evangelizing (1492–1519) in the Antilles relied principally on the collaboration of lay Spaniards in the Crown's vision of Christianization. While Columbus initially sought to simply "convert by love" as he traded gifts with Taínos, the preferred setting for Christianizing became the encomienda.[139] As legislated by the Laws of Burgos, the Indigenous people in encomienda were to be edified by the Spaniards' example of the Christian way of life and instructed in the Christian faith by their encomenderos. This hoped-for peaceful method of Christianization would be supported and supplemented by itinerant clergy who served the religious needs of the Spaniards in the missions and churches that were constructed on the islands.[140]

However, the encomienda proved to be, as Las Casas charged, "the most grave obstacle" to conversion because the maltreatment of and harm done to Indigenous people fostered hate and scandal rather than imitation of the Christian way of life.[141] Additionally, adequate instruction was not done, even though *Inter Caetera II* had also mandated that "the sovereigns were to dispatch virtuous and God-fearing men endowed with training, experience, and skill, to instruct the natives and to imbue them with Christian faith and sound morals." Encomenderos proved to be incompetent and also unwilling to instruct the Indigenous natives in the faith; frequently secular *curas* were not very knowledgeable in Christian doctrine.[142]

During this first phase, mendicant friars also came to serve in the Antilles. In 1505, Franciscans from the Province of Picard in Belgium arrived, followed in 1510 by the Spanish Dominicans from San Esteban. In 1511, the Hispaniola Dominicans and Picard Franciscans initiated the first peaceful evangelization in the Indies in Cuba, before the conquest of that island.[143] The second attempt at peaceful conversion by the mendicant friars was in 1515 on Tierra Firme, where the Dominicans erected a mission in Chiribichí, and the Franciscans established a community in the small port of Cumaná.[144] Later, in 1521, Las Casas also began his own experiment of peaceful evangelization on Tierra Firme at Cumaná. However, during this early period, great inroads were not made: evangelization in Cuba was slow, all three missions on Tierra Firme ended in disaster, and the Indigenous populations were quickly declining because of diseases and increasing destruction of their way of life.

The second phase of evangelization began in Mexico after the fall of Tenochtitlan with systematic proselytizing by the mendicant orders, particularly the Franciscans and Dominicans whose assignments were requested by Cortés. Part of the reason for these appointments was because Cortés believed that religious clergy were better educated, had higher moral standards, and more experience in evangelization than did secular *curas*.[145]

Upon their arrival in Mexico in 1524, the Spanish Franciscans immediately embraced the practical geo-religious implications of the "discovery."[146] With mass conversions forefront in their minds, these millenarian-oriented friars began evangelizing in large areas of the central plateau in pursuit of their utopian plan to create a new form of Christianity in the Indies that would be better and purer than the one they left behind in Europe. Animating their efforts was their conviction that Indigenous peoples possessed the capabilities for absorbing the Christian religion because of their advanced social and political institutions.

Figure 4.3 Las Casas and Dominicans Preaching. Painting found in the Cathedral of Mexico City.
Source: Photo by David Orique.

Accelerating their methods of conversion was their belief in the imminent eschaton that would take place when all the Indigenous people have been baptized (Figure 4.3).[147]

With their arrival in 1526, the Dominicans engaged in evangelization activities in the Valley of Mexico, what are now the provinces of Tlaxcala, Toluca, Puebla, and Morelos, and the Zapotec and Mixtec lands with the city of Antequera (Oaxaca) as the center.[148] In many of these areas, the Franciscans were already present and had established houses in many places. The Dominicans pioneered in those places that their Franciscan confreres had not claimed, for example, in Oaxaca, or they filled in around the edges in areas in which the Franciscans were in charge, or they took over earlier Franciscan zones that became available with territorial changes in ecclesiastical jurisdiction. Some differences in pastoral perspectives also existed. Unlike the Spanish Franciscans, the Spanish reformed Dominicans did not, for the most part, subscribe to the imminent Second Coming of Christ. However, both mendicant orders regarded their missionary work as a return to the Age of the Apostles and sought to exemplify the *modo de ser* of their apostolic forebearers by the poverty and simplicity of their individual and communal lives.[149]

The Franciscans and the Dominicans espoused other ways of spreading the gospel of Christ.[150] For example, both initially targeted Indigenous rulers and native priests; the Franciscans also pursued this "upper-class" outreach by extending educational opportunities to the sons of Indigenous nobility.[151] For the masses, both groups of friars used pedagogical devices such as songs and theater in addition to capitalizing on feast-day celebrations. Both sought to eradicate idolatry—although the Franciscans were more overtly active and even violent in their early suppression of idol worship. Major differences between them emerged in the sacramental realm, and particularly with respect to pre- and post-baptism instruction. In pre-baptism instruction, the Franciscans limited themselves to the strictly essential, which greatly facilitated baptisms *en masse*. At one time, they allegedly consisted of baptizing "fourteen thousand daily," which meant that only the indispensable part of the rite was performed.[152] In contrast, the Dominicans generally insisted on more thorough catechesis prior to receiving baptism, which was administered in the fullness of its rite. Similarly, the Franciscans' post-baptism instruction was less frequent than that done by the Dominicans (Figure 4.4).[153]

Underlying these techniques for evangelism, administering the Sacrament of Baptism, and catechism were implicit assumptions about the degree to which the would-be converts and neophyte Christians could exercise agency in the process of their conversion. These assumptions

Figure 4.4 Pope Clement VII and Emperor Charles V on horseback under a canopy by Jacopo Ligozzi, c. 1580 (Pope and the Emperor entering Bologna in 1530, where Charles was crowned Holy Roman Emperor by the Pope).

Source: Wikipedia.

ranged on a continuum from zero agency to full agency. Those ascribing no agency to Indigenous people included Spaniards who assumed that the Indigenous people were incapable of receiving the faith. Such was the conviction of a member of the Council of Castile in 1517 during evangelization in the Antilles.[154] Similarly, not too many years later, Friar Domingo de Betanzos, Provincial of the Dominican province in Mexico, adamantly proclaimed that "Indigenous people could never become Christians ... even though the Emperor, the Pope, the Virgin, and all the celestial orders intervened on their behalf."[155] Others assumed limited agency on the part of the Indigenous people in the process of conversion. For example, some Franciscans (and also secular Bishop Vasco de Quiroga in Michoacán) paternalistically advocated tutelage in order to supplement the "childlike" capabilities of Indigenous people so that they might join the ranks of Christians on their own. Some, such as Sepúlveda, asserted the cultural inferiority of the Indigenous peoples, and therefore trivialized and deprecated Indigenous agency; from his perspective, governance of these people by a "superior" and "cultured" people would compensate for their second-class status by guiding and assisting their conversion (albeit forcefully) to the superior Roman Catholic religion.[156] Those who ascribed full agency to Indigenous people included those who welcomed and lauded the papal pronouncement of Paul III in *Sublimis Deus*, such as Bishops Garcés and Zumárraga and many other mendicant missionaries.[157] As in the papal decree, the basis of their judgment was the equality of all peoples and the belief that all persons are rational, free, and social human beings made in the image and likeness of God and redeemed by Christ. This was also Las Casas's position.

However, accompanying the different techniques and ways of preaching the gospel and of instructing the faith that the mendicants utilized was the specter of warfare. Ever since Ovando first waged battle against Indigenous people in Hispaniola, waves of wars ebbed and flowed across the islands and mainlands of the Indies. In addition to the Christian belief in the mandate to preach the gospel to the whole world, the attitude prevailed—even in 1530 at the level of the papacy—that the only way to prepare the inhabitants of the Indigenous lands for the preaching of the gospel was through military and then political conquest.[158] For example, in the Sepúlveda-Las Casas debate at Valladolid about warfare prior to evangelizing, Sepúlveda argued that wars can be waged "so that once the path has been totally cleared for the preachers of the gospel, the Christian religion may be spread."[159] He also argued, as did Major (his mentor), that the Indigenous people would not otherwise receive Christianity since they did not understand the Spanish language. Moreover, success in warfare against the Indigenous people would allow the Spaniards to build fortified Christian settlements on the lands so that the Indigenous inhabitants could become accustomed to and knowledgeable about the Christian way of life.[160]

Las Casas's Peaceful and Persuasive Missiology

As will be shown in the following chapter, Las Casas and others rejected such wars as a transgression of the gospel message of peace because the method of evangelization must be peaceful and rational.[161] His juridical approach to this method of evangelization was articulated in his thrice-redacted treatise, *De unico vocationis modo universas gentes ad veram religionem* (The Only Way to Call all People to the True Religion).[162] From natural law, Las Casas explicated that the "one way only" established by God for people to receive the true religion was "the way that wins the mind with reasons, that wins the will with gentleness, with invitation."[163] Given the equality of all persons and of all nations, he contended that the method of preaching must be common among all people regardless of distinction. In the *Brevísima relación*, he inferred to these criteria when he asserted—as he had done since his early years in Hispaniola—that the Indigenous peoples were "of lively understanding, [as well as] very apt and tractable for all fair doctrine."[164] In *De unico vocationis modo*, Las Casas also had recourse to the ecclesial juridical tradition. He drew copiously on divine law and on the examples of Christ and his apostles to demonstrate the only acceptable method of preaching the gospel.[165] He presented teachings of the Church Fathers and canonical directives about, as well as papal endorsements for, the peaceful conversion of subjected people. In this and at length, he cited Gratian, the *Decretales*, the Fourth Council of Toledo (663 CE), and pontiffs such as Leo I, the Great (440–461), Nicholas I, the Great (858–867), and Paul III.[166] Using natural, divine, and canon laws, he explicated and denounced "false evangelization" and "wars of conversion" because these "violated the mind and the will," "contradicted the way of Christ," of the apostles, and of Christianity, as well as were condemned by papal decrees.[167]

In addition to these juridical rationales in *De unico vocationis modo*, Las Casas argued in his debate with Sepúlveda for a textual re-interpretation of the Alexandrine Bulls of Donation.[168] He called for limiting the violent meaning of the word "*subiicere*" [to subject] in the 1493 *Inter caetera* bulls, and for understanding this word rather as "a subjection that will be born of the mild and gentle preaching of the divine word."[169] He insisted that the word (*subiicere*) must be taken in this sense because the pontiff could not have meant violent subjection. To this end, he had recourse to Gratian's dictum that "words should serve the intent, not the intent the words," and quoted the juridical maxim from *De Regulis Iuris, c. Intelligentia* that "the understanding of what is said is to be taken from the things that caused them to be said, because reality is not subject to speech, but speech to reality."[170] In the spirit of this recasting of the narrative of the bull, Las Casas reminded the monarch as he did in the Prologue of the *Brevísima relación* of what "God and the Church" had conceded and trusted "to the King and Queen of Castille": the Indigenous peoples' peaceful conversion "to belief in Christ and the Holy Catholic Church."[171]

The above-listed missiological challenges—ignorance of the Other, inversion of the primary and secondary goals, and diversity in methods of conversion—had consequences for the ultimate goal for the presence of the Spaniards in the Indies, which was, in Christian belief, the salvation of the Indigenous people. The first challenge provoked the recognition that the gospel had not been proclaimed to *all* the world; hence, the salvific plan of God was more extensive than initially imagined, and Christendom was potentially larger than previously asserted in ancient texts and attested by age-old experience. The second challenge resulting from the subordination of evangelization to political and economic goals could result in the forfeiture of salvation for the Indigenous people insofar as the so-called Christians repeatedly scandalized and brutally deprived the would-be Christians of their personal freedom and collective liberty. The third challenge with its defective ways of evangelizing impeded and/or obfuscated the only peaceful and rational way of bringing Indigenous people to the attainment of eternal salvation in accord with Christian teaching.

Ultimate Goal of Salvation and Las Casas's Soteriology[172]

This soteriological concern for the eternal salvation of the Indigenous people was present and paramount in Las Casas's writings from the beginning of his labors on their behalf.[173] In his 1516 *Memorial,* Las Casas clearly stated that "the principal goal for which all has been ordained, or might be ordained" and "the ultimate and final end" of the Spanish presence in the Indies was "the salvation of [its native inhabitants]." He further asserted that royal authority had legislated that the salvation of the Indigenous inhabitants was "to be effected through the Christian doctrine that His Highness commands to be imparted to them."[174] In the 1530s, his two major *cartas* reiterated how the Alexandrine Bulls of Donation with their crucial condition, Queen Isabel's Last Testament, and royal legislation all decreed the conversion of the Indigenous people in order that their souls might be saved.[175] Las Casas was adamant that only through peaceful, rational, and persuasive evangelization would the Indigenous people embrace and live the faith, and so attain eternal salvation after their deaths.

The scenario, however, was that countless Indigenous *neoinfideles* had died or were dying "without the Faith and the sacraments," as Las Casas contended in the *Brevísima relación.*[176] According to the ecclesial teaching of *Extra Ecclesiam Nulla Salus,* which was derived from divine law, these Indigenous people would be "cast into hell" because "outside of the church there was no salvation."[177] That is, salvation was considered impossible without baptism and the explicit confession of the Christian faith.[178] While this soteriological position implied that infidels could not attain salvation unless they converted (and Las Casas did state prior to his pre-Dominican formation that Aristotle was "burning in hell" because he was "a pagan"), the seeming employment of this predominantly Augustinian position needs examination.[179] Arguably, this earlier posture of Las Casas changed as he expanded his theoretical study—especially of Aquinas, and integrated his practical experience from the Indies, first as a Dominican friar and then as a bishop. As a result, in his later soteriology position, Las Casas proposed several pathways to salvation without explicit faith and the sacraments.

First, in his *Apología*, Las Casas argued that the Indigenous people were what Cajetan categorized as "negative infidels," meaning those who, unlike "positive infidels," had never heard of—let alone rejected—Christ.[180] This was also in accord with Aquinas's teachings about "unbelief by way of pure negation [or deprivation] in those who have heard nothing about the Faith."[181] Las Casas built on this classification and distinction in *The Only Way* when he asserted: "It is clear as clear as clear can be that the nations of our Indies fall into [a special category of infidels]. They are of the fourth kind of infidels [far away non-hostile pagans], no one can doubt it."[182] For Las Casas, theirs was an invincible and non-culpable ignorance; as such, Indigenous people could not have been condemned because they were infidels—they would be saved.[183]

Second, Las Casas addressed and clarified the Indigenous peoples' relationship to Christ in terms of the ecclesial and civil juridical tradition. In the *Tratado comprobatorio*, he asserted that—in ways known to God alone according to eternal law—the Indigenous people were "in Christ *in actu*" because Christ is the head of all creation. Las Casas supported this with divine, canon, and civil laws as well.[184] In *De thesauris*, he cited divine law to reiterate that they were also members of Christ's flock *in actu*, that is, of the invisible Church—the "mystical body of Christ."[185] As part of the human family, the Indigenous people were imbued with God's salvific grace.[186] However, according to divine law, they were in Christ's Church (the visible body of Christ) only "*in potentia*."[187] Moreover, in the trans-temporal eternal moment of the Day of Judgment and in accord with eternal law, potency will become actuality: everyone will be *in actu* in the Church of Christ—some saved, some damned.[188]

Third, Las Casas added deliberations based on natural law with aspects of the ecclesial tradition as an avenue of salvation for the Indigenous people. Justin Martyr (103–165 CE), in addition to Aquinas, had argued that salvation was attainable by those who lived before Christ to the extent that they lived according to the natural law—doing what was reasonable, pursuing the good, and avoiding evil.[189] For Aquinas, this way of life indicated either implied belief in the existence of a provident God—who rewards those who seek God or an implicit belief in the reality of a mediator—Christ.[190] In the sixteenth century, Spanish scholastics such as Domingo de Soto applied this teaching in their contention that the Indigenous peoples' natural knowledge of God generated implicit faith in Christ and was sufficient for their salvation.[191] During the early years after the encounter, Palacios Rubios also argued that Indigenous people who "lived according to natural law might be saved through the gospel even before they came to know it."[192] Humanists, who like the Thomists believed in humans' inherent goodness and in meritorious action, also posited a broader optic of entrance into the salvific plan: love is the path to salvation, whether living according to natural law that prevailed from Adam to Moses, or according to the Mosaic law from the time of Moses to Christ, or according to the law of grace established with Christ's coming.[193] As such, Juan Ginés de Sepúlveda, the prominent humanist scholar, took the position that Aristotle and other pagan philosophers were not in hell. With respect to those born after Christ's coming, Sepúlveda cited Aquinas's teaching that if they followed the natural law, they were saved, but with much more difficulty. However, believing that the Indigenous people were inferior people and did not live in conformity with the natural law, Sepúlveda contended that they were "headed for certain downfall" or, in other words, for eternal damnation.[194] Las Casas countered this judgment by upholding the Indigenous peoples' conformity to natural law.

Fourth, Las Casas drew on the doctrine about grace. According to eternal law, Divine Providence always "provides all that is necessary for salvation," Christ's grace is "exceedingly sufficient" for all, and "grace does not destroy nature." Moreover, given the "singular care" that God's Providence has for all, God exercises divine freedom in God's response to circumstances of the human condition.[195] In the *Brevísima relación*, Las Casas offered the possibility of God's intervention with respect to the attainment of salvation when he narrated that a "most wretched captain" who died "in a state of sinfulness and perdition, without confession… is now sunk in the very maw of hell, save perhaps that God has secretly not sent him there, as His divine mercy… do dictate."[196] The implication was that God, whose providential glance sees the heart and probes the intention, may have chosen to save "the tyrant." So too Indigenous people may be saved by God's justice, generosity, and mercy, or—according to Aquinas's novel examples—by miraculous instruction.[197]

According to traditional Christian teaching, the ultimate desired goal of the salvation of Indigenous people was not being accomplished. Instead, as claimed by Las Casas, the killings of them—through the bondage and warfare to which certain Spaniards subjected them—resulted in their being "cast into hell" because they "die without Faith."[198] However, given the soteriological considerations offered by Las Casas and the alternative avenues of salvation that he proposed, the ultimate judgment about "the ultimate end" of the Indigenous people would be determined by God's eternal law or Providence—by God's plan for and God's governance of all of creation.[199]

As such, the soteriological issue of salvation highlighted theological understandings about the tension between God's eternal, divine, infinite, uncreated freedom—and women and men's temporal, human, limited, created freedom. According to Christian doctrine, salvation constituted the pivotal point where God's freedom meets human freedom. Las Casas's soteriological views reflected this understanding. On the one hand, he asserted that God's grace expressed in the free encompassing salvific action of Jesus Christ gave all people what was necessary for salvation. On the other hand, he held that free will gave all people the ability to rationally choose the good in virtuous actions and to avoid evil.[200] Las Casas's appreciation for human freedom came from his academic training, his admiration of the religious culture of non-Christian Indigenous peoples, and his firsthand experience in the Indies. Ultimately, this appreciation of freedom led the Dominican friar and bishop to entertain the question of the possibility of salvation outside the visible frontiers of the Church.[201] Nevertheless, whether to become a Christian, whether to become a member of Christ's Church *in actu*, is intimately related to freedom. The decision must be one of conscious free choice. However, as will be seen in the next chapter, the economic institutions of bondage, as well as what Las Casas saw as the tyrannical exercise of political *dominium*, militated against such free choice.

Notes

1 Fray Bernardino de Sahagún, Florentine Codex, in *Latin American Philosophy: An Introduction with Readings*, eds. Susana Nuccetelli and Gary Seay (Upper Saddle River, NJ: Pearson Education Inc., 2004), 26; Fray Ramón Pané, *Relación acerca de las antigüedades de los indios*, notes, José Juan Arrom, Decimotercera edición (México, DF: Siglo XXI Editores S.A. de C.V., 2004), 48.

2 Álvar Núñez Cabeza de Vaca, *The Narrative of Cabeza De Vaca*, ed., trans., intro., Rolena Adorno and Patrick Charles Pautz (Lincoln: Univ. of Nebraska Press, 2003), 157; Alonso de la Vera Cruz, *The Writings of Alonso de la Vera Cruz: II*, ed., trans. Ernest J. Burris (Rome: Jesuit Historical Institute, 1968), 133.

3 Although the neologism anthropo-status is employed to avoid confusion with the focus of the modern discipline of anthropology, even so philosophical, theological, and Christian discourse also employs anthropological considerations. Philosophical anthropology studies the human being as a knowing, moral, and political animal; theological anthropology, which builds upon philosophical anthropology, examines humans as humans in the light of revelation, and human's relationship to the divine or to the Absolutely Other; Christian anthropology, which builds on the analysis of philosophical and theological anthropology, studies human beings as made in the image and likeness of God, and redeemed by Jesus Christ, God incarnate.

4 These discourses seemingly did not take into account the Indigenous point of view with respect to how they conceived of or would represent their own humanity. Most available sources from within the Indies were written after the initial conquests of different territories and kingdoms.

5 At Contact, the Antilles were populated by numerous groups, such as the Ciboney, Taíno, Arawak, Carib, and Kalingo. See Esteban Mira Caballos,

El Indio Antillano: Repartimiento, Encomienda y Esclavitud (1492–1542) (Seville: Múñoz Moya, 1997), 21, 31.

6 Martín Fernández de Navarrete, *Colección de los viajes y descubrimientos que hicieron por mar los españoles* (Madrid: Atlas, 1825), 217; Bartolomé de las Casas, *An Account, Much Abbreviated, of the Destruction of the Indies*, trans. Andrew Hurley, intro. and ed. Franklin W. Knight (Indianapolis, IN: Hackett, 2003), 47–48 (hereafter, Knight, *An Account*).

7 In his 1498 letter to Doña Juana, Columbus narrated how he had sailed farther south on his third journey to Trinidad and Venezuela where he encountered the mouth of the Orinoco River. He believed that its source, as well as the source of the three other rivers (the Euphrates, Nile, and Ganges), was the Garden of Eden—the highest point of the earth, and also believed that the Caribbean was an approach to this paradise. Miles H. Davidson, *Columbus Then and Now: A Life Reexamined* (Norman: Univ. of Oklahoma Press, 1997), 419–20.

8 José Luis Abellan, "Los Orígenes Españoles del Mito del 'Buen Salvaje': Fray Bartolomé de Las Casas y su antropología utopica" (Madrid: Institut G. Fernández de Oviedo C.S.I.C., 1976), 157–58.

9 Hilaire Kallendorf, "A Myth Rejected: The Noble Savage in Dominican Dystopia," *Journal of Latin American Studies* 27, no. 2 (May 1995): 449–70.

10 José Rabasa, "The Noble Savage as Utopian Figure?" in *Approaches to Teaching the Writings of Bartolomé de Las Casas*, eds. Santa Arias and Eyda Merediz (New York: Modern Language Association of America, 2008), 121.

11 Jose Luis Abellan contended that the image of "the noble savage" was developed in Spain by men such as Juan Vives, Antonio de Guevara, and, most especially, by Las Casas. See his *Historia crítica del pensamiento español*, 2 vols. (Madrid: Espasa-Calpe, 1986), 2:422. Other scholars who argued that Las Casas helped develop "the noble savage" portrayal of the Indigenous people include Marcel Bataillon and André Saint-Lu. See their *El Padre Las Casas y la defensa de los Indios*, trans. Javier Alfaya y Bárbara McShane (Barcelona: Ariel, 1976), 193–94. Pérez Fernández vehemently rejects this ascription; see Bartolomé de las Casas, *Brevísima relación de la destruicion de las Indias*, ed. Isacio Pérez Fernández, vol. 3 (Bayamon, Puerto Rico: Centro de Estudios de los Dominicos del Caribe and Universidad Central de Bayamon, 1999), 3:632–34, note 23 (hereafter cited as Pérez Fernández, *Brevísima*).

12 Knight, *An Account*, 5.

13 Alberto M. Salas, *Tres cronistas de Indias: Pedro Mártir de Anglería, Gonzalo Fernández de Oviedo, Bartolomé de Las Casas* (México, DF: Fondo de Cultura Económicas, 1959), 46–47; Vasco de Quiroga, 1535 "Información en derecho," in Vasco de Quiroga, *La utopía en América*, ed. Paz Serrano Gassent (Madrid, 1992), 217; Silvio Zavala, *Sir Thomas More in New Spain: A Utopian Adventure of the Renaissance* (London: Canning House, 1955), 8; Abellan, "Los Orígenes Españoles del mito del 'Buen Salvaje'," 160.

14 See Quiroga's 1535 "Información en derecho," in *La utopia*, 98–99, 203; Toribio de Motolinía, *History of the Indians of New Spain*, trans., ed., Elizabeth Andros Foster (Berkeley: The Cortés Society, 1950), 193–94; John Leddy Phelan, *The Millennial Kingdom of the Franciscans in the New World: A Study of the Writings of Gerónimo de Mendieta (1525–1604)* (Berkeley: Univ. of California Press, 1956), 40, 44–45; Knight, *An Account*, 5. Las Casas first referred to the Indigenous peoples as the major part of the human lineage in his "Carta al Consejo de las Indias" (1531), in *Obras Escogidas: Opúsculos, cartas, y memoriales*, ed. Juan Pérez de Tudela Bueso (Madrid: Biblioteca

de autores españoles, 1958), 5:43b, 45b (hereafter cited as *O.E.*). Also see his "Carta a un personaje de la Corte" (1535), in *O.E.*, 5:60b; Also see Manuel M. Martínez, "Las Casas on the Conquest of America," in *Bartolomé de Las Casas in History: Toward an Understanding of the Man and His Work*, eds. Juan Friede and Benjamin Keen (DeKalb: Northern Illinois Univ., 1971), 337ff. He first referred to them as the primitive church in his 1518 *Memorial de remedios*, in *O.E.*, 5:38a.

15 Bartolomé de las Casas, *Diario del primer y tercer viaje de Cristóbal Colón* in *Obras Completas* (Madrid: Alianza, 1998), 14:57 (hereafter cited as *O.C.*); Samuel Wilson, *Hispaniola: Caribbean Chiefdoms in the Age of Columbus* (Tuscaloosa: Univ. of Alabama Press, 1990), 7, 63; Abellan, "Los orígenes españoles del mito del 'Buen Salvaje'," 138; Kallendorf, "A Myth Rejected," 458–99.

16 Knight, *An Account*, 11, 38, 64–65, 84, 85.

17 Pérez Fernández contended that Las Casas would have understood that the word "innocent" is derived from the Latin *in-nocens*, which meant "without prejudice or harm," and that, after becoming a Dominican friar, Las Casas consistently used this scriptural metaphor in his writings. *Brevísima*, 34, 640–41.

18 "Carta que escribieron varios Padres de las Órdenes de Santo Domingo y San Francisco, residentes en la isla Española, a Mr. de Xevres," in Miguel Angel Medina, *Una Comunidad al servicio del Indio: la obra de Fr. Pedro de Córdoba, O.P. (1482–1521)* (Madrid: Instituto Pontificio de Teología, 1983), 271 (hereafter cited as *Una Comunidad al servicio*); Alfonso X El Sabio, "Aquí se comienza la estoria de espanna que fijo el muy noble Rey don Alfonsso, hijo del Noble Rey don Ffernando et de la Reyna donna Beatriz," in *Alfonso X El Sabio, Estoria de españa: antologia*, ed. Reinaldo Ayerbe-Chaux (Madrid: Talleres Gráficos Purrúa, 1982), 206.

19 Kallendorf points out that in Columbus's third and fourth diaries, he wrote of the murderers that there "are no people so evil as are cowards," and that, after learning about many of their customs, Columbus came to regard both the Taínos and the Caribs simply as "savages." See his "A Myth Rejected," 458, 465.

20 Christopher Columbus, *Cristóbal Colón: Diario de navegación y otros escritos*, eds. Joaquín Balaguer, Ramón Menéndez Pidal; notes, Carlos Esteban Deive, vol. 1 (Santo Domingo: Ediciones de la Fundacion Corripio, 1988), 342.

21 Oviedo wrote that "these people are by nature lazy and vicious, of little faith, melancholic, cowardly, of low and evil inclinations, liars and of little memory and constancy." See Gonzalo Fernández de Oviedo, *Historia general y natural de las Indias*, 5 vols. (Madrid: BAE, 1959), 1:31, 67–8, 112, 124; Francisco López de Gómara, *Historia general de las Indias* (Barcelona: Iberia, [1569] 1954), 1:49–51; D.A. Brading, "Prophet and Apostle: Bartolomé de Las Casas and the Spiritual Conquest of America," in *Christianity and Missions, 1450–1800*, ed. J.S. Cummins (Brookfield, VT: Ashgate, 1997), 121.

22 See James Lockhart and Stuart B. Schwartz's categorization of sedentary peoples as "imperial" and "non-imperial" peoples, in their *Early Latin America: A History of Colonial Spanish America and Brazil* (Cambridge: Cambridge Univ. Press, 1983), 37–52.

23 For descriptions of the grandeur of Indigenous civilizations in Peru, see also the writings of Francisco López de Jerez, "Verdadera relación de la conquista del Perú y la provincia de Cuzco, llamada la Nueva Castilla, 1534"; Henríquez Ureña, *Los corrientes literarias en la América Hispánica* (México, DF: Fondo de Cultura Económica, 1949), 26.

24 Bernal Díaz de Castillo, *The History of the Conquest of New Spain*, ed. and intro. Davíd Carrasco (Albuquerque: Univ. of New Mexico Press, 2008), 156–58, 171, 175, 177. Pérez Fernández adroitly chronicled the Spaniards' disesteem of the Indigenous people in note 38 of his *Brevísima relación*, 717–19.

25 Phelan, *The Millennial Kingdom of the Franciscans*, 40.

26 This Western classical tradition was teleological and intellectualist in its approaches, and variously articulated by the Greeks (e.g. Socrates, Plato, Aristotle, and the Stoics), by the Romans (e.g. Cicero, Seneca, and Marcus Aurelius), and by jurists such as Justinian, as well as others whose work was enshrined in the *Corpus Juris Civilis: Gaius, Paulus, and Uplian*. Medieval jurists from Inerius to Accurius focused on determining and glossing the common elements of different legal traditions, while medieval canonists incorporated philosophy and theology with legal thought. The medieval Christian tradition, which absorbed classical and medieval jurisprudential and philosophic thought into Christian theology, began with St. Paul and the Church Fathers, followed by twelfth-century scholastic theologians, and, for the purposes of this study, in particular, the teachings of Thomas Aquinas. Francis H. Eterovich, *Approaches to Natural Law from Plato to Kant* (New York: Exposition Press, 1972), 16–17, 19–86; Michael Bertram Crowe, *The Changing Profile of the Natural Law* (The Hague: Martinus Nijhoff, 1977), 6–51, 54–71, 72–100.

27 Bartolomé de las Casas, *Historia de las Indias*, ed., André Saint-Lu (Caracas: Biblioteca Ayacucho, 1986), 3:360, chap. 99 [hereafter cited as *Historia* (Ayacucho)].

28 According to Aquinas, to be made in the image of God meant to reflect the supreme Intellect and Will of God. Because humans were created with intellect and will, they were capable of knowing and loving; through the exercise of these rational faculties, humans participate in God's rationality. Thomas Aquinas, *Summa Theologica* (New York: Benziger Brothers, Inc, 1947), 1a, q. 93, a. 1–8, (hereafter *S.T.*). To be made in the likeness of God meant to participate in God's being by existence, that is, humans were made in the likeness of God insofar as they exist. *S.T.* 1a, q. 93, a. 9.

29 Monotheistic natural theology, a philosophical study which establishes the existence of one God by reason, was inseparable from revealed theology, which consists of faith-based knowledge of God as well as of humans' creation in a supernatural state, their redemption from sin, and their eternal destiny.

30 Francis Oakley, *Natural Law, Laws of Nature, Natural Rights: Continuity and Discontinuity in the History of Ideas* (New York: Continuum International Publishing Group, 2005), 103.

31 Thomists regarded these ontological considerations, which constituted a "metaphysics of morality," as foundational for their moral theology and, accordingly, for their approach to the issues surfacing in the Indies. Anthony J. Lisska, *Aquinas's Theory of Natural Law: An Analytic Reconstruction* (Oxford: Clarendon Press, 1996), 192–95.

32 However, Major (1469–1550), a professor at the University of Paris who was inclined to nominalism, Scotism, and humanism, had published his lectures by 1510, that is, before the Spaniards encountered the elaborate civilizations of the Aztecs, Maya, and Incas. While Major was only briefly concerned with the epistemological challenge, his thesis had great influence on the debate in Spain and on the treatment of the Indigenous inhabitants in the Indies. Gustavo Gutiérrez, *Las Casas: In Search of the Poor of Jesus Christ* (Maryknoll, NY: Orbis Press, 1995), 492n39; Anthony Pagden, *European*

Encounters with the New World: From Renaissance to Romanticism (New Haven: Yale Univ. Press, 1993), 94.

33 Aristotle, *Politics*, book I, chap. 5. Aristotle's theory of slavery, albeit notoriously complex, is found in Book I, chapters 3 through 7 in his *Politics*, and in Book VII of his *Nicomachean Ethics*. However, nowhere does Aristotle state how a natural slave is to be identified. See the lecture delivered by G. L. Huxley on "Aristotle, Las Casas, and the American Indians," at the Royal Irish Academy, June 26, 1979, published as George Leonard Huxley, "Aristotle, Las Casas, and the American Indians" (Dublin Royal Irish Academy, 1980). See also Isacio Pérez Fernández, "La doctrina de Santo Tomás en la mente y en la acción del Padre Las Casas," *Communio* 27 (1987): 289.

34 Mesa stated that "para unos, el indio es un holgazán, un ser bruto e irracional." Antonio Sacoto, "Fray Bartolomé de Las Casas: paladín de la justicia social," *Cuadernos Americanos* CCIII, 6 (Noviembre–Diciembre 1975): 139–40. According to Las Casas's account, Gregorio stated that "cómo son estos indios, que todos dicen, son como animales que hablan." Las Casas, *Historia* (Ayacucho), bk. 3, chap. 9, pp. 32–35, chap. 12, p. 46. Porter also pointed out that by construing nature as creation and as part of salvation history, theologians such as Paz (and Christians) gained a "necessary interpretive key" to integrate and make sense of the differing approaches to human nature they encountered. Jean Porter, *Nature as Reason: A Thomistic theory of natural law* (Grand Rapids, MI: Eerdmans, 2005), 58–60.

35 Matías de Paz was the first European scholar to argue against applying the Aristotelian theory of natural slavery to the Amer-Indigenous people. Fray Matías de Paz, O.P., *Del dominio de los reyes de España sobre los Indios*, in *Juan López de Palacios Rubios, De las islas del mar Océano*, into. Silvio Zavala, trans. and notes, Agustina Millares Carlo (México, DF: Fondo de Cultura Económica, 1954), 217–19, 221–22, 228; Las Casas, *Historia* (Ayacucho), bk. 3, chap. 8, p. 31.

36 Las Casas, "Memorial de remedios para las Indias (1516)," in *O.E.*, 5:9a.

37 Juan López de Palacios Rubios, *De las islas del mar Océano*, intro. Silvio Zavala, trans. Agustín Millares Carlo (México, DF: Fondo de Cultura Económica, 1954), 25–39. Gutiérrez, *Las Casas*, 282–83.

38 Isacio Pérez Fernández, *El Derecho Hispano-Indiano: dinámica social de su proceso histórico constituyente* (Salamanca: San Esteban, 2001), 97–101.

39 Natural law or, as stated by Socrates, "the natural rules dictated by reason" was "discovered" by the Stoics during the first century before the Common Era. Included in the ancient orations about natural law were the admonitions of Epicurius to "follow nature," and Cicero's conviction that this law, which all humans by reason can know and obey, applied to all, is eternal and unchangeable, and must not be violated by human law. After the fall of Rome, the knowledge of natural law was kept alive by the church, and subsequently formalized by jurists and theologians during the early medieval period.

40 Jean Porter, "From Natural Law to Human Rights: Or, Why Rights Talk Matters," *The Journal of Law and Religion* 14, no. 1 (1999–2000): 81.

41 José María Iraburu, *Hechos de los apóstoles* (Pamplona: Fundación Gratis Date, 1992), 60.

42 Miguel Luque Talaván, *Un universo de opiniones: la literatura jurídica Indiana* (Madrid: Consejo Superior de Investigaciones Científicas Instituto de Historia, 2003), 253–54.

43 Gratian, *Decretum*, Distinction 86, c.21, Distinction 42 ante c.1, C.12, Q.1 c.2, Distinction 47, c.8. The doctrine of *miserabiles personae* was in keeping

with scripture, the ordinances of Constantine and the Siete Partidas, as well as in Aquinas's teachings. Brian P. Owensby, *Empire of Law and Indian Justice in Colonial Mexico* (Stanford: Stanford Univ. Press, 2008), 55–56.

44 See Brian Tierney, "The Origins of Natural Rights Language," in *Rights, Laws and Infallibility in Medieval Thought* (Aldershot: Ashgate, 1977), II:615–46.

45 As Tierney pointed out, embedded in human nature was the ability rooted in reason and free will to discern what was right and to act rightly. Brian Tierney, "The Idea of Natural Rights: Origins and Persistence," *Northwestern University Journal of International Human Rights* 2, no. 1 (April 2004): 1–13, accessed July 19, 2020 https://scholarlycommons.law.northwestern.edu/cgi/viewcontent.cgi?referer=https://www.bing.com/&httpsredir=1&article=1005&context=njihr.

46 Bartolomé de las Casas, "Memorial de remedios para las Indias (1516)," Spanish and English versions, in *Bartolomé de las Casas and Thomas More's Utopia: Connections and Similarities*, trans. Victor N. Baptiste (Culver City, CA: Labyrinthos, 1990), 25, 57–58; Bartolomé de las Casas, "Memorial de remedios (1516)," in *O.E.*, 5:10a, 26b.

47 Knight, *An Account*, 28, 44.

48 Las Casas, "Memorial de remedios (1516)," in *O.E.*, 7ab.

49 "Vivir en policía y ser doctrinados e instruidos, and a ser oidos para su régimen jurídico." Las Casas, "Memorial de remedios (1516)," in *O.E.*; Manuel Giménez Fernández, *Bartolomé de las Casas: delegado de Cisneros para la reformación de las Indias 1516–1517* (Madrid: Consejo Superior de Investigaciones Científicas, 1984), 183 (hereafter *Las Casas: Delegado*).

50 Knight, *An Account*, 5–6, 7, 44; Ramón Jesús Queralto Moreno, *El pensamiento filosófico-político de Bartolomé de las Casas* (Seville: Escuela de Estudios Hispano-Americanos de Sevilla, 1976), 102.

51 "Vivir, estar y conversar los unos con los otros"; Las Casas, "Memorial de remedios (1516)," in *O.E.*; Giménez Fernández, *Las Casas: Delegado*, 183. That humans need one another for their subsistence, development, and perfection as persons, both individually and collectively, was part of the ontological foundation of human nature "discovered" in Roman times, as well as of the epistemological framework of Thomism, which was studied by the Hispaniola Dominicans as well as adhered to by scholars in the *Escuela Española*.

52 For example, see Knight, *An Account*, 5, 7, 10. 12, 22, 23, 47, 66, 70, 74.

53 Las Casas, "Memorial de remedios (1516)," in *O.E.*, Giménez Fernández, *Las Casas: Delegado*, 183.

54 Las Casas, "Memorial de remedios (1516)," in *O.E.*, 9. While much scholarly debate and textual glossing has taken place during and since the twelfth century as to whether divine and natural laws were identical, the common reading among canonists was to equate the two laws as Gratian did in his *Decretum*, Distinction 1, C.1.

55 Gratian, *Decretum*, Distinction 1, Part 1.

56 Gratian, *Decretum*, Distinction 4, C.2.

57 Las Casas, "Memorial de remedios (1516)," in *O.E.*, 10a.

58 "Carta del Vice-Provincial [Pedro de Córdoba] y sacerdotes del convento de Santo Domingo, dirigida a los muy reverendos padres (Avril/Mayo 1517)," Miguel Angel Medina, *Una Comunidad al servicio*, 248–51 (hereafter cited as *Una Comunidad al servicio*).

59 Knight, *An Account*, 3; "Carta del Vice-Provincial (1517)," Medina, *Una comunidad al servicio*, 249.

60 Such considerations were also implied in the responses of jurists and theologians—in particular from the *Escuela Española*, to the ethical-epistemological challenges of the time as they too gradually began to associate a doctrine of rights with predominantly Thomistic principles and to spell out the accompanying legislative implications.

61 Porter, *From Natural Law to Human Rights*, 89–90.

62 This ancient-medieval ideal, which also implied the common supernatural destiny of all people, came from Cicero whom Las Casas directly quoted. Bartolomé de las Casas, *Witness: Writings of Bartolomé de las Casas*, trans. and ed. George Sanderlin (Maryknoll, NY: Orbis Books, 1971), 174–76; John Leddy Phelan, "The Apologetic History of Fray Bartolome de las Casas," *Hispanic American Historical Review* 49, no. 1 (February 1969): 96.

63 For the definition of natural law, see Gratian, *Decretum*, Distinction 1, C. 7. 2.

64 With respect to equality, see Las Casas, *Historia* (Ayacucho), bk. 3, chap. 149, p. 546. Las Casas wrote about the encounter with the bishop of Darien in lengthy detail in Book 3, chapters 147–52 of his *Historia*.

65 Las Casas, *Historia* (Ayacucho), bk. 3, chap. 149, p. 546. Las Casas also charged that the bishop's interpretation of Aristotle's *Política* was erroneous.

66 Patricia Seed, "'Are These Not Also Men?': The Indians' Humanity and Capacity for Spanish Civilization," *Journal of Latin American Studies* 25, No. 3 (October 1993): 637n30.

67 Knight, *An Account*, 8; Gutiérrez, *Las Casas*, 292.

68 Betanzos's primary purpose in going to Rome was to petition the erection of a new Dominican Province in New Spain (with himself as the new Provincial) and to recruit personnel for the new Province. On his deathbed, he retracted his indophobic position, and explained that he had acted in "ignorance." Phelan, *The Millennial Kingdom*, 94–95. According to canon law, to plead invincible ignorance was an acceptable excuse, and automatically secured one mercy. See Gratian, *Decretum*, Distinction 8, c.8.2.b.

69 Anthony Padgen, *The Fall of Natural Man: The American Indian and the Origins of Comparative Ethnology* (Cambridge: Cambridge Univ. Press, 1982), 100; Lewis Hanke, *All Mankind Is One: A Study of the Disputation Between Bartolomé de Las Casas and Juan Ginés de Sepúlveda in 1550 on the Intellectual and Religious Capacity of the American Indians* (De Kalb: Northern Illinois Univ. Press, 1974), 18.

70 Fuenleal graduated from Valladolid in canon law, was bishop of Santo Domingo and President of the Audiencia of Santo Domingo from 1528 to 1531. He was also President of the second Audiencia of New Spain from January 10, 1531 to April 16, 1535. Later, he was a member of the Council of the Indies.

71 Gil Fernando and Ricardo Corleto, "Fr. Bernardino de Minaya y la Sublimis Deus," (2003), accessed April 3, 2010, http://usuarios.advance.com.ar/pfernando/DoclglLA/MinayaFelipell.htm; Jesús Angel Barreda, "Encuentro de dos absolutos el hombre y el Evangelio: proyecto misionero lascasiano," *Studium* 32, no. 1 (1992): 127; A. Lobato Casado, "El obispo Garcés O.P. y la bula Sublimis Deus," in *Los Dominicos y el nuevo mundo, Actas del Congreso Internacional* (Madrid, 1988): 739–95.

72 Parish and Weidman published the complete Latin text and Spanish translation of *Sublimis Deus*—a papal bull that some considered as the *Magna Carta* of Indigenous Rights Helen. Rand Parish and Harold E. Weidman, *Las Casas en México: Historia y obra desconocidas* (México DF: Fondo de Cultura Económica, 1992), 310–12. This document proved to be a powerful weapon in the hands of the pro-Indigenous forces. Charles H Lippy,

Robert Choquette, and Stafford Poole, *Christianity Comes to the Americas: 1492–1776* (New York: Paragon House, 1992), 83–84. See also Lewis Hanke, "Pope Paul III and the American Indians," *The Harvard Theological Review* 30, no. 2 (April 1937): 65–102.

73 Francisco de Vitoria, *Doctrina sobre los Indios*, edición facsimilar, 2nd ed., trans. Ramón Hernández Martín (Salamanca: Editorial San Esteban, 1992), 109, 115–16, 128–30, 133–35; Mauricio Beuchot, *La Querella de la Conquista: Una polémica del Siglo XVI* (Mexico, DF: Siglo XXI editores, 2004), 28; Brian Tierney, "Aristotle and the American Indians–Again: Two Critical Discussions," in *Rights and Laws and Infallibility in Medieval Thought* (Aldershot, UK: Ashgate Publishing, 1997), V:312, 314.

74 Sepúlveda had requested a debate with two distinguished Dominican theologians from Salamanca and Valladolid, namely, Melchior Cano and Bartolomé Carranza. Apparently, because of Las Casas's experience and his writings, which were earlier than those of his confreres, the decision was made to have Las Casas debate Sepúlveda.

75 Anthony Grafton, April Shelford and Nancy Siraisi, *New Worlds, Ancient Text: The Power of Tradition and the Shock of Discovery* (Cambridge, MA: The Belknap Press of Harvard Univ. Press, 1992), 136; Gutiérrez, *Las Casas*, 292.

76 Eduardo Andújar, "Bartolomé de Las Cases and Juan Ginés de Sepúlveda: Moral Theology versus Political Philosophy," in *Hispanic Philosophy at the Age of Discovery*, ed. Kevin White (Washington, DC: The Catholic Univ. of America Press, 1997), 76.

77 Juan Ginés de Sepúlveda, *Demócrates Segundo*, ed. and trans. Angel Losada, 2nd ed. (Madrid: CSIC, 1984), 29, 33, 36; Vasco de Quiroga, *Información en derecho del licenciado Quiroga sobre algunas provisiones del Real Consejo de las Indias*, ed., Paulino Castañeda Delgado (Madrid: José Porrúa Turanzas, 1974), 142, 200.

78 See Sepúlveda's "Prólogo" in Las Casas, "Aquí se contiene una disputa o controversia," in *O.C.*, 10:141. Aquinas treats of this in *In Librum Secundum Sententiarum, Distinction* 34, q. 1, a. 8.

79 Las Casas, *Apología*, in *O.C.*, 9:57; Bartolomé de las Casas, *In Defense of the Indians: the Defense of the Most Reverend Lord, Don Fray Bartolomé de las Casas, of the Order of Preachers, late Bishop of Chiapa, against the Persecutors and Slanderers of the Peoples of the New World Discovered Across the Seas*, trans. Stafford Poole (DeKalb: Northern Illinois Univ. Press, 1974), 12 (hereafter cited as Las Casas, *In Defense*); Sepúlveda, *Demócrates Segundo*, 33.

80 Quiroga also espoused this contention, which was ironic because the seemingly "barbaric Indigenous" people of Michoacán affectionately called their prelate "Tata Vasco." Nevertheless, Quiroga adamantly insisted that the Tarascans lived without law and king (*sin ley y sin rey*). See his *Información en derecho*, 168; Gutiérrez, *Las Casas*, 65, 294.

81 See Sepúlveda's "Prólogo," in *Las Casas*, "Aquí se contiene una disputa o controversia," in *O.C.*, 10:132–33, 143.

82 David Brion Davis, "Constructing Race: A Reflection," *The William and Mary Quarterly* 54, no. 1 (January 1997): 7–18; Rabasa, "The Noble Savage as Utopian Figure," 121.

83 Lyle N. McAlister, *Spain and Portugal in the New World, 1492–1700* (Minneapolis: Univ. of Minnesota Press, 1984), 52–55.

84 Carina L. Johnson, "Idolatrous Cultures and the Practice of Religion," *Journal of the History of Ideas* 67, no. 4 (October 2006): 597.

85 Ibid., 610–11.

86 Las Casas's refutation of Sepúlveda on the basis of *derecho* is contained in his *Apología*, which he designated at the first part of his rebuttal.
87 Las Casas drew particularly from Cicero's *De legibus*. Also see his *Apologética historia sumaria*, in *O.C.*, 7, chap. 48 and especially pages 536–38.
88 Las Casas, *In Defense*, 34–35; Las Casas, *Apología*, in *O.C.*, 9:91–93; Tierney, "The Idea of Natural Rights-Origins and Persistence," 278.
89 Las Casas, *Apologética historia sumaria*, in *O.C.*, 8, chap. 266, and the *Epílogo* on pages 1590–91; Las Casas, *Apología*, in *O.C.*, 9:93–95; Las Casas, *In Defense*, 35–36.
90 Aquinas, *De Veritate*, q. 18, a. 6; Las Casas, *Apología*, *O.C.*, 9:123–25; Las Casas, *In Defense*, 35, 53; Las Casas, "Aquí se contiene una disputa o controversia," in *O.C.*, 10:141.
91 This fourth category was articulated in *The Only Way*. Las Casas, *Apología*, in *O.C.*, 9:131–33; Las Casas, *In Defense*, 55.
92 José María Chacón y Calvo, "La experiencia del Indio," in *El Padre Las Casas y los Cubanos*, eds. Ana Cairo and Amavri Gutiérrez (Puerto Rico: Universidad Central de Bayamón, 2007), 173–74.
93 Las Casas, *Apología*, in *O.C.*, 9:111–17; Las Casas, *In Defense*, 46, 48.
94 Las Casas, *Apología*, in *O.C.*, 9:127–29, 153–55, 159, 255–57; Las Casas, *In Defense*, 54, 69, 72.
95 Las Casas, *Apología*, in *O.C.*, 9:367, 443–45, and chaps. 34, 35, 37. Las Casas, *In Defense*, 188, 223–35, 243 and chaps. 34–37. Davíd Carrasco offers a supportive interpretation from another wisdom tradition asserting that it is the god-image and not the human image that is killed and transformed into creative energy, in his "Human Sacrifices/Debt Payments from the Aztec Point of View," in Díaz del Castillo, *The History of the Conquest of New Spain*, 458–65.
96 Las Casas, *Apología*, in *O.C.*, 9:153–55, 299–301; Las Casas, *In Defense*, 69, 151; Las Casas, *Apologética história sumaria*, *O.C.*, 7, chap. 73.
97 See his *Apologética historia sumaria*, in *O.C.*, 7: chaps. 75–78, 103–18 about idolatry in ancient times, chaps. 147–162 about ancient human sacrifice, and chaps. 120–26 about idolatry in the Indies.
98 In the *Apología*, Las Casas had referred to the second part of his rebuttal, which would consist of *los hechos* in contrast to *los derechos*. The voluminous *Apologética historia sumaria* was this second part. Las Casas, *Apología*, in *O.C.*, 9, chaps. 53–56; Las Casas, *In Defense*, 326–41.
99 Las Casas, *Aqui se contiene*, in *O.C.*, 10:166; Las Casas, *Apología*, in *O.C.*, 9:109–13, chaps. 57–58; Las Casas, *In Defense*, 45–46, 343–48.
100 Las Casas, *Apología*, in *O.C.*, 9:105–09; Las Casas, *In Defense*, 43–44; Las Casas, *Aqui se contiene*, in *O.C.*, 10:165.
101 James Lockhart and Enrique Otte, eds. and trans, *Letters and People of the Spanish Indies: Sixteenth Century* (Cambridge: Cambridge Univ. Press, 1976), 231.
102 Las Casas, *Apología*, in *O.C.*, 9:107–109; Las Casas, *In Defense*, 44.
103 Díaz del Castillo, *The History of the Conquest of New Spain*, 156.
104 Vitoria, *Doctrina sobre los Indios*, 115; Las Casas, *Apología*, in *O.C.*, 9:259.
105 Las Casas, *Apología*, in *O.C.*, 9:105–09; Las Casas, *In Defense*, 41–43. See the following chapters of Las Casas's *Apología* for his descriptions of Indigenous cities: 49 (New Spain), 50–51 (Mexico), 52 (other New Spain, Guatemala, Honduras, Yucatan), 53 (Jalisco, Cíbola, and others), 54 (Iquique, Quibira, Coza), 55 (in the provinces of Cumaná, Darién, and Nueva Granada), and 56 (in Peru).
106 Benjamin Keen, "The Legacy of Bartolomé de las Casas," *Ibero-Americana Pragensia* 2 (1977): 59–60; Berta Ares Queija, "La *Apologética historia sumaria* y el debate sobre la naturaleza del indio," in *O.C.*, 6:201–14; Anthony

Pagden, *The Fall of Natural Man: The American Indian and the origins of comparative ethnology* (Cambridge: Cambridge Univ. Press, 1999), 120, 144. See also Sebastián Robiou Lamarche, *Taínos y Caribes: Las culturas aborígenes antillanas*, prologue Ricardo E. Alegría (San Juan, Puerto Rico: Editorial Punto y Coma, 2005).

107 Las Casas, *Apología*, in *O.C.*, 9:259; Tierney, "Aristotle and the American Indians," V: 305.

108 Las Casas, *Apología*, in *O.C.*, 9:107; Las Casas, *In Defense*, 43.

109 Tierney, "Aristotle and the American Indians," V:316. For Las Casas's assessment of the cultural complexity of the *ciudades* of Mexico, New Spain, Guatemala, Honduras, Yucatan, Jalisco, Cíbola, Ciquique, Quibara, Coza, and, among others, those in Cumaná, Darien, Reino de Granada, the kingdom of Peru, and especially in Cuzco, see his *Apologética historia sumaria*, in *O.C.*, 7, chaps. 49–58.

110 *Apologética historia sumaria*, in *O.C.*, 7:606, chap. 65. This insight anticipated the teaching of Vatican II in *Lumen Gentium*.

111 Tierney, "Aristotle and the American Indians," V:315–17; George Sanderlin suggested that Las Casas's idea of progress placed him in an intermediate position between Aquinas and Jean Jacques Rousseau; see his *Bartolomé de Las Casas: A Selection of His Writings* (New York, Alfred A. Knopf, 1971), 112.

112 Keen, "The Legacy of Bartolomé de las Casas," 60.

113 Talaván, *Un Universo de Opiniones*, 251.

114 Las Casas, *Apología*, in *O.C.*, 9:667.

115 Las Casas, "Diario del primer y tercer viaje de Cristóbal Colón," in *O.C.*, 14:41; Peggy K. Liss, *Isabel the Queen: Life and Times*, rev. ed. (Philadelphia: Univ. of Pennsylvania Press, 2004), 316–17; Henry Kamen, *Empire: How Spain Became a World Power 1492–1763* (New York: Harper Collins, 2003), 14; Luis N. Rivera, *A Violent Evangelization: The Political and Religious Conquest of the Americas* (Louisville, KT: Westminster/John Knox Press, 1992), 55.

116 George Mariscal, "Bartolomé de las Casas on Imperial Ethics and the Use of Force," in *Reason and Its Others: Italy, Spain, and the New World*, eds. David Castillo and Massimo Lollini (Nashville, TN: Vanderbilt Univ. Press, 2006): 260–1; Phelan, *The Millennial Kingdom of the Franciscans*, 17–23.

117 Pope Alexander IV, *Inter Caetera II* (May 4, 1493).

118 Knight, *An Account*, 3, 6, 8, 22, 47, 50–51, 59, 86.

119 Johnson points out that pastoral discourse emphasized "the distance between true Christianity and false sects, conflating pagan, Muslims, Jews, and heretics." See her "Idolatrous Cultures," 620.

120 Antonio Rumeu de Armas, *La Política Indigenista de Isabel la Católica* (Valladolid: Instituto "Isabel la Católica" de História Eclesiastica, 1969), 9–28.

121 Thomas Benjamin, *The Atlantic World: Europeans, Africans, Indians, and Their Shared History, 1490–1900* (Cambridge: Cambridge Univ. Press, 2009), 107–9; Lewis Hanke, "The Theological Significance of the Discovery of America," in *First Images of America. The Impact of the New World on the Old*, ed. Fredi Chiappelli (Berkeley: Univ. of California Press, 1976), 364–71.

122 Theoretically, these fundamental human inquiries derive from Western classifications of the disciplines of epistemology, ethics, and politics, respectively. Osvaldo F. Pardo, *The Origins of Mexican Catholicism: Nahua Rituals and Christian Sacraments in Sixteenth-Century Mexico* (Ann Arbor: Univ. of Michigan Press, 2006), 2.

123 Laureano Robles, "El Pensamiento filosófico de España," in *Filosofía iberoamericana en la época del Encuentro*, ed. Laureano Robles (Madrid: Ed. Trotta, S.A., 1992), 15–49; Cirilo Flórez Miguel, "La Ciencia Europea Antes de 1492," in *Filosofía iberoamericana*, 51–78.

124 Miguel León-Portilla, "El Pensamiento Nahuatl," in *Filosofía iberoamericana*, 79–98; Enrique Florescano, *Memory, Myth, and Time in Mexico: From the Aztecs to Independence*, trans. Albert G. Bork and Kathryn R. Bork (Austin: Univ. of Texas Press, 1997), 1–64; Mercedes de la Garza, "El Pensamiento Maya," in *Filosofía iberoamericana*, 99–125; María Luisa Rivara de Tuesta, "El Pensamiento Incaico," in *Filosofía iberoamericana*, 127–53.

125 A similar conception is found in Greek thought. Enrique Florescano, "Concepciones de la Historia," in *Filosofía iberoamericana*, 309–29; Elsa Cecilia Frost, "La Visión Providencialista de la História," in *Filosofía iberoamericana*, 331–32.

126 Between 1524 and 1572, mendicant orders printed at least 109 books pertaining to evangelization in various Amerindian languages, including 80 Franciscan texts, 16 Dominican texts, 8 Augustinian texts, and 5 anonymous texts. See Bernardino Verástique, *Michoacán and Eden: Vasco de Quiroga and the Evangelization of Western Mexico* (Austin: Univ. of Texas Press, 2000), 106. For a complete listing of these texts by the mendicants, see Robert Ricard, *The Spiritual Conquest of Mexico: An Essay on the Apostolate and the Evangelization Methods of the Mendicant Orders in New Spain: 1523–1572* (Berkeley: Univ. of California Press, 1966), 406–14 (hereafter *The Spiritual Conquest*). Concerning other linguistic considerations, also see Lippy, Choquette, and Poole, *Christianity Comes*, 33–7; Matthew Restall, *The Seven Myths of the Spanish Conquest* (Oxford: Oxford Univ. Press, 2003), 14–5; Ricard, *The Spiritual Conquest*, 39–60; Alain Milhou, "Misión, Represión, Paternalismo e Integración para un Balance de un Siglo de Evangelización en Iberoamérica (1520–1620)," in *Los Conquistadores: 1492 y la población indígena de las Américas*, ed. Heraclio Bonilla (Santa Fé de Bogotá, Columbia: Tercer Mundo Editores, 1992), 282.

127 Owensby, *Empire of Law*, 26.

128 Pérez Fernández, *Brevísima*, 237–38; Pope Alexander IV, *Inter Caetera I* (May 3, 1493); Pope Alexander IV, *Inter Caetera II* (May 4, 1493).

129 Knight, *An Account*, 3.

130 Rumeu de Armas, *La Política Indigentista*, 129.

131 Knight, *An Account*, 17.

132 Pope Alexander VI, *Eximiae Devotionis I*, May 3, 1493.

133 Anthony Pagden, *Lords of all the World: Ideologies of Empire in Spain, Britain and France, c. 1500–c.1800* (New Haven, CT: Yale Univ. Press, 1995), 1.

134 Pérez Fernández, *Brevísima*, 261.

135 Reportedly, Hatüey and his people even tried to rid themselves of their own gold, hoping that in so doing they would also be rid of the evil followers of the Christian god. "Carta que escribieron varios padres de las órdenes de Santo Domingo y San Francisco, residentes en la Isla Española, a Mr. de Xèvres, 4 de Junio de 1517," Medina, *Una comunidad al servicio*, 285; Knight, *An Account*, 19.

136 Enrique Otte, "Un episodio desconocido de la vida de los cronistas de Indias, Bartolomé de las Casas y Gonzalo Fernández de Oviedo," *Ibero-Amerikanisches Archiv*, Año 3 (1977): 130.

137 Knight, *An Account*, 86.

138 Rivera, *A Violent Evangelism*, 201, 207–16.

139 Las Casas, *Diario del primer y tercer viaje de Cristóbal Colón*, in *O.C.* 14:56. This was also in accord with the Catholic Monarchs' instructions to lead the Indigenous peoples "by the example of good works and love." Bartolomé de las Casas, *Las Casas on Columbus: Background and the Second and Fourth Voyage*, ed. and trans. Nigel Griffin, intro. Anthony Pagden, Repetorium Columbianum, vol. VII. (Turnhout, Belgium: Brepols Publishing, 1999), 7:83.

140 Subsequent papal bulls addressed matters related to the establishment of the church in the Indies. For example, *Eximiae Devotionis II* (November 16, 1501) empowered the Spanish monarchs to receive all tithes levied from the inhabitants with the condition that a portion be given for the maintenance of the church. Later, Julius II's *Universalis Ecclesiae* of 1508 gave the Crown the right of formal presentation of candidates for all ecclesiastical offices in the Indies. J. H. Parry, *The Spanish Seaborne Empire* (Berkeley: Univ. of California Press, 1966), 153–54.

141 The fourth reason of Las Casas's *El octavo remedio* reiterated the requirements by divine law of the Christian life in order to attain eternal life, namely, keeping the commandments, participating in "the divine cult," and receiving the sacraments. *O.C.*, 10:304–05.

142 See the third reason of Las Casas's *El octavo remedio*. However, while this may have been true most of the time, religious priests (as was Las Casas at this time) tended to be prejudiced toward the secular clergy. Yet, Schwaller does point out that during the early years, conqueror-priests (who were usually secular clergy) "became caught up in the adventure of conquest, seeking personal benefits, along with fulfilling spiritual obligations [to the Spaniards]." John Frederick Schwaller, *The Church and Clergy in Sixteenth Century Mexico* (Albuquerque: Univ. of New Mexico Press, 1987), 226.

143 Although conversions were slow, the diocese of Cuba was erected (perhaps prematurely) in 1516 and the first resident bishops were Dominicans. Álvaro Huerga, "Los Dominicos y la evangelización de Cuba," in *Cuadernos del Aula: Fray Bartolomé de las Casas* (Havana: 1998), 85–93; José Luís Espinel, *San Esteban de Salamanca: historia y guía (siglos XIII-XX)*, 2nd ed. (Salamanca: Editorial San Esteban, 1995), 59.

144 Manuel Giménez Fernández, *Bartolomé de las Casas: capellán de S.M. Carlos I, poblador de Cumaná 1517–1523* (Madrid: Consejo Superior de Investigaciones Científicas, 1984), 686, 679; Pérez Fernández, *Brevísima*, note 205, 852–53; Francisco Morales Valerio, "México: La evangelización fundante (Siglo XVI), in *Historia de la Iglesia en Hispanoamérica y Filipinas (Siglos XV–XIX)*, vol. 2: Aspectos regionales, ed., Pedro Borges (Madrid: Biblioteca de Autores Cristianos, 1992), 132–33.

145 Schwaller contends that the secular clergy were "quite worldly," and suffered from an image of being "less spiritual," more "venal [and] rapacious" than their religious counterparts. See his *The Church and Clergy*, 165, and also Sarah Cline, "The Spiritual Conquest Reexamined: Baptism and Christian Marriage in Early Sixteenth-Century Mexico," *Hispanic American Historical Review* 73, no. 3 (1993): 455; Ricard, *Spiritual Conquest*, 20–1.

146 The first three Franciscans to arrive in 1523 were Flemish; twelve Spanish Franciscans arrived in 1524. See Charles H Lippy, Robert Choquette, and Stafford Poole, *Christianity Comes to the Americas: 1492–1776* (New York: Paragon House, 1992), 31–41. After the death of their founder—Francis of Assisi (1226)—the Franciscans disagreed about how to live according to Francis's ideal of poverty. In 1517, two independent Franciscan branches were established: the Friars Minor of Regular Observance, who adopted an austere lifestyle, and the Friars Minor Conventuals, who adapted poverty to the needs of the time.

147 Georges Baudot, *Utopia and History in Mexico: The First Chroniclers of Mexican Civilization, 1520–1569*, trans. Bernard R. Ortiz de Montellano and Thelma Ortiz de Montellano (Niwot, 1995), 77; Phelan, *The Millennial Kingdom of the Franciscans*, 22. Although not easy, conversions were more rapid in the central plateau because of the population density and proximity to Mexico City. Morales Valerio, "México: La evangelización fundante," 132. See also Jose M. Maravall, "La utopía político-religiosa de los franciscanos

en Nueva España," *Estudios Americanos* 1, no. 2 (1949): 201–03; Pardo, *The Origins of Mexican Catholicism*, 2–3.

148 According to Fernández Rodríguez, the first group of Dominicans to arrive in Mexico from Spain consisted of two professed friars and four novices; they were followed later by numerous others. Pedro Fernández Rodríguez, *Los Dominicos en el contexto de la primera evangelización de México, 1526–1550*, Monumenta Histórica Iberoamericana de la Orden de Predicadores, vol. 3 (Salamanca: San Esteban, 1994), 95, 109–10; Lippy, Choquette, and Poole, *Christianity Comes*, 33–40.

149 Ricard, *The Spiritual Conquest*, 128–34.

150 See Morales Valerio, "México: La evangelización fundante," 133–40.

151 Cline, "The Spiritual Reconquest Revisited," 478. In their outreach to Indigenous persons of highest rank, Franciscans used the Bible as the basis of dialogue, and Dominicans used their books of *Doctrina*.

152 Ricard, *The Spiritual Conquest*, 91. In his 1537 papal bull, *Altitudo divini consilii*, Paul III prohibited the omission of any part of the rite of baptism.

153 Ricard, *The Spiritual Conquest*, chaps. 4–6; Pardo, *The Origins of Mexican Catholicism*, 42–48.

154 Las Casas, *Historia* (Ayacucho), bk. 3, chap. 99. Hanke, "Pope Paul III," 67–68.

155 Hanke, *All Mankind is One*, 18.

156 Owensby pointed out that the Indigenous peoples' second-class status in the colonial system left conversion as "equals" before God a theoretical abstraction rather than a practical application. *Empire of Law*, 55; Luciano Vicente Pereña, *Misión de España en América, 1540–1560* (Madrid: Instituto Francisco de Vitoria, 1954), 15.

157 The papal pronouncement affirmed the position, for example, of Julian Gárces, Dominican bishop of Tlaxcala, that Indigenous people were capable of receiving the faith because they were rational creatures made in the image of God. Lobato Casado, "El obispo Garcés O.P. y la bula *Sublimis Deus*," 48–49.

158 In his 1530 bull, *Intra Arcana*, Clement VII advocated an aggressive militaristic approach to evangelization, which included conversion "by force and arms, if needful." Paul III countered this position in his 1537 *Sublimis Deus*.

159 Hanke, *All Mankind is One*, 66–67; Las Casas, *Apología*, in *O.C.*, 9, chap. 42, 501; Las Casas, *In Defense*, chap. 42, 267.

160 Las Casas, *Apología*, *O.C.*, 9, chap. 53, 601–3; Las Casas, *In Defense*, chap. 53, 326–27.

161 Pérez Fernández, *Brevísima*, 250, 264. Although there were differences and conflicts among the mendicants, there were also continuities. For example, in Mexico and Guatemala, Las Casas continued the missionary approach of his Dominican mentors on Hispaniola; in Peru, Domingo de Santo Tomás was a disciple of Las Casas. Milhou, "Misíon, Represión, Paternalismo e Interiorización," 264.

162 Las Casas began writing *The Only Way* during his Dominican *studium* and published his first version in Latin in 1534 in response to Betanzos's defamation of the Indigenous peoples and to the revocation of the 1530 anti-slavery law. This first version, which was published in Latin in Santo Domingo, Hispaniola, was entitled *De unico trahendi modo universas gentes ad veram religionem*, and is translated as *Del único modo de atraer a todos los pueblos a la verdadera religion* (The Only Way to Draw all People to the True Religion). According to Helen Rand Parish's interpretation of Chapter 11, Book 3, of Las Casas's *Historia*, "*religionem*" meant "a living faith" in the

sense of "doing" the work of religion by deeds that bring about the divine plan of salvation. Helen Rand Parish, interview by the author, February 12, 2001, tape recording. In 1536, Las Casas wrote a summary of the first version of the treatise in Spanish, entitled Of the Promulgation of the Gospel to all Peoples, for the use of conquerors, governors, and other officials in the New World who could not read Latin. In 1539, Las Casas prepared a second version of The Only Way entitled How the Kings of Spain must care for the World of the Indies namely, [by] the Only Way of calling all people to a Living Faith (*De cura habenda regibus Hispaniorum circa orbem Indianum et [sic sc.] de unico vocationis modo omnium gentium ad veram religionem*). Sometime between 1552 and 1559, Las Casas prepared a third version entitled *De unico vocationis modo omnium gentium ad veram religionem*, at the College of San Gregorio at the University of Valladolid. See Bartolomé de las Casas, *The Only Way*, ed. Helen Rand Parish, trans. Francis Patrick Sullivan (New York: Paulist Press, 1992), 211–21 (hereafter cited as Las Casas, *The Only Way*); Isacio Pérez Fernández, *Cronología documentada de los viajes, estancias y actuaciones de Fray Bartolomé de las Casas*, vol. 2 (Bayamón, P.R.: Centro de Estudios de los Dominicos del Caribe, 1984) 510; Isacio Pérez Fernández, *Inventario documentado de los escritos de Fray Bartolomé de las Casas*, vol. 1, Estudios Monográficos. Ed. Helen Rand Parish. Bayamón, P.R.: Centro de Estudios de los Dominicos del Caribe, 1981, 272; Luis Ortega Iglesias, *Bartolomé de Las Casas: Cuarenta y cuatro años infinitos* (Seville: Fundación José Lara, 2007), 325; Paulino Castañeda, "Las Doctrinas Sobre la Coacción y el 'Idearium' de Las Casas," in *O.C.*, 2:xxvii. Parish asserts that the first four chapters are missing (and allegedly removed by Las Casas) from the only known manuscript. The surviving manuscript contains the basic thesis and an attached conclusion. In addition, the reconstruction of the tract also benefited from two published seventeenth-century summaries. See *The Only Way*, 63, 222–43.

163 Las Casas, *The Only Way*, 68.

164 Knight, *An Account*, 29, 5–6. In his critical edition of the *Brevísima*, Pérez Fernández discussed the various aspects that Las Casas presented in his Introduction about the Indigenous people. With respect to the mental capacity of the Indigenous people, see his note 24, 634–38; concerning their aptness for Christian doctrine, see his note 25, 638–40.

165 Las Casas, *The Only Way*, 69–108.

166 Ibid., 109–16.

167 Ibid., 117–57.

168 Las Casas, *Apologia*, in *O.C.*, 9, chaps. 61–62; Glen Carman, "On the Pope's Original Intent: Las Casas Reads the Papal Bulls of 1493," *Colonial Latin American Review* 7, no. 2 (1998): 193–204.

169 Las Casas, *Apologia*, in *O.C.*, 9:661.

170 Ibid., 9:661.

171 Ibid., 9:657; Knight, *An Account*, 3.

172 In addition to the following discussion, also see David Orique, "To Heaven or Hell: An Introduction to the Soteriology of Bartolomé de Las Casas," *Bulletin of Spanish Studies: Hispanic Studies and Researches on Spain, Portugal and Latin America* (May 2016): 1–32.

173 Soteriology (soteria, salvation, logos, discourse) is the study of the doctrine of salvation. In the Christian theology, soteriology examines the question of the separation of people from God due to sin and their possible reconciliation with—and salvation from God—through the salvific action of the incarnation, life, death, and resurrection of Jesus Christ.

174 Las Casas, "Memorial de remedios para las Indias" (1516), in *O.E.*, 20a.
175 "Carta al Consejo de las Indias" (1531), in *O.E.*, 44a, 47b; "Carta a un personaje de la Corte" (1535), in *O.E.*, 62a, 63b; Martínez, "Las Casas on the Conquest," 337ff. So important was this principal end that Las Casas attached a copy of the relevant papal bull to his 1531 *Carta* to the Council of the Indies.
176 Knight, *An Account*, 18, 86.
177 That there was no salvation apart from the Catholic Church was first asserted by Cyprian, bishop of Carthage (248–58 CE); by this, he meant to emphasize the oneness of the church in the path to salvation. A more rigorous theological view was developed by Augustine (354–430 CE), which held that salvation required explicit faith and the reception of the sacraments. Adding to the complexity of the debate about preaching of the gospel in the Indies, profound changes were beginning to take place in European Christianity. Although previous reforming waves had washed ashore in Christendom, the Reformation was a tidal wave that battered the notion of *Orbis Christianus*; its ideas delivered a profound shock to Christian religious understanding, especially as related to salvation. The ensuing soteriological argument at the heart of the religious conflict propelled the process of confessionalization that ultimately divided sixteenth-century Europe into Catholic and Protestant camps. Stuart B. Schwartz, *All Can be Saved: Religious Tolerance and Salvation in the Iberian Atlantic World* (New Haven: Yale Univ. Press, 2008), 2.
178 Explicit confession of faith included belief in the three pillars of belief in Christianity: the Incarnation, the Redemption, and the Trinity. Because of the need for these beliefs and for baptism, German Emperor Maximilian was told by the priest Trithemius in response to the monarch's query about how to regard the "dwellers of these recently discovered islands in the Ocean" that "there will be no Indians in heaven." Gutiérrez, *Las Casas*, 243.
179 Augustine and his followers believed that few could be saved because of humans' depravity due to original sin. This theological orientation also eventually became the basis of the Calvinist doctrine of predestination. Luther and the Jansenists also adhered to a strict Augustinian interpretation of doctrine that God did not will to save everyone. Hanke, "The Theological Significance," 364; Gutiérrez, *Las Casas*, 241–48. Las Casas was also deeply influenced by Augustine's vision of the permanent discord between the Earthly City and the City of God—a discord born of the oppositional factors of self-love and the love of God, and present between the unbridled desire for dominion and Christian obedience. For Augustine's influence on Las Casas, see D.A. Brading, *The First America: The Spanish Monarchy, Creole Patriotism, and the Liberal State 1492–1867* (New York: Cambridge Univ. Press, 1991), 76–100. For his appraisal of Aristotle, see Las Casas, *Historia* (Ayacucho), bk. 3, chap. 149, p. 546.
180 Positive infidels were those who refused to hear the preaching of the faith, who fought against those proclaiming the faith, and who after having heard the gospel message refused to believe. See Cajetan's *De iustitia et iure* cited in Jesús Angel Barreda, *Ideología y pastoral misionera en Bartolomé de las Casas, O.P.* (Madrid: Instituto Pontificio de Teología, 1981), 151–52, 152n676.
181 Aquinas, *S.T.*, IIa–IIae, q. 10, a. 1.
182 Las Casas, *The Only Way*, 66.
183 Las Casas, *In Defense*, 130.
184 Las Casas, *Tratado comprobatorio del imperio soberano*, in *O.C.*, 10:402.
185 Romans, chap. 12; *De thesauris*, in *O.C.*, 11.1:41; *Tratado comprobatorio del imperio soberano*, in *O.C.*, 10:401.

186 Gutiérrez, *Las Casas*, 255.
187 I Corinthians 12:12–13; *Tratado comprobatorio del imperio soberano*, in *O.C.*, 10:402.
188 Las Casas, *Tratado comprobatorio del imperio soberano*, in *O.C.*, 10:403. Las Casas drew this from Aquinas's *Super Epistolas S. Pauli, Super Epistolam ad Philippenses, and Super Epistolam ad Hebraeos.*
189 Schwartz, *All Can be Saved*, 36.
190 Aquinas, *S.T.* 2a–2ae, q. 2, a. 7, q. 1, a. 7.
191 See De Soto's *De natura et gratia* (1549). Given the change in the historical situation of the church in the sixteenth century because of the breach in Christendom and the encounter with new peoples, soteriological understandings were both under siege and expanding. Gutiérrez, *Las Casas*, 266. For example, some theologians distinguished two ways of being *in actu* in the church—*in re* ("in thing") and *in voto* ("in desire") and, as such, proposed that implicit faith consisted of baptism by desire—as expressed in intention and manifested in action. Schwartz, *All Can be Saved*, 36, 39.
192 Schwartz, *All Can be Saved*, 38.
193 These distinctions were made by Spanish humanist Luis Vives. See Gutiérrez, *Las Casas*, 244. Church functionaries in the Indies, such as Juan de Zumarraga, OFM, don Vasco de Quiroga, Alonso de Vera Cruz, OSA, Juan Ramírez, OP, and Las Casas also drew from such humanistic trends. Mauricio Beuchot, "Filósofos Humanistas Novohispanos," in *Filosofía iberoamericana*, 281. Also see Lippy, Choquette, and Poole, *Christianity Comes*, 32.
194 Gutiérrez, *Las Casas*, 248–50, 292.
195 Las Casas, *Tratado comprobatorio*, in *O.C.*, 10:402–03; Las Casas, *Apología*, in *O.C.*, 9:275; Aquinas, *S.T.* 2a–2ae, q. 10, a. 10.
196 Knight, *An Account*, 71.
197 In two of his early works (*De Veritate and Commentarium super Epistolam ad Romanos*), Aquinas discussed the hypothetical case of a person reared in the wilderness, where the gospel was totally unknown. Thomas reasoned that God could make it possible for him to become a Christian believer, either through an inner illumination or by sending a missionary to him. Additionally, Aquinas's example about Cornelius involved instruction by an angel as recorded in Acts 10. Hanke, "The Theological Significance," 364.
198 Knight, *An Account*, 22, 84, 68, 48, 64, 86, 8, 18, 63.
199 Gutiérrez, *Las Casas*, 253–54.
200 Ibid., 253–54.
201 Ibid., 270.

5 The Articulation of Las Casas's Juridical Voice

Debates about Economic Institutions and Political Dominium

In 1514, fifty-six percent of 26,189 Indigenous people on the Island of Hispaniola were granted as laborers to eighty-three encomenderos.[1] From 1521 until 1535, the average price for an adult Indigenous female slave was 8.54 *pesos de oro*, and 8.16 for Indigenous girls, while adult Indigenous male slaves were sold for 5.32 *pesos de oro*.[2] In 1521, in the Year Three House, "the lord Quauhtemoctzin was installed as ruler of Tenochtitlan in Izcalli … when the Spaniards still occupied Tlaxcala."[3] In 1529, the *Audiencia* accused Hernando Cortés of waging war on and making slaves of peaceful Indigenous people without using the *requerimento*.[4]

The above narrative snippets gesture to two additional kinds of major debates that emerged from Spain's presence in the Indies. In this chapter, the first section addresses the economic institutions of encomienda and slavery that were generated by the colonial system and its commercial interests. The second section explicates political issues about the legitimacy of the Spaniards' *dominium* and of the exercise of this jurisdiction through warfare, as well as Las Casas's assessment of Indigenous wars and *dominium*, and his juridical criteria for Spanish sovereignty. The chapter concludes with a summary statement about the range of Las Casas's juridical voice.

Economic Debate

Initial Economic Development

The economic goals of the Spanish Crown and others at the end of the *quattrocento* constituted an important impetus for subsequent mercantile development in the Indies. Among these objectives was the desire to open trade routes to Asia (to the west of Iberia) in response to Portuguese advances into the Atlantic, and to the Islamic control of eastern land routes.[5] Accordingly, economic enterprises were an initial and enduring interest in the "discovered" Indies, which turned out to be the reality of what lay to the west.[6] Consequently, Columbus immediately (and obsessively) searched for gold and other precious metals (the most desired commercial commodity) in 1492 and during his subsequent trips.[7] In response to the ever-increasing flow of and demand for trade

Figure 5.1 Codex Kingsborough (aka Codex Tepetlaoztoc) is a sixteenth-century Mesoamerican pictorial manuscript that was part of a lawsuit against the Spanish encomenderos for mistreatment.

commodities (including bullion), the Crown expeditiously regulated this traffic by establishing the *Casa de Contratación* in 1503. Additionally, maritime trade and economic development in the Antilles was also fostered by erecting mercantile colonies, which were in accord with previous patterns of settlement in the Mediterranean world, namely, of the Phoenicians, Romans, Venetians, and Genoese-Spaniards (Figure 5.1).[8]

Emergence and Development of Encomienda

In Hispaniola, economic enterprises initially faltered. The Spanish colonists were generally unable and/or unwilling to provide for their own subsistence, to produce trade commodities, and—as royal vassals—to pay their tribute to the Crown.[9] Nor were many of them content to become salaried employees of a proposed monopoly company on the island.

Consequently, in 1497, about half of the colonists migrated to western Hispaniola where they created a system of *repartimiento*, which Columbus reluctantly endorsed in 1499.[10] By this method of individual shares, the Spaniards divided up the Taínos in individual allotments to serve as work crews in the fields and the mines.[11]

In 1502, the situation was further complicated when twenty-five-hundred Spaniards arrived in Hispaniola with the second governor, knight *comendador* Nicolás de Ovando.[12] These would-be settlers included twelve-hundred from Extremadura, *hidalgos* from Andalusia, two hundred families, and many poor men who emigrated because of their uncertain economic futures in Castile. Among the passengers on the twenty-seven ships were women, servants, and artisans, seventeen Franciscan friars and four secular priests, as well as fiscal personnel for the island and the various ships' crews. Because Ovando had many more people than could be cared for, the Spaniards began to starve. Moreover, lacking the skills and labor force needed for production, they were unable to meet the tribute assessments.[13] Furthermore, while the Taínos of the islands initially "provided an adequate immediate basis of support for a substantial European population," this support diminished as new demands in type and amount of labor were foisted upon them, such as in the Spaniards' large-scale mining operations.[14] As well, Indigenous people routinely resisted the activities that accompanied the Spaniards' presence in their world (Figure 5.2).[15]

Figure 5.2 Caribbean sugar cane mill. Engraving by Theodor de Bry (1528–1598).

To facilitate communication and association of Indigenous people with the Spaniards, as well as to respond to the earlier agitation among the colonists who went westward, Governor Ovando requested the reduction of the Taínos into pueblos. Consequently, in the royal *cédula* of December 20, 1503, Queen Isabel mandated that Indigenous people were to live in pueblos, and that each pueblo would be entrusted to a "good Spaniard" for whom they could work moderately and voluntarily, and from whom the native laborers would receive payment.[16] However, what was established was contrary to Isabel's mandate as well as to her previous instructions in 1502 that the Indigenous inhabitants, as her royal vassals, were to be "governed as free peoples caringly, benignly, and with justice and charity."[17] Instead, mimicking the colonists' early *repartimiento*, Ovando instituted the *encomienda indiana* in a manner that continued to force and exploit Indigenous labor for economic gain.

This Hispano-Indiano juridical institution constituted an intertwining of contemporaneous and medieval practices.[18] First, the Ovando-Isabelline institution exploited the traditional authority of the caciques, and the autochthonous Taíno *repartimiento* system of assigning groups of Indigenous people as laborers for specific communal tasks, to secure and allocate the workers needed by the encomenderos.[19] Second, the Ovando-Isabelline institution was also similar to the "encomienda" of medieval military orders. Just as knight *comendadores* collected the required royal tribute, encomenderos in the Antilles collected tribute from the Indigenous people held in encomienda as delegates of the Crown.[20] Additionally, just as the medieval serfs received "*pan y protección*" in return for their services, so too Indigenous people (at least in theory) were to be provided for and protected. However, unlike the serfs of the Christian military orders, the Indigenous, whom many Spaniards characterized as "primitive" and "pagan," were also to be Christianized and "civilized" by their overlords.[21]

This intertwining of precedents and practices lends credence to Lockhart's revisionist scholarship about the presence of "two strands of institutional development" in the emergent encomienda system that were economic in nature: governmental delegation to the encomendero of "the right to collect and enjoy the royal tribute," and the assignment of Indigenous laborers to work on the encomendero's property.[22] Accordingly, through these two aspects of the 1503 Ovando-Isabelline encomienda, and—for the most part—of subsequent encomiendas, the Indigenous people were forced to contribute to Spaniards' economic gain by tribute in the form of goods and metal, as well as by labor in mining, agriculture, transport, domestic, or other services.[23] In the *Brevísima relación*, Las Casas recorded how under the governorship of "the tyrant-major [*comendador*]," meaning Ovando, certain Spaniards

> were not content with what the Indigenous people gave them willingly, … and parceled [them] out among themselves, giving one

> thirty, another forty, another a hundred and two hundred … and sent the men into the mines to dig out gold … and the women they sent to work on their *estancias*.[24]

The degree to which encomiendas focused on labor service and/or tribute varied in the different regions of the Indies. In the Antilles, changes in the terms of the labor services especially contributed to the escalating maltreatment of Indigenous laborers.[25] For example, in August of 1509, two to three years of service were required of the workers; in November of that year, the length of service became indefinite. To curb the increasing abuse suffered by the Indigenous and to respond to the 1511 outcry of the Hispaniola Dominicans, the 1512 Laws of Burgos legislated reforms; for example, the length of service in the mines was reduced to six months.[26] Sadly, these interventions came too late for all too many of the inhabitants of Hispaniola, where the population had drastically declined.[27] However, due in part to the prevailing Spanish attitude about the "inferior" nature of Indigenous people, the mistreatment of the island populations in the labor force continued. Indeed, the Laws of Burgos had in fact strengthened the encomienda, and resulted in more *repartimientos* of Indigenous people being granted in places like Cuba and Darien to colonists' wives and children, as well as to clergy (such as Las Casas in early 1514) and to non-settlers.[28]

Beyond the Antilles, for example in Mexico in 1523, Cortés also instituted encomiendas of Indigenous, and declared them perpetual vassals of the encomenderos, to whom Indigenous people were obligated to pay tribute directly and rendered service personally.[29] This was typical of Spanish colonialist practices, in general. In the *Brevísima relación*, Las Casas wrote that this turn of events "exceeded and surpassed in violence and tyranny" of what transpired in the Antilles.[30] In 1532, Fuenleal, as the president of New Spain's Second *Audiencia*, first substantiated that the Indigenous people were vassals of the king and not of the conquistadores or other Spaniards. Fuenleal also suppressed the encomiendas that Beltrán Nuño de Guzmán had formed when he was the president of the First New Spain *Audiencia*. In the *Brevísima relación*, Las Casas claimed that these encomiendas were characterized by "such great evils, so many sins, so many cruelties, thefts, and abominations that it could not all be believed [in order] to take from the Indians gold and tributes."[31] In the Crown-controlled centralized system of Indian government that was subsequently established, Indigenous tribute was paid for the *corregidor*'s salary. In the still existing encomiendas, the Indigenous tribute that was paid directly to the encomenderos was however limited by the *Audiencia*. Even so, Las Casas charged, they continued in Mexico to "slay the Indian with their infernal tributes."[32] Later legislation obligated only a "simple" tribute that was to be decided by the appropriate *Audiencia* and paid to royal officials rather than to encomenderos; this ordinance disallowed the use of Indigenous people for personal labor service of any kind for the entire Spanish "domain" in the Indies, and specifically commanded that Indigenous inhabitants who "are alive on the Islands of Hispaniola, Cuba, and San Juan ... be not troubled or molested with tributes or other services ... [but] be allowed to rest."[33] In reality, this legislative clause was never very effective and, in Peru, led to a revolt of encomenderos and other Spaniards.

As indicated above, accompanying this trajectory of variations in tribute and labor obligations was the stark reality of the horrendous subjection and inhumane treatment of the Indigenous encomendados. Cruel maltreatment occurred under Columbus's watch, during Ovando's management of the emergent encomienda system, and beyond. In the *Brevísima relación*, Las Casas repeatedly contended that the maltreatment increased over time in degree and form, and that Indigenous people served the Spaniards "day and night, without respite or rest" until they were "consumed."[34]

This seems to suggest that Las Casas regarded the treatment of Indigenous persons held in encomienda as equal to that of slaves, which position was initially held by some scholars, but is no longer tenable.[35] Older scholarship that equates the encomienda and slavery ignores several facts: that the encomienda system was characterized by greater complexity and variations as it moved beyond the islands, that Indigenous peoples often had a traditional expectation from their own cultures that they would need to serve their conquerors and overlords in some way.[36] Additionally, in the colonial period, Indigenous people also went to court to seek a reduction of their obligations. Furthermore, there were legal distinctions between these two institutions. The encomienda gave the Spaniards rights to Indigenous labor and tribute; slavery gave them ownership of the person of the slave.[37] Unlike slaves, Indigenous people held in encomienda were not to be bought or sold, bequeathed to future generations, or moved out of the geographic area; that is, the encomendero's rights were to be limited by trading, inheritance, and relocation restrictions, at least theoretically.[38] Nevertheless, in the stark reality of the maltreatment of the Indigenous peoples, both the encomienda and, as will be seen, slavery constituted what Las Casas referred to in the *Brevísima relación* as "the hardest, harshest, most heinous bondage to which men or beast might be bound."

Emergence and Development of Slavery

While the Crown initially prohibited slavery in the Antilles, precedents for this institution existed in the Mediterranean region, where greater religious and linguistic diversity (as compared with northern Europe) increased the sense of difference between peoples, which, in turn, aided the acceptance and vitality of slavery. In Iberia, another form of slavery developed when slaves from Sub-Saharan Africa were introduced. Initially, these male and female slaves, who were considered "prestige items," rendered personal and/or household service as determined by the gender ideology of the time. Subsequently, slave labor became essential in commercial enterprises—first in Cypress and Sicily, then westward to the expanding Atlantic island colonies of Portugal and Spain. Unlike the eastern Mediterraneans who enslaved Moors, the Portuguese (and later Spaniards) exploited Sub-Saharan Africans to meet the growing labor demands in the production of sugar.[39] Meanwhile, across the Atlantic, slavery among Indigenous peoples also existed long before the Spaniards arrived in the Antilles. Native slaves were generally those captured in war, and those purchased or owned by ruling classes.[40]

Queen Isabel opposed slavery in the Indies. In her response in 1500 to Columbus's transport of Indigenous persons to Spain to sell as slaves, she insisted on their freedom as her royal vassals, and demanded that all of the Indigenous people taken to Spain be returned, repatriated, and compensated.[41] Clearly, Isabel did not perceive Indigenous people as slaves by nature. Instead, she considered them her vassals "in whom Christianity must be instilled."[42] Given their juridical status as vassals of the Spanish Crown, the Indigenous people were also equal to Spaniards and obligated to pay royal tribute.[43] Consequently, if Indigenous people were made slaves, their tribute payment would go to those to whom they belonged instead of to the Crown.[44] Nevertheless, the Crown's Spanish vassals continued to have recourse to slavery to augment the labor force as well as the revenue needed for different economic enterprises of the colonized islands (particularly in the fringe areas), even though the Crown persisted in reiterating, as in the royal *cédula* of June 21, 1511, that Indigenous people were not to be made slaves.[45] Moreover, as addressed in the previous chapter, slavery was not in keeping with Las Casas's conviction about the full humanity of the Indigenous peoples, and especially about their right to liberty and their equality to the Spaniards in personhood and nationhood.

Slavery of Indigenous peoples persisted in the Caribbean but was less prolonged and less widespread in the mainland. This was because the mainland populations were denser, and rotational draft labor was preferred (and was known in pre-Contact times and was also less deadly). The atrocities of the first decades and the outcry (such as that of Las Casas) also helped to stem the use of Indigenous slavery in the central areas and in some intermediate regions. However, in the periphery, slavery persisted longer.

Spaniards made slaves of Indigenous people principally through war and trade (*rescate*).[46] Similar to the pre-Contact pattern in the Indies, *esclavos de guerra* consisted of those captured in battles and/or suppressed in rebellions. *Esclavos de rescate* were of several kinds. They included Indigenous people held in ransom by some Spaniards in exchange for gold, examples of which Las Casas cited in his narrations in the *Brevísima relación* about Venezuela, Santa Marta, and Peru.[47] They also included Indigenous persons who, according to ancient custom, had already been made slaves among their own people, and whom some Spaniards simply "took," or demanded in "trade off" for payment of tribute and/or in exchange for goods.[48]

The *Brevísima relación* constituted a shocking litany of the "infinite abominable and infernal wars" through which countless *esclavos de guerra* and *esclavos de rescate* were obtained, as well as a gripping narrative of the cruel commerce and horrific treatment to which the enslaved were subjected. For example, Las Casas told of how during the first irregular phases of the conquest of the Yucatán beginning in 1527, the conquistadors from the Montejo family, a trio of father, son, and nephew, sold Indigenous people as slaves to waiting "ships in exchange for wine and clothing and other things."[49] Pedro de Alvarado and Cristóbal de Olid did the same in the Yucatán and en route to Naco and Honduras.[50] Las Casas learned of this commerce through his close friend, Friar Jacobo de Tastera, OFM, who also informed him about the enslavement of children when there were no legal slaves to give nor riches to be found in the land. In this enslavement of children, which also allegedly took place in Nicaragua and Guatemala, Las Casas wrote that "whoever had two would give one child, and who had three gave two."[51] He also told of how, in 1525 in Pánuco, Nuño de Guzmán reportedly purchased a mare for the price of eighty enslaved Indigenous persons, and how slaves were mercilessly branded with searing irons, for example, in Tierra Firme, Guatemala, Jalisco, and Venezuela.[52]

In 1530, the Crown attempted to stop the slave trade (of Indigenous people) by the Anti-Slavery Act. That the monarch clearly intended to eradicate all forms of Indigenous slavery was evidenced in the royal *cédula* of January 25, 1531, to Nicaraguan officials, which mandated the freedom of all slaves—those captured in war and in rebellions, those purchased, and those that Spaniards may have acquired who were slaves by Indigenous custom or law. According to Sherman's study of forced native labor, the anti-slavery legislation had various consequences: some Spaniards "suffered" without Indigenous slaves, and some others refused to obey the law; many territories were not pacified and, given that the Indigenous peoples could not be enslaved for rebellion, caciques were emboldened to revolt.[53]

Because of these and other considerations, Charles V revoked the Anti-Slavery Act in 1534. Opinions of the *Escuela Española* further legitimated the revocation; for example, in his 1535 treatise, *De Dominio*, Domingo de Soto defined legal slaves as those captured in a just war, and as those who freely chose to sell themselves.[54] Nevertheless, episcopal authorities at the 1536 ecclesiastical junta in Mexico City challenged the revocation by issuing an *acta* generally referred to as *Seis Verdades* (Six

Truths), which questioned the justice of both the Spanish and the Indigenous practices of taking *esclavos de guerra* and *esclavos de rescate*—and which, significantly, bore Las Casas's signature.[55]

As implied above in broad narrative strokes, the history of slavery and of the corresponding positions of the Crown was exceedingly complex.[56] From an economic perspective, the choices and trade-offs were paradoxically difficult. On the one hand, there was the need for labor and trade, which led to "person-purchase" and "ransom-trading" that, in turn, benefited many Spaniards in the Indies and Spain. The emperor himself was pressed for money to finance his European imperial ambitions. On the other hand, the amassing of wealth and the possible creation of a rich and distant aristocracy of Spanish conquistadors and colonizers constituted an economic threat to the king. Due in part to the need to halt these kinds of enrichments at the economic expense of the Crown—as well as to mitigate the toll on the Indigenous labor force, Emperor Charles promulgated the New Laws of 1542, which abolished both the encomienda and the slavery. With respect to the encomienda, the emperor legislated that:

> We do furthermore order and command that no viceroy, governor, *Audiencia*, discoverer, or any other person may henceforth possess Indians in *encomienda* through any new provision or through any renunciation or donation or sale or any other manner whatever, nor through vacancy or inheritance.[57]

With respect to slavery, the monarch proclaimed that:

> Furthermore, we do order and command that from this time forward, no cause of war or other reason, even under title of rebellion or for rescue or in any other manner, shall justify making a slave of any Indian whatsoever, and that it is our will that they be treated as subjects of the crown of Castile, for so they are. No person may employ Indians as personal servants … or in any other way against their will.[58]

Las Casas's Juridical Assessment and Condemnation

During the months of deliberations in which Las Casas participated that led to the legislation of the New Laws (which will be addressed in more length in Chapter 6), the Dominican friar addressed in detail and denounced without compromise the bondage of the institutions of encomienda and slavery.[59] Part of his contribution to the discussions was his *El octavo remedio* (*The Eighth Remedy*) in which he articulated twenty reasons from divine, natural, canonical, and civil laws for the elimination of the encomienda.[60] Another part of his contribution in the forming of the New Laws consisted of his arguments for the abolition of slavery.[61] However, because he was not pleased that the promulgated New Laws "accepted the so-called proof that various Indians had been legitimately enslaved," he formulated another major treatise, *Se han hecho esclavos* (*They Have Been Made Slaves*), to prove the unlawfulness of all slavery in the Indies using "many juridical reasons and authorities."[62]

In keeping with his juridical approach, both of these texts, *El octavo remedio* and *Se han hecho esclavos*, were published in 1552 as *tratados*—a legal genre of juristic writing, which consisted of monographs on some aspect of civil and/or canon law. However, *El octavo remedio* also belonged to the genre of *memoriales* by reason of its being a request based on *hechos* and *derecho*, and its origin in the original 1542 *Memorial de remedios*. *Se han hecho esclavos*, a document requested by the Council of the Indies, consisted of a compendium of slavery's historical and legal trajectory, as well as of an *alegato*—which genre of plea obligated the monarchical and ecclesial arms to eradicate this institution. In both of these major *tratados*, Las Casas's arguments persistently had recourse to the law as well as to natural rights.

In his recourse to the law in *El octavo remedio*, Las Casas pointed out that the early encomiendas were established without royal approval and were "never ordered by the Laws of Castile": Columbus and Ovando disobeyed Isabel's instructions, and Cortés disregarded Charles's prohibition.[63] Furthermore, both kinds of encomienda violated the juridical status and rights of Indigenous people as vassals of the Crown.[64] In addition to their failure to obey royal directives, encomenderos and officials in the Indies flouted the recommendations of the *Consejo Real* and various juntas of *letrados* and theologians, particularly those of 1523 and 1528, upon whose counsel the monarchs often based their legislative actions.[65] In the *Brevísima relación*, Las Casas charged that information about the destruction in the Antilles had been "kept from the Queen," and that a "disservice" was being done to the king. He quoted from a letter to the emperor written by Fray Juan Fernández de Ángula, Bishop of Santa Marta, alleging that Spaniards in that region publicly proclaim "that they have come here upon orders of Your Majesty" as they "steal, destroy, kill, and burn."[66]

Many of the reasons in *El octavo remedio* that Las Casas gave for abolishing the encomienda were related to the maltreatment of Indigenous people—first, about its underlying origin in many Spaniards' greed and, second, about its manifestations in intolerable services and tyrannical violence—all of which, he argued, violated divine, natural, and human laws. In his juridical appraisal of greed, Las Casas cited scriptural, philosophical, and canonist authorities to demonstrate the danger of giving rule to those whose goal was to become rich: namely, Ecclesiastes about the pursuit of riches never ending; Boecio and Aristotle about the similarity of the appetite for riches to that for happiness; Aristotle and Ambrose about the "infinite augmentation" in "the blind passion of greed."[67] In the *Brevísima relación*, Las Casas persistently alleged that the Spanish were "filled" with "eagerness and avidity for the gold and riches."[68]

In his condemnation in *The Eighth Remedy* of the intolerable services and tyrannical violence, Las Casas turned to the discourses of learned jurists as well as to texts of the Justinian Code and the *Corpus Iuris Canonici* to demonstrate how the maltreatment of Indigenous people violated natural justice as well as Roman and canon laws; as well, he drew copiously from divine law as articulated in the New Testament about the mandate of charity in human relationships.[69] He laid out the negative consequences of the encomienda for the Indigenous people, for the Crown, and for Spain. As he narrated in the *Brevísima relación*, Indigenous people die "little by little, the King is robbed of temporal goods," and "my native land" risks destruction.[70] He argued for its replacement by the "good governance" of *corregidores* instead of by greedy encomenderos, and by human law that "defends and conserves" the Indigenous, and that would have many positive consequences for all—for the Indigenous people, the Crown, and Spain.[71] (Little did he know that the *corregidores* would later earn a reputation as corrupt, greedy, and self-serving officials.) Las Casas ended his treatise as he began it: this *octavo remedio* was the principal and most crucial of all the remedies suggested. This is because Las Casas held that the encomienda violated Indigenous peoples' basic humanity and particularly their fundamental natural right to liberty, as well as their juridical and ontological status as equal to Spaniards; he was convinced that without the abolition of the encomienda, all other remedies would be of no value and all hope for a total remedy would be lost, and the Indigenous peoples will be destroyed.[72]

In his recourse to law in *Se han hecho esclavos*, Las Casas drew on *ius gentium* to assert a major premise as he did in the *Brevísima relación*: "not one Indian has been justly enslaved in the Indies since the discovery."[73] While *ius gentium* allowed the enslavement of those captured in just war, Las Casas argued that the Spaniards' causes for waging war on Indigenous people were never just because the Spaniards lacked royal authorization and just cause.[74] He alleged that "it was manifest" that certain Spaniards disobeyed "the mandates, laws, ordinances, and instructions of the Catholic monarchs, and of [the Emperor]" by the taking of Indigenous slaves and issuing of licenses. He maintained that, "even if mandated by the crown," any ordinance or permission to enslave would be unlawful because human law cannot violate the prohibitions of natural or divine law and, as such, such ordinances would have to be disobeyed.[75] Just cause was also lacking because, as Las Casas contended both in the *Very Brief Account* and in *Se han hecho esclavos*, Indigenous people had never harmed the Spaniards. Las Casas qualified this absolutist position in his *Brevísima relación*, when he wrote that Indigenous people have "never done any wrong or evil to any Christian without first having received wrongs and thefts and acts of treachery from them."[76] However, both of these assertions that Las Casas made about the non-bellicose nature of the Indigenous inhabitants could have been easily countered by those who did not share this opinion because of their own experiences. As will be discussed later, these assertions are also seemingly related to Las Casas's penchant as a legal advocate for the Indigenous people to present them in the best possible light.

To further substantiate his premise that Indigenous people had unjustly been made slaves, Las Casas then presented the geographic trajectory of slavery by specific descriptions of such enslavement in the Antilles, Nicaragua, Honduras, and Mexico, as well as referred to archived official and unofficial documents (*probanzas*, *relaciones*, *pleitos*, and *cartas*) in support of "all that I said."[77] He further demonstrated that all of the methods through which Spaniards acquired Indigenous slaves were against divine and natural laws, and therefore illegal, whether in wars or raids, whether through deception, demands, or provocation, whether as payment of tribute or as trade commodities.[78] He condemned their ill treatment and especially the branding with irons.[79] Drawing on natural law, he also claimed that some Indigenous societies made slaves of their own people illicitly.[80] In addition to his own condemnation of this "most grievous servitude" of "perpetual bondage," he asked his readers in the *Brevísima relación* "to consider whether they [the Indigenous people] have justly been made slaves"—just as he had asked the readers of *Se han hecho esclavos* to do.[81]

Las Casas also addressed the nemesis of the New Laws governing slavery (and the encomienda), which was the fact that this legislation permitted those who had slaves (and *encomendados*) to retain them, and he further argued that those who still held Indigenous persons in such bondage did so in bad conscience.[82] Given that these Indigenous people "were made [slaves] by fear, force, threats, cruel, and inhumane treatment," he contended that their owners were in conscience "obliged to doubt" whether they were taken legally.[83] Las Casas's concern about the specific issue of the retention of slaves then "adduced a torrent of juridical arguments and Latin citations" from his pen, which were based on divine, natural, canon, and Roman laws as well as on Thomism and ancient philosophy. (This juridical assessment totaled some twenty-three folios.) He ended the treatise with three lengthy appended corollaries based on divine precept.[84] First, the king was obliged to liberate all Indigenous slaves, or there "would be no Indians to sustain the land." Second, bishops were obliged to "insist and negotiate importunely" at Crown and diocesan levels for the liberation of these slaves, and to "risk their lives if necessary." Third, confessors were obliged to withhold absolution from anyone owning slaves. This requirement, which reflected sixteenth-century demands for restitution, constituted a novel enforcement of this right and need for restitution and compensation for the wrongs that were done by making slaves of the Indigenous inhabitants.[85] In the *Brevísima relación*, Las Casas prayed that God may "give understanding to those who may and ought to right these wrongs."[86]

In summary, with respect to the encomienda and slavery, Las Casas did indeed persistently apply the law and also had recourse to specific natural rights in his assessment of these institutions. He condemned the violation of the Indigenous peoples' right to life's necessities, such as the failure to feed slaves as was the slaves' right by canon and civil laws.[87] Drawing on property ordinances in Cicero's *De Officiis*, he upheld the right of Indigenous peoples to both communal and personal property, that is, to "their haciendas, … lands, … [and] houses," and demanded that the Spanish "robbers and thieves" be treated in accord with laws articulated in the *Corpus Iuris Civilis*.[88] As he had done since 1516, Las Casas insisted that all those who exploited, enslaved, or harmed Indigenous people in any way were bound to make restitution, and based his judgment, for example, on civil law in the *Digest* about *furtum* (plunderous thievery), on canon law in Gratian's *Decretum*, the *Libro Sexto*, and the commentaries on the *Decretales*, as well as on divine law in the *Book of Exodus*.[89]

However, for Las Casas, after the right to life, the right to liberty was the most fundamental. He characterized liberty as the "most precious and valued" and as the most "*favorecido*" (advantageous) of all rights, as well as "the highest of all temporal goods" and "the most loved" by all rational beings.[90] Accordingly, his argument against slavery and the servitude of the encomienda first based the right to liberty in humans' rational nature. From this, he asserted that, according to natural law and *ius gentium*, "all the people and all the nations of that world [the Indies] are free."[91] Then, he drew on the philosophical distinctions about essence and accident. From Aristotle, Gratian, and Aquinas, he argued that "liberty is a right by necessity and *per se*"; from the *Institute* and *Digest* of the *Corpus Iuris Civilis*, he demonstrated that slavery and the servitude of the encomienda were "something accidental … by circumstance or chance … imposed or prescribed … and does not have a natural cause."[92] Finally, he pointed out the protection, given the right to liberty in civil and canon laws.[93]

Finally, Las Casas's juridical arguments that the encomienda and slavery violated natural rights and natural law, as well as the dictates of civil and canon laws, also flesh out other premises contained in the *Brevísima relación*. These premises were (1) that the way "the destruction of the Indies" took place (and continued) was because Spaniards' subjected the native inhabitants of the Indies to the bondage of the encomienda and slavery, (2) that Indigenous people had been made slaves unjustly in unjust wars, and (3) that certain Spaniards became increasingly cruel in their treatment of Indigenous people.[94] Undergirding these statements was, however, Las Casas's fundamental premise asserting the natural right to liberty and life—as well as its attendant ancillary rights. Freedom would also remain the crucial and deciding factor in Las Casas's understanding of the legitimacy of Spanish political *dominium* in the colonized Indies.

Political Debate

Issue of Legitimacy

The political goals of the Spanish Crown at the moment of the "encounter" were contoured by centuries of intermittent warfare with Islam that culminated in the reconquest of Granada in 1492.[95] Other important influences include the ongoing restlessness of the noble classes who resisted the monarchy's political centralization and consolidation of their Iberian domains, as well as the emerging and potential jurisdictional claims of rival European powers in the expanding Atlantic world. Given such considerations and the Spanish presence in the Indies, the legitimacy of Castile's political *dominium* and of conquest as a mechanism for establishing jurisdiction became the paramount political issue.[96]

Declarations and Initial Assessments of Dominium

Declarations of possession initiated Spain's claim to *dominium* in the Indies.[97] In 1492, Columbus raised flags and planted crosses in the Antilles to assert the political authority of Isabel and Ferdinand "como señores que son de las dichas mares océanas" (as lords that they are of the said ocean seas).[98] In 1493, the Catholic monarchs requested and received papal approbation from Alexander VI through a series of bulls. These so-called Bulls of Donation articulated the papal intent to "give, grant, and assign to you [the Catholic monarchs] and your heirs and successors, kings of Castile and León, forever, together with all the dominions, cities, camps, places, and villages, and all rights, jurisdictions, and appurtenances of all islands and mainlands found and to be found, discovered and to be discovered."[99]

Both procedures reflected the medieval European notion of double jurisdiction—one being the authority of the pope, and the other, the power of the monarch. A hierarchical notion of jurisdiction developed from the intellectual framework for diverse interpretations of papal authority that Gratian produced in the 1140s by his reduction of papal decrees into systematized codified canon law. According to this jurisdictional hierarchical framework, authority proceeded from God to the pope as Christ's vicar on earth, and then to the monarch as the pope's delegate; as such, the pope had full temporal and spiritual power, or *plenitudo potestatis*.[100] Accordingly, by the mid-thirteenth century, Christian society was canonically unified with papal authority as supreme.[101] In keeping with this medieval canonical tradition, Columbus's declaration reflected royal authority, and the monarchs' request for a papal bull recognized the higher ecclesial authority.

However, ongoing Christian European interaction during the Middle Ages with non-Christian populations and territories generated reconsiderations about the supremacy of papal dominion over those outside the *Orbis Christianus*.[102] For example, the march of reconquest across Iberia needed a juridical rationale for the subjection of non-Christian peoples, and for the expropriation of their lands.[103] Two opposing interpretations emerged in canonistic debates about *who* had *what dominium* in the sense of the right to rule (jurisdiction) and the right to own (possession).[104] Pope (and eminent canonist) Innocent IV (1243–1254) argued that, by natural law and *ius gentium*, non-Christians had legitimate *dominium*—that is, the right to political sovereignty and to the possession of property.[105] He also insisted that, even though infidels were not members of Christ's Church, they were part of Christ's flock, and as such were subject to the spiritual authority of the pope as Christ's vicar.[106] Moreover, those in non-Christian domains could have recourse to papal authority and to the pope's intervention, if needed or desired, because spiritual authority was above any secular authority.[107] However, Cardinal Hostiensis (1200–1271), a famous decretalist and Innocent IV's former student, rejected his teacher's argument, and instead followed the writings of Alanus Anglicus about the *dominium* of infidels. Accordingly, for Hostiensis, the Incarnation of Christ had irreversibly changed human history: all *dominium* belonged to the faithful alone since the coming of Christ, and there was no legitimate secular power outside the Church.[108] Indeed, those who did not accept the Christian faith were regarded as "unworthy and incapable" of political sovereignty. Because non-Christians therefore lost any legitimate right to rule and to own, their lords were only *de facto* and not *de jure* rulers.[109]

Assessments about Spanish *dominium* in the Indies first began in the halls of learning at the University of Paris in a series of lectures by John Major that were subsequently printed in 1510 as *The Commentaries on the Second Book of Sentences*.[110] In contrast to Hostiensis, the Scottish philosopher argued that neither the pope nor the monarch had temporal power over non-Christians.[111] This position was not shared by two prominent Castilian royal counselors, Matías de Paz and Juan López de Palacios Rubios. In response to Montesinos's 1511 outcry, Paz advised the king that Spaniards had "no right to burst in like robbers, seize what they liked, and proclaim that they had 'conquered' [the Indigenous domains]."[112] In his response to Ferdinand's request for a theological opinion about Spanish *dominium* in the Indies, Paz drew from both Innocent IV and Hostiensis in his treatise, *De Dominio Regnum Hispaniae super Indos* (Concerning the Rule of the King of Spain over the Indies).[113] Like

Innocent IV, Paz contended that, even though the Indigenous peoples had legitimate natural *dominium*, they belonged to Christ's flock and, as such, were subject to the pope who, as Christ's vicar, had direct albeit limited temporal power over all the world. Accordingly, Paz contended that "only by authorization of the Pope [would] it be lawful for the King to govern these Indians politically and annex them forever to his Crown."[114] Like Hostiensis, Paz also believed that once Indigenous people were converted, their natural *dominium* passed to Christ as the Lord of the world, spiritually and temporally, who delegated this supreme *dominium* to the pope. In any case, the pope had a say about the *dominium* of the Indigenous inhabitants of the Indies.

Palacios Rubios shared the essential thesis of Paz that Spain's right to rule the Indies was established through the papal donation. In his *De las islas del mar Océano*, Palacios Rubios also took the Hostiensian position, which was common for most canonists of the time, that the pope (as vicar of Christ's Church) had spiritual authority as well as direct temporal power over the world.[115] With respect to the right to own, traditional historiography as articulated by Anthony Pagden claimed that Palacios Rubios and Paz dismissed that right by their recourse to the Roman legal definition of civil society as one based on property relations; simply put, for Palacios Rubios and Paz, the Indigenous inhabitants in the Caribbean were not property owners because they lived in open spaces.[116] This perspective of two individuals who had never been in the Indies was erroneous, because the Taínos were non-imperial sedentary people.[117]

These initial assessments of the legitimacy of Spain's political *dominium* drew on traditions of medieval theological and canonistic thought that envisioned the expansion of the *Orbis Christianus* and adhered to a framework of hierarchical power wherein the pope was supreme. Accordingly, for Paz and Palacios Rubios, the papal donation rightfully bestowed *dominium* in the Indies to the Spanish monarchs. However, as Las Casas pointed out, the Indigenous people were unlike the non-Christian peoples (such as Jews and Muslims) with whom the Spaniards were familiar; Indigenous people had never heard of Christ, and (as was premised in the *Brevísima relación*) they had never harmed the Christians.[118] The new and novel complexities of this reality were seemingly not taken into account, especially in the mechanisms that the Spaniards used to claim and exercise jurisdiction.

Establishment of Dominium through Conquests

The legitimacy of establishing *dominium* through conquests constituted another aspect of the paramount political issue of the time. For the expansion of its reign, Castile typically engaged in "conquests of the classic kind," wherein *dominium* was achieved through warfare rather than rights.[119] As first practiced by Moors and then by Christians, such military conquests were followed by the establishment of permanent settlements of immigrants, formal jurisdiction, and collection of tribute.[120] That is, Castile's royal system of governance sought to absorb the conquered land and people, that is, to colonize them politically and to convert them religiously.[121] This was, however, the ideal; the reality was sometimes different as, for instance, in the Yucatán and Guatemala.

In the Indies, the initial phases of conquest involved easy *entrada* and the assumption of quick control by capturing the caciques and ruling through the caciques if they were pliable.[122] Having a role for the Indigenous leaders in local rule was a very significant strategy, as well as qualifies the meaning (and our understanding) of conquest. Under the governorship of Ovando, Indigenous rebellions and non-compliance were ruthlessly suppressed through a series of bloody campaigns, such as was observed in the Hispaniola province of Higuey (which Las Casas also witnessed and recorded in his *Very Brief Account*).[123] With the development of the initial and subsequent *entradas*, three different objectives became discernible: wealth, status, and Christianization.[124] In time, an inner circle of those who had attained both riches and prestige developed among the invaders. This precipitated a southward trajectory of *entradas* in 1509 to Tierra Firme as newly arriving and would-be conquistadores and colonists searched for new lands on which to enrich themselves and hopefully attain social prestige. In the *Brevísima relación*, Las Casas censured the objectives of these Spaniards "to stuff themselves with riches … and to raise themselves to high estates."[125] Meanwhile, those intent on Christianization included the Hispaniola Dominicans whose collective outcry in 1511 against the maltreatment of Indigenous people marked the beginning of critical attitudes with respect to Spain's presence in the Indies and generated concern on the part of the Crown about guaranteeing the legitimacy of Spain's rule in the face of the conquests that were taking place.[126]

The issue became procedural: were the seizures of power conducted "legitimately"? Historical precedents for legitimizing conquests existed in Europe. In the Greek and Roman traditions about waging war, a messenger was sent out prior to attack; in Spanish-Muslim jurisprudence about conducting *jihad*, a messenger was sent to read a summons to submit and to offer liberal treatment to them before initiating the attack.[127] Castile adopted the protocol used in Muslim Spain that was based on the teachings of Mãliki who emphasized the ritual and religious aspects of jurisprudence, and whose works were available in Spain through Averroes's summaries of the Mãlikian tradition.[128] Accordingly, in 1512, Spanish authorities commissioned Palacios Rubios to compose the text of just such a "formal invitation" to be read to the Indigenous inhabitants prior to every *entrada*.[129] This invitation to submit to the king of Spain as their "universal sovereign lord" and to receive the Christian faith was known as the *requerimiento*. As a political ritual that proclaimed divine, papal, and royal authority, the *requerimiento* asserted Spain's political *dominium*; in this, the document textually concretized previous patterns of behavior utilized in Spain's claiming of the Canary Islands and in Columbus's planting of flags and crosses. As a military ritual that outlined strategy, the *requerimiento* was laden with orders to obey and with threats of brutal attack for non-compliance.[130] In effect, both the text and the execution of "the invitation" seemingly gave rights to invade the particular Indigenous territory as well as to attack and subdue its inhabitants.

Or, did the document simply furnish Spaniards with "excuses"? While Anthony Pagden (and Las Casas) assumed that the *requerimiento* embodied Hostiensis's contention that non-Christian peoples do not have dominion, the revisionist scholarship of James Muldoon offers another perspective. Muldoon argues that the reason for issuing the *requerimiento* was because Castilians—following the views of Innocent IV—believed that Indigenous people as infidels did have *dominium* and, accordingly, that "the Spanish had to justify their invasions by demonstrating the unwillingness of the Indians" to comply with the demands made in God's, the pope's, and the monarch's names.[131] Moreover, the Crown may have feared the charge of heresy if the Spaniards' conquests were perceived as based on the condemned doctrine of John Wyclif who taught that infidels had no right to *dominium* because only those in the state of grace can have *dominium*; additionally, judging from Wycliffe's teachings about the papacy, the *dominium* of the Indigenous peoples could certainly not be bestowed by papal authority.[132] Given these concerns, as Pérez Fernández pointed out, the document and its legal ritual was politically astute from a theoretical standpoint.[133]

However, in its practical application, the *requerimiento* was farcical: the juridical document was read in Spanish "to give unbelievers an opportunity to come to Christ of their own free will," but in reality it was employed to satisfy the conscience of those about to wage wars of conquest.[134] Confronted with the ridiculous yet tragic juridical quality of the *requerimiento*, Las Casas confessed that he did not know whether to laugh or cry.[135] His summary characterization of the text of the *requerimiento* in the *Brevísima relación* substantially reproduced its shocking content.

> *Caciques* and Indians of this Terra Firma of such-and-such a village, we do hereby give you notice that there is a God and a pope, and a King of Castile who is lord of these lands. Come then to give him obedience, &c. For if you do not, know ye that we shall wage war upon you, and shall slay you and capture you, &c.[136]

Earlier and sometime before 1519, Martín Fernández de Enciso (c. 1470–1528) had recorded the reaction of the caciques in Cenú when the *requerimiento* was proclaimed; the Indigenous lords stated that "the pope must have been drunk when he did this—given that he gave away what he did not possess, and that the monarch who asked for and received this *merced* must have been somewhat crazy since what he asked for belonged to others."[137] A description of the bizarre and horrific execution of this would-be legitimizing document, which Restall called "a paragon of miscommunication," was also included by Las Casas in his treatise wherein he wrote:

> Spaniards go at night to within a half a league of the village, while the Indians were in their villages and in their houses fearing no harm, and there, that night, they should read out the *requerimiento* to themselves
>
> … And at the fourth watch [at dawn], while the innocent Indians were sleeping with their women and children, they would rush upon the village, putting fire to the houses, which generally were of straw, and burning the children and women and many of the others alive, before they knew what was upon them.[138]

Although the *requerimiento* was conceived at the time when the Spaniards' sole "possessions" were a handful of islands in the Caribbean and some territory on Tierra Firme, the *requerimiento* became the principal and enduring means of asserting and exercising *dominium* until the legislation of the New Laws in 1542 (Figure 5.3).[139]

Protests, Pronouncements, and Critiques

As wars intensified in 1514 and moved southward from Tierra Firme to Panama and eventually to Peru in 1531, as well as northwest from Cuba to Mexico in 1519, so did voices of opposition and protest. Initially through *memoriales* and *cartas*, the Hispaniola Dominicans supported by the Picard Franciscans in the Antilles as well as by the Hieronymite monk Bernardino de Manzanedo, OSH, protested and condemned the cruelties, killings, and bondage caused by the wars conducted for *entrada* and punishment, and/or for slaves and *rescate*.[140] Agents of the Crown, such as Baltasar de Castro—agent of the king in San Juan (1520), and Juan Martínez de Ampíes—governor of Santo Domingo's colony on Tierra Firme (1527–1529) also addressed and denounced "the harms that are always done."[141] Nevertheless, the various kinds of war continued, and often did so with explicit crown approval. For example, in a 1526 royal *cédula*, Charles V ordered the pronouncement of *requerimientos* to resisting Indigenous inhabitants in Cuba and authorized the commencement of "the judicial process of war … against them," as well as instructed them that the failure "to obey and to submit to royal authority … would result in their being taken captive and enslaved."[142] Ten years later in a letter to a member of the Council of Castile, Las Casas—now a

CAROLVS·V·IMPERATOR · REX ISPANIE·

Leyes y ordenanças nueuamẽte hechas por su Magestad/pa la gouernacion de las Indias y buen tratamiento y conseruacion de los Indios: que se han de guardar en el consejo y audiẽcias reales q̃ en ellas residen: y por todos los otros gouernadores/juezes y personas particulares dellas.

Con priuilegio imperial.

Figure 5.3 Cover of the "Leyes Nuevas" of 1542.

Dominican friar—adamantly condemned all wars as "tyrannical, unjust, and against all law."[143] In the *Brevísima relación*, he called these "cruel and bloody" wars "invasions," and refused to call them conquests.[144]

Another wave of critiques about both Spanish *dominium* and the conquests also emerged from both ecclesial and academic institutions. For example, in an effort to legislate over the extant temporal power of the monarch, the 1536 ecclesiastical junta of bishops called on the higher spiritual power of the pope. In his reply in the 1537 papal bull, *Sublimis Deus*, Paul III decreed that "the Indians ... outside the faith though they be ... are to have, to hold, to enjoy ... *dominium* freely, lawfully ... [and] are not to be deprived of their liberty or the right to their property ... [nor] enslaved." The pontiff further decreed that "should anything different be done, it is void, invalid, of no force, no worth."[145]

In the academic arena, indofile scholastics in the emerging *Escuela Española*—consisting of Vitoria (its founder), his pupils, and his followers—engaged key issues related to the Indies and Europe that needed original solutions. For example, issues during this crucial moment in politics and economics pertained to the endless wars among Christian monarchs, the extension of Islam, the expansion of rival European powers, the emergence of the modern state, and the escalation of transatlantic commerce, as well as to the exacerbation of fractures in the *Orbis Christianus*, and to the examination of Spanish *dominium* in Europe and in the Americas.[146]

With respect to *dominium* in the Indies, many were confronted with the firsthand practical consequences of Spanish rule, ownership, and conquests; in Iberia, Vitoria and other indofile scholastics tackled the speculative rationales. Although, for the most part, Spain's claim to *dominium* was a *fait accompli*, the ever-increasing arrival in Spain of the tragic news of the bloody invasions into the lands on the other side of the Atlantic, such as the Inca empire of Peru, compelled Vitoria to speak out through his lectures and their publications.[147]

Vitoria made a Copernican turn in theological perspectives about *dominium*. While maintaining the connection of temporal power to the transcendent order, Vitoria moved away from the medieval theocratic notion of *dominium* as hierarchical political authority given by God to the pope who, in turn, delegates authority to the monarch toward the recognition of a separation of the authorities of the pope and of the sovereign. Accordingly, in the teachings of Vitoria, both the power of the pope and of the monarch proceeded from God because "all *dominium* has its origins in divine authority." For these and other Thomists such as Paz and de Soto, the pope's authority proceeded immediately and directly from God, whereas the ruler's authority derived from God-given natural law and consequent society (in the form of *ius gentium*).[148] From this perspective, scholastics argued that the pope could not wield temporal authority (except for spiritual ends if necessary) and, as such, the papal donation could not serve as the basis of Spanish *dominium* in the Indies, because the "pope has no temporal or spiritual authority over infidels."[149] Furthermore, neither the pope nor the emperor was the lord of the whole world. These teachings further challenged the theory of *dominium* that was based on the notion of the world as *Orbis Christianus*.[150]

Accordingly, and using the teachings of Innocent IV and Aquinas, Vitoria unequivocally stated that Indigenous people "undoubtedly possessed true *dominium*, both public and private, as any Christian does; … they cannot be robbed of their property, either as private citizens or as princes, on the grounds that they were not true masters."[151] He then refuted the seven "titles" (arguments) conventionally used to justify the Spaniards' subjection of Indigenous peoples and their dispossession of Indigenous property.[152] He subsequently offered arguments based on natural law and *ius gentium* that would legitimate the Spanish presence in the Indies; with this line of thinking, Vitoria laid out the basis for international law—for international solidarity based on rights.[153] Vitoria argued that since the social nature of human beings demands association, and since all humans were citizens of nations that together constitute a globalized community, sociability required commerce, trade, travel (and so forth), in, into, and among different nations. Spaniards could also come to the islands and mainlands to preach the faith, defend converts, defend the innocent, and so forth.[154] However, if the Indigenous peoples refused to allow any of these legitimate activities, or demonstrated gross ineptitude in attempting to do so, Vitoria contended that wars of conquest and the imposition of Spanish rule would be justified.[155] Conversely, the Indigenous peoples' "true and voluntary choice" of Spaniards as their rulers would also be legitimate.

Nevertheless, Vitoria stridently condemned the excesses of the conquest, its consequences and character as unjust wars.[156] Utopically, he envisioned wars being conducted *sine dolo y fraude* (without suffering and fraud).[157] He argued that war must be conducted in "good faith" by both parties, that is, in accord with the law and justice. Drawing from old roots of philosophical and theological discourse about just war, Vitoria contended that the only cause of a just war was grave injury.[158] Its motives included self-defense, the common good, "just vengeance," and the abolition of tyranny.[159] Vitoria stressed that while there may be a just cause for going to war, the question always needed to be asked: should a nation go to war? His response was that it depended on the conscience of the king and of the republic.

Las Casas's Assessment of Indigenous and Spanish Dominium

Las Casas was in the thick of this now mid-century political-ideological debate that canopied the Spanish presence in the Indies.[160] As one of many sixteenth-century thinkers who adapted civil and canon law concepts to political theory, he espoused the position of Innocent IV (that legitimate secular power exists outside of the Church) as early as 1531 in his *Carta al Consejo de las Indias* wherein he contended that the Indigenous peoples had both the right to rule and the right to own.[161] Indeed, all the rest of his politico-juridical arguments pivoted on this premise, which was also stated in the *Brevísima relación*, that the *dominium* of Indigenous people was legitimate and just.[162] As such, in Las Casas's juridical approach to the political issue of the legitimacy of Spanish *dominium* in the Indies and of the conquests as the means to exercise this *dominium*, his derived premises also included (1) that the Indigenous people had just cause for war, and that they had never done anything wrong, (2) that all the wars of conquest were unjust, (3) that the papal donation was the sole juridical basis for the sovereignty of the monarch in the Indies, and (4) that the sovereign lordship of the king of Spain was currently only *de jure*.

Las Casas based the premise that Indigenous people had legitimate *dominium* on natural law and *ius gentium*, as did Paz, Vitoria, and other scholars of the *Escuela Española*. However, Las Casas also went beyond this philosophical approach to anchor this premise on laws from the civil and ecclesial traditions as well as on jurisprudential commentaries, especially those of Bartolus and Baldus de Ubaldis (1327–1400). Recognizing the full humanity of Indigenous people as rational, free, and social, Las Casas addressed their right to rule and their right to own.

As exemplified in his *tratado* titled *Principia Quaedam*, he copiously cited "the law" and *comentaria* about jurisdiction.[163] He also devoted two-hundred-and-forty-five chapters (that is, from chapter twenty-three onward) in the *Apologética historia sumaria* to demonstrate that Indigenous people were capable of self-government "insofar as it is possible by the natural and human way and without the light of Faith."[164] In the *Brevísima relación*, Las Casas asserted the Indigenous peoples' *dominium* by explicit reference to the jurisdiction (right to rule) of Indigenous lords and princes. For example, he described Indigenous lords as "possessors of vassals and lands," as well as recognized that the five principal kingdoms on Hispaniola were ruled by supreme lords and secondary lords.[165] Also significantly, he consistently used the word "territory" throughout his tract to designate the different areas in which the Indigenous peoples lived (and that the Spanish and Germans "invaded") and did so according to its legal definition, which meant "the totality of lands within the borders of each locality where one has a right to rule."[166]

In addition to this jurisdictional *dominium*, the Indigenous peoples' right to ownership was clear in Las Casas's mind. Again, throughout the *Brevísima relación*, he referred to Indigenous people as the "inhabitants" of the lands as well as explicitly stated that they were "in possession of their own lands."[167] In this, Las Casas applied the legal understanding of the concepts "to have" and "to possess" in accord with Castilian jurisprudence to refer "non-redundantly" to the Indigenous peoples' "*de facto* and *de jure* possession over their princedoms, kingdoms, states, high offices, territorial jurisdictions, and domains."[168] His conviction about and his juridical arguments for the legitimacy of Indigenous *dominium* were laced throughout his writings, such as in the *Apología*, and *Tratado comprobatorio*, as well as succinctly asserted in Proposition Ten of his *Treinta proposiciones muy jurídicas*, and explicitly addressed in *Doce dudas* and *De thesauris*, wherein he argued his premise from divine law in the Old and New Testaments, from natural justice and canonical authorities of the Church Fathers, in particular Augustine and John Chrysostom, as well as from Aquinas and Paul III.[169]

Indigenous Wars and Wars of Conquest

A second premise—that the Indigenous peoples had just cause for war and had "always waged the most just and defensible war against the Christians"—also formed part of Las Casas's legal assertions in his writings.[170] For example, in his narration in the *Brevísima relación* of the battle initiated by the Aztecs at Tenochtitlán during the *noche triste* that "killed a great number of Christians on the causeways," Las Casas judged this warfare as "most high and just," indeed, as "most exceedingly just … [as] any reasonable fair man must acknowledge."[171] While this must not have been a very popular stance to take at the time, Las Casas boldly based his assertion on the Christian understanding of just warfare. This Christian perspective, which built on the teachings of Plato, Aristotle, and Cicero, as well as Augustine, distinguished between *ius ad bellum* (which considered whether it would be just to go to war), and *ius in bello* (which addressed how to conduct war justly).[172] The Thomistic criteria for a just war, which Las Casas specifically applied, can be subsumed within these two categories.[173] The category related to *ius ad bellum* consisted of (1) just cause—to repair an injustice or injury, (2) declaration by competent authority, and (3) right intention—to do good and avoid evil. The category pertaining to *ius in bello* consisted of the criteria of proportionality, war as a last resort, protection of the innocent, and reasonable possibility of success.

Using the criteria for *ius ad bellum* and speculating from narrations of the battle on the causeway, the Aztecs' cause was self-defense; their competent authority was the new lord and captain they appointed to replace Moctezuma, and their intention was their freedom. With respect to *ius in bello*, the battle was certainly one of last resorts, given that the Aztecs' demonstrations of hospitality had been so grossly manipulated, and there were no "innocent" Spaniards to protect. While proportionality from the European point of view was lacking in their methods of killing (e.g. cutting out the Spaniards' hearts), the Aztecs probably had reasonable prospects for success, given that the Spaniards on the causeway were trying to escape at night and were burdened down with caches of plunder.

In this causeway battle, the Aztecs engaged in a classical (and justifiable) kind of warfare: self-defense. In his writings, Las Casas pointed out that war in self-defense was "a common rule among the *legistas*," as well as approved in the *Libro Sexto* of canon law, and in the commentaries of Innocent IV and "other doctors."[174] In the *Brevísima relación*, Las Casas periodically narrated how Indigenous people both defended themselves by "taking up arms" and battled to "recover their wives and children," and to "cast [the Spaniards] from their lands."[175] In this, Las Casas attributed human agency to them, and did not, as had his detractors, characterize them as barbaric, violent, or semi-human.

Avengement of wrongs was another classical type of warfare, which Las Casas addressed in the *Brevísima relación* when he spoke about the "desire for vengeance" as a "sin" that was "reserved for punishment by God alone." He attributed this avenging cause for war only to those "very few Indians" who were "more impetuous and hard."[176] However, later he also regarded the slaying of two Dominican friars by the Indigenous inhabitants of Chiribichí as "just vengeance" because the secular Spaniards had not returned their captured cacique within four months as the friars had seemingly promised.[177] Furthermore, in his *De thesauris*, Las Casas argued that Indigenous inhabitants of Peru could justly avenge the wrongs done to them. In support, he presented laws from the Justinian *Codex* to demonstrate that vengeance was licit.[178] At first glance, these assertions seem contradictory, because vengeance is a right of God alone. Yet, their actions were licit according to Roman law as well as in conformity with the criteria of "just cause" in just war theory. The "injury" was that the Spaniards had taken the Chiribichí cacique, and had stolen from the Inca graves. However, Las Casas persistently claimed that the Indigenous people always had "just cause," because they "never did any wrong or evil to the Christians without first having received wrongs and thefts and acts of treachery from them."[179] For him, theirs was a "just vengeance." In Aquinas's teachings, vengeance is lawful if the act is to obtain some good or its primary aim is "the good." That is, vengeance is "just" and does not usurp what belongs to God when, for example, the vengeful act restrains or corrects the evildoer.[180] Then, there is no sin. Seemingly, Las Casas espoused this interpretation, and was adamant that the Indigenous people "did not commit against the Christians, as far as I can believe or conjecture, a single mortal sin punishable by man."[181]

Las Casas's judgment that the Indigenous inhabitants of Chiribichí exercised "just vengeance" by killing his two confreres needs contextualization within the larger framework of canon law and Christian beliefs. In his narration of this incident, Las Casas pointed out that these Indigenous people did not and could not distinguish between the raiding Spaniards and the evangelizing friars at that time (although, according to Las Casas, they did so later). As noted in the previous chapter with respect to Betanzos's error due to ignorance about the Indigenous peoples' level of humanity, canon law regarded ignorance as an acceptable excuse. (Recall as well that Las Casas had asserted that Indigenous people were sinless in their interaction with Spaniards.) Additionally, Christian teaching held that preaching the gospel entailed total giving of oneself, which meant, as Las Casas noted, that the friars "would have given their lives to prevent injustice." Such Christian commitment frequently entailed "suffering unjustly" as the friars did, which Las Casas acknowledged and added that they were "true martyrs." Seemingly, Las Casas attempted to reconcile the justice and injustice of the incident by recourse to an even larger framework: the Day of Judgment, at which he asserted "all shall be made more clear."[182]

With respect to the conquistadors' wars of conquest, Las Casas enunciated his radical judgment of this warfare in another premise in the *Brevísima relación*: "all the wars that have been fought [by the Spaniards] in the Indies" were "iniquitous, diabolical, tyrannical and infinitely unjust." He opined that such wars of conquest were "much worse than those conducted by the Turks against the Christians."[183] He was adamant that the Spaniards' reasons for going to war (*ius ad bellam*) lacked just cause. There were no grave injuries done to them by Indigenous people that required reparation and/or avenging. Moreover, the six circumstances under which Christians could wage war against infidels did not apply to the unbelievers in the Indies. These circumstances were (1) if the infidels unjustly held Christian lords in captivity, (2) if they practiced idolatry in a previously Christian country, (3) if they knowingly blasphemed, (4) if they attacked Christian territories (since Christians also had the right of self-defense), and (5) if they harmed the innocent.[184] By applying these criteria, Las Casas harkened back to his persistent refusal to see Castilian territorial claims as legitimate.

Furthermore, Las Casas contended that competent authority had not declared wars of conquest: Alexander VI did not have temporal jurisdiction to do so, and, in Las Casas's assessment, the monarchs did not authorize them, although the *requerimiento* could be regarded as implicit royal authorization to begin the process of war.[185] Nevertheless, as Las Casas alleged in the *Brevísima relación*, the first wars were "kept from the knowledge of the Queen." He further charged that the conquistadors consistently lied or "feigned obedience" to the monarch as did Francisco de Montejo who was subsequently rewarded for his loyalty with the position of governor of the Yucatán.[186] Although Las Casas admitted that some Spaniards thought that "their evil wars were just," he believed that they did not act with right intention; rather, their invasions into Indigenous territories were wars of expansion whose main purpose was to exploit material and human resources. At times, their "hellish" wars were also punitive, such as against the Cholulans, when thousands were massacred by Cortés's orders in order to "set a terrorizing example" for other groups who might deceive and/or plot against the Spaniards.[187]

Las Casas condemned all these wars as violations of the most elementary rights of the inhabitants of these lands, of the Old and New Testaments' messages of peace, and of canon law.[188]

With respect to *ius in bello*, the Spaniards' manner of conducting war consisted of two main components: the *requerimiento* and violence. Their consistent use of the *requerimiento*, which Las Casas charged was "unjust, iniquitous, [and] absurd" as well as "against all law and reason, and … the gospel of Jesus Christ," violated the criteria of only using war as a last resort, because in actuality its use disallowed any other negotiations.[189] The pervasive brutality of the "violent invasions by cruel tyrants" violated the criteria of proportionality and of protection of the innocent.[190] Indeed, in *De unico vocationis modo*, Las Casas alleged that the viciousness of these wars mimicked the "Mohammedan wars on infidels" because they wrested power "by slash and slaughter of the sword, by the rape and robbery of a people's livelihood, by captivity of parent and child, [and] by the outright murder of many, never mind their sex or age."[191]

Las Casas's condemnation of the Islamic manner of warfare is not surprising. Bartolemé was aware of the ongoing tensions and wars between Muslims and Christians in mainland Europe and the Mediterranean, including the 1529 Siege of Vienna during the expansion of the Ottoman empire's imperial power. Indeed, as Rolena Adorno asserts, "all Europe—all of Christendom—was engaged in defensive war against Islam," which, as Las Casas insisted, was justly waged war.[192] However, in addition to the atrocities of Islamic wars, the primary reason for the Dominican friar and bishop's condemnation of the Islamic wars was to declare unequivocally that conquests waged in the manner of Islamic wars violated the rational and persuasive method of evangelization. Accordingly, because of the absolute necessity of this kind of peaceful Christianization, he condemned all forced and violent *entradas* on the basis of the right to liberty, because without freedom the intellect can neither be convinced nor the will be attracted to the gospel. And, in accord with his ever-present juridical approach, Las Casas further condemned such manner of warfare by recourse to the doctrines of jurists and to canon law.[193]

Las Casas's Juridical Criteria for Spanish Sovereignty

Because of the Spaniards' violations of the criteria for just war, Las Casas alleged that "from the discovery until now, … all that the Spaniards had done in the Indies was illegal and invalid, and therefore, null"; he believed that their tyrannical wars of conquest gave no legitimate rights to the kings of Castile over the inhabitants and lands of the Indies.[194] To solve with a bold stroke the intractable situation of the Spaniards' illegal, illicit, and invalid presence in the Indies, Las Casas had recourse to two more premises. First, he argued that the pope, as Christ's vicar, had jurisdiction over infidels in spiritual matters to the extent that he had the obligation by divine law to preach the faith to all nations and, as such, to institute Christian rulers who would oversee the accomplishment of this mandate to spread the faith, which mandate would have significant temporal consequences.[195] Second, he argued that the "juridical and substantial" basis of the Spanish monarch(s)'s *dominium* and sovereign title in the Indies derived solely from "the authority, concession, and donation of the Holy Apostolic See, … [that is] from divine authority."[196] Only in this manner did the Spanish monarch receive the "most just title" of universal lordship over the Indies. These two premises were referenced in the *Brevísima relación,* succinctly formulated as Proposition Seventeen of the *Treinta proposiciones muy jurídicas*, and subsequently elaborated at great length and with copious references to divine, canon, and civil laws in his *Tratado comprobatorio del imperio soberano.*[197] The juridical basis of Las Casas's political doctrine, which he centered on human freedom and its political consequences, was then expounded with *hechos* and *derechos* in his dense and detailed juridical trilogy of *De regia potestate* (On Royal Power), *Doce dudas* (Twelve Doubts), and *De thesauris* (On Treasures).

Universal lordship was part of both Indigenous and Iberian political structures as well as of legal tradition. In the *Brevísima relación*, Las Casas referred to such supreme lordship, for instance, in Hispaniola, the Yucatán, and New Spain, and later wrote that there was "no contradiction between the high, universal, and sovereign lordship of supreme princes belonging to the kings of Castile, and the lesser and direct lordships of the ancient kings and lords of the Indians," especially in New Spain, Peru, and the New Kingdom of Granada.[198] In Iberia, the "monarchy" was an association of multiple kingdoms that retained "complete independence in government, laws, coinage, and armed forces," … but "rendered obedience to a common sovereign" or accepted this sovereign ruler as their "Lord." Las Casas pointed out that the Crown's supreme jurisdiction was "not contradicted in Spain by the lordships of the counts, dukes, and other particular lords."[199] In jurisprudential tradition, the *dominium* of a sovereign lord—of "one person over others"—was, as Las Casas argued, "introduced or imposed by natural law," contained in divine law recorded in scripture, "perfected or confirmed in practice by the law of nations," and supported in the *Corpus Iuris Civilis* as explained, for example, in the commentaries of Baldus.[200]

The role of the Supreme Lord was, according to Las Casas, to be a "rector," a "counselor and administrator," a "servant [of the people and nations]… who must rule for the common good" as one who, according to Bartolus's commentary on *dominus mundi* in the Justinian Code, has the highest power to make laws.[201] In addition to these roles, Las Casas coined a new right on which to base the Spanish title: that of protector—both of the Indigenous inhabitants and of the Spanish colonies—and probably did so because of Vitoria's concern that marauding foreign nations might descend upon the Indies.[202]

The institution of the Spanish king's sovereign *dominium*—and the consequent juridical status of Indigenous people as royal vassals—did not take away Indigenous *dominium* because, as Las Casas argued, "they cannot be deprived of this according to natural law, the law of nations, scripture, and divine law."[203] For him, native kings ruled by just title and their "liberty is not lost by admitting and having [the Spanish monarch] as universal lord."[204] Additionally, he contended that the Alexandrian Bulls "did not intend to prejudice the freedom [of the Indigenous populace]," nor "to dispossess the native peoples of their lands," nor "to dispossess the native lords, or to abrogate their right to rule."[205]

What was so innovative about Las Casas's thought was his contention that the pontiff only instituted sovereign lordship of the king of Spain *de jure*.[206] In order for the Spanish monarch to become universal lord *de facto,* Las Casas argued that the consent of the Indigenous inhabitants was required.[207] This line of reasoning drew from the radical and innovative introduction of an egalitarian concept as the basis for legal and philosophical theories of government by consensus, which augmented the old notion of hierarchical governance that was considered necessary for an orderly society.[208] Consensus doctrine held that more wisdom inheres in the community than in one outstanding individual, and that political authority should remain accordingly with the whole community.[209] Like Spanish scholastics of the sixteenth century, Las Casas also believed that sovereignty resides first in the people.[210] In support of this, he had recourse to the Roman maxim known as *Quod omnes tangit* that had been incorporated into the *Decretales*, and that stated "what affects all must be known and approved by all."[211] Las Casas incorporated an example of the exercise of this right of the governed when, in the *Brevísima relación*, he narrated what he was told by Jacobo de Tastera, one of the Franciscan friars who went to Champotón and Campeche, a region of the Yucatán that had been abandoned by the tyrants in 1534. Las Casas recounted how "twelve or fifteen lords, possessors of many vassals and lands," gathered together their respective peoples and, after receiving the approval of their peoples, "subjected themselves of their own will to the rule of the monarchs of Castile, taking the emperor, as the king of Spain, for their supreme and universal lord."[212] According to the Dominican friar, this was "a thing that never before in the Indies had been done, or to this day has been done again."[213] Again, Las Casas presented this right to institute rulers by consent as ancillary to the right of liberty.[214]

The validity of the title of universal lord both *de jure* and *de facto* thus depended on the papal donation and on consent in the form of the Indigenous peoples' voluntary acceptance of the Spanish sovereign lordship. By virtue of the papal donation, the Spanish monarch had title to the Indies *ius ad rem* (right toward a thing), but not a right of actually ruling the Indigenous peoples, that is, not *ius in re* (right over a thing).[215] However, because of the "hellish" warfare, nothing had changed with respect to the papal concession: the principal requirement of Christianization was not accomplished, was "still pending," or, as Las Casas also charged, was "permanently suspended."[216] Furthermore, with or without the title, in his view the Indigenous people never consented to the presence of Iberians in their world.

To remedy the calamitous situation, Las Casas articulated a radical reform plan in his final trilogy of writings. This was the fruit of his thoughts and labors since 1515, and was based on his firm belief in the Indigenous peoples' right to restitution. Las Casas understood this right in the canonical sense of *compositio* or settlement for the evils and harm done, just as did Paz in 1512 and their confreres, the Dominican theologians at San Gregorio—Domingo de Soto and Bartolomé de Carranza.[217] Las Casas's voice was unwavering: the Spaniards were obliged by law to make restitution—"to give everything back … because neither the Pope nor any prince on earth … can strip or deprive Christians or infidels of their lordship, royal preeminence, jurisdiction, and public or private properties without legitimate cause."[218] However unrealistic as his grand reform plan might have seemed, Las Casas was no stranger to revolutionary ideas. As Arias pointed out, he had sought the abolition of the encomienda and of slavery, had championed natural rights, and had insisted on the sovereignty of the people.[219] Yet, even Las Casas admitted that, for example, full restitution was an impossible task, and suggested that the Andean people be persuaded to accept an agreed-upon "small amount" as sufficient recompense for the "boatloads of gold and silver" garnered by Spain.[220] Even though his grand scheme had little chance of success at the time, his grand scheme is admirable in the boldness of its recommendations and in the justice of its arguments.

Las Casas's plan was as follows. First, political freedom must be restored before Christianity can be shared with them. For example, the king was obliged to restore the living heirs of the last Inca ruler, Titu Cussi Yupanqui and Tupac Amaru, to positions of authority over their lands and people.[221] Second, Indigenous republics must be restored and/or new Indigenous states must be organized directly under the Crown and under the direction of the religious clergy. With this oversight, any defects in the Indigenous republics would be corrected and eliminated by the supreme lordship of the monarch, which would greatly improve the Indigenous peoples' liberty and, as mentioned previously, Las Casas mused that the Spaniards might also learn something from the Indigenous republics.[222] Third, all property that the Spaniards had unjustly plundered or seized must be restored. Here, he brought to bear one of the fundamental principles of late medieval jurisprudence: the idea of due process, which he claimed was lacking since the first encounter with the Indigenous inhabitants of the Indies, and which must be followed in disputes over the Indigenous peoples' rights to property as well as in other matters pertaining to them.[223] Fourth, those who profited from Indigenous life and labor must make restitution. Indeed, Las Casas made restitution an indispensable condition for sacramental absolution for those who had taken or still took up arms (the conquistadors), for those who still held Indigenous people in bondage (the encomenderos and slave owners), and for the merchants who supplied arms or materials for wars against the Indigenous inhabitants.[224] Fifth, rather than abandoning the Indies, Spaniards would stay there but "in a certain manner." That is, they could settle in geographic areas that were acceptable to the Indigenous peoples and in areas where the Indigenous inhabitants had converted to the faith. Their presence would be to support and conserve the faith by Christian example, to voluntarily watch out for the good of the Indigenous peoples, to live peacefully, and to pay for the expenses of preaching the gospel to them.[225] Finally, friars and bishops (with the help of lay auxiliaries) would organize and conduct peaceful evangelization in Indigenous territories, as well as any needed penetration of the region.

Accordingly, and in addition to the eventual consent of the Indigenous inhabitants of the Indies to the monarch's universal lordship (*de jure* and *de facto*), the hoped-for subsequent conversion of Indigenous people would associate them with the Spanish sovereign by another title—that of universal lord of Christians—and (if converted) now as members of Christ's Church, their lands would become part of the *Orbis Christianus*.[226] Toward this end, Las Casas reminded his hearers and readers that the Catholic monarchs had made a "solemn promise," known in the *Digest* as a "*pollicitatio*." In Las Casas's view, this sacred pact entailed a two-fold juridical procedure: first, of *débito per se*, meaning single-minded commitment toward the goal and, second, of *débito propter aliud,* meaning to do what was necessary to accomplish the goal, which—for the Spanish presence in the Indies—was peaceful evangelization in order to facilitate the conversion and salvation of the Indigenous peoples.[227]

Range of Las Casas's Juridical Approach

Chapters 4 and 5 constituted a broad-stroke presentation and examination of Las Casas's juridical responses to the major debates of the time to substantiate his well-honed ability to take a juridical approach. His encyclopedic knowledge of and persistent inquiry into the law were amply demonstrated by his contributions to contemporaneous issues.[228] In this, he drew on the ecclesial juridical tradition by his recourse to eternal, divine, and canon laws, as well as on the civil juridical traditions of natural and Roman laws. His depth of penetration and juxtaposition of the components of this wide range of law was interwoven with a nuanced Thomism. As such, his arguments were based on principles of medieval jurisprudence and substantiated with philosophy and theology.

In his juridical approach, Las Casas's "essential achievement was to graft a doctrine of rights" that was "discernible by reason independent of revelation" on to teachings about natural law.[229] Within this doctrine of rights, the right to freedom was foundational in Las Casas's juridical responses, and is found *in nuce* in all of his major works.[230] For him, liberty was the "most precious" root of all other rights and of all law, and derived from humans' rationality, which was "the most noble and perfect of all things created."[231] This foundational right generated all the ancillary rights—those to life's necessities and sociocultural self-determination, to property and to self-defense, to *dominium* and to consent, to due process and to restitution, to hear the gospel preached, and to attain salvation. For the most part, each of these rights was explicitly or inferentially included in the *Brevísima relación.*

However, Las Casas's juridical contributions by virtue of his knowledge and expertise as well as his theoretical achievements in the study of law do not exhaust the dynamism and evidence of the juridical nature of the *Very Brief Account.* As will be addressed in the next chapters, his recourse to the juridical is also discernible in the circumstances surrounding the development and publication of his treatise, as well as in the legal character and content of the published tract.

Notes

1 Esteban Mira Caballos, *El Indio Antillano: Repartimiento, Encomienda y Esclavitud* (1492–1542) (Seville: Múñoz Moya, 1997), 126–27, 28.
2 Ibid., 280.
3 Don Domingo de San Antón Muñon Chimalpahín, "The Death of Cuauhtemoc," in *Victors and Vanquished: Spanish and Nahua Views of the Conquest of Mexico*, ed. and intro. Stuart B. Schwartz, The Bedford Series in History and Culture (Boston, MA: St. Martin's Press, 2000), 230.
4 Bartolomé de las Casas, *Brevísima relación de la destruicion de las Indias*, ed. Isacio Pérez Fernández, vol. 3 (Bayamon: Centro de Estudios de los Dominicos del Caribe and Universidad Central de Bayamon, 1999), 3:789 (hereafter cited as Pérez Fernández, *Brevísima*).
5 Jocelyn Hunt, *Spain 1474–1598* (London: Routledge, 2001), 42–44.
6 For an explication of how colonial enterprises produced capital through precious metal mining, trade, and agriculture, as well as through the "primitive accumulation" of forced labor, see J. M. Blaut, "Fourteen Ninety-two," in *1492: The Debate on Colonialism, Eurocentrism, and History*, ed. J. M. Blaut, (Trenton, NJ: Africa World Press, 1992), 38–49.
7 Columbus's diary referred sixty-five times to this search during the three months after the "discovery"; Dennis O. Flynn, "Fiscal Crisis and the Decline of Spain (Castile)," *Economic History* 42, no. 1 (March 1982): 140.
8 In 1510, royal ordinances augmented the task of this first Hispano-Indiano institution from regulations about maritime traffic and commerce to and from Spain to tasks related to emigrant services, including passenger lists and the utilization of Santo Domingo as the port of entry. Isacio Pérez Fernández, *El derecho Hispano-Indiano: dinámica social de su proceso histórico constituyente* (Salamanca: San Esteban, 2001), 27, 28 (hereafter *El derecho Hispano-Indiano*)

9 Alfonso de Diego García-Gallo, "El encomendero indiano," *Revista de estudios políticos* 55 (1951): 143.
10 Lockhart and Schwartz, *Early Latin America: A History of Colonial Spanish America and Brazil* (Cambridge: Cambridge Univ. Press, 1983), 31.
11 Hugh Thomas, *Rivers of Gold: The Rise of Spanish Empire, from Columbus to Magellan* (New York: RandomHouse, 2003), 176–80 (hereafter cited as *Rivers of Gold*); Alfonso de Diego García-Gallo, "El encomendero Indiano," *Revista de estudios politicos* 55 (1951): 142–43.
12 Thomas, *Rivers of Gold*, 205–6.
13 Troy Floyd, *The Columbus Dynasty in the Caribbean 1492–1526* (Albuquerque: Univ. of New Mexico Press, 1973), 53–54. Lesley Byrd Simpson, *The Encomienda in New Spain: The Beginning of Spanish Mexico*, first pub. 1950, rev. ed. (Berkeley: Univ. of California Press, 1982), 7. The tribute paid to the royal treasury included one-third of goods such as cotton, and one-half of the gold mined. In 1504, this assessment for the gold was reduced first to one-third and then to one-fifth. Bartolomé de las Casas, *Historia de las Indias*, ed. André Saint-Lu (Caracas: Biblioteca Ayacucho, 1986), bk. II, chap. 6, p. 31 [hereafter cited as *Historia* (Ayacucho)].
14 Lockhart and Schwartz, *Early Latin America*, 50–51; Floyd, *The Columbus Dynasty*, 65, 74, 95.
15 For example, Columbus's assignment of Taínos to labor in gold mines triggered open revolt in 1494. David M. Traboulay, *Columbus and Las Casas: The Conquest and Christianization of America, 1492–1566* (New York: Univ. Press of America, 1994), 26–27; Pérez Fernández, *El derecho Hispano-Indiano*, 31. See also García-Gallo, "El encomendero Indiano," 142; John Edwards, *The Spain of the Catholic Monarchs: 1474–1520* (Oxford: Blackwell, 2000), 286–87; Mira Caballos, *El Indio Antillano*, 101, 325–41.
16 The stated purpose of the mandated arrangement was the conversion of the Indigenous inhabitants; as such, that they were to be instructed in the Catholic faith was included in the eight points of this cédula. Las Casas, *Historia* (Ayacucho), bk. II, chap. 12. Even so, the Spanish monarchs reluctantly approved the institution of the encomienda because of geographic distances and administrative complexities. Simpson, *The Encomienda*, ix
17 Bartolomé de las Casas, *El octavo remedio* in *Obras Completas* (Madrid: Alianza, 1998), 10:f. 33 (hereafter cited as *O.C.*). Brian P. Owensby, *Empire of Law and Indian Justice in Colonial Mexico* (Stanford: Stanford Univ. Press, 2008), 134.
18 James Lockhart, "Encomienda and Hacienda: The Evolution of the Great Estate in Spanish Indies," *The Hispanic American Historical Review* 49, no. 3 (August 1969): 411–29.
19 Lynne Guitar, "No More Negotiation: Slavery and the Destabilization of Colonial Hispaniola's Encomienda System," accessed August 18, 2020, http://cai.sg.inter.edu/revista-ciscla/volume29/guitar.pdf. This system was destabilized in the Antilles as a result of the severe population decline. However, the practice to "rule through the *caciques*" continued to be encouraged and even mandated by the Crown throughout the Spanish colonies until as late as 1547. Simpson, *The Encomienda*, xiii; Lockhart and Schwartz, *Early Latin America*, 68–69.
20 García-Gallo, "El encomendero Indiano," 142. This would remain the encomenderos' responsibility until the 1542 New Laws. Simpson, *The Encomienda*, xiii; Lockhart and Schwartz, *Early Latin America*, 19–22.
21 Guy Stair Saintly, "The Military Order of Calatrava," 9, accessed September 5, 2010, http://www.chival ricorders.org/orders/Spanish/calatrav.htm; Simpson, *The Encomienda* ix; Robert S. Chamberlain, "Castilian Backgrounds of

the Repartimiento-Encomienda," in *Contributions to American Anthropology and History* 5, no. 25 (June 1939): 33–45.

22 Lockhart, "Encomienda and Hacienda," III–524.

23 Recent scholarship suggests that tribute referred to labor as well as to goods, metal, and money. Timothy J. Yeager, "Encomienda or Slavery? The Spanish Crown's Choice of Labor Organization in Sixteenth-Century Spanish America," *The Journal of Economic History* 55, no. 4 (December 1995): 843.

24 Bartolomé de las Casas, *An Account, Much Abbreviated, of the Destruction of the Indies*, trans. Andrew Hurley, intro. and ed. Franklin W. Knight (Indianapolis: Hackett, 2003), 8, 16 (hereafter cited as Knight, *An Account*).

25 Isacio Pérez Fernández, "Fray Bartolomé de las Casas en torno a las leyes nuevas de Indias: su promotor, inspirador y perfeccionador," *Ciencia Tomista* 102 (1975): 456 (hereafter "En torno"); Las Casas contended that the oppressions began to increase after the death of Isabel in 1504. Knight, *An Account*, 17.

26 García-Gallo, "El encomendero Indiano," 143–44; Gustavo Gutiérrez, *Dios o el oro en las Indias* (Lima, Perú: Instituto Bartolomé de Las Casas, 1989), 27–30, 33–41.

27 Lockhart and Schwartz, *Early Latin America*, 64. Las Casas contended that the original three million "souls" on Hispaniola and the six hundred thousand on San Juan and Jamaica were reduced to some two hundred on each island as a consequence of the Spaniards' exploitation and brutality in the encomienda system and as a consequence of warfare, because with them came economic and social dislocations as well as high mortality and reduced fertility rates. Las Casas did not take disease into account. However, as Livi-Bacci pointed out, "the unsettling normality of conquest itself was sufficient cause" for the demographic collapse. Massimo Livi-Bacci, "Return to Hispaniola," *Hispanic American Historical Review* 83, no. 1 (February 2003): 51.

28 After his conversion during the summer of 1514, Las Casas attempted to generate correctives in the treatment of the Indigenous population through the fourteen remedies and three projects that he proposed from 1516 to 1522. These correctives included the Las Casas-Cisneros plan for the communities of the Island of Hispaniola and of Tierra Firme, the farmer-settler proposal, and the Cumaná project. Hans Magnus Enzensberger, *Fray Bartolomé de Las Casas: una retrospectiva al futuro*, prologue and trans. Christian von Randow, Textos de Humanidades (México, DF: UNAM, 1987), 29.

29 Hans Roskamp, *Los Códices de Cutzio y Huetamo: Encomienda y Tributo en la Tierra Caliente de Michoacán, Siglo XVI* (Michoacán: El Colegio de Michoacán, 2003), 77–87.

30 The Crown did not desire a replication of what happened in the Antilles, wherein the depopulation resulted in the loss of royal revenue. Simpson, *The Encomienda*, 66–69. In New Spain, the demand for tribute was sometimes satisfied by giving Indigenous slaves to the encomenderos. However, this early practice did not become the norm in New Spain. García-Gallo, "El encomendero Indiano," 149. Owensby, *Empire of Law*, 13. Knight, *An Account*, 29.

31 Knight, *An Account*, 44, 46.

32 Ibid., 87.

33 Ibid., 101; García-Gallo, "El encomendero Indiano," 149–51; Pérez Fernández, "En torno," 456. Through these tribute changes, and as ownership of many encomiendas reverted to the Crown, an increasingly greater share of Indigenous tribute went to the royal treasury. Charles Gibson, *The Aztecs under Spanish Rule: A History of the Indians of the Valley of Mexico, 1519–1810* (Stanford: Stanford Univ. Press, 1964), 61–62.

34 Knight, *An Account*, 17, 27, 38, 46, 64–65.

35 Enzensberger, *Fray Bartolomé de Las Casas: una retrospectiva al futuro*, 27; J. H. Elliott, *Imperial Spain 1496–1716* (New York: St. Martin's Press, 1963), 69.

36 For a discussion of the development of the encomienda in Puerto Rico, see Eugenio Fernández Méndez, *Las encomiendas y esclavitud de los indios de Puerto Rico, 1508–1550* (Seville: Escuela de Estudios Hispano Americanos, 1966). For primary documents from the sixteenth century to the late seventeenth about the encomienda in Nuevo Reino de León, see Eugenio del Hoyo, *Esclavitud y Encomiendas de Indios en el Nuevo Reino de León, Siglos XVI y XVII* (Monterrey, N.L.: Archivo General del Estado de Nuevo León, 1985). For a comprehensive discussion of the institution of the *encomienda* in Peru, see José de la Puente Brunke, *Encomienda y Encomenderos en el Perú: Estudio social y político de una institución colonial*, Sección Historia V Centenario del Descubrimiento de América, no. 14 (Seville: Diputación Provincial de Sevilla, 1992).

37 Rolena Adorno, "Discourses on Colonialism: Bernal Díaz, Las Casas, and the Twentieth-Century Reader," *Modern Language Notes* 103 (1988): 252.

38 Yeager, "Encomienda or Slavery?," 842–43; 856–57.

39 Lockhart and Schwartz, *Early Latin America*, 17–19, 26–28. For a succinct portrayal of the institution of slavery in Spain in the *quattrocento*, as well as in the sixteenth century when King Ferdinand was "literally surrounded" by white (Muslim) and black slaves, see Hugh Thomas, *The Slave Trade: The Story of Atlantic Slave Trade 1440–1870* (New York: Touchstone, 1997), 83–86, 93.

40 William L. Sherman, *Forced Native Labor in Sixteenth-Century Central America* (Lincoln: Univ. of Nebraska Press, 1979), 15–19 (hereafter cited as *Forced Native Labor*).

41 Columbus brought 500 Indigenous persons to Spain in 1495, 300 in 1496, 600 in 1498, and 300 in 1499. Las Casas, *Historia* (Ayacucho), 1: chaps. 102, 113, 150, 154, 159, 176. For the text of Isabel's instructions, see M. Elena Ginobili de Tumminello and Elvira Germano de Volpe, *El derecho a la cultura Indígena en el Testamento de Isabel la Católica* (Argentina: Ediciones Utopía, 1992), 15–16.

42 Peggy K. Liss, *Isabel the Queen: Life and Times*, rev. ed. (Philadelphia: Univ. of Pennsylvania Press, 2004), 339.

43 Pérez Fernández, *El Derecho Hispano-Indiano*, 52–53, 56; Patricia Seed, *Ceremonies of Possession in Europe's Conquest of the New World, 1491–1640* (Cambridge: Cambridge Univ. Press, 1995), 81.

44 Columbus seemingly believed that the profit gained from the sale of Indigenous slaves in Castile would be given to the Spaniards who settled in the Islands. Tzvetan Todorov, *The Conquest of America: The Question of the Other*, trans. Richard Howard (New York: Harper Colophon Books, 1995), 47.

45 This 1511 ordinance was also circumvented, for example, when the corrupt First *Audiencia de Santo Domingo* allowed Spaniards to charge four *pesos* for the "expenses of transfer" of an Indigenous person "for sale" as well as fifty to one hundred pesos for his *camisa*; Bartolomé de las Casas, *Brevísima relación de la destruición de las Indias*, ed. and intro. José Miguel Martínez Torrejón (Alicante: Universidad de Alicante, 2006), 244n51 (hereafter Torrejón, *Brevísima relación*).

46 While the issue of African slavery is significant in Latin American history, the complexities of the issue prohibit its study in this book. Even so, a few comments are important to mention here about how African slavery was related to Indigenous slavery. In 1510, King Ferdinand was the first to

officially order that African slaves (two hundred in number) be sent to the New World, although some assert that Columbus may have been the first to bring African slaves to the Indies. With the decline of the Indigenous population, African slaves were believed to be more capable of enduring the demanding labor, especially in the mines. Thomas, *The Slave Trade*, 14, 92. Also, in 1516, because of his concern about the plight of the Indigenous people, Las Casas suggested importing "twenty black or other slaves to work in the mines." See the eleventh remedy of his "Memorial de remedios para las Indias (1516)," *Obras Escogidas: Opúsculos, cartas, y memoriales*, ed. Juan Pérez de Tudela Bueso (Madrid: Biblioteca de autores españoles, 1958), 9b (hereafter cited as *O.E.*). However, when in 1546, Las Casas learned that African slaves were being captured in unjust wars; he realized that he erred in ignorance of the facts, quickly condemned this practice, and compared the Africans' unjust capture to that of the Amerindians. See Isacio Pérez Fernández, *Fray Bartolomé de las Casas, O.P., Brevísima relación de la destruición de África* (Salamanca: Editorial San Esteban, 1989); Isacio Pérez Fernández, *Fray Bartolomé de las Casas, O.P. de defensor de los Indios a defensor de los Negros* (Salamanca: Editorial San Esteban, 1995); Juan Comas, "Fray Bartolomé: la esclavitud y el racismo," *Cuadernos Americanos* 205, no. 2 (Marzo–Abril 1976). For a nineteenth-century denunciation of Las Casas—of "that very very notorious avaricious Catholic priest or preacher and adventurer with Columbus"—as the cause of African slavery in America, see David Walker, *Appeal to the Coloured Citizens of the World*, ed., intro., annot., Peter P. Hinks (University Park: Pennsylvania State Univ. Press, 2000), 37–45, 119–20.

47 Knight, *An Account*, 66, 74.

48 See William L. Sherman's chapters on pre-Hispanic slavery, slavery after the conquest, slaves of *rescate*, and the slave trade in his *Forced Native Labor*.

49 Knight, *An Account*, 48; Torrejón, *Brevísima relación*, 167n232.

50 Knight, *An Account*, 37–38.

51 Ibid., 28, 42, 52.

52 Knight, *An Account*, 44, 24, 41, 46, 58. According to Sherman, in his *Forced Native Labor* (35, 64–67), brands were seared on the faces of those whose parents were slaves, and on the thighs of those who were sold or given out of need as slaves. While the official royal brand was *ROC*, the irons for branding were varied. For example, slaves captured in war were branded with a *G* for *guerra*; in Jalisco, those enslaved for rebellion had columns burned into their faces; in the Yucatán, the Montejos seared a cross on their chins; in Mesoamerica, brands included *C* for Cortés, and R for *rescate*. Face brands were sometimes canceled by burning "libre" on the already scarred face.

53 Sherman, *Forced Native Labor*, 33–38.

54 All Spanish scholastics approved of slavery as long as it was based on juridically recognized titles. Gustavo Gutiérrez, *Las Casas: In Search of the Poor of Jesus Christ* (Maryknoll, NY: Orbis Press, 1995), 569n59 (hereafter Gutiérrez, *Las Casas*). Domingo de Soto distinguished legal slavery and natural slavery—the latter being against divine and natural laws as well as human liberty. Mauricio Beuchot, *La Querella de la Conquista: Una polémica del Siglo XVI* (Mexico, DF: Siglo XXI editores, 2004), 44–46. The *Siete Partidas* allowed three kinds of slaves: captives taken in war, those who sold themselves, and the offspring of female slaves. Agustín Parise, "Slave Labor and Labor Activities during the Spanish Colonial Period: A Study of the South American Region of Rio de la Plata," *Rutgers Law Record* 32, no. 1 (Spring 2008): 3.

55 While this *Acta* bore the signature of "Fray Juan de Zumárraga, Obispo de México," its purported author was Las Casas. This designation derives from a notation by Las Casas as well as his signature on an amplified version of the Acta that is conserved at the National Library of Paris. See the original "Parecer ampliado con seis verdades sobre esclavos indios (1536)" in Helen Rand Parish and Harold E. Weidman, *Las Casas en México: Historia y obra desconocidas* (México, DF: Fondo de Cultura Económica, 1992), 255–60, and Isacio Pérez Fernández, *Inventario documentado de los escritos de Fray Bartolomé de las Casas*, vol. 1, Estudios Monográficos, ed. Helen Rand Parish. (Bayamón, P.R.: Centro de Estudios de los Dominicos del Caribe, 1981), note 98, 257.

56 Sherman, *Forced Native Labor*, 20–63; Lockhart and Schwartz, *Early Latin America*, 68–72.

57 "New Laws of the Indies," in Knight, *An Account*, 98.

58 Ibid., 95.

59 Pérez Fernández was the first to contend that "it can be said straight out that the one who made the New Laws was Father Las Casas, and nobody else."[... se puede decir a boca llena que quien hizo las Leyes Nuevas fue el Padre las Casas, y nadie más.] *El Derecho Hispano-Indiano*, 259. For a complete portrayal of Las Casas's prominent role in the initiation, development, and legislation of the New Laws, see David Orique, "New Discoveries about an Old Manuscript: The Date, Place of Origin, and the Role of the Parecer de fray Bartolomé de las Casas in the Making of the New Laws of the Indies," *Colonial Latin American Review* 15, no. 4 (Fall 2006, published in 2010): 1–23.

60 Las Casas, *El octavo remedio*, in *O.C.*, 10:291–360, folios 1–53v. This treatise is also known as *Entre los remedios* and is the only existing manuscript from the original *Memorial de remedios* that contained at least sixteen and possibly twenty remedies, of which the eighth remedy called for the abolition of the encomienda.

61 See *Parecer de fray Bartolomé de las Casas*, transcription and trans. by David Orique, Jay I. Kislak Collection, Library of Congress, Fall 2008, accessed September 5, 2009, https://www.loc.gov/rr/rarebook/kislak.html. See Kislak 244.

62 The treatise is also titled *Este es un tratado que el Obispo de la Ciudad Real de Chiapa, don fray Bartolomé de las Casas, o Casaus, compuso, por comisión del Consejo Real de las Indias, sobre la material de los indios que se han hecho en ellas esclavos; el cual tiene muchas razones y autoridades jurídicas, que pueden aprovechar a los lectores...* Las Casas, *Se ha hecho esclavos*, in *O.C.*, 10:219–84, folios 1–36. Wagner and Parish offered another motive for Las Casas to write this *tratado*: while bishop-elect in 1544, Las Casas encountered great difficulty with the *Casa de Contratación* in Seville in his efforts to return the remaining Indigenous slaves from Andalusia back to their native land. Henry Raup Wagner and Helen Rand Parish, *The Life and Writings of Bartolomé de Las Casas* (Albuquerque: Univ. of New Mexico Press, 1967), 126–27 (hereafter cited as *The Life and Writings*); Juan Friede, "Las Casas and Indigenism in the Sixteenth Century," in *Bartolomé de Las Casas in History: Toward an Understanding of the Man and His Work*, eds. Juan Friede and Benjamin Keen (DeKalb: Northern Illinois Univ. Press, 1971), 165.

63 Las Casas, *El octavo remedio*, in *O.C.*, 10:f. 33, 35v, 48v.

64 Ibid., 10:f. 8v, 34, 34v.

65 Ibid., 10:f. 48v–50.

66 Knight, *An Account*, 17, 55–56.

67 Las Casas, *El octavo remedio*, in *O.C.*, 10:f. 16v–24.
68 Knight, *An Account*, 50.
69 Las Casas, *El octavo remedio*, in *O.C.*, 10:f. 24v–32v.
70 Knight, *An Account*, 88, 68, 86.
71 The negative consequences highlighted by Las Casas were the killings of Indigenous people and the resultant depopulation, as well as "inestimable losses for the crown"; these were addressed in reasons 10, 12, and 13 of the *El octavo remedio*. Positive aspects of the abolition of encomiendas included joy, comfort, security, and good governance for the Indigenous inhabitants as well as a needed *merced* for the Spaniards in the Indies and in, O Spain to liberate them from sin; these were addressed in reasons 17, 18, and 20 of the *El octavo remedio*, in *O.C.*
72 Las Casas, *El octavo remedio*, in *O.C.*, 10:f. 2, 53.
73 Knight, *An Account*, 59, 68; Las Casas, *Se han hecho esclavos*, in *O.C.*, 10: f. 2, 2v, 3, 3v. *Ius gentium* consisted of principles that were reasonable, common to all people, and equally applicable to all humankind.
74 Las Casas, *Se han hecho esclavos*, in *O.C.*, 10:f. 3.
75 Ibid., 10:f. 3, 3v, 17v; Pérez Fernández, *El Derecho Hispano-Indiano*, 119–21.
76 Pérez Fernández, *El Derecho Hispano-Indiano*, 86.
77 Las Casas, *Se han hecho esclavos*, in *O.C.*, 10:f. 8–9v.
78 Ibid., 10:4v–7v, 9v, 17v.
79 Las Casas, *Se han hecho esclavos*, in *O.C.*, 10:f. 5.
80 Las Casas pointed out that while the Indigenous people lacked knowledge of the true God and of the gospel, they were still obliged by natural law. He presented the scenario of rich and poor Indians during a time of hunger. He claimed that the rich (who have corn and, in New Spain, wheat) would persuade the poor to give them a son or a daughter in exchange for corn or wheat for the rest of their families to eat. He condemned this as against natural law which obliges all to give food gratuitously or at least to loan food to the poor. He also claimed that rich Indians left corncobs outside, and that when poor Indians take them, the rich Indians capture and keep them as slaves. This too was against natural law. He stated that his sources were "the religious," and especially those who know the language(s). Las Casas, *Se han hecho esclavos*, in *O.C.*, 10:f. 10v–12v.
81 Knight, *An Account*, 16, 83, 59.
82 Las Casas, *Se han hecho esclavos*, in *O.C.*, 10:f. 10–11v.
83 Ibid., 10:f. 16, 18, 19–19v, 21–24v.
84 Ibid., 10:f. 25–27, 27v–34v, 35–36.
85 Because of the inviolable nature of the sacrament of penance, nothing learned or heard in the internal forum can be disclosed or discussed in the external forum. In his diocese and in his *Confesionario*, Bishop Las Casas made it a requirement for confession that, prior to entering into the sacrament (internal forum), any penitent holding Indian slaves and/or benefiting from them had to have a legally binding document drawn up certifying that the penitent will make restitution for these injustices committed, that is, to give one's slaves freedom and compensation. Las Casas also required the penitent to again make the pledge of restitution before receiving absolution. By this method, Las Casas preserved the seal of confession, as well as combined and concretized in practice the personal and social dimensions of the sacrament. David Thomas Orique, *To Heaven or to Hell: Bartolomé de Las Casas's Confesionario* (University Park: Penn State University Press, 2018), 64–65, 83n17, 92. See also Carlos Josaphat Pinto de Oliveira, *Las Casas: Todos os Direitos Para Todos* (San Paulo: Edições Loyola, 2000), 127–128.

86 Knight, *An Account*, 83, 56.
87 Las Casas, *Se han hecho esclavos*, in *O.C.*, 10:f. 23v–24; Knight, *An Account*, 42.
88 See the eighth and ninth reasons of Las Casas, *El octavo remedio*, in *O.C.*, 10:f.25v, 27v; Las Casas, *Se han hecho esclavos*, in *O.C.*, 10:f. 3v; see Las Casas, *The Only Way*, ed. Helen Rand Parish, trans. Francis Patrick Sullivan (New York: Paulist Press, 1992), 172 (hereafter cited as Las Casas, *The Only Way*).
89 Las Casas, *Se han hecho esclavos*, in *O.C.*, 10:f.10, 16–16v; Las Casas, *De thesauris*, in *O.C.*, 11.1: f.9; Exodus, chap. 20.
90 Las Casas, *Se han hecho esclavos*, in *O.C.*, 10:f. 15–15v; Las Casas, *El octavo remedio*, in *O.C.*, 10:27v.
91 Las Casas, *El octavo remedio*, in *O.C.*, 10:f. 26v.
92 Gratian, *Decretum*, Distinction 1. c.7, Aristotle, *Physica*, 2.5, and Aquinas, *S.T.* 1a–1ae q. 72., a.1 cited in *De regia potestate*, in *O.C.*, 12:35–37.
93 From civil law, Las Casas cited *Libertas inestimabilis res est, Libertas omnibus rebus este favorabilior, Digesto*, and *De regulis iuris*; from canon law, he cited *De re iudicata*, *Ex literis*, and *De probationibus* in Gregory's *Decretales*. See his *El octavo remedio*, in *O.C.*, 10:239; *Se han hecho esclavos*, *O.C.*, 10:327.
94 Knight, *An Account*, 29, 28, 59, 68, 17, 27.
95 Antonio Carreño, "Una guerra 'sine dolo et fraude': el P. Las Casas y la lucha por la dignidad del Indio en el siglo XVI," *Cuadernos Americanos* 193, no. 2 (Marzo–Abril 1974): 126–27.
96 The term *dominium* means both political sovereignty and ownership and will be used in place of "dominion" in this book. The usage of this term is common in scholarship about medieval law and was also used synonymously with "jurisdiction" and "imperium" in the Middle Ages. In the fifteenth and sixteenth centuries, these terms continued to be used interchangeably. Francesco Maiolo, *Medieval Sovereignty: Marsilius of Padua and Bartolus of Saxoferrato* (Delft: Eburon Academic Publishers, 2007), 156, 159; Canonists also used the term as referring to the "perfect community." Anthony Pagden, *Lords of all the World: Ideologies of Empire in Spain, Britain and France, ca. 1500—ca. 1800* (New Haven, CT: Yale Univ. Press, 1995), 2; in his *Principia Quaedam*, Las Casas also stated that "jurisdiction is the same as *dominium*" in *O.C.*, 10:555.
97 Symbolic actions to establish authority differed from one European nation to another. For example, English tradition required landing on the discovered lands, whereas Spanish regulations (judging from Columbus's "drive-by acquisition" without always going ashore) entailed declaring and naming. Seed, *Ceremonies of Possession*, 10–11.
98 *Capitulación de Santa Fe, 17 de abril, 1492*, accessed September 23, 2010, http://webs.advance.com.ar/ pfernando /DocsIglLA/CapsSantaFe.htm. For a discussion of the geopolitical impact of this first entrance into the Indies, see Salvador Morales's "1492 y población Indígena del caribe," in *Los Conquistadores: 1492 y la población indígena de las Américas*, ed. Bonilla, Heraclio (Santa Fé de Bogotá, Columbia: Tercer Mundo Editores, 1992), 147–64.
99 Pope Alexander VI, *The Papal Bull Inter Caetera May 4, 1493*, accessed July 24, 2020, http://www.let.rug.nl/usa/documents/before-1600/the-papal-bull-inter-caetera-alexander-vi-may-4-1493.php. The Bulls of Donation, *Inter Caetera I* (May 3, 1493), *Inter Caetera II* (May 4, 1493), *Eximiae Devotionis* (May 3, 1493), and *Dudum Siquidem* (September 25, 1493), were issued by Alexander VI (Rodrigo de Lanzòl-Borgia, a notorious figure), who was the second Spanish pope and the nephew of the first Spanish pope, Callixtus

III (Alonzo de Borgia). *Inter Caetera I* was quickly followed by *Inter Caetera II* to clarify the area of the newly "discovered" lands that were "given" to Spain. *Dudum Siquidem* was initially issued to assert Spanish claims in India; this document was revoked after the 1493 Treaty of Tordesillas. J. H. Parry, *The Spanish Seaborne Empire* (Berkeley: Univ. of California Press, 1966), 153–54.

100 In theology and canon law, the idea of a double order of jurisdiction (*duplex ordo jurisdictionis* or *divisa jurisdictio*) functioned as a heuristic base for all jurisdictions. Francesco Maiolo, *Medieval Sovereignty: Marsilius of Padua and Bartolus of Saxoferrato* (Delft: Eburon Academic Publishers, 2007), 148.

101 A second interpretation of *potestatis*, which derived from medieval constitutionalism, attributed this power not to the pope individually but to the Church collectively. Brian Tierney, "The Canonists and the Medieval State," *The Review of Politics* 15, no. 3 (July 1953): 378–88; Quentin Skinner, *The Foundations of Modern Political Thought: Vol. 1 The Renaissance; vol. 2 The Age of Reformation* (Cambridge: Cambridge Univ. Press, 1978), 1:14–15 (hereafter cited as *The Foundations of Modern Political Thought*).

102 The medieval concept of the "Orbis christianus" was the historical and spiritual foundation of Spanish ethics in that Christianity was at that time both a religious and political entity. For Europeans, the notion of "*Orbis christianus*" became a password for the conquest of the world, since its worldview had as its purpose the propagation of the kingdom of Christ under the twin banners of the pope and of the emperor. Joseph Hoffner, *La ética colonial española del siglo de oro: cristianismo y dignidad humana* (Madrid: Ediciones Cultura Hispánica, 1957), 4–6.

103 James A. Brundage, "The Teaching and Study of Canon Law in the Law Schools," in *The History of Medieval Canon Law in the Classical Period, 1140–1234: From Gratian to the Decretals of Pope Gregory IX*, eds., Wilfried Hartmann and Kenneth Pennington, pp. 98–120 (Washington, DC: Catholic Univ. of America Press, 2008), 163 (hereafter cited as *The History of Medieval Canon Law*).

104 Recall that *dominium* referred both to jurisdiction (the right to rule) and to ownership (the right to own). Brian Tierney, *The Idea of Natural Rights: Studies on Natural Rights, Natural Law and Church Law 1150–1625*, Emory University Studies in Law and Religion 5 (Atlanta: Scholars Press, 1997), 117; James Muldoon, *The Americas in the Spanish World Order: The Justification for the Conquest in the Seventeenth Century* (Philadelphia: Univ. of Pennsylvania Press, 1995), 15.

105 Kenneth Pennington, "Bartolomé de Las Casas and the Tradition of Medieval Law," in *Popes, Canonists and Texts, 1150–1550*, ed. Kenneth Pennington, XIII:1–17 (Aldershot: Ashgate Publishing, 1993), XIII: 4–5 (hereafter cited as "Bartolomé de Las Casas and the Tradition of Medieval Law").

106 Las Casas, *Tratado comprobatorio del imperio soberano*, in *O.C.*, 10:f.2v–28v.

107 In this capacity, the pope was the authority of final recourse for adjudicating otherwise irresolvable disputes between different jurisdictions. However, as Innocent III advised, which perspective was held by Innocent IV, "the pope could not routinely legitimize temporal affairs," and can exercise temporal jurisdiction only if the party or parties agree to the action. Kenneth Pennington, "Innocent III's Views on Church and State: A Gloss to Per Venerabilem," in *Popes, Canonists and Texts* (Aldershot: Ashgate Publishing, 1993), IV:12, 18–25.

108 Pennington, "Bartolomé de Las Casas and the Tradition of Medieval Law," in *Popes, Canonists and Texts*, XIII: 5–6.

109 James Brundage, *Medieval Canon Law* (London: Longman, 1995), 164; Pérez Fernández, *Brevísima*, 196.
110 In *Libros Sententiarum primum et secundum commentarium*.
111 Thomas, *Rivers of Gold*, 297–8; Nicolás Wey Gómez, *The Tropics of Empire: Why Columbus Sailed South to the Indies* (Cambridge, MA: Massachusetts Institute of Technology Press, 2008), 102; Traboulay, *Columbus and Las Casas*, 95.
112 Matías de Paz, *El dominio de los Reyes de España sobre los Indios*, in Juan López de Palacio Rubios, *De las Islas del mar Océano : Del dominio de los Reyes de España sobre los indios*, intro. Zavala. trans. and annot. Agustín Millares Carlo (México, DF: Fondo de Cultura Económica, 1954), 222; Henry Kamen, *Empire: How Spain Became a World Power 1492–1763* (New York: Harper Collins, 2003), 96.
113 Matías de Paz, *El dominio de los Reyes de España sobre los Indios*, 223. For the circumstances, see Ramon Hernandez's comment in Las Casas's *Tratado comprobatorio del imperio soberano*, in *O.C.*, 10:399n6.
114 Lewis Hanke, *The Spanish Struggle for Justice in the Conquest of America* (Dallas: Southern Methodist Univ. Press, 2002), 28; Carreño, "Una guerra 'sine dolo et fraude'," 127.
115 Pennington, "Bartolomé de Las Casas and the Tradition of Medieval Law," in Pennington, *Popes, Canonists and Texts*, XIII: 9.
116 Imagine the Spaniards' surprise when they arrived in Mexico and Peru! Anthony Pagden, *Spanish Imperialism and the Political Imagination: Studies in European and Spanish-American Social and Political Theory 1513–1830* (New Haven, CT: Yale Univ. Press, 1990), 15.
117 Sebastián Robiou Lamarche, *Taínos y Caribes: Las culturas aborígenes antillanas*. prologue Ricardo E. Alegría (San Juan: Editorial Punto y Coma, 2005), 69–75; Lockhart and Schwartz, *Early Latin America*, 50–51.
118 Knight, *An Account*, 13. Citing Cajetan's distinction between the different classes of infidels, Carro pointed out that relationships between infidels and Christians would differ depending on whether they were subjects of the Christian princes, like the Jews and Moors in Europe, or who occupied lands wrested from Christians, as happened in the Holy Land as well as in parts of Africa and Hungary. Venancio D. Carro, "The Spanish Theological-Juridical Renaissance and the Ideology of Bartolomé de Las Casas," in *Bartolomé de Las Casas in History*, 269.
119 Seed, *Ceremonies of Possession*, 7.
120 Lockhart and Schwartz, *Early Latin America*, 19.
121 James Muldoon, *Popes, Lawyers, and Infidels* (Philadelphia: Univ. of Pennsylvania Press, 1979), 140; Seed, *Ceremonies of Possession*, 7.
122 Lockhart and Schwartz, *Early Latin America*, 80. At least that was the idea; reality was sometimes different as, for example, in the invasions of the Yucatán and Guatemala.
123 Knight, *An Account*, 15–16.
124 Steve J. Stern, "Paradigms of Conquest: History, Historiography, and Politics," *Journal of Latin American Studies* 24, Quincentennary Supplement: The Colonial and Post-Colonial Experience (1992): 10.
125 Knight, *An Account*, 8.
126 Seed, *Ceremonies of Possession*, 72.
127 Ibid., 74–76.
128 The school of Mãliki of Medina (d. 795) was one of four schools of jurisprudence that developed within Sunni Islam. According to Seed, Christian theologians and canon lawyers did not use the Old Testament to justify Christian methods or aims of warfare outside of the Iberian World, but

instead Spaniards borrowed from the Spanish Muslim school of jurisprudence founded by Mãliki. On the Iberian peninsula, Mãlikian jihad meant war based on proper legal principles, and constituted warfare ordained by God. Castile's recourse to Muslim jurisprudence helps to explain why Las Casas insisted in several of his writings that the wars of conquest fought by the Spaniards in the Indies were inspired by Islamic ideas. Seed, *Ceremonies of Possession*, 73–74, 92–93; Las Casas, *The Only Way*, 146–7; *Historia* (Ayacucho), bk 3, chap. 58, pp. 213–16.

129 Seed, *Ceremonies of Possession*, 72, 74, 91ff.

130 Ibid., 70.

131 Muldoon, *Popes, Lawyers, and Infidels*, 140–43.

132 James Muldoon, "John Wyclif and the Rights of the Infidels: The *Requerimiento* Re-Examined," *The Americas* 36, no. 3 (January 1980): 301–16. Muldoon, *Popes, Lawyers, and Infidels*, 141–42. John Wyclif was one of the earliest opponents of papal authority influencing secular power.

133 Pérez Fernández, *El Derecho Hispano-Indiano*, 130–31.

134 While there was "legal" compliance insofar as the Requerimiento was indeed read, the legal intention was hardly fulfilled. Because of this, Pérez Fernández contended that one might better understand the future "obedezco pero no cumplo" ["I obey but do not comply"] attitude of Spaniards in the Indies toward undesired legal requirements. *El Derecho Hispano-Indiano*, 130–1; Owensby, *Empire of Law*, 2.

135 Las Casas, *Historia* (Ayacucho), bk 3, chap. 58, p. 216; Seed, *Ceremonies of Possession*, 71.

136 Knight, *An Account*, 23.

137 Isacio Pérez Fernández, "Las conquistas de Indias fueron, en sí mismas, injustas y antisignos de la evangelización," *Studium* 32, 1 (1992): 42. Enciso was an *abogado* and geographer who was instrumental in colonizing the isthmus of Darien after he had accumulated a fortune in Hispaniola where he had practiced law until 1508. His *Suma de Geografía que trata de todas las partidas del mundo* was the first account in Spanish about the lands discovered by the Spaniards up to 1519. The Cenú Indians of the northern lowlands of Colombia became extinct under Spanish rule; their territory was *Modern Spain* (Chicago: Univ. of Chicago Press, 2010), 120.

138 Knight, *An Account*, 23; Matthew Restall, *Seven Myths of the Spanish Conquest* (Oxford: Oxford Univ. Press, 2003), 94.

139 Pérez Fernández, *El Derecho Hispano-Indiano*, 131; Seed, *Ceremonies of Possession*, 70, 72, 95.

140 "Carta del vice-provincial y sacerdotes del convento de Santo Domingo, dirigida a los muy reverendos padres [Jerónimos] invitados por el Comisario Fr. Bernardino Manzanedo, c. Abril/Mayo de 1517," in Miguel Angel Medina, *Una comunidad al servicio del Indio: la obra de Fr. Pedro de Córdoba, O.P. (1482—1521)* (Madrid: Instituto Pontifício de Teología, 1983), 248–51; "Carta latina de Dominicos y Franciscanos de las Indias a los regentes de España, 27 de Mayo de 1517," in Medina, *Una comunidad al servicio*, 252–62; "Carta al Rey del padre fray Pedro de Córdoba, vice-provincial de la orden de Santo Domingo, 28 de Mayo de 1517," in Medina, *Una comunidad al servicio*, 263–68; "Carta que escribieron varios padres de las órdenes de Santo Domingo y San Francisco, residentes en la Isla Española, a Mr. De Xèvres, 4 de Junio de 1517," in Medina, *Una comunidad al servicio*, 269–87; "Carta del padre fray Pedro de Córdoba al padre fray Antonio Montesino, 26 de Septiembre de 1517," in Medina, *Una comunidad al servicio*, 288–91; "Memorial de fray Bernardino de Manzanedo de las Islas al emperador, 1518," in *Colección de documentos inéditos, relativos al descubrimiento,*

conquista y organización de las antiguas posesiones españolas de América y Oceanía, sacados de los archivos del reino, y muy especialmente de las Indias, eds., Francisco de Cárdenas y Espejo, y Luis Torres de Mendoza (Madrid: Ministerio de Ultramar, 1864–84), XI:298–321 (hereafter cited as *Colección de documentos inéditos*).

141 "Carta al emperador de Baltasar de Castro de Santo Domingo de la Española, 16 de Noviembre de 1520," in *Colección de documentos inéditos*, 1:429–30; "Carta del factor de Santo Domingo, Juan de Ampíes, a Su Majestad, avisando lo que hizo con los indios que habían venido a la Isla Española de las islas inmediatas a Tierra Firme, 1527," in *Colección de documentos inéditos*, 1:431–36.

142 This royal cédula was addressed to Gonzalo de Guzmán, Lieutenant Governor of Cuba from 1526 to 1530 (which was also known as Isla Juana, and then Isla Fernandina), ratified by Secretario Universal Francisco de los Cobos, and signed by Canciller Mercurino Arborio Gattinara, Juan García Loaysa, OP (bishop of Osma 1514–1530), Doctor Lorenzo Galíndez de Carvajal, Luis Cabeza de Vaca (bishop of Canaria 1523–30), Doctor Diego Beltrán, and Gonzalo Maldonado (bishop of Ciudad Rodrigo 1525–30). See *Colección de documentos inéditos*, 1:351–2.

143 Las Casas, "Carta a un personaje de la corte," in *O.E.*, 5:61a.

144 Knight, *An Account*, 29, 17, 19, 70, 84.

145 Las Casas, *The Only Way*, 114–15.

146 Juan Belda Plans, *La Escuela de Salamanca y la renovación de la teología en el siglo* XVI (Madrid: Biblioteca de Autores Cristianos, 2000), 313; Gutiérrez, *Las Casas*, 342–44.

147 Vitoria's first *relecciones* from 1528 to 1534 focused on civil and ecclesiastical power in general. Then in 1537, his lectures on restraint addressed politics in the Indies. In 1539, he delivered his famous *Relecciones sobre los Indios*, in which he contributed to the origins of international law. Ramón Hernández, *Derechos humanos en Francisco de Vitoria: antología* (Salamanca: Editorial San Esteban, 1984), 73–78, 159–78; Ramón Hernández, *Francisco de Vitoria, O.P.: síntesis de su vida y pensamiento* (Caleruega: Editorial OPE, 1983); Carreño, "Una guerra 'sine dolo et fraude'," 126.

148 Francisco de Vitoria, *Doctrina sobre los Indios*, 2nd ed., trans. Ramón Hernández Martín (Salamanca: San Esteban, 1992) 109; gleaned from Domingo de Soto's *De justitiae et jure*, as cited in André Alves Azevedo and José Manuel Moreira, *The Salamanca School*, Major Conservative and Liberation Thinkers Series, vol. 9 (New York: Continuum, 2010), 58.

149 Vitoria, *Doctrina sobre los Indios*, 125; Christopher R. Rossi, *Broken Chain of Being: James Brown Scott and the Origins of Modern International Law* (The Hague: Martinus Nijhoff Publishers, 1988), 121–23; Hanke, *The Spanish Struggle for Justice*, 151.

150 Belda Plans, *La Escuela de Salamanca*, 380–81.

151 Vitoria, *Doctrina sobre los Indios*, 116; Aquinas, *S.T.* 2a–2ae, q. 10, a. 10; André Alves Azevedo and José Manuel Moreira. *The Salamanca School.* Major Conservative and Liberation Thinkers Series, vol. 9 (New York: Continuum, 2010), 96. Vitoria seemingly endorsed Aquinas's theory of political society that the right to hold property was derived from natural law. Skinner, *The Foundations of Modern Political Thought*, 2:153.

152 Vitoria, *Doctrina sobre los Indios*, 116–36; John P. Doyle, "Hispanic scholastic philosophy," in *The Cambridge Companion to Renaissance Philosophy*, ed. James Hankins (Cambridge: Cambridge Univ. Press, 2007), 251; James Brown Scott, *The Spanish Origin of International Law: Francisco de Vitoria and his Law of Nations* (Oxford: Clarendon Press, 1932), 116–35.

153 Brown Scott, *The Spanish Origin of International Law*, 136–72.
154 Vitoria, *Doctrina sobre los Indios*, 136–47; Alves Azevedo and Moreira, *The Salamanca School*, 97; Carro, "The Spanish Theological-Juridical Renaissance," 258–63.
155 Alves Azevedo and Moreira, *The Salamanca School*, 97.
156 Doyle, "Hispanic scholastic philosophy," 251; Brown Scott, *The Spanish Origin of International Law*, 130–31.
157 Carreño, "Una guerra 'sine dolo et fraude'," 120–21.
158 Vitoria drew from Aquinas's teachings on just war in *S.T.* 2a–2ae, q. 40, a.1. Ádam Szásdi Nagy, "Los justos títulos y la guerra justa a la luz del Tratado de las Alcázovas," in *Iglesia y Sociedad: 500 Años en Puerto Rico y el Caribe, Siglo XVI*, eds., Manuel Alvarado Morales and Marie Minette Díaz Burley (San Juan de Puerto Rico: Nomos Impresores, S.A., 2008), 123–41.
159 Ramón Hernández, *Derechos humanos en Francisco de Vitoria: antología* (Salamanca: Editorial San Esteban, 1984), 189–203. On vengeance, see also Aquinas, *S.T.* 2a–2ae, q. 108, a. 1–4.
160 Isabel Monal, *Ensayos Americanos* (Havana: Editorial de Ciencias Sociales, 2007), 58–59.
161 Las Casas, "Carta al Consejo de las Indias (1531)," in *O.E.*, 5:44a, 45b, 49b, 53b.
162 Pennington, "Bartolomé de Las Casas and the Tradition of Medieval Law," in *Popes, Canonists and Texts*, XIII: 3–4; Knight, *An Account*, 15.
163 The full title of this Latin treatise was "Some principles of those necessary to take into account in all the controversy about justice for the Indians." Las Casas, *Principia Quaedam*, in *O.C.*, 10:569–71.
164 Wagner and Parish, *The Life and Writings*, 203.
165 Knight, *An Account*, 12–15, 51, 74; Las Casas, *Doce dudas*, in *O.C.*, 11.2:f. 138.
166 Las Casas, *Apología*, in *O.C.*, 9:181; J.S. Davidson, "The Rights of Indigenous Peoples in Early International Law." *The Canterbury Law Review* 5 (1994): 414; Angel Losada, "The Controversy between Sepúlveda and Las Casas in the Junta of Valladolid" in *Bartolomé de Las Casas in History*, 282–88.
167 Knight, *An Account*, 23, 9.
168 Rolena Adorno, *The Polemics of Possession in Spanish American Narrative* (New Haven, CT: Yale Univ. Press, 2007), vii.
169 Las Casas, *Apología*, in *O.C.*, 9: chap.51; Las Casas, *Doce dudas*, in *O.C.*, 11.2:75–89; Las Casas, *De thesauris*, in *O.C.*, 11.1: chap. 6. Las Casas, *Treinta proposiciones muy jurídicas*, in *O.C.*, 10:f. 4v.
170 Knight, *An Account*, 16. Las Casas, *De thesauris*, in *O.C.*, 11.1:335–37; Las Casas, *Historia* (Ayacucho)., bk.1, chap. 104, p. 435; "Memorial de Fray Bartolomé de las Casas y Fray Rodrigo de Andrada al Rey (1543)," in *O.E.*, 5:191a–193b; Bartolomé de las Casas, *In Defense of the Indians: the Defense of the Most Reverend Lord, Don Fray Bartolomé de las Casas, of the Order of Preachers, late Bishop of Chiapa, against the Persecutors and Slanderers of the Peoples of the New World Discovered Across the Seas*, trans. Stafford Poole (DeKalb: Northern Illinois Univ. Press, 1974), 355; Las Casas, *The Only Way*, 163.
171 Knight, *An Account*, 34–35.
172 The chronological evolution of just war theory is presented in the revised dissertation of Frederick H. Russell published as *The Just War in the Middle Ages*, Studies in Medieval Life and Thought Series, 3rd ed., vol. 8 (Cambridge: Cambridge Univ. Press, 1975).
173 Aquinas utilized the traditional rules of just war that originated in the work of Augustine and that he supplemented with canonistic interpretations. *S.T.*

2a–2ae, q. 60, q. 40, a. 1. Las Casas fully adhered to these rules. See his *Apología*, in *O.C.*, 9:387–89, 653–55, chaps. 30, 60; *Tratado comprobatorio del imperio soberano*, in *O.C.*, 10:445, Las Casas, *Historia* (Ayacucho), bk.1, chap. 25; Pérez Fernández, *Brevísima*, 191–211.

174 Las Casas, *De thesauris*, in *O.C.*, 11.1: chap. 36, and especially p. 389.

175 Knight, *An Account*, 14, 9, 31, 39, 25.

176 Ibid., 16.

177 Ibid., 60.

178 Las Casas, *De thesauris*, in *O.C.*, 11.1:151.

179 Knight, *An Account*, 86; Pérez Fernández, *Brevísima*, note 39.

180 Aquinas, *S.T.* 2a–2ae, q. 108, a. 1–4.

181 In moral theology, mortal sin requires serious matter, full knowledge, full consent, and the freedom to do so. Knight, *An Account*, 16.

182 Knight. *An Account*, 61.

183 Ibid., 16, 29–30; Pérez Fernández, *Brevísima*, 191–211, 746.

184 Las Casas, *In Defense*, 118ff, Ramón Jesús Queralto Moreno, *El pensamiento filosófico-político de Bartolomé de las Casas* (Seville: Escuela de Estudios Hispano-Americanos de Sevilla, 1976), 278; Losada, "The Controversy," 292–93. However, there was no obligation to rescue the innocent from human sacrifice if this would mean that larger numbers would perish; in this case, the lesser of the two evils should be chosen, i.e. human sacrifice over war.

185 "Representación al Emperador Carlos V (1542)," in *O.E.*, 5:124a, 125b, 128a.

186 Knight, *An Account*, 17, 47, 64.

187 Ibid., 47, 30–31, 28.

188 Las Casas cited glosses on the *Decretales* in his *De thesauris*, in *O.C.*, 11.1:381; Alves Azevedo and Moreira, *The Salamanca School*, 61–62; Pérez Fernández, *Brevísima*, 264–65.

189 "Memorial de Fray Bartolomé de las Casas y Fray Rodrigo de Andrada al Rey (1543)," in *O.E.*, 5:197b.

190 Knight, *An Account*, 29.

191 Las Casas, *The Only Way*, 147; Las Casas, *De unico vocationis modo*, in *O.C.*, 2:445.

192 Adorno, *The Polemics of Possession*, 66.

193 From the *Corpus Iuris Civilis*, Las Casas specifically cited jurists in the Roman Codex, and authoritative commentaries on the *Digest* that were written by Bartolus, in his *Sumaria de la ley and Liber Feudorum*, and by Andrés de Isernía in his *De Prohibita Feudi Alienativo* on the *Digest*'s *De locate conducti*, and by Baldus (Baldo in Spanish). From canon law, he cited *De Legibus*, which was written by Durandus of Saint Pourçain. Las Casas, *De thesauris*, in *O.C.*, 11.1:149, 151, 153, 155.

194 Las Casas, *De thesauris*, in *O.C.*, 11.1:369–77; Pérez Fernández, *Brevísima*, note 66.

195 Las Casas never doubted the validity of papal power to legislate in spiritual affairs, including over non-Christian rulers, while Vitoria held that the pope has neither temporal nor spiritual authority over infidels. Drawing from theologians, the Church Fathers, canonists, and jurists in the Codex, Las Casas pointed out that "the pope can intervene only with true and necessary cause," and presented reasons why the Indigenous people as the fourth kind of infidel were not subject to any other kind of papal intervention. *Doce dudas*, in *O.C.*, 11.2: chap. 7, especially pp. 51–52. Vitoria, *Doctrina sobre los Indios*, ed. Ramón Hernández Martín (Salamanca: Editorial San Esteban, 1992), 125; Rossi, *Broken Chain of Being*, 121–23; Hanke, *The Spanish Struggle for Justice*, 151.

196 Las Casas, "Aqui se contienen treinta proposiciones muy jurídicas" (1552), in *O.C.*, 10:208 (hereafter "Treinta proposiciones"; Las Casas, *Tratado comprobatorio del imperio soberano*, in *O.C.*, 10:465, 477; *Doce dudas*, in *O.C.*, 11.2: chap. 7.
197 Knight, *An Account*, 3; Las Casas, "Treinta proposiciones," in *O.C.*, 10:208; *Tratado comprobatorio del imperio soberano*, in *O.C.*, 10:399–400.
198 Knight, *An Account*, 74; Las Casas, *Tratado comprobatorio del imperio soberano*, in *O.C.*, 10:442. Las Casas's comment does, however, reflect a value implicit hierarchy when comparing the Spanish king with Indigenous kings.
199 Henry Kamen, *Golden Age of Spain*, 2nd ed. Studies in European History Series (New York: Palgrave MacMillian, 2005), 9; "Memorial de Fray Bartolomé de las Casas y Fray Rodrigo de Andrada al Rey (1543)," in *O.E.*, 5:184a. Las Casas also compared this with Charlemagne's *dominium* over Jerusalem, as well as that of Portugal and Castile over Africa in his *Tratado comprobatorio del imperio soberano*, in *O.C.*, 10:442.
200 Las Casas, *Tratado comprobatorio del imperio soberano*, *O.C.*, 10:453–55; Las Casas, *Principia quaedam*, in *O.C.*, 10:555–559. In his argument, Las Casas specifically cited Proverbs 11:14 and Ecclesiastes 17, 14; however, the latter citation did not correspond to the topic.
201 Las Casas, *Principia quaedam*, in *O.C.*, 10:555, 571; Las Casas, *De regia potestate*, *O.C.*, 12: chap. 12; Skinner, *The Foundations of Modern Political Thought*, 1:9–10.
202 Las Casas, *De Regia Potestate*, in *O.C.*, 12:49, 51, 145.
203 "Memorial de Fray Bartolomé de las Casas y Fray Rodrigo de Andrada al Rey (1543)," in *O.E.*, 5:184a; Las Casas, *Tratado comprobatorio del imperio soberano*, in *O.C.*, 10:451.
204 Las Casas, *El octavo remedio*, in *O.C.*, 10:330.
205 Las Casas, *Doce dudas*, in *O.C.*, 11.2: chaps 8, 11.
206 Las Casas, *De thesauris*, in *O.C.*, 11.1:325.
207 Las Casas, *Tratado comprobatorio del imperio soberano*, in *O.C.*, 10:455–56; Las Casas, *De thesauris*, in *O.C.*, 11.1:315–18.
208 Brain Tierney, "Hierarchy, Consent, and the "Western Tradition," *Political Theory* 15, no. 4 (1987): 650.
209 Ibid., 649.
210 Las Casas, *In Defense*, 338, 383.
211 Las Casas, *De thesauris*, in *O.C.*, 11.1:199; Tierney, *The Idea of Natural Rights*, 283–84; Kenneth Pennington, "Law, legislative authority and theories of government, 1150–1300" in *The Cambridge History of Medieval Political Thought*, 449.
212 The penetration and conversions were reportedly accomplished by Jacobo de Tastera, OFM, and four Franciscan confreres. Torrejón and Pérez Fernández surmise that Las Casas heard about this from Tastera, as well as read the report containing the friars' testimony that was sent to the emperor. Parish also discovered supporting documents, which she reported in her *Las Casas as Bishop*, nn30, 31. See also Parish and Weidman, and Harold E Weidman. *Las Casas en México: historia y obra desconocidas* (México, DF: Fondo de Cultura Económica, 1992), 101n59b. Mendieta also reported this incident in his *Historia ecclesiástica indiana,* IV, vi. Pérez Fernández, *Brevísima*, notas 182, 183; Torrejón, *Brevísima relación*, 171n246; 292n244.
213 Knight, *An Account*, 50–51.
214 Las Casas, *De regia potestate*, in *O.C.*, 12:87; Tierney, *The Idea of Natural Rights*, 279.
215 Las Casas, *De thesauris*, in *O.C.*, 11.1:316–17, 325, 327, 357; Brian Tierney, "Aristotle and the American Indians–Again: Two Critical Discussions," in

Rights and Laws and Infallibility in Medieval Thought (Aldershot: Ashgate Publishing, 1997), V:300–04.

216 Las Casas, *De thesauris*, in *O.C.*, 11.1:355, 369–77, 507–09.

217 Hanke, *The Spanish Struggle for Justice*, 28–29.

218 Las Casas, *Tratado de doce dudas*, in *O.E.*, 5:501–4; 531; Las Casas, *De thesauris*, in *O.C.*, 11.1:405, 411.

219 Santa Arias, "Las Casas as Genealogical Keystone for Discourse on Political Independence," in *Approaches to Teaching the Writings of Bartolomé de Las Casas*, eds. Santa Arias and Eyda Merediz (New York: Modern Language Association of America, 2008), 168.

220 Las Casas, *Tratado de doce dudas*, in *O.E.*, 5:535a.

221 Among others, Las Casas referred to these two Incas *señores*; see his *Doce dudas*, in *O.C.*, 11.2:f. 217.

222 Las Casas, *Principia quaedam*, in *O.C.*, 10:581; Las Casas, *El octavo remedio*, in *O.C.*, 10:326.

223 Las Casas, *De thesauris*, in *O.C.*, 11.1:311; Kenneth Pennington, *The Prince and the Law, 1200–1600: Sovereignty and Rights in the Western Legal Tradition* (Berkeley: Univ. of California Press, 1993), 272–73, 272n10. According to this idea generated from natural law—and (according to medieval jurists) as exemplified in the Genesis account of God summoning Adam before rendering judgment, decisions should not be made until all parties had been consulted. This principle also applied to the pontiff and the monarch—both must act with due process.

224 Las Casas, *Aquí se contienen unos avisos y reglas para los confesores que oyeren confesiones del los españoles que son o han sido en cargo a los indios de las Indias del mar Océano, colegidas por el Obispo de Chiapa don fray Bartolomé de la Casas o Casaus, de la orden de Santo Domingo*, [also known as *El Confesionario*], in *O.C.*, 10:369, 374, 383.

225 Las Casas, *De thesauris*, in *O.C.*, 11.1:393, chaps. 36, 42, 45.

226 See Las Casas's Proposition 19 in his "Treinta proposiciones." in *O.C.*, 10:209, and *De thesauris*, 11.1:471. The recent scholarship of David A. Lupher addressed this "Christian-Roman universalism," which held that, once converted, the Indigenous people were *ipso facto* members of the "Holy Roman Empire"—now as Christians and not merely as vassals of Charles V. See his *Romans in a New World: Classical Models in Sixteenth-Century Spanish America* (Ann Arbor: Univ. of Michigan Press, 2003).

227 Las Casas, *De thesauris*, in *O.C.*, 11.1:475–76; Las Casas, *Principia quaedam*, in *O.C.*, 10:583.

228 Vidal Abril Castelló, "Estudio preliminar," in *Apologética historia sumaria*, in *O.C.*, 6:163.

229 Tierney, *The Idea of Natural Rights*, 276.

230 Luis Iglesias Ortega, *Bartolomé de Las Casas: Cuarenta y cuatro años infinitos* (Seville: Fundación José Lara, 2007), 325ff.

231 Las Casas, *Apología*, in *O.C.*, 9:97.

6 The Focus of Las Casas's Juridical Voice

Context and Legal Character of the *Brevísima Relación*

In May of 1540, after almost twenty years of absence from Spain, Las Casas returned to his native land to present the monarch with "a very necessary account" [about] "most important matters of great service and utility for the *Estado real* [in the Indies] related to the universality of that new world that God [had] put under [the emperor's] administration."[1] In April of 1542, Las Casas had several audiences with Charles V to inform the emperor of what he saw as the evils and harm done to Indigenous people by Spaniards. In December of 1542, for the benefit of the young Prince Philip, Las Casas produced the *Brevísima relación* as a "very brief" summary of his "very long" official report to the emperor and special junta.[2] This chapter first focuses on the specific juridical context that generated the *Very Brief Account*. As such, the following are initially explicated: the confluence of contemporaneous juridical circumstances that occasioned Las Casas's return to Spain in 1540, that generated the initial writing of the *tratado* in 1542, and that precipitated its publication in 1552. Then, this chapter focuses on the text of the *Brevísima relación* to assess and establish its legal character.

Confluence of Legislative Circumstances

The trajectory of circumstances that eventually produced the *Brevísima relación* began in 1539 when, at the behest of the 1538 Chapter of the Dominican Province of Santiago de México, Las Casas and his Dominican confrere Rodrígo de Ladrada prepared to return to Spain to recruit more friars.[3] For Las Casas, his "most cherished dream" and ardent desire, which he articulated several times since becoming a friar, was to return to Spain to lobby at court on behalf of the Indigenous people.[4] His central motivation was that the Indigenous inhabitants of the Indies would not perish, temporally and eternally.[5] As such, he wanted to return to Spain to speak directly to the emperor about "the tragic, disastrous, and pitiful situation in which the Indians found themselves" because of the "excesses of particular Spaniards" and, above all, because of the corruption of royal officials on both sides of the Atlantic.[6]

Additional circumstances in the Indies compelled Las Casas to appeal to the monarch. These included the revocation of the anti-slavery legislation, the desolation of the land in the backwaters of Nicaragua, the transportation of fifty thousand slaves from upper Central America to Panama and Peru, the devastation wrought by armed forays into Indigenous territories, the premature deaths of Indigenous laboring in Mexican mines—in addition to informing the emperor about the slow tortures and ghastly executions of Indigenous people by Nuño de Guzmán in Michoacán, Pánuco, and Jalisco.[7]

Out of their experiences in other territories, other friars and bishops as well as laity had informed or were also informing the sovereign of the atrocities taking place. For example, writing from Darien in 1513/15, Vasco Núñez de Balboa wrote about the ill-treatment given to Indigenous people by governors Diego de Nicuesa and Alonso de Hojeda.[8] Writing from Cuzco in 1539, Vicente Valverde, OP, wrote of the offenses suffered by the Indigenous inhabitants, as did *Bachiller* Luis de Morales in 1541. In 1531 from Nueva Granada (Columbia-Venezuela), Tomás Ortiz, OP—first bishop of Santa Marta and first protector of the Indigenous inhabitants of Nueva Granada—reported to the king the harm committed by the entradas of the Spanish Christians. His successors Alonso de Tobes, OFM (who challenged governor Fernández de Lugo) and Juan Fernández de Ángulo, OFM (who appealed to the emperor in 1540) followed Ortiz's lead. In the same year, the bishops of Mexico, Michoacán, Antequera, and Guatemala sent their assessments of what "was necessary" for good governance. From Lima in 1541, *letrado* Alonso Pérez de Santoyo—as the municipal *assessor*—sent an official account to Spain of matters that "must be remedied in the kingdoms of Perú."[9]

In preparation for his hoped-for audience with the emperor, and while staying at the Dominican convent in Oaxaca from May until August of 1539, Las Casas drafted an extensive account of what he saw as the atrocities that occurred and continued to take place in the Indies. His sources were his own experience, the drafts of his *Historia de las Indias* and his *Apologética historia sumaria*, as well as the *cartas* and experiences that others had penned over the years, allegedly notarized *probanzas*, and other official records. Las Casas's written draft, which was based on these data, would become the *Larguísima relación de la destruición de las Indias*.[10] This title, as well as its summary as the *Brevísima relación*, resembles (and was perhaps deliberately taken by Las Casas from) the titles of early Spanish accounts in medieval times about "la destruición de España" occasioned by the Arab invasion and conquest of Spain in 711.[11] Las Casas's use of the trope of "destruction" will be discussed in Chapter 7.

Return to Spain

In 1540, more than twenty years after Las Casas's pro-Indigenous work began at court, he and Ladrada arrived in Spain. These two confreres were highly recommended in letters to the emperor that they carried from the bishops of Mexico City, Michoacán, Oaxaca, Tlaxcala, and Guatemala, as well as from civil authorities: Alonso de Maldonado, *oidor* of the first *Audiencia de Guatemala*; Pedro de Alvarado, governor of Guatemala (whom Las Casas would eventually condemn as a "tyrant"), and the city councils of Santiago (Guatemala) and of Trujillo (Honduras).[12] For example, in Francisco Marroquín's laudatory letter of recommendation to Charles V, this Guatemalan bishop wrote that Las Casas and Ladrada "are servants of God ... [and] I have lived with them for more than three years, and daily I have seen their hearts and minds growing in solicitude for the welfare and salvation of these people." The prelate added that "through an experience of more than thirty years, they have come to know and appreciate the hardships these people suffer and what must be done for their relief."[13]

Together in Spain, Las Casas and Ladrada completed their recruitment of friars and other duties.[14] Having been instructed by Charles to await his return—an order prompted by Las Casas's request for an audience, the emperor's knowledge of Las Casas's defense of the Indigenous people, and the Hapsburg monarchical policy of programmatic conciliarism—the two friars prepared for their presentations to Charles and his court.[15] Accordingly, during this interim period, Las Casas completed the *Larguísima relación*—a report of what he deemed horrific events that would become an integral part of his juridical arguments for new reform legislation in the Indies.[16] In this very long account, he identified the names of the conquistadors, encomenderos, and royal officials, whom he consistently called "tyrants." He described the "hellish" conquests and "infernal" bondage in horrendous detail and in chronological and geographic sequence. He condemned their accompanying "evils and harm" as violations of divine, natural, and human laws. At this time, Las Casas also continued composing another very lengthy juridical treatise—a *Memorial de remedios*.[17] In this *Memorial*, he proposed the suppression of the encomiendas, the incorporation of the Indigenous inhabitants of the Indies as vassals of the Crown, the colonization of territories in the Indies by farmers, the abolition of Indigenous slavery, the cessation of armed conquests, the "reduction" or relocation of Indigenous inhabitants by friars in settlements, and the evangelization of the Indigenous people by rational and peaceful methods.

Events of 1542

In mid-April of 1542 during several audiences with Charles V, Las Casas read both the *Larguísima relación* and his *Memorial de remedios* to the emperor and discussed their content.[18] Already suspicious of the corruption and now, as reported by Las Casas, seemingly shocked by the rampant injustices, the emperor immediately convened an extraordinary junta to which he assigned the task of studying the situation and of drafting new ordinances to govern the Indies.[19] Las Casas was invited by the emperor to participate in the junta sessions.[20] Before this legislative assembly with the emperor present, Las Casas again orally presented the *Larguísima relación* and its complementary *Memorial de remedios.*[21] According to the *Crónica del Emperador Carlos V*, Las Casas's *Very Long Account* was delivered over a period of "many days at a certain hour until the friar read [it] in its entirety."[22] Throughout his half-read and half-oral delivery of the "very lengthy" *Larguísima relación*, Las Casas documented his roster of atrocities with "a stack [allegedly three-feet high] of sworn and notarized statements" (*probanzas*) from both Indigenous individuals and Spaniards in the New World.[23] However, since these *probanzas* have not as yet been discovered, their specific content and authors are unknown. In addition to this, the fact that they were "notarized" could simply mean that a notary wrote them or that the document was a true rendition of the words of those who produced or dictated the document. For these reasons, conclusions about the veracity of these *probanzas* are premature. Nevertheless, according to Las Casas's description in the *Brevísima relación*, those assembled sat motionless during the presentation of the data and spellbound in "a manner of ecstasy and suspension of spirit in his hearers."[24]

Subsequently, Las Casas "was begged and importuned" by Juan Martínez del Guijo, a member of the junta and tutor of Prince Philip, to write a brief summary of the *Larguísima relación* for the purpose of educating the fifteen-year-old future leader of the Spanish realms.[25] This request, which was recorded in the opening Argument and Prologue of the published *Very Brief Account*, constituted the genesis of the *Brevísima relación de la destruición de las Indias*. However, Las Casas did not begin to draft this summary document until September of 1540. Finished on December 8, 1542, this *Brevísima relación* consisted in Las Casas's narration of only "some—a very few—examples that in days past [he] had collected from among the countless numbers that [he] could in truth declare."[26] This first writing of the *Brevísima relación* in 1542 was augmented in 1546 and again in 1552 when the text was published in Seville, Spain (Figure 6.1).

Decade of Struggle: 1542–1552

The specific context that generated the publication of the 1552 version of the *Brevísima relación* was shaped by the not-unexpected non-compliance with the New Laws in the colonies, as well as by Las Casas's continuous appeals for justice from 1542 to 1552. After having contributed to the New Laws' legislation for a "total remedy" in the New World, Las Casas was offered the wealthy bishopric of Cuzco, Peru—which he refused, and

Aqui se cōtienē tre
ynta proposiciones muy juridicas: en
las quales sumaria y succintamente se
tocā muchas cosas pertenecietes al de
recho q̄ la yglesia y los principes chri
stianos tienen/o puedē tener sobre los
infieles de qual quier especie que sean.
Mayormente se assigna el verdadero
y fortissimo fundamento en que se assi
enta y estriba: el titulo y señorio supre
mo y vniuersal que los Reyes d Casti
lla y Leon tienen al orbe de las que lla
mamos occidētales Indias. Por el ql
son constituydos vniuersales señores y
Emperadores en ellas sobre muchos re
yes. Apuntā se tambien otras cosas cō
cernientes al hecho acaecido en aql or
be notabilissimas: y dignas d ser vistas
y sabidas. Colijo las dichas treynta p
posiciones El obispo dō Fray Bartho
lome de las Casas/o Casaus: Obispo
q̄ fue d la ciudad Real de Chiapa: cier
to Reyno de los de la nueua España.

Año. 1552.

Figure 6.1 Aquí se contiene treynta proposiciones muy jurídicas: en la quales sumaria y succintamente se toca[n] muchas cosas pertenecie[n]tes al derecho q[ue] la yglesia y los principes christianos tienen, o puede[n] tener sobre los infieles … 1552.

then the impoverished See of Chiapa, which he accepted.[27] This offer of an episcopal position was in keeping with the Crown's attempt to undergird the New Laws by naming bishops in the Indies who would support the spirit of the new legislation.[28] However, the promotion of his episcopal nomination could also have been a strategy on the part of his enemies to co-opt him or to remove him from his position of influence at court since, at the time, Chiapa was a very remote posting.[29] In any case, in 1544, Bishop Bartolomé de Las Casas returned to the Indies, and in 1545 "took possession" of the diocese of Chiapa—an ecclesiastical territory that included most of the modern Mexican State of Chiapas and part of Guatemala.[30] Las Casas was determined to use his new ecclesiastical position and its canonical juridical power to enforce the New Laws and to develop a model diocese in one of the poorest regions (by Spanish standards) and a fringe area of the Indies.[31]

In addition to his new episcopal role, Las Casas's presence in the Indies afforded him eyewitness experience of how the New Laws were met with hostility, ridicule, and anger, as well as with non-compliance. This would not have been unusual since compliance with the law was always sketchier in fringe areas than in the centers. Even the bishop of Antequera, Juan López de Zárate who, in 1530 had highly recommended Las Casas, wrote the emperor on October 5, 1543, protesting the News Laws on the basis of the need to continue perpetual *repartimientos* as much for the benefit of Spaniards as for the Indigenous populace, as well as for mixed-race families.[32] The Peruvian viceroy, Blasco Núñez Vela, was murdered by angry encomenderos when he tried to enforce the New Laws.[33] The viceroy of New Spain, Antonio Mendoza, refused to apply the New Laws until the Crown had replied to an appeal to rescind them, because, according to legal and legislative process, an appeal would provoke (or was assumed to provoke) the suspension of the disputed law. The appeal was sent to Spain by encomenderos and civil authorities, as well as surprisingly supported by the superiors of the three mendicant orders out of concern for commerce, Christianization of "lazy" Indians, and the king's revenue.[34] In Las Casas's concluding statement (or "Final Testament") at the end of the 1552 *Brevísima relación*, he referred to this appeal as a "refusal to obey the laws …under the colour of appealing them." He pointed out that after the New Laws were published, many officials (including some "within the court") "submitted documents in support of the tyrants" and were "very much aggrieved by those [New] Laws" because their portion of "the spoils of the Indies" would be taken away. Las Casas charged that even "the new judges who came to carry them out" were complicit in this rejection of the New Laws.[35]

Las Casas was cognizant of the economic, political, socio-religious, and legal revolution implied by the New Laws—a revolution that would not come easily. In his own diocese, he used ecclesiastical measures in the form of pastoral letters, excommunication, and threats of excommunication to enforce the ordinances about the encomiendas and the enslavement of Indigenous people.[36] In this, he wielded the independent ecclesiastical arm as well as applied canonical principles that, for example, stipulated that "repentance demands restitution of what belongs or had been done to another."[37] Along with the bishops of Guatemala and Nicaragua, he informed the *Audiencia de los Confines* that, according to "sacred canons," bishops can intervene on behalf of *miserabiles personae* whether or not secular authorities do their part in amelioration of their situation because bishops are obliged by divine law to aid and defend them.[38] In his subsequent *Corrolarium* about the office of a prelate, Las Casas forcefully asserted the "superiority" of a bishop's "spiritual power and jurisdiction, by divine and canon laws, over all people, great and small, and over all temporal power that in whatever form may exist in his diocese."[39] Coupled with a series of complicated events and grave problems, Las Casas's efforts to exert his episcopal jurisdiction—and consequently indirect control—in civil matters resulted in prolonged and bitter embattlements, in insults, sarcasms, calumnies, reprisals, and even death threats from those who opposed him.[40]

Las Casas's reform efforts to bring about change in Church and society in Chiapa were both embraced and rejected. In Tierra de Verapaz, the bishop was welcomed by the Indigenous inhabitants with fiestas and palms. In most other parts of his diocese, he was met with resistance predominantly from Spaniards, including from the secular clergy and the Mercedarians, a religious order that had not participated in the reforms of religious orders that had taken place in Spain.[41] Even the newly formed *Audiencia de los Confines* rejected Las Casas's request to place the Indigenous inhabitants under the jurisdiction of the Church.[42] In sum, the difficulty of implementing the New Laws and of exercising his episcopal functions in the diocese became painfully evident. The depth of the bishop's anguish—and of his faith—was revealed in the prayer he reportedly uttered in 1545:

> Lord, you know what I am trying to do and you see what I gain: hunger, thirst, fatigue, everyone's hate; if I am deceived, I am deceived by your Gospel; but to the degree that I believe it, I believe that I am not deceived; but if I do not understand it, enlighten me, Lord, so that I may not be the scandal that I am in this world.[43]

Disheartened but not defeated, Las Casas left his diocese in the hands of the vicar general, canon Juan de Perera, on May 14, 1546, and traveled to Mexico City where he participated in two ecclesiastical juntas, one of the bishops, another of the friars.[44] At the assembly of bishops, he secured the unanimous support of his episcopal confreres for a declaration legislating moderate application of the doctrine of restitution. He also persuaded them to petition the emperor for ecclesiastical immunity for all bishops. These episcopal and canonical actions were of official character and carried official weight.[45]

At the assembly of friars, he rallied the mendicant missionaries to condemn the enslavement of Indigenous people and to declare all slave titles illegal. Furthermore, in 1545, he challenged the public law that had revoked the prohibition about inheriting encomiendas, by using the private seal of confession (and the privacy of conscience) to compel all confessors of his diocese to follow his orders and example: they were to withhold absolution from those who did not obey the New Laws.[46]

Once again, Las Casas's activities and directives met with outrage and opposition from conquistadors, encomenderos, merchants, civil authorities, and the royal *visitador*. In his experiences in Mexico City and those in his diocese, Las Casas concluded that "the most serious obstacle … to the implementation of the New Laws was the fact that the royal officials who were entrusted with their enactment had been corrupted by self-interest." Even *corregidores*, whom at one time he considered potential allies, had become "tyrants."[47]

Las Casas was convinced that the majority of the royal functionaries in the Indies was involved in economic exploitation and, therefore, generally did not intend to enforce the New Laws. As a result, he again realized that the political struggle could only be won at court.[48] Consequently, in May of 1547, Las Casas returned directly from Mexico to Spain to voice his assessments to Prince Philip. Back at court, and assured of the heir-apparent's support (even of his episcopal directives in Chiapa), Las Casas continued promoting and engaging in new ways to achieve justice.[49] In addition to advising the prince, the bishop of Chiapa presented three reports to the council: one that again condemned slavery; one that amply clarified the monarch's rights in the Indies; and one that again questioned the lawfulness and justice of war against the Indigenous inhabitants of the Indies.[50]

Once more, Las Casas was not alone in the struggle for justice for the Indigenous people. Pro-Indigenous letters and accounts continued to arrive in Spain especially from bishops in the Indies. For example, in 1544, Francisco de Benavides Velasco, OSH, bishop of Cartagena, stressed the obligation of restitution. In 1547, Martín de Calatayud, OSH, bishop of Santa Marta, resigned as "Protector of the Indians" in protest of the abuses of many Spaniards. In 1548, Juan de Valle, bishop of Popayán, expressed in "strong terms" his defense of the Indigenous populace. In 1550, Domingo de Santa Tomás, OP, bishop of Charcas (Peru), wrote "a terrible *carta*" to the king about the barbarous cruelty of certain Spaniards. Supported during this period by these kinds of pro-Indigenous stands, Las Casas contributed to legislative changes: namely, ordinances about restitution were generalized, laws against abuses were strengthened, orders against slavery were legislated (1548), and further conquests were prohibited (1549).

In addition, Las Casas devoted time to writing his *tratados*, *cartas*, *memorials*, and *obras mayores*, as well as recruited missionaries and attended to diocesan matters *en absentia* until his six-year assignment as resident bishop expired in 1550, at which time he resigned the bishopric of Chiapa.[51] That same year and into the next—in two sessions of a special legislative junta assembled by the emperor, Las Casas and Sepúlveda debated the ethical-political issue of whether the wars of conquest were just.[52] According to Pérez Fernández, the failure of the assembled jurists, theologians, and royal officials to resolve the issue, along with the ongoing evils and harm done that Las Casas had painfully witnessed and that others continued to report, constituted the specific context that compelled the retired bishop of Chiapa to revise and publish the *Brevísima relación* in 1552.[53]

There were also other motives for its publication. As stated in the tract, Las Casas claimed that he was personally "persuaded [to do so] by some notable persons resident in this court, zealous for God's honour and compassionate toward the afflictions and calamities of their fellow beings."[54] He was individually motivated to publish the *Brevísima relación*, because "I myself had conceived the same purpose... to set down [in print] an accounting of the hell that is the Indies... but had not put it to work on account of my constant occupations."[55] To be silent would have been "tantamount to becoming an accomplice."[56]

Moreover, he was intentionally disposed to ascertain whether Prince Philip had read or might re-read the *Very Brief Account*. In the *tratado*, he diplomatically stated that he printed it so that ostensibly "His Highness might read [it] with greater ease" than the 1542 handwritten copy. In the *Brevísima relación*, Las Casas suggested that "it may be that ... Your Highness did not read that account [of 1542] or has forgotten that Your Highness has it."[57] The possibility that Philip might not have shared his tutor's enthusiasm for the 1542 version is significant, and may give some indication of the prince regents' concern about the activities of "the tyrants." Surely, Philip was aware of Spain's dependence on the revenues of the colonies for its financial well-being. This dependence constituted a double-edged sword. On the one hand, he had to be concerned about the survival of the Indigenous populace as the needed labor force; on the other hand, he needed the institutions that channeled that labor (and tribute) into the royal treasury. Although he may have wished to abolish the encomienda, he could not afford to do away with the tribute system. Additionally, the concerns of the then twenty-six-year-old prince extended to European issues such as the Reformation, and the Spanish royal house's loss of control over German lands, as well as his father's ailing health which lessened the emperor's engagement with the daily requirements of rule. Las Casas seemingly recognized these burdens of office (or pending office) when, in the Prologue of the *Very Brief*

Account, he acknowledged the busy travel and occupations incumbent on the prince regent.

André Saint-Lu suggested another motive for publishing the *Brevísima relación*. He contended that Las Casas wanted "to cause the greatest possible impact and to make obvious the urgency of a radical reform of the Indies."[58] If so, his intended audience would extend beyond Charles V, Prince Philip, and members of the Council of the Indies to Salamanca theologians, as well as *letrados* and bishops in the Indies.[59] As Giménez Fernández points out, Las Casas also wanted the friars (and confessors) to take the printed *tratado* to the Indies for use there.[60] Accordingly, the greatest—or, at least a greater—social impact would be achievable by distributing the *Brevísima relación* to people in Spain beyond the royal court as well as to missionaries in the Indies.[61] Additionally, more weight would be given to the tract if the *Brevísima relación* was an official publication.

Legal Character of the *Brevísima relación*

The character of the text as a piece of juristic writing will now be established by examining its juridical attributes, functions, and features as they relate to genres of the civil juridical tradition, namely, *relaciones*, *denuncias*, and *peticiones*, as well as by contextualizing these juristic writings in the hegemonic legal culture of the early colonial period (Figure 6.2).

Publication

According to traditional Lascasian scholarship, two avenues for officially publishing the *Brevísima relación* were available to Las Casas. Hernández pointed out what was available within the ecclesial juridical tradition: bishops had magisterial and doctrinal authority as well as juridical power to print *tratados*—their own or those of others.[62] That Las Casas included his ecclesiastical rank in the title of the "Presentation" or Prologue of the *Brevísima relación*, wherein he wrote "Presentation by Bishop don Fray Bartolomé de las Casas," suggests possible utilization of this episcopal privilege to publish his tract.[63] Hernández also contended that there was at least "private" royal permission for the publication.[64] In this respect, Pérez Fernández pointed out that Philip's royal chronicler, Antonio de Herrera, had recorded that Las Casas's *tratados* were "printed in Seville with privilege in 1552."[65] Pérez Fernández also uncovered criteria from the civil juridical tradition about the different licenses at that time for publishing that further supported his conclusion that the tract was indeed published "with royal privilege."[66] This special license meant that the publication of the tract (with the royal coat of arms on the cover) as well as its distribution in the Indies had been pre-approved by the Council of the Indies.[67]

Figure 6.2 Woodcut from 1568. Shows printers removing a page from the press and inking text-blocks.
Source: Wikipedia.

However, recent scholarship by the medieval historian and theologian Fernando Domínguez Reboiras conjectures that Las Casas lacked a license, and published his *Brevísima relación* along with seven other *tratados* in 1552 in Seville with financial support garnered through his Dominican confreres at San Pablo convent, from members of the *Consejo de las Indias*, and from the *Casa de Contratación*. The Dominicans in this Andalusian city consisted of friars of all ages and experiences who were opposed to the colonial system that Las Casas so consistently condemned and who gave Las Casas their unconditional support. Additionally, the friars were well-connected as confessors and counselors of affluent Sevillians. Apparently, because many of this financially secure class became rich by commercial enterprises in the Indies, their "guilt feelings" may have compelled them to help fund the publications of the Universal Protector of the Indigenous people. Furthermore, during this period, an influential member of the *Consejo de las Indias*, Hernán Pérez de la Fuente, was conducting a *visita* in Seville and, reportedly, personally interacted with Las Casas. In addition to reorganizing the *Audiencia* in that port city, Fuente established better business practices in the *Casa de Contratación*.[68] Reboiras suggests that Fuente may have used his position to secure funding from the *Casa de Contratación* as well as from the *Consejo de las Indias* for Las Casas's printing costs.[69]

With respect to the license issue, Reboiras contends that Las Casas had the guarantee of the *Tribunal de la Inquisición* that the Holy Office would ignore any charges that might be brought against the Dominican bishop of Chiapa or his patrons for publishing without a license, just as was done previously when his *Confessionario* was reported to the Tribunal.[70] Several factors allegedly facilitated this "protection." The Tribunal had relocated to Seville at this time, thus allowing Las Casas greater access. The *Inquisidor-General* was the archbishop of Seville, don Fernando de Valdés y Salas (1483–1568), who was a former professor of canon law at Salamanca. The Dominicans (for a hundred years) were closely linked to the *Tribunal de la Inquisición*, and served as examiners in *autos de fe* and as Inquisitors-General. Furthermore, Las Casas was under a time constraint, because he wanted to send printed *tratados* to the Indies with the thirty-two friars that he had recruited to work in Chiapa and who were due to sail that summer. Because he could not wait for a license to be issued, the Inquisition arrangement offered him an alternative.

Reboiras conjectures that not only was financial support available, but more importantly, if the *Tribunal de la Inquisición* and the *Consejo de las Indias* supported Las Casas's ambitious and costly project—directly or indirectly, the normal route for publication could have been skirted, and Charles's coat of arms (with its implied license to print) could have been printed without concern on the cover of the *Very Brief Account*. This perspective, however, weakens other scholars' contention that the *Brevísima relación* was an official publication. However, this alternative approach seems plausible, given Philip's apparent indifference at the time. Moreover, even though Philip was probably more or less in charge, the *Consejo* also exercised a lot of authority in the name of the often-absent Charles V.

Whatever the route Las Casas took to publish, Pérez Fernández forcefully contends that the *Brevísima relación* was published as "a tract on law."[71] Similarly, Arías convincingly opines that the tract was "a legal document meant to be read aloud," as well as points out that Las Casas consistently used the word "*item*" (meaning "therefore" or "whereas") to distinguish the different points in the tract as was common in legal documents of the time.[72]

Evidence

The types of authoritative evidence that Las Casas employed also serve to demonstrate the general legal character of the *Brevísima relación*. Spanish jurisprudential practice built on Roman and canon procedures. Initially, in Roman legal procedures, both documentary evidence and oral testimony were considered, although the former carried more weight.[73] Later, in canonistic legal procedures, Innocent III both preferred and standardized documentary evidence, although canonists remained wary of written evidence. His successor, Innocent IV, who favored oral testimony, reportedly opined that it was "contrary to nature to trust the skin of a dead animal more than the voice of a living [person]."[74]

Documentary evidence for the *Brevísima relación* was derived from the fact that this tract was a summary of the *Larguísima relación*, which (as previously noted) was alleged to be "a heavily authenticated report," based on *probanzas*. Although Las Casas did not include statements from or the actual *probanzas* in the *Brevísima relación*, he did refer to these sworn testimonies.[75] He also included documentary evidence in his tract in the form of written eyewitness testimony from Fray Marcos de Niza, OFM, and bishop Juan Fernández de Ángulo, OFM.[76] The chronicle of the Franciscan friar was also counter-signed by Bishop Zumárraga, OFM, a credible witness who testified to the document's veracity; the excerpt from the *carta al emperado* of the Franciscan bishop of Santa Marta (and, as such, a "Protector of the Indigenous people") also lent credence to Las Casas's allegations.

Oral testimony included that of others, as well as Las Casas's first-hand eyewitness account of what he firmly believed were the evils and harm done. The testimonial force of this tract resided in Las Casas's declaration that "I saw."[77] He certified the truth of his statements by reference to his episcopal position. In medieval law, the social status of the witness lent credibility to the testimony. He also referred to his years of living in the Indies, which was another important factor found in medieval law that was related to credibility.[78] Additionally, he did not simply affirm his account of the facts but he "vowed" to their veracity and, in this, seemed to take recourse to Roman law wherein the oath constituted further evidence.[79] Additionally, his inclusion of the testimonies of his episcopal confreres might also have been because he knew that, according to canonical standards, oral proof was the greatest if corroborated by two credible witnesses.[80] Furthermore, for those territories in which he had not lived, Las Casas included—indeed, textually borrowed—information from, for example, Cabeza de Vaca about Xalisco (or Nueva Galicia, as it was known officially), as well as appended the "piece of a letter" that described the "atrocious" expedition of captain Sebastián de Benalcázar into the Quito region or in what had been the northern Inca empire.[81] (These Xalisco and Quito regions were widely separated as well as culturally and geographically distinct.) The "piece of a *carta*" was written by an unknown conquistador who had participated in the expedition of Sebastián de Benalcázar as they returned from Acerma to Calí, Popayán and Quito. The excerpt narrates how licenses were given to take Indigenous persons as prisoners, and how the captives died en route of hunger and/or were "killed like cattle" when they collapsed with fatigue. Indeed, as Adorno contended, the *Brevísima relación* was "one of the only *printed* works that offered … authoritative evidence" about the considerable destruction of the Indies by Christian Spaniards.[82]

Relación

In addition to the publication of the *Very Brief Account* with at least royal and/or ecclesia-related consent as well as its documentation with sworn and eyewitness testimony, evidence that this *tratado* was a piece of juristic writing also derives from its function "to inform," which corresponds to the genre of the civil juridical tradition that was culturally recognized as a *relación*. This function and genre are confirmed in the title of both the *Larguísima relación* and its brief summary, the *Brevísima relación*, which included the word "*relación*," a term that meant "an official account."[83] González-Echevarría contends that, in the sixteenth century, the genre of legal writing known as the *relación* was an official narration, report, deposition, or letter that bore witness to something that had happened.[84] This, however, may be too narrow a definition of *relación*. Some writings that were dubbed *relaciones* were little more than narrations of events.

Indeed, until 1574, *relaciones* constituted a large and diverse body of fact-oriented writings that shared the quality of informing, but did so in different ways and for different purposes.[85] For example, the 1513 *relación* detailing the triumphal entry of Ferdinand of Aragon into Valladolid functioned to inform the populace of the ideals of kingship, of ancient and modern heroes, and of the king's life, his fortunes, and virtues; the narrative efforts at royal image-making also informed as propaganda aimed at obtaining recognition of the Aragonese-born monarch as Christian king of Castile.[86] In 1519, treasurer Núñez de Guzmán sent fiscal information to the Crown, whereas the *relaciones* of Pané (1496) and Cabeza de Vaca (1542) described geographic features of the territories as well as provided ethnographic data about Indigenous lifestyles such as those recorded in Alcalá's 1540 *Relación de Michoacán*.[87] In the *Brevísima relación*, Las Casas also included information about the geographic trajectory of the *entradas*—territory by territory—as well as ethnographic material to demonstrate the rational capacity of Indigenous people.[88] In contrast, Bishop Diego de Landa, OFM, generated information about the arrival of conquistadors and clergy to one region, as well as ethnographic data on Mayan religion and on the Mayan glyphs in his 1566 *Relación de las cosas de Yucatán*.[89] Beginning in 1564, accounts that reported predominantly geographic and/or ethnographic information were supplemented (and to some degree replaced) by *relaciones geográficas*, which were to be written according to a standardized format to produce more detailed and systematic information about the territories and peoples of the Indies.[90] For example, the 1577 *Relación geográfica de San Miguel* carefully responded to fifty questions contained in the Crown's instructions.[91] However, the actual information found in *relaciones geográficas* was often anything but "standardized," in part because of local influences and interpretations, in part because not all of the questions were actually answered.[92]

Information in narratives and *relaciones* about encounters and conquests abounded over the years since the *entradas* began.[93] For example, Gaspar de Espinoza began his 1516 account about Tierra Firme with Quintilian prose lauding the marvels and riches encountered followed by very lengthy narration of the pacification measures that were taken.[94] Other Spaniards recorded their *viajes* (journeys) to unknown islands and peoples.[95] Royal scribes were the mouthpiece for many: in 1534, Alonso Vehedor drew up a very official report of "the things that happened [including acquiring *esclavos de rescate*] in the *armada* of Simon de Alcazaba" as it traveled along the coast of what is now South America; in 1540, Sardella penned the account of Robledo's expeditions in the provinces of Antiochia (Colombia).[96] From 1519 to 1526, Hernándo Cortés wrote five *relaciones* that reported and justified the conquests of Nueva España; decades later, a former member of Cortés *entrada*, Fray Francisco de Aguilar, OP, dictated an eight-*jornada* report in his *Relación breve de la conquista de la Nueva España*, and *oidor* Alonso de Zorita finished his lengthy *Relación de la Nueva España* about the origins and development of the Spanish *señorío* and tribute systems from the initial conquests onward.[97] Circa 1546, Pascual de Andagoya wrote of the conquest of Tierra Firme—from Nicaragua to Peru—and of his "evangelizing executions" in territories previously torched and brutalized by Benalcázar.[98] In 1559, Gutiérrez de Santa Clara also wrote "a certain and true *relación*" in retrospect about the civil wars in Peru. In that same year, three conquistadors of Río de la Plata and Paraguay recorded the many and persistent difficulties they personally experienced in their *viajes* and *entradas*.[99]

Information in Las Casas's 1552 *Brevísima relación* constituted a global synopsis about the conquests—about what he saw as the underside of the expansionist expeditions: "destruction" in the sense of increasing devastation and depopulation of the Indies. Other *relaciones* (sometimes labeled *cartas*, *informaciones*, and/or *testimonios*) also informed the authorities about the underside of the conquests, such as the *cartas* that the Hispaniola Dominicans and the Picard Franciscans sent to the Crown between 1516 and 1519, and the report that the *oidores* of the *Audiencia de Santo Domingo* filed after their visit in 1522 about how cruelly a band of Spanish soldiers treated and punished the Indigenous inhabitants in Sancti-Spiritus (Cuba).[100] Speaking out of forty years of experience in New Spain, Fray Pedro de Gante, OFM, informed the emperor in his 1552 *relación* about what he perceived as the imminent destruction of the Indigenous population, and the possibility of Mexico becoming "as deserted as the [Caribbean] Island," in the event that "a solution is not forthcoming." The Franciscan narrated the personal and collective physical tolls as well as the temporal and spiritual consequences of "the destruction of these people."[101] Las Casas also chronicled what he perceived (and predicted) as the "*destruición de las Indias*" as a result of fifty years of Spanish presence. To temper as well as contradict narratives about the "heroic conquest," both he and Gante offered a counter-discourse.

In addition to these substantive differences, the distinctiveness of Las Casas's *Brevísima relación* was its fundamental character as a juridical instrument. Other *relaciones* reflecting this same character consisted of the reports of investigations of colonial officials resulting from *visitas* and *residencias*.[102] *Visitas* were periodic, and sometimes unexpected, investigations of the conduct of an official, often stemming from complaints made about them. *Residencias* pertained to investigations carried out at the end of the tenure of an official in a particular administrative post. As in Las Casas's *relación*, these reports were deliberately legal in their presentation of witness testimony, out of which was generated the *relación*. Arguably, since Las Casas was aware of these official investigations, his *Brevísima relación* may be regarded as a kind of collective *residencia* of conquistadors, encomenderos, and colonial officials, using eyewitness experiences as well as written and oral testimony from witnesses. This highlights a major difference between the *Very Brief Account* and the accounts from *visitas* and *residencias*: the former was territorially all-inclusive; the latter emerged from territorially restricted investigations.

Denuncia

In addition to the function of the *Brevísima relación* "to inform" was Las Casas's employment of his data "to denounce" the evils and harm done. The salience of this denunciatory function of the *tratado*—and of its correspondence to the civil juridical genre of *denuncia*—can also be gleaned from the original title of the very lengthy official report that Las Casas gave the emperor and the junta in 1542: *Larguísima relación de denuncias de la destruición de las Indias*.[103]

Denuncias, first understood in an archaic sense as a warning or announcement of impending threat, were part of both juridical procedures and juristic writing. Las Casas's law studies would have familiarized him with the *denunciatio* that originated as an alternative to the *accusatio*, which was the standard form of procedure for medieval jurists and borrowed from Roman jurisprudence.[104] In sixteenth-century criminal procedure, the *denunciatio* brought information of wrongdoing (supported by oath) to a judge's attention; in canonical jurisprudence, this also complied with the gospel admonition that "if someone does something wrong … and refuses to listen, … report it to the community."[105] Accordingly, in the *Brevísima relación*, Las Casas declared that the wrongdoings must be "reported" [read, "denounced"] so that the monarch has "notice of them."[106] (Yet, the monarch was under no formal obligation to take "notice of" the reported wrongdoings.) Furthermore, this denunciatory report to the prince and emperor also exemplifies that the *Very Brief Account* was radically juridical in that it sidestepped the administrative and jurisprudential structures that had developed since the conquest, and presented a denunciation directly and immediately to the font of justice itself.

Las Casas was also familiar with *denuncias* as a form of legal communication as evidenced in the fact that, as a young cleric in 1516, he began writing denunciatory documents about the wrongdoings of certain Spaniards on both sides of the Atlantic: namely, his *Representación a los regentes Cisneros y Adriano*, and his *Memorial de denuncias*.[107] During the course of his lifetime, Las Casas's denunciations ranged in subject matter from the *abusos* of crown officials to the *agravios* (offenses) of conquistadors, encomenderos, and merchants. The repertoire of genres of Las Casas's condemnatory juristic writings extended from his *cartas*, his *tratados* about the encomienda and slavery, his 1543 *Memorial al emperador*, to the 1550–1551 *controversía* with Sepúlveda, which was quickly followed by the publication of the *Very Brief Account* denouncing the deeds of the "tyrannical" conquistadors, encomenderos, and royal officials that contributed to devastation and depopulation of the Indies.[108] Other Spaniards also wrote in the tenor of this widely used form of censorial juridical writing: for example, Felipe Gutiérrez from Cuzco in 1540 denounced the offenses of a conquistador; Antonio de Aguayo from Mexico City in 1554, those of an *oidor*; Diego de Ibarra from Ciudad de los Reyes (Lima) in 1557, those of a governor. The conquistador was accused of bad governance and maltreatment of Indigenous people, especially by the thefts and killings, as well as taking away the encomendero's Indians. The *oidor* was charged with poisoning the *juez de residencia*, his wife, and family. The governor was also culpable of bad governance and of his administration of the royal estates.[109] Indigenous people also made denunciations. For example, in 1552, the Nahua-speaking *cabildo* of Tlaxcala articulated their concerns about land and labor changes that would result in native nobles living as commoners; in 1560, they denounced the effects of the Spaniards' intended congregation of people on the homes, horticulture, animals, and so forth that those relocated would leave behind.[110]

Several scholars likened the denunciations of the *Brevísima relación* to a *Memorial de agravios*.[111] Just as *memoriales* combined *hechos* and *derechos*—albeit to address more particularized issues, so too *denuncias* made accusations that laid blame for the facts (*hechos*) of wrongdoing as well as made judgments that condemned the wrongdoing on the basis of laws (*derechos*). However, the difference was that Las Casas denounced not just one of many issues, but rather the entire project of conquest and colonization—that is, the many-faceted acts that could lead to the *destruición de las Indias*.

Saint-Lu regarded the *Brevísima relación* as "the prototype" of Las Casas's accusatory writings.[112] In this *tratado*, as previously demonstrated, the authoritative strength of his accusations derived from the collective and corroborative proof that he offered in *probanzas* and others' eyewitness testimonies.[113] The criteria for his condemnation of the accused Spaniards were divine, natural, and human laws, and the basis of the legal charge (*querella*) that he laid against them was their violation of this tripartite scheme of law.[114] As such, throughout the *Brevísima relación*, Las Casas accused "the tyrants" and condemned the "evils" of their conquests and the enslavement. For Las Casas, these "evils" included the "slayings, depopulation, injustices, acts of violence, havoc, and great sins … of greed … of idolatry of gold," the deleterious effects on the evangelization and salvation of the Indigenous peoples, and the conquistadors' use of an "exceedingly unjust" human law—the *requerimiento*. He charged that "all these things … are iniquitous, tyrannous, condemned, detested, and accursed by all natural, divine, and human law."[115]

Petición

In addition to the functions of "to inform" and "to denounce," a third function of the *Brevísima relación* was "to petition." *Peticiones*, which in the writings of Cicero and Quintilian connoted a right of claim, were simply written requests made to an authority figure on a certain matter. From their acceptance in the thirteenth century as a tolerated practice, petitions gradually evolved during the first half of the sixteenth century into a meaningful objective juridical right. Accordingly, aggrieved persons began, for example, to ask for redress on the basis of abridged liberties or of justice.[116]

Petitions varied greatly in subject matter and, given their ubiquity, were an important and valuable source of information.[117] Indeed, petitions became one of the most common genres of colonial writings, and were drawn up in favor of all types of peoples, races, and ethnicities, as well as by all social classes. For example, scholarship has indicated how Indigenous peoples, such as in Mexico and Peru, enthusiastically and quickly adopted these petitions for their own purposes, for example, to report the alleged abuses of Spanish officials in charge of tribute labor systems, of certain priests, and of their own reportedly dishonest town leaders.[118] In this manner, petitions also constituted a mechanism for Indigenous people to demonstrate and gain agency and influence. As well, the use of petitions by Indigenous people of New Spain to argue against any "total destruction" of the Indies may be implied. Spaniards also submitted diverse kinds of petitions. For example, in 1520, the petition of Hernándo de Arguello reiterated his request (that he had made twice previously) for an extension of a shipbuilding contract in Darien. That same year, the *Audiencia* of Santo Domingo petitioned for the construction of a fort at Cumaná and contextualized this request by information on the larger scenario of current and future relationships with different Indigenous peoples.[119] In the *Brevísima relación*, Las Casas also petitioned the prince "not [to] concede licenses [for new *entradas*] nor allow those terrible things that the tyrants did invent, pursue, and have committed against those peaceable ... Indians," and to fortify the New Laws, especially those disallowing the inheritance of encomiendas and the continuation of slavery.[120] In a way, the *Very Brief Account* constitutes a multi-topic book-length version of the plethora of more mundane and localized petitions, in which Las Casas condenses these legal instruments in effect to one request: stop the conquests and the maltreatment.

Mixed and Similar Genres

Given the above functions and their corresponding legal genres, the *Brevísima relación* is simultaneously a *relación*, a *denuncia*, and a *petición*. According to González-Echevarría, intermingling of different genres of juridical discourse in a single text was "nothing new" at the time.[121] In similar vein, Pennington and Müller contend that, even in the works of thirteenth-century Decretists, texts mixed "what seemed to be" several different types of writing, which Las Casas probably knew.[122] Additionally, genre scholarship contends that individual texts rarely if ever have all the characteristic features of a genre and that, even when they did, not all of these aspects were included to the same degree.[123] This lack of uniformity was in keeping with the fluidity of texts during this period.[124]

A commonly used example of the intersection of texts as well as of functions is found in a humble legal genre rooted in feudalism wherein ordinary people told of their accomplishments and petitioned rewards for their services.[125] Such official accounts, which combined autobiographical narrative with a bureaucratic request for some benefit as a result of one's "great" service to the monarch, were referred to as *relaciones de méritos y servicios*.[126] By the time of the conquest, these accounts were also called *probanzas de méritos* (proof of merit), which was a more familiar kind of *probanza* that was dispatched by conquistadors and other vassals (including Indigenous people) to request favors and grants on the basis of their services to the Crown.[127] By combining an official report of their feats with a petition, the initial "discoverers," conquerors, and settlers in the colonial economy also sought to benefit from the principle of *mercedes* (royal favors) as a reward for them and their descendants.[128] Accordingly, by virtue of these two functions—"to inform" of their respective expeditions and "to petition" recognition and favors for their accomplishments and services as loyal royal vassals, official accounts such as Cortés's five *relaciones* and Cabeza de Vaca's *Relación de naufragios y comentarios* belonged to two juridical genres, that of *relación* and that of *petición*.[129]

There are numerous examples of this tendency—indeed, this practice—of mixing discursive types. As such, the *Brevísima relación* was not unique. In addition to the 1517 *Carta de los dominicos y franciscanos* to Chancellor Xèvres in which the friars informed the Crown of the facts, denounced the *abusos* and *agravios*, as well as petitioned legislative action (which *Carta* was also strikingly similar in its descriptions to those in the *Very Brief Account*), several documents written during and after 1552 also consisted of the same blend of genres as in the *Brevísima relación*.[130]

One is a 1555 *Relación de agravios* signed by Don Francisco Tenamaztle, an Indigenous lord, in which he narrated the harm done by Nuño de Guzmán particularly during the Mixton war and pinpointed their source in unjust wars and cruel treatment; as well, he informed the monarch of the misdeeds of royal officials. Cacique don Francisco denounced the Spaniards' deeds, including that of the viceroy, who sent him as a prisoner to Spain; he justified his actions on natural law and on the right of resistance against a "tyrant." He petitioned restitution as well as material provisions and ecclesiastical personnel to conduct peaceful evangelization in the territories of the unconquered and unevangelized Acaltecas and Coachilcas.[131] Salvador Álvarez conjectured that Las Casas had drafted this *relación*.[132] That Las Casas, or someone else, might have done so is plausible, given the conventions of the time. This is also possible, given that Las Casas visited with Tenamaztle in Spain, and that the bishop of Chiapa was held in high regard by Indigenous leadership. This regard was later demonstrated by communications from Indigenous leaders in 1556, first to the emperor from Indigenous leaders in New Spain requesting the appointment of Las Casas as their advocate—a juridical appointment described in the *Siete Partidas* (3.6.1, 2); then from Indigenous leaders in Peru notifying Philip II that Las Casas (and friar Domingo de Santo Tomás) had *poder legal* (power of attorney) to act in their names.[133]

Another document whose functions and genres corresponded to those of the *Brevísima relación* was the 1552 account of the Flemish Franciscan, Fray Pedro de Gante, to his countryman and long-time friend, Charles V.

He informed the emperor about the injustices taking place in New Spain, denounced the outrageous hiring practices, mine labor, and excessive tributes demanded of the Indigenous people, and condemned the governor and judges for not implementing royal decrees. He petitioned remedies in the form of "expeditious justice," "good judges," prohibition of lawsuits by Indigenous people, financial support for schools, hospitals, and chapels, as well as the assignment of more friars. Gante wanted the cessation of lawsuits by the Indigenous inhabitants because he asserted that the Spanish notaries were corrupt and that the caciques had become "avid litigants" off the "sweat of the Indian commoner, whose belongings are sold in order to litigate."[134] Similarly, in 1552, Juan Fernández, *fiscal* for the *Audiencia de Lima*, wrote an official account of the uprisings that took place in Peru after the death of Viceroy Mendoza, of *lo malo y lo bueno* (the good and the bad), named and condemned the traitors, and listed the loyal Spaniards, as well as petitioned remedies.[135] An official account about the devastation in Nueva Granada penned in 1560 by Fray Francisco de Carvajal, OP, also contained the same amalgam of *relación*, *denuncia*, and *petición*.[136]

The *relación* that most closely resembled Las Casas's *Very Brief Account* in its functions and juridical character was a *Memorial sobre la despoblación y destruición de las Indias* penned a month after Las Casas's death in 1566 by Luís Sánchez, a retired cleric. At the request of the president of the Council of the Indies, Sánchez narrated and denounced the injustices perpetrated by secular and ecclesial judges, by clergy and friars, and by conquistadors and encomenderos. As was one of Las Casas's dying wishes, Sánchez petitioned for a *junta magna* consisting of the monarch and the Council of the Indies, with theologians "as judges," as well as "good religious" and other "virtuous people" who have experience in the Indies, to "study the facts in order to determine the law." In his *Memorial*, Sánchez spoke with high regard for the bishop of Chiapa and the bishop of Popayán (Colombia); he had served under Bishop Juan de Valle in Popayán, and retired to Mexico after the bishop's death. Like Las Casas, Sánchez attributed the cruel unjust wars and the enslavement of the Indigenous inhabitants to the Spaniards' greed, which he claimed resulted in the depopulation and destruction of the peoples and their lands. Among the problems that allowed this to happen that Sánchez listed were the distance from Spain, as well as the fact that those making legislation had—in his opinion—never visited the Indies, and were also misinformed. (Sánchez' assertion that legislators never visited the Indies is not entirely true, because gradually the *Consejo de las Indias* and other administrative bureaucratic organs were staffed with at least some people who had "American" experience.) Furthermore, while Sánchez acknowledged that there were a small number of *gente de bien* and good religious, he blamed what he characterized as the continuing destruction of the Indigenous peoples and their lands on ecclesial and secular judges, on certain religious and other priests, and on conquistadors and encomenderos.[137]

While the above examination indicates that the genres of the text are juridical, and that mixing of genres was typical at the time, there were other features of the genres of *relaciones*, *denuncias*, and *peticiones* that also gave the *Very Brief Account* legal weight. Two of these features pertained to notarial conventions and obligatory connotations.[138]

Notarial Conventions

An important legal feature in juristic writing were formulary notarial conventions such as the mode of reporting and autobiographical data.[139] While the generally prescribed style of writing was in the first-person singular, which constituted a form of personal enfranchisement no matter the "ego" revelations of the document, many documents were mediated through scribes.[140] In *relaciones*, autobiographical information tended to be biographical, genealogical, and territorial. As González-Echeverría pointed out, the writer of an official account included his name, lineage, and/or place of origin, as well as his claim to knowledge of the topic through his years of experience and/or residence in the territory.[141] For example, in his 1496 *relación*, Pané wrote, "I, Fray Ramón Pané, poor hermit of the Order of St. Jerome"; the writer for Jorge Robledo's 1540 *relación* identified himself as "I, Juan Baptista Sardella, experienced scribe."[142] In the final testament of his 1542 written summary, Las Casas wrote, "I, Fray Bartolomé de las Casas or Casaus, friar of the Order of Saint Dominic."[143] This biographical information contributed toward establishing the legitimacy of the narrator of the account—Pané as an exclaustrated hermit, Sardella as a registered scribe, and Las Casas as a seasoned friar and a possible descendant of the French noble "House of Casaus."[144] For legitimation by territorial experience, Pané mentioned his residence in Magdalena and La Isabela (Hispaniola); Sardella indicated his presence during the expeditions in Antiochia; Las Casas underscored his "fifty years and more" spent in the Indies.[145] Through these autobiographical details, these narrators asserted three pillars of legal credibility for their official accounts, namely, "I saw … "; "I originated … "; "I resided …"

Denuncias and *peticiones* also used both first-person and mediated reporting, but identification of the author was usually as vassal and *criado* (subject, servant, underling) of the monarch.[146] Some identified themselves according to a significant role they played. For example, Antonio de Aguayo cast himself as "one of the first conquistadores of the New Kingdom of Galicia in New Spain."[147] Genealogical information seemed limited in *denuncias* and *peticiones* to, for example, the statement that the author was the child of a *criado* and/or of one *tan antigua* (of many years). Territorial experience to legitimize the author of the *denuncia* and/ or *petición* frequently took the form of references in the text to the length of time or the number of years that the author had, for example, "walked all the land in these provinces."[148]

These biographical, genealogical, and territorial formulary notarial conventions correspond to information about professional identity or social status, cultural roots or family background, and residence or experience. These kinds of information assert the character and credentials of the writers in order to bolster the legal credibility of the authors and their statements. Use of these conventions also connotes the enfranchisement of the author, and constitutes links to the source of power, such that their civil and cultural being is expressed in legal language.

Obligatory Connotations

Another important feature that gave a legal character to documents, including the *Brevísima relación*, pertained to implied obligations. First, vassals and *criados* were obliged to give service to their lord(s). In his *tratado*, Las Casas explicitly clarified that dutiful vassals and *criados* are only those "who desire to serve purely and solely to further the public will and the prosperity of the royal estates."[149] He further charged that the king was "receiving no service" from certain conquistadors, encomenderos, and royal officials, that the atrocities they committed were "not in service of the king"; indeed, he charged that their "service" in the Indies consisted in "destroying those monarchs' kingdoms and rendering naught all the right that the monarchy has to all the Indies."[150] In contrast, he lauded the "great service ... to the king and queen of Castile" rendered by the supreme lords of the five Indigenous kingdoms on Hispaniola, and extolled their peoples' "immense benefices to the Spaniards," at first given freely, then forced to serve in hard labor, as beasts of burden, as personal servants, and so forth.[151]

Second, *relaciones* were also obligatory insofar as these texts complied with a request from the Crown (or from royal intermediaries), or insofar as one's position demanded such an account.[152] For example, in response to the mandate of the Catholic monarchs to *hacer entera relación*, Columbus prepared and submitted an account of his travels.[153] Pané wrote his *relación* at the bidding of Columbus—*del ilustre señor Almirante, virrey y gobernador de las Islas y Tierra Firme*—the intermediary of the Crown.[154] Fray Jerónimo de Alcalá recorded the *Relación de Michoacán* at the order of Viceroy Mendoza.[155] Las Casas penned the *Brevísima relación* in compliance with an official request from the prince's tutor.[156]

In addition to *relaciones* that were requested, official accounts were also expected from all royal appointees. Las Casas's appointment by

Cisneros in 1516 to the royal position of "Protector of all of the Indigenous people in the Indies" carried both the obligation and the right to submit an official account to the Crown.[157] After becoming a bishop in 1544, Las Casas's obligation to the Crown doubled by virtue of the *Patronato real*; accordingly, the duty of making reports corresponded to his position as both Universal Protector and bishop.[158] Other royal appointees also submitted such *relaciones*: for example, treasurer Pedro Núñez de Guzmán sent accounts to the Crown about the amount of gold produced in the Cuban mines; *oidores* Licentiate Espinosa and Licentiate Zuazo dispatched an account to the emperor about the repopulation of Hispaniola.[159] Additionally, among office-holders obliged to render an account to the Crown could be Hernándo Cortés—the rogue-conquistador who, as the mayor of the city of Veracruz (that he established), sent *relaciones* to the emperor chronicling and justifying his "service."[160] In any case, such first-hand accounts were tantamount to legal depositions, and the *Brevísima relación* was one such deposition that was both officially requested and obligatorily required.

Third, *denuncias* and *peticiones* carried obligations for those in authority. For example, *denuncias* implied future action on the part of authorities. Las Casas contended in the *Brevísima relación* that "the mere notice of wrong or malefaction suffices … for not a single moment could [the king] tolerate them" and, moreover, that "it is the duty of the king … to root them out."[161] With respect to *peticiones*, all petitions had to be read and considered—although not necessarily approved—by the designated jurisdictional authority.[162] Whether in the form of denunciations or requests, the general right to approach the authorities was protected by the royal mandate of August 15, 1509, wherein King Ferdinand ordered that "no official can prevent anyone from sending to the king, or anyone else, letters and other information which concerned the welfare of the Indies."[163] Furthermore, authority was in theory "obliged" by documents—including *denuncias* and *peticiones*—that presented the need for remedial action since, according to the canonist principle of equity, "no wrong should be without a remedy."[164]

Hegemony of Juristic Discourse

The foregoing assessment of the legal character of the *Brevísima relación* requires contextualization in the institutional juridical reality through which the Spaniards penetrated and governed the Indies. Although, as Kathleen Ross contends, the legal character of this reality and its history have tended to be overlooked for the most part by historians and legal scholars, scholarship by Miguel Luque Talaván, Robert González-Echevarría, and others has generated insightful perspectives about this dimension of colonial history.[165]

González-Echevarría pointed out that "América" existed as a legal document before it was "encountered."[166] Indeed, the birth of América (according to Spaniards) and of Hispano-Indiano law for the Indies can be precisely pinpointed as *el 17 de abril de 1492* when the Catholic monarchs signed the *Capitulaciones de Santa Fe*, which juridically asserted the monarchs' territorial rights as well as Columbus's reward-laden titles over any discovered land—over any *tierra firme*.[167] These legal claims were further buttressed the following year by the papal donation to the monarchs of legal title under the condition of their Christianizing the "discovered" people. These two documents were the foundational juridical texts of the encounter, conquest(s), colonization, and governance of the Indies. The subsequent preeminence of the juridical was apparent—indeed, unmistakable—not only in litigations involving Columbus and his heirs, Cortés, Pizarro, and other conquistadors, but in the establishment of encomiendas and of crown towns, in the declarations of war by *requerimiento*, in the issuing of licenses for slaving expeditions, in the regulation of commercial traffic, in the reliance on discourses of *letrados*, and in the decisions of juntas about legitimacy. Accordingly, from the first founding juridical document in 1492 and onward, a "stupendous" proliferation of *cédulas*, edicts, laws, and legal writings allegedly crossed the Atlantic in both directions as the juridical narrative expanded from contract to contact to conquest to colonization.[168] In any case, according to González-Echevarría, the predominant form of discourse at the beginning of and during the early colonial period was legal writing, or, as he coined it, "the law of the letter."[169] The existence of multi-dimensional poly-discursive documents of a legal character, including the *Brevísima relación*, mirrored this discourse and reflected how deeply ensconced was the Castilian legal tradition out of which the different genres of juristic writing originated and Hispano-Indiano law was born.

The hegemony of legal discourse in the Castilian tradition—and subsequently in the Indies—derived in part, as explicated earlier, from Castile's establishment and cultivation of the study of Roman and canon laws in the *Facultades de Leyes* of *studia generalia*.[170] Accordingly, almost four centuries before the "encounter," students of jurisprudence were examining legal forms of writing such as *distinctiones* (to present solutions to textual contradictions) that they incorporated into their glosses and commentaries, which *summas* later generated *tratados* (monographs on a selected topic), *argumenta* (to articulate all observations relevant to a particular place in a legal text), *generalia* (to argue for and against a particular legal principle), *quaestiones* (to solve logically a legal problem) that evolved into *quaestiones disputationes* (to inquire by syllogistic debate), *consilia* (to give authoritative advice on an actual case), and *casus* (to explicate the specific contents of a law, decree, decretal, or constitution).[171] As such, by the dawn of the encounter, common juridical texts included—among others—*relaciones, exhortos, memoriales, demandas, denuncias, querellas, suplicatorios, requerimientos, peticiones*, and *exposiciones*.[172] Moreover, during the reign of the Catholic monarchs, Spain excelled in the abstract field of jurisprudence and the practice of law, which was in great demand in that "very litigious society."[173] This jurisprudential expertise would carry over into the governance of the Indies.

The hegemony of legal discourse ultimately derived from its embodiment in Spain's juxtaposition of two institutional forms of governance: patrimonial and bureaucratic.[174] In their centralization of power, the Catholic monarchs labored to curtail the sphere of domestic power that derived from land-based lordship of paternal and patriarchal lords who, in adherence to tradition, ruled through bonds of kinship and *patrón*-ship. The monarchs attempted to replace any semblance of these kinds of bonds in the Indies by a barrage of legal directives as exemplified in their establishment of the encomienda, wherein laws were also geared to prevent the development of an aristocracy of nouveau-riche conquistadors. In their centralization of power, the monarchs also structured the governance of Spain and its possessions in a bureaucratic fashion that was characterized by functional rationality as manifested in a vertical hierarchy of authority, in different levels of royal jurisdiction in geographic and administrative areas through *corregidores, audiencias*, and viceroys (along with mechanisms for supervision and appeal) as would be structured in the Indies, as well as in a conciliar system of decision-making.[175] Equally important in the bureaucratic system was the Crown's employment of professionals—especially of *letrados*—in administrative positions. Consequently, not only did *letrados* help dislodge aristocratic power in Castile, they also eroded the power of conquistadors in the Indies or, as González-Echevarría phrased it, they "re-conquered" the territories for the Crown. Most importantly, in the colonial period, *letrados* were the "keepers of writing" as learned men who knew and lived by the letter of the law. As well, they accompanied *entradas* in their official capacity as scribes, as did others who, however, were not *letrados*.[176]

Furthermore, the increasing bureaucratic centralization redefined the relationship between the individual and the body politic in legal terms: one's civil status as vassal became one's master status (except for those of recognized higher status). While the subordinate status of vassal was equalizing for the populace, vassalage was also impersonal. Indeed, as Charles V once counseled his wife, Isabel of Portugal (1503–1539) and later his son, Philip, do not be "overly respectful of anyone's personal wishes."[177] Control of individuals through their civil status as vassals (whether Spanish or Indigenous) also undergirded and sustained the development of Hispano-Indiano law, insofar as a function of law is the ordering of human relationships.[178] The Spaniards' (and later the Indigenous peoples') internalization of this master status was manifested in their consistent self-identification as vassals in their *cartas* and other communications to royal authority. This self-identification became the standard and expected formula.[179]

In a bureaucratic form of governance, and given the distance of Spain from the Indies, official business was necessarily conducted on the basis of written documents. Indeed, for writers in the Indies, texts were "a necessary part" of the prevailing exchange of legal discourse, and were "the only way of saying what they had to say, and the most effective way to give their writings an immediate political impact."[180] As such, an overwhelming mass of meticulous documentation was generated in the sixteenth century, because everything had to be ordered, regulated, documented, and received in writing.[181] As a legal instrument of governance, writing gradually became a more regulated activity as the Crown imposed its interpretations and goals. For example, the format and content of *Relaciones geográficas* during the reign of Philip II enabled the monarch to ascertain the customs and resources, etc., of the different communities and regions of the Indies.

The hegemony of legal discourse was also legitimized by the Thomistic tradition and the *Escuela Española* and, in this, overtly reflected the religious-ethical dimension of Hispano-Indiano law.[182] Just as the Crown and jurists had recourse to theologians with respect to the moral dimensions of the Spaniards' presence in the Indies, theologians dedicated themselves to juridical issues from a theological perspective, since the field of action for the "science of God" (theology) was all that was human. Contributors to this "discourse community" ranged from mendicant friars in the Indies who were trained in Thomism (eventually including the canonist Las Casas) to theologians and philosophers in Spain such as Vitoria and de Soto, whose works initiated the *Escuela Española*.[183] In particular and as explicated in Chapters 5 and 6, these representatives of the Thomistic tradition of the Dominican Order and of the institutions of Salamanca and Valladolid addressed three major juridical issues: the question of the treatment of the Indigenous people as rational, free, and social human beings created by God and redeemed by Christ; the question of the legitimacy of Castile's political *dominium* and of conquest as a means for exercising jurisdiction; and the question of war as a method of evangelization.

Such was the hegemonic legal discourse that canopied the genesis, writing, publication, and legal character of the *Brevísima relación*. As a canon lawyer and one trained in theology, Las Casas enjoyed "genre literacy." He knew what and how to compose and publish a legal text. He needed to inform, to accuse and condemn, as well as to petition a remedy.[184] He wrote the *Very Brief Account* with a clear audience in mind, with a definitive purpose at its core. As will be demonstrated in the next chapter, he had a specific structural arrangement in mind, which was fleshed out by an epistemological rationale, and guided by an analytic framework based on the tripartite scheme of divine, natural, and human laws.

Notes

1 "Carta al Emperador" (15–12–1540), in *Obras Escogidas: Opúsculos, cartas, y memoriales*, ed. Juan Pérez de Tudela Bueso (Madrid: Biblioteca de autores españoles, 1958), 5:69a (hereafter cited as *O.E.*). Also see Isacio Pérez Fernández, *Inventario documentado de los escritos de Fray Bartolomé de las Casas*, vol. 1, Estudios Monográficos, ed. Helen Rand Parish (Bayamón, P.R.: Centro de Estudios de los Dominicos del Caribe, 1981), 1:284–286 (hereafter *Inventario*); Isacio Pérez Fernández, *Cronología documentada de los viajes, estancias y actuaciones de Fray Bartolomé de las Casas*, vol. 2 (Bayamón, P.R.: Centro de Estudios de los Dominicos del Caribe, 1984), 2:534–39 (hereafter cited as *Cronología*).

2 The *Brevísima relación* was a summary of the *Larguísima relación de la destruición de las Indias* (A Very Long Account of the Destruction of the Indies). Bartolomé de las Casas, *An Account, Much Abbreviated, of the Destruction of the Indies*, intro. and ed. Franklin W. Knight, trans. Andrew Hurley (Indianapolis, IN: Hackett, 2003), 87 (hereafter, Knight, *An Account*). Philip, the son of Emperor Charles and Empress Isabel of Portugal, became prince regent in 1543, and ascended to the throne as Philip II in 1559 upon the abdication of his father.

3 Rodrígo de Ladrada, OP (who came from Nueva Granada) joined Las Casas (who came from Hispaniola) in Nicaragua. Later, along with Pedro de Ángulo, OP (who came from Mexico) and Luis Cáncer, OP (who came from Nicaragua), they worked together in Guatemala. In 1538, the Dominican Provincial Chapter in Mexico City gave permission to Las Casas, Ladrada, and Cáncer to return to Spain to recruit missionaries. Las Casas and Ladrada arrived in Spain in May of 1540; Cáncer went to Spain earlier and returned to Guatemala with the friars he recruited, while Las Casas and Ladrada waited in Spain for the emperor's return from Flanders. Ladrada remained a life-long friend and faithful companion of Las Casas.

4 Bartolomé de las Casas, "Carta al Consejo de las Indias (30–4–1534)," in *O.E.*, 56–59, which was written in Santo Domingo; also see Las Casas, "Carta a un personaje de la Corte (15–10–1535)," in *O.E.*, 59a, 63b, which was written in Nicaragua. Also see Pérez Fernández, *Inventario*, 1:284–286.

5 This central motive as well as his hope that "God would have compassion" and not destroy Spain was explicitly stated in the *Brevísima relación*. Knight, *An Account*, 86.

6 "Carta al Emperador (15–12–1540)," in *O.E.*, 69ab. This letter was hand-delivered by Jacobo de Testera, OFM, to the emperor who at that time was in Flanders attending to issues in Ghent. See Isacio Pérez Fernández, "Autenticidad, sentido histórico y valor capital de este documento," in *Conclusiones sumarias sobre el remedio de las Indias* (Madrid: Biblioteca Nacional, 1992), Sign.: Mss 22605 (124):6.

7 Helen Rand Parish, "Introduction," in Bartolomé de las Casas, *The Only Way*, ed. Helen Rand Parish, trans. Francis Patrick Sullivan (New York: Paulist Press, 1992), 36–38 (hereafter cited as *The Only Way*). While the conditions in the mines were poor indeed in Mexico, Las Casas did not take into account that the Spaniards did not uniformly rely on forced Indigenous labor. Rather, he seems to equate the Mexican situation with that of the islands. See Robert Haskett, "'Our Suffering with the Taxco Tribute': Involuntary Mine Labor and Indigenous Society in Central New Spain," *Hispanic American Historical Review* 71, no. 3 (1991): 447–75.

8 In his letter, Balboa reiterated what he had reported to the Crown twice previously about Pedrárias Davila, again denounced the conqueror's actions,

and requested action; see his "Carta del adelantado Vasco Núñez de Balboa, 16 Octubre 1513/1515," in *Colección de documentos inéditos, relativos al descubrimiento, conquista y organización de las antiguas posesiones españolas de América y Oceanía, sacados de los archivos del reino, y muy especialmente de las Indias*, eds. Francisco de Cárdenas y Espejo, y Luis Torres de Mendoza (Madrid: Ministerio de Ultramar, 1864–84), 2:526–38 (hereafter cited as *Colección de documentos inéditos*).

9 "Carta al rey de los obispos de Nueva España," in *Epistolario de Nueva España 1505–1818* (México, DF: Antigua Librería Robredo de José Porrúa e Hijos, 1940): 4:8–18.

10 Lewis Hanke, "Estudio Preliminar," in Bartolomé de las Casas, *Historia de las Indias*, ed. Augustín Millares Carlo (México, DF: Fondo de Cultura Económica, 1951), 1:lxxv; Anthony Pagden, "Introduction," in Bartolomé de las Casas, *An Account, Much Abbreviated, of the Destruction of the Indies*, ed. and trans. Nigel Griffin, intro. Anthony Pagden (London: Penguin Books, 1992), xxxviii.

11 Pagden, "Introduction," in Bartolomé de las Casas, *An Account, Much Abbreviated, of the Destruction of the Indies*, ed. and trans. Nigel Griffin, intro. Anthony Pagden (London: Penguin Books, 1992), xxxviii; Elizabeth Sauer, "Las Casas and Early Modern Spanish and English Colonialist Discourses," in *Approaches to Teaching the Writings of Bartolomé de Las Casas*, eds. Santa Arias and Eyda Merediz (New York: Modern Language Association of America, 2008), 215.

12 Pérez Fernández, *Cronología*, 2:518.

13 Carmelo Sáenz de Santa María, *El licenciado don Francisco Marroquín, primer obispo de Guatemala, 1499–1563* (Madrid: Ediciones Cultura Hispánica, 1964), 162.

14 Las Casas's lobbying at court during this time was greatly facilitated by Jacobo de Tastera, OFM, and by the companionship and insights of Ladrada, his Dominican assistant. Pérez Fernández, *Inventario*, 518; Manuel Giménez Fernández, "Fray Bartolomé de Las Casas: A Biographical Sketch," in *Bartolomé de Las Casas in History: Toward an Understanding of the Man and His Work*, eds. Juan Friede and Benjamin Keen (DeKalb: Northern Illinois Univ., 1971), 92–94 (hereafter *Las Casas in History*); Charles H. Lippy, Robert Choquette, and Stafford Poole, *Christianity Comes to the Americas: 1492–1776* (New York: Paragon House, 1992), 85; Las Casas, *The Only Way*, 40.

15 While Las Casas requested that the emperor order him to remain in Spain until the monarch had returned from Flanders, another reason why Charles V would want to see him was related to the fact that Charles knew Las Casas well both as a secular priest and as a Dominican friar, and that his Flemish officials in Spain (co-regent Adrian of Utrecht—who later became Pope Adrian VI, chancellor Jean le Sauvage, and chancellor Mercurino Arborio de Gattinara) had worked closely with Las Casas from 1516 to 1521. Additionally, and in keeping with the monarchical policy of programmatic conciliarism, which was characteristic of the Hapsburg administrations (in contrast to the pragmatic absolutism of the later Bourdon kings), as well as to better govern the Indies, the emperor welcomed the varios and conflicting voices of his subjects. Moreover, in addition to the Crown's engagement in economic and political problems as well as with ecclesiastical and humanitarian issues on both sides of the Atlantic, Charles was also concerned about the threat of colonial feudalism in the Indies, the diminishment of royal interests by independent, self-serving conquistadors, and the dangers of political instability in New Spain, Peru, and other Indigenous territories. See Manuel Giménez Fernández, "Fray Bartolomé

de Las Casas: A Biographical Sketch," in *Las Casas in History*, 75, 77–79; Lippy, Choquette, and Poole, *Christianity Comes*, 54–55.

16 Santa Arias, *Retórica, Historia y Polémica: Bartolomé de las Casas ya la tradición intelectual renacentista* (Lanham, MD: Univ. Press of America, 2001), 78.

17 This *Memorial de remedios* was drafted by Las Casas and Ladrada between December 1541 and April 1542, purportedly in Valladolid. Pérez Fernández, *Inventario*, 1:276–77, note 107, 296–98, note 121. The *memorial* is also referred to as the *Memorial de veinte remedios para reformación de las Indias*, or as the "Remedies for the Existing Evils with Twenty Reasons Thereof," and also as the *Memorial de dieciséis remedios para reformación de las Indias*. Pérez Fernández stated that there had to be twenty, not sixteen, remedies because Las Casas referred to the "seventeenth and following" remedies of that *Memorial* in his *Entre los remedios. Inventario*, 296–97.

18 In addition, Las Casas gave the emperor a copy of the second version of his work, *De unico modo*, which he had drafted from September to December in 1538, and from May to August in 1539 also in preparation for his return to Spain. This expanded version, titled *De cura habenda regibus Hispaniarum circa orbem Indiarum et de unico vocationis modo omnium gentium ad veram religionem* (How the Kings of Spain Must Care for the World of the Indies [by] the Only Way of Calling All People to True Religion), expounded how rational and peaceful evangelization was a royal duty. Las Casas hoped to move the conscience of the king through this treatise.

19 The fifteen members of the junta included members of the Council of the Indies (Cardinal García de Loaysa, OP, president of the Council; Dr. Diego Beltrán, *oidor*; Lic. Juan Suárez de Carvajal, bishop of Lugo; Dr. Juan Bernal de Luco, *oidor*; Lic. Gutierre Velásquez, *oidor*), experts in colonial issues (D. García Fernández Manrique, count of Osorno and president of the *Consejo de los Órdenes*; D. Sebastián Ramírez de Fuenleal, bishop of León and later of Cuenca as well as ex-president of the *Audiencia de Santo Domingo* and of the second *Audiencia de México*; Lic. Pedro Mercado de Peñalosa, *oidor* and ex-councilor; Lic. Juan de Salmerón, ex-*oidor* of the *Audiencia de Nueva España* and of the *Chancillería de México*), jurists (Dr. Juan de Figueroa, regent, member of the Council of Castile; Dr. Hernando de Guevara, *oidor*; Lic. Gregorio López, fiscal; Dr. Jacobo González de Arteaga, *oidor*), and two persons in whom the king had the highest confidence (D. Francisco de los Cobos, titular secretary of the Council of the Indies; D. Juan de Zúñiga, *comendador mayor de Castilla*). Pérez Fernández, *Cronología*, 2:573; and Giménez Fernández, "Fray Bartolomé de Las Casas: A Biographical Sketch," in *Las Casas in History*, 95.

20 Pérez Fernández contended that Las Casas functioned as a reformer in the junta and was mandated to intervene in this way by the emperor. *Cronología*, 2:574; *Brevísima*, 3:399. In addition to his participation in the votes and deliberations of the junta with its interrogations, witnesses, and requested *parecers* (opinions), Las Casas was requested to write a summary of the *Memorial de remedios*, which he entitled *Conclusiones sumarias sobre el remedio de las Indias*; in mid-summer, he delivered (with Ladrada) a *memorial* on the need for restitution [see his "Representación al Emperador Carlos V (1542)," in *O.E.*, 5:123–33], as well as submitted a very short to-the-point written *parecer* at the eleventh hour—just before the New Laws were formulated in late autumn of 1542. See also David Orique, "New Discoveries about an Old Manuscript: The Date, Place of Origin, and Role of the *Parcer de fray Bartolomé de las Casas* in the Making of the New Laws of the Indies." *Colonial*

Latin American Historical Review 15, no. 4 (Fall 2006—published in 2010): 419–41.

21 After orally proposing the needed *remedios*, Las Casas also distributed written copies of *El octavo remedio* to the junta as well as his second version of *De unico modo*, in which specifically he addressed the duties of the Crown.

22 This account, which was lost, was referred to in the writings of the royal scribe, Alonso de Santa Cruz. In Santa Cruz's reference to the *Larguísima*, he also included comments about the Spanish encomenderos, conquistadores, and officials who perpetrated evils and harm in the Indies. Alonso de Santa Cruz, *Crónica del Emperador Carlos V* [1551], 5 vols. (Madrid: 1920–223), 4:217; see Bartolomé de las Casas, *Brevísima relación de la destruicion de las Indias*, ed. Isacio Pérez Fernández, vol. 3 (Bayamon: Centro de Estudios de los Dominicos del Caribe and Universidad Central de Bayamon, 1999), 3:60–62 (hereafter cited as Pérez Fernández, *Brevísima*). Helen Rand Parish and Henry Raup Wagner, *The Life and Writings of Bartolome de las Casas* (Albuquerque: Univ. of New Mexico), 109.

23 This "stack" of documents was allegedly three feet high. Unfortunately, the sources documenting this statement by Helen Rand Parish are not available due to her untimely death. Interview by the author, David Orique, February 12, 2001, tape recording, Berkeley, CA. Although Motolinía observed that the amount of *probanzas* that Las Casas took back with him to Spain required using "twenty-seven to thirty-seven" Indigenous people to carry the *probanzas* from Mexico City to Honduras from whence Las Casas set sail for Spain in 1540, the Franciscan friar was not known for his numerical accuracy. With respect to the content of the *probanzas*, Motolinía also contended that "the greatest part of what they were carrying was accusations against the Spaniards." "Father Fray Toribio de Motolinía to Charles V, January 2, 1555" in Lesley Byrd Simpson, *The Encomienda in New Spain: The Beginning of Spanish Mexico*, first pub. 1950, rev. ed. (Berkeley: Univ. of California Press, 1982), 238. Pérez Fernández's investigation, supported by other records, revealed that each of the Indigenous individuals was probably carrying a few kilograms of *probanzas* each. Isacio Pérez Fernández, *Fray Toribio Motolinía, OFM, frente a Fray Bartolomé de las Casas, OP: Estudio y edición crítica de la carta de Motolinía al Emperador* (Tlaxcala, a 2 de Enero de 1555) (Salamanca: Editorial San Esteban, 1989), 158–64; Pérez Fernández, *Inventario*, 1:n.108; Pérez Fernández, *Cronología*, 2:511.

24 Knight, *An Account*, 1. According to Arias, the persuasive force of the *Brevísima relación* was rooted in its rhetorical and oral structure, which linked the past with the present and eliminated the spatial-temporal distance between the audience and the events in order that they might experience the destruction. See her *Retórica, historia y polémica*, 75–76.

25 Juan Martínez del Guijo, also known as Guijarro and as Silíceo, became the prince's tutor in 1535, and bishop of Cartagena in 1540. He was named archbishop of Toledo in 1546 and cardinal in 1555. He died on May 11, 1557. Knight, *An Account*, 1, 3; Pérez Fernández, *Brevísima*, 381n9.

26 Knight, *An Account*, 3.

27 Las Casas was nominated for the See of Chiapa on December 20, 1543, and consecrated bishop of Chiapa in Seville, Spain, on March 31, 1544. Las Casas was Chiapa's first resident bishop. Prior to him, two other bishops were assigned to the diocese of Chiapa: Juan de Ortega (who refused the position) and Juan de Arteaga (who died en route to Chiapa). Francesca Cantú, "Documentos lascasianos," *Historiografía y Bibliografía Americanista* 19, no. 20 (1975–76): 127–55.

28 In addition to Las Casas's nomination to a bishopric in 1543, Charles V nominated the following prelates: Antonio de Valdivieso, OP, for Nicaragua in 1544. Cristóbal de Pedraza for Honduras in 1545, Pablo de Torres, OP, for Panamá in 1547, and Juan del Valle for Popayán in 1548. Enrique Dussel, *A History of the Church in Latin America: Colonialism to Liberation*, trans. Alan Neely (Grand Rapids, MI: W.B. Eerdmans Publishing, 1981), 51.

29 Las Casas's enemies in official circles in Spain included the deposed Cardinal Loaysa. Helen Rand Parish, *Las Casas as Bishop: A New Interpretation based on his Holograph Petition in the Hans P. Kraus Collection of Hispanic American Manuscripts* (Washington, DC: Library of Congress, 1980), xiiiab.

30 Bishop Las Casas arrived in Santo Domingo, Hispaniola, on September 9, 1544, in the Yucatán on January 6, 1545, and in Chiapa on March 9, 1545.

31 The goals of his episcopate were threefold: to peacefully convert and reduce the unconquered Indians, to strengthen the ecclesiastical arm and the protectorate, as well as to promote colonization by farmers. Parish, *Las Casas as Bishop*, xva–xviiib. Las Casas also wanted all clergy of his diocese to follow the Rule of Saint Augustine with the hope that they would be examples of holiness and service. Bishop Zumárraga of Mexico City also considered engaging in this kind of clerical reform, which was based on the Decretals of Gregory IX and compiled by Raimundo de Peñafort in 1234. Isacio Pérez Fernández, "San Agustín y Fray Bartolomé de las Casas, La regula apostólica y la reforma del clero secular en Hispano-América," *Augustinus* 26 (1981): 82–86.

32 "Carta al rey del obispo de Antequera, en el valle de Oaxaca, don Juan López de Zárate, con ocasión de la promulgación de las Leyes Nuevas (1542) con especial referencia a la encomienda perpetua y hereditaria," Archivo general de Indias, Audiencia de México, Legajo 357, in Enrique Dussel, *El episcopado hispanoamericano: institución misionera en defensa del indio, 1504–1620*, Apéndice documental, Tomos 1–9 (Cuernavaca: CIDOC, 1970), 8:147–52.

33 Brian P. Owensby, *Empire of Law and Indian Justice in Colonial Mexico* (Stanford: Stanford Univ. Press, 2008), 14–15.

34 Giménez Fernández, "A Biographical Sketch," in *Las Casas in History*, 101; Simpson, *The Encomienda in New Spain*, 132–44.

35 Knight, *An Account*, 88.

36 Parish, *Las Casas as Bishop*, xxiiiab.

37 According to Miguel Concha Malo, Bishop Las Casas's use of canonical principles constituted an "alternative use of the law," of law that belongs to the Church and demands the compliance of the faithful. See his "El uso alternativo del derecho en Bartolomé de las Casas," in *Dominicos en Mesoamérica: 500 Años* (México, DF: Analogía Revista de Filosofía, 1992), 57–75.

38 "Representación a la Audiencia de los Confines (19–10–1545)," in Bartolomé de las Casas, *Obras completas*, vol. 1: *Vida y Obras*, ed. Álvaro Huerga (Madrid: Alianza Editorial, 1998), 13:199 (hereafter *O.C.*). Five days later, Marroquín issued a statement in which he "abandoned" his position in this *Representación* in favor of giving full secular power to the *Audiencia de los Confines.* Carlos Sempat Assadourian presents the many issues on which Las Casas and Marroquín differed, the complexity of their relationship, and the relevant documents in his "Fray Bartolomé de Las Casas obispo: la naturaleza miserable de las naciones indianas y el derecho de la Iglesia: un escrito de 1545," in *Historia mexicana* 40, no. 3 (Enero–Marzo, 1991): 387–451.

39 "Corrolarium de episcoporum officio (6–1546?)," in *O.C.*, 13:228–33. Enrique Dussel's dissertation documents the habitual manner in which

informes from bishops were requested by the Crown and how these reports gave bishops an avenue to govern indirectly in civil matters of their dioceses. See his *El episcopado hispanoamericano*, 1:vii–xii.

40 Of particular sensitivity was Las Casas's episcopal directive that confessors had to send the penitent Spaniard to Bishop Las Casas for the absolution of any sins related to holding Indigenous people in encomienda or in other forms of slavery. See David Thomas Orique, *To Heaven or to Hell: Bartolomé de Las Casas's Confesionario* (University Park: Penn. State Univ. Press, 2018).

41 Isacio Pérez Fernández, *Brevísima relación de su vida, diseño de su personalidad, síntesis de su doctrina* (Caleruega: Editorial OPE, 1984) 58; Isacio Pérez Fernández, "San Augustín y Fray Bartolomé de las Casas, la regula apostólica y la reforma del clero secular en Hispano-América." *Augustinus* 26 (1981): 86–95; Venancio Diego Carro, *Carta abierta a D.R. Menéndez Pidal* (Madrid: Librería OPE, 1962), 11.

42 Las Casas's request was based on canonistic tradition to care for the poor or *miserabiles personae*, and his conviction that the Indigenous people were "the poorest of the poor" and "the most wretched of the wretched." Gustavo Gutiérrez, *Las Casas: In Search of the Poor of Jesus Christ* (Maryknoll, NY: Orbis, 1995), 316–19.

43 Translated by the writer from the following prayer:

> !Señor, tú sabes lo que yo pretendo en esto y ves lo que de esto gano: que son hambres, sed, cansancio, aborrecimiento de todos; si me engaño, por tu Evangelio me engaño; pero en el grado que lo creo, creo que no me engaño; pero si yo no lo entiendo, tú me alumbras, Señor, para que yo no sea el escándalo que en este mundo soy!.
>
> Pérez Fernández, *Brevísima relación de su vida*, 58

44 Pérez Fernández, *Cronología*, 2:695–704.

45 In his discussion of these official and published documents, Carro elucidated the influence and mark of Las Casas's hand. Carro Venancio Diego, *Carta abierta a D.R. Menéndez Pidal* (Madrid: Librería OPE, 1962), 12.

46 Orique, *To Heaven or to Hell*, 1–2, 16, 27–28, 41, 42, 75, 91. Others also contributed their ideas about how to better implement the New Laws, such as Diego Fernández, in his *Crónicas del Peru*, estudio preliminar y ed., Juan Pérez de Tudela Bueso (Madrid: Atlas, 1963), 1:6.

47 Giménez Fernández, "Fray Bartolomé de Las Casas: A Biographical Sketch," in *Las Casas in History*, 105–06.

48 Ibid., 104.

49 However, Philip seemed to turn against Las Casas since the monarch ordered the confiscation of Las Casas's work after the retired bishop died.

50 These reports were seemingly drafts of the *tratados* that he published in 1552, such as *Se han hecho esclavos*, *Tratado comprobatorio del imperio soberano*, and *Principia Quaedam*. See also Ramón Jesús Queraltó Moreno, *El pensamiento filosófico-político de Bartolomé de las Casas* (Seville: Escuela de Estudios Hispano-Americanos de Sevilla, 1976), 88–89.

51 Note that even though a bishop may resign from his position in a diocese, he nevertheless remained a bishop. Pérez Fernández, *Inventario*, 1:463–87. For a detailed chronology of Las Casas's tenure as bishop of Chiapa, see Pérez Fernández, *Cronología*, 2:651–85.

52 See the discussion of this debate in Chapter 4. Also see, Lewis Hanke, "The Great Debate at Valladolid, 1550–1551," in *The Roman Catholic Church in Colonial America*, ed. Richard E. Greenleaf (New York: Alfred E. Knopf, 1971), 47–52; Fernando Domínguez Reboiras, "'Y hasta agora no es

poderoso el rey'. Sobre monarquía y elites de poder en los orígenes de la Brevíssima," in *Talleres de la memoria—Reivindicaciones y autoridad en la historiografía de los siglos XVI y XVII*, eds. Robert Folger and Wulf Oesterreicher (Münster: LIT, Druck, 2005), 53 (hereafter "Y hasta agora no es poderoso el rey" and *Talleres de la memoria*).

53 Pérez Fernández *Brevísima*, 117. The published *tratado* consisted of ninety-two pages and was printed in gothic letters. By an analysis of the dates of seven other documents that Las Casas also published in 1552, Pérez Fernández arrived at the conclusion that this *opusculo* was probably published at the end of November in 1552. *Brevísima*, 118, 123, 911.

54 Knight, *An Account*, 86. Although Las Casas does not mention these individuals, it can be presumed that one of them was Philip's tutor, Martínez del Guijo.

55 Ibid., 86.

56 Cynthia L. Stone, "Confronting Stereotypes: The *Brevísima relación* as Homily, Not History," in *Approaches to Teaching the Writings of Bartolomé de Las Casas*, 67.

57 Knight, *An Account*, 3. The question could be asked whether Philip supported Las Casas's *relación*, given that he (as a teenager) perhaps had not read or did not want to read the 1542 version. Pérez Fernández did not infer this; rather, he seemed to indicate that the printed version improved the likelihood that the prince would indeed read it or re-read it, especially given that Las Casas included a dedication to the prince in the Prologue. *Brevísima*, note 12, 565.

58 "Introducción," in Bartolomé de las Casas, *Brevísima relación de la destruición de las Indias*, ed. André Saint-Lu (Cátedra: Quinta Ediciones, 1991), 56 (hereafter Las Casas, *Brevísima*).

59 José Alejandro Cárdenas Bunsen, "Escritura y derecho canónico en la obra de fray Bartolomé de las Casas" (Ph.D. diss., Yale Univ., 2008), 75.

60 Huerga concurs with Giménez Fernández that Las Casas was motivated to publish the *Brevísima relación* because he wished to send the *tratado* to the Indies for distribution among the missionaries and also because, by their use of it, Las Casas would continue to be present and active in those land. See *O.C.*, 1:284.

61 The intended audience of the *relación* would understand the message conveyed by the tract, especially if juridically trained. From the intended audience to the unintended audience (as in the case of the Black Legend), the information of the *Brevísima relación* thus expanded to an ever-increasingly literate public, although this cohort was a relatively small percentage of the population at this time. Tess Knighton and Carmen Morte García, "Ferdinand of Aragon's Entry into Valladolid in 1513: The Triumph of a Christian King," 18 *Early Music History* (1999): 142–43.

62 Ramón Hernández, "Los tratados impresos por Bartolomé de las Casas," in *O.C.*, 10:8–11.

63 Knight, *An Account*, 2.

64 The *Pragmática* of 1502 ordered that books published in Castile were obliged to obtain a royal license. Reboiras, "Y hasta agora no es poderoso el rey," 65. Furthermore, the *pase regio* of 1539 mandated that all episcopal petitions to the Holy See had to pass through the Crown. At first, imperial policy continued the tradition of patronizing and protecting certain works favored by the Crown or at least pro-active involvement in disseminating information. Hernández contended that Charles V, who had listened to the *Larguísima relación*, privately approved the summary account. See his "Los tratados impresos por Bartolomé de las Casas," in *O.C.*, 10:8–11. However,

the Crown's policy gradually became one of censure and oppression. For example, in 1556, four years after the publication of the *Brevísima relación*, no books about the Indies could be published without a royal license. Ralph Bauer, *The Cultural Geography of Colonial Latin American Literatures: Empire, Travel, Modernity* (Cambridge: Cambridge Univ. Press, 2003), 40.

65 Isacio Pérez Fernández, "Estudio Preliminar," in Bartolomé de las Casas, *Brevísima relación de la destruición de las Indias*, ed. Pérez Fernández (Madrid: Editorial Tecnos, 1992), xiii.

66 Royal privilege included the obligation to present the original manuscript to the authorities and to give a printed copy to them for comparison with the original, and for examination of the printed license. Pérez Fernández, *Brevísima*, 140–55, 911. Keen maintained that this publication was given crown approval because "royal fear of a colonial feudalism [was] more dangerous to the Crown than the shattered power of the Indigenous kings and states." Benjamin Keen, "The Black Legend Revisited: Assumptions and Realities," *Hispanic American Historical Review* 49, no. 4 (1969): 704.

67 Reyes Cano contended that the *Consejo de las Indias* probably did support the publication, or at least did not impede it as they could have; see his "Introducción" in *Brevísima relación de la destruición de las Indias*, ed. and intro. J.M. Reyes Cano (Barcelona: Planeta, 1994), xliii. Varela also noted that the royal coat of arms on the cover indicated crown approval; see his "Introducción," in Las Casas, *Brevísima relación*, 29. Interestingly, using Charles V's coat of arms for a text originally handwritten for Philip provides some indication of Las Casas's intention to trade off of his connections with royal power in printing and distributing this tract widely. That is, seemingly, Las Casas could demonstrate to readers beyond princely and other court circles that he had influence and power, as well as the ear of the king-in-waiting, Prince Philip. Consuelo Varela. "Introducción," in Bartolomé de las Casas, *Brevísima relación de la destruición de las Indias* (Madrid: Castalia, 1999).

68 "Los Consejeros de Carlos V," in *La Corte de Carlos V, segunda parte: Los Consejos y los consejeros de Carlos V*, dir., José Martínez Millán (Madrid: Sociedad Estatal para la Conmemoración de los Centenarios de Felipe II y Carlos V, 2000), 333–35.

69 Reboiras, "Y hasta agora no es poderoso el rey," 61–66.

70 Ibid., 66–73.

71 Pérez Fernández, *Inventario*, 1:xxii.

72 Santa Arias, *Retórica, história y polémica*, 77–78.

73 According to Mousourakis, these forms of evidence were present from the pre-classical period onward, which eras he classified as (1) pre-classical: Rome's ascendancy as the dominant power in the ancient world beginning in mid-third century BCE and ending in the first century BCE with the establishment of the imperial era under Augustus (63 BCE–14 CE), (2) classical: the first 250 years of the Common Era during which Roman law and Roman legal science reached a high degree of perfection, and (3) post-classical: from the reign of Diocletian (284–305 CE) to the codification of Roman law under Justinian (483–565 CE). George Mousourakis, *The Historical and Institutional Context of Roman Law* (Burlington, VT: Ashgate, 2003) 308, 370.

74 James A. Brundage, *Medieval Canon Law* (London: Longman, 1995), 133. Of the various kinds of evidence in Roman and canon laws, *confessio in iure* carried special weight. Mousourakis, *The Historical and Institutional Context of Roman Law*, 370. Torture had been part of classical Roman law but was abandoned in the early Middle Ages; this flawed method of proof was unfortunately reemployed in the thirteenth century with the revival

of Roman law. Kenneth Pennington, *The Prince and the Law, 1200–1600: Sovereignty and Rights in the Western Legal Tradition* (Berkeley: Univ. of California Press, 1993), 42–43.

75 Knight, *An Account*, 67, 78, 80. In his published tract, he reminded readers that the *probanzas* were now with the Council of the Indies.

76 Ibid., 75–77, 55–56. According to Torrejón, Niza accompanied Pedro de Alvarado's expedition to northern Peru. See Torrejón, *Brevísima*, 208n346, 316–17n346.

77 Arias, *Retórica, historia y polémica*, 77.

78 Mousourakis, *The Historical and Institutional Context of Roman Law*, 370n71.

79 Knight, *An Account*, 30, 55; Mousourakis, *The Historical and Institutional Context of Roman Law*, 370.

80 Brundage, *Medieval Canon Law*, 132. Mousourakis contended that oral testimony by a single witness carried no weight at all. *The Historical and Institutional Context of Roman Law*, 370.

81 Pérez Fernández stated that the *carta*, written on or before November 30, 1550, was part of a set of manuscripts bound by a bookseller and sold to conquistador and chronicler, Pedro de Cieza de León, who also used the *carta* in his *La Conquista de Perú. Brevísima*, notes 288 and 289, 907–10, 538. Cieza de León had also participated in that expedition.

82 Italics mine. Rolena Adorno, "Novedades en el estudio actual de la cronística peruana: Las Casas, Guaman Poma y el padre Oliva," accessed March 25, 2006, https://sites.fas.harvard.edu/~icop/rolenaadorno.html.

83 Bartolomé de las Casas, *A Short Account of the Destruction of the Indies*, ed. and trans. Nigel Griffin, into. Anthony Pagden (London: Penguin Books, 1992), xxxi.

84 Roberto González-Echevarría, *Myth and Archive: A theory of Latin American narrative* (Durham: Duke Univ. Press, 1998), 10; Javier Díaz Noci, "Los raíces de los géneros periodísticos interpretativos" accessed Oct. 27, 2019, https://revistas.ucm.es/index.php/ESMP/article/view/ESMP0000110135A/12925. Ramón Menéndez Pidal has a succinct synopsis of the *relaciones* of well-known and other conquistadors and writers of the early colonial period in his Introduction to the *Historia general de las literaturas Hispánicas*, dir., Guillermo Díaz-Plaja (Barcelona: Editorial Barna, S.A., 1953), 311–18.

85 Mignolo denoted the time from the discovery until 1574 as "the unofficial period" of "official reports," that is of *relaciones*. See his "Cartas, crónicas y relaciones del descubrimiento y la conquista," in *Historia de la literatura hispanoamericana, epoca colonial*, coord. Luis Iñigo Madrigal (Madrid: Catedra, 1982) 59, 70; González-Echevarría, *Isla a su vuelo fugitiva*, 20–1; Brenda Danet, "Language in the Legal Process," in *Law and Society Review* 14, no. 3 (Spring 1980): 508; Ramon Menéndez Pidal, "Introduction," in *Historia General de las Literaturas Hispánicas*, dir. Guillermo Díaz-Plaja, 6 vols. (Barcelona: Editorial Barna, 1953), 3:312.

86 This *Relación que se hizo al rey … don Fernando … en la valle de Valladolid … víspera de la epifanía deste año de 1513*, which was ordered by the Bishop of Córdoba, is an early printed example of this genre. The long-established entry ritual was used by Ferdinand in Naples 1506, Valencia 1507, Seville 1508, outside the city walls of Valladolid 1509, and in Valladolid 1513. Luis de Soto, who wrote the 1509 *relación* of entry into Valladolid, confined his account to the celebrations outside of the city walls, which included dances, songs, and eulogies about Ferdinand as king; de Soto justified his account as "very right that the King should be received

with the triumphal entry appropriate to His Majesty." Tess Knighton and Carmen Morte García. "Ferdinand of Aragon's Entry into Valladolid in 1513: The Triumph of a Christian King," *Early Music History* 18 (1999): 119–28, 131, 134.

87 The *Relación de naufragios y comentarios*, published in 1542, presented historical events, descriptions of people, flora and fauna, as well as the vexing paradoxes of survival during the ten-year period. Published in 1540, the *Relación de Michoacán* described pre-Conquest customs of the inhabitants of Michoacán, Mexico.

88 Stephanie Merrim, "The First Fifty Years of Hispanic New World Historiography: The Caribbean, Mexico and Central America," in *The Cambridge History of Latin American Literature*, eds. Roberto González Echevarría and Enrique Pupo-Walker (Cambridge: Cambridge Univ. Press, 1996), 1:94–95. Santa Arias, "Empowerment through the Writing of History: Bartolome de Las Casas's Representation of the Other(s)," in *Early Images of the Americas: Transfer and Invention*, eds. J. M. Williams and R. E. Lewis (Tucson: Univ. of Arizona Press, 1993), 165.

89 Allen Wells, (1996), "Forgotten Chapters of Yucatán's Past," *Estudios Mexicanos* 12, no. 2 (1996): 201; Diego de Landa Calderón, *Relación de las cosas de Yucatán*, accessed April 8. 2011, http://www.wayeb. org/download/resources/landa.pdf.

90 James Lockhart and Stuart B. Schwartz, *Early Latin America: A History of Colonial Spanish America and Brazil* (Cambridge: Cambridge Univ. Press, 1983), 121. In 1574, standardized *Relaciones geográficas de las Indias* were mandated in response to the growing need for information for Spain's expanding and demanding imperial project, and provided narrations for political, ethnographic, and philosophical consideration. Rolena Adorno, *The Polemics of Possession in Spanish American Narrative* (New Haven, CT: Yale Univ. Press, 2007), 198. The narrations were produced by an official questionnaire that was confected and distributed by the *Consejo de las Indias.* Because of its pragmatic and organizational features, the resultant relación more closely and directly transmitted and organized information. Walter Mignolo, "Cartas, crónicas y relaciones del descubrimiento y la conquista," 1:59, 70.

91 Germán Latorre, ed., "Relación geográfica de San Miguel de las Palmas de Tamalameque, Gobernación de Santa Marta, Audiencia de Nueva Granada, Virreinato del Perú (hoy República de Colombia) (1577)," in *Relaciones geográficas de las Indias* (Sevilla: Tip. Zarzuela, 1919), 1–29.

92 Mignolo, "Cartas, crónicas y relaciones del descubrimiento y la conquista," 73–75.

93 Knighton and García pointed out that the intent of many such relaciones was both judicial and historical. See their "Ferdinand of Aragon's Entry into Valladolid," 134.

94 "Relación hecha por Gaspar de Espinosa, alcalde mayor de Castilla Del Oro, dada á Pedrárias de Avila, lugar teniento general de aquellas provincias, de todo lo que le sucedió en la entrada que hizo en ellas, de órden de Pedrárias," in *Colección de documentos inéditos*, 2:467–522.

95 "Relación del viaje hecho á las Molucas ó de la Especieria por la armada á las órdenes del Comendador García Jofre de Loaysa, hecha por el Capitán Andrés de Urdaneta," in *Colección de documentos inéditos*, 5:5–67; "Relación hecha por Vicencio de Pápoles, del viaje que hizo la armada que Hernán Cortés envió en busca de las Islas de la Especieria," in *Colección de documentos inéditos*, 5:68–97.

96 "Relación de las cosas que sucedieron en la armada de Simón de Alcazaba, el cual iba por Gobernador á las provincia de León por parte de la Mar Del Sur, el cual habia de pasar por el Estrecho de Magallanes … una copia que de lo susodicho tenia fecho Alonso Vehedor, escribano de S.M.," in *Colección de documentos inéditos*, 5:97–116; "Relación del descubrimiento de las provincias de Antiochia por Jorge Robledo," in *Colección de documentos inéditos*, 2:291–355.

97 Vittorio Salvadorini, "Las 'Relaciones' de Hernán Cortés," accessed November 11, 2010, https://cvc.cervantes.es/lengua/thesaurus/pdf/18/TH_18_001_085_0.pdf, Fray Francisco de Aguilar, *Relación breve de la conquista de Nueva España*, ed. Jorge Gurría Lacroix (México, DF: UNAM, 1977); Alonso de Zorita, *Relación de la Nueva España*, 2 vols. (México, DF: Consejo Nacional para la Cultura y las Artes, 1999).

98 "Relación de los sucesos de Pedrarias Dávila en las Provincias de Tierra Firme o Castilla del Oro, y de lo ocurrido en el descubrimiento de la mar del sur y de costas del Perú y Nicaragua," in *Pascual de Andagoya: Relación y documentos*, ed. Adrián Blázquez (Madrid: Historia, 1986); also see Álvaro Félix Bolaños, "A Place to Live, a Place to Think, and a Place to Die: Sixteenth Century Frontier Cities, Plazas, and 'Relaciones' in Spanish America," in *Mapping Colonial Spanish America: Places and Commonplaces of Identity, Culture, and Experience*, eds. Santa Arias and Mariselle Meléndez (Lewisburg, PA: Bucknell Univ. Press, 2002), 280–83.

99 Pedro Gutiérrez de Santa Clara. *Quinquenarios o Historia de las guerras civiles del Perú (1544–1548) y de otros sucesos de Las Indias* (Madrid: Ediciones Atlas, 1963), 133–388; "Verdadera relación de lo que sucedió al Gobernador Jaime Rasquin en el viaje que intentó para el Río de la Plata en el año 1559, hecha por Alonso Gómez de Santoya, Alférez del Maestre de Campo, D. Juan de Villandrando," in *Colección de documentos inéditos*, 4:147–190.

100 "Testimonio remitido por los oidores de la Audiencia de Santo Domingo que fueron á la isla Fernandina, de la declaración tomada á Vasco Porcallo de Figueroa, sobre las alteraciones en la villa de Sancti-Spiritus; crueles castigos á los indios; intervención en los sucesos del licenciado Zuazo. 13 Marzo 1522," in *Colección de documentos inéditos, relativos al descubrimiento, conquista y organización de las antiguas posesiones españolas de ultramar*, Segunda serie, vol. 1, *Isla de Cuba* (Madrid: Publicada por la Real Academia de la Historia, 1885), 1:119–26 (hereafter cited as *Colección de documentos inéditos, Isla de Cuba*).

101 While this report is called a "Letter," Gante referred in the text to his document as a "relación." "Fray Pedro Gante's Letter to Charles V, Mexico City (1552)," in *Colonial Latin America: A Documentary History*, eds. Kenneth Mills, William B. Taylor, and Sandra Lauderdale Graham (Wilmington, DE: Scholarly Resources Books, 2002), 105–112.

102 Charles Gibson, *Spain in America* (New York: Harper and Row, 1966), 100.

103 The published epítome of the "*destruición*" did not include the phrase "*de denuncias*"; even so, the denunciatory function of the document and its character as a form of juristic writing that corresponds to the genre of *denuncias* remains. Pérez Fernández, *Brevísima*, 61–2.

104 In the thirteenth century, the accusatory procedure carried with it the high risk of the accuser being punished in the same manner as the accused if the defendant won in court. Brundage, *Medieval Canon Law*, 143. In Roman law from the last century of the republic, the citizen was both the accuser and the denouncer.

105 R.H. Helmholtz, *The Spirit of Classical Canon Law* (Athens: Univ. Of Georgia Press, 1996), 294–95; Matt. 18:15–17; cf. Lev. 19:17.

106 Knight, *An Account*, 2–3.

107 Las Casas, "Representación a los regentes Cisneros y Adriano (1516)," in *O.E.*, 5:3–5; Las Casas, "Memorial de denuncias presentado al Cardenal Cisneros (1516)," in *O.E.*, 5:27–30.

108 John M. Swales, *Genre Analysis: English in Academic and Research Settings* (Cambridge: Cambridge Univ. Press, 1990), 58; André Saint-Lu, "Bartolomé de Las Casas en sus escritos," in *España y América en una perspectiva humanista: Homenaje a marcel Bataillon*, ed. Joseph Pérez (Madrid: Casa de Velázquez, 1998) 110.

109 "Carta de Felipe Gutiérrez al Emperador, pidiendo justicia de los agravios que le había hecho don Francisco Pizarro, 30–12–1540," in *Colección de documentos inéditos*, 3:202–204; "Carta al emperador de Antonio de Aguayo dando aviso a las injusticias y agravios que hacía el licenciado Lebrón, oidor de la Audiencia de Guadalajara, y acusándole de haber hecho envenenar al licenciado Villagar, juez de residencia y a su mujer, 25-Octubre-1554," in *Epistolario de Nueva España 1505–1818*" (doc. 411), 7:272–76; "Carta al rey de Diego de Ibarra, dando aviso de los abusos que cometía el gobernador de Los Reyes y del desorden en que estaba la real hacienda, 1-Septiembre-1557," in *Epistolario de Nueva España 1505–1818* (doc. 450), 8:135–38.

110 "Concerns over the Sale of Nahua Noble's Land, Tlaxcala, 1552," in *Mesoamerican Voices: Native-Language Writings from Colonial Mexico, Oaxaca, Yucatan, and Guatemala*, eds. Matthew Restall, Lisa Sousa, and Kevin Terraciano (Cambridge: Cambridge Univ. Press, 2005), 102–03; "Complaints against Congregation from the Nahua Cabildo of Tlaxcala, 1560," in *Mesoamerican Voices: Native-Language Writings*, 75–77.

111 See, for example, Merrim, "The First Fifty Years," 95–96; Saint-Lu, "Fray Bartolomé de Las Casas," I:122–23; Jean-Paul Duviols, "Introducción," in *Brevísima relación de La Destruyción De Las Indias*, ed. and intro. Jean-Paul Duviols (Barcelona, Linkgua Ediciones S.L., 2009), xxvi; Consuelo Varela, "Introducción," in *Brevísima relación de la destruición de las Indias*, intro. Consuelo Varela (Madrid: Castalia, 1999), 34.

112 André Saint-Lu, *Las Casas indigeniste: Études sur la vie et l'oeuvre du défenseur des Indiens* (Paris: L'Hammattan, 1982), 21.

113 Adorno, *The Polemics of Possession*, 6–7; 142–43, 176–77. Mignolo considered a text, such as the *Brevísima relación*, as the collective memory of what was denounced in the Indies. See his "*Cartas, crónicas y relaciones del descubrimiento y la conquista*," 57. Juan Durán Luzio pointed out that Las Casas spoke "with great authority" in his accusations. See his *Bartolomé de las Casas ante la conquista de América: las voces del historiador* (Heredia, C.R.: EUNA, 1992), 125.

114 Knight, *An Account*, 3. While difficult to translate into English, a *querella* is similar to a suit that is privately instigated, and is a *derecho* (right), while the *denuncia* is a *deber* (obligation or duty) for anyone who is aware of the *agravios* and abusos. See Enrique Alcaraz Varó and Brian Hughes, *El Español Jurídico* (Barcelona: Editorial Ariel, S.A., 2008), 281; Manuel Giménez Fernández, *Instituciones jurídicas en la Iglesia Católica*, vol. 2 (Seville: Socieda Anónima Española de Traductores y Autores, 1942) 2:273.

115 Knight, *An Account*, 3, 23.

116 Julie M. Spanbauer, "The First Amendment Right to Petition Government for a Redress of Grievances: Cut from a Different Cloth," *Hastings Constitutional Law Quarterly* 15 (Fall 1993): 26–34.

117 Stephen A. Higginson, "A Short History of the Right to Petition," *Yale Law Journal* 96, no. 1 (November 1986): 145.

118 Robert S. Haskett, "'Our Suffering with the Taxco Tribute': Involuntary Mine Labor and Indigenous Society in Central New Spain," *Hispanic American Historical Review* 71, no. 3 (1991): 447–75; Steve Stern, "New

Approaches to the Study of Peasant Rebellion," in *Resistance, Rebellion, and Consciousness in the Andean Peasant World, 18th to 20th Centuries*, ed. Steve Stern (Madison: Univ. of Wisconsin Press, 1987).

119 "Petición presentada por Hernando de Arguello, á nombre de Vasco Núñez de Balboa, sobre que se le prorrogue el término que se le había dado para la construcción de unos navíos, que intentaba hazer, á fin de ir á la población de acla, en la provincia del Darién (5 Marzo 1520)," in *Colección de documentos inéditos*, 2:556–58; "Petición a sus Majestades de los oidores é officiales reales de la Audiencia de Santo Domingo (14 Noviembre 1520)," in *Colección de documentos inéditos*, 1:422–27. The latter *petición* included plans to conduct expeditions against the Caríbes and to continue negotiations with Indigenous people friendly to the Spaniards, namely, the *guatiaos.*

120 Knight, *An Account*, 2, 4, 87. Especially in New Spain and Peru, the Spaniards continued to ask the king for licenses and authority. Pérez Fernández, *Brevísima*, 375.

121 Beatriz Pastor Bodmer, *The Armature of Conquest: Spanish Accounts of Discovery of America, 1492–1589*, trans. Lydia Longstreth Hunt (Stanford, CA: Stanford Univ. Press, 1992), 66; Arias, *Retórica, Historia y Polémica*, 111; González-Echevarría, *Myth and Archive*, 55; Walter D. Mignolo, "El metatexto historiográfico y la historiografía Indiana," *Modern Language Notes* 96 (1981): 359n2.

122 Kenneth Pennington and Wolfgang P. Müller, "The Decretists: The Italian School," in *The History of Medieval Canon Law in the Classical Period, 1140–1234: From Gratian to the Decretals*, eds. Wilfried Hartmann and Kenneth Pennington (Washington, DC: Catholic Univ. of America Press, 2008), 163.

123 Alastair Fowler, "Genre," in *International Encyclopedia of Communications*, ed. Erik Barnouw (New York: Oxford Univ. Press, 1989), 2:215; Christine Gledhill, "Genre," in *The Cinema Book*, ed. Pam Cook (London: British Film Institute, 1985), 60; Kathryn Burns also maintained that texts ranged from close to loose conformity with the general genre templates. See her "Notaries, Truth and Consequences," *The American Historical Review* 110, no. 2 (April 2005): 350–79.

124 Mignolo, "Cartas, crónicas y relaciones del descubrimiento y la conquista," 71.

125 Stephanie Merrim. "The Counter-Discourse of Bartolomé de Las Casas," in *Early Images of the Americas: Transfer and Invention*, eds. Jerry M. Williams and Robert E. Lewis (Tucson: Univ. of Arizona Press, 1993), 159n2.

126 However, Folger maintained that these accounts could also become tactical manipulations of personal (private) memories for public gain. González-Echevarría contended that Cortés manipulated reality in his historical narrative in order to achieve his overarching purpose of gaining the favor of the king. Robert Folger, "Alonso Borregán Writes Himself: The Colonial Subject and the Writing of History in Relaciones de méritos y servicios," in *Talleres de la memoria*, 267–68; Roberto González-Echevarría, *Isla a su vuelo fugitiva* (Madrid: José Porrúa Turanzas, 1983), 21.

127 Matthew Restall, *The Seven Myths of the Spanish Conquest* (New York: Oxford Univ. Press, 2003), 12–14.

128 After the initial economic "rewards" from conquest plunder, Spaniards pursued ongoing financial compensation from colonization through the reservoir of *mercedes*—be they tributes, land, labor, and/or offices. More permanent and basic rewards consisted of encomiendas and concomitant benefits such as large residences in the nearest Spanish "city," etc., James Lockhart and Enrique Otte, eds. and trans. *Letters and People of the*

Spanish Indies: Sixteenth Century, Cambridge Latin American Studies Series (Cambridge: Cambridge Univ. Press, 1976), 43, 47, 52; Anthony Pagden, "Introduction," Las Casas, *An Account*, xxxii; Folger, "Alonso Borregán Writes Himself," 269.

129 Cabeza de Vaca became governor of Río de Plata (Paraguay); his *relación* was written in 1537 from a series of reports penned during and after the expedition that began in Florida. Álvar Núñez. Cabeza de Vaca, *The Narrative of Cabeza de Vaca*, ed. trans. and intro. Rolena Adorno and Patrick Charles Pautz (Lincoln: Univ. of Nebraska Press, 2003), 22–24. Bernal Díaz del Castillo's historical account was also a petition for recognition of his years of service that he documented, as well as an attempt to correct errors that were published about him especially by López de Gómara. Karl Kohut, "Crónicas y teoría historiográfica," in *Talleres de la memoria*, 154–55. Such favors were also petitioned in *relaciones* that were written on behalf of others, such as did Cortés's soldier, Andrés de Tapia, whose *relación* was a panegyric of Cortés. Andrés de Tapia, "Relación de algunas cosas de las que acaecieron al muy ilustre señor don Hernándo Cortés, marqués del valle, desde que se determinó a ir a descubrir tierra en la tierra Firme del mar Océano," in *Colección de documentos para la historia de México*, ed. Joaquín García Icazbalceta (Alicante: Biblioteca Virtual Miguel de Cervantes, 1999), 2:554–94.

130 Juan Durán Luzio, *Bartolomé de las Casas ante la conquista de América: las voces del historiador* (Heredia, Costa Rica: EUNA, 1992), chap. 2. Arias also contended that Las Casas's *Brevísima relación* gave rise to similar texts of legal discourse but did not identify these. *Retórica, historia y polémica*, 78.

131 "Lo que Suplica Don Francisco y relación que hace de agravios," in Lewis Hanke, "Un Festón de documentos lascasianos," *Revista Cubana* 16 (Julio–Diciembre 1941): 196–203. Tenamaztle was born in Nueva Galicia, educated by the Franciscans, and recognized as a *cacique* of Nochistlán by the Spaniards; as well, he was the successor of Aguano, the cacique who governed before the *entradas* of Núño de Guzmán. Tenamaztle participated in the Mixton war, was captured, and sent to Spain by Viceroy Mendoza where he met Las Casas. No documents exist telling of the fate of the Indigenous lord and/or his petition. According to a *relación* by Pedro de Ahumada, these "tribes" were still rebelling in 1562.

132 Salvador Álvarez, "Conquista y encomienda en la Nueva Galicia durante la primera mitad del siglo XVI: 'bárbaros' y 'civilizados' en las fronteras americanas," *Relaciones* 116, vol. XXIX (Otoño 2008): 180–81.

133 The letter requesting that Las Casas be protector and advocate for the Indigenous lords in their efforts to secure a remedy for the harm done to them by the Spaniards (as well as requesting the emperor to give them his help and support) was signed by seven *señores principales*: don Estevan de Guzmán, don Hernando Pimentel, don Antonio Cortés, don Juan de Cuyoacan, don Pedro de Moteucçuma (the son of Moctezuma II), don Alonso Ytztapalapa, don Diego de Mendoça, don Balthasar de San Gabriel; by three *alcaldes*: Christóval de Guzmán, Miguel Sánchez, don Jerónimo del Águila; and by two *regidores* in the name of all *regidores*: don Pedro de la Cruz and Pedro Almán. See "Carta de los señores y principales de la Nueva España al emperador Carlos V: en español, Tlacopan, 2 mayo 1556," in *La Nobleza Indígena del centro de México después de la conquista*, eds. Emma Pérez-Rocha y Rafael Tena (México, DF: Instituto Nacional de Antropología e Historia, 2000), 199–200. For the letter from Peru, see "Poder legal dado por Indios Peruanos á fray Bartolomé de Las Casas y Domingo de Santo

Tomás (19 Octubre 1556)," in Lewis Hanke, "Un Festón de documentos lascasianos," *Revista Cubana* 16 (Julio–Diciembre 1941): 204–08. Regarding advocacy for the Indigenous people, see James A. Brundage, *The Profession and Practice of Medieval Canon Law* (Hampshire: Ashgate/Variorum, 2004), II:243, V:533, XIV, 171.

134 However, cessation of such lawsuits would have robbed the Indigenous people of voice and agency. See Fray Pedro de Gante's "Letter to Charles V, Mexico City (1552)," in *Colonial Latin America: A Documentary History*, ed. Kenneth Mills, William B. Taylor, and Sandra Lauderdale Graham (Wilmington, DE: Scholarly Resources Books, 2002), 104–12; also see Owensby, *Empire of Law*, 19, 43.

135 "Relación cierta y breve de los desasosiegos sucedidos en Perú después de la muerte del Sr. Virrey D. Antonio de Mendoza, y de las causas de donde procedieron, por el licenciado Juan Fernández, Fiscal de Audiencia de Lima (1552)," in *Colección de documentos inéditos*, 3:246–71.

136 Fray Francisco de Carvajal. "Los males e injusticias, crueldades, robos y disensiones que hay en el Nuevo Reino de Granada," in José María Iraburu, *Hechos de los apóstoles en América* (Pamplona: Fundación Gratis Date, 1992), 39.

137 "Memorial que dió el bachiller Luis Sánchez, residente en Chillaron de Pareja, al Presidente Espinosa, en Madrid (26 Agosto 1566)," in *Colección de documentos inéditos*, 11:163–68.

138 Carolyn Miller, "Genre as Social Action," *Quarterly Journal of Speech* 70, no. 2 (1984): 151–76.

139 Kathleen A. Myers, "The Representation of New World Phenomena," in *Early Images of the Americas: Transfer and Invention*, edited by J. M. Williams and R. E. Lewis, 183–213 (Tucson: Univ. of Arizona Press, 1993), 183.

140 Anthony Pagden, "Ius et Factum: Text and Experience in the Writings of Bartolomé de Las Casas," in *New World Encounters*, ed. Stephen Greenblatt (Berkeley: Univ. of California Press, 1993), 88, 91–92; González-Echevarría, "The Law of the Letter: Garcilaso's Commentaries and the Origin of the Latin American Narrative," *The Yale Journal of Criticism* 1, no. 1 (1987): 109. The Dutch historian Jacob Presser coined the term "ego document" to describe texts written in the first-person singular ("I," "Ego"), which denomination does carry a negative connotation.

141 Roberto González-Echevarría, *Myth and Archive: A theory of Latin American narrative* (Durham: Duke Univ. Press, 1998), 56–60.

142 Fray Ramón Pané, *Relación acerca de las antigüedade de los indios*, notes and appendices, José Juan Arrom, Decimotecera edición (México, DF: Siglo XXI Editores S.A. de C.V., 2004), 3, 43, 45; "Relación del descubrimiento de las provincias de Antioquia por Jorge Robledo (1540)," in *Colección de documentos inéditos*, 2:291–356.

143 In his opening *argumento* written in 1552, Las Casas also wrote "Casas or Casaus." As was the case with other *tratados* that he published, Las Casas also wrote the *argumento* using third-person reporting. Knight, *An Account*, 1, 86.

144 Las Casas seemingly referred to this lineage to deflect the reader's attention from his alleged Jewish ancestry. Saint-Lu conjectured that Las Casas wished to distinguish himself from the Las Casas merchants of Andulasía—many of whom were *conversos*. "Introducción" in Las Casas, *Brevísima relación*, 28. See also Durán Luzio, *Bartolomé de Las Casas ante la Conquista*, 285.

145 Pané, *Relación acerca de las antigüedade de los indios*, 41–44; "Relación del descubrimiento de las provincias de Antiochia por Jorge Robledo," in *Colección de documentos inéditos*, 2:291; Knight, *An Account*, 3, 8, 10, 21.

146 *Criado* has several meanings, including someone who was raised doing service at court, someone who is under the protection of the Crown, or someone who served as a "lackey" for a conquistador.
147 "Carta al Emperador de Antonio de Aguayo," in *Epistolario de Nueva España 1505–1818*, 7:272.
148 "Carta de Felipe Gutiérrez al Emperador," in *Colección de documentos inéditos*, 3:202.
149 Knight, *An Account*, 4.
150 Ibid., 36, 56, 77, 80.
151 Ibid., 15.
152 Arias, *Retórica, historia y polémica*, 112, 147n10; Horst Pietschmann, "El desarrollo de la práctica del gobierno Indiano durante el Siglo XVI: novedades, relaciones personales, narrativa, simbolismo, normas y burocracia," in *Talleres de la memoria*, 9.
153 Mignolo, "Cartas, crónicas y relaciones del descubrimiento y la conquista," 71.
154 Pané, *Relación acerca de las antigüedades de los indios*, 3.
155 *Relación de las ceremonias y ritos y población y gobernación de los Indios de la provincia de Mechuacan, hecha al ilustrísimo señor don Antonio de Mendoza, virrey y gobernador desta Nueva España por su majestad … (1541)*, Reproducción facsímil del M. C. IV. 5 de El Escorial, Transcripción por José Tudela (Morelia: Balsal Editores S.A., 1977), IV, folio 3.
156 Knight, *An Account*, 3.
157 After Ferdinand I died, Spain was governed by two co-regents: Adrian of Utrecht, Charles's Flemish designee, and Cardinal Francisco Jiménez de Cisneros, OFM, Ferdinand's Spanish designee. On September 17, 1516, Cisneros appointed Las Casas to the official position of "Universal Protector of all the Indigenous people in the Indies." Lewis Hanke and Manuel Giménez Fernández, *Bartolomé de las Casas Bartolomé de las Casas 1474–1566: bibliografía crítica y cuerpo de materiales para el estudio de su vida, escritos, actuación y polémicas que suscitaron durante cuatro siglos*. Santiago de Chile: Fondo Histórico, 1954, 5; Manuel Giménez Fernández, *Bartolomé de las Casas: delegado de Cisneros para la reformación de las Indias 1516–1517*, vol. 1, Reprint of 1953 (Madrid: Consejo Superior de Investigaciones Científicas, 1984), 2:486.
158 Pietschmann, "El desarrollo de la práctica del gobierno Indiano," 8n12.
159 "Relación del oro que se fundió para la Hacienda Real en el mes de mayo 1519," in *Colección de documentos inéditos, Isla de Cuba*, 1:89–91; "Relación de los Oidores de la Audiencia de Santo Domingo, Espinosa y Zuazo, sobre lo que podría proveerse para la población de aquellas tierras (1528)," in *Colección de documentos inéditos*, 11:342–62.
160 However, Cortés was not with "the King's army," which—as Restall pointed out—did not exist. See *Cartas y relaciones de Hernán Cortés al emperador Carlos V*, colegidas y ilustradas por don Pascual de Gayangos (París: Imprenta Central de los Ferro-Carriles, 1866); Restall, *Seven Myths of the Spanish Conquest*, 33–43. For the *tratado* as a requested and required disposition, see Mignolo, "Cartas, crónicas y relaciones del descubrimiento y la conquista," 70; Patricio Edgardo Boyer, "Empire and American Visions of the Humane" (Ph.D. diss., Yale University, 2006), 25.
161 Knight, *An Account*, 2–3.
162 Higginson, "A Short History of the Right to Petition," 142–66. Note that petitions differ from *súplicas*, which are an appeal to a higher authority to overturn the decision of a lower authority. For example, *licenciado* Lorenzo Lebrón wrote a "Carta o Petición" to the prince—the highest authority—to

supplicate the "unequal judgments" rendered against him by the *Audiencia*. See *Epistolario de Nueva España 1505–1818*, 7:255–59.

163 By 1521, the practice of reporting to and/or appealing to authority became a standard procedure, which indicated that there was some level of freedom of speech and of expression in the New World and in Spain—whether in writing, in person, or through someone else. See Lewis Hanke, *Bartolomé de Las Casas: An Interpretation of His Life and Writings* (The Hague: Martinus Nijhoff, 1951), 42–3; Queralto Moreno, *El pensamiento*, 46–50.

164 A.R. Everton, *What is Equity About?* (London: Butterworth, 1970), 8.

165 Kathleen Ross, "History of the Conquest and Colonization of the New World: 1550–1620)," in *Cambridge History of Latin American Literature*, 104. See especially González-Echevarría, *Myth and Archive*; González-Echevarría, "The Law of the Letter," 107–32; Miguel Luque Talaván, *Un Universo de Opiniones: La Literatura Jurídica Indiana* (Madrid: Consejo Superior de Investigaciones. Científicas Instituto de Historia, 2003); Javier Barrientos Grandon, *La Cultura Jurídica en la Nueva España (Sobre la recepción de la tradición jurídica europea en el virreinato)* (México, DF: UNAM, 1993); Ripodas Ardanaz, "Los Indios y la Figura Jurídica del Rey durante el Quinientos," in *Justicia, Sociedad, Economía en la América Española (Siglos XVI, XVII, XVIII)* (Valladolid: Seminario Americanista de la Universidad de Valladolid, 1983), 275–322; Elizabeth Mertz pointed out that there is also "an exciting convergence" among a number of disciplinary specialties such as legal anthropology, linguistics, and critical legal theorists in their focus on law. See her "Legal Language: Pragmatics, Poetics, and Social Power," *Annual Review of Anthropology*, 23 (1994): 435–55.

166 González-Echevarría, "The Law of the Letter," 108. However, if it is taken into account that "America" was unknown in April of 1492, a more precise reference would have been to lands encountered "in India" or "the East" or "South Asia." By stipulating "America," González-Echevarría in effect endows those involved with prophetic insight!

167 The Catholic monarchs referred to themselves as the lords of any discovered lands and granted the titles of admiral, governor, and viceroy of these lands to Columbus. Alfonso de Diego García-Gallo, "El desarrollo de la historiografía jurídica Indiana," *Revista de estudios políticos* 70 (1953): 164.

168 González-Echevarría, *Myth and Archive*, 50.

169 González-Echevarría, "The Law of the Letter," 108.

170 González-Echevarría, *Myth and Archive*, 41.

171 Pennington and Müller, "The Decretists," 161–72; Antonio García y García, *En el entorno del derecho común* (Madrid: Editorial Dykinson, 1999), 79–83, 112–17.

172 María Paz Marín García, "Propuesta de Ramas y Géneros para los Documentos en la Traducción Jurídica," *Jornades de Foment de la Investigación* (Castellón de la Plana: Universitat Jaume, 2001), accessed July 29, 2020, https://core.ac.uk/download/pdf/61427355.pdf; Talaván, *Un Universo de Opiniones*, 229–54.

173 González-Echevarría, *Myth and Archive*, 48; Richard Kagan, *Lawsuits and Litigants in Castille, 1500–1700* (Chapel Hill: Univ. of North Carolina Press, 1981).

174 This segment relies on the scholarship of González-Echevarría, in his *Myth and Archive*, 41, 52–54.

175 Ripodas Ardanaz, "Los Indios y la Figura Jurídica del Rey," 306–07.

176 Kagan, *Lawsuits and Litigants*, 111–14; González-Echevarría, *Myth and Archive*, 41, 46–48, 52–54.

177 Kagan, *Lawsuits and Litigants*, 155.

178 Medieval jurisprudence also recognized the existence of higher, equal, and subordinate ranks or statuses in its delineation of the three divisions of law. See Alfonso X, *Las Siete Partidas del rey Don Alfonso el Sabio 1268.* (Madrid: Imprenta Real, 1807), 1:1.1.3.

179 About the shifting and complex relationship of the individual with central power, see Mertz, "Legal Language: Pragmatics, Poetics, and Social Power," 441: González-Echevarría, *Myth and Archive*, 39, 48; J. H. Parry, *The Spanish Theory of Empire in the Sixteenth Century* (New York: Octagon Books, 1940), 2; Danet, "Language in the Legal Process," 449.

180 González-Echevarría, *Myth and Archive*, 147.

181 J.H. Elliott, *Spain and its World: 1500–1700* (New Haven, CT: Yale Univ. Press, 1989), xi.

182 Talaván, *Un universo de opiniones*, 203–04.

183 Swales characterized these communities as having common goals, expertise, and mechanisms for information exchange and participation, *Genre Analysis*, 24–29, 58; Talaván, *Un universo de opiniones*, 205–06.

184 María Angeles Orts Llopis, María, "Legal Genres in English and Spanish: Some Attempts of Analysis," *Ibérica* 18 (2009): 113–14.

7 The Focus of Las Casas's Juridical Voice

Content of the *Brevísima Relación*

In 1552, Las Casas wrote in the prologue to his *Historia*: "Since about the year 1500, I have seen and traversed these Indies, and I know what I write"[1] (Figure 7.1).

This chapter focuses on the content of the *Very Brief Account* as a juridically based text and demonstrates that Las Casas maintained a juridical approach in its structural components, epistemological rationale, and analytic framework. Accordingly, this chapter will first elucidate the juridical character discernible in the structural components of the treatise, followed by an explication of the law-based theoretical rationale canopying his assessments, and concluding with an explication of the analytic framework that Las Casas employed in his condemnation of what he denominated as the destruction wrought by certain Spaniards (and Germans) in the Indies.[2] This analysis is concluded by elucidating the ethical-juridical basis of his approach, which was justice coupled with equity.

Juridical Structural Components

The structure of the content of the *Brevísima relación* consists of two introductory sections—an argument and a prologue, followed by the body of the treatise, and three segments of concluding statements. In this construction of the published *Very Brief Account*, Las Casas used what can be identified as juridical components, although modern equivalents for some of these genres are not known.[3] An initial indication of a juridical component is found in Las Casas's employment of *declarationes titulorum* (declarations of titles) to clearly distinguish and denominate his 1552 additions to the original 1542 text, namely, the titles of *Argument of the present epitome*, and *Prologue by Bishop don Fray Bartolomé de las Casas or Casaus, to the most high and potent lord Prince of all the Spains, don Felipe, our lord.*[4] By its formulaic reference to the prince as "the most high and potent lord," the title of the prologue also conveys the intention

Figure 7.1 Cover of the *Brevísima relación de la destruición de las Indias*. Published in 1552 in Seville.

to elicit action from him and also to imply that he will serve as judge in the matter at hand. Additionally, in the title of his *Argumento*, Las Casas referred to the 1552 version as an "*epítome*"—thus employing what Pennington and Müller regarded as the oldest form of juristic writing—a genre designed to convey the magnitude of the content of the report in spite of its brevity.[5] Further evidence of Las Casas's employment of components of juristic writing is found in the content of the *Argumento* and *Prólogo.*

The first structural component of the published *Very Brief Account* was the *Argumento*, which directed attention to juridical considerations to be taken into account.[6] Employing *argumento por analogía* (argument by analogy)—one of the forms of juridical argumentation, Las Casas first contrasted the epic aspect of "the marvelous discovery ... [and its] extraordinary ... incredible" feats with the epic proportions of the subsequent "slaughters and ruins of innocent people" as well as devastations and "depopulations of [Indigenous] villages, provinces, and kingdoms."[7] Again by this, Las Casas juxtaposes good and evil, this time in epic and perhaps exaggerated proportions. Then, after reminding the reader of his previous intervention that brought this ethical-juridical issue before the junta in 1542 and resulted in the New Laws, Las Casas reiterated the *querella* he had made at that time—that "men of reprobate mind" committed and continue to commit "these wicked deeds out of greed and ambition." He concluded with a *petición* to Prince Philip to read the treatise and to deny these Spaniards both licenses and authority for conquest and slave-trading.[8] In this development of the *Argumento*, Las Casas also followed the parameters of the *exordium* from the organizational scheme of juridical writing that was refined by Cicero and Quintilian.[9] As in the civil and canonistic legal genre of the *argumento*, the purpose of an *exordium* was to lay out and narrow down the issue and also to evoke sympathy for the cause.[10]

The second structural component of the published *Brevísima relación* was the *Prólogo*, which corresponded in several ways to fifteenth-century exemplars of prologues and *exordia*. For example, by directly addressing the twenty-six-year-old prince-regent, this section began with a dedication of the *tratado* that, according to Carmen Codoñer, was typical for such texts.[11] Furthermore, as an *exordium*, this prologue to the prince also included exhortatory references to kingly attributes and royal responsibilities—references that were encomiastic of Philip as future king and judge.[12] In accord with the civil and canonical ethical-juridical norm of equity, he allocated primary responsibility to the king to remedy any wrongs brought to his attention. As will be seen, he does not blame the monarch for the wrongdoings. Then, as was fundamental in all *exordia* as well as in prologues, Las Casas presented himself as a credible authority by citing his "fifty years and more [of] experience ... in these lands"; he further acknowledged that he was duty-bound to speak up, or become an accomplice himself. Subsequently, Las Casas alleged that "if the *tiranos* be allowed [licenses], these evil men shall, most surely, commit once more [these] iniquitous [and] tyrannous [deeds] of the conquest." He accused these Spaniards of the most serious of *querellas*: their deeds were violations of "all divine, natural, and human law." Continuing this line of argument based on higher principles of the law (*argumento a partir de principios del derecho*) and especially in accord with the juridical norm of justice, Las Casas warned the prince that if he gave permission for licenses for conquest to these Spaniards, he would violate "divine and natural law," as well as commit "most grave mortal sin" punishable by "eternal torment."[13] Note that Las Casas's warning means "in the future," and thus he ignores any culpability that may already reside with the monarch for having approved conquering expeditions in the past. Finally, in his conclusion, Las Casas had recourse to a legal procedure known as the *exhorto*, which consisted of one authority asking another of equal authority over the same jurisdiction to comply with a request. Accordingly, at the end of the prologue, Las Casas encouraged and petitioned Prince Philip "to persuade His Majesty [his father, Charles V]" not to allow such "noxious and detestable enterprises."[14]

The third structural component of the published *Very Brief Account* constituted the body of the treatise, which encompassed the complete text of the original 1542 *epítome*, including its untitled introduction, twenty chapters, and the initial concluding testament.[15] As a *relación* of the facts and a *denuncia* of the evils and harm done, this section of the *tratado* clearly reflected juridical genres as have been explicated in Chapter 6. In its internal structure, this body of the text began with an introduction that first lauded the beauty of the land and the goodness of the Indigenous inhabitants. This was followed by a depiction of what he characterized as the evil deeds of conquistadors during their *entradas*, the subsequent wars and forms of bondage that he believed had devastated and depopulated the lands, and which Las Casas charged were motivated by greed and ambition. This contrast of the good and the evil mirrors the sequencing of the *argumento*, and functions first to elicit sympathy for the Indigenous people (*ab nostra persona*) and then to remove any sympathy for their Spanish adversaries (*ab adversariorum persona*). This kind of oppositional depiction was common in jurists' constructions of their arguments and also in Quintilian juridical writing, and it was utilized by Las Casas both in his general introductory statement and in the twenty chapters that followed.[16]

Accordingly, the individual chapters, which presented the territory by territory trajectory of the *entradas*, were structured according to three categories of information, although not necessarily narrated in an identical sequence. Similar to the introduction, each of the official accounts about a territory consisted of more specific laudatory data about the lands and people of the region, information about the *entradas* and of the destructions the invaders wrought, as well as examples of their overwhelming cruelty. However, in these *relaciónes* of the facts in the body of the tract, Las Casas distanced himself from the particularized tangle that would constitute a history of the Indies to bring to light what he saw as general principles underlying events—such as "the greater the discoveries, the greater the cruelties," or as a single governing matrix—such as that of the Indigenous peoples' goodness abused by certain Spaniards' evilness. Las Casas's ability to do this reflected what Mousourakis identified as a unique quality of a jurist: "the ability to look beyond the accidental elements of the individual case, the *species facti*, and to define the relevant legal problem as a *quaestio iuris*, that is, as a question of justice."[17]

Accordingly, the denunciations contained in the chapters tended to be based predominantly on considerations of justice. One was justice in the sense of "what was due" the Indigenous people by reason of their human attributes, their salvific entitlements, and fundamental shared unities (as persons and as nations). Another was the injustice of encomienda and slavery in addition to the injustice of conquests, compulsory vassalage, and forced conversion. To strengthen these premises that anchor the *Very Brief Account* and to remind its readers of the need to correct these injustices, Las Casas's *denuncias* were intermittently intertwined with requests for divine or royal intervention, and sometimes both. Consequently, the chapters of the *Brevísima relación* can also be regarded as Pagden maintained, as "a series of overlapping depositions" that stated the facts as Las Casas perceived them, denounced the injustice, and petitioned for redress.[18]

The fourth structural component of the *tratado* consisted of two sets of concluding statements. In the initial concluding statement of the tract, Las Casas disclosed his personal motivations for writing the original 1542 *relación de denuncias*; he asserted that two of his guiding life-goals were that the Indigenous inhabitants of the Indies may "know their Creator and be saved," and that God may not punish and destroy "my native land."[19] As well, he expressed his hope that the emperor, as "lover and cultivator of justice," might "bring an end to so many evils and bring relief to that new world, which God has given him."[20] These motivations and sentiments, which were geared to evoke agreement with Las Casas's assessments, generally corresponded to the *peroratio* (conclusion) of juridical writing.[21]

In the second conclusion or *post scriptum* penned in 1546, Las Casas added information of a juridical nature about the promulgation of the New Laws and about many Spaniards' refusal "to obey the Laws." He ended this summation with two indictments intended to move the prince to act: the injustices "dishonor God" and they "rob and destroy the King."[22] (Here, too, the monarch is cast as a victim and not as a perpetrator of injustices.) As a final plea, Las Casas appended additional contemporaneous evidence, in the form of "an excerpt of a letter" written by the unknown conquistador "so that the prince may know and be certain of what [certain] Spaniards have done since the discovery to this day."[23]

Finally, in recent discussions related to the juridical components of this treatise, the question was asked whether the major and minor juristic components that Las Casas employed in the *Brevísima relación* might be similar to those used in an oral or written court record. In court procedures in the Spanish colonial world, each side drew up depositions and gathered witness testimony separately (with a notary writing down responses to a set of questions).[24] All the documents produced would be read and adjudicated by the judge. In a very real way, the *Very Brief Account* resembles a one-sided deposition and its partisan testimony. Moreover, as a canon lawyer or *fiscal*, Las Casas was no doubt familiar with the components of legal proceedings and, as a legal advocate, he would have utilized the full armature of jurisprudential defense for the Indigenous people. Furthermore, utilizing juridical building blocks in his treatise would have been highly appropriate for an official report (*relación*) and denunciation (*denuncia*) of the evils and harm done. Additionally, the juridical structural components of the *Very Brief Account* were also both canopied and permeated by an epistemological rationale that utilized the building blocks of the legal order established by divine providence.

Epistemological Rationale

The epistemological rationale for the content of the *Brevísima relación* was based on Aquinas's understanding of divine providence—that is, of God's relationship to the world. Two dimensions of providence are discernible in this Thomistic theological-philosophical understanding: one horizontal, in its interpretation of history as the unfolding of God's plan and governance in the world; the other vertical, in its conception of the universe as a divinely ordered whole.[25] This conception of providence—and, in particular, of providence as divine governance and as an ordering of the world in accord with eternal, divine, natural, and human laws—constituted the epistemological basis of the juridical approach that Las Casas took in his articulations and assessments in the *Very Brief Account*. To understand the significance of this theoretical rationale, first, this section will elucidate providential interpretations of history in ancient Greco-Roman and Jewish thought that influenced the Christian perspective, followed by explication of Las Casas's and others' providentialist interpretations of the "discovery" and conquest. Next, the two dimensions of the Thomistic understanding of divine providence will be explicated to elucidate the juridical basis of the meta-narrative of divine providence employed by Las Casas in the *Brevísima relación*.

The Judeo-Christian providential interpretation of history was influenced by articulations in ancient Greco-Roman thought about the design and governance of the universe.[26] Plato introduced the expression "divine providence" as a metaphysical first principle, which Stoics identified initially as a material first principle and subsequently as an end-directed *logos* (order) permeating the universe, and which Middle Platonists combined with the idea of a religious first principle identified with God.[27] By introducing history as the history of salvation that began at the moment of creation, the Jewish meta-narrative of God's providence became an "expiatory pilgrimage" after the original sin of Adam and Eve, and posited the people of Israel as God's chosen agents to prepare for the coming of the redeeming Messiah.[28] The early Christian meta-narrative continued the interpretation of history as the history of salvation but radically changed it because of the belief in the advent of God-made-human in the person of Jesus Christ, who is destined to return in the Second Coming. In this Judeo-Christian providentialist plan of the eternal-distant-and-abstract God who became temporal-near-and-concrete, the transcendent God is the exemplar of beauty, truth, goodness, justice, equity, and temperance par excellence. While Christian notions in the Latin West about God's providence were most famously associated with Augustine's teachings, these beliefs were most fully developed in the High Middle Ages by Aquinas.[29] In the Christian meta-narrative in the teachings of the "Angelic Doctor," the course of history was guided by the divine plan or exemplar for all of creation that emanated from the divine intellect, and by the divine governance that directed all creation through the divine will.[30]

However, from the early modern Christian meta-narrative about the providential character of the *Orbis Christianus*, which flowed from contemporaneous (including Habsburg) understandings of the collective Christian world, Spain embraced a "universal, progressive, and providential conception of history."[31] The universalistic dimension was derived from medieval theology that conceived of Christianity as worldwide even though Christendom constituted only a small part of the known world.[32] The progressive dimension was bolstered by the *translatio imperii* with its political connotations of imperial expansion and its religious considerations of messianism and eschatology. The providential dimension was quickened by the unforeseen discovery of new lands and of until-then-unknown civilizations.[33] These three dimensions of Spain's conception of history coalesced in the opportunities engendered by the "discovery" of the Indies for Spain to write a providentialist-imperialist history. That is, the discovery as a manifest act of divine providence also resulted in another perceived providential act: the initiation of the Spanish empire.[34]

In the *Brevísima relación*, Las Casas extolled the "marvelous discovery" of the Indies as an "episode of salvation history."[35] In contrast, Oviedo viewed the "discovery" as a "stellar episode" in universal providential-imperialist history.[36] That is, Las Casas focused on God's providential plan for the Indies within the Judeo-Christian framework of salvation history, while Oviedo focused on God's providential plan for Spain and its empire within the framework of a "universal" providentialist-imperialist history as did Oviedo. Nevertheless, from the perspective of the Spanish Crown and the Spanish people (including Las Casas), the "discovery" was indeed a manifest act of divine providence. Accordingly, Isabel and Ferdinand informed Columbus prior to his second journey that "it pleased God our Lord in his great mercy to grant the discovery of those islands and mainlands to the King and Queen."[37] Spaniards saw themselves as the "chosen people," and faced the dual task of a papal-decreed providential mission to Christianize the inhabitants and of a crown-perceived providential opportunity to expand its embryonic empire. The first task obliged catechizing in word and deed; the second task generated conquests by lethal violence and maltreatment by forced labor.

Las Casas's response to these tasks in the *Brevisíma relación* was providentialist-soteriological in its focus on God's plan for the Christianization and salvation of the Indigenous people, and concomitantly in its rejection of the conquest and enslavement mode of imperialist expansion.[38] Columbus's and Cortés's responses to the dual task generated different providential interpretations of history. For example, Columbus's response contained a providentialism akin to a personal messianism in which he viewed himself as a chosen instrument of divine providence; his response also consisted of expansionist activities linked to trade and other commercial interests; however, his eventual enslavement and seizure of many Caribbean natives would have been contrary to perceived providentialist endeavors.[39] Cortés's response can also be regarded as a personal-messianic kind of providentialism—a stance that was sustained by the providentialist-messianic-millenarianism of Friar Toribio de Motolinía, OFM, and other Franciscan mendicants.[40] However, rather than being simply an instrument of providence, the conqueror of the Nahuatl-speaking Mexica (Aztec) viewed himself as a protagonist of history, for whom divine providence was simply a medium to strengthen and aid human's aspirations and actions.[41] Cortés justified his actions by using providential narrative and symbols, while his self-ascribed protagonistic role subverted God's providential agency.[42] In addition, his expansionist aims and activities derived from strongly held military, political, and material interests, which resulted in conquests and enslavement that many Christian Spaniards perceived as part of the providential plan for unification under the civil crown and ecclesial mantle.[43] Such notions of providentialist unfolding tended to be typical of Spanish Habsburg historiography at that time.

Las Casas's providentialist-soteriological focus in the *Brevísima relación* drew from the horizontal dimension of the Thomistic understanding of divine providence in the course of history as the divine plan conceived by the divine intellect, and as divine governance exercised by the divine will. Las Casas first elucidated two observable features of

God's providential plan (or exemplar) of salvation history in the Indies: the creation of these lands and its diverse peoples, and the proper supernatural destiny of the inhabitants. As such, in the untitled introduction to the body of the *Very Brief Account*, he wrote "God did set down upon those lands …the greatest part of the entire human lineage," and inhabitants "of all kinds" for these lands, who were "a simple people … most humble … pacific … slow to take offense."[44] Later, in his descriptions of the inhabitants of New Spain, and particularly of the Yucatec Maya, Las Casas declared that "God set in those leagues … so great populations" that were "prudent in policía," which perhaps implicitly recognized the complex political organization of these more advanced societies.[45]

Surely, Las Casas knew that all the Indigenous inhabitants of the Indies were not "simple" and "pacific" people and that, for example, the Aztecs were sophisticated and militaristic people. Why would Las Casas choose to describe highly complex state-level and imperialistic societies in such seemingly simplistic terms? Perhaps he wrote the treatise as a concise chronology; his narration in the *Brevísima relación* began apparently with the Taínos. Moreover, by 1542 when he initially produced the *tratado*, he was also working on his *Historia*, which began with the first two decades of the Spanish presence in the Indies. Furthermore, since the body of the narrative of the 1552 published *Very Brief Account* was virtually identical to the 1542 summary account, detailed information about the interim decade was not for the most part included. Another possibility might have been his wish to give priority to his trope of "good Indigenous people" and certain "evil Spaniards," and thus was silent in this treatise about differentiations, which he made in his other writings about Indigenous peoples. Related is the possibility that he wanted the treatise to be a "short read"; consequently, he did not include a lot of distinctions or other nuances so as to focus primarily on his core message. Another possibility may have been his desire to persistently assert God's continuing providence, such as he did when writing about New Spain and the Yucatán. Furthermore, Las Casas may also have been intent on driving home his conviction that the "simple" and "prudent" and "good" Indigenous people were also specially favored by God as "the poorest of the poor," as Gustavo Gutiérrez contended. Finally, Las Casas's portrayal of the Indigenous people as "simple, … humble, … and pacific" may be an indicator of his possible tendency to "objectify" them, an issue that will be addressed in the concluding chapter.

In his characterization of the Indigenous peoples, Las Casas also drew on Aquinas's teaching that, in accord with the divine exemplar, all created things were given natural dispositions and existential conditions as a means to achieve their proper proximate ends, which for human beings—as rational, free, and social creatures possessing intellect and will—would lead them ultimately to eternal salvation.[46] Believing that the divine plan for the Indigenous included these needed proximate means and conditions in addition to their ultimate salvation, Las Casas asserted that the Indigenous were of "lively understanding, [and] very apt and tractable for all fair doctrine."[47] Moreover, as he had maintained all his life, the principal reason for the Spaniards' presence among the Indigenous was their evangelization and eternal salvation. Gutiérrez observed that Las Casas espoused a predestination orientation that was proper in his time; accordingly, in his assessments about the Indigenous peoples, the Sevillian truly believed that "God must have disposed" these people with what was natural and needed—including a capacity for doctrine and grace—for their advancement and salvation, as well as had in mind a pre-planned time for their calling and conversion.[48]

Subsequently, Las Casas drew from Thomistic teaching that God's providence also extended, through the divine will, to the governance of the created order. Accordingly, at the very beginning of the Prologue to Prince Philip, Las Casas invoked God's will for the governance of the Indies by stating, "Divine providence has ordered in this world that, for the direction and common utility of the human lineage, the world be constituted by Kingdoms and peoples."[49] For the Dominican, these kingdoms that God's providence ordained also included the Indigenous kingdoms. Accordingly, throughout the text, Las Casas consistently referred to the Indigenous territories as kingdoms, which also implied, as he publicly proclaimed in the 1550–1551 debate with Sepúlveda, that the Indigenous were capable of governing themselves. (As indeed they demonstrated through the *cabildo* and later the *ayuntamiento.*)

In the Thomistic understanding of the divine scheme of things, because God willed to share governance with all created things in accordance with their nature, humans participated in the governance of "Kingdoms and peoples."[50] The king was preeminent among the intermediaries to whom God delegated governance.[51] In the Roman and canonist traditions, the monarch was an intermediary of God's will governed by divine right, and was the sole legislator and ultimate authoritative interpreter of the law.[52] In the Christian perspective of sixteenth-century Spain, God governed the temporal order through the Spanish monarchs (and, Las Casas would add, in the Indies through the natural lords) and their representatives. Indeed, in his *Crónica de los Señores Reyes Católicos Don Fernando y Doña Isabel de Castilla y de Aragón*, diplomat and historian Fernando del Pulgar (c. 1436–c. 1492) claimed that the actions of the monarchs were manifestations of the will and governance of God. In his *Historia general*, Oviedo noted that the universal monarchy of Charles V was "providentially inspired" and, in his *Historia ecclesiástica indiana*, Gerónimo de Mendieta, OFM (1525–1604) regarded the monarchs as apostles.[53] This delegation of divine authority through monarchs and their representatives was part of contemporaneous understanding about the divine hierarchical ordering of the world by providence, in addition to legitimizing existing royal governments and monarchs.

This conception of a divinely ordered world constituted the vertical dimension of the Thomistic understanding of divine providence, and consisted of four kinds of law that were hierarchically arranged: eternal, divine, natural, and human.[54] The supreme law was eternal law, which corresponded to the preexisting exemplar (plan) and governance of divine providence.[55] Since eternal law was the preexisting rational plan in God's mind and was the ultimate source of all law, all other plans of governance must be derived from eternal law.[56] As such, each type of law in the tripartite scheme of divine, natural, and human laws was derived from and participated in some manner in this eternal law or, in other words, in God's providence.[57]

Divine law, which pertained to the supernatural order of grace, was enacted by God, and participated most perfectly in eternal law because it "directed humans to their supernatural end, that is, their eternal salvation."[58] In the Judeo-Christian tradition, divine law was made known to humankind through revelation in the scriptures and most fully in the person of Jesus Christ, God-made-flesh, through whom the Church was founded.[59] In the *Brevísima relación*, Las Casas employed what "Jesus Christ… had commanded in his Law" as the criterion for judgment.[60] In Aquinas's teachings, divine law was necessary because human laws could only govern external actions, whereas divine law guarded against errors in human judgment, and regulated both internal dispositions and external acts. Moreover, given that human law could not prohibit or punish all evil action without removing much good as well, divine law was required so that ultimately no evil would go unpunished.[61]

Natural law, which pertained to understanding God's designs and ordinances for creation, was derived from God as supreme intellect and will—as supreme rationality. By the natural law divinely implanted in human nature, women and men participated in the eternal law through their rational faculties of intellect and will.[62] These divinely endowed rational components of human nature inclined humans to act reasonably and justly in accord with God's intrinsically rational exemplar, and to seek the good in accord with God's inherently just will.[63] Reason, as a unique human ability in the order of creation, was the foundation of natural law.[64] Las Casas inferred this primacy of reason in natural law by his reference in the *Brevísima relación* to the tripartite scheme of law as "of God, reason, and human law" instead of his usual "divine, natural, and human law."[65] Natural law also imbued humans with abilities to discern good and evil, and—in accord with the innate first principle of natural law—"to do good and to avoid evil." In this manner and out of this knowledge and also by virtue of the human attributes of rationality, freedom, and sociability, humans were to choose to conform their lives to the divine universal rational order and to the objective moral order (natural law) built into human nature.[66] In these components, abilities, and attributes as well as in the knowledge of what ought to be observed, natural law was everlasting, immutable, and universal. However, the abilities to fulfill "secondary goods," that were related to preservation of life, worship of God, procreation and education of offspring, pursuit of knowledge and truth, and establishment of civil social orders, were mutable and depended on the justice of human law.[67]

Human law, which pertained to law actually enforced or positive law, participated in eternal law and was derived from natural law insofar as these ordinances "partook of right reason."[68] As the social dimension or as an externalization of natural law, human law must promote the application and fulfillment of the natural law.[69] As an enactment promulgated by legitimate authority and supporting the common good, human law must be compatible with natural justice.[70] The fundamental determinant of the justice or injustice of human law was rationality; human law that was "just" both shared in God's rationality and expressed humans' unique rational nature.

Aquinas also distinguished various divisions of positive human law.[71] The law of nations (*ius gentium*) pertained to unchangeable and universal customs dictated by natural reason and by humans' social nature; this law bound people together in societal arrangements by virtue of the social need, for example, for government, trade, and ownership.[72] Civil law (*ius civilis*) was, however, both mutable and contextual because its promotion and application of natural law was dependent on the particular geographic, historical, and social circumstances of the community or society.[73] Of the various forms of human law, the law of nations (*ius gentium*), civil law, and ecclesial law were among those that Las Casas also took into account in his *Brevísima relación*.

Within Aquinas's hierarchy of laws, the promulgation of human laws was necessary to govern personal behavior and to regulate humans' relationships with others. As understood in Christian thought, the practical shaping of human law that was reasonable and just must be guided by natural and divine laws. To accomplish this, these two higher levels of law functioned as theoretical quarries from which to extract knowledge and understanding of the natural and supernatural orders. In effect, these three levels of law—human, natural, and divine—were mortared together epistemologically in a hierarchical manner in accord with God's intellect and will, that is, in accord with eternal law. Human law must be compatible with natural and divine laws. Natural law necessarily reflected the rationality of eternal law and the pursuit of the good as known through natural revelation. Divine law legislated aspects of the plan and will of God that are known through supernatural revelation and dictate ordinances for the Christian life and for the attainment of humans' ultimate end: union with God by eternal salvation. From this structuring, Aquinas posited the tripartite scheme of divine, natural, and human laws that governed all of temporal life. Las Casas employed this tripartite construct of the meta-narrative of divine providence in his condemnation of what he saw as the evils and harm done in the Indies.

From a review of samples of literature covering fifty years of the Spaniards' presence in the Indies, recourse to this tripartite scheme of law was not typical in the communications of bishops and friars to the Crown. However, one undated *relación* written by Bishop Garay, OC, about the usury taking place in the Antilles forthrightly used the tripartite scheme to condemn the activities of Spanish vendors, who purchased commodities such as wheat, fish, and bread cheaply and sold them at high prices, and of money-lenders who charged exceedingly high interest rates.[74] In his framing of usury in terms of the tripartite of law, Bishop Garay charged that these Spaniards' lack of "fear of God" violated divine law. Their over-charging also violated the seventh commandment of divine law and the mandate of natural law to do good. Their theft of the royal *rentas* violated human law.

For the most part, the tripartite construct seemed to have been employed primarily in the writings of Dominicans. This is not surprising because, for example, Franciscans would draw from Scotist scholasticism, and Dominicans from Thomistic scholasticism, especially in view of their order's reform legislating the study of their medieval confrere Aquinas. Accordingly, Pedro de Córdoba (Las Casas's mentor) and his Dominican confreres in Santo Domingo employed this framework of divine, natural, and human laws in their 1517 letter to the Hieronymites about the devastation in Hispaniola.[75] Sometime after 1534, Vicente Valverde, Dominican bishop of Cuzco, used the same framework when he informed the emperor about ecclesial and general governance in Peru.[76] This is not to infer, however, that non-Dominican Church functionaries and laypersons in the Indies did not make reference to and/or deliberate on eternal, divine, natural, or human laws. Rather, they tended to describe the obligations and/or infractions of one or another of these laws in their discourses but did not utilize the Thomistic tripartite framework. This kind of recourse to one or another of these laws was also evident in Spain in the articulation of grievances in terms of natural law and freedom, as well as of biblical ideas of equality during the 1520–1521 *Communeros*' revolt in Castile and, before this, in the 1462–1486 Catalan war of the *Remences*.[77] The Castilian communities failed to accomplish their goals, but the Catalan enserfed peasants achieved the official abolition of servitude.

Studied employment of the tripartite scheme of law is found, however, in the writings of the *Escuela Española*, in particular, those of de Soto and of Vitoria.[78] Domingo de Soto devoted the first three volumes of his ten-volume *De justitia y iure*, to an in-depth study of eternal, divine, natural, and human laws, with particular emphasis in the latter on *ius gentium* and on justice.[79] Vitoria systematically employed the tripartite scheme of law in his *Relecciones*.[80] Beyond these scholastic arenas of discourse, sixteenth-century wisdom literature also utilized the Thomistic distinctions of law as, for example, in Cardano's *De Sapientia* in 1544 wherein the Italian scholar treated the tripartite framework of laws as interrelated kinds of wisdom.[81]

In Lascasian scholarship, the tripartite scheme of law has not been identified nor explicated as part of the genre of Thomistic scholasticism. For example, while Saint-Lu contended that the *Very Brief Account* constituted a "very clearly formulated juridical refutation" of some Spaniards' violation of "natural and divine law," he did not develop this as belonging to the ecclesial juridical tradition.[82] While Reyes Cano discussed how the Thomistic interpretation of divine law was the core of the treatise's legal reflection, he did not address its relationships to other kinds of law present in Aquinas's scheme.[83] Similarly, Waldegaray regarded the *Brevísima relación* as a *denuncia* of the violations of divine, natural, and human laws but did not develop this insight in her literary analysis of the treatise.[84]

In contrast, this study locates the tripartite scheme of divine, natural, and human laws as part of the vertical dimension of divine providence in the Christian meta-narrative as explicated by Aquinas. This scheme of law belonged to the genre of Thomism, which, like the general genre of scholasticism, was part of the juridical and ideational tradition of the medieval and early modern Church.[85] Las Casas's utilization of this law-based epistemology was in keeping with his penchant for the juridical. Moreover, this approach was enhanced by his knowledge of canon law, which as practical theology was a composite of divine, natural, and human laws. As will be shown in the next section, Las Casas employed Aquinas's systematized tripartite scheme of law—canopied by God's eternal law that guides the history of salvation—as the specific analytic and juridical framework for his articulation and assessment of the evils and harm done in the Indies.

Analytic Framework

In Las Casas's assessment of the course of salvation history, which he interpreted in accord with the meta-narrative of divine providence, certain conquistadors, encomenderos, and royal officials disregarded and disesteemed the providential exemplar and governance of God in the Indies. Las Casas charged that their deeds had resulted in the *"destruición" de las Indias*. Accordingly, in his *Very Brief Account*, he articulated what he perceived as widespread "destruction," as well as certain specific details of the cruelties and related events that took place. Prior to examining the juridical approach that Las Casas employed in writing his treatise, the trope of destruction needs to be parsed, and the way in which he presents "facts" and narratives of events also needs to be addressed.

With respect to the trope of destruction, a careful examination of the text reveals that Las Casas never used the trope to mean "total destruction." He never employed any type of qualifying adjective that specified or inferred "total destruction." Moreover, there was never total "destruction of the Indies," nor was the "destruction" the same everywhere. Destruction may be an acceptable interpretation to describe what took place in the Caribbean islands and in some lowland tropical areas, given the combination of brutal military conquest, the introduction of previously unknown forms of labor and consequent changes in lifestyle, in addition to the advent of disease and epidemics among already weakened Indigenous populations. In this way, some Indigenous peoples and cultures were decimated. However, in other more heavily populated and more temperate areas, such as Central and Southeastern Mesoamerica and much of the Andean zone, this kind of complete destruction did not take place. Instead, there was death, dislocation, and destruction of particular things; yet, there was also cultural change, evolution, and survival.[86] Proof that there was never "total destruction of the Indies" in these regions is also found in the many groups today that identify themselves as Nahuas, Zapotecs, Purepechas, Mixtecos, Otomies, Aymara, Quechua, Quiche, Tzutujil, and so forth. In the more remote areas, many of these peoples still govern their own communities, speak their own languages, eat much of the same food, and use the same herbal remedies as in 1491. Finally, most Spaniards (including most conquistadors) did not want to destroy the Indigenous people. They needed them for labor.

Considering the above explanations, what Las Casas probably meant by "destruction" was at best massive damage or perhaps multi-faceted destructive acts that might lead to eventual destruction in a "total" sense. Why then would Las Casas use this trope of destruction? Four reasons can be conjectured. The first relates to his knowledge of a time period that encompassed the worst and most sustained destructive elements after the Spaniards' initial encounters with the Indigenous inhabitants of the Indies. He spoke from extensive personal experience and drew on information from others who lived in these and other territories and regions. The second pertains to his sense of a God-given mission whereby he felt compelled in conscience to stop the destruction by seeking a total remedy for the injustices the Indigenous inhabitants suffered. This urgency also extended in conscience to his native land, which he feared would be destroyed by God because, if for no other reason, all Spaniards (from the monarch(s) on down) had benefited and were benefiting from ill-gotten goods. The third stems from his profound conviction that divine providence would not ordain the deaths, much less the destruction, of a "lineage of humankind." Instead, as he penned in the prologue, he believed that "divine providence had ordained that … the world would be constituted by kingdoms and peoples." The fourth relates to his well-honed skills, including in rhetoric. Did Las Casas employ a rhetorical device by titling his treatise in a manner that resembled the title of medieval accounts about "the destruction of Spain" (although Spain was never destroyed) to bring closer to home the horrific experiences related to conquest? Is Las Casas's use of the term "destruction" a rhetorical device that uses exaggeration for effect? Perhaps to present his case in the starkest and most forceful way possible, he deliberately wrote in a compelling polemical manner (as could be demonstrated by other literary devices and strategies he employed in the treatise).

For example, in Las Casas's account about the imprisonment of Motecuhzoma, he wrote that

at the entrance to the city, [Motecuhzoma] himself came out in person

> ... to receive [Cortés and his men], and he accompanied them to the palaces in which he ordered that they be lodged, that same day, as I have been told by some who were there present, but with some feigning they were sure, the Spaniards took the great king Motenzuma (*sic*) and set eighty men to guard him, and afterward they put him in irons.[87]

Las Casas was accurate about the "facts" that the first encounter between Hernando Cortés and Motecuhzoma took place at the entryway to the city of Tenochtitlán, and that the Spaniards were lodged as guests in the palace. However, Las Casas's account differed from standard accounts in the statement that "on that same day," the "great king" was taken prisoner. Two notable accounts by Bernal Díaz and Fray Francisco de Aguilar allocated a longer period of time between the Spaniards being lodged as guests and Motecuhzoma being made prisoner by them: a week or more according to Bernal Díaz; five days according to Fray Aquilar.[88] Unless this difference is due to misinformation from "those who were there present," Las Casas's collapsed time in his presentation of the "facts." He may have done this as a rhetorical device to create a starker and more shocking event that emphasized the "evil" Spaniards who were so duplicitous as compared to the "good" Aztecs who were so hospitable. This same tendency and ability to report events (and facts) in emotionally compelling ways was also evident in Las Casas's narration about the massacre at Cholula. According to Saint-Lu's study that compared Las Casas's account with that in the Florentine Codex, the details were identical but not the sentiment. Both accounts narrated that Cortés's party—although allegedly welcomed by the Cholulans—killed a great number of the Indigenous inhabitants there, including their lords. The accounts differed in that the sentiment expressed in the Codex account was one of sheer bottomless grief, whereas Las Casas's account, which mirrored the deep sorrow, voiced vehement outrage as well.[89]

Another consequence of Las Casas's collapsing of the time period between Motecuhzoma's welcome and his imprisonment relates to the omission of details. For example, Bernal Díaz wrote about how the Spaniards prayed, and asked and received permission from Motecuhzoma to construct a chapel in their guest quarters where Mass was celebrated (until the wine ran out). Furthermore, both Bernal Díaz and Fray Aguilar told of the rumor from other "good Indians" (friendly to the Spaniards) that Motecuhzoma had been advised to allow the Spaniards to enter and lodge in the city so that the "good Aztecs" could kill them later. For Las Casas to have included such details would have contradicted and weakened the trope of the "good Indigenous people" and "evil Spanish people" that pervaded his *Very Brief Account.*[90]

From these examples, two of the various rhetorical strategies that Las Casas employed in his *tratado* are observable: his evident re-shaping of the narrative about events by collapsing time, and his selective presentation of facts by omitting certain details. While such rhetorical strategies have implications for the historical accuracy of his *relación* (and will be addressed in the next chapter), Las Casas apparently used these strategies at times to support his counter-discourse (or anti-heroic narrative) about the conquest, which was that the actions of certain "evil" Spaniards (and Germans) were destroying lands, possessions, and populations of the "good" Indigenous people. However, he did not limit his treatise to a portrayal of the "destruction" wrought, or to a description of the "evil actions" in the events he narrated and facts he marshaled. He also denounced and condemned them on the basis of the canonistic and Thomistic tripartite scheme of law. This evaluative juridical architecture frames the dramatic counter-narrative of the *Brevísima relación.*

As such, this study focuses on the juridical approach taken by Las Casas in this treatise, which is based on his ethical-juridical judgment that "the evils and harm" committed by certain Spaniards against the Indigenous inhabitants of the Indies are violations of "all divine, natural, and human law."[91] In the Prologue to Prince Philip, this juridical *querella* was explicitly stated twice as well as implicitly several times in the descriptive narrative.[92] Although Las Casas did not systematically develop this juridical contention in the text, he did present ample descriptive evidence, albeit selective, and also significant narrative commentary to support his judgment.[93] That is, what underscored the evidence and commentary that Las Casas presented about the "destruction" of the Indies was a purposive analytic framework based on considerations of divine, natural, and human laws.

To explicate this analytic framework, this study will employ the juridical figure of tyranny. Utilizing this composite of tyranny is particularly appropriate for several reasons. First, Las Casas regarded the presence of certain Spaniards (and Germans) in the Indies as totally tyrannical.[94] The *Brevísima relación* is replete with descriptions and designations of tyrannous behaviors, attitudes, and persons. Indeed, this trope of tyranny, as will be shown, pervades the content of the *Very Brief Account.* Second, Las Casas modified the manuscript for the 1552 publication by deleting the names of the offenders, of the captains and/or conquistadors, encomenderos, German merchants, governors, *oidores* of New Spain and Hispaniola, other officers of the king, and the "highest and foremost bishop."[95] By removing the names of the specific offenders, he transformed the text from one of particularized accusations to one of broad indictments. Accordingly and in keeping with what Pérez Fernández described as Las Casas's "calculated and measured" use of language, he employed the composite construct of tyranny and, throughout the entire text, referred to all the offenders as "tyrants."[96] While so denominating all the offenders and thus not differentiating them may have constituted another of Las Casas's juridical tactics, he did at times refer to "tyrants" such as Nuño de Guzmán and the Germans as especially cruel. Third, utilization of the juridical figure of tyranny facilitates inclusion, as will be shown, of all the premises discernible in Las Casas's condemnatory assessment of what he regarded as the depopulation and devastation of the Indies, and anchors the torrent of facts that he selected and marshaled to make his case. Fourth, tyranny was a consistent subject in Las Casas's writings after he became a Dominican friar: for example, he denounced tyranny as "the epitome of evil," and repeatedly condemned the "tyrannical government … [and] … conquistadors," as well as the "tyrannous wars" in the Indies and their law-perverting consequences, which generated "tyrannous behaviors and attitudes."[97]

In addition to this appropriateness in Las Casas's mind, the juridical figure of tyranny is theoretically significant because the concept and assessment of tyranny was part of centuries-old intellectual discourse, a font of knowledge with which Las Casas was familiar. In medieval theological, ancient philosophical, and Roman-ecclesial canonical traditions, tyranny was essentially lawlessness and had many referents. Aquinas defined tyranny as "oppressive power," and regarded tyrannical law as a perversion of law—or "not a law"—because it was not in accord with reason.[98] Aristotle addressed tyranny as one form of government.[99] Medieval canonists deliberated the merits and demerits of the tyrannical ruler.[100] For his understanding of tyranny, Las Casas relied on Aquinas's teachings, especially on his *Treatise on Law*, on Aristotle's *Politics* and *Ethics*, and, in particular, on Bartolus's treatise about tyranny.[101] Bartolus had expanded the notion of tyranny beyond that of "bad government" to include "tyranny of the people, tyranny of a group, and tyranny of one person"; indeed, in his assessment of his native land, he had written: "today Italy is full of tyrants," and he advised looking to jurists for guidance "in matters touching tyranny."[102] Las Casas seemingly took Bartolus's advice to heart, and, as Pérez Fernández pointed out, used the juridical figure of tyranny in a manner calculated to denounce and indict the culpable Spaniards as "tyrants."[103]

Furthermore, utilization of the juridical figure of tyranny is theoretically significant because the tyranny of the conquistadors, as well as of many encomenderos and royal officials, constituted a discourse of lawlessness that was flagrantly counter to the meta-narrative of providence in salvation history, wherein God is the eternal law-giver—the giver of law as an ordinance of reason promulgated for the good of the community by the one who has care of that community.[104] The juridical figure of tyranny thus highlights a deeper dimension of Las Casas's ethical-juridical judgment, that of God's eternal law.[105] As will be shown, this supreme law of divine reason and divine will canopy Las Casas's explication of the deeds of certain Spaniards (and Germans) in terms of violations of the tripartite scheme of law.

Las Casas located the source of tyranny in the personhood of the offending Spaniards and presented his characterization of them at the very beginning of his *Very Brief Account*. In the *Argumento* and *Prólogo*, he did not refer to the offending conquistadors, encomenderos, and royal officials as "Spaniards." Rather, he portrayed them first in terms of an attribute of human nature: they were irrational or "insensible men." He charged that, as a result of the vices of greed and inordinate ambition, their humanity had degenerated to a sub-human level; later in the text, he likened their behavior to that of ravenous wolves, tigers, and lions.[106] Given his providentialist-soteriological perspective, he next described them as "of reprobate mind," which, as Aquinas taught, consisted of a turning away from humans' supernatural end of eternal salvation to pursue lesser and/or perverted ends. While this violated divine law, providence permitted such reprobation because humans have free will.[107] At the end of the prologue, Las Casas concluded this introductory description by calling them "evil [and] tyrannical men."[108] Then, later in the treatise, he characterized how irrational and reprobate some conquerors had become by referring to them as "demons incarnate."[109]

After clearly stipulating this source of tyranny in the Indies, Las Casas then condemned the deeds of these individuals as violations of divine, natural, and human laws, and subsequently offered what he regarded as evidence of their tyranny in the body of his treatise. To explicate Las Casas's juridical approach in his condemnation of the tyranny, this study now examines the content of the *tratado* to elucidate three spheres of tyranny that existed in the Indies: the political, the moral, and the theological.[110]

Political Tyranny

The sphere of political tyranny refers to institutionalized tyrannical practices in which certain conquistadors, encomenderos, and royal officials engaged at the political and socio-economic level of society. In the Indies, political tyranny was manifested in the wars of invasion and subjugation, and in the institutions of encomienda and slavery. In the *Brevísima relación*, Las Casas identified and condemned these as "two forms of infernal tyranny," namely, "wars and bondage," that existed since the "discovery."[111]

These forms of political tyranny were condemnable by natural and divine laws. Accordingly, in the *tratado*, Las Casas condemned the killings and enslavement as transgressions of the Indigenous peoples' natural right to life, to life's necessities, and to liberty, as well as of the divine commandment "You shall not kill" and the divine precept to love one's neighbor as one's self.[112] Similarly, he showed that, through their wars and bondage, certain Spaniards (and Germans) intentionally neglected the common good as required by natural and divine laws. He drew from Thomistic thought in his assessment that the "tyrannical government" that was established in the Indies did not result in the good of the "governed," that is, in the continued "prosperity" of the Indigenous peoples, but only benefited those who "governed," that is, the Spaniards and the Crown.[113]

Prominent in Las Casas's particular assessment of the conquests was his assertion that the "violent invasions by cruel tyrants ... [were] condemned ... by all human laws."[114] In the *Very Brief Account*, Las Casas addressed violations of ecclesial and royal positive law in addition to *ius gentium*. For Las Casas, ecclesial positive law was violated by some Christian Spaniards because the crucial condition of the ecclesial legislation known as the papal donation consisted, as he informed the prince in the prologue, of the mandate to "convert [the Indigenous inhabitants] to belief in Christ and the Holy Catholic Church, and give them to prosper temporally and spiritually."[115] As was previously shown, Las Casas believed that the ecclesial donation never ordered "submission" through war, as was done through what he referred to as the "tyrannical warfare" of the conquests.[116] He charged that instead of effecting the Indigenous peoples' temporal and spiritual welfare, the "slaughters and perditions" of the conquests, for example, in the subjected kingdoms of Panamá, left "neither trace nor sign that any village ever was, or man born, there."[117] While this may be an over-statement for rhetorical purposes of the devastation wrought by the warfare, Las Casas was correct in his judgment that ecclesial positive law had been violated.

According to Las Casas, royal human law was also violated by the bellicose *entradas* in which certain conquistadors engaged, and which he believed transgressed the guidelines for peaceful *entradas* as stipulated in the Laws of Burgos and in the 1526 Ordenanzas de Granada. Las Casas's judgment does not, however, take into account expectations rooted in the *reconquista*, and then the invasion and occupation of the Canaries, which assumed military conquests and occupation, and/or were part of royal *Capitulaciones* and *Instrucciones*.[118] Nevertheless, Las Casas did charge that the *entradas* were not peaceful and, in support of this, asserted that from the Antilles to "the great kingdoms and great provinces of Perú," the conquerors' "accursed *entradas* caused many murders and destroyed divers villages … and subjected [the Indigenous inhabitants] through fears and terrors."[119] Drawing on his knowledge of juristic writing and jurisprudential procedure, he also contended that unless the monarch was informed through *denuncias* about the injustices of such conquests and consequently would cease to grant licenses, the "devastation and depopulation of the Indigenous kingdoms would continue."[120] Referring to another matter of royal positive law, Las Casas also condemned what he perceived as the widespread disobedience of royal directives and flagrant disregard of crown authority on the part of some Spaniards and which he called "rebellion" and "acts of tyranny."[121] Other sixteenth-century *relaciones* also recorded such rebellious acts and referred to the perpetrators as "tyrants," for example, those in Venezuela and on the Isle of Margarita near the coast of Nueva Granada.[122] Ironically, an ordinance of Hispano-Indiano law that the conquistadors did obey was the *Requerimiento,* which juridical instrument Las Casas condemned as irrational in concept and evil in execution.[123]

Las Casas also contended that the law of nations (*ius gentium*) was violated by the conquests. This law, which emerged from the seminal thought of Vitoria in the *Escuela Española* and was based on natural law, asserted the natural right of association and communication among nations by virtue of the attribute of sociability that inhered in all persons.[124] In his *Very Brief Account*, Las Casas did not question the Spaniards' right to travel to, trade with, and settle in what Las Casas referred to as the Indigenous "nations."[125] He did, however, condemn "tyrannical *entradas*" for the purpose of subjugating people who are "reasonable … and free," as well as "in possession of their lands."[126] Although the "visiting" Europeans could wage war if their right of natural association and communication were impeded by the Indigenous peoples, Las Casas had recourse to his premise that the natives of the Indies had "never done harm" to the Spaniards, and he corroborated this with narrations about the welcomes that the Spanish strangers received.[127] That this hospitality sometimes occurred is significant, and implies that not all stages of all *entradas* were violent. Nevertheless, Las Casas unequivocally denounced the Spanish expansionist wars of conquest as unjust.[128] He based his *denuncias* on considerations about the equality of all human persons and of all nations and, from this, also asserted that Indigenous people had legitimate and just *dominium*.[129] Indeed, throughout the *Very Brief Account*, whenever Las Casas used the term "vassal," he did so only with respect to the Indigenous people in reference to their being vassals of their native lords.[130] Indeed, in many places, the Indigenous populations continued to be vassals of their Indigenous lords (for better or for worse) when their lords agreed to cooperate with the Spanish invaders and thereby retained local authority. Las Casas also juxtaposed these Spaniards' violation of embryonic-international law with that of ecclesial legislation. Maintaining another premise that the papal donation only gave *de jure* jurisdiction to the Spanish king, he charged these Spaniards with imposing *de facto* jurisdiction by their unjust wars of expansion, which imposition was in violation of the natural right of all people to institute their rulers by consent.

In addition to these jurisdictional considerations, the *Brevísima relación* chronicled further violations of *ius gentium* that were related to the harm done to the Indigenous peoples' expressions of their human nature as social beings: their political, economic, and socio-cultural institutions. Accordingly, Las Casas contended that by the invading Spaniards' establishment of *de facto* jurisdiction, which he deemed unjust and forced, they usurped and disrupted the political structures of Indigenous peoples. For example, he reported that some Spaniards tortured and killed many legitimate native rulers, such as the caciques in Marién on Hispaniola and in Michoacán, as well as the universal Indigenous lords such as Atahualpa in Peru and Bogotá in Nueva Granada.[131] He charged that in some kingdoms, such regicide resulted in the loss of the succession of their nobility.[132] He pointed out that, in many provinces, for example in Cuba, Jalisco, Venezuela, and Nueva Granada, large areas of "fertile land remained untilled," which he attributed to the death of the inhabitants through warfare; however, he did not mention the role of disease epidemics in this population decrease.[133] He also charged that the conquests devastated and ravaged the Indigenous peoples' socio-cultural networks of families and communities in, for example, Hispaniola and Guatemala, and also pointed out that "many tongues [but fortunately not all] were lost" in Venezuela.[134] Based on this evidence of the violations of the *de jure* and *de facto* jurisdiction of Indigenous peoples as well as of their ways of life and their lands, Las Casas asserted his premise that the Indigenous inhabitants of the Indies had just cause for war.[135] To support this, he explained the principle of "just cause" from canonistic and Thomistic just war theory, which taught that "divine and human law," and "all justice" gave Indigenous peoples the right to resist and to defend themselves.[136] He also made reference to the principle of proportionality from the doctrine of just war; he pointed out that Taínos in Hispaniola and Incas in Peru who "took up arms"—using "weak and useless weapons"—were "no match for the Christians' horses, swords, pikes, and lances."[137] However, he did not mention that Indigenous allies of Spaniards also apparently used traditional weapons.

In Las Casas's juridical assessment of the conquests, he also charged that the "violent invasions by cruel tyrants … [were] condemned … by the law of God."[138] In this, he had recourse to the highest law that canopied the tripartite of law: the eternal law of God's plan for humankind. In his narrations about the "kingdoms and peoples" of New Spain, he explicitly spoke of how the divine providential plan was foiled by the conquests. He wrote that "God set [the Indigenous peoples] in those leagues of lands," and related how their "four or five kingdoms," their "cities," and "great populations" were severely impacted by the "slaughters and devastations" that had taken place "from the moment of their *entrada* … in 1518 until 1530."[139] Las Casas may, however, be overstating the impact because widespread destruction in New Spain did not happen. Nevertheless, his recourse to eternal law is significant, because such "slaughters and devastations" wrought by the conquests imply violation of God's supreme law, as well as of divine, natural, and just human laws.[140] Indeed, nowhere in the text does Las Casas explicitly refer to non-compliance with God's eternal law except with respect to the conquests.

In his juridical assessment of the political tyranny in the institutions of encomienda and slavery, Las Casas charged that "after the deaths and devastations of the wars, [certain Spaniards] bound the people … who had escaped the slaughter … into most grievous servitude."[141] He pointed out that this subsequent "tyrannical bondage" extinguished any future hope of freedom on the part of those who survived.[142] For the most part, Las Casas combined his descriptions, assessments, and condemnations of the encomienda and slavery in his *Very Brief Account*, apparently because both constituted a form of enslavement. However, by this combining, he equated two institutions that were not in fact equivalent, and to this extent was historically inaccurate. Nevertheless, Las Casas's juridical assessment of both institutions of bondage was that they were condemnable by "natural, human, and divine law"—that is, by "the divine precepts of love for God and man," and by "Christians who know something about God, reason … and human laws."[143]

Accordingly, he condemned the encomienda as an "intrinsic evil," which violated their liberty, as well as fragmented and mutated their economic activities, which had sustained their ways of life. In addition, the encomienda fractured their social systems as men, women, and children were "divided up" or assigned on a rotational basis to serve the conquistadors and encomenderos.[144] He denounced the commerce of human persons, which deepened as Indigenous people were "taken" or demanded as slaves, branded, and "put in irons" in the slave trade or captured in "tyrannical raids."[145] As Fray Pedro de Gante, OFM, wrote at the same time as Las Casas's publication, "even those who were overlords of the whole land are now slaves," in the sense of having lost their political authority.[146] Reiterating his premise that all the conquests were unjust wars, Las Casas also called on the doctrine of just war to declare that any captives that the Spaniards took by war in the Indies violated the requirements of authorization by competent authority (because neither the pope nor the monarchs, so he claimed, had authorized these wars), of just cause (since the Indigenous people had done no wrong), and of right intention (meaning "doing good" by Christianizing and not "tyrannizing").[147] In Las Casas's condemnation of the "mortal enslaving oppression" of the encomienda and the "perpetual bondage" of slavery, he repeatedly insisted that the Indigenous peoples were "free as all," as "truly free as I."[148]

Related to the institutions of the encomienda and of slavery was the tribute system that Las Casas also denounced in his *Brevísima relación*. This system was initially instituted as a tribute to the Crown that was allocated, in turn, to the encomendero as a *merced* from the monarch. However, this royal tribute became indistinguishable in principle from extra levies for private gain.[149] In his denunciation of the tribute system, Las Casas charged that the Crown's vision for the encomienda was quickly corrupted beginning in Ovando's governorship, as the labor of men was required in the mines "to dig out gold, which is intolerable work," and of women in the fields "to till the land, which is not labor for women but for strong men."[150] By this assertion, Las Casas could be ignoring or ignorant of gender ideologies among Indigenous peoples wherein fieldwork may be acceptable. Las Casas also charged that services in transport as "beasts of burden" were exacted even of "pregnant and suckling women" in Nicaragua, and that slaves were demanded as tribute payment in Guatemala.[151] The Franciscan friar, Pedro de Gante, corroborated the Dominican's assessment and called the emperor's attention to "the long history of the difficulty [indeed, the impossibility] of meeting the tribute requirements."[152] Whether held in encomienda or in slavery, Las Casas insisted that "the infernal tributes slay [the Indigenous inhabitants] little by little" and, as Gante and Las Casas both contended, was "one of the main reasons for the destruction of these people."[153] However, both friars, lacking contemporary scientific understanding, ignored the devastating effects of European diseases, such as smallpox on the Indigenous populations; however, both must have been aware of pandemics, such as those in Santo Domingo in 1518–1519, and in New Spain in 1545.

Hispano-Indiano law was also violated by royal officials who, Las Casas accused, failed to uphold the law—an accusation also echoed in Gante's report to the emperor.[154] For example, Las Casas charged that the Council of Indies did not examine the *probanzas*, which allegedly detailed the crimes committed, and that the *oidores* of the *Audiencias* of Hispaniola and New Spain favored the encomenderos and slave raiders who were under their jurisdiction.[155] Allocating their irresponsibility to bribes received, culpable ignorance, and/or perverse motivations, Las Casas charged that such officials were accomplices to the tyranny because they did not punish the offenders or, as with the New Laws, they "did the work of the tyrants" by appealing (and thereby temporally suspended) the legislation about the encomienda and slavery.[156]

Reboiras contended that political tyranny could only be diminished and/or eliminated by legal procedures. Yet, no law actually ended them, although slavery was halted temporarily by crown legislation in 1530, as were encomiendas in perpetuity in 1542 and conquests in 1547. Conquests stopped for various reasons; by the mid-sixteenth century, there were no viable places left to conquer in the eyes of most Spaniards, except for lesser conquistadors such as Lope de Aguirre sought to conquer the mythical El Dorado. Nevertheless, Las Casas continued to lobby for the eradication of these forms of tyranny through human laws that were just. However, from his canonistic-Thomistic training, he knew that the justice of human law—civil and ecclesial—was dependent on the correspondence of these laws with natural and divine laws. Evidence in the *Very Brief Account* based on Las Casas's use of a juridical approach shows that the offending Spaniards (and Germans) also violated these "higher" laws of nature and of the supernatural order, and that this tyranny was also rampant in these spheres of morals and theology.

Moral Tyranny

The sphere of moral tyranny pertains to dispositions and actions that disregard and/or pervert the moral codes knowable by natural law independent of divine revelation. Lascasian scholarship contends—as did Las Casas—that moral tyranny in the Indies was borne of some Spaniards' greed and inordinate ambition.[157] According to Aquinas's teachings on human behavior, action always originated from some desire.[158] Some Spaniards' desire for riches and prestige was recognized by Montesinos and his Dominican confreres in their 1511 pulpit condemnation.[159] Similarly, in 1516, Las Casas asserted that "the majority [of the Spaniards] came [to the Indies] with the sole concern of making money." Most would not have questioned this goal (which is still shared by immigrants today in their desire to find a place where they can enjoy more prosperity among other things). A year later in 1517, the mendicant friars of Hispaniola also informed Chancellor Xèvres that "those who came here, or the majority of them, are the dross of Spain—a greedy marauding people."[160] Even conquistador Bernal Díaz acknowledged that the Spaniards came "because there was wealth."[161] Sánchez also maintained that the Spaniards had "come with the intention of returning very rich to Spain."[162] In the *Very Brief Account*, Las Casas repeatedly denounced the conquistadors, encomenderos, and certain royal officials as "avaricious tyrants" for their "eagerness and avidity for the gold" and other precious metals and gems. Like Balboa in 1515, Las Casas particularly condemned their "infinite greed" in the pearl-diving enterprise in Cubagua that began in 1514.[163] Additionally, he denounced their "unquenchable" ambition to "hold offices and positions," to "raise themselves to high estates," and so "to become grand and rich lords."[164] Ambitions for social mobility were common among many, if not most, immigrant groups. However, the difference with respect to those who went to the Indies was their concern to secure higher status, albeit on the backs of an unjustly (in Las Casas's view) subjugated people.

Las Casas assessed the moral consequences of this inordinate pursuit of wealth and prestige in terms of the Thomistic understanding of natural law. By this law that is embedded in peoples' nature as rational, free, and social beings created in the image of God and equal to one another (which premise Las Casas also adamantly posited with respect to the Indigenous inhabitants of the Indies), people have the capacity for moral agency and moral judgment. Central to moral agency is humans' ability for rational self-direction. Fundamental for moral judgment is human's capacity to distinguish between good and evil. This capacity derives from people's natural inclination to the good, which is guided at a general level by the first principle of natural law "to do good and avoid evil." As such, the basis of morality is humans' commitment to non-malfeasance. The natural inclination to the good also guides humans' pursuit of secondary goods necessary for "the good life" as individuals and in society. Living as moral agents and making moral judgments promotes the full development of humans' capacities, and results in the attainment of humans' proper temporal end, namely, happiness. This end is nurtured and attained by adherence to the Golden Rule of natural moral law and by the practice of virtue.[165] However, a virtuous life must be oriented to more than an individual's overall good. As social beings, the truly virtuous person is characterized by regard for and pursuit of the good of others.

Given this Thomistic understanding of natural law, the inordinate pursuit of riches and prestige by some Spaniards (and Germans) would have made impossible their living as virtuous moral agents and making moral judgments that would promote the common good. Instead, these Spaniards (and Germans) were disposed to vices in the form of inclinations, actions, and habits contrary to humans' nature. In Aquinas's teachings, the source of inordinate dispositions and acts was covetousness.[166] Indeed, in both the *Siete Partidas* and the *Summa Theologiae*, covetousness was regarded as "the root of all evils" because the intellect of covetous persons "cleaves to evil, becomes blind to the good" and "unreasonable."[167] Moreover, covetous persons give unreasonable priority to irrational pursuit of a secondary good, that of wealth, which violated the common good and vitiated the moral basis of civic society. Applying these teachings, Las Casas declared that, "owing to the covetousness they have," the conquistadors, encomenderos, and certain crown officials—including some of the lettered "ministers of justice" in the Council of the Indies and in the *Audiencias*—became as "men made blind and unreasonable by ambition and diabolic greed."[168] He even more harshly denounced the German merchants in Venezuela, and declared that they were "more blind and [more filled with] wrathful avarice … and more unreasonable … than all those who went before."[169] Nevertheless, for both the offending Spaniards (and Germans), Las Casas argued that their covetousness, blindness, irrationality, and inordinate ambitions constituted the source of the moral tyranny that spread throughout the Indies.[170]

Las Casas's emphasis on the pervasiveness of moral tyranny is understandable, given that, according to both the *Siete Partidas* and the

Summa Theologiae, covetousness was a "capital vice" consisting of unregulated interior dispositions that "cannot refrain from things prohibited."[171] That is, from a canonistic-philosophical-theological perspective, covetousness led to other vices in the sense of dispositions, actions, and habits that were inclined to evil and vicious (meaning vice-generated, or immoral) acts that became second nature or were chosen by the individual's will out of malice and/or for "pleasure."[172] From an analysis of the *Brevísima relación*, the data showed that Las Casas held that the vice of covetousness disposed the greedy Spaniards (and Germans) to commit three discernible kinds of vicious acts against the Indigenous inhabitants of the Indies. These acts, which were characterized by violence, cruelty, and injustices, consisted of bodily injury (and often death), emotional harm, and material losses.

Deeds of bodily injury, from a Thomistic perspective, were moral violations because those acts violated the physical integrity of the human body, the tranquility of sensory experience, and freedom of movement. Violations of the substantial integrity of the human body that are recorded in the *Very Brief Account* ranged from killing innocent Indigenous people by sword or torch or gallows (which violated the basic right to life), to brutal maiming, cruel torture, violent mutilation, and slow starvation (which militated against their attainment of the most basic of secondary goods, the preservation of life and development of their human potential). The narrative of the *tratado* contains alleged instances of maiming by severing the victims' legs, feet, and/or hands. According to both Las Casas and the Hispaniola mendicant friars, this practice began in Hispaniola where some Spaniards cut off the hands of some Taínos and then maliciously ordered them to deliver some "letters"; Nuño de Guzmán engaged in this same practice in Jalisco.[173] The scorching of body parts was also an allegedly common practice of torture. For example—and as reported in both the *Very Brief Account* and the *Relación about Michoacán*—the feet of the Tarascan *cazonci* (king) were held over fire and "wetted with oil ... from time to time ... to roast the flesh the better" in order to force him to disclose the location of the gold to Guzmán.[174] In a similar manner, the last Aztec emperor Cuauhtémoc and King Bogotá in Nueva Granada were also tortured.[175] Seemingly purposeless malice (or purposive intimidation) also prompted some Spaniards in Hispaniola and Nueva Granada to allegedly "open the belly of a pregnant woman with one stroke of their blade," or "to rip [the Indians'] bellies open, and hack so many to pieces."[176] Among this "great harm ... and cruelties ... to their bodies," as Sánchez also denounced them, were those that Las Casas reported was the invaders' practice in Jalisco, the Yucatán, Florida, Peru, and Nueva Granada of cutting off the noses, lips, and/or chins of their victims, and then "laughing as though it were not more than pulling hair."[177] With similar cruelty and violence, as both Las Casas and the Hispaniola mendicant friars claimed, the invading Spaniards in

Hispaniola, Jalisco, the Yucatán, Michoacán, and Nueva Granada also used "ferocious dogs" to attack on command and also fed them infants and children—limb from limb.[178] Starvation was also an ever-present and slower form of death that the Indigenous people suffered because the conquistadors, for example, in Nicaragua and Peru and on Hispaniola, "gave them no food," or "took all their food," and/or depleted their storehouses.[179]

In addition to these violations of the physical integrity of the body, alleged deeds of bodily injuries reported in the *Very Brief Account* included the infliction of brutal sensory pain in the form of "whippings and floggings ... [with] lashes, rods, and smitings" ... "sticks and cudgels" ... "and other insufferable treatments" ... with "fists and slaps," and "teeth knocked out by the shafts of swords."[180] This disregard and disesteem for the full humanity of Indigenous people was also confirmed by Fray Pedro de Gante who, like Las Casas, denounced "the many acts of mistreatment [that they] received ... [as] beasts of burden," and who charged that "a kick, a hair-pulling, or a clubbing was never lacking."[181] Such brutal behavior was also reported in 1517 by the Hispaniola friars and, according to Gante and Tenamaztle, still continued albeit not in widespread form in the mid-1500s.[182]

Deeds of bodily injuries also included restricting the free movement of some Indigenous people by imprisonment and by the use of chains and shackles. Las Casas reported that conquering Spaniards imprisoned caciques to extort gold from them, and that the Germans in Venezuela allegedly employed a "new and foreign" method to restrict movement. They imprisoned the Indigenous people in a "great corral" with the promise to release those who paid a ransom for themselves—and for their spouses and children. However, because of some Spaniards' purported obsession to extract riches to more quickly pay off Spain's debt to German bankers, these Spaniards were "licensed" by the German governor to "re-corral" the Indigenous people and force them to pay "two or three times" more in ransom before being released.[183] Later in Peru, according to Las Casas, similar reneging on promises took place with respect to Atahualpa, whom Las Casas and other Spanish residents in Peru such as Espinosa (in 1533) and Friar Niza (in 1534) referred to as the "Universal Lord of the Incas."[184] (However, his lordship as well as its legitimacy had actually been contested by another faction within the Inca ruling class headed by Huascar.) Although the demanded ransom was delivered, Pizarro did not release Atahualpa from prison even though "eleven million castellanos more" than the original ransom price was apparently paid.[185] According to Mercedarian friar Martín de Murúa, the required ransom was paid by a "quantity of gold, silver, jars, and valuable pottery."[186]

Confinement of Indigenous people by chains and shackles was first reported in the captures on Hispaniola of two Indigenous supreme lords: King Guarionex of the province of Maguá, and King Caonabó of the province of Maguaná. According to Las Casas, Guarionex was "very obedient and virtuous, naturally peaceable, and devoted to the king and queen of Castile" and, as Torrejón points out, a friend of Christopher Columbus. Guarionex's vassals had faithfully paid the tax imposed by Columbus in 1495 of one gourd filled with gold every three months for every person over fourteen years of age who lived near the mines.[187] When eventually in 1497 his people were unable to fulfill this contract because they "did not know how to extract the gold," Guarionex offered in exchange to till the five leagues of farm land between Santo Domingo and Isabela. The response of Francisco Roldán, mayor of Isabela, to this offer was to rape Guarionex's wife. Enraged, the Indigenous supreme lord took refuge in the territory of one of his secondary caciques to organize how he would avenge this crime. Eventually learning of Guarionex's whereabouts, Roldán declared war on the territory, slaughtered many Taínos, and captured the Taíno supreme lord. Bartolomé Colon imprisoned and restrained Guarionex with chains and shackles for three years.[188] In 1503, still chained and shackled, he was transferred to a ship bound for Castille and then drowned when the ship subsequently sank in the Atlantic.[189]

According to Sebastián Robiou Lamarche, Caonabó exceeded all other supreme lords in prestige and stately ceremony.[190] His name meant "Lord of the House of Gold." He reportedly was "manly and vigorous" and a Carib. His wife was Anacaona, *cacica* (ruler) of the province of Xaragua. However, Columbus and others suspected that Caonabó was responsible for the massacre of the Spaniards in the settlement of Navidad. Consequently, in time, Captain Alonso de Hojeda was able to capture Caonabó by making him believe that the shackles and handcuffs that Hojeda put on the *cacique* were ornaments worn only by the Castilian monarch. Thus, in 1495 and bound by irons, Canaobó was taken to a ship returning to Castile, which vessel also sank during a storm.[191]

From this early period onward, and given the slave trade and forced labor, such restriction of movement by chains and shackles was increasingly commonplace, and forthrightly denounced by Las Casas as "cruel and against nature." In the *Very Brief Account*, Las Casas particularly condemned the Germans in Venezuela for their particularly cruel and "new and foreign" methods. For example, instead of removing the collar of the shackle from the neck of an exhausted worker or slave in the chain gang, the Germans reportedly simply severed his head.[192] However, as reported in the predominantly geographic *relación* of Cristóbal de Pedraza, some Spaniards in Honduras also had chain gangs and treated any exhausted Indigenous "beast of burden" in the same way.[193] Both Venezuela and Honduras were frontier zones where one would expect more brutal and lawless behavior of this sort. This practice was not, however, reported in Las Casas's narratives about the central regions of Mexico and Peru.

The second kind of vicious actions committed by some covetous Spaniards (and Germans) pertained to emotional harm. In the *Very Brief Account*, Las Casas narrated how certain Spaniards (and Germans), for example, threatened Indigenous people with "long-extended tortures" if they did not obey, and how they deceived and confused the people with promises on which they reneged, as well as intimidated and tyrannized them with "intolerable and unjust *vejaciones* (vexations)."[194] For an understanding of the core emotional harm done, the employment of the term *vejaciones* is significant. First, this term was commonly used in sixteenth-century *cartas* in reference to the plight of the Indigenous peoples. For example, Tenamaztle, in addition to bishops and the native *señores* and *principales* of New Spain, called attention to the "many and great vexations" that were "done to the Indigenous people" or were "received by them."[195] Second, the etymology of the word "vexations" (*vejaciones*) is important. In one sense, the term meant "shock, jolt, upheaval, disturbance," which surely the Indigenous people experienced. In Old Spanish (Castilian), the term meant "the sacrifice of damage to one's person or interests in order to avoid greater harm."[196] In the context of the emotional (and physical) sufferings that Indigenous people bore, the latter meaning of the term conveys their endurance of lesser evils in order to avoid (and, in some measure, to control) the infliction of greater evils. Thus, the vexations endured resulted in fear of the greater evil that the Indigenous people wanted to avoid and of the power of certain Spaniards to inflict the greater *mal*. Both Las Casas and the New Spain bishops recognized that the powerlessness of some Indigenous people to repel the evil caused a "great loss of spirit" in them.[197] (Others, of course, resisted and found ways to carry on.) All this, Las Casas insisted, played into the invaders' designs to instill "fear and terror" and "to dispirit [the Indigenous populace] and cause them to fear … [so] that they would … give them gold and tribute."[198] A pernicious example of the consequence of what Las Casas maintained were the offending Spaniards' evil deeds and power—which Indigenous people feared, is found in the raping of women, which was reported by Las Casas and the Hispaniola mendicants in addition to the native *señores* and *principales*.[199] Contemporaneous accounts about rape confirm such abuse. In central areas, accounts of rape of Indigenous noblewomen were noted by Bernal Díaz and in the Florentine Codex. However, instances of rape in these areas were apparently reduced in frequency by the development of colonial "social mores and penal codes," except in frontier areas.[200] Irrespective of the locale, because of such instances of moral tyranny—and out of emotional fear of greater physical violence, women were forced to suffer violation of and to sacrifice damage to their persons and interests, as well as to live in fear and terror, as did the men and children. Such moral tyranny, which reflected asymmetrical gender power relations of Spanish patriarchal cultural norms, also contributed to the degrading and disruption of what Karen Powers referred to (in another context) as gender-parallel and gender-complementary spheres of Indigenous society.[201] This disruption included the virtual emasculation of men who were unable to protect their women from rape and harm.

The third kind of vicious action committed by some Spaniards (and Germans), and referred to by Las Casas, pertained to material losses that Indigenous inhabitants of the Indies suffered and that resulted from conquests. Material losses from robbery varied depending on the area or region. For instance, in New Spain and Peru, there were too few Spaniards to carry out widespread destruction and/or taking of the material possessions of the Indigenous inhabitants. As such, larceny in these regions was a gradual and complicated process. In his *tratado*, Las Casas characterized this kind of larceny as violent, coercive, unjust, and greed-motivated raids.[202] In doing so, he employed the Thomistic and jurisprudential definitions of robbery as "the use of force and violence to openly and unjustly take what belongs to another," and the Roman legal understanding of robbery as "oriented toward profit," which was typical of *rapina* (plunder).[203] Another kind of larceny, which Las Casas denounced and which Thomism and jurisprudence distinguished, consisted of stealing "secretly and stealthily."[204] For example, after hearing about gold in some villages on Terra Firme, greedy Spaniards went at night to take the coveted metal.[205] However, how widespread and persistent this practice was is not discernible from the text of Las Casas's summary *Very Brief Account*.

According to Las Casas, both overt robbery and surreptitious theft were frequently accompanied by *furtum*—an aspect of larceny that extended well beyond the seizure of goods. First articulated in Roman law and applied by Cajetan in sixteenth-century discourse about stolen goods in the Old and New worlds, *furtum* included all forms of trickery and fraud that deprived owners of their possessions.[206] Whether utilized in robbing or stealing, Las Casas stridently condemned the invaders' craftiness and guile. An example of this is found in a narrative in the *Very Brief Account* about the Indigenous lords of the province of Xaragua on Hispaniola and the settlement at Cumaná on Terra Firme.[207] In addition to the deceitful manner (previously discussed) in which Alonso de Hojeda shackled and handcuffed King Caonabó, these Spaniards also enticed Caonabó's brother-in-law, King Bechecio, and most of his secondary lords to enter a large house of straw, to which they quickly set fire. Governor Ovando, who gave the instructions to do this, later tried to justify his actions by contending that the caciques were guilty of treason.[208] The alleged craftiness of such invaders was also shown in what Las Casas claimed happened in Chiribichí—the settlement on Cumaná where the Hispaniola Dominicans were conducting peaceful evangelization. During a time when the friars had temporarily departed the settlement, a Spanish slave ship came to port and enticed the cacique, Don Alonso, his wife, and seventeen other villagers, to board the ship for a fiesta. Once on board, the ship took off for the slave trade market in Santo Domingo. Even though the friars had promised that no Spaniards would come to the settlement, the invaders gave only lip service to the agreement, which contract, of course, lay Spanish Christians had not made, and which circumstance would not excuse their actions today.[209]

In the *Brevísima relación*, Las Casas also presented the moral tyranny in each territory as a clustering and amassing of the different kinds of vicious actions in which some Spaniards (and Germans) engaged. This is exemplified in what allegedly occurred in Paría on the peninsula of Venezuela. Higueroto, the native lord of a village, set up a "refuge and hostelry for all men," including for those Spaniards who had fled from other provinces where they "had done many acts of tyranny and evil doing," and had need of food, rest, and ship repair. This hospitality of peaceful Indigenous people, which, from a Thomistic perspective, would be in accord with the natural inclination "to do good," was truncated, Las Casas wrote, when another "wretched tyrant" heard of "the inn." This malefactor journeyed to Paría where he tricked the unsuspecting "good" lord, Higueroto, and his "virtuous" people to board his ships (as they had done previously with Spanish ships in need or in distress). Once the Indigenous people were on board, the ships of the "wretched tyrant" sailed to the slave markets on the island of San Juan; later, the same Spaniards returned to Paría where they pillaged and plundered the village for its gold and possessions.[210] This example combines the vicious actions of bodily injury (enslavement), emotional harm (shock), and material loss (larceny).

However, the narrations of morally tyrannous acts that are in the *Very Brief Account* are, according to Las Casas, only a sampling of what he declared could be told about the magnitude of the tyranny precipitated by covetousness. At the end of his treatise, he claimed that he had "not said in quantity or quality the ten-thousandth part of what has been done and is still being done today."[211] Fray Pedro de Gante also informed Charles that he "could talk about [these deeds] without end."[212]

Nevertheless and significantly, in his sampling of tyrannous deeds, Las Casas articulated and demonstrated a "Rule" generated by his experience and knowledge, which he periodically repeated throughout the *Very Brief Account*: "that the longer and more thoroughly the Spaniards discovered people and lands and destroyed them and laid them waste, the more heinous became the cruelties and iniquities against God and their neighbors (*prójimos*)."[213]As defined in a gloss in the *Decretum*, a "Rule" was whatever lays down some general principle—without any exceptions. Accordingly, Las Casas asserted (as did the Hispaniola mendicant friars) that, without exception, in each region and beginning with Hispaniola, the Spaniards employed "more and greater and newer forms of torture."[214] Some of his assertions were as follows. In New Spain since 1518, their "outrageous and hellish deeds have grown worse and greater." In Nicaragua since "1522 or 1523," they "exceeded all the injustices … done in Hispaniola." In Guatemala since 1524, they "exceeded all slaughters and acts of robbery, burning, and stealing and destroying."[215] In Jalisco since 1525, they used "cruelties and torments such as never before heard." In Santa Marta beginning in 1523 and intensely in 1529, they engaged in "ever more exorbitant cruelties and iniquities." In Venezuela since 1526, they "entered into those lands with more incomparable cruelty than any of the other tyrants." In Florida beginning in 1510/1511 and especially in 1538, their deeds were "most heinous" and, in Peru since 1531 with the third expedition of Francisco Pizarro to the Inca empire, they were "more savage yet and cruel." In Nueva Granada since 1539, "the tyranny and violence and injustices against [the Incas] grew greater in harshness and inhumanity and evil-doing day by day."[216]

Some may consider Las Casas's assertions about this "Rule" that cruelty increased in each region as exaggerated for effect, over-simplified, and even erroneous. For example, most scholars now regard the conditions in New Spain as having gradually improved, rather than "grown worse and greater."[217] This improvement was in part because those peoples of New Spain who had allied with the Spaniards fared well compared to, for example, the Taínos and inhabitants of Nicaragua and other more peripheral areas. Las Casas must have been aware of that improvement since, at the end of his treatise when writing about the conditions in 1542, he asserted that "Mexico and its territory is a little less bad [in violence, tyranny, etc.]." He claimed that "there and no other place there is some justice (however little it may be)," and attributed that to the work of the friars.[218]

Throughout the *Very Brief Account*, Las Casas contended that all these vicious actions and trends had the character of injustice. According to Aquinas, injustice was a special vice that militated against the common good, because harm to a member (or a part of a member) of a community also harmed the common good of that community.[219] Maimed, traumatized, and impoverished persons cannot contribute fully to the greater community. Neither could the vice-filled Spaniards (and Germans) contribute to the good of others or to the common good of the Indies or of their native lands, because vice was also directly contrary to virtue. As Aquinas taught, only virtue consisted of dispositions, actions, and habits "befitting one's rational nature, and only virtue rendered 'good' its possessors and their activities."[220] Accordingly, Las Casas declared that because of their lack of virtue, the "tyrants [had] no pity … [nor] mercy … [nor] compassion."[221]

In summary, Las Casas's condemnations of and narratives about the moral tyranny in the Indies are framed by the canonistic-Thomist understanding of natural law. He used this understanding in his judgment that certain conquistadors, encomenderos, and royal officials had violated natural law by their covetous dispositions, vicious actions, and cruel habits, which, in turn, resulted in bodily injuries, emotional harm, and material losses for Indigenous people. He charged that these greedy Spaniards (and Germans) were fundamentally immoral in their total lack of reasonableness and therefore of moral agency, as well as in their flagrant mockery of moral judgment by their pursuit of riches and prestige through evil means. While his juridical approach from the perspective of natural law condemned the culpable Spaniards (and Germans) for their disregard of any inclination to do good, and thus their undermining of the natural basis of morality, he went beyond his judgment based on natural law, to denounce and condemn their violations of the moral imperatives generated by divine law.

Theological Tyranny

Theological tyranny pertains to violations of divine law, that is, of the revealed supernatural order of grace that surpassed the endowed natural order of reason. In the *Argumento*, Las Casas drew on Thomistic teachings to charge that the source of the theological tyranny in the Indies was because so many Spaniards (and Germans) became of "reprobate mind," in the sense of deliberately choosing to sin.[222] According to Aquinas, this turning away from God resulted from the vice of covetousness as well as other vice-filled dispositions, actions, and habits that, according to divine law, were mortal sins. As such, by their reprobation, they put themselves outside the order of grace, and, according to Las Casas, were "allowed [by God] to fall ever lower and to hurl themselves ever deeper into accursed judgment" and thus engaged in increasingly "tyrannical actions and infernal works."[223] Continuing his juridical approach, Las Casas condemned the resultant forms of theological tyranny as violations of the three fundamental precepts of divine law. The first two divine precepts concerned Christians' obligations to God and to others: namely, the biblical precepts to love God and to love one's neighbor. These general mandates are made more specific in the Decalogue, a genre of Old Testament writings. The third divine precept encompassed the New Testament mandate of Christ to proclaim the gospel to all nations. Las Casas applied these theological precepts to the behavior of the certain Spaniards (and Germans) in the following ways.

The offending Spaniards (and Germans) sinned against the first general precept of divine law "to love God above all things" and the first three specific commandments of the Decalogue. In their lawlessness, they violated divine law by their lack of fear of God, idolatry, apostasy, blasphemy, and heresy. Echoing the assertion of the Hispaniola mendicant friars and the teachings of Aquinas, Las Casas claimed that these Spaniards (and Germans) had "no fear of God" in the sense of exhibiting no fear of offending God, of God's punishment for sins committed, and/

or of separation from God.[224] Whether conducting expeditions such as those into New Spain or refusing to implement the New Laws, he alleged that they had lost "both fear and love of God," and variously designated them (ironically) as "Christians," or differentiated them as "the great" or "the more unreasonable tyrant," or identified them as "those who did the work of the tyrants and many of them were at the time within the court."[225] He also recognized that they even thought "God was on their side," as was common in the depressingly age-old way of conquerors and those waging war.

Las Casas's condemnation of their sins of idolatry was based on their pursuit of gold as their "ultimate end."[226] Accordingly, he charged that they perverted the supreme goal of all creation—the glory of God, and rejected the supremacy of God by their worship of gold, which was—he declared—"the only god they adore."[227] As reported by both the Hispaniola mendicants and Las Casas, even cacique Hatüey in Cuba recognized this idolatry when he filled a small basket with gold and gems, and told his vassals that "this is a god [the Spaniards] worship and love much."[228] Their idolatrous turning away from God also specifically violated the First Commandment of the Decalogue, which was, Las Casas unequivocally proclaimed, that "one God alone be worshipped."[229] He also asserted that their reprobation was compounded by their apparent promotion of apostasy or "backsliding" among the Indigenous people. For example, while not a common practice, the sacrilegious commerce of idols by thirty conquistadors in the Yucatán allegedly enticed converted Indigenous persons to again worship idols.[230] In his condemnation of such activities and drawing on scriptural tradition, Las Casas likened these conquistadors to Judas who "betrayed and sold Jesus Christ," and charged that they too "many times, yea infinite times … sold and still today do sell and deny Jesus Christ, time and time again."[231]

Las Casas also condemned the reprobate Spaniards (and Germans) for their blasphemy, as sin against the general divine precept to love God and the Second Commandment of the Decalogue to "not take God's name in vain." Although many inexact definitions of blasphemy existed among the early canonists, including that of Alfonso X who regarded the offense as "insults to God, Holy Mary, and the saints … in word and deed," the *Escuela Española* popularized the Thomistic understanding of blasphemy as a "vilification of God's excellence and goodness."[232] Employing this definition, Las Casas accused the reprobate Spaniards (and Germans) of several manifestations of what he regarded as blasphemous conduct. For example, he decried how they attributed their conquest victories to God because, as Aquinas taught, God cannot be the author of moral evil; in this, Las Casas likened them to "those thieving tyrants … of whom the prophet Zacharias spoke," who praised God for their ill-gotten riches.[233] The *Very Brief Account* also reported (as did the Dominican and Franciscan friars) the blasphemous vilification of the goodness of God's design for salvation history when, on the island of Hispaniola, some reprobate invaders bound Indigenous persons on gibbets in lots of thirteen to burn "in honor and reverence, they said, of Our Redeemer and the Twelve Apostles."[234] Las Casas was equally appalled by the blasphemy, although not detailed in the *tratado*, of the German Lutherans in Venezuela as indicated in his charge about their "many blasphemies [and] infamies against God and His Law, ... because of the greed and inhumanity of those 'aleman' [German] or 'animal' tyrants."[235] As was typical of sixteenth-century discourse about blasphemy, Las Casas equated blasphemy with heresy in his assessments of the presence and activities of the Germans. First, he inferred that the German merchants were heretics because, as he assumed, they were all Lutherans. In this, he followed the Thomistic understanding of heresy as "a species of unbelief" that "assented to Christ, but not to all that Christ handed down."[236] Second, Las Casas explicitly asserted that the German governor was a heretic, because he disobeyed the Third Commandment of the Decalogue to "keep holy the Sabbath day," and did not allow "many others to hear [Mass]."[237] In Las Casas's outrage about this and "other signs of Lutheranism that were found out," he then denounced all the Germans in the Indies as "enemies of God."[238]

In addition to denouncing these sins against the God-related precept of love, Las Casas drew on theological teachings to condemn violations of the precept to "love your neighbor as yourself." This second divine precept enhanced the Golden Rule embedded in natural law, and elevated humans' care for one another to the domain of God's gratuitous grace. The last seven commandments of the Decalogue also provided Christian moral norms to govern humans' relationships with others. Again, these commandments supplemented and made more specific the general moral directives implanted in human nature and mandated by the natural order of reason: namely, "to do good," "to do unto others as you would have others do unto you," and "to give to others their due."

Accordingly, Las Casas charged that these Spaniards (and Germans) sinned against "the divine commandment ... that humans should love one another."[239] He also based his understanding of this precept on the writings of the Apostle Paul, whom he quoted, that love of neighbor meant to "fulfill the Law" and to keep the commandments.[240] In Las Casas's narrations about each region of the Indies, he persistently included and condemned the invaders' sins against certain specific commandments of the Decalogue that pertained to love for one's neighbor, namely, you shall not kill, ... commit adultery, ... steal, ... bear false witness, ... covet. Violation of these Christian injunctions to do no harm constituted sin against both "God and neighbor (*prójimo*)."[241]

The violations of the injunctions of the Decalogue by some Spaniards (and Germans) were fundamentally against justice—justice toward God and toward neighbors. The first three commandments of the Decalogue required rendering due reverence to God; the other seven commandments required rendering others their due. Although the norms of the Decalogue spelled out what constitutes justice as "right relationships" with God and others, the two-fold injunction to love God and neighbor is the essence of justice because love is an expression of the supernatural dynamisms of grace. In the supernatural order, humans have the ability to love and act justly because they partake of the divine life of God Who is Love and Justice Itself.[242] Given their "fall from grace," these reprobate Spaniards (and Germans), in Las Casas's theological assessment, could not love God nor act lovingly toward others, nor could they render what was due to either God or neighbor. Consequently, although redeemed by Christ, he judged that their "inhumane and bestial hearts" could not be perfected by grace.[243] Furthermore, by the many injustices they committed in disregarding the Christian requirements necessary for moral living, he charged that they jeopardized their attainment of the supernatural goal of eternal salvation and, according to the general Christian understanding of the time, they "cast" unconverted Indigenous people into the "fires of hell" because they "perish without faith or the sacraments."[244]

Consequently, Las Casas maintained that these reprobate Spaniards (and Germans) also sinned against the third precept of divine law, which mandated Christians to "go and teach all nations" the message of and means to eternal salvation: faith in Jesus Christ.[245] They obstructed the proclamation of the gospel by behavior that was counter to the peaceful and rational method of evangelization as mandated by divine, ecclesial, and royal authority, and which he championed all his life. They prohibited the preaching of the gospel as, for example, in Nueva Granada where they allegedly "forbid the men of the cloth … to preach to those people and those nations."[246] They impeded the conversion of the Indigenous peoples by their scandalous behavior, for example, in "the harsh and cruel maltreatment … done in the name of Christianity."[247] They undercut evangelization efforts by invading mission territories such as Chiribichí and Cumaná.[248] Furthermore, and very significant for Las Casas, these Spaniards perverted "the principal goal" of their presence in the Indies (which was the salvation of the Indigenous inhabitants) by their pursuit of gold and glory as "their ultimate aim" for being in the Indies. Because of these kinds of violations of the third divine precept, Las Casas bitterly concluded from his theological perspective that "today in all the Indies, there is no more knowledge of God, whether He is made of wood, or sky, or earth, than there was one hundred years ago among those people."[249]

These considerations about theological tyranny underscore the Thomistic conception of morality as a combination of natural and divine laws. Aquinas refined Gratian's equation of natural law with divine law, that is, with "what is contained in the Law and the Gospel." Aquinas taught that natural law was only a part of the divine law, and that "whatever belongs to natural law is fully contained in the Law and the Gospel."[250] From this Christian faith perspective, natural law was intrinsic to the character of the human soul as made in the image of God. However, according to Las Casas's canonistic-philosophical-theological understanding, he held that, although people—including the Indigenous—were created by God as rational, free, and social beings and redeemed by Jesus Christ, moral knowledge at the rational level was both limited and corrupted by the pervasive effects of sin. Accordingly, he judged that the covetous and reprobate conquistadors, encomenderos, and royal officials became lawless in their immorality. So intense was Las Casas's yearning for a remedy (which was the purpose of his *tratado*) that he rhetorically declared that in their dispositions, actions, and habits, and in the institutional arrangements in the Indies, there was "no law" and that these reprobate Spaniards (and Germans) "never had law ... of any kind."[251] He supported this statement that allowed for no exceptions by pointing out that, instead, there was "cruel and pestilential, ... harsh and vehement and diabolic tyranny," which, as he further charged, consisted of "all the disorder that Lucifer could sow."[252] As elucidated in this study, Las Casas employed the juridical figure of tyranny to narrate dramatically and to condemn clearly certain Spaniards (and Germans) and their reign of terror. Employing canonistic and Thomistic genres from the ecclesial tradition, he denounced and condemned the political, moral, and theological tyranny that underlay the evils and harm done to the Indigenous people by some Spaniards (and Germans), and that were condemned by "all divine, natural, and human law."

Basis of Las Casas's Juridical Voice

The basis for Las Casas's judgment, and the remedy for the all-pervasive tyranny, was justice. The central position of justice in Las Casas's appraisals of law (and of lawlessness) was in keeping with the conscious medieval development of the concept of justice, as well as with the dictum in the *Decretum* that "no one may act without consideration of justice."[253] Three interlocking dimensions characterized the Thomistic and canonistic understanding of justice to which Las Casas subscribed. These were natural justice as "right order" established by God, general justice as a virtue, and particular justice as a distinctive moral virtue. Each of these three dimensions reflected justice as "right relationship"; general and particular justice related to humans' relations in general with others and as individuals, respectively.

Natural justice emanated from the divine order of justice, which reflected in the original design of God who was posited as Justice *par excellence*. This overarching order of justice was implanted as natural law in humans. As creatures whose nature was rational, free, and social, humans must act in their relations with others in accord with this established order of natural justice. That is, this objective "right order" was inherent in human nature, and the first obligation of natural justice was "to do good and to avoid evil."[254] So incensed was Las Casas with the comportment of the conquistadors, encomenderos, and royal officials who thwarted natural justice that he rhetorically declared that "in the Indies, there was never any order or justice." While this particular hyperbolic charge refers to the lack of "order or justice" in the dispositions, actions, and habits of the offenders, his judgment reflected this theological-philosophical perspective of the Christian faith.[255]

General justice, in Thomistic teaching, was a virtue directed to the common good in humans' relations to others in general. General justice also governed the exercise of all the virtues insofar as they were oriented toward this good. This justice sought the good of humanity by its promotion of secondary goods such as self-preservation and the necessities of life, the preservation of the human species by procreation and human development of various kinds, as well as by civic association in community and in accord with *ius gentium*. This justice was denominated legal justice when law regulated the common good. In terms of general justice, the reprobate Spaniards (and Germans) lacked civic virtue and failed to conform to laws, such as those related to *ius gentium*, that regulated the common good. Again, out of Las Casas's conviction that these Spaniards (and Germans) failed to act in accord with general justice, he charged that they undercut the common good of what he regarded as "the greatest part of the entire human lineage."[256]

Particular justice consisted of the distinctive moral virtue of rendering to other persons their due by a "constant and perpetual will."[257] That is, in accord with the divine structuring of right relationships among individuals as equals, humans must respect the rights of other individuals, and do what was objectively "right"; they must, as Las Casas (and Aquinas) stated, do "the just thing."[258] According to this fundamental ideal of social justice, two types of dues were owed. Distributive justice allocated to each individual a due share of the goods held in common by society. Commutative justice governed exchanges between individuals.[259] When justice faltered in these human relations—such as in the relationships of the Spaniards (and Germans) with the Indigenous inhabitants—restoration and recompense were characteristic ways of making restitution, and were demanded of the "tyrants" by Las Casas in his *Very Brief Account*.[260]

However, to function as a moral virtue, particular justice went beyond the juridical norm of justice, albeit rational and authoritative, to include the moral evaluation of equity. This ethical dimension pinpointed what was intrinsically necessary to meet the demands of justice in a changing or changed human reality, which in Las Casas's time was that of the Indies. Equity, a term denoting fairness, was variously regarded over time as "applied justice," as "a supreme part of justice," or as justice itself.[261] Aquinas regarded equity as a higher rule of human moral action that "sets aside the letter of the law so that that which is just in itself can be attained."[262] Thus, the virtue of justice (augmented by the virtue of equity) went beyond the strict juridical norm of justice. Las Casas insisted on equity in his battle for justice for the Indigenous peoples. In justice, he demanded adherence to the maxim of equity that "no wrong should be without an adequate remedy" and, in the spirit of this directive, he repeatedly petitioned the monarch, as he did in the *Very Brief Account*, to right the wrongs done to the Indigenous peoples. Furthermore, according to canonistic teaching, the supreme role of equity was to foster humans' spiritual welfare, which makes more understandable Las Casas's central focus on the conversion and salvation of the Indigenous peoples, in addition to his appreciation of their own beliefs.[263] The above considerations also indicate why he focused solely in his *Very Brief Account* on what he regarded as necessary for the temporal and spiritual welfare of the Indigenous peoples and not on the Spaniards' well-being, other than articulating his concern with respect to their salvation. By this coupling of the juridical norm of justice with the moral norms of equity, the basis for Las Casas's judgment about the tyranny in the Indies was eminently ethical-juridical, and further demonstrates his persistent recourse to genres of inquiry from the Thomistic and canonistic juridical traditions.

Notes

1 Bartolomé de las Casas, *Historia de las Indias*, 3 vols., ed. André Saint-Lu (Caracas: Biblioteca Ayacucho, 1986), 1:19 [hereafter cited as *Historia* (Ayacucho)].

2 While this analysis relies primarily on Knight's English version of the *Brevísima relación*, the Spanish versions published by Pérez Fernández, Torrejón, and Saint-Lu, and also in the *Obras Completas*, were periodically consulted for verification and contextualization of the English translation. Bartolomé de las Casas, *An Account, Much Abbreviated, of the Destruction of the Indies*, trans. Andrew Hurley, intro. and ed. Franklin W. Knight (Indianapolis, IN: Hackett, 2003) (hereafter, Knight, *An Account*).

3 Antonio García y Garcia, *En el entorno del derecho común* (Madrid: Dykinson, 1999), 79, 82. Given Las Casas's studies in canon law and at San Miguel, his knowledge of and abilities in juristic writing would have included *ars notaria*, which developed out of *ars dictamis* taught in cathedral schools.

4 *Declarationes titulorum* referred to the titles that divided legal texts and that explicated the meaning or content of the section; see García y Garcia, *En el entorno del derecho común*, 80. Others, such as Bartolomé de Vega, also began their legal texts with an *Argumento* and *Prólogo*. Bartolomé de Vega, "El tratado de doce dudas," in *Obras Completas*, ed. J. B. Lassegue, OP, intro. and notes, J. Denglos (Madrid: Alianza Editorial, 1992), 11.2:13–32 (hereafter *O.C.*).

5 Kenneth Pennington and Wolfgang P. Müller, "The Decretists: The Italian School," in *The History of Medieval Canon Law in the Classical Period, 1140–1234: From Gratian to the Decretals of Pope Gregory IX*, ed. by Wilfried

Hartmann and Kenneth Pennington (Washington, DC: Catholic Univ. of America Press, 2008), 123. Bartolomé de las Casas, *Brevísima relación de la destruición de las Indias*, ed. and intro. Isacio Pérez Fernández (Madrid: Editorial Tecnos, 1992), 3:551 (hereafter, Fernández, *Brevísima*). Bartolomé de las Casas, *Brevísima relación de la destruición de las Indias*, ed. and intro. José Miguel Martínez Torrejón (Alicante, España: Universidad de Alicante, 2006), 101n2 (hereafter Torrejón, *Brevísima relación*).

6 In jurisprudence, the *argumento* encapsulated the core considerations that supported the case being made. James Brundage, *Medieval Canon Law* (London: Longman, 1995), 133.

7 Knight, *An Account*, 1; Pérez Fernández, *Brevísima*, 553–55; Brundage, *Medieval Canon Law*, 133. Juan Antonio Cruz Parcero and Roberto Lara Chagoyán contend that the central role of *argumentación jurídica* has been almost forgotten in legal studies since the eighteenth century; they offer ten kinds of interpretive arguments, including *argumento por analogía*, that were formerly part of juristic practice and writing. See their "Argumentación Jurídica," in *Enciclopedia Jurídica Latinoamericana* (México, DF: Editorial Porrúa, SA de CV, 2006), 1:481–90.

8 Knight, *An Account*, 1–2.

9 Although a thorough examination of the juridical rhetoric (in speech and in writing) that Las Casas may have used is beyond the boundaries of this book, judging from the bibliographic entries and textual citations about Cicero and Quintilian in Las Casas's writings, the bishop of Chiapa was very familiar with classical modes of oral and written discourse. Torrejon, *Brevísima relación*, 240n31.

10 The terms *exordium* (in Latin) and *exordio* (in Spanish) come from the Latin term meaning "to urge forward."

11 Carmen Codoñer, "Tres cronístas reales: Alfonso de Palencia, Antonio de Nebrija y Lucio Marineo Sículo," *Cronica* 37, no. 1 (Fall, 2008): 117.

12 Ibid., 117.

13 Knight, *An Account*, 3–4; Juan Antonio Cruz Parcero and Roberto Lara Chagoyán, "Argumentación Jurídica," in *Enciclopedia Jurídica Latinoamericana* (Mexico: Editorial Porrúa, SA de CV, 2006), 1:489–90.

14 Knight, *An Account*, 3–4.

15 According to Pérez Fernández, Las Casas was in too much of a hurry to print the *Very Brief Account* in 1552 that he did not designate the first part of the 1542 written material as an introduction—which it clearly is. *Brevísima*, 384.

16 Torrejon, *Brevísima relación*, 240n31; Manlio Bellomo, *The Common Legal Past of Europe: 1000–1800* (Washington, DC: Catholic Univ. of America Press, 1995), 144.

17 George Mousourakis, *The Historical and Institutional Context of Roman Law* (Burlington, VT: Ashgate Publishing, 2003), 305.

18 Anthony Pagden, "Ius et Factum: Text and Experience in the Writings of Bartolomé de las Casas," in *New World Encounters*, ed. Stephen Greenblatt (Berkeley: Univ. of California Press, 1993), 95.

19 Knight, *An Account*, 86.

20 Ibid., 87.

21 Stephanie Merrim, "The First Fifty Years of Hispanic New World Historiography: The Caribbean, Mexico and Central America," in *The Cambridge History of Latin American Literature*, eds. Roberto González Echevarría and Enrique Pupo-Walker (Cambridge: Cambridge Univ. Press, 1996), 1:66. Cicero taught that a *peroratio* can sum up an argument, and/or cast anyone who disagrees with it in a negative light, and/or evoke sympathy for the case.

22 Knight, *An Account*, 88; Pérez Fernández, *Brevísima*, 529, 531.

23 See the text related to endnote 81 of Chapter 6 for the content and source of this letter.

24 With respect to the availability of such "briefs" for future analysis, see Silvio Zavala, *Tributos y servicios personales de indios para Hernán Cortés y su familia. Extractos de documentos del siglo XVI* (México: AGN, 1984); Woodrow Wilson Borah, *Justice by insurance: The General Indian Court of Colonial Mexico and the legal aides of the half-rea*l (Berkeley: Univ. of California Press, 1983).

25 Aquinas's philosophy constituted a redevelopment of elements of Aristotle's teachings in a Christian framework that was in accord with biblical and early Christian tradition, which had already drawn elements from Roman law and from Platonic and Stoic philosophies. See André Azevedo Alves and José Manuel Moreira, *The Salamanca School*, Major Conservative and Liberation Thinkers Series, vol. 9. (New York: Continuum, 2010), 26–27.

26 In non-Christian belief systems, providential interpretations of history were first articulated in the ideational meta-narratives of ancient western thought by pre-Socratic thinkers who posited various natural determinants as movers of history.

27 Peter Frick, *Divine Providence in Philo of Alexandria* (Tübingen: Mohr Siebeck, 1999), 5–6. Aristotle's sense of providence was less explicit, and Epicurius's notion of history as "pure chance" completely denied the existence of any providence. For Aristotle, providence corresponded to the superlunary realm; for Epicurius, events of history were ultimately based on the interactions of atoms moving in empty space. Roman philosophers, such as Cicero who drew on Greek sources, regarded God as the "designer and enactor" of history; indeed, the glory of the reign of Emperor Augustus (63 BCE–44 BCE) was attributed to the teleological process predetermined by God that, as Emperor Marcus Aurelius (161 CE–180 CE) later wrote, constituted "divine providence as ... the nature of the universe hath appointed." Mousourakis, *The Historical and Institutional Context of Roman Law*, 25n70; Jorge Checa, "Cortes y el espacio de la Conquista: la Segunda carta de relación", *MLN* 111, no. 2 (March 1996): 209; Marcus Aurelius Antoninus, *Meditations Book XII.*

28 The expression "providence" does not, however, appear in the Old Testament until the Books of Job (10:12) and Wisdom 6:7; 14:3; 17:2. Ernst Niermann, "Providence," in *Encyclopedia of Theology*, ed. Karl Rahner (New York: Crossroad, 1986), 1313–15. See also Elsa Cecilia Frost, "La visión providencialista de la historia," in *Filosofía iberoamericana en la época del Encuentro*, ed. Laureano Robles (Madrid: Ed. Trotta, S.A., 1992), 332; Peter Frick, *Divine Providence in Philo of Alexandria* (Tübingen: Mohr Siebeck, 1999), 12–15.

29 Saint Augustine, *The Happy Life; Answer to Skeptics; Divine Providence and the Problem of Evil Soliloquies* (Washington, DC: Catholic Univ. of America Press, 2008); Jorge Gurría Lacroix, "Estudio Preliminar," in *Fray Francisco de Aguilar, Relación breve de la conquista de la Nueva España*, edición, estudio preliminar, notes and appendix by Jorge Gurría Lacroix (México, DF: UNAM, 1980), 37–48.

30 Aquinas, *S.T.* 1a, q. 19, a. 1, 2; q. 93, a. 1. The exemplar and the governance were simultaneous expressions of both God's divine knowledge and divine reason. Divine reason was frequently referred to as divine will or "the will of God." The entire panorama of the universe was one moment to God—who just "Is." This was because, as Aristotle taught, "the First Mover" was pure act. There was no potentiality in God—no movement from potentiality to

action, from unknowing to knowing. As such, God was considered the pure expression of creator, of divine pathos, of love, of being itself.

31 Enrique Florescano, *Memory, Myth, and Time in Mexico: From the Aztecs to Independence*, trans. Albert G. Bork and Kathryn R. Bork (Austin: Univ. of Texas Press, 1997), 76.

32 Ibid., 76.

33 Roberto González-Echevarría, *Isla a su vuelo fugitiva* (Madrid: José Porrúa Turanzas, 1983), 19.

34 D.A. Brading, *The First America: The Spanish Monarchy, Creole Patriotism, and the Liberal State 1492–1867* (New York: Cambridge Univ. Press, 1991), 96.

35 Knight, *An Account*, 1. Others also employed this interpretation. For example, in reference to Peru, Cieza de León wrote "to think that God should have permitted something so great to remain hidden from the world for so long in history, unknown to men, and then let it be found, discovered." See Pedro de Cieza de León, *The Discovery and Conquest of Peru: Chronicles of the New World*, eds. Alexandra Parma Cook and Noble David Cook (Durham, NC: Duke Univ. Press, 1998), 37.

36 Juan Villegas, SJ, "Providencialismo y denuncia en la 'Historia de las Indias' de fray Bartolomé de las Casas," in *Bartolomé de las Casas (1474–1974) e historia de la iglesia en América Latina,* Chiapas CEHILA Conferencia (Barcelona: Editorial Nova Terra, 1976), 23; Luis N Rivera Pagán, *A Violent Evangelization: The Political and Religious Conquest of the Americas* (Louisville, KT: Westminster/John Knox Press, 1992), 60. Enrique Florescano, *Memory, Myth, and Time in Mexico: From the Aztecs to Independence,* trans. Albert G. Bork and Kathryn R. Bork (Austin: Univ. of Texas Press, 1997), 79. Another possible indication of this providentialist-imperialist orientation might be the observation reportedly by Mendieta that the discovery was "rendered more striking" by its temporal proximity to the Fall of Granada and the expulsion of the Jews. Brading, *The First America*, 115–16.

37 Richard Konetzke, *Colección de documentos para la historia de la formación social de Hispanoamérica, 1493–1810* (Madrid: Consejo superior de Investigaciones Científicas, 1953), 1:1.

38 As reported in Chapter 6, other documents highlighted the centrality of evangelization and salvation, and condemned the conquests, such as those of Fray Pedro de Gante, don Francisco Tenamaztle, and Fray Francisco de Carvajal.

39 Leonard I. Sweet also called attention to Columbus's dream of an expanding Christianity in his "Christopher Columbus and the Millennial Vision of the New World," *The Catholic Historical Review* 72, no. 3 (July 1986): 369–82. Also see Brading, *The First America*, 13; Sarah H Beckjord, *Territories of History: Humanism, Rhetoric, and the Historical Imagination in the Early Chronicles of Spanish America* (University Park, PA: Pennsylvania State Univ. Press, 2007), 113; David Brading, "Prophet and Apostle: Bartolomé de Las Casas and the Spiritual Conquest of America," in *Christianity and Missions, 1450–1800*, ed. J.S. Cummins, An Expanding World Series 28 (Brookfield, VT: Ashgate Publishing, 1997), 120.

40 Cortés "opened the door" for the friars to preach the Gospel in New Spain, and, in accord with Joaquin Fiore's teaching about the Age of the Holy Spirit that would herald Christ's Second Coming, to build a "friars' church" and an Indian church akin to the early apostolic church. John Leddy Phelan, *The Millennial Kingdom of the Franciscans in the New World: A Study of the Writings of Gerónimo de Mendieta (1525–1604)* (Berkeley: Univ. of

California Press, 1956), 14–15; Rivera, *A Violent Evangelization*, 55, 57; David E. Timmer, "Providence and Perdition: Fray Diego de Landa justifies his Inquisition against the Yucatecan Maya," *Church History* 66, no. 3 (September 1997): 477–88.

41 Vittorio Salvadorini, "Las 'Relaciones' de Hernán Cortés," accessed November 11, 2010, http://cvc.cervantes.es/lengua/thesaurus/pdf/18/TH_18_001_085_0.pdf, 95–96. For a Nahuatl account—albeit it written from the 1540s to the 1570s—of the conquest of Tenochtitlan (Mexico City), see Matthew Restall, Lisa Sousa, and Kevin Terraciano, eds., *Mesoamerican Voices: Native-Language Writings from Colonial Mexico, Oaxaca, Yucatan, and Guatemala* (Cambridge: Cambridge Univ. Press, 2005), 25–44.

42 Cortés reportedly engaged in what Bodmer called "discourse of mythification" in his redefinition of his rebellion as service. Accordingly, Cortés used standard God-referent clichés to present his actions as under the purview of providence, such as "God gave us such victory …" or "if God had not mysteriously desired to save us, it would have been impossible to escape." See Beatriz Pastor Bodmer, *The Armature of Conquest: Spanish Accounts of Discovery of America, 1492–1589*, trans. Lydia Longstreth Hunt (Stanford CA: Stanford Univ. Press, 1992), 78; also see Merrim, "The First Fifty Years," 76; Florescano, *Memory, Myth, and Time in Mexico*, 78–79.

43 Florescano, *Memory, Myth, and Time in Mexico*, 79.

44 Knight, *An Account*, 5. Las Casas first referred to the Indigenous peoples as the major part of the human lineage in his "Carta al Consejo de las Indias" (1531), in *Obras Escogidas: Opúsculos, cartas, y memoriales*, ed. Juan Pérez de Tudela Bueso (Madrid: Biblioteca de autores españoles, 1958), 43b, 45b (hereafter cited as *O.E.*). Also see his "Carta a un personaje de la Corte" (1535), in *O.E.*, 60b; also cf. Manuel María Martínez, "Las Casas on the Conquest of America," in *Bartolomé de Las Casas in History: Toward an Understanding of the Man and His Work,* eds. Juan Friede and Benjamin Keen (DeKalb: Northern Illinois Univ., 1971), 337ff.

45 Knight, *An Account*, 29, 47.

46 Queralto Moreno, *El pensamiento*, 363; Aquinas, *S.T.* 1a, q. 1, a. 1; q. 44, a. 4.

47 Knight, *An Account*, 29, 5–6.

48 Gustavo Gutiérrez, *Las Casas: In Search of the Poor of Jesus Christ* (Maryknll, NY: Orbis, 1995), 253–54.

49 Knight, *An Account*, 2.

50 Aquinas, *S.T.* 1a, q. 22, a. 3.

51 This temporal governance was subject, however, to the authority of the pontiff. Francesco Maiolo, *Medieval Sovereignty: Marsilius of Padua and Bartolus of Saxoferrato* (Delft: Eburon Academic Publishers, 2007), 257.

52 Charles Casassa, "Magister Vacarius 'Hic En Oxonefordia Legem Docuit': An Analysis of the Dissemination of Roman Law in the Middle Ages," Department of History, University of Kansas, November 26, 1991, pages 2, 5, accessed January 6, 2010, http://history.eserver.org/dissemination-of-law.txt.

53 Fernando del Pulgar, *Crónica de los Señores Reyes Católicos Don Fernando y Doña Isabel de Castilla y de Aragón* (Alicante: Biblioteca Virtual Miguel de Cervantes, 2003); Vittorio Salvadorini, "Las 'relaciones' de Hernán Cortés," in *Thesaurus* 18, no. 1 (1963): 95; Brading, *The First America*, 44, 67; Phelan, *The Millennial Kingdom of the Franciscans*, 11.

54 Aquinas, *S.T.* 1a–2ae, q. 91, a. 1–6.

55 Eternal law was a very ancient concept, rooted in the Stoic and Platonic ideas of the immanent reason in things or universal logos; this concept was absolutized in God's wisdom and personified in the Christian religion as

the second person of the Trinity. Eternal law was the so-called because it was not subject to time, although, in the created world, its implementation takes place in time. God alone knew eternal law or divine providence. While humans did not have direct knowledge of eternal law, all women and men had a notion of eternal law as indicated in their propensity for virtue or their fear of God. Aquinas also taught that eternal law was recognized by all (*lex aeterna omnibus* nota). See Aquinas, *S.T.* la–2ae q. 93, a.1, 3; George Mousourakis, *The Historical and Institutional Context of Roman Law* (Burlington, VT: Ashgate Publishing, 2003), 25, 25n70.

56 Aquinas, *S.T.* la–2ae, q. 93, a. 3.

57 Every law ultimately derived from eternal law insofar as the law was reasonable. Aquinas, *S.T.* la–2ae, q. 93, a. 3. While the four types of law were differentiated in the way humans perceived and participated in them, they were—in their essence—a unity and, to the extent that divine, natural, and human laws reflected eternal law, they worked harmoniously together in a properly ordered human community. Aquinas, *S.T.* la–2ae, q. 90–91.

58 Aquinas, *S.T.* la–2ae, q. 91, a. 4.

59 In his treatise on peaceful evangelization, Las Casas argued that because Jesus Christ "was divine law" and God-made-flesh in human form, "the words and deeds of Jesus Christ have equally the force of law." Bartolomé de las Casas, *The Only Way,* ed. Helen Rand Parish, trans. Francis Patrick Sullivan (New York: Paulist Press, 1992), 88. In the Old Testament, divine law emphasized the governance of human relationships and divine institutions. This law contained useful juridical precepts regarding form of government, the role of judges and witnesses, ownership and transference of goods, treatment of foreigners, women and children. In the New Testament, divine law focused chiefly on the grace of the Holy Spirit: certain external actions (sacraments) were prescribed that lead to grace; certain external actions that weaken or destroy grace were prohibited. Edward J. Gratsch, *Aquinas' Summa: An Introduction and Interpretation* (New York: Alba House, 1985), 132–33.

60 Knight, *An Account*, 23.

61 Aquinas taught that divine law, which is found in grace, does not destroy human law, which stems from natural reason. Aquinas, *S.T.* 2a–2ae, q. 10, a.10; la–2ae, q. 91, a. 4. See also Jane E. Ruby, "The Ambivalence of St. Thomas Aquinas's View of the Relationship of Divine Law to Human Law," *Harvard Theological Review* 48, no. 2 (April 1955): 101–28.

62 Rationality or human reason (composed of intellect and will) pursues the true and the good, respectively. The intellect presents the true to the will, which the will perceives as a good. Human intelligence possesses simple direct knowledge of the truth, which reason gradually apprehends, as the intellect proceeds from one known thing to another. The will necessarily seek what is good; that is, what fulfills desire and gives happiness. However, the will is free to choose among particular goods that are presented to it by the intellect. Concerning the human intellect, see Aquinas, *S.T.* la, q. 79, a. 3, 4, 8; concerning the human will, see *S.T.* la–2ae, q. 8, a. 1, 2; q. 10, a. 1. For an understanding of the intellect as engaged in speculative or abstract reasoning and in practical reasoning (that deals with things that have to be done), and of the will as an inclination to action, see *S.T.* la, q. 79, a. 11; la–2ae, q. 91, a. 2. Reason dictated the course of action in this pursuit of the good.

63 Aquinas, *S.T.* la–2ae, q. 94, a. 2, 3, 4. Skinner provides a very concise explanation of this dual essence of natural law in his *The Foundations of Modern Political Thought*, 2:147–48. Quentin Skinner, *The Foundations of Modern*

Political Thought: Vol. 1 The Renaissance; *Vol. 2 The Age of Reformation* (Cambridge: Cambridge Univ. Press, 1978), 2:147–48 (hereafter cited as *The Foundations of Modern Political Thought*).

64 Aquinas, *S.T.* la–2ae, q. 95, a. 2.

65 Knight, *An Account*, 36.

66 All acts of virtue pertain to natural law. Although natural law directed all creation toward the good, moral evils or habits of vice can undermine the good. However, natural knowledge of general moral principles can never be completely undermined, although secondary principles can be. Aquinas, *S.T.* la–2ae, q. 94. a. 1, 5, 6.

67 Aquinas, *S.T.* la–2ae, q. 94, a. 2; q. 91, a. 3.

68 Aquinas, *S.T.* la–2ae, q. 90, a. 1; q. 92, a. 1; q. 93, a. 3; q. 95, a. 2, 3.

69 Aquinas, *S.T.* la–2ae, q. 95, a. 3, 4. Medieval canonists added another dimension to this Thomistic notion. For them, the "just social arrangements" obliged by law must "acquire, through the common good, that which is needed by humans to achieve their proper transcendental end." Manuel Giménez Fernández, *Instituciones jurídicas en la Iglesia Católica*, vol. 1 (Seville: Sociedad Anónima Española de Traductores y Autores, 1940), 1:108.

70 Aquinas, *S.T.* la–2ae, q. 95, a. 2.

71 Aquinas, *S.T.* la–2ae, q. 95, a. 4. As understood in Aquinas's thought, *ius gentium*, civil, and ecclesial laws are all considered positive law insofar as they are posited by reason and will over and above what humans know naturally. As such, positive law is the rational and willed decision of the lawmaker(s). In the case of *ius gentium*, this "law" (which can be understood as an overarching theoretical construct to understand and compare the law of societies) represents the reasoned and willed decisions of lawmakers of various societies. See *S.T.* la–2ae, q. 95, a. 4, a. 1.

72 Aquinas, *S.T.* 2a–2ae, q. 57, a. 3.

73 Aquinas, *S.T.* la–2ae, q. 94, a. 6; q. 95, a. 4.

74 Information about Bishop Garay is very limited. Apparently, he was a monk in the Order of Cistercians (OC), and a member of the royal household. At the time of writing, he was residing in Valladolid since he refers to it as "this here city." Since this report was addressed to the emperor who ruled from 1519 to 1556, as well as made reference to the prevailing Laws of Burgos, it must have been written after 1519 and before the 1542 New Laws. El Obispo Garay, OC, "Informe dado por el Obispo Garay al Emperador, de las cosas de Indias," in *Colección de documentos inéditos, relativos al descubrimiento, conquista y organización de las antiguas posesiones españolas de América y Oceanía, sacados de los archivos del reino, y muy especialmente del de Indias*, Competentemente autorizada, eds. Joaquín Francisco Pacheco, Francisco de Cárdenas y Espejo, and Luis Torres de Mendoza, vol. 11 (Madrid: Ministerio de Ultramar, 1864–84) 11:233–43 (hereafter *Colección de documentos inéditos*).

75 Pedro de Córdoba, OP, "Carta del vice-provincial y sacerdotes del convento de Santo Domingo, dirigida a los reverendos padres" in Miguel Angel Medina, *Una Comunidad al servicio del Indio: la obra de Fr. Pedro de Córdoba, O.P. (1482–1521)* (Madrid: Instituto Pontificio de Teología, 1983), 249.

76 Vicente Valverde, OP, "Carta del Obispo del Cuzco al Emperador sobre asuntos de su iglesia y otros de la gobernación general de aquel país," in *Colección de documentos inéditos*, 3:97.

77 The Catalan word "Remeça" is from the Latin word for redemption. J.H. Elliott, *Imperial Spain 1469–1716* (London: Penguin Books, 1963), 148–60; Teofilo Ruiz, *Spanish Society, 1400–1600*, A Social History of Europe Series

(Harlow: Pearson Education Limited, 2001), 192–94; Joseph Pérez, *La revolución de las comunidades de Castilla (1520–1521)*, trans., Juan José Faci Lacasta (Madrid: Siglo Veintiuno Editores, 1998), 451–566; Paul Freedman, "The German and Catalan Peasant Revolts," *American Historical Review* 98, no. 1 (February 1993): 39–54.

78 Both of these scholars (and other scholastics) were well-known to Las Casas and frequently cited by him. Las Casas also referred to Vitoria as a "most orthodox and ingeniously clear teacher." See his "Tratado Comprobatorio," in *O.C.*, 10:folio 20v.

79 De Soto's three-volume study about the tripartite scheme of law is known as *De Legibus*. Vitoria's application of this scheme extended to the rights of the Indigenous people, the power of kings in the temporal order, and the jurisdiction of the monarchy and the Church in the spiritual realm. Juan Belda Plans, *La Escuela de Salamanca y la renovación de la teología en el siglo XVI* (Madrid: Biblioteca de Autores Cristianos, 2000), chap. 5, and especially pages 489–500. See also S. Lyman Tyler, ed., *Concerning the Indians Lately Discovered: The Indian Cause Before the Law of Nations: Colonial Period* (Salt Lake City, UT: American West Center/Univ. of Utah, 1980), 11–130.

80 Francisco de Vitoria, *Doctrina sobre los Indios*, 2nd ed., trans. and trans. Ramón Hernández Martín (Salamanca: San Esteban, 1992), 103–147.

81 Girolamo Cardano, "De Sapientia," in *Opera Omnia*, 10 vols. ed., C. Spohn (New York and London: Johnson, 1967), 1:493–580. Girolamo Cardano (1501–1576), son of an Italian jurist, became a prominent mathematician, astrologer, physician (and gambler!), whose writings spanned many fields of knowledge during the early modern period—including the field of wisdom literature. (Of note—his multifaceted scholarship generated offers of employment from Pope Paul III.) The origins of wisdom writing date back to the Instructions of Shuruppak to the World of Ahiqar in Mesopotamia in 2600 BCE. Wisdom literature addressed humans' capacity for right judgment in the choice of means and ends in life and conduct; that is, wisdom denoted the pursuit of the best ends by the best means. Cardano's wisdom writings built on Aquinas's understanding of law-like behavior in the world of humanity and in the cosmos. Aquinas became regarded as one of the most thoughtful Western writers on wisdom, which he equated with sacred doctrine, and linked to Aristotle's teachings about *sapientia* and *prudentia*. *S.T.* 1a–2ae, q. 57, a. 1, 2.

82 André Saint-Lu, "Introducción," in Bartolomé de las Casas, *Brevísima relación de la destruición de las Indias*, ed. André Saint-Lu (Madrid: Ediciones Cátedra S.A., 1991), 30.

83 Reyes Cano, "Introducción," in Bartolomé de las Casas, *Brevísima relación de la destruición de las Indias*, ed. and intro. J. M. Reyes Cano (Barcelona: Planeta, 1994), xxx, xxxi, xlii, xlv (hereafter Las Casas, *Brevísima relación*).

84 Marta Inés Waldegaray, "Discours et relations de sociabilité dans La Brevísima Relación de las Indias de Bartolomé de Las Casas," *Caravelle: Cahiers du Monde Hispanique et Luso-Brésilien* 82 (2004): 19, 24, 37.

85 Aquinas devoted twenty-one questions to his "treatise on law" in addition to one each on providence and predestination in his *S.T.* 1a–2ae, q. 93–114, q. 22, q. 23.

86 See Chapter 6, "The Indians Are Coming to an End: The Myth of Native Desolations," in Matthew Restall, *The Seven Myths of the Spanish Conquest* (Oxford: Oxford Univ. Press, 2003), 100–30.

87 Knight, *An Account*, 32–33.

88 Bernal Díaz del Castillo, *The History of the Conquest of New Spain*, ed. and intro. Davíd Carrasco (Albuquerque: Univ. of New Mexico Press, 2008),

161–90; Fray Francisco de Aguilar, *Relación breve de la conquista de la Nueva España,* ed. Jorge Gurría Lacroix (Mexico, DF: UNAM, 1980), 78–83.

89 See especially his chapter entitled "Le cri de tant de sang: Les massacres d'Indiens relatés par Las Casas," in André Saint-Lu, *Las Casas indigéniste: Études sur la vie et l'oeuvre du défenseur des Indiens* (Paris: L'Harmattan, 1982), 45–54.

90 For a recently published scholarly examination of the encounter, see Matthew Restall's *When Montezuma Met Cortes: The True Story of the Meeting that Changed History* (New York: HarperCollins Publishers, 2018).

91 While Pérez Fernández identified Las Casas's ethical-juridical judgment about the violations of the tripartite scheme of law as the dominant element in the text's expository account, he did not systematically examine this dimension in his colossal and important critical edition of the tract. *Brevísima*, 326–33.

92 Knight, *An Account*, 3, 30, 36, 47. In addition to these specific references to the tripartite scheme of divine, natural, and human laws, Las Casas also referred, at times, to one or another of the three laws as he made his assessments.

93 Carozzo noted that Las Casas's views are difficult to synthesize because they are "characterized by a litigator's focus on the practical result sought in the dispute at hand." Paolo Carozzo, "From Conquest to Constitutions: The Latin American Tradition of the Idea of Human Rights," *Human Rights Quarterly* 25, no. 2 (May 2003): 292.

94 Because of the emperor's monetary problems, including financing the quelling of heresy and revolt in Germany, Charles V owed large debts to German bankers, and especially to the Welser family. Under pressure from the German banking houses, the Crown allowed German merchants to trade but not to settle in the Indies. This contract, which was signed on December 10, 1522, constituted an exemption from the general rule that prohibited foreigners from engaging in colonial trade. V. Afanasiev, "The Literary Heritage of Bartolomé de Las Casas," in *Bartolomé de las Casas in History*, 574n62; Elliott, *Imperial Spain*, 196–7; Blanca De Lima Urdaneta, "Alemanes en la provincia de Venezuela durante el siglo XVI," Conference paper, 53rd International Congress of Americanists: "The People of the Americas: Continuity and Change," Mexico City, July 19–24, 2009. Las Casas presented his perception of the consequences of Spain's agreement with the Germans in his and Ladrada's "Memorial de Fray Bartolomé de las Casas y Fray Rodrigo de Andrada al Rey" (1543), in *O.E.*, 188a.

95 Some identifying information of the alleged tyrants along with the relevant page numbers from Knight's edition of the *Brevísima relación* is as follows: captains and/or conquistadores: Francisco de Valenzuela who raped cacique Enrique's wife, 13; Pedrarias Dávila, capitán or conqueror of Panamá, 21; Pedro de Alvarado, the "great tyrant of a captain" in the kingdom of Guatemala, 36–38; Cristobal de Olid in the kingdoms of Naco and Honduras, 36–37; the "tyrannical captain-major" in the kingdom of Nueva Granada, 79; encomenderos, 79; merchants and the powerful German Welser family in Venezuela, 64–67, governors: Nicolás de Ovando, "the tyrant-major" governor of Darien, 15–16; the governors that succeeded Pedrarias, 24; the governor of Nicaragua, 28; the governors in the provinces of New Spain, Pánuco, and Jalisco, 44; Francisco de Montejo in the kingdom of Yucatán, 47; the German governor in Venezuela, 66; the governor of Río de la Plata, 72; Jiménez de Quesada in the kingdom of Nueva Granada, 78; *oidores* (judges) of New Spain, 44, and of Hispaniola who authorized the Tierra Firme slave raids, 60; as well as other officers of the king in Cuba, 21; and

Juan de Quevedo, the "highest and foremost bishop" of Darien, 24. Pérez Fernández suggested that the title of this treatise ought to have been the *Brevísima relación de la destruyción de las Indias por los cristianos españoles seglares (o por los conquistadores, encomenderos y mercaderes) movidos por la codicia y ambición y para saciarlas*. See his *Brevísima*, 552.

96 Pérez Fernández, "La doctrina de Santo Tomás en la mente y en la acción del Padre las Casas," *Communio* 18 (1985): 286.

97 Bartolomé de las Casas, *The Only Way*, ed. Helen Rand Parish, trans. Francis Patrick Sullivan (New York: Paulist Press, 1992), 127, 158, 164; "Carta al Consejo de las Indias" (1531), in *O.E.*, 48; "Carta a un personaje de la Corte" (1535), in *O.E.*, 61a, 64b. During the 1530s, Las Casas particularly censured the actions of the *Audiencia of Hispaniola* (1532), the German merchants invading Venezuela (1531) as well as the governments of Nicaragua (1535) and Guatemala (1539) as tyrannical. See Henry Raup Wagner and Helen Rand Parish, *The Life and Writings of Bartolomé de Las Casas (*Albuquerque: Univ. of New Mexico Press, 1967), 264; Pedro Borges, *Quién era Bartolomé de las Casas* (Madrid: Ediciones RIALP, 1990), 174–75; Isacio Pérez Fernández, *Inventario documentado de los escritos de Fray Bartolomé de las Casas*, vol. 1, Estudios Monográficos, ed. Helen Rand Parish (Bayamón, P.R.: Centro de Estudios de los Dominicos del Caribe, 1981), 220–79; José Alejandro Cárdenas Bunsen, "Escritura y derecho canónico en la obra de fray Bartolomé de las Casas" (Ph.D. diss., Yale University, 2008), 77.

98 Aquinas, *S.T.* 1a–2ae, q. 92. a.1, obj. 4; q. 96, a. 4.

99 Aristotle, *Politics*, bk V, chap. 10.

100 Brundage, *Medieval Canon Law*, 105–10. On issues related to judging and deposing a tyrannical ruler, see Kenneth Pennington, *The Prince and the Law, 1200–1600: Sovereignty and Rights in the Western Legal Tradition* (Berkeley: Univ. of California Press, 1993).

101 Brading, *The First America*, 98. Aquinas's teachings on tyranny and government are also found in his *De Regno sive de Regimine Principum ad Regem Cypri*, which tract was completed after Aquinas's death (1274) by Ptolemy de Lucca. Cardenas Bunsen also explicates Las Casas's recourse to these fonts of knowledge in his "Escritura y derecho canónico en la obra de Bartolomé de las Casas." José Alejandro Cárdenas Bunsen, "Escritura y derecho canónico en la obra de fray Bartolomé de las Casas" (Ph.D. Diss., Yale University, 2008), 122–23.

102 Bartolus de Saxoferrato, *De regimine civitatis*, cited in Maiolo, *Medieval Sovereignty*, 268–69, 272–73. Also in Bellomo, *The Common Legal Past*, 201.

103 Pérez Fernández, "La Doctrina de santo Tomás," 286–87.

104 Aquinas, *S.T.* 1a–2ae, q. 90, a. 4.

105 Aquinas, *S.T.* 1a–2ae, q. 93, a. 1–6; q. 91, a. 1.

106 Knight, *An Account*, 1, 6.

107 Ibid., 1, 46, 50; Romans 1:28–29. According to Aquinas, providence both permits and punishes reprobation. Aquinas, *S.T.* 1a, q. 23, a. 4.

108 Knight, *An Account*, 3.

109 Ibid., 50, 65.

110 Reboiras Fernando Domínguez, "'Y hasta agora no es poderoso el rey'. Sobre monarquía y élites de poder en los orígenes de la *Brevísima*," in *Talleres de la memoria—Reivindicaciones y autoridad en la historiografía de los siglos XVI y XVII*, eds. Robert Folger and Wulf Oesterreicher (Münster: LIT, Druck, 2005), 56.

111 Knight, *An Account*, 7. In Tenamaztle's *relación* in 1555, he too denounced the conquests and the institutions of bondage, as did Sánchez a decade later.

"Lo que suplica Don Francisco y relación que hace de agravios (1555)," in Lewis Hanke, "Un Festón de documentos lascasianos," *Revista Cubana* 16 (Julio-Diciembre 1941): 197–99; "Memorial que dió el bachiller Luis Sánchez, residente en Chillaron de Pareja, al Presidente Espinosa, Madrid (26 Agosto 1566)," in *Colección de documentos inéditos*, 11:163–64.

112 Knight, *An Account*, 62.

113 Ibid., 17, 26, 63; Aquinas, *S.T.* 2a–2ae, q. 42, a. 2, obj. 3. Maiolo pointed out that the practice of seeking one's own good was viewed at that time as contrary to God's will; he also cited Bartolus's teaching that tyrants "inevitably recede from pursuing the common good." See Miaolo's *Medieval Sovereignty*, 284. See Bartolomé de las Casas, *Doce Dudas*, in *O.C.*, 11.2:f. 177v, 178.

114 Knight, *An Account*, 29–30.

115 Ibid., 3.

116 Las Casas insisted that Alexander VI and also Queen Isabel understood the term "*subiicere*" to mean "to subject by meek and gentle means" so that the Indians will "be disposed" to "submit" to the gospel. See Pérez Fernández, *Brevísima*, 246–59.

117 Knight, *An Account*, 25, 54, 67.

118 From Pérez Fernández's study of *Capitulaciones* for the Indies, licenses and agreements initially were "to discover and to settle"; then requests began to be made and permission given "to discover, to conquer, and to settle." Pérez Fernández alleged that the discovery of gold in Cuba was a major factor in granting permission for conquests, which, however, as he opined, resulted in wholesale slaughters and in the enslavement of those who survived the killings. See his *El derecho Hispano-Indiano: dinámica social de su proceso histórico Constituyente* (Salamanca: Editorial San Esteban, 2001), 193, and his *Brevísima*, chaps. 7, 8.

119 Knight, *An Account*, 36, 72–73. For the Ordenanzas de Granada, and the kinds of licenses granted, see Pérez Fernández, *El derecho Hispano-Indiano*, 110–19, 62–72, 192–237.

120 Knight, *An Account*, 2–3, 6–7, 83.

121 Ibid., 26, 60, 61, 78.

122 See "Relación verdadera de todo lo sucedido en el Río del Marañón … y el comienzo de los tiranos …" 4:215–67; "Relación de la llegada del dicho tirano á la provincia de Venezuela," 4:268–74; "Carta que escribió el tirano al Rey," 4:274–282, in *Colección de documentos inéditos*. Brading contended that the contemporaneous usage of the term "tyrant" was loosely employed to describe leaders of rebellions against the Crown; Las Casas contended that the tyrants also usurped Indian lands and crown authority, thus exercising illegitimate power between the Crown and the Indigenous people. Brading, *The First America*, 98–99.

123 Knight, *An Account*, 23.

124 Tyler, *Concerning the Indians Lately Discovered*, 87–130.

125 Knight, *An Account*, 83, 86.

126 Ibid., 26, 35, 65, 73, 7, 28, 46, 23.

127 Ibid., 8, 20, 25, 57, 58, 61, 70, 75, 86. Other just reasons for war, according to *ius gentium*, would be to rescue Indigenous from any tyrannical native rulers, to defend any converted Indigenous individuals who needed protection, or to conquer those who prohibited the preaching of the gospel in their lands.

128 Knight, *An Account*, 7, 14, 16, 74.

129 Ibid., 34, 75, 77.

130 Ibid., 12, 13, 34, 51, 52, 55, 74, 75, 77.
131 Ibid., 51, 13, 44, 74, 79.
132 Ibid., 34.
133 Ibid., 21, 46, 65, 84.
134 Ibid., 16, 43, 65.
135 Ibid., 16, 35, 46–47.
136 Ibid., 47. See also Brundage, *Medieval Canon Law*, 105; Alves Azevedo and Moreira, *The Salamanca School*, 34.
137 Knight, *An Account*, 9, 14.
138 Ibid., 29–30.
139 Ibid., 29.
140 Ibid., 54.
141 Ibid., 15, 16, 36, 84.
142 Ibid., 24.
143 Ibid., 36, 63, 68.
144 Ibid., 27, 60.
145 Ibid., 15, 24, 45, 46, 47, 58–59, 60–62, 65, 66, 68, 73.
146 "Fray Pedro Gante's Letter to Charles V, Mexico City (1552)," in *Colonial Latin America: A Documentary History*, eds. Kenneth Mills, William B. Taylor, and Sandra Lauderdale Graham (Wilmington, DE: Scholarly Resources Books, 2002), 105–12.
147 Knight, *An Account*, 37, 46, 59, 84.
148 Ibid., 16, 27, 28, 46.
149 Pérez Fernández, *El derecho Hispano-Indiano*, 191; Brian Owensby, *Empire of Law and Indian Justice in Colonial Mexico* (Stanford: Stanford Univ. Press, 2008), 15, 36.
150 Knight, *An Account*, 16.
151 Ibid., 27, 41–42.
152 "Fray Pedro Gante's Letter to Charles V," 106–07.
153 Knight, *An Account*, 38, 87, 88; "Fray Pedro Gante's Letter to Charles V," 106.
154 Knight, *An Account*, 78, 88; "Fray Pedro Gante's Letter to Charles V," 109.
155 Knight, *An Account*, 26, 44, 60, 67, 68, 78, 80.
156 Ibid., 47, 67, 68, 88; Pérez Fernández, *Brevísima*, 529, 531.
157 Reboiras, "Y hasta agora no es muy poderoso el rey," 56; Knight, *An Account*, 1, 8, 60, 86.
158 Aquinas, *S.T.* 1a–2ae, q. 9, a. 1, ad. 2; 2a–2ae, q. 47, a. 4.
159 Las Casas, *Historia* (Ayacucho), 3:13–14, chap. 4.
160 Las Casas, "Memorial de remedios (1516)," in *O.E.* 5:27b; "Carta que escribieron varios Padres de las Ordenes de Santo Domingo y San Francisco, residentes en la isla Española, a Mr. de Xevres (presumably on 4 Dec. 1519)," in Medina, *Una Comunidad al servicio del Indio: la obra de Fr. Pedro de Córdoba, O.P. (1482—1521)*, 281, 272, 278, 283, 285. Fifty years later, Sánchez informed the authorities that so many provinces were depopulated and millions of people died because of the greed of the Spaniards. "Memorial que dió el bachiller Luis Sánchez … (26 Agosto 1566)," in *Colección de documentos inéditos*, 11:165. One hundred years later, Felipe Guamán Poma de Ayala continued to denounce this same greed and ambition. See his *Primer nueva corónica y buen gobierno*, ed. J. Murra and R. Adorno, 3 vols (México, DF: Siglo xxi, 1980), 372, 374, 391.
161 Bernal Díaz del Castillo, *The History of the Conquest of New Spain*, ed. and intro. Davíd Carrasco (Albuquerque: Univ. of New Mexico Press, 2008), 311–14.
162 "Memorial que dió el bachiller Luis Sánchez … (26 Agosto 1566)," 11:163, 165.

163 Carta del adelantado Vasco Nunez de Balboa, 16 Octubre 1513/1515," in *Colección de documentos inéditos*, 2:530–31; Knight, *An Account*, 50, 63, 68.
164 Knight, *An Account*, 8, 71, 47.
165 In addition to the explication of virtues in the *Summa Theologiae* and for a thorough discussion of natural law and morality, see Jean Porter's *Natural and Divine Law: Reclaiming the Tradition for Christian Ethics* (Grand Rapids, MI: Saint Paul Univ. Press, 1999). Also see Skinners's explication of advice books written for the prince, which reflected the initial humanist ideal of virtue in the pursuit of honor, glory, and fame, and constituted admonitions related to component virtues. Later, as Skinner explains, humanists' teachings about virtue were less a listing of virtuous behavior and more of an emphasis on "a broad sense of public commitment" coupled with an absence of private ambition and dedication to equality as the basis of a stable and lasting political society. Skinner, *The Foundations of Modern Political Thought*, 1:175.
166 Aquinas, *S.T.* 1a–2ae, q. 84, a. 1.
167 Alfonso X, *Las Siete Partidas*, 5 vols, trans. by Samuel Parsons Scott, ed. Robert I. Burns (Philadelphia, PA: Univ. of Pennsylvania Press, 2001), 1.5.58, 2.3.4; Aquinas, *S.T.* 1a–2ae, q. 84, a. 1–4, q. 78.2, q. 79, a. 3. Aquinas also taught that vices (or bad habits) do not corrupt the reason altogether. See also the admonition of Paul in 1 Timothy 6:10.
168 Knight, *An Account*, 22–23, 35, 36, 44, 48, 50, 67, 87. Pérez Fernández noted that the blind governors and legislators were "lettered" Spaniards, whereas the conquistadors were generally "unlettered." He also pointed out that the Spaniards were blind in their prior violent actions toward the Moors and Turks, and he suggested that the blindness of the "tyrants" was a mental set "received in antiquity." *Brevísima*, 801, 828–29. Before his own prophetic conversion in 1514, Las Casas also had been spiritually blind insofar as he did not see the injustices being done to the Indigenous people. Shortly thereafter, at the time of his failed 1516–1517 reform plan, he encountered the blindness of the Hispaniola colonists, conquistadors, and officials. Twenty-five years later, he continued to be confronted with their blindness.
169 Knight, *An Account*, 65. According to Venancio D. Carro, Las Casas was the first to alert the emperor of the dangers of the concessions made to the German bankers. See his "The Spanish Theological-Juridical Renaissance and the Ideology of Bartolomé de Las Casas," in *Bartolomé de las Casas in History*, 273.
170 Knight, *An Account*, 22, 23, 65; "Carta que escribieron varios padres de las órdenes de Santo Domingo y San Francisco, … a Mr. de Xèvres, 4 de Junio de 1517," in*La nobleza indígena del centro de México después de la conquista*, coord. Emma Pérez-Rocha and Rafael Tena (México, DF: Instituto Nacional de Antropología e Historia, 2000), 279.
171 Alfonso X, *Siete Partidas*, 1.5.58; Aquinas, *S.T.* 1a–1ae, q. 78. a. 3, q. 84, a. 1–4.
172 Aquinas, *S.T.* 1a–2ae, q. 78, a. 4.
173 Knight, *An Account*, 9–10, 46; "Carta que escribieron varios Padres de las Ordenes de Santo Domingo y San Francisco, residentes en la isla Española, a Mr. de Xevres (presumably on 4 Dec. 1519)," in Medina, *Una Comunidad al servicio del Indio: la obra de Fr.Pedro de Córdoba, O.P.(1482–1521)*, 275, 283.
174 Knight, *An Account*, 44–45; *Relación de las cerimonias y ritos y población y gobernación de los indios de la provincia de Mechuacan*, eds. Jerónimo de Alcalá and Moisés Franco Mendoza (Gobierno del Estado de Michoacán, 2000), 272–73.
175 Knight, *An Account*, 19.

176 Ibid., 9, 82.
177 "Memorial que dió el bachiller Luis Sánchez … (26 Agosto 1566)," in *Colección de documentos inéditos*, 11:165–66; Knight, *An Account*, 15, 46, 49, 50, 70, 76, 80, 82–82. Rigoberta Menchu reported these same kinds of cruelties in Guatemala in the 1980s. See her *I, Rigoberta Menchu: An Indian Woman in Guatemala*, 2nd ed. (Verso, 2010).
178 Knight, *An Account*, 11, 40, 45, 46, 48, 76, 80, 82–85; "Carta que escribieron varios padres de las órdenes de Santo Domingo y San Francisco, … a Mr. de Xèvres, 4 de Junio de 1517," 275.
179 Knight, *An Account*, 26–28, 62, 73.
180 Ibid., 8, 38, 56.
181 Ibid., 86; "Fray Pedro Gante's Letter to Charles V," 108.
182 The Dominicans and Franciscans described how the Indigenous people were used and treated as "brute animals" in the transport of both goods and the Spaniards. See their "Carta que escribieron varios padres de las órdenes de Santo Domingo y San Francisco, … a Mr. de Xèvres, 4 de Junio de 1517," 273, 286; "Fray Pedro Gante's Letter to Charles V," 108. Also see "Lo que Suplica Don Francisco y relación que hace de agravios (1555)," 199.
183 Knight, *An Account*, 66; Blanca De Lima Urdaneta, "Alemanes en la provincia de Venezuela durante el siglo XVI," conference paper, 53rd International Congress of Americanists: "The People of the Americas: Continuity and Change," Mexico City, July 19–24, 2009, 19.
184 Knight, *An Account*, 74–75; "Carta del Licenciado Espinosa a S. M. con las nuevas de los descubrimientos y conquistas que hacía Francisco Pizarro," in *Gobernantes del Perú: cartas y papeles, siglo XVI*, dirigida por D. Roberto Levillier (Madrid: Sucesores de Rivadeneyra S.A., 1921), 2:15–30.
185 Knight, *An Account*, 66.
186 Fray Martín de Murúa, *Historia general del Perú*, ed. Manuel Ballesteros (Madrid: Cofás, S.A., 2001), 210–11.
187 According to the contract with the caciques, Indigenous persons, ten years and older, who did not live near the mines were each taxed an *arroba* (a unit of Spanish weight equal to twenty-five lbs) of cotton or food every three months. When soon the people could not meet the quotas, the requirements were reduced by one half. Torrejón, *Brevísima relación*, 116n71.
188 Roldán's animosity may have been fueled by Guarionex's friendship with his rival, Columbus. Bartolomé Colon's complicity is less easy to explain.
189 Knight, *An Account*, 12, 14; Thomas Benjamin, *The Atlantic World: Europeans, Africans, Indians, and Their Shared History, 1490–1900* (Cambridge: Cambridge Univ. Press, 2009), 127–28; Pérez Fernández, *Brevísima relación*, notes 52, 53; Torrejón, *Brevísima relación*, 116n71, 117n73, 249n71. In his critical edition, Torrejón also drew from Anglería's *Décadas*, Oviedo's *Historia general*, and Las Casas's *Historia*.
190 About the three levels of caciques that lived on Hispaniola: namely, the supreme lord or "His Highness," the secondary lords or "Their Lordships," and the lords of the villages or "Their Graces." Sebastián Robiou Lamarche, *Taínos y Caribes: Las culturas aborígenes antillanas*, prologue by Ricardo E. Alegría (San Juan, Puerto Rico: Editorial Punto y Coma), 2005, 71–72
191 Knight, *An Account*, 14; Benjamin, *The Atlantic World*, 126; Torrejón, *Brevísima relación*, 117n73, 118n76; 250n76.
192 Knight, *An Account*, 45, 67, 70.
193 Pedraza, Cristóbal de Pedraza, "Relación de la Provincia de Honduras y Higueras," in *Relaciones histórico-geográficas de las provincias de Yucatán*, 2 vols., Madrid (*Colección de documentos inéditos relativos al descubrimiento, conquista y organización de las antiguas posesiones españolas de Ultramar*, segunda serie, 11, 13) Editado por Asencio, José María (1898–1900): 378–436.

194 Knight, *An Account*, 30, 36, 88.

195 "Carta al rey de los obispos de Nueva España," in *Epistolario de Nueva España 1508–1818*, 16 vols., compiled by Francisco del Paso y Troncoso (México, DF: Biblioteca Historica Mexicana, 1940): 4:10. "Carta de los señores y principales de la Nueva España al emperador Carlos V: en español, Tlacopan, 2 mayo 1556," in *La nobleza indígena del centro de México después de la conquista*, 199; "Lo que suplica Don Francisco [Tenamaztle] y relación que hace de agravios (1555)," 199.

196 Enrique Alcaraz Varó, Enrique y Brian Hughes, *Diccionario de Términos Jurídicos* (Inglés-Español; Spanish-English) (7 edición. Madrid: Ariel, 2003).

197 "Carta al rey de los obispos de Nueva España 1540," 10. Las Casas also narrated how some in Cuba "in desperation and lack of hope" hanged themselves. Knight, *An Account*, 21.

198 Knight, *An Account*, 30, 36, 38, 46, 65.

199 Ibid., 9, 13, 43, 45; "Carta que escribieron varios padres de las órdenes de Santo Domingo y San Francisco, ... a Mr. de Xèvres, 4 de Junio de 1517," 283; "Carta de los señores y principales de la Nueva España al emperador Carlos V: en español, Tlacopan, 2 mayo 1556," 199.

200 Stephanie Wood, *Transcending Conquest: Nahua Views of Spanish Colonial Mexico* (Norman: Univ. of Oklahoma Press, 1997), 68–69.

201 In gender-parallel societies, women and men operate in two separate but equivalent spheres, and each gender enjoys autonomy in its own sphere. In gender-complementary relationships, women and men complement one another as separate parts that together make up a composite whole. The existence of these two forms of gender relationships in pre-Contact Indigenous societies strongly indicates that there was greater gender equality in these societies as compared with that of societies infused with a highly dominant-subordinate gender ideology such as that brought from Europe to the Indies. Richard C. Trexler, *Sex and Conquest: Gendered Violence, Political Order, and the European Conquest of the Americas* (Cambridge: Polity Press, 1995), 7; Karen Vieira Powers, "Andeans and Spaniards in the Contact Zone," *American Indian Quarterly* 24, no. 4 (Fall 2000): 521–37; Karen V. Powers, *Women in the Crucible of Conquest: The Gendered Genesis of Spanish American Society, 1500–1600* (Albuquerque: Univ. of New Mexico Press, 2005).

202 Knight, *An Account*, 22, 29, 54, 66, 72.

203 Aquinas, *S.T.* 2a–2ae, q. 66, a. 8; Alfonso X, *Siete Partidas* 1.18.2, 7.13.1; *Institutes* 4.2. Thomas M. Izbicki, "Cajetan on the Acquisition of Stolen Goods in the Old and New Worlds," *Rivista di Storia del Cristianesimo* 4, no. 2 (2007): 505.

204 Knight, *An Account*, 88.

205 Ibid., 23.

206 Izbicki, "Cajetan on the Acquisition of Stolen Goods in the Old and New Worlds," 504–05.

207 Knight, *An Account*, 15, 59–61.

208 Ibid., 15; Torrejón, *Brevísima relación*, 250n79, 251n82. Torrejón also cited Oviedo's *Historia general*, Anglería's *Décadas*, and Las Casas's *Historia*; see Gonzalo Fernández de Oviedo y Valdés, *Historia general y natural de Las Indias, Islas y tierra-Firme del Mar Oceano (1535)*, ed. José Amador de los Rios (Madrid: R. Academia de la historia, 1851–1855); also see Las Casas, *Historia de las Indias*, in *O.C.*, vols. 3, 4, 5.

209 Knight, *An Account*, 59–61; Torrejón, *Brevísima relación*, 183n277, 184n279.

210 Knight, *An Account*, 61.

211 Ibid., 85; see also 30, 61.

212 "Fray Pedro Gante's Letter to Charles V," 108.
213 Knight, *An Account*, 70.
214 Ibid., 17; "Carta que escribieron varios padres de las órdenes de Santo Domingo y San Francisco, … a Mr. de Xèvres, 4 de Junio de 1517," 279.
215 Knight, *An Account*, 38.
216 Ibid., 29, 27, 38, 46, 54, 64–65, 70, 77, 84.
217 This is based on decades of research that included the use of native-language texts as sources of information.
218 Knight, *An Account*, 87.
219 Aquinas, *S.T.* 2a–2ae, q. 59, a. 1.
220 Aquinas, *S.T.* la–2ae, q. 71, a. 1–6; q 56, a. 4.
221 Knight, *An Account*, 31, 36, 54, 56.
222 Knight, *An Account*, 46, 45, 50.
223 Ibid., 17, 23; Aquinas, *S.T.* la–2ae, q. 79, a. 3.
224 Knight, *An Account*, 29; "Carta que escribieron varios padres de las órdenes de Santo Domingo y San Francisco, … a Mr. de Xèvres, 4 de Junio de 1517," 271; *S.T* 2a–2ae, q. 19, a. 2.
225 Knight, *An Account*, 29, 54, 64–65, 77, 88.
226 Ibid., 5. As explicated in the *Siete Partidas*, they were like Christians who revere riches more than they eschew sin. Alfonso X, *Siete Partidas*, 1.5.58.
227 Knight, *An Account*, 45.
228 Ibid., 18–19; "Carta que escribieron varios padres de las órdenes de Santo Domingo y San Francisco, … a Mr. de Xèvres, 4 de Junio de 1517," 286.
229 Knight, *An Account*, 53.
230 Ibid., 50–52; Aquinas, *S.T.* 2a–2ae, q. 12, a. 1.
231 Knight, *An Account*, 52.
232 R.H. Helmholtz, *The Spirit of Classical Canon Law* (Athens: Univ. of Georgia Press, 1996), 266–69; Alfonso X, *Siete Partidas*, 5.28.1; Aquinas, *S.T.* 2a–2ae, q.13, a. 1.
233 Aquinas, *S.T.* la, q. 19, a. 9; Knight, *An Account*, 47; Zacharias, 11:4–5.
234 Knight, *An Account*, 47; "Carta que escribieron varios padres de las órdenes de Santo Domingo y San Francisco, … a Mr. de Xèvres, 4 de Junio de 1517," 272.
235 Knight, *An Account*, 68. Here Las Casas is using a play on words.
236 Aquinas, *S.T.* 2a–2ae, q. 11, a. 1–4. At that time, Luther's doctrine also included charges that the "fullness of power" ascribed to the pope was blasphemous since only God could hold such power. Helmholz, *The Spirit of Classical Canon Law*, 267.
237 Knight, *An Account*, 66.
238 Ibid., 66, 68. Las Casas's apparent obsession with *luteranismo* could have been related to Luther's rejection of the pope's fullness of power. Indeed, forty years after the publication of the *Brevísima relación*, the bishop of Cuzco, Gregorio Montalvo de Coca, OP, also adamantly condemned as "Lutheranism" the royal directive that required all papal communications to pass through the Council of Castile and the Council of the Indies. Joseph M. Barnadas, "Una contribución a la historia del lascasismo," in *Bartolomé de las Casas (1474—1974) e historia de la iglesia en América Latina*, Chiapas CEHILA conferencia (Barcelona: Editorial Nova Terra, 1976), 96n15.
239 Knight, *An Account*, 62.
240 Romans 13:8–10.
241 Knight, *An Account*, 63, 70.
242 Aquinas, *S.T.* la–2ae, q. 100, a.3.
243 Knight, *An Account*, 39.

244 Ibid., 85, 86.
245 Ibid., 23.
246 Ibid., 86.
247 Ibid., 55.
248 Ibid., 59–60, 61.
249 Ibid., 86.
250 Aquinas, *S.T.* 1a–2ae, q. 94, a. 4, reply obj. 1.
251 Knight, *An Account*, 88.
252 Ibid., 83, 86, 88.
253 Bellamo, *The Common Legal Past*, 50; Gratian, *Decretum*, Distinction 12, 1.
254 Aquinas, *S.T.* 1a, q. 21, a. 1–2. Brian Tierney, *The Idea of Natural Rights: Studies on Natural Rights, Natural Law and Church Law 1150–1625*, Emory U. Studies in Law and Religion 5 (Atlanta, GA: Scholars Press, 1997), 21.
255 Knight, *An Account*, 72.
256 Ibid., 5, 11, 30, 54.
257 Aquinas, *S.T.* 2a–2ae, q. 58, a. 1.
258 Knight, *An Account*, 7, 14, 23; Aquinas, *S.T.* 2a–2ae, q. 57, a.1. Justice, as a virtue as well as over and above other virtues, had its own special proper object: the "right."
259 Aquinas, *S.T.* 2a–2ae, q. 61, a. 1–4.
260 Ibid.
261 A.R. Everton, *What is Equity About?* (London: Butterworth, 1970), 8. In the evolution of the legal system, the strictness of rules of law was tempered by the moral evaluation of equity, which ethical dimension was then incorporated into the juridical norm of justice. In this sense, equity was considered the source or "mother of justice." Accordingly, equity allowed judges to adjust the laws according to the particular situation, because justice seemed to require departure from strict observance of the law. Bellamo, *The Common Legal Past*, 160–61; Brundage, *Medieval Canon Law*, 61.
262 In this, Aquinas drew from the canonistic teaching of Isidore of Seville. Aquinas, *S.T.* 2a–2ae, q. 120, a. 1–2.
263 Peter Landau, "Aequitas in the Corpus iuris canonici," *Syracuse Journal of International Law and Commerce* 20 (1994): 94.

8 Peroratio

In July 1566, shortly before the Dominican Bishop of Chiapa died, King Philip II received Las Casas's request to the Council of the Indies that

> His Majesty ... order an assembly of learned theologians and jurists ... to examine the [eight] premises included in this document, their proofs, reasoning, and authorities, and ... to do justice to the [Indigenous] peoples who are so enormously aggrieved, for the safeguarding of the conscience of all.[1]

Las Casas was unrelenting. In 1514, after meditating on a passage from *Ecclesiasticus*, he was compelled in conscience to leave a comfortable encomendero's life and embark upon the afflicted life of a prophet.[2] Prophets are unwelcome; they speak the uncomfortable truth and demand hard solutions. His prophetic life as a cleric, friar, and bishop proclaimed the full humanity and complete dignity of the Indigenous peoples, and Las Casas demanded justice for them even to the point of possibly losing his life, as did his episcopal and Dominican confrere Antonio de Valdivieso. During the fifty-two years of Las Casas's prophetic life, he, too, gave completely of his life defending them, and wrote about them:

> ... in the Indies, Jesus Christ our God scourged, and afflicted and buffeted and crucified, not once but millions of times on the part of Spaniards who ruin and destroy these people and deprive them of the space they require for their conversion and repentance, and rob them of life before their time.[3]

Yet, he never gave up (Figure 8.1).

Figure 8.1 Statue of Bartolomé de las Casas, outside Cathedral in Mexico City.
Source: Photo by David Orique.

Concluding Synopsis and Discussion of the Argument

The main argument and organizing principle of this book contended that the *Brevisima relación* was an intricately reasoned piece of juristic writing, which belonged to the genres of the early modern legal tradition and constituted the product of Las Casas's erudite and persistent employment of a juridical approach. This concluding chapter first summarizes the previously presented contextual and textual support for this argument, as well as addresses questions generated about whether Las Casas homogenized or objectified the Indigenous people, or deemed them inferior or superior. The next section discusses three plausible foci of future scholarship: the issue of historical accuracy and historical truth, the relationship of Las Casas's corpus of writings to the *Brevísima relación*, and Las Casas's possible recourse to another sphere of ecclesial jurisdiction, the Inquisition. Lastly, this chapter presents other "Las Casas types," and concludes with what distinguished Las Casas as the conscience of Spain.

Contextual Support for Las Casas's Juridical Approach

As explicated in Chapters 2–6, contextual support for this book's argument was garnered from his formation within the historical matrix of Las Casas's native land, in the academic disciplines of canon law and theology, as well as in the Dominican *studium*, from his contributions to certain major debates, and from the circumstances surrounding the genesis and publication of the *Brevisima relación*.

The historical matrix of fifteenth-century and early sixteenth-century Renaissance Spain, in which Las Casas was born and lived, generated intellectual and cultural developments that provided the young Bartolomé with an opportunity to benefit from established curricular programs and academic institutions. Accordingly, Las Casas was educated in *estudia humanitatis* subjects (including grammar and Latin, oral and written rhetoric, humanistic moral philosophy) and in preparatory courses in theology and canon law at San Miguel in Seville, one of the most accomplished Castilian cathedral schools. His education then extended to the study of canon law likely at the academically prestigious University of Salamanca. Additionally, Spain's social history exposed Las Casas to ethnically diverse populations, and generated labor systems that were reflected in the early colonial institutions of the encomienda and *repartimiento.* Seville's urban landscape provided the young Bartolomé with exposure to mercantile, artisanal, and nautical skills. Seville's trade center also constituted the blueprint for the future *Casa de la Contratación*, which regulated trade in the Indies. Similarly, Castile's centralized system of government constituted the framework for the administration of the early Spanish colonial system, which consisted of governors, the *Audiencia de Santo Domingo*, and the Council of the Indies (later augmented by *audiencias*, viceroys, *corregidores*, *alcaldes mayores*, and so forth). In accord with the Catholic monarchs' vision of a geo-politically re-unified

Hispania, governance was to be conciliar in decision-making, peace-oriented, and "godly." The religious zeal and political ambitions of Isabel and Ferdinand for *ecclesia*, *patria*, and *orbis* also generated the Inquisition, reform of religious orders and monasteries, initial peaceful methods of evangelization in Granada, as well as a sense of messianic mission that Columbus also promoted. In the Indies in 1516, the young Padre Las Casas requested the establishment of the Inquisition, promoted peaceful evangelization, and shared Spain's sense of mission. Columbus's "discovery" and "possession" of the Indies opened a new horizon for Spain and for Las Casas. As a child, Bartolomé saw Taínos in Seville and lived in Taíno territory while he was, initially, a *doctrinero* and provisioner. Later in Hispaniola and Cuba, where he was both a cleric and an encomendero, Las Casas experienced a profound change of heart and perspective that led him to initiate a law-based "total remedy" for the "evils and harm" done to Indigenous people that would occupy him for the rest of his life.

Las Casas's intellectual formation consisted of canon law studies at the *bachiller* and *licenciado* levels, which the young cleric applied explicitly in his response to the Laws of Burgos and forcefully in his defense of the full humanity, religious capacity, and supernatural destiny of Indigenous people. His subsequent formation in Thomistic theology and in the charism of the Dominican Order—coupled with his canonistic expertise—enabled him to take a comprehensive approach to issues of the time. This ability to combine canonistic, philosophical, and theological teachings on law anchored his approach. For example, his distinctively juridical voice drew on Bartolian methodology and on the progressive nature of canon law: he applied age-old principles of law to new situations; he sought to reform law (*los derechos*) by attention to the facts (*los hechos*); he derived a doctrine of natural rights from natural law. As friar and bishop, Las Casas employed this juridical approach in his contributions to the ongoing anthropo-status and religious, and also economic and political debates. As explicated in Chapters 4 and 5, in these discourses (as well as in the *Brevísima relación*), he articulated the following uncompromising juridical premises. With respect to the full humanity and dignity of the Indigenous people, he asserted that Indigenous persons were rational, free, and social human beings, created by God and redeemed by Jesus Christ, and equal to other human beings, including the Spaniards. As well, they were part of the human family that constituted nations.[4] With respect to Christianization, he claimed that the method of evangelization must be peaceful and persuasive, and that the conversion of the Indigenous people and their salvation were the respective primary and ultimate reasons for the presence of the Spaniards in the Indies.[5] On the basis of these human attributes, fundamental unities, and salvific entitlements, as well as on *ius gentium* and canon law, Las Casas condemned the encomienda and slavery as institutions of the "hardest, harshest, and most heinous bondage." Out of his accumulated knowledge and experience with respect to complicated manifestations and historical precedents of such bondage, he generated the "Rule" that the Spaniards became increasingly cruel, and the premise that Indigenous peoples were made slaves unjustly in unjust wars.[6] With respect to *dominium*, he held that the Indigenous lords had legitimate *dominium* over their people and lands, that the only legal basis for the universal lordship of the king of Spain was the papal donation (which authorized sovereignty *de jure*) coupled with the consent of the people (which was required for sovereignty *de facto*).[7] With respect to the exercise of *dominium*, he asserted that all of the expansionist wars of conquest were "iniquitous, diabolical, tyrannical, and infinitely unjust," that the Indigenous people had never done any wrong or evil to the Christians, and that they had just cause for war against the Spaniards.[8]

The specific circumstances surrounding the genesis, writing, and publication of the *Very Brief Account* (as explicated in Chapter 6) also reflected Las Casas's eminently juridical approach. He submitted *los hechos* upon which he based his perception of the ongoing depopulation and devastation of the Indies to the highest civil authority and participated in the promulgation of the New Laws as a "total remedy" for the wrongs that, according to canon law, must be righted. He applied the force of ecclesial power to stem the tide of opposition to and non-conformity with the new *derechos*. Before the special junta in 1542, he argued that using "conquest to convert" was unjust, and subsequently published the *Very Brief Account*.

From among the kinds of support garnered in this book to demonstrate Las Casas's juridical approach, the premises underlying his substantive arguments in defense of Indigenous people need revisiting to address the question of their agency. In these premises, which Las Casas articulated in the debates of the time and also included in the *Brevísima relación*, he asserted their agency in several ways. He contended that Indigenous people had the right to institute (to choose) the Spanish monarch as their supreme lord—a right that was apparently exercised by fifteen Indigenous lords in the Yucatán. He asserted that Indigenous people also had the right to resist in addition to having just cause for war. They exercised this right through various modes of resistance as exemplified in the narrations in his *relación* about their battling to recover their spouses and children, and rising in revolt and rebellion as done in the Andean region. In this, the Indigenous people demonstrated their ability to struggle, which, along with their overall survival in the Indies, further suggests agency. Of perhaps singular importance for the Dominican was the right of Indigenous people to choose whether or not to become Christian. Las Casas was very clear that the duty of the Spanish Christians was to preach the Gospel, and to do this through rational and peaceful methods both in word and in deed. For him, conversion was not to be forced nor undertaken lightly. For him, liberty was "the most precious" attribute of rational human beings and must not be compromised, not by economic and political practices, or in matters of religion. For Las Casas, as he amply explicated in the larger corpus of his writings, religious freedom was a given. Considerations of Indigenous agency in whether or not to convert also had significant ramifications for the *entradas*. The idea of a "peaceful" *entrada* was based on the notion that if properly approached and persuaded (which meant with adequate knowledge, in accord with rules of *ius gentium*, and with free consent), the local inhabitants would still have the choice to object to the situation and even go to war. Thus, even if the Indigenous inhabitants of the Indies were left more peacefully by themselves, Las Casas would respect their choice to question (or reject) Christianity. For him, this was fundamental to religious freedom. Also, Las Casas was convinced of the power of the gift of faith from the Creator-Redeemer; acceptance and nurturing of this free gift depended on humans' free will. Nevertheless, Las Casas also lamented that many Indigenous people died (at the hands of certain Spaniards and Germans) without faith and the sacraments. Thus, he shared the hope of the time that "all should be one" (at least eventually) in "the only true Faith"—an ethnocentric consideration that will be discussed later in this chapter.

Textual Support for Las Casas's Juridical Approach

As elucidated in Chapters 6 and 7, study of the context, character, and content of the text has also generated significant indicators of the intricately juridical nature of the *Brevisima relación*. Evidence of the legal character of the treatise is found in its official publication with seeming pre-approval, special privilege, and/or influential support, in addition to its integrity as a report based on *probanzas* and other evidentiary sources. The correspondence of its functions to three genres of the civil juridical tradition—*relaciones*, *denuncias*, and *peticiones*—further ascertains its character as a piece of juristic writing, which was in keeping with the flourishing of hegemonic legal discourse and the "law of the letter"—as was typical of Spain's bureaucratic form of governance.

Evidence of the legal content of the treatise is further revealed in the variety of structural components of a juridical quality that characterize the *Argumento*, *Prólogo*, body of narrative, and *Peroratio*. The overarching meta-narratives of Providence as divine exemplar and divine governance as well as of the hierarchy of eternal, divine, natural, and human laws constitute a law-based epistemological rationale for the treatise. The analytic framework for the narrative of the text delineates Las Casas's intricate employment of divine precepts, natural law principles, and human law ordinances. According to these criteria, he presented and judged what he deemed the rampant political, moral, and theological tyranny in the Indies, which had caused (and continued to cause) premature and unjust deaths as well as untold suffering due to the violations of divine entitlements, natural rights, and just human law. Underlying Las Casas's recourse in the text to Thomistic, canonistic, and scriptural genres of the ecclesial juridical tradition is the basis of his ethical-juridical voice: the juridical norm of justice coupled with the moral norm of equity.

Questions Raised

Study of the content of the treatise also raises three questions about Las Casas's portrayal of Indigenous peoples: the seeming tendency to homogenize, the alleged issue of objectification, and the manifest question of equality.

Homogenization or overgeneralization did characterize Las Casas's portrayal of Indigenous peoples in his *Very Brief Account*, beginning with his initial description of them as a "simple people." He made no clear distinctions to demarcate the complexity of and differences between the various Indigenous societies, whether nomadic, semi-sedentary, or sedentary, whether state-level imperialist or militarist. Instead, he collapsed their differences under one general category for the native inhabitants of the Indies: the Indigenous people. His purpose was clear: to portray that the Indigenous people are "all the same" in their simplicity, their innocence, their abilities, their suffering, and so forth, which depiction served to support the trope of good and evil that he employed. Yet, his portrayal of the Indigenous people was not one of complete homogenization as indicated in the *tratado* by his inclusion of some individual exceptions. His ability to see the individual was exemplified, for example, when he asserted that some individual Indigenous persons might belong to Aristotle's third category, and that some Indigenous persons might be hard-hearted enough to wrought sinful vengeance on the Spaniards for their deeds.

The tendency to homogenize was also evident in Las Casas's use of the trope of "tyrant," in which he generally did not allow for differentiation between the especially cruel individuals and others, or between the leaders and followers (who might have been too intimidated to object), although he did at times distinguish the leader or the especially perverse from the rest of them. (Recall, however, that the *Larguísima relación* apparently contained names and other identifying information.) In like manner, he generally denoted Spaniards as "evil," meaning especially the "secular" or lay Spaniards and some clergy, but not the "good" friars and bishops, the monarch, and some crown authorities.

However, these kinds of homogenization of population cohorts and of differential tropes are understandable as rhetorical strategies and juridical tactics that Las Casas, as a "lawyer," would have used in order to unambiguously impart his *querella* that the Indigenous inhabitants of the Indies had suffered great evils and harm at the hands of some Spaniards. Because of his need to present a narration that was neither encumbered by minute detail nor obfuscated by complex distinctions, he deliberately collapsed diversity. Yet, in the larger corpus of his writings, and especially in the *Apologética historia sumaria*, *Apología*, and *Historia de las Indias*, Las Casas did present a very complex and sophisticated portrayal of Indigenous societies and clearly demonstrated his understanding of their different ways of life.

However, in addition to Las Casas's tendency in the *Very Brief Account* to homogenize his portrayal of Indigenous peoples, was he also "objectifying" them? Was he making them the objects of his own actions and authority, and/or treating them impersonally? True, the Indigenous people were the object of his battle for justice on their behalf—and he took them (seemingly without their request or consent) as his "client," and lobbied for them at court. If it can be argued that by this he had objectified them, was there evidence in the "*Very Brief*" summary that he treated them impersonally? He did, after all, include narrations about specific Indigenous persons, calling them by name and describing part of the situation in which they found themselves. Indeed, the narrative of the *Brevisima relación* elucidated a different source of objectification: those Spaniards who made Indigenous people the objects of their greed, their reprobation, and their lawlessness. These Spaniards (and Germans) disallowed and otherwise prohibited the consequently subjugated natives from becoming and being the subjects of their own lives. These Europeans disallowed the agency of the Indigenous people. However, agency mitigates objectification because, with agency, people become subjects of their lives. Consequently, given the level of agency of Indigenous people asserted by Las Casas, any charge of objectification on his part would be lessened.

In addition to prompting examination of Las Casas's ability to homogenize strategically and allegedly to objectify Indigenous people, study of the content of the *Brevisima relación* raises the question of equality. In his presentation, were Indigenous people equal to the Spaniards? Ontologically, as rational, free, and social beings, yes. Theologically, as created by God and redeemed by Jesus Christ, yes. But were they equal culturally? Obviously, Las Casas desired that these people, who never heard of Christ, become Christians. The questions then become: Did Las Casas mean that they needed to be acculturated into Spanish Christianity? Or, did he intend for them to become Christians within their own culture, thus forming an autochthonous Christianity (which gradually and eventually did happen in all of Latin America)? Would this Indigenous Christianity be different from the Franciscans' hoped-for Indian Church? (Additionally, would not Christianity in effect disrupt traditional Indigenous cultures?) These kinds of questions suggest an assertion of the Christian culture's superiority as compared with Indigenous culture. Moreover, in Las Casas's employment of a cultural evolutionary scheme, he did maintain that Christianity perfects culture. Yet, he also insisted that the Spaniards could learn some things from the cultures of Indigenous peoples, which both connotes superiority and indicates that the culture of the Spanish Christians in the Indies had much to be desired. Seemingly, for Las Casas, the ideal culture was one infused with the Christian culture wherein by word and deed, the Gospel would be proclaimed and lived.

Another example of the ascription of inferiority on Indigenous people is implied in Las Casas's categorization of them as *miserabiles personae.* Jurisprudential canons—civil and ecclesial, and especially scriptural—stipulated care for the most "wretched," as Las Casas described the Indigenous people in his *Brevisima relación.* In the Indies, the Indigenous people qualified for categorization as *miserabiles personae* precisely because of the "wretched" circumstances of their lives, which were made so by some Spaniards (who were not living in accord with Christian norms and beliefs). Their ascribed inferiority did not, however, jeopardize the rights of Indigenous people in accord with applied justice, that is, equity. In "fairness," the wrongs that precipitated the "wretched" condition of their lives must be remedied, and their spiritual welfare must be fostered.

These rationales emit ethnocentric European thought (and action), and Las Casas was not immune to them. He had a certain ethnocentrism precisely because he was part of his time and his culture. This ethnocentrism was tempered, however, by his acquired knowledge of Indigenous peoples and by his insistence on their agency. For him, agency trumped ethnocentrism. The agency he asserted for the Indigenous peoples was more important than this ethnocentric bias, because, for him, human freedom was the highest value. For Las Casas, fully exercising agency and freely choosing faith were supreme.

Plausible Foci of Future Scholarship

During the late nineteenth century and through most of the twentieth, Lascasian scholarship was underdeveloped and, for the most part, reflected the conflicted nature of Lascasian historiography. Much tension existed between over-vilification and over-encomiastic perspectives of Las Casas's role in the critique of the conquest and colonization. As fuller access to edited versions of the corpus of Las Casas's writings became available and scholars began to more critically examine his works, a better understanding of his life, labor, and legacy developed. This growth in understanding holds three important implications for this study and future scholarship. At the same time, more scholarship about the early colonial era, and about what came after, provides a more accurate understanding of the strengths and limitations of the *Brevísima relación* as history.

Historical Accuracy and Historical Truth

This book invites refocusing on the issue of historical accuracy and historical truth in the *Brevísima relación.* According to Torrejón, the issue of historical accuracy has not been adequately addressed in the many editions of the *tratado* and in other Lascasian scholarship.[9] Some of the most recent scholarship has inquired into this issue. For example, Comas compared scholars' evaluations of Las Casas's data but did not discuss specific events, population figures, and sources employed in the text.[10]

Similarly, Hanke demonstrated the range of oral and written testimony to which Las Casas had access, but did not apply these to Las Casas's specific narrations.[11] To bridge the subsequent lacuna in Lascasian scholarship about this issue, Torrejón undertook and recently published an extensively annotated edition of the *Brevísima relación* that places Las Casas's narrations in their historical contexts. On the basis of his impressive study, Torrejón claims that ninety percent of the facts in the *Very Brief Account* are confirmed by contemporaneous accounts.[12]

While Torrejón's detailed and comprehensive critical edition of the *Very Brief Account* with its copious footnotes and *notas complementarias* (complementary notes) is of tremendous interpretive and documentary value in its identification of the "tyrants" and other actors, as well as the sources Las Casas used, there are additional considerations to take into account to assess the historical accuracy—particularly of the remaining ten percent of the data.

One consideration is the fact that the *Brevisima relación* originated from the *Larguísima relación*, a report which, according to the Chronicles of Emperor Charles V, did exist and was a much longer, more detailed, and fuller portrayal of events, people, and populations.[13] While this *Larguísima relación* and its supporting documents have yet to be discovered, this *Very Long Account* arguably had some level of credence at court. (The length and gravity of this report could have also been a tactic to alarm or persuade its audience.) The report was delivered to the emperor and the special junta; it also became an important component in the genesis of the New Laws. Additionally, the report also apparently included a scrupulously veridical presentation of a "stack of *probanzas*," and other evidentiary sources. Yet, certainly other reports from civil authorities, conquerors, encomenderos, and so forth also existed, which presented events in a different light, even though they may not have directly addressed Las Casas's charges. Furthermore, the contents of the *probanzas* Las Casas collected are unknown. Neither do we know whether he used them selectively. However, to the best of my knowledge, no one at the time discredited, disputed, or disparaged this official report. To the contrary, as detailed earlier, other friars and bishops also submitted supportive evidence to the emperor at this same time. In any case, since the *Brevisima relación* was derived from the longer report, its general accuracy can also be implied, albeit indirectly, until the original "working papers" are found. Even so, these "working papers" would still represent Las Casas's choice of facts, style of reporting, and priority of endeavors, and also may contain weaknesses in the evidence, potential biases, and possible exaggerations.

A second consideration derives from the fact that the *Very Brief Account* was merely a summary. As such, Las Casas did not frequently include detailed descriptions of the particular events such as those he narrated about the Inn at Paría or about the consent of the Yucatán Mayans to become *de facto* vassals of the Spanish monarch. Indeed, Las

Casas was "silent" about many activities, structures, and processes pertaining to the ways of life of Indigenous peoples that if included would have resulted in a fuller portrayal of the first five decades of life in the Indies. For example, although he addressed the injustice of the colonial tribute system, he did not refer to nor assess the tribute system of Indigenous peoples. Nor did he acknowledge that there were Indigenous encomenderos. In his assessments about warfare, he does not address inter-ethnic wars (and how, for example, in Guatemala, Alvarado played one Indigenous group off the other), nor does he consider whether the Indigenous people waged just war among themselves. Las Casas also omitted any information about Indigenous allies of the Spaniards. Inclusion of the above kinds of information would, of course, have undermined the trope of good Indigenous peoples and evil Spaniards. References to pre-Contact political structures and hierarchy were largely absent. He merely identified the five kings of Hispaniola and Atahualpa (Peru) as supreme lords, and also recognized the developed polity in New Spain and the Yucatán. With respect to pre-Contact socio-cultural aspects, he said little about gender roles and ideology. Similarly, he did not entertain Indigenous cosmological ideas to probe how they understood themselves and what was their concept of human nature. He only used European categories. The net result was a one-sided-summary report, which was compounded by exaggerated statistics, a general phenomenon of the epoch.[14] Additionally, the written sources that he chose to retain in the summary may have included questionable second-hand materials that were not necessarily based on eyewitness testimony even though the documents seemingly carried reliable approbation from authorities, such as that given by Bishop Zumárraga to Niza's chronicle.

A third consideration in addressing the issue of historical accuracy is particularly relevant to this book and more directly related to this historical investigation of Las Casas's juridical approach: the fact that the *Very Brief Account* was written by a canon law advocates for the *miserabiles personae*—the Indigenous people. Las Casas may have simply been functioning as a "lawyer." As such, he would have been inclined to emphasize certain things, to leave out others, and/or to exaggerate for effect. He would have selected, described, and presented evidence that supported his contentions. That is, he needed to present "a case" that would "win" in court—even if it meant "erring" in, what Torrejón contended would be, ten percent of his data. To address this, future scholarship might pursue comparative research on contemporaneous legal processes and briefs, as well as on the accuracy of claimants' accounts.

Furthermore, to interpret Las Casas's choices of *los hechos* and of evidence as part of a prosecutor's strategy to argue his "case" constitutes an attempt to historicize the treatise, and to focus attention away from mythologizing elements such as his use of tropes and feigned language, as well as its place in Golden Age literature or polemical texts. Since multiple opinions can be held about the same event, more historical research is needed to determine how they may differ from Las Casas's interpretations. More research is needed on what others perceived and articulated as "the truth" of the event(s) and what would be the appropriate remedy.

Recall also that Las Casas needed to convince his intended audience of the need for drastic reforms. He needed to create a stark undeniable picture of tyranny and abuse that was beneath the dignity of Spaniards, of the non-"tyrants," of the majority of the Spaniards who were essentially good people. Torrejón opined that Las Casas "transformed information to make a coherent story," and that the details "blur into one another" in the Dominican's "repetitious account of [this] blurred reality" in order to convey the "enormity and uniformity" of the rampant tyranny. Again, this suggests that Las Casas acted as a "lawyer," stressing the shocking and habitual tyrannous events, and making his "clients" (the Indigenous people) as appealing and understandable as possible. (Torrejón's characterization of the *Brevísima relación* as a "blurred reality" also evokes questions about his ninety percent argument.)

Torrejón also suggested that this "coherent story," although in places not necessarily factually true, was "morally, essentially true."[15] A quarter of a century earlier, scholars also pointed out this kind of "truth" in the *Brevísima relación*. Carreño contended that Las Casas did not err in the essential truth: the cruelty toward the Indigenous peoples, and the depopulation of their communities.[16] (Yet, much of this depopulation was unintentional as a result of disease especially in Hispaniola, New Spain, Peru, and later other colonial areas.) Sacoto also claimed that Las Casas presented *la verdad vivida*—the lived truth or the real-life truth.[17] These contentions imply a distinction between historical accuracy and historical truth.

Any assessment of historical truth in the *Brevísima relación* must take into account that Las Casas had a specific understanding of the source of truth: he extrapolated the truth from the available facts (*los hechos*). Furthermore, to speak the truth was for him a duty of conscience. Accordingly, out of his well-informed conscience on which he radically relied, he "spoke the truth … as he knew it," which is the only truth that anyone can speak.[18] His intent in the *Very Brief Account* was to speak the truth—as derived from *los hechos* and as he understood it—and, as he stated, he "could not be silenced."[19]

The kind of truth that Las Casas articulated in the *Very Brief Account* can be conceptualized as a meta-truth—the overarching truth about the injustice of the conquests and colonization, which resulted in devastation of some Indigenous peoples and their lands, and which constituted violations of divine, natural, and human laws.[20] Las Casas articulated this meta-truth persistently in each territory as he presented the trajectory of conquests from Hispaniola and Tierra Firme to Peru and Nueva Granada. Even though by 1542 the conquests "of the last known sedentary people" were completed, the consequences of conquests continued: in the enslavements in the periphery (but not in the centers), in the dislocations, which varied in type and intensity from place to place and over time.[21] By distilling what was essential from *los hechos*, Las Casas universalized this truth about the injustice. This meta-truth was more valuable and important than any detailed event. Proclaiming this meta-truth was of far greater impact than narrating particulars.[22] Las Casas's articulation of this historically transcendent truth was also intricately coupled with the Christian meta-narrative of the hierarchy of law (which meta-narrative was explicated in Chapter 7). However, further research is also needed on how this kind of historical truth was understood in the philosophical, theological, and legal structures of discourse of the time. Indeed, even if we understand how and why meta-truths were created, our cultural expressions of them cannot be left untested.

Commentaria on the Brevísima Relación

This book also invites inquiry into the relationship of Las Casas's corpus of writings to the *Brevísima relación*. Examination of Las Casas's contributions to the debates addressed in Chapters 4 and 5 of this study revealed that his *memoriales*, *cartas*, *tratados*, and *obras mayores* seemed to function as jurisprudential *commentaria* on the premises contained in the *Brevísima relación*. Judging from his repeated citations of judicial commentaries, Las Casas was very familiar with this textual form and also with how Bartolus (and others) utilized this juristic form of writing.

The characteristics of this legal genre suggest that the corpus of his writings did serve as commentaries for the *Brevísima relación*. Unlike other legal genres, *commentaria* were a type of exposition that presented a personal re-elaboration of a variety of issues while at the same time being relatively homogenous in content.[23] Las Casas's writings also addressed a variety of issues, for example, those related to the encomienda, slavery, conversion methods, and governance; the basis of his interpretations, reinterpretations, and arguments was always from the perspective of law. That is, the homogeneity in Las Casas's writings consisted in his approach to issues from a juridical framework of rights and laws. Jurisprudential commentaries also functioned to explicate the law, namely, to clarify and to apply the universal principles of law to new circumstances, to modify the law when necessary, and to build a unified body of law. These functions were also typical components of Las Casas's approach in the corpus of his writings. Furthermore, *commentaria* also varied in form and in documentation, as did Las Casas's written works.[24] For these reasons, interpreting Las Casas's writings as juridical commentaries on the various premises in the *Brevísima relación* seems to offer another plausible law-related interpretation of the text, which could be the focus of future research.

Possible Invitation to Ecclesial Intervention

This book also invites reassessment of the degree of trust that Las Casas placed in royal justice. In the text of the *Brevísima relación*, Las Casas presented the juridical figure of the king in three ways: as monarch of "all the Spains," enactor of legislation, and guardian of justice.[25] In the Prologue, after addressing the twenty-six-year-old prince-regent as the "most high and potent lord of all the Spains," Las Casas reminded the heir-apparent that the king, as the monarch of Spain, was simultaneously "father and shepherd," and the "most noble and generous member of the republic."[26] Projecting (or perhaps assuming) the "undoubtedly just character" of the monarchy, Bartolomé reiterated the kingly attributes of "innate and natural virtue," specifically those of "rectitude, ... study, and vigilant industry," which he declared must be coupled with knowledge gleaned from reports that are "true" in order to distinguish right from wrong.[27] He further admonished that "the mere notice of wrong or malefaction suffices ... for not a single moment could [the monarch] tolerate them."[28]

Las Casas's characterization of the king as an enactor of legislation and as a guardian of justice drew on assessments he added to the original 1542 written *Brevísima relación* in 1547.[29] His depiction of the king as "giver of laws" corresponded to the attributes of the royal lawmaker articulated in the *Siete Partidas*, which stipulated that the king must change and amend laws if due reason was given and the common good was served.[30] In the *Very Brief Account*, Las Casas recalled how Philip's father did this when he legislated the New Laws "after many gatherings of persons of great authority, letters, and conscience, and also debates and conferences," as well as with their consent.[31] Las Casas also depicted the emperor as the "lover and cultivator of justice," which implied the medieval notion of the king as the fountainhead or source of justice.[32] By these characterizations of the king as "giver of laws," and "guardian of justice," the friar-bishop had recourse to the traditional Castilian ideal of the monarch as *rey justiciero*.[33] Given Las Casas's repeated recourse to the highest authority, he surely believed in this ideal as well as regarded at least the Habsburg monarchs as kings intent on this role. Yet whether they were or not is debatable, but the discourse that would appeal to them in this way was expected. Richard Kagan also argues that Charles V (and later Philip II) "worked hard to become more than a *rey justiciero* in name only" and, as such, to achieve justice through an effective rule of law.[34] However, some observers of the atrocities of the Spanish conquering expeditions would lay part of the blame at the monarchs' feet, which Las Casas would not do because he was appealing to them for their help in reversing the situation.

Moreover, while Las Casas was scathing and unflinching in his censuring of the Spaniards and Germans in the *Brevísima relación*, as was common in the era in which he lived, he did not denounce the king. Rather, Bartolomé's denunciations of the tyranny were based on the premise that "the evils and harm were done against the will of the monarchs and their royal orders."[35] This kind of assessment that blames the "wicked tyrants" (including the "wicked ministers") seems to reflect the myth of the benevolent king. This notion was seemingly generated by the Renaissance recovery of classical Roman and Greek models of rulers as benign dispensers of the good and was further promoted by humanists' advice books to the prince. Yet, the Spanish monarch must have been aware of the rampant tyranny taking place in the Indies. As Davidson pointed out, the covetous conquistadors, encomenderos, and royal officials were appointed and/or licensed by the emperor and, as such, either Charles himself was a "tyrant" or he condoned the use of tyranny as an instrument of governance and expansion in the Indies.[36] If so, was Charles guilty of what Bartolus denominated "veiled and tacit tyranny"? Did Charles deliberately ignore the "open and manifest tyranny" of many of the Spaniards and Germans?[37] Perhaps Charles simply did not see some of these things as tyranny, which is more likely because they profited the crown and allowed Charles to act as the champion of Catholic Christianity in the wars of the Reformation and Counter-Reformation, those against the Ottomans, and those attendant to his duties as Holy Roman Emperor. In his deliberations on this issue, Carro suggested that inevitably there would be instances in monarchical decisions where the lesser of two evils was chosen, and that the monarch tolerated some failures on the part of his subjects to conform to the law, including those incompatible with Christian morality. Carro insisted that "to tolerate is not to approve."[38]

However, in the *Peroratio* of the *Brevísima relación*, after first referring to the monarch as just, Las Casas provocatively observed that the king was unable to bring about justice.[39] He explicitly stated: "there has been no justice of the king to punish [the tyrants]," and then forthrightly asserted that "to this day, the king is not powerful enough to put an end to this [tyranny]."[40] The implicit message was that the king failed as *rey justiciero*. Perhaps this encoded message about the exercise of royal jurisdiction in the Indies was to prompt Philip (and to provoke his father) to act (perhaps by shaming them), or perhaps to marshal others to action in Las Casas's long-desired juridical goal of a just remedy for the wrongs done and being done. In my opinion, by publishing the *Brevísima relación* in 1552, Las Casas intended to position the Church to effect a remedy for the tyrannous situation in the Indies.

Consider the long-standing precedent in canon law, first promulgated by Innocent III, that "if justice is not available in the temporal forum, jurisdiction may be transferred to ecclesiastical judges … [to] do justice themselves."[41] This superiority of the spiritual over the temporal and, accordingly, of ecclesiastical jurisdiction over secular jurisdiction was upheld and reaffirmed by the Council of Trent (1545–1563).[42] Recall also that Las Casas had appealed (unsuccessfully) for a "total remedy" from three monarchs. His Dominican mentor, Pedro de Córdoba, had cautioned him that their goals of just treatment of the Indigenous inhabitants of the Indies would not be achieved as long as Ferdinand lived.[43] While Las Casas's views were seemingly greatly valued by Charles V, the Dominican encountered both resolute support and ferocious opposition from royal officials at the court of the cosmopolitan emperor.[44] Although Las Casas was apparently a confidant of the youthful Prince Philip, he experienced the frustrating undulations precipitated by the transitions of power after the promulgation of the New Laws. Indeed, royal officials were perhaps pleased with the growing riches from the colonies; while the gold had largely played out by 1540, it was replaced by significant silver finds. Additionally, these experiences may also suggest that the monarchs wanted to control the Spanish Church in many ways, and not be controlled by it—even (or especially) by the Andalusian friar-bishop.

Consider also Las Casas's knowledge and employment of episcopal powers, such as excommunication and interdict. As bishop of Chiapa and as "Protector of All the Indians," he knew that ecclesiastical jurisdiction also extended to the welfare of *miserabiles personae* (in the Indies, of the Indigenous people) and to matters of restitution.[45] In his diocese, he had wielded the ecclesial juridical arm by edicts of excommunication and by withholding absolution in the Sacrament of Confession, but even these church-based efforts did not succeed in generating a total remedy and instead caused much resentment. Later in Spain, the bishop of Chiapa experienced more disappointments. The law prohibiting perpetual encomiendas was revoked. "Conquests" were abolished, but "pacification" was allowed. In spite of his detailed and lengthy arguments, the special junta of 1550–1551 did not make a public statement about whether "conquest prior to conversion" was disallowed.

Consider that, since 1516, Las Casas had adhered to and promoted a plan for the peaceful penetration of Indigenous lands by friars and bishops to preach the Gospel to the autochthonous people, with the hope of their free-willed conversion and eventual salvation. (Could it be that he lacked what might be called "diplomatic skills"?) While his attempts to actualize this plan failed in Cumaná (1521–1522), he carried it out in Tierra de Guerra (Land of War) (1537–1539) with such success that this Guatemalan territory was renamed *Vera Paz* (True Peace). His subsequent plan (presented in Chapter 5) proposed the restoration of Indigenous republics under the leadership of religious clerics and friars, a plan that was not particularly realistic in the political context of the time. This plan, first articulated in 1543, was devised as a way to Christianize large populations of Indigenous peoples in, for example, New Spain, Peru, and New Granada. However, in these plans promoting clergy-based-leadership, Las Casas did not address how those he denominated "tyrants" could be stopped and punished.

Yet, both the content of the *Brevísima relación* and perhaps the circumstances of its publication gesture toward a way to do this that would have recourse to another arena of ecclesiastical jurisdiction: the Office of the Inquisition. Consider that the *Very Brief Account* was replete with allegations and condemnations of the "tyrants" that constituted fodder for inquisitional inquiry, namely, their idolatry, blasphemy, heresy, apostasy, and other violations of divine, natural, and human laws. Moreover, according to canon law, the Church's jurisdiction also extended to homicide, arson, adultery, theft, usury, forgery, and simony. While these crimes (and sins) were dealt with according to criminal law in ecclesiastical courts, blasphemy, apostasy, idolatry, and heresy were regarded as worse than murder and so forth, because of their direct affront to God.[46] In any case, the charges and the best evidence that Las Casas could assemble were all there in the *Very Brief Account*. Names and the crimes and sins committed, in addition to any other needed information, were available from the *Larguísima relación*. All that remained was for the Office of the Inquisition to summon, prosecute, and punish the idolatrous, greedy, and disobedient Spaniards. Was this perhaps what Las Casas had in mind as he readied the *tratado* for publication?

Whether (and how) the *Tribunal de la Inquisición* as part of ecclesiastical jurisdiction may have been involved is at this point pure speculation. However, during his stay in Seville prior to publishing the *Brevísima relación*, Las Casas lived at the Dominican convent of San Pablo where his confrere, Domingo de Soto, also resided and functioned as an examiner for the Inquisition.[47] As Reboiras discovered (and was reported in Chapter 6), by that time, the Tribunal of the Inquisition was located in Seville, and its Inquisitor-general was the archbishop of Seville. There was ample opportunity and time for these clerics to consider the possibility of dealing with the "tyrants" by wielding the arm of ecclesial jurisdiction, especially since the authority of the Church prevailed in matters of faith.[48] Perhaps research in the archives of the *Tribunal de la Inquisición*, the *Consejo de las Indias*, or of the Archdiocese of Seville may contain information that would verify or reject this enticing possibility. If so, this might also open a new arena of research about the Inquisition that focuses more on prosecution of objectionable (and sinful) forms of behavior such as violence and maltreatment, rather than predominantly on sexual deviance, witchcraft, and blasphemy.

Voices of Conscience

Was the *Brevísima relación* the only publication that proposed and sought a total remedy? Perhaps. Was Las Casas the only voice raised on behalf of the Indigenous people? Absolutely not. In different ways, many promoted and lent their voices to the defense of the *miserabiles personae* in the Indies. Consider the institutional foci of Vasco de Quiroga and the Franciscans. From a humanist and utopian perspective that Quiroga derived from Erasmus and Thomas More, the bishop of Michoacán established the Santa Fe hospital-pueblos, which became the model for later mission compounds in Alta California and Paraguay.[49] Although trained like Las Casas in canon law, Bishop Quiroga, as a secular cleric, did not have Las Casas's expertise in Thomistic scholasticism, which may explain why Quiroga agreed with Sepúlveda that the

Indigenous people were not capable of self-governance and civil society, but rather needed the supervision of the Spaniards. (Or, Quiroga could simply have shared the general Spanish prejudices, as did many friars and priests who thought Indigenous peoples were worthy but still inferior to Spaniards.) New Spain's vanguard and senior mendicant order, the Spanish Franciscans, focused on the erection of centers of learning (including the University of Mexico) and of edifices for worship, which Las Casas did not. These reform spiritualist Franciscans—such as Motolinía, also known as Toribio of Benavente, OFM (1482–1568); Bernardino de Sahagún (1499–1590); and later Gerónimo de Mendieta (1528–1604)[50]—wrote catechetical books, *Historias*, proto-ethnographies and *doctrinas* (as did Franciscan Bishop Zumárraga). In contrast, Las Casas wrote *El unico vocationis modo* as a tract for any and all missionaries. [However, his three-volume *Apologética historia sumaria*, a detailed account of Indigenous way of life, was similar in its extensive data to the accounts of Indigenous religions and history written by Sahagún, Motolinía, and the Dominican Diego de Durán (1537–1588).] The Franciscans' radical poverty combined with their emphasis on teaching and preaching also underscored their urgency in building an Indian Church before the imminent Second Coming of Christ; their approach was characterized (like Quiroga) by a benevolent yet coercive paternalism in actions and authority, which, however, diminished the agency of Indigenous people. Because of their paternalist approach and their perceived immediate territorial needs, both Quiroga and the Franciscans opposed the New Laws in their abolition of the encomienda, whereas Las Casas chose to disregard any particularized (and positive) consequences of Indigenous people as encomendados (and, as previously noted, also the fact that there were "good" encomenderos in addition to Indigenous encomenderos). Perhaps the Spanish Franciscans' tendency to focus on localized, particularized, and predominantly catechetical questions was because they had a different philosophical-theological training compared to the Dominicans. Nevertheless, recall that Las Casas had drafted *Las Seis Verdades* for Zumárraga—a Franciscan and the first archbishop of Mexico. What distinguished Las Casas was his ability to universalize the needs and problems of the entire Indies beyond those simply of New Spain or of any other particular territory.

Also recall that the learned Hispaniola Dominicans (and Picard Franciscans) first articulated the framework for a comprehensive remedy for the sufferings endured by Indigenous people. Consider further the contributions of Dominican bishops to articulate the urgent need for the universal Church to address the issue of the level of humanity of Indigenous people and the proper methods of Christianization. Julian Gárces, bishop of Tlaxcala (1527–1542), who exemplified this broader approach by his appeal to Paul III, also built schools and churches. Domingo de Santo Tomás, bishop of Charcas, Bolivia (1562–1570), who wrote the first

Quechua language and grammar book, also took an all-encompassing approach. Like the Hispaniola Dominicans and Las Casas, Santo Tomás called for radical restitution by amending the wrongs done, returning the encomienda lands—and even the whole country—to the Indigenous peoples.[51]

By the mid-1550s and beyond, others from the ranks of secular clergy were also lending their voices to broader issues related to the Indigenous peoples. Juan López de Zárate, bishop of Antequera (1535–1555), upheld the full humanity of Indigenous people and their needs, in addition to peaceful methods of instruction and conversion. In 1551, Zárate denounced the lack of zeal of many religious, the Franciscans' custom of whipping some Indigenous persons, as well as the unchristian interests of the colonizers. Subsequently, he informed Prince Philip that the diocese was so large that "whole provinces do not know the true God."[52] Juan del Valle, bishop of Popoyán (1549–1561), wielded the arm of ecclesiastical jurisdiction as did Las Casas by excommunicating and interdicting Spaniards in his diocese who were not complying with the legislation protecting the Indigenous people.[53] His colleague, Juan de Simancas, bishop of Cartagena (1557–1570), also struggled in vain to convince local authorities to enforce the New Laws and, like Las Casas, requested papal permission to no longer reside in his diocese.[54]

In 1566, the retired secular cleric, Luis Sánchez, also raised his voice in assessments, denunciations, and proposals related to the threatened destruction of the Indigenous peoples and their lands. Like Las Casas, Sánchez attributed the cruel unjust wars and enslavement of Indigenous people to the Spaniards' greed. Among the problems Sánchez cited was the distance from Spain, as well as the fact that legislators had never visited the Indies and were grossly misinformed. While acknowledging that there were a small number of *gente de bien* and good religious, just as Las Casas did in his *Confessionario*, Sánchez blamed what he considered the continuing destruction on ecclesial and secular judges who did not pursue justice; on religious and other priests who granted absolution without demanding restitution; and on conquistadors and encomenderos, whose sins were destroying the Indigenous peoples temporally and spiritually. The remedy Sánchez petitioned was identical to that of Las Casas in his last *Memorial* to the Council of the Indies: that a grand junta be convened consisting of the monarch, the *Consejo de las Indias*, and *letrados* in theology and canon law.[55]

Others published to disseminate their message. Cristóbal de Pedraza, bishop of Comayagua, Honduras (1541–1553), wrote a scathing critique of the conquistadors and requested a remedy from Charles V in his "Relación de la provincia de Honduras y Higueras." Bartolomé Frías de Albornoz, Spanish lawyer and professor of civil law at the University of Mexico, condemned the slave trade in his 1556 *Arte de los contratos* and questioned the morality of "saving souls" through enslavement, as well as of making slaves of prisoners of wars. In his 1569 *Suma de tratos y contratos*, Dominican friar Tomás de Mercado decried the vile conditions endured by Indigenous and African slaves on ships, and declared that involvement in the slave trade incurred "deadly sin."[56] All these defenders of Indigenous peoples, from the first mendicant friars on Hispaniola to others in multiple places, were exponents of a reform movement to prevent *la destruición de las Indias*, and were supported in this by Spaniards in governmental circles and in other parts of society such as the *Escuela Española*. These pro-Indigenous individuals functioned as a leaven by their insistence on judging Spain's policies and the Spaniards' deeds. Lay Spaniards in the Indies and Indigenous people were also part of the chorus of voices intent on ameliorating conditions. For example, the son of conquistador Diego de Aguero distributed four hundred pesos in gold to hospitals in the Andes in compensation for the excessive tribute that his deceased father had collected from the native people on his encomienda. Conquistador Lorenzo de Aldana bequeathed his extensive holdings to the Andean people in Arequipa.[57] Indigenous authorities such as the town council of Huejotzingo expressed their concerns and needs in letters to the monarch.[58] To its credit, Spain's political system allowed voices to be raised that demanded that its actions be just. No nation, as Hanke declared, made "so continuous or so compassionate an attempt to discover what was just treatment for the native people under its jurisdiction."[59]

Outside of Spain, there were also other "Las Casas types." For example, in 1555, the Portuguese cleric (and former Dominican) and humanist, Fernão Oliveira, mirrored Las Casas's position in his *Arte de Guerra no mar* (The Art of Maritime War). In a rare denunciation of slavery, Oliveira contended that non-Christians were outside of papal authority, war against them was unjustified, and enslaving them was manifest tyranny.[60] Rodrigo de Betanzos defended the Guanches in the Canary Islands.[61] Individuals such as these were part of the "conscience of European Christianity," as was Las Casas.[62]

In the Indies, Las Casas became one of "the authentic representatives … of the conscience of Spain," its "public conscience," and "the paradigmatic voice of the historical moment."[63] As this voice of conscience, Las Casas's dedication, experience, and knowledge of the New World were unparalleled. His interactions extended to the highest levels. He addressed three monarchs: Ferdinand II, Charles V, and Philip II. He personally knew Adrian VI, Paul III, and Pius V—three of the fourteen popes who reigned during this lifetime.[64] His vision encompassed the whole of the Indies. His arguments combined the canonistic, philosophical, and theological, and were anchored in his understanding of *los hechos* and *los derechos*. Las Casas thought and acted "with-knowledge," that is, *cum-ciencia*, with knowledge enlightened by faith and in accord with reason and eternal, divine, and just human law. This distinguished him as the conscience of Spain.

Las Casas raised his juridical voice by means of the written word in his *Very Brief Account* to explicate the crisis of conscience of Spain that had reached its zenith in the Indies in the mid-sixteenth century.[65] The emotive tenor of Las Casas's voice in the text echoes the voice of Spain's "tormented conscience," one of outrage, frustration, and disbelief.[66] Yet, the text's concomitant juridical tenor, with its distinctive, wide-ranging, and justice-based approach, gives credence to his stature as a jurist, to his persistent employment of a juridical approach, and to the presence of this approach in his famous and infamous *Brevísima relación de la destruición de las Indias* (Figures 8.2 and 8.3).

Figure 8.2 Portrait of Bartolomé de Las Casas (c. 1484–1566).
Source: Unidentified painter.

Figure 8.3 Signature of Bartolomé de las Casas, former bishop of Chiapa. In a letter dated November 1559, Las Casas donated the manuscript of his *Historia de las Indias* to the Dominican friars' convent of San Gregorio in Valladolid, Spain (*Preserved at the Biblioteca Nacionalde España*).

Notes

1 "Memorial al Consejo de las Indias [July, 1566]," in *Obras escogidas de Fray Bartolomé de las Casas*: *Historia de las Indias*, ed. Juan Pérez de Tudela Bueso, vol. 3, Biblioteca de Autores Españoles (Madrid: Ediciones Atlas, 1957), 5:537b; Henry Raup Wagner and Helen Rand Parish, *The Life and Writings of Bartolomé de Las Casas* (Albuquerque: Univ. of New Mexico Press, 1967), 236–38, 297n78.

2 Ecclesiasticus 34:18–22:

> Unclean is the offering sacrificed by an oppressor. [Such] mockeries of the unjust are not pleasing [to God]. The Lord is pleased only by those who keep to the way of truth and justice. The Most High does not accept the gifts of unjust people; He does not look well upon their offerings. Their sins will not be expiated by repeat[ed] sacrifices. The one whose sacrifice comes from the goods of the poor is like one who kills his neighbor. The one who sheds blood and the one who defrauds the laborer are kin and kith.
>
> Bartolomé de las Casas, *The Only Way*, ed. Helen Rand Parish, trans. Francis Patrick Sullivan (New York: Paulist Press, 1992), 188

3 Bartolomé de las Casas, *Historia de las Indias*, 3 vols., ed. André Saint-Lu (Caracas: Biblioteca Ayacucho, 1986), 3:510, chap. 138 [hereafter *Historia* (Ayacucho)].

4 Bartolomé de las Casas, *An Account, Much Abbreviated, of the Destruction of the Indies*, trans. Andrew Hurley, intro. and ed. Franklin W. Knight (Indianapolis, IN: Hackett, 2003), 44, 46, 7, 50, 64, 4 (hereafter Knight, *An Account*, 28).

5 Ibid., 22, 59, 60, 63, 86.

6 Ibid., 7, 17, 27, 29, 36, 46, 59, 68.
7 Ibid., 9, 23, 51, 3.
8 Ibid., 16, 29–30, 47, 34–35.
9 José Miguel Martínez Torrejón, "Bartolomé de Las Casas's *Brevísima Relación* as Weapon and Victim," *Literatura e Pluralidade Cultural*, Actas do 3 Congresso Nacional da Associacão Portuguesa de Literatura Comparada (Lisbon: Edicões Colibri, 1999), 402.
10 Juan Comas, "Historical Reality and the Detractors of Father Las Casas," in *Bartolomé de Las Casas in History: Toward an Understanding of the Man and His Work*, eds. Juan Friede, Juan and Benjamin Keen (DeKalb: Northern Illinois Univ., 1971), 487–537.
11 Lewis Hanke, Bartolomé de Las Casas, Historian: An Essay in Spanish Historiography (Gainesville: Univ. of Florida Press, 1952), 77–88.
12 Torrejón, "Bartolomé de Las Casas's *Brevísima Relación* as Weapon and Victim," 403.
13 Alonso de Santa Cruz, *Crónica del emperador Carlos V, compuesta por Alonso de Santa Cruz, su cosmógrafo mayor*, eds. Ricardo Beltrán y Rózpide and Antonio Blázquez y Delgado-Aguilera (Madrid: Imprenta del Patronato de Huérfanos, 1920): part IV, chap. 42, 216–17.
14 Juan Comas, "Historical Reality and the Detractors of Father Las Casas," in *Bartolomé de las Casas in History*, 502–4.
15 Torrejón, "Bartolomé de Las Casas's *Brevísima Relación* as Weapon and Victim," 404.
16 Antonio Carreño, "Una guerra 'sine dolo et fraude': el P. Las Casas y la lucha por la dignidad del Indio en el siglo XVI," *Cuadernos Americanos* 193, no. 2 (Marzo–Abril 1974): 135.
17 Antonio Sacoto, "Fray Bartolomé de las Casas: paladín de la justicia social," *Cuadernos Americanos* 193, no. 6 (Noviembre–Diciembre 1975): 145.
18 Cited from the November 15, 1963, letter of Bolivian historian, Gunnar Mendoza, to Lewis Hanke, in his "More Heat and Some Light on the Spanish Struggle for Justice in the Conquest of America," *The Hispanic American Historical Review* 44, no. 3 (August 1964): 335, 336n137.
19 Knight, *An Account*, 3; Bartolomé de las Casas, *Fray Bartolomé de Las Casas: brevísima relación de la destruicion de las Indias*, vol. 3, Estudios monográficos, ed. Isacio Pérez Fernández, O. P. (Bayamón, P.R.: Centro de Estudios de los Dominicos del Caribe, 1999), note 11 (hereafter Pérez Fernández, *Brevísima*).
20 Recent scholarship does demonstrate that "the unsettling normality of conquest was a sufficient cause" for the depopulation of Hispaniola because the deep economic and social dislocations that resulted created conditions for high mortality and reduced fertility. Massimo Livi-Bacci, "Return to Hispaniola: Reassessing a Demographic Collapse," *Hispanic American Historical Review* 83, no. 1 (February 2003): 3–52. 50–51.
21 James Lockhart and Stuart B. Schwartz, *Early Latin America: A History of Colonial Spanish America and Brazil* (Cambridge: Cambridge Univ. Press, 1983), 120.
22 J.M. Reyes Cano, "Introducción," in Bartolomé de las Casas, *Brevísima relación de la destruición de las Indias*, ed. and intro. Reyes Cano (Barcelona: Planeta, 1994), L–LI.
23 Manlio Bellomo, *The Common Legal Past of Europe: 1000–1800*, Washington, DC: Catholic Univ. of America Press, 1995, 147–48.
24 For example, in the treatise on papal and princely power, on evangelization and governance, that Las Casas titled *Treinta proposiciones muy jurídicas*, he logically structured and succinctly enunciated his propositions without

a barrage of citations; then, he developed the seventeenth and eighteenth propositions about Spanish and Indigenous *dominium* into a very lengthy, detailed, and copiously documented treatise—the *Tratado comprobatorio del imperio soberano.*

25 Daisy Ripodas Ardanaz, "Los Indios y la Figura Jurídica del Rey durante los Quinientos," in *Justicia, Sociedad, Economía en la América Española (Siglos XVI, XVII, XVIII)* (Valladolid: Seminario Americanista de la Universidad de Valladolid, 1983): 275–322.

26 Knight, *An Account*, 2. Las Casas's reference to the monarch as "father and shepherd" in the Homerian sense of the terms is an indication of humanistic influence. Torrejón suggests that Las Casas took his cue from Erasmus's writings about the Iliad. In Greek mythology, the father of the gods and of humans was Zeus; the shepherd was Hector who, as the noblest of heroes, was the courageous, peace-loving, and brave defender of the fatherland. Bartolomé de las Casas, *Brevísima relación de la destruición de las Indias*, ed. and intro. José Miguel Martínez Torrejón (Alicante: Universidad de Alicante, 2006), 103n13. Aquinas, who echoed the *Siete Partidas*, defined the shepherd as one who guides the formation of "a perfect community." Brian Owensby, *Empire of Law and Indian Justice in Colonial Mexico* (Stanford: Stanford Univ. Press, 2008), 32–33. Another possible understanding that Las Casas, as a Christian, would have had was that of Christ as Shepherd and of God as Father. Finally, flattering the monarch was also a formula in sixteenth-century letters to the king.

27 About the monarch's duty to distinguish right from wrong, see Alfonso X, *Las Siete Partidas*, 5 vols., trans. by Samuel Parsons Scott, ed. Robert I. Burns (Philadelphia: Univ. of Pennsylvania Press, 2001), 1:1.1.9.

28 Knight, *An Account*, 2–3.

29 Ibid., 87–88.

30 Alfonso X, *Las Siete Partidas*, 1:1.1.11.

31 Knight, *An Account*, 87.

32 Charles H. Lippy, Robert Choquette, and Stafford Poole, *Christianity Comes to the Americas: 1492–1776* (New York: Paragon House, 1992), 88.

33 Knight, *An Account*, 87; Richard Kagan, *Lawsuits and Litigants of Castile, 1500–1700* (Chapel Hill: Univ. of North Carolina Press, 1981), 15; J.H. Elliott, *Imperial Spain 1469–1716* (London: Penguin Books, 1963), 95–96.

34 Kagan, *Lawsuits and Litigants of Castile*, 150–60.

35 Knight, *An Account*, 87; Venancio D. Carro, "The Spanish Theological-Juridical Renaissance and the Ideology of Bartolomé de Las Casas," in *Bartolomé de las Casas in History*, 273.

36 J. S. Davidson, "The Rights of Indigenous Peoples in Early International Law," *The Canterbury Law Review* 5 (1994): 403.

37 Francesco Maiolo, *Medieval Sovereignty: Marsilius of Padua and Bartolus of Saxoferrato* (Deft: Eburon Academic Publishers, 2007), 268–69.

38 Venancio D. Carro, *Carta abierta a D.R. Menéndez Pidal* (Madrid: Librería OPE, 1962), 9.

39 Angélica Prieto Inzunza, *La pasión en las crónicas.* (Xalapa, Veracruz, México: Universidad Veracruzana, 2008), 57–58.

40 Knight, *An Account*, 88.

41 *Decretales* 10:2.2.10–11, cited in R.H. Helmholtz, *The Spirit of Classical Canon Law* (Athens: Univ. of Georgia Press, 1996), 119; see the complete explication of ecclesiastical jurisdiction in his chapter 5.

42 During this time of tension between the civil and ecclesial orders, the Council also affirmed the papal right to intervene in temporal affairs. Helmholtz, *The Spirit of Classical Canon Law*, 141.

43 Las Casas, *Historia* (Ayacucho), 3:297.

44 Isacio Pérez Fernández, *Fray Bartolomé de Las Casas: brevísima relación de su vida, diseño de su personalidad, síntesis de su doctrina* (Caleruega, Burgos: Editorial OPE, 1984), 42.

45 Helmholtz, *The Spirit of Classical Canon Law*, 93–115, 128–32.

46 Helmholtz, *The Spirit of Classical Canon Law*, chap. 10.

47 Isacio Pérez Fernández, *Cronología documentada de los viajes, estancias y actuaciones de Fray Bartolomé de las Casas*, vol. 2, Estudios Monográficos (Bayamón, P.R.: Centro de Estudios de los Dominicos del Caribe, 1984), 2:839.

48 Gratian, *Decretum*, Distinction 11, c. 9. While some may argue that the ability of the Holy Office in Seville to apprehend and prosecute "tyrants" who lived in the Indies was a doubtful project, because the Tribunal was not established until later in the sixteenth century, remember that the bishops could also be authorized to conduct inquisitorial inquiries and *autos de fe*.

49 David T. Orique, "Journey to the Headwaters: Bartolomé de Las Casas in a Comparative Context," *The Catholic Historical Review* 95, no. 1 (January 2009): 1–24.

50 Enrique Florescano, *National Narratives in Mexico: A history* (Norman: Univ. of Oklahoma Press, 2006), 142.

51 Lockhart and Schwartz insightfully denominated this post-New-Laws era as the "last wave of 'radical restitution'." See their *Early Latin America*, 120.

52 Charles Braden, *Religious Aspects of the Conquest of Mexico* (Durham, NC: Duke Univ. Press, 1930), 170, 246, 321.

53 Bishop del Valle was a disciple of Las Casas, although, according to Friede, not a theoretician. Juan Friede, "Las Casas and Indigenism of the Sixteenth Century," in *Bartolomé de Las Casas in History*, 127–28.

54 Interestingly, Bishop Las Casas and Bishop del Valle were the co-consecrators at the ceremony that elevated Bishop-elect Simancas to the episcopacy. Juan Friede, "Las Casas and Indigenism of the Sixteenth Century," in *Bartolomé de Las Casas in History*, 127.

55 In his *Memorial*, Sánchez spoke with high regard for the Bishop of Chiapa and the Bishop of Popayán (modern Columbia). He served as a secular priest in Bishop del Valle's diocese, and retired to Mexico after the bishop's death. See his "Memorial que dió el bachiller Luis Sánchez, residente en Chillaron de Pareja, al Presidente Espinosa, en Madrid (26 Agosto 1566)," in *Colección de documentos inéditos, relativos al descubrimiento, conquista y organización de las antiguas posesiones españolas de América y Oceanía, sacados de los archivos del reino, y muy especialmente del de Indias*, eds. Joaquín Francisco Pacheco, Francisco de Cárdenas y Espejo, and Luis Torres de Mendoza (Madrid: Ministerio de Ultramar, 1864–1884), 11:163–68.

56 Hugh Thomas, *The Slave Trade: The Story of Atlantic Slave Trade 1440–1870* (New York: Touchstone, 1997), 146. Cristóbal de Pedraza, "Relación de la Provincia de Honduras y Higueras," in *Relaciones histórico-geográficas de las provincias de Yucatán*, 2 vols., ed. José María Asencio (Colección de documentos inéditos relativos al descubrimiento, conquista y organización de las antiguas posesiones españolas de Ultramar, segunda serie, 11, 13) (Madrid: 1890–1900), 378–436.

57 Regina Harrison, "Teaching Restitution: Las Casas, the *Rules for Confessors*, and the Politics of Repayment," in *Approaches to Teaching the Writings of Bartolomé de Las Casas*, eds. Santa Arias and Eyda Merediz (New York: The Modern Language Association of America, 2008), 135.

58 See this public letter in Lockhart and Otte, *Letters and People, Letters and People of the Spanish Indies: Sixteenth Century*, ed and trans. James Lockhart and Enrique Otte, Cambridge Latin American Studies Series (Cambridge: Cambridge Univ. Press, 1976), 165–172.
59 Lewis Hanke, *Aristotle and the American Indians: A Study in Race Prejudice in the Modern World* (Bloomington: Indiana Univ. Press, 1975), 139.
60 Stuart B Schwartz, *All Can be Saved: Religious Tolerance and Salvation in the Iberian Atlantic World* (New Haven, CT: Yale Univ. Press, 2008), 162; Lúcia Helena Costigan, "Bartolomé de Las Casas and His Counterparts in the Luso-Brazilian World," in *Approaches to Teaching the Writings of Bartolomé de Las Casas*, 236–37; David Orique, "A Comparison of Bartolomé de Las Casas and Fernão Oliveira: Just War and Slavery," *E-journal of Portuguese History*, 12, no. 1 (June 2014): 87–118.
61 Antonio Rumeu de Armas, *La Política Indigentista de Isabel la Católica* (Valladolid: Instituto "Isabel la Católica" de História Eclesiastica, 1969), 94–96.
62 Anthony Pagden, "Introduction," in *Bartolomé de Las Casas. An Account, Much Abbreviated, of the Destruction of the Indies*, ed. and trans. Nigel Griffin (London: Penguin Books, 1992), xiii.
63 Lewis Hanke, *The Spanish Struggle for Justice in the Conquest of America* (Dallas: Southern Methodist Univ. Press, 2002), 177; Elsa Cecilia Frost, "Fray Bartolomé de las Casas: Conciencia de España," in *Symposium Fray Bartolomé de las Casas: Trascendencia de su Obra y Doctrina* (México, DF: UNAM, 1985), 172; Paolo Carozzo, "From Conquest to Constitutions: The Latin American Tradition of the Idea of Human Rights," *Human Rights Quarterly* 25, no. 2 (May 2003): 291; Pagden, "Introduction" in Las Casas, *An Account*, xxvii.
64 Las Casas's life spanned the long ecclesial history of the papacies of Sixtus IV (d. 1484); Innocent VIII (d. 1492); Alexander VI (d. 1503); Pius III (d. 1503); Julius II (d. 1513); Leo X (d. 1521); Adrian VI (d. 1523); Clement VII (d. 1534); Paul III (d. 1549); Julius III (d. 1555); Marcellus II (d. 1555); Paul IV (d. 1559); Pius IV (d. 1565); and Pius V (d. 1572).
65 Santa Arias, *Retórica, história y polémica: Bartolomé de Las Casas y la tradición intelectual renacentista* (Lanham, MD: Univ. Press of America, 2001), 72–73.
66 Lewis Hanke, "More Heat and Some Light on the Spanish Struggle for Justice in the Conquest of America," *The Hispanic American Historical Review* 44, no. 3 (August 1964): 335, 336n137.

Bibliography

Primary Sources

Actas generales de los capítulos provinciales Dominicanos. Querétaro: Archivos Generales de los Dominicos de la Provincia de Santiago de México, 1540–1570.

Alfonso X el Sabio. *Estoria de España.* Selecciones por Reinaldo Ayerbe-Chaux. Madrid: José Porrúa Turanzas, S.A., 1982.

———. *Las Siete Partidas.* 5 vols. Translated by Samuel Parsons Scott. Edited by Robert I. Burns. Philadelphia: Univ. of Pennsylvania Press, 2001.

———. *Las Siete Partidas del rey Don Alfonso el Sabio 1268.* Madrid: Imprenta Real, 1807. [text online]. (Accessed August 30, 2020).

Alexander VI: The Papal bull Inter Caetera May 4, 1493. [text online]. (Accessed September 1, 2020).

Aguilar, Fray Francisco de. *Relación breve de la conquista de la Nueva España.* Edición, estudio preliminar, notas y apéndices por Jorge Gurría Lacroix. Mexico, DF: UNAM, 1980.

Aquinas, Thomas. *Summa Theologiae.* New York: Benziger Brothers, 1947.

———. *Summa Theologiae: A Concise Translation.* Edited by Timothy McDermott. Westminster, MD: Christian Classics, 1989.

———. *The Summa Contra Gentiles.* 3 vols. Translated by Dominican Fathers. London: Burns, Oates and Washbourne, 1924.

———. *The Trinity and the Unicity of the Intellect.* Translated by Sr. Rose Emanuella Brennan, S.H.N. London: B. Herder Books, 1946.

Aristotle. *Poetics.* Translated by Gerald F. Else. Ann Arbor: Univ. of Michigan Press, 1967.

Aurelius Antoninus, Marcus. *Meditations Book XII.* [book online]. (Accessed September 1, 2020).

Beltrán de Heredia, Vicente. *Bulario de la Universidad de Salamanca 1219–1549.* 3 tomos. Acta Salamanticensia. Historia de la Universidad 12, 13, 14. Salamanca: Universidad de Salamanca, 1967.

Biblia Sacra Vulgata. Stuttgart: Württembergische Bibelanstalt, 1969.

Cabeza de Vaca, Álvar Núñez. *The Narrative of Cabeza de Vaca.* Edited, translated and introduction by Rolena Adorno and Patrick Charles Pautz. Lincoln: Univ. of Nebraska Press, 2003.

"Carta al emperador de Antonio de Aguayo dando aviso a las injusticias y agravios que hacía el licenciado Lebrón, oidor de la Audiencia de Guadalajara, y acusándole de haber hecho envenenar al licenciado Villagar, juez de residencia y a su mujer, 25 Octubre 1554." In *Epistolario de Nueva España*

1505—1818." 16 tomos. Recopilado por Francisco del Paso y Troncoso, 7:272–276. México, DF: Biblioteca Historica Mexicana, 1940.

"Carta al rey de Diego de Ibarra, dando aviso de los abusos que cometía el gobernador de Los Reyes y del desorden en que estaba la real hacienda, 1 Setiembre 1557." In *Epistolario de Nueva España 1505—1818*." 16 tomos. Recopilado por Francisco del Paso y Troncoso, 8:135–138. Mexico, DF: Biblioteca Historica Mexicana, 1940.

"Carta al rey del obispo de Antequera, en el valle de Oaxaca, don Juan López de Zárate, con occasión de la promulgación de las Leyes Nuevas (1542) con especial referencia a la encomienda perpetua y hereditaria." Archivo general de Indias, Audiencia de México, Legajo 357. In Enrique Dussel, *El episcopado hispanoamericano: institución misionera en defensa del indio, 1504–1620*. 9 tomos. Apéndice documental, 8:147–152. Cuernavaca: CIDOC, 1970.

"Carta al rey, del Padre Fray Pedro de Córdoba, vice-provincial de la Orden de Santo Domingo (28 Mayo 1517)." In Medina, *Una Comunidad al servicio del Indio: la obra de Fr. Pedro de Córdoba, O.P. (1482—1521)*, 263–268.

"Carta de Felipe Gutierrez al Emperador, pidiendo justicia de los agravios que le habia hecho don Francisco Pizarro, 30-12-1540." In *Colección de documentos inéditos*, 3:202–204.

"Carta de Fray Pedro de Ángulo a l'empereur Charles Quint, (Guatemala, 19 de Febrero de 1542)." In *La Vera Paz: Esprit Évangelique et Cólonisation*. Reproduction pour André Saint-Lu, 451–454. Paris: Centre de Recherches Hispaniques, 1968.

"Carta de Fray Pedro de Córdoba a Bartolomé de las Casas (1518/1519)." In Medina, *Una Comunidad al servicio del Indio: la obra de Fr. Pedro de Córdoba, O.P. (1482—1521)*, 292.

"Carta de Fray Pedro de Gante al emperador don Carlos V, exponiéndole el sensible estado a que tenía reducidos a los indios el servicio personal de San Francisco de México, 15 de febrero de 1552." [text online]. (Accessed August 30, 2020).

"Carta de los señores y principales de la Nueva España al emperador Carlos V: en español, Tlacopan, 2 mayo 1556." In *La nobleza indígena del centro de México después de la conquista*. Coordinado por Emma Pérez-Rocha y Rafael Tena, 199–200. México, DF: Instituto Nacional de Antropología e Historia, 2000.

"Carta del adelantado Vasco Nunez de Balboa, 16 Octubre 1513/1515." In *Colección de documentos inéditos*, 2:526–538.

"Carta del Licenciado Espinosa a S. M. con las nuevas de los descubrimientos y conquistas que hacía Francisco Pizarro." In *Gobernantes del Perú: cartas y papeles, siglo XVI*. Dirigida por D. Roberto Levillier, 2:15–30. Madrid: Sucesores de Rivadeneyra S.A., 1921.

"Carta del vice-provincial y sacerdotes del convento de Santo Domingo, dirigida a los muy reverendos Padres (Abril-Mayo 1517)." Original en AGI, Patronato, 171, no. 2, ramo 5. 248–251.

"Carta Latina de Dominicos y Franciscanos de las Indias a los regentes de España (27 de Mayo de 1517)." Original en AGI, Patronato, 171, no. 2, ramo 5. In Medina, *Una Comunidad al servicio del Indio: la obra de Fr.Pedro de Córdoba, O.P. (1482—1521)*, 258–262.

"Carta que escribieron varios Padres de las Ordenes de Santo Domingo y San Francisco, residentes en la isla Española, a Mr. de Xevres (presumably on 4 Dec. 1519)." Original en AGI, Patronato, 174, ramo 12. In Medina, *Una Comunidad al servicio del Indio: la obra de Fr. Pedro de Córdoba, O.P. (1482—1521)*, 269–287.

Cartas y relaciones de Hernán Cortés al emperador Carlos V, collegidas y ilustradas por don Pascual de Gayangos. Paris: Imprenta Central de los Ferro-Carriles, 1866.

Carvajal, Fray Francisco de. "Los males e injusticias, crueldades, robos y disensiones que hay en el Nuevo Reino de Granada." In José María Iraburu, *Hechos de los apóstoles en América*. Pamplona: Fundación Gratis Date, 1992.

"Certificación del pago por el Tesorero Dr. Sancho de Matienzo de 10.00 mrs. a Juan Fernández por el pasaje y flete de Bachiller Bartolomé de las Casas. Seville, 6 de avril, 1517." In *Bartolomé de las Casas: delegado de Cisneros para la reformación de Las Indias 1516–1517*. Vol. 1. Reimpresión de 1953, 571. Madrid: Consejo Superior de Investigaciones Científicas, 1984.

Cieza de León, Pedro de. *The Discovery and Conquest of Peru: Chronicles of the New World Encounter*. Edited and translated by Alexandra Parma Cook and Noble David Cook. Duke Univ. Press, 1998.

Colección de documentos inéditos, relativos al descubrimiento, conquista y organización de las antiguas posesiones españolas de América y Oceanía, sacados de los archivos del reino, y muy especialmente del de Indias. Competentemente autorizada. Editado por Joaquín Francisco Pacheco; Francisco de Cárdenas y Espejo; Luis Torres de Mendoza. Vols. 1, 2, 3, 4, 5 y 11. Madrid: Ministerio de Ultramar, 1864–84.

Colección de documentos inéditos, relativos al descubrimiento, conquista y organización de las antiguas posesiones españolas de ultramar: Isla de Cuba. Segunda serie. Vol. 1. Madrid: Publicada por la Real Academia de la Historia, 1885.

Colón, Fernando. *Historia del Almirante (year 1571)*. 4 vols. Edited by Luis Arranz Marquez. Globus Madrid, 2000.

"Complaints against Congregation from the Nahua Cabildo of Tlaxcala, 1560." In *Mesoamerican Voices: Native-Language Writings from Colonial Mexico, Oaxaca, Yucatan, and Guatemala*. Edited by Matthew Restall, Lisa Sousa, and Kevin Terraciano, 75–77. Cambridge: Cambridge Univ. Press, 2005.

"Concerns over the Sale of Nahua Noble's Land, Tlaxcala, 1552." In *Mesoamerican Voices: Native-Language Writings from Colonial*. Edited by Matthew Restall, Lisa Sousa, and Kevin Terraciano, 102–103. Cambridge: Cambridge Univ. Press, 2005.

Córdoba, Pedro de. *Doctrina Cristiana para Instrucción de los Indios: Redactada por Fray Pedrode Córdoba, O.P. y otros religiosos doctos de la misma Órden. Impresa en México, 1544 y 1548*. Editado y introducción por Miquel Ángel Medina. Salamanca: Editorial San Esteban, 1987.

Cristóbal Colón: Diario de navegación y otros escritos. Editado por Carlos Esteban Deive. Biblioteca de Clásicos Dominicanos. Vol. 1. Santo Domingo, 1988.

Crónica del emperador Carlos V, compuesta por Alonso de Santa Cruz, su cosmógrafo mayor. [text online]. Publicada por Ricardo Beltrán y Rózpide, y Antonio Blázquez y Delgado-Aguilera, 4:217. Madrid: Imprenta del Patronato de Huérfanos, 1920. [text online]. (Accessed September 1, 2020).

Crónicas del Perú. Diego Fernández, Pedro Gutiérrez de Santa Clara, Juan Cristóbal Calvete de Estrella, Pedro Pizarro. 5 vols. Madrid: Ediciones Atlas, 1963–1965.

D'Ailly, Pierre. *Imago Mundi*. Texte en latin et traduction française des quarte traités cosmographiques de d'Ailly et des notes marginales de Christophe Colomb. Etude sur les sources de l'auteur. Tomo II. Libraire Orientale et Américaine Maisonneuve Fréres Étiteurs. Paris, 1930.

———. *Imago Mundi*. With annotations by Christopher Columbus. Boston, MA: Massachusetts Historical Society, 1927.

———. *Imago Mundi y Otros Opúsculos*. Preparado pro Antonio Ramírez de Verger; y revisado por Juan Fernández Valverde y Francisco Socas. Madrid: Alianza Editorial, 1992.

Díaz del Castillo, Bernal. *The History of the Conquest of New Spain*. Edited and introduction by Davíd Carrasco. Albuquerque: Univ. of New Mexico Press, 2008.

———. *The Conquest of New Spain*. Translation and introduction by J.M. Cohen. London: Penguin Books, 1963.

Digest of Justinian. 4 vols. Translated by Alan Watson. Philadelphia: Univ. of Pennsylvania Press, 1985.

El Obispo Garay OC. "Informe dado por el Obispo Garay al Emperador, de las cosas de Indias." In *Colección de documentos inéditos*, 11:233–243.

Epistolario de Nueva España 1508–1818. 16 tomos. Recopilado por Francisco del Paso y Troncoso. México, DF: Biblioteca Historica Mexicana, 1940.

Erasmus, Desiderius. *The Education of a Christian Prince*. Edited by Lisa Jardine, Neil M. Cheshire, and Michael J. Heath. Cambridge: Cambridge Univ. Press, 1997.

"Estatuto ordenando por el Capítulo provincial dominicano de Burgos mandando que no se reciban el hábito a descendientes de raza judía, Burgos 16 de Setiembre 1506." In *Cartulario de la universidad de Salamanca*. Edición patrocinada y sufragada por la fundación Calouste Gulbenkian de Lisboa, 262. Salamanca, 1972.

Felipe Guamán Poma de Ayala. *El primer nueva corónica y buen gobierno*. 3 vols. Edited by John V. Murra, Rolena Adorno, and Jorge Urioste. Colección América nuestra, 31. México, DF: Siglo Veintiuno, 1980.

Fernández de Oviedo y Valdés, Gonzalo. *Historia general y natural de Las Indias, Islas y tierra-Firme del Mar Oceano (1535)*. Editado por José Amador de los Rios. Madrid: R. Academia de la historia, 1851–1855.

Fortin, Ernest L. *Classical Christianity and the Political Order: Reflections on the Theologico-Political Problem*. Edited by J. Brian Benestad. New York: Rowman & Littlefield, 1996.

Fray Juan José de la Cruz Moya (1706ca. – 1760). *Historia de la Santa y Apostólica Provincia de Santiago de Predicadores de México en la Nueva España*. Introducción e índices de Gabriel Saldívar. Tomo 1. México, DF: Documentos Mexicanos, 1955.

Fray Martín de Murúa. *Historia general del Perú*. Edición de Manuel Ballesteros. Madrid: Cofás, S.A., 2001.

"Fray Pedro Gante's Letter to Charles V, Mexico City (1552)." In *Colonial Latin America: A Documentary History*. Edited by Kenneth Mills, William B. Taylor, and Sandra Lauderdale Graham, 105–112. Wilmington, DE: Scholarly Resources Books, 2002.

Gratian, The Treatise on Laws (Decretum DD. 1–20) with the Ordinary Gloss. Studies in Medieval and Early Modern Canon Law. Vol. 2. Introduction by Katherine Christensen. Translated by Augustine Thompson and James Gordley. Washington, DC: Catholic Univ. of America Press, 1993.

Gutiérrez de Santa Clara, Pedro. *Quinquenarios o Historia de las guerras civiles del Peru (1544–1548) y de otros sucesos de Las Indias.* Madrid: Ediciones Atlas, 1963.

Indian Freedom: The Cause of Bartolomé de las Casas, 1484–1566, A Reader. Translated and annotated by Patrick F. Sullivan. Kansas City, MO: Sheed & Ward, 1995.

Landa Calderón, Diego de. *Relación de las cosas de Yucatán.* Translated by A.M. Tozzer. Cambridge: Cambridge Univ. Press, 1941.

Las Capitulaciones de Santa Fe. [text online]. (Accessed September 1, 2020).

Las Capitulaciones del Almirante don Cristóbal Colón. [text online]. (Accessed September 2, 2020).

La Carpeta Real, Kraus mss. 129, 138, Washington, DC: Library of Congress.

Las Casas, Bartolomé de. *A Short Account of the Destruction of the Indies.* Edited and translated by Nigel Griffin. Introduction by Anthony Pagden. London: Penguin Books, 1992.

———. *An Account, Much Abbreviated, of the Destruction of the Indies.* Edited and translated by Nigel Griffin. Introduction by Anthony Pagden. London: Penguin Books, 1992.

———. *An Account, Much Abbreviated, of the Destruction of the Indies.* Translated by Andrew Hurley. Introduction and edited by Franklin W. Knight. Indianapolis, IN: Hackett, 2003.

———.*Apologética historia sumaria.* In *Obras completas.* Vols. 6, 7.

———.*Apología.* In *Obras completas.* Vol. 9.

———. "Aqui se contienen treinta proposiciones muy jurídicas." 1552. In *Obras completas,* 10:197–214.

———. "Aquí se contienen unos aviosos y reglas para los confesores." 1552. In *Obras escogidas,* 235–249; *Obras completas,* 10:367–390.

———. "Aquí se tiene una disputa o controversia." 1552. In *Obras escogidas,* 293–348; *Obras completas,* 10:101–196.

———. *Breve relación de la destrucción de las Indias Occidentales: presentada a Felipe II siendo príncipe de Asturias por Don fray Bartolomé de las Casas (Del Orden de Predicadores, Obispo de Chiapa).* Notas del licenciado Ignacio Romerovargas Yturbide. México, DF: Libros Luciernaga, 1957.

———. *Brevísima relación de la Destruccion de Indias.* Introducción por Manuel Ballesteros Gaibrios. Madrid: Alcalá, 1977.

———. *Brevísima relación de la destruición de las Indias.* Edición de André Saint-Lu. Cátedra: Quinta Ediciónes, 1991.

———. *Brevísima relación de la destruición de las Indias.* Editado e introducción por Isacio Pérez Fernández. Madrid: Editorial Tecnos, 1992.

———. *Brevísima relación de la destruición de las Indias.* In *Obras completas* 10: 29–96. Editado por Ramón Hernández, 1992.

———. *Brevisima relación de la destrucción de las Indias.* Editado e introducción por J.M. Reyes Cano. Barcelona: Planeta, 1994.

———. *Brevísima relación de la destrucción de las Indias.* Con los grabados de la edición latina de Jean Théodore y Jean Isräel de Bry Frankfurt, 1598.

Edición de Andrés Moreno Mengíbar. Secunda edición. Sevilla: Editorial A. Er. Revista de Filosofía, 1994.
———. *Brevísima relación de la destruícion de Las Indias*. Vol. 3. Estudios monográficos. Primera Edición Crítica por Isacio Pérez Fernández, O.P. Bayamón, PR: Centro de Estudios de los Dominicos del Caribe, 1999.
———. *Brevísima relación de la destruición de las Indias*. Introducción por Consuelo Varela. Madrid: Castalia, 1999.
———. *Brevísima relación de la destruición de las Indias*. Editado e introducción por José Miguel Martínez Torrejón. Alicante, España: Universidad de Alicante, 2006.
———. "Carta a los Dominicos de Chiapa y Guatemala (1564)." In *Obras Completas*, 13:353–364.
———. "Carta a un personaje de la Corte (15–10–1535)." In *Obras escogidas*, 5:59–68.
———. "Carta al Consejo de Indias (20–1–1531)." In *Obras escogida*, 5:43–55.
———. "Carta al Consejo de las Indias (30–4–1534)." In *Obras escogidas*, 5:56–59.
———. "Carta al Emperador (15–12–1540)." In *Obras escogidas*, 5:68–119.
———. "Corrolarium de episcoporum officio (6–1546?)." In *Obras Completas*, 13:228–233.
———. *De Thesauris*. In *Obras Completas*, vol 11.1.
———. *De unico vocationis modo omnium gentium ad veram religionem*. In *Obras Completas*, 2:13–557.
———. *Diario del primer y tercer viaje de Cristóbal Colón*. In *Obras Completas*, vol. 14.
———. *Doce Dudas*. In *Obras Completas*, vol. 11.2.
———. "El octavo remedio." In *Obras Completas*, 10:291–358.
———. "Entre los remedios." In *Obras Completas*, 10:291–358.
———. "Este es un tratado… sobre la materia de los indios que se han hecho esclavos." In *Obras completas*, 10:219–286.
———. *Historia de las Indias*. 3 vols. Editado por André Saint-Lu. Caracas: Biblioteca Ayacucho, 1986.
———. *Historia de las Indias*. In *Obras completas*, vols. 3, 4, 5.
———. *In Defense of the Indians: The Defense of the Most Reverend Lord, Don Fray Bartolomé de las Casas, of the Order of Preachers, late Bishop of Chiapa, against the Persecutors and Slanderers of the Peoples of the New World Discovered Across the Seas*. Translated by Stafford Poole. DeKalb: Northern Illinois Univ. Press, 1974.
———. "Memorial al Consejo de Indias [July, 1566]." In *Obras escogidas*, 5:536a–538b.
———. "Memorial de denuncias presentado al Cardenal Cisneros (1516)." In *Obras escogidas*, 5:27–30.
———. "Memorial de remedios para Las Indias (1516)." In *Obras completes*, 13:23–48; *Obras escogidas*, 5:5–27.
———. "Memorial de remedios para las Indias (1516)." In *Bartolomé de Las Casas and Thomas More's Utopia: Connections and Similarities*. Translation and study by Victor N. Baptiste, 15–59. Culver City, CA: Labyrinthos, 1990.
———. "Memorial de remedios para Las Indias (1518)." In *Obras escogidas*, 5:31–39.

———. *Obras escogidas de Fray Bartolome de las Casas: Historia de las Indias.* Editado por Juan Pérez de Tudela Bueso. Vol. 3. Biblioteca de Autores Españoles. Madrid: Ediciones Atlas, 1957.

———. *Obras escogidas de Fray Bartolome de las Casas: opúsculos, cartas y memoriales.* Editado por Juan Pérez de Tudela Bueso. Vol. 5. Biblioteca de Autores Españoles. Madrid: Ediciones Atlas, 1958.

———. *Obra indigenista.* Introdución y edición de José Alcina Franch. Madrid: Alianza Editorial, 1985.

———. *Obras completas.* 14 vols. Edición Crítica por Álvaro Huerga. Madrid: Alianza Editorial, 1998.

———. *Parecer de fray Bartolomé de las Casas 1542.* Washington, DC: Library of Congress. [text online]. (Accessed September 1, 2020).

———. *Principia Quaedam.* In *Obras completas,* 10:549–583.

———. *Quaestio theologalis.* In *Obras Completas,* vol. 12.

———. "Representación a los regentes Cisneros y Adriano (1516)." In *Obras escogidas,* 5:3–5.

———. "Representación al Emperador Carlos V (1542)." In *Obras escogidas,* 5:123–133.

———. "Se han hecho esclavos." In *Obras completas,* 10:219–286.

———. *The Devastation of the Indies: A Brief Account.* Introduction by Bill M. Donovan. Translation by Herma Briffault. Baltimore, MD: Johns Hopkins Univ. Press, 1992.

———. *The Only Way.* Edited by Helen Rand Parish. Translated by Francis Patrick Sullivan. New York: Paulist Press, 1992.

———. "Tratado comprobatorio del imperio soberano." In *Obras completas,* 10:395–546.

———. *Très Brève Relation de la Destruction des Indes.* Introducion de Roberto Fernandez Retamar. Traduit de l'espagnol par Fanchita Gonzalez Batlle. Paris: François Maspero, 1980.

———. *Witness: Writings of Bartolomé de las Casas.* Translated and edited by George Sanderlin. Maryknoll, NY: Orbis Books, 1971.

Las Casas on Columbus: Background and the Second and Fourth Voyages. Edited and translated by Nigel Griffin. Introduction by Anthony Pagden. Repetorium Columbianum, Vol. VII. Turnhout: Brepols Publishing, 1999.

Letters and People of the Spanish Indies: Sixteenth Century. Edited and translated by James Lockhart and Enrique Otte. Cambridge Latin American Studies Series. Cambridge: Cambridge Univ. Press, 1976.

"Lo que Suplica Don Francisco y relación que hace de agravios." In Lewis Hanke, "Un Festón de documentos lascasianos." *Revista Cubana* 16 (Julio-Diciembre, 1941):196–203.

Manuscritos holográficos en favor y en contra de Bartolomé de las Casas (circa de 1516). Originales en AGI, Patronato, 252, Ramo 1\1\1–4; Patronato, 252, Ramo 1\2\1–2; Patronato, 252, Ramo 1\3\1–8; Patronato, 252, Ramo 3\1\1–11; Patronato, 252, Ramo 3\1\12–31; Patronato, 252, Ramo 3\1\32; Indiferente, 420, Leg. 10\1\472–474. Fotocopiados en Sevilla.

"Memorial que dió el bachiller Luis Sánchez, residente en Chillaron de Pareja, al Presidente Espinosa, Madrid (26 Agosto 1566)." In *Colección de documentos inéditos,* 11:163–168.

Palacio Rubios, Juan López de. *De las Islas del mar Océano: Del dominio de los Reyes de España sobre los indios.* Introducción de Silvio Zavala. Traducción, notas y bibliografía de Agustín Millares Carlo. México, DF: Fondo de Cultura Económica, 1954.

Pané, Fray Ramón. *Relación acerca de las antigüedade de los indios.* Nueva versión con estudio preliminar, notas y apendices por José Juan Arrom. Decimotecera edición. México, DF: Siglo XXI Editores S.A. de C.V., 2004.

Pedraza, Cristóbal de. *Relación de la Provincia de Honduras y Higueras.* In *Relaciones histórico-geográflcas de las provincias de Yucatán.* 2 vols. (Colección de documentos inéditos relativos al descubrimiento, conquista y organización de las antiguas posesiones españolas de Ultramar, segunda serie, 11, 13). Editado por Asencio, José María (1898—1900): 378–436. Madrid: Ministerio de Ultramar, 1864–84.

Madrid.

Peña, Juan de la. *De Bello Contra Insulanos Intervención de España en America: Escuela Española de la Paz Segunda generación, 1560–1585, Testigos y Fuentes.* Elaborado bajo la dirección de Luciano Pereña. Corpus Hispanorum de Pace, Vol. 9. Madrid: Consejo Superior de Investigaciones Cientificos, 1982.

"Petición presentada por Hernándo de Arguello, á nombre de Vasco Nuñez de Balboa, sobre que se le prorrogue el término que se le habia dado para la construcción de unos navios, que intentaba hazer, á fin de ir á la población de acla, en la provincia del Darien (5 Marzo 1520)." In *Colección de documentos inéditos*, 2:556–558.

"Poder legal dado por Indios Peruanos á fray Bartolomé de Las Casas y Domingo de Santo Tomás (19 Octubre 1556)." In Lewis Hanke, "Un Festón de documentos lascasianos." *Revista Cubana* 16 (Julio-Diciembre, 1941):204–208.

Provisiones cedulas instrucciones para el gobierno de la Nueva España. Editado por el doctor Vasco de Puga. Madrid: Ediciones Cultura Hispánica, 1945.

Quiroga, Vasco de. *Información en derecho del licenciado Quiroga sobre algunas provisiones del Real Consejo de las Indias.* Edited by Paulino Castañeda Delgado. Madrid: Ediciones José Porrúa Turanzas, 1974.

Remesal, Antonio de. *Bartolomé de Las Casas (1474–1566) in the pages of Father Antonio de Remesal.* Translated and annotated by Felix Jay. Lewiston, NY: E. Mellen Press, 2002.

———. *Historia general de las Indias occidentales y particular de la gobernación de Chiapa y Guatemala.* Editado por Carmelo Sáenz de Santa María. Madrid: Ediciones Atlas, 1964.

"Relación cierta y breve de los desasosiegos sucedidos en Perú despues de la muerte del Sr. Virey D. Antonio de Mendoza, y de las causas de donde procedieron, por el licenciado Juan Fernandez, Fiscal de Audiencia del Lima (1552)." In *Colección de documentos inéditos*, 3:246–271.

"Relación de agravios hechos por Núño de Guzmán de don Francisco Tenamaztle (1552)." Introducción y notas por Salvador Reinoso. *Colección Siglo XVI.* Mexico, 1959.

Relación de las cerimonias y rictos y población y gobernación de los indios de la provincia de Mechuacán. Editado por Jerónimo de Alcalá y Moisés Franco Mendoza. Gobierno del Estado de Michoacán, Mexico, 2000.

Relación de las ceremonias y ritos y población y gobierno de los Indios de la provincial de Michoacán, hecha al ilustrísimo Señor Don Antonio de Mendoza, virrey y gobernador desta Nueva españa por su majestad, (1541). Reproducción facsímil del M. C. IV. 5 de El Escorial. Transcripción por José Tudela. Morelia, MC: Balsal Editores S.A., 1977.

"Relación del descubrimiento de las provincias de Antiochia por Jorge Robledo (1540)." In *Colección de documentos inéditos*, 2:291–356.

"Relación de los Oidores de la Audiencia de Santo Domingo, Espinosa y Zuazo, sobre lo que podría proveerse para la poblacion de aquellas tierras (1528)." In *Colección de documentos inéditos*, 11:342–362.

"Relación de los sucesos de Pedrarias Dávila en las Provincias de Tierra Firme o Castilla del Oro, y de lo ocurrido en el descrubrimiento de la mar del sur y de costas del Peru y Nicaragua." In *Pascual de Andagoya: Relación y documentos*. Editado por Adrian Blázquez. Madrid: Historia, 1986.

"Relación del oro que se fundió para la Hacienda Real en el mes de mayo 1519." In *Colección de documentos inéditos, Isla de Cuba*, 1:89–91.

"Relación del viaje hecho á las Molucas ó de la Especieria por la armada á las órdenes del Comendador Garcia Jofre de Loaysa, hecha por el Capitán Andrés de Urdaneta." In *Colección de documentos inéditos*, 5:5–67.

"Relación geográfica de San Miguel de las Palmas de Tamalameque, Gobernación de Santa Marta, Audiencia de Nueva Granada, Virreinato del Perú (hoy República de Columbia) (1577)." In *Relaciones geográficas de Indias*. Colectado y publicado por Germán Latorre, 1–29. Sevilla: Tip. Zarzuela, 1919.

"Relación hecha por Vicencio de Pápoles, del viaje que hizo la armada que Hernan Cortés envió en busca de las Islas de la Especieria." In *Colección de documentos inéditos*, 5:68–97.

Saint Augustine. *The Happy Life; Answer to Skeptics; Divine Providence and the Problem of Evil Soliloquies*. Washington, DC: Catholic Univ. of America, 2008.

Stabler, Arthur P. and John E. Kicza. "Ruy González's 1553 Letter to Emperor Charles V, An Annotated Translation." *The Americas* 42, no. 4 (April, 1986): 473–487.

Tapia, Andrés de. "Relación de algunas cosas de las que acaecieron al muy ilustre señor don Hernándo Cortés, marqués del valle, desde que se determinó a ir a descubrir tierra en la tierra Firme del mar Océano." In *Colección de documentos para la historia de México*. Edited por Joaquín García Icazbalceta, 2:554–594. Alicante: Biblioteca Virtual Miguel de Cervantes, 1999.

"Testimonio remitido por los oidores de la Audience de Santo Domingo que fueron á la isla Fernandina, de la declaración tomada á Vasco Porcallo de Figueroa, sobre las alteraciones en la villa de Sancti-Spiritus; crueles castigos á los indios; intervención en los sucesos del licenciado Zuazo. 13 Marzo 1522." In *Colección de documentos inéditos, Isla de Cuba*, 1:119–126.

Vega, Bartolomé de. "El tratado de doce dudas." In *O.C.*, 11.2:13–32.

"Verdadera relación de lo que sucedió al Gobrnador Jaime Rasquin en el viaje que intentó para el Rio de la Plata en el año 1559, hecha por Alonso Gomez de Santoya, Alferez del Maestre de Campo, D. Juan de Villadrando." In *Colección de documentos inéditos*, 4:147–190.

Vicente Valverde OP, "Carta del Obispo del Cuzco al Emperador sobre asuntos de su iglesia y otros de la gobernación general de aquel país." In *Colección de documentos inéditos*, 3:92–137.

Victors and Vanquished: Spanish and Nahua Views of the Conquest of Mexico. Edited and introduction by Stuart B. Schwartz. The Bedford Series in History and Culture. Boston, MA: Bedford/St. Martin's, 2000.

Vitoria, Francisco de. *De Indis De Jure Belli.* Edited by Ernest Nys. New York: Oceana Publications Inc., 1964.

———. *Doctrina sobre los Indios*, 2nd ed. Transcripción y traducción por Ramón Hernández Martín. Salamanca: San Esteban, 1992.

———. *Relectio de Indis or libertad de los Indios.* Editado por L. Pereña y J.M. Pérez Prendes. Madrid: CSIC, 1967.

Vera Cruz, Alonso de la. *The Writings of Alonso de la Vera Cruz: II.* Edited and translated by Ernest J. Burris. Rome: Jesuit Historical Institute, 1968.

Walker, David. *David Walker's Appeal to the Coloured Citizens of the World.* Edited and New Introduction and Annotations by Peter P. Hinks. University Park: Pennsylvania State Univ. Press, 2000.

Witness: Writings of Bartolomé de las Casas. Translated and edited by George Sanderlin. Maryknoll, NY: Orbis Books, 1971.

Zorita, Alonso de. *Relación de la Nueva España.* 2 vols. México: Consejo Nacional para la Cultura y las Artes, 1999.

Secondary Sources: Books

Abulafia, David. *The Discovery of Mankind: Atlantic Encounters in the Age of Columbus.* New Haven, CT: Yale Univ. Press, 2008.

Actualidad de Bartolomé de Las Casas. Conferencia del V Centenario de su Nacimiento. Fomento Cultural Banamex, A.C. México, DF: Editorial Jus, S.A., 1975.

Adams, Nicholson B. and John E. Keller, *Spanish Literature: A Brief Survey.* Paterson, NJ: Littlefield, Adams & Co., 1960.

Adorno, Rolena. *De Guancane a Macondo: Estudios de Literatura Hispanoamericana.* Sevilla: Iluminaciones Renacimiento, 2008.

———. *The Polemics of Possession in Spanish American Narrative.* New Haven, CT: Yale Univ. Press, 2007.

Andrés Martín, Melquiades. *La teología española en el siglo XVI.* Madrid: La Editoria Católica, 1976.

Alcaraz Varó, Enrique y Brian Hughes. *Diccionario de Términos Jurídicos (Inglés-Español;Spanish-English).* 7th ed. Madrid: Areil, 2003.

———. *El Español Jurídico.* Barcelona: Editorial Ariel, S.A., 2008.

Alegría, Ricardo E. *Las Primeras Representaciones Gráficas del Indio Americano, 1493–1523.* 2nd ed. San Juan: Centro de Estudios Avanzados de Puerto Rico, 1986.

Allen, Prudence. *The Concept of Women. Vol 2: The Early Humanist Reformation 1250–1500.* Grand Rapids, MI: Wm. B. Eerdman Publishing, 2002.

Álvarez Villar, Julián. *La Universidad de Salamanca: Arte y Tradiciones.* 4th ed. Vol. 3. Salamanca: Universidad de Salamanca, 1990.

Álvaro Rubio, Joaquin. *La Esclavitud en Bancarrota y Salvaleón en el Período Moderno (Siglos XVI-XVIII).* España: Diputación Provincial de Badajoz, 2005.

Alves Azevedo, André and José Manuel Moreira. *The Salamanca School.* Major Conservative and Liberation Thinkers Series, vol. 9. New York: Continuum, 2010.

André-Vicent, Philippe-Ignace. *Bartolomé de Las Casas, prophète du Nouveau Monde.* Paris: Edicion Tallandier, 1980.

Ann Meyers, Kathleen. *Fernández de Oviedo's Chronicle of America: A New History for a New World.* Translated by Nina M. Scott. Austin: Univ. of Texas Press, 2007.

Aporta García, Fernando. *Fray Bartolomé de las Casas y su vinculación a Sevilla.* Malaga: Gráficas Anarol, 2002.

Arias, Santa. *Retórica, história y polémica: Bartolomé de Las Casas y la tradición intelectual renacentista.* Lanham, MD: Univ. Press of America, 2001.

——— and Mariselle Meléndez. *Mapping Colonial Spanish America: Places and Commonplaces of Identity, Culture, and Experience.* Lewisburg, PA: Bucknell Univ. Press, 2002.

Arroyo González, Esteban. *Los misioneros dominicos de Chiapas: entre lobos y corderos.* Querétaro: Instituto Dominicano de Investigaciones Históricas Provincia de Santiago de México, 1997.

Aznar Vallejo, Eduardo. *La Integración de las islas Canarias en la Corona de Castilla (1478–1526): Aspectos administrativos, sociales, y económicos.* Sevilla: Univ. de Sevilla, 2009.

Bannon, John Francis. *The Spanish Borderlands Frontier, 1513–1821.* Histories of the American Frontier Series. Albuquerque: Univ. of New Mexico Press, 1974.

Barreda, Jesús Angel. *Ideología y pastoral misionera en Bartolomé de las Casas.* Madrid: Institutos Pontifícios de Filosofía y Teología, 1981.

Barrenecnez, Raúl Porras. *Los Cronistas del Perú (1528–1650) y Otros Ensayos.* Edición y prólogo de Franklin Pease, et al. Lima: Biblioteca Peruana, 1986.

Barrientos Grandon, Javier. *La Cultura Jurídica en la Nueva España (Sobre la recepción de la tradición jurídica europea en el virreinato).* México, DF: UNAM, 1993.

Bataillon, Marcel. *Estudios Sobre Bartolomé de las Casas.* Barcelona: RIGSA, 1976.

——— y André Saint-Lu. *El Padre Las Casas y la defensa de los Indios.* Traducción de Javier Alfaya y Bárbara McShane. Barcelona: Editorial Ariel, 1976.

Batiffol, Pierre. *History of the Roman Breviary.* Translated by Atwell M.Y. Baylay. London: Longmans, Green and Compay, 1912.

Battles, Ford Lewis. *Study Outline Number 15: Peter Lombard.* Pittsburgh, PA: Pittsburgh Theological Union, 1973.

Baudot, Dom. *The Breviary Its History and Contents.* Translated by the Benedictines of Stanbrook. Catholic Library of Religious IV. St. Louis, MO: Sands and Company, 1929.

Beckjord, Sarah H. *Territories of History: Humanism, Rhetoric, and the Historical Imagination in the Early Chronicles of Spanish America.* University Park: Pennsylvania State Univ. Press, 2007.

Belda Plans, Juan. *La Escuela de Salamanca y la renovación de la teología en el siglo XVI.* Madrid: Biblioteca de Autores Cristianos, 2000.

Bellomo, Manlio. *The Common Legal Past of Europe: 1000–1800.* Washington, DC: Catholic Univ. of America Press, 1995.

Benítez-Rojo, Antonio. *The Repeating Island: The Caribbean and the Postmodern Perspective.* Translated by James Maraniss. Durham, NC: Duke Univ. Press, 1992.

Benjamin, Thomas. *The Atlantic World: Europeans, Africans, Indians, and Their Shared History, 1490–1900.* Cambridge: Cambridge Univ. Press, 2009.

Beuchot, Mauricio. *Bartolomé de las Casas (1484–1566).* Madrid: Ediciones del Orto, 1995.

———. *La Querella de la Conquista: Una polémica del Siglo XVI.* Colección América Nuestra, Siglo XXI. Mexico, DF: Siglo XXI Editores, 2004.

———. *Los fundamentos de los derechos humanos en Bartolomé de las Casas.* Barcelona: Editorial Anthropos, 1994.

———. *The History of Philosophy in Colonial Mexico.* Translated by Elizabeth Millían. Forward by Jorge J.E. García. Washington, DC: Catholic Univ. of America Press, 1997.

Blaut, J.M. *1492: The Debate on Colonialism, Eurocentrism, and History.* Trenton, NJ: Africa World Press, 1992.

Bodmer, Beatriz Pastor. *The Armature of Conquest: Spanish Accounts of Discovery of America, 1492–1589.* Translated by Lydia Longstreth Hunt. Stanford CA: Stanford Univ. Press, 1992.

Bonilla, Heraclio, ed. *Los Conquistadores: 1492 y la población indígena de las Américas.* Santa Fé de Bogotá, Columbia: Tercer Mundo Editores, 1992.

Bonniwell, William. *A History of the Dominican Liturgy, 1215–1945.* New York: Joseph F. Wagner, Inc., 1945.

Borah, Woodrow Wilson. *Justice by Insurance: the General Indian Court of Colonial Mexico and the Legal Aides of the Half-Real.* Berkeley: Univ. of California, 1983.

Borges, Pedro. *Misión y Civilización en América.* Madrid: Editorial Alhambra, 1987.

———. *Quién era Bartolomé de las Casas.* Madrid: Ediciones RIALP, 1990.

———. *Religiosos en Hispanoamérica.* Colección Iglesia Católica en el Nuevo Mundo. Madrid: MAPFRE, 1992.

Boxer, C.R. *The Church Militant and Iberian Expansion 1440–1770.* Baltimore, MD: Johns Hopkins Univ. Press, 1978.

Boyd-Barrett, Oliver and Chris Newbold, eds. *Approaches to Media: A Reader.* London: Arnold/Gray Publishing, 1995.

Boyer, Patricio Edgardo. "Empire and American Visions of the Humane." Ph.D. Diss. Yale University, 2006.

Braden, Charles. *Religious Aspects of the Conquest of Mexico.* Durham, NC: Duke Univ. Press, 1930.

Brading, D.A. *The First America: The Spanish Monarchy, Creole Patriotism, and the LiberalState 1492–1867.* New York: Cambridge Univ. Press, 1991.

Brice, Angel Francisco. *Simón Bolívar y Fray Bartolomé de las Casas ante sus críticos.* Caracas: Italgráfica, C.A., 1969.

Brundage, James A. *Medieval Canon Law.* London: Longman, 1995.

———. *The Profession and Practice of Medieval Canon Law.* Hampshire: Ashgate/Variorum, 2004.

Burkholder, Mark. A. and Lyman L. Johnson. *Colonial Latin America.* 6th ed. New York: Oxford Univ. Press, 2008.

Cardano, Girolamo. *Opera omnia.* Edited by August Buck, Charles Spon, and Gabriel Naudé. Stuttgart-Bad Cannstatt: F. Frommann (G. Holzboog), 1966.

Cárdenas Bunsen, José Alejandro. "Escritura y derecho canónico en la obra de fray Bartolomé de las Casas." Ph.D. Diss. Yale University, 2008.

Carlin, Robert A. *A Paleographic Guide to Spanish Abbreviations: 1500–1700.* USA: Universal Publishers, 2003.

Carmona, María de los Ángeles Guajardo-Fajardo. *Escribanos en Indias Durante la Primera Mitad del Siglo XVI.* 2 tomos. Madrid: Consejo General del Notariado, 1995.

Carro, Venancio Diego. *Carta abierta a D.R. Menéndez Pidal.* Madrid: Librería OPE, 1962.

———. *Los postulados teológico-juridicos de Bartolomé de las Casas: sus aciertos, sus olvidos y sus fallos, ante maestros Francisco de Vitoria y Domingo de Soto.* Sevilla: Estudios Hispano-Americanos, 1966.

Castillo Mattasoglio, Carlos. *Libres para Creer: La Conversión según Bartolomé de Las Casas en la História de las Indias.* Lima: Pontificia Univ. Católica del Perú, 1993.

Castro, Daniel. *Another Face of Empire: Bartolomé de Las Casas, Indigenous Rights, and Ecclesiastical Imperialism.* Durham, NC: Duke Univ. Press, 2007.

Chiappelli, Fredi, ed. *First Images of America: The Impact of the New World on the Old.* Vol. 1. Berkeley: Univ. of California Press, 1976.

Collin, P.H. and Lourdes Melicon, eds. *Spanish Law Dictionary/Diccionario De Terminos Juridicos: Spanish-English English-Spanish/Espanol-Ingles.* Peter Collin Publishing, 1999.

Comerford, Kathleen M. and Hilmar M. Pabal, eds. *Early Modern Catholicism: Essays in Honor of John W. O'Malley, S.J.* Toronto: Univ. of Toronto Press, 2001.

Cowans, Jon, ed. *Early Modern Spain: A Documentary History.* Philadelphia: Univ. of Pennsylvania Press, 2003.

Crosby, Alfred W. Jr. *The Columbian Exchange: Biological and Cultural Consequences of 1492.* Forwards by J.R. McNeil and Otto von Mering. Westport, CT: Praeger Publishing, 2003.

Crow, John A. *Spain: The Root and the Flower: An Interpretation of Spain and the Spanish People.* 3rd ed. Los Angeles: Univ. of California Press, 1985.

Dávila Padilla, Fray Agustín. *Historia de la fundación y discurso de la provincial de Santiago de México, de la Orden de Predicadores.* México, DF: 1955.

Defourneaux, Marcelin. *Daily Life in Spain: In the Golden Age.* Translated by Newton Branch. Stanford, CA: Stanford Univ. Press, 1979.

Denevan, William M., ed. *The Native Population of the Americas in 1492.* 2nd ed. Madison: Univ. of Wisconsin Press, 1992.

Díaz-Plaja, Guillermo. *Historia general de las literaturas hispánicas.* 3 vols. Barcelona: Editorial Barna, S.A., 1953.

———. *The History of Spanish Literature.* Edited and translated by Hugh A. Harter. New York: New York Univ. Press, 1971.

Diffe, Bailey W. and George D. Winius. *Foundations of the Portuguese Empire, 1415–1580.* Europe and the world in the Age of Expansion, vol. 1. Minneapolis: Univ. of Minnesota Press, 1977.

Durán Luzio, Juan. *Bartolomé de las Casas ante la conquista de América: las voces del historiador.* Heredia: EUNA, 1992.

Dussel, Enrique. *A History of the Church in Latin America: Colonialism to Liberation.* Translated by Alan Neely. Grand Rapids, MI: Wm. B. Eerdman Publishing, 1981.

———. *El encubrimiento del otro: hacia el origen del mito de la modernidad.* Quito: Ediciones ABYA-YALA, 1994.

———. *El episcopado hispanoamericano: institución misionera en defensa delindio, 1504–1620.* Apéndice documental. 9 tomos. Cuernavaca: CIDOC, 1970.

Dutto, L.A. *The Life of Bartolomé de Las Casas and the First Leaves of American Ecclesiastical History.* St. Louis, MO: B. Herder, 1902.

Edwards, John. *The Spain of the Catholic Monarchs: 1474–1520.* Oxford: Blackwell Publishers, 2000.

El Padre Las Casas y Los Cubanos. Selección de Ana Cairo y Amavari Gutiérrez. Aula "Fray Bartolomé de Las Casas." Puerto Rico: Univ. Central de Bayamon, 2007.

El Siglo de Frai Luis de León: Salamanca y el Renacimiento. Coordinated by Mercedes Aznar López and Luz de Gaztelu y Quijano. Madrid: Junta de Castilla y León, 1991.

Elliott, J.H. *Imperial Spain 1469–1716.* London: Penguin Books, 1963.

———. *Spain and Its World: 1500–1700.* New Haven, CT: Yale Univ. Press, 1989.

Enciclopedia jurídica latinoamericana. Instituto de investigaciones jurídicas. 10 tomos. México: UNAM; Buenos Aires: Rubinzal-Culzoni Editores, 2006.

En el V Centenario de Bartolomé de las Casas. Instituto de Cooperación Iberoamericana. Madrid: Ediciones Cultura Hispánica, 1986.

Enzensberger, Hans Magnus. *Fray Bartolomé de las Casas: una retrospectiva al futuro.* Mexico: UNAM, 1987.

Espinel, José Luís. *San Esteban de Salamanca: historia y guía (siglos XIII-XX).* 2nd ed. Salamanca: Editorial San Esteban, 1995.

Evans, G.R. *Law and Theology in the Middle Ages.* London: Routledge, 2002.

Everton, A.R. *What Is Equity about?* London: Butterworth, 1970.

Fernández Méndez, Eugenio. *Las encomiendas y esclavitud de los indios de Puerto Rico, 1508–1550.* Sevilla: Escuela de Estudios Hispano Americanos, 1966.

Fernández Rodríguez, Pedro. *Los Dominicos en el contexto de la primera evangelización de México, 1526–1550.* Monumenta Histórica Iberoamericana de la Orden de Predicadores. Vol. 3. Salamanca: San Esteban, 1994.

Fernández-Santamaría, J.A. *Natura Law, Constitutionalism, Reason of State, and War: Counter-Reformation Spanish Political Thought.* Vol. 1: Renaissance and Baroque: Studies and Texts, no. 32. New York: Peter Lang Publishing, 2005.

Fiske, John. *The Discovery of America with Some Account of Ancient America and the Spanish Conquest.* Vol. 2. Boston, MA: Houghton Mifflin, 1892.

Florescano, Enrique. *Memory, Myth, and Time in Mexico: From the Aztecs to Independence.* Translated by Albert G. Bork and Kathryn R. Bork. Austin: Univ. of Texas Press, 1997.

Floyd, Troy S. *The Columbus Dynasty in the Caribbean, 1492–1526.* Albuquerque: Univ. of New Mexico Press, 1973.

Folger, Robert and Wulf Oesterreicher, eds. *Talleres de la memoria—Reivindicaciones y autoridad en la historigrafía de los siglos XVI y XVII.* Münster: LIT, Druck, 2005.

Frades Gaspar, Eduardo. *El uso de la Biblia en los escritos de Fray Barolomé de Las Casas.* Caracas: Instituto Universitario Seminario Interdiocesano Santa Rosa de Lima, 1997.

Franco, José Luis. *500 Años de evangelización e história: Una comemoración litúrgica.* México, DF: Centro Antonio de Montesinos, 1992.

Frick, Peter. *Divine Providence in Philo of Alexandria.* Tübingen: Mohr Siebeck, 1999.

Friede, Juan and Benjamin Keen, eds. *Bartolomé de Las Casas in History: Toward an Understanding of the Man and His Work.* DeKalb: Northern Illinois Univ., 1971.

García de Cortázar, J.A. *Historia de España Alfaguara II: La época medieval.* Madrid: Alianza Editorial, 1973.

García y García, Antonio. *Derecho común en España: los juristas y sus obras.* Murcía: Secretarido de Publicaciones, 1991.

———. *En el entorno del derecho comun.* Madrid: Editorial Dykinson, 1999.

Gibson, Charles. *Spain in America.* New York: Harper and Row, 1966.

———. *The Aztecs under Spanish Rule: A History of the Indians of the Valley of Mexico, 1519–1810.* Stanford, CA: Stanford Univ. Press, 1964.

Gil, Juan. *Mitos y utopías del descubrimiento.* 3 vols. Madrid: Alianza Editorial, 1989.

Giménez Fernández, Manuel. *Bartolomé de las Casas: delegado de Cisneros para la reformación de las Indias 1516–1517.* Vol. 1. Reimpresión de 1953. Madrid: Consejo Superior de Investigaciones Científicas, 1984.

———. *Bartolomé de las Casas: capellán de S.M. Carlos I, poblador de Cumaná 1517–1523.* Vol. 2. Reimpresión de 1960. Madrid: Consejo Superior de Investigaciones Científicas, 1984.

———. *Fray Bartolomé de las Casas: "Padre de América."* Estudio biográfico-crítico. Madrid: La RAFA, S. L. Abato, 1958.

———. *Instituciones jurídicas en la Iglesia Católica.* Vol. 1. Sevilla: Sociedad Anónima Española de Traductores y Autores, 1940.

———. *Instituciones jurídicas en la Iglesia Católica.* Vol. 2. Sevilla: Sociedad Anónima Española de Traductores y Autores, 1942.

Ginobill de Tumminello, M. Elena and Elvira Germano de Volpe. *El Derecho a la Cultura Indigena en el Testamento de Isabel la Católica.* Argentina: Ediciones Utopia, 1992.

González-Echevarría, Roberto. *Isla a su vuelo fugitiva.* Madrid: José Purrúa Turanzas, 1983.

——— and Enrique Pupo-Walker. *Myth and Archive: A Theory of Latin American narrative.* Durham, NC: Duke Univ. Press, 1998.

———, eds. *The Cambridge History of Latin American Literature.* Cambridge: Cambridge Univ. Press, 1996.

González, Justo L. *The Story of Christianity.* Vol. 1, *The Early Church to the Dawn of the Reformation.* Vol. 2, *The Reformation to the Present Day.* San Francisco, CA: Harper Collins, 1985.

González-Reviriego, Donato. *En Torno Al Monasterio de Santo Tomás de Ávila.* Avila: Industrias Gráficas Abulenses, S.L., 2006.

Grafton, Anthony, with April Shelford and Nancy Siraisi. *New Worlds, Ancient Text: The Power of Tradition and the Shock of Discovery.* Cambridge, MA: The Belknap Press of Harvard Univ. Press, 1992.

Greenblatt, Stephen, ed. *New World Encounters.* Berkeley: Univ. of California, 1993.

Greenleaf, Richard E., ed. *The Roman Catholic Church in Colonial America.* New York: Alfred E. Knopf, 1971.

Gratsch, Edward J. *Aquinas' Summa: An Introduction and Interpretation*. New York: Alba House, 1985.

Gula, Richard M. *Reason Informed by Faith: Foundations of Catholic Morality*. New York: Paulist Press, 1989.

Gutiérrez, Gustavo. *Dios o el oro en las Indias*. Lima: Instituto Bartolomé de Las Casas, 1989.

———. *En busca de los pobres de Jesucristo: el pensamiento de Bartolomé de las Casas*. Lima: Instituto Bartolomé de las Casas, 1992.

———. *Las Casas: In Search of the Poor of Jesus Christ*. Maryknoll, NY: Orbis, 1995.

Hacking, Ian. *The Emergence of Possibility*. Cambridge: Cambridge Univ. Press, 1975.

Handbook of Middle American Indians: Guide to Ethnohistorical Sources. Edited by Robert Wauchope, Howard Cline, John B. Glass. Austin: Univ. of Texas, 1973.

Hanke, Lewis. *Bartolomé de Las Casas: An Interpretation of His Life and Writings*. The Hague: Martinus Nijhoff, 1951.

———. *Bartolomé de Las Casas: Bookman, Scholar and Propagandist*. Philadelphia: Univ. of Pennsylvania Press, 1952.

———. *Bartolomé de Las Casas, Historian: an Essay in Spanish Historiography*. Gainesville: Univ. of Florida Press, 1952.

——— and Manuel Giménez Fernández. *All Mankind Is One: A Study of the Disputation between Bartolomé de Las Casas and Juan Ginés de Sepúlveda in 1550 on the Intellectual and Religious Capacity of the American Indians*. De Kalb: Northern Illinois Univ. Press, 1974.

———. *Aristotle and the American Indians: A Study in Race Prejudice in the Modern World*. Bloomington: Indiana Univ. Press, 1975.

———. *Bartolomé de las Casas 1474–1566: bibliografía crítica y cuerpo de materiales para el estudio de su vida, escritos, actuación y polémicas que suscitaron durante cuatro siglos*. Santiago de Chile: Fondo Histórico, 1954.

———. *The Spanish Struggle for Justice in the Conquest of America*. Dallas, TX: Southern Methodist Univ. Press, 2002.

Hankins, James, ed. *The Cambridge Companion to Renaissance Philosophy*. New York: Cambridge Univ. Press, 2007.

Hanks, William F. *Converting Words: Maya in the Age of the Cross*. Berkeley: Univ. of California Press, 2010.

Hartmann, Wilfried and Kenneth Pennington, eds. *The History of Medieval Canon Law in the Classical Period, 1140–1234: From Gratian to the Decretals of Pope Gregory IX*. Washington, DC: Catholic Univ. of America Press, 2008.

Helmholtz, R.H. *The Spirit of Classical Canon Law*. Athens: Univ. of Georgia Press, 1996.

Hernández, Ramón. *Derechos humanos en Francisco de Vitoria: antología*. Salamanca: Editorial San Esteban, 1984.

———. *Francisco de Vitoria, O.P.: síntesis de su vida y pensamiento*. Caleruela, Burgos: Editorial OPE, 1983.

Henríquez Ureña, Pedro. *Las corrientes literarias en la America hispánica*. Mexico, DF: Fondo de Cultural Economica, 1949.

Heschel, Abraham J. *The Prophets*. 2 vols. New York: Harper and Row, 1962.

Historia de la Iglesia in Hispanoamérica y Filipinas (Siglos XV-XIX). 2 tomos. Madrid: Biblioteca de Autores Cristianos, 1992.

Historia de la Universidad de Salamanca. 3 vols. Coordinado por Luis Enrique Rodríguez-San Pedro Bezarez. Salamanca: Ediciones Univ. de Salamanca, 2002.

Historia de la Universidad de Valladolid. Transcrita del Libro de Bezerro (1757) por Vicente Velázquez de Figueroa. Valladolid: Imprenta Castellana, 1918.

Hoberman, Louisa Schell and Susan Midgen Socolow, eds. *Cities and Society in Colonial Latin America*. Albuquerque: Univ. of New Mexico Press, 1986.

Homza, Lu Ann. *Religious Authority in the Spanish Renaissance*. Baltimore, MD: Johns Hopkins Univ. Press, 2000.

Horst, Ulrich. *The Dominicans and the Pope: Papal Teaching Authority in the Medieval and Early Modern Thomist Tradition*. Translated by James D. Mixson. The Conway Lectures in Medieval Studies. Notre Dame, IN: Univ. of Notre Dame, 2002.

Hoyo, Eugenio del. *Esclavitud y Encomienas de Indios en el Nuevo Reino de León, Siglos XVI y XVII*. Monterrey: Archivo General del Estado de Nuevo León, 1985.

Huerta, José Luis Burguet, José Barrado Barquillo, y Bernardo Fueyo Suárez. *Influencia Lascasiana en el Siglo XVI: VIII Congreso de Historiadores Dominicos*. Salamanca: Editorial San Esteban, 2006.

Humphreys, K.W. *The Book Provisions of the Mediaeval Friars, 1215–1400*. Amsterdam: Erasmus Booksellers, 1964.

Hunt, Jocelyn. *Spain, 1474–1598*. London: Routledge, 2001.

Iñigo Madrigal, Luis, coordinador. *Historia de la literatura hispanoamericana, epoca colonial*. Madrid: Catedra, 1982.

Iraburu, José María. *Hechos de los apóstoles de América*. Pamplona: Fundacion Gratis Date, 1992.

Justicia, Sociedad y Economia en America Española (Siglos XVI, XVII y XVIII). Editado por Casa-Mueso de Colón Seminario Americanista de la Universidad de Valladolid. Trabajos del VI Congreso del Instituto Internacional de Historia del Derecho Indiano. Valladolid: 1983.

Kagan, Richard L. *Lawsuits and Litigants in Castille, 1500–1700*. Chapel Hill: Univ. of North Carolina Press, 1981.

———. *Students and Society in Early Modern Spain*. Baltimore, MD: Johns Hopkins Univ. Press, 1974.

Kainz, Howard P. *Natual Law: An Introduction and Re-examination*. Chicago, IL: Open Court Publishing, 2004.

Kamen, Henry. *Empire: How Spain Became a World Power 1492–1763*. New York: Harper Collins, 2003.

———. *Philip of Spain*. New Haven, CT: Yale Univ. Press, 1997.

———. *Golden Age of Spain*. 2nd ed. Studies in European History Series. New York: Palgrave MacMillian, 2005.

———. *The Spanish Inquisition: A Historical Revision*. New Haven, CT: Yale Univ. Press, 1997.

Kelley, Donald. *Foundations of Modern Historical Scholarship: Language, Law, and History in the French Renaissance*. New York: Columbia Univ. Press, 1970.

Kinneavy, Gerald. *A Voice in the Wilderness: The Story of Bartolomé de Las Casas*. Denver, CO: Outskirts Press, 2007.

Konetzke, Richard. *Colección de documentos para la historia de la formación social de Hispanoamerica, 1493–1810.* 3 vols. Madrid: Consejo Superior de Investigaciones Científicas, 1953–58.

Kraye, Jill, ed. *The Cambridge Companion to Renaissance Humanism.* Cambridge: Cambridge Univ. Press, 1988.

Kristeller, Paul Oskar. *Medieval Aspects of Renaissance Learning: Three Essays by Paul Oskar Kristeller.* Edited and translated by Edward P. Mahoney. Durham, NC: Duke Univ. Press, 1974.

———. *Renaissance Thought and Its Sources.* Edited by Michael Mooney. New York: Columbia Univ. Press, 1979.

La Universidad de Salamanca. 3 volúmenes. Directado por Manuel Fernández Álvarez. Salamanca: Ediciones Universidad de Salamanca, 1989/1990.

———. *Renaissance Thought: The Classic, Scholastic, and Humanistic Strains.* New York: Harper Torchbooks, 1961.

Latorre, Octavio. *Thomás de Berlanga y el Descubrimiento de Galápagos.* Quito: Consejo Nacional de Cultura, 1996.

Latin American Philosophy: An Introduction with Readings. Edited by Susana Nuccetelli and Gary Seay. Upper Saddle River, NJ: Pearson Education, 2004.

Lehfeldt, Elizabeth A. *Religious Women in Golden Age Spain: The Permeable Cloister.* Hampshire: Ashgate Publishing, 2005.

León-Portilla, Miguel. *Francisco Tenamaztle: Primer Guerrillero de América. Defensor de los Derechos Humanos.* Mexico, DF: Editorial Diana, 2005.

Lippy, Charles H., Robert Choquette, and Stafford Poole. *Christianity Comes to the Americas: 1492–1776.* New York: Paragon House, 1992.

Liss, Peggy K. *Isabel the Queen: Life and Times.* Revised edition. Philadelphia: Univ. of Pennsylvania Press, 2004.

Lockhart, James and Stuart B. Schwartz. *Early Latin America: A History of Colonial Spanish America and Brazil.* Cambridge: Cambridge Univ. Press, 1983.

———. *Of Things in the Indies: Essays Old and New in Early Latin American History.* Stanford, CA: Stanford Univ. Press, 1999.

———. *Spanish Peru, 1532–1560: A Social History.* 2nd ed. Madison: Univ. of Wisconsin Press, 1994.

Lombard, Peter. *The Sentences, Book 1: The Mystery of the Trinity.* Translated by Giulio Silano. Medieval Sources in Translation 42. Toronto: Pontifical Institute of Medieval Studies, 2007.

López Grigera, Luisa. *La rétorica en la España del siglo de oro.* Salamanca: Ediciones Universidad de Salmanca, 1994.

Luengo Celada, Gregorio. *Tomás de Aquino, testigo y maestro de la fe.* Salamanca: Editorial San Esteban, 1999.

Lynch, John. *Spain, 1516–1598.* Oxford: Blackwell, 1991.

Mabry, Donald J. *Colonial Latin America.* Coral Springs, FL: Lumina Press, 2002.

MacLachlan, Colin M. *Spain's Empire in the New World: The Role of Ideas in Institutional and Social Change.* Berkeley: Univ. of California Press, 1988.

MacNutt, Francis Augustus. *Bartholomew de Las Casas: His Life, His Apostolate and His Writings.* Cleveland: Arthur H. Clark, 1909.

Maiolo, Francesco. *Medieval Sovereignty: Marsilius of Padua and Bartolus of Saxoferrato.* Delft: Eburon Academic Publishers, 2007.

Márquez de la Plata y Fernández, Vicente María. *Mujeres Renacentistas en la corte de Isabel la Católica*. Madrid: Editorial Castalia, 2005.

Martí, José. *El padre Las Casas*. Edición crítica. Investigación, cronología, estudio valorativo y notas por Ana Cairo. La Habana: Centro de Estudios Martianos, 2001.

Martin, Henri-Jean. *The Coming of the Book: The Impact of Printing, 1450–1800*. Translated by Geoffrey Nowell-Smith and David Wootton. London: Atlantic Highlands Humanities Press, 1976.

Martínez, Manuel M. *El obispo Marroquín y el Franciscano Motolinía, enemigos de las Casas*. Madrid: La Rafa, 1954.

———. *Fray Bartolomé de las Casas: el gran calumniado*. Madrid: La Rafa, 1955.

———. *Fray Bartolomé de las Casas: Padre de América*. Estudio biográfico-crítico. Madrid: La Rafa, 1958.

Martínez Millán, José. *La Corte de Carlos V*. 5 vols. Madrid: Sociedad Estatal para la Comemoración de los Centenarios de Felipe II y Carlos V, 2000.

Marías, Julián. *Understanding Spain*. Translated by Frances M. López-Morilla. Ann Arbor: Univ. of Michigan Press, 1990.

McAlister, Lyle N. *Spain and Portugal in the New World, 1492–1700*. Europe and the World in the Age of Expansion Series. Minneapolis: Univ. of Minnesota Press, 1984.

McGonigle, Thomas D., and James F Quigley. *A History of the Christian Tradition: From Its Jewish Origins to the Reformation*. New York: Paulist Press, 1988.

———. *A History of the Christian Tradition: From the Reformation to the Present*. New York: Paulist Press, 1996.

Medieval Iberia: An Encyclopedia. Edited by E. Michael Gerli, Samuel G. Armistead, et al. New York: Routledge, 2003.

Medina, Miguel Angel. *Una Comunidad al servicio del Indio: la obra de Fr. Pedro de Córdoba, O.P. (1482—1521)*. Madrid: Instituto Pontifício de Teología, 1983.

Mejía de Fernández, Abigail. *Historia de la literatura castellana: estudio histórico crítico que comprende la literatura hispano-americana*. Barcelona: Araluce, 1934.

Menéndez Pidal, Ramón. *El Padre Las Casas: su doble personalidad*. Madrid: Espasa-Calpe, 1963.

Mills, Kenneth, William B. Taylor, and Sandra Lauderdale Graham. *Colonial Latin America: A Documentary History*. Wilmington, DE: Scholarly Resources, 2002.

Mira Caballos, Esteban. *El Indio Antillano: Repartimiento, Encomienda y Esclavitud. (1492–1542)*. Sevilla: Biblioteca Americana, 1997.

Monal, Isabel. *Ensayos Americanos*. La Habana: Editorial de Ciencias Sociales, 2007.

Mousourakis, George. *The Historical and Institutional Context of Roman Law*. Burlington, VT: Ashgate Publishing, 2003.

Muldoon, James. *Popes, Lawyers, and Infidels*. Philadelphia: Univ. of Pennsylvania Press, 1979.

———. *The Americas in the Spanish World Order: The Justification for the Conquest in the Seventeenth Century*. Philadelphia: Univ. of Pennsylvania Press, 1995.

Muñoz Iglesias, Salvador. *Introducción a la lectura del Antiguo Testamento.* Madrid: Taurus, 1955.

———. *Los generos literarios y la interpretacion de la Biblia.* Madrid: Casa de la Biblia, 1968.

Nader, Helen. *Liberty in Absolutist Spain: The Habsburg Sale of Towns, 1516–1700.* Baltimore, MD: Johns Hopkins Univ. Press, 1990.

Nauert, Jr, Charles G. *Humanism and the Culture of Renaissance Europe.* Cambridge: Cambridge Univ. Press, 1995.

Neale, Stephen. *Genre.* London: British Film Institute, 1980.

Nebrija, Antonio de. *Gramática de la lengua Castellano (1492).* Editado por I. González-Llubera. New York: Oxford Univ. Press, 1926.

Nolasco, Flérida de. *Clamor de Justicia en la Española, 1502–1795.* Santo Domingo, República Dominicana: Sociedad Dominicana de Bibliófilos, 2008.

O'Daniel, V.F. *Dominicans in Early Florida.* Monograph Series XII. New York: United States Catholic Historical Society, 1930.

Olivera, Otto. *Relatos y Relaciones de Hispanoamérica Colonial.* Austin: Univ. of Texas Press, 2004.

Oquendo, Ángel R., ed. *Latin American Law.* New York: Foundation Press, 2006.

Ortega Iglesias, Luis. *Bartolomé de Las Casas: Cuarenta y cuatro años infinitos.* Sevilla: Fundación José Lara, 2007.

Owensby, Brian. *Empire of Law and Indian Justice in Colonial Mexico.* Stanford, CA: Stanford Univ. Press, 2008.

Pagden, Anthony. *European Encounters with the New World: From Renaissance to Romanticism.* New Haven, CT: Yale Univ. Press, 1993.

———. *The Fall of Natural Man: The American Indian and the Origins of Comparative Ethnology.* Cambridge: Cambridge Univ. Press, 1982.

———. *Lords of all the World: Ideologies of Empire in Spain, Britain and France, ca. 1500—ca 1800.* New Haven, CT: Yale Univ. Press, 1995.

———. *Spanish Imperialism and the Political Imagination: Studies in European and Spanish-American Social and Political Theory 1513–1830.* New Haven, CT: Yale Univ. Press, 1990.

Pardo, Osvaldo F. *The Origins of Mexican Catholicism: Nahua Rituals and Christian Sacraments in Sixteenth-Century Mexico.* Ann Arbor: Univ. of Michigan, 2006.

Parish, Helen Rand. *Las Casas as Bishop: A New Interpretation Based on His Holograph Petition in the Hans P. Kraus Collection of Hispanic American Manuscripts.* Washington, DC: Library of Congress, 1980.

———. María Concepta Maciel, and Gustavo Gutiérrez. *Bartolomé de Las Casas:Liberation of the Oppressed.* San Jose, CA: San José Dominican Sisters, 1984.

——— and Harold E Weidman. *Las Casas en México: historia y obra desconocidas.* México, DF: Fondo de Cultura Económica, 1992.

Parry, J.H. *The Spanish Seaborne Empire.* Berkeley: Univ. of California Press, 1966.

———. *The Spanish Theory of Empire in the Sixteenth Century.* Cambridge: Cambridge Univ. Press, 1940.

Pensamiento Novohispano. Compilado por Noé Esquivel Estrada, et al. México, DF: UNAM, 2003.

Pennington, Kenneth and Robert Somerville, eds. *Law, Church, and Society: Essays in Honor of Stephen Kuttner.* Philadelphia: Univ. of Pennsylvania Press, 1977.

———. *Popes, Canonists and Texts, 1150–1550.* Hampshire: Ashgate Publishing, 1993.

———. *The Prince and the Law, 1200–1600: Sovereignty and Rights in the Western Legal Tradition.* Berkeley: Univ. of California Press, 1993.

Pereño Vicente, Luciano. *Misión de España en América 1540–1560.* Madrid: Consejo Superior de Investigaciones Cientificas, 1956.

Pérez, Joseph. *La revolución de las comunidades de Castilla (1520–1521).* Translated by Juan José Faci Lacasta. Madrid: Siglo Veintiuno Editores, 1998.

Pérez, Juan-Manuel. *Estos ¿no son hombres? Lectura actual del Proyecto Apostólico de la Primera Comunidad de Dominicos en el Nuevo Mundo.* Santo Domingo, Republica Dominicana: Fundación García-Arévalo, 1984.

———. *Evangelio y Libertad: Primeros dominicos en América.* 2nd edición. Cusco: Centro Bartolomé de Las Casas, 1998.

Pérez Fernández, Isacio. *Bartolomé de las Casas en el Perú: el espíritu lascasiano el la primera evangelización del imperio incaico (1531–1573).* Cuzco: Centro de Estudios Rurales Andinos, 1986.

———. *Bartolomé de Las Casas viajero por dos mundos: su figura, su biografía, su personalidad.* Archivos de Historia Andina 30. Cuzco: Centro de Estudios Regionales Andinos Bartolomé de Las Casas, 1998.

———. "Conclusiones sumarias sobre el remedio de las Indias." Edición facsímil del manuscrito y doble comentario del mismo por el Padre Isacio Pérez Fernández. Madrid: Biblioteca Nacional, 1992.

———. *Cronología documentada de los viajes, estancias y actuaciones de Fray Bartolomé de las Casas.* Vol. 2, Estudios Monográficos. Bayamón, PR: Centro de Estudios de los Dominicos del Caribe, 1984.

———. *Don Quijote de la Mancha y Don Quijote de Las Casas: Fray Bartolomé de Las Casas clave histórica de la obra inmortal de Cervantes.* Sevilla: Convento de Santo Tomás de Aquino, 2002.

———. *El derecho Hispano-Indiano: dinamica social de su proceso histórico constituyente.* Salamanca: Editorial San Esteban, 2001.

———. *Fray Bartolomé de Las Casas: brevísima relación de su vida, diseño de su personalidad, síntesis de su doctrina.* Caleruega, Burgos: Editorial OPE, 1984.

———. *Fray Bartolomé de Las Casas: brevísima relación de la destruicion de las Indias,* Vol. 3, Estudios monográficos. Primera Edición Crítica por Isacio Pérez Fernández, O.P. Bayamón, PR: Centro de Estudios de los Dominicos del Caribe, 1999.

———. *Fray Bartolomé de las Casas, O.P., brevísima relación de la destruición de Africa.* Salamanca: Editorial San Esteban, 1989.

———. *Fray Bartolomé de las Casas, O.P.: de defensor de los Indios a defensor de los Negros.* Salamanca: Editorial San Esteban, 1995.

———. *Fray Toribio Motolinía, O.F.M., frente a Fray Bartolomé de las Casas, O.P.: estudio y edición crítica de la carta de Motolinía al Emperador (Tlaxcala, 2 de Enero de 1555).* Salamanca: Editorial San Esteban, 1989.

———. *Inventario documentado de los escritos de Fray Bartolomé de las Casas.* Vol. 1, Estudios Monográficos. Revisado por Helen Rand Parish. Bayamón, PR: Centro de Estudios de los Dominicos del Caribe, 1981.

———. *Itinerario Espiritual de Fr. Bartolomé de las Casas.* Querétaro: Instituto Dominicano de Investigaciones Históricas, 1996.

Pérez Villanueva, Joaquin and Bartolomé Escandell Bonet, eds. *Historia de la Inquisición en España y América.* 3 vols. Madrid: Biblioteca de Autores Cristianos, Centro Estudios Inquisitoriales, 1984.

Phelan, John Leddy. *The Millennial Kingdom of the Franciscans in the New World: A Study of the Writings of Gerónimo de Mendieta (1525–1604).* Berkeley: Univ. of California Press, 1956.

Pintado, Feliciano Barrios, ed. *Derecho y Administración Pública en las Indias Hispánicas: Actas del XII Congresso International de Derecho Indiano (Toledo, 19 a 21 de octubre de 1998).* 2 vols. Cuenca, España: Universidad de Castilla-La Mancha, 2002.

Pinto de Oliveira, Carlos Josaphat. *Contemplação e Liberação: Tomás de Aquino, João da Cruz, Bartolomeu de Las Casas.* São Paulo: Editora Ática, 1995.

———. *Las Casas: Todos os direitos para todos.* São Paulo, Brasil: Ediçoes Loyola, 2000.

———. *Tomás de Aquino ea Nova Era do Espírito.* São Paulo, Brasil: Ediçoes Loyola, 1998.

Pita Moreda, Maria Teresa. *Los Predicadores Novohispanos del Siglo XVI.* Los Dominicos y América, vol. 9. Salamanca: San Esteban, 1992.

Plancarte, Gabriel Méndez. *Humanismo Mexicano del Siglo XVI.* Biblioteca del Estudante Universidad, 63. México, DF, UNAM, 1946.

Porter, Jean. *Natural and Divine Law: Reclaiming the Tradition for Christian Ethics.* Grand Rapids, MI: Saint Paul Univ. Press, 1999.

Powers, Karen Vieira. *Women in the Crucible of Conquest: The Gendered Genesis of Spanish American Society, 1500–1600.* Albuquerque: Univ. of New Mexico Press, 2005.

Predicadores de la gracia: Los Dominicos el la República Dominicana. Coordinados por Javier Atienza y Jesús Espeja. Salamanca: San Esteban, 2006.

Prescott, William H. and John Foster Kirk. *History of the Conquest of Mexico.* New York: J. B. Lippincott, 1891.

Prieto Inzunza, Angélica. *La pasión en las crónicas.* Xalapa, Veracruz, México: Universidad Veracruzana, 2008.

Puente Brunke, José de la. *Encomienda y Encomenderos en el Perú: Estudio social y político de una institución colonial.* Centenario del Descubrimiento de América, no. 14. Sevilla: Diputación Provincial de Sevilla, 1992.

Queralto Moreno, Ramón Jesús. *El pensamiento filosófico-político de Bartolomé de las Casas.* Sevilla: Escuela de Estudios Hispano-Americanos de Sevilla, 1976.

Quintana, Manuel José. *Fray Bartolomé de las Casas.* Buenos Aires: Editorial Poseidon, 1943.

Rabasa, José. *Inventing America: Spanish Historiography and the Formation of Eurocentrism.* Norman: Univ. of Oklahoma Press, 1993.

Rahner, Karl, ed. *Encyclopedia of Theology.* New York: Crossroads, 1986.

Ratzinger, Joseph Cardinal. *Church, Ecumenism and Politics.* New York: Crossroads, 1988.

Rausch, Jane M. *A Tropical Plains Frontier: The Llanos of Colombia, 1531–1831.* Albuquerque: Univ. of New Mexico Press, 1984.

Renaissance Philosophy: New Translations, Lorenzo Valla (1407–1457), Paul Cortese (1465–1510), Cajetan (Thomas de Vio) (1469–1534), Tiberio Baccillieri (c.1470–1511), Juan Luis Vives (1492–1540), Peter Ramus (1515–1572). Edited by Leonard A. Kennedy. Chicago, IL: Mouton, 1973.

Restall, Matthew. *The Seven Myths of the Spanish Conquest.* New York: Oxford Univ. Press, 2003.

———. Lisa Sousa, and Kevin Terraciano. *Mesoamerican Voices: Native-Language Writings from Colonial Mexico, Oaxaca, Yucatan, and Guatemala.* New York: Cambridge Univ. Press, 2005.

Ricard, Robert. *La conquista espiritual de México: ensayo sobre el apostolado y los métodos misioneros de las Ordenes en la Nueva España de 1523–1524 a 1572.* México, DF: Fundo de Cultura Económica, 1986.

———. *The Spiritual Conquest of Mexico: An Essay on the Apostolate and the Evangelization Methods of the Mendicant Orders in New Spain: 1523–1572.* Berkeley: Univ. of California Press, 1966.

Rivera Pagán, Luis N. *A Violent Evangelization: The Political and Religious Conquest of the Americas.* Louisville, KT: Westminster/John Knox Press, 1992.

———. *Entre el oro y la fe: el dilema de América.* San Juan: Universidad de Puerto Rico, 1995.

Robiou Lamarche, Sebastián. *Taínos y Caribes: Las culturas aborígenes antillanas.* Prólogo por Ricardo E. Alegría. San Juan: Editorial Punto y Coma, 2005.

Rodríquez, Francisco. "La *'Brevísima relación'* del Padre Las Casas: Textos y Subtextos." Ph.D. Diss. University of California, Davis. 1995.

Romero, Fernando y Mauricio Beuchot. *Los Derechos Humanos y Los Dominicos.* México, DF: Cuadernos "Oasis", 1998.

Romero Galván, José Rubén. *Contextos y Texto de una Crónica: Libro Tercero de la Historia Religiosa de la Provincia de México de la Órden de Santo Domingo de Fray Hernando Ojea, O.P.* México, DF: UNAM, 2007.

Rorty, Amélie Oksenberg. *Essays on Aristotle's Poetics.* Princeton, NJ: Princeton Univ. Press, 1992.

Roskamp, Hans. *Los Códices de Cutzio y Huetamo: Encomienda y Tributo en la Tierra Caliente de Michoacán, Siglo XVI.* Michoacán: El Colegio de Michoacán, 2003.

Rossi, Christopher R. *Broken Chain of Being: James Brown Scott and the Origins of Modern International Law.* The Hague: Kluwer Law International, 1998.

Roys, Ralph L. *The Book of Chilam Balam of Chumayel.* Washington, DC: Carnegie Institution, 1933.

Ruiz, Teofilo. *Spanish Society, 1400–1600.* A Social History of Europe Series. Harlow: Pearson Education Limited, 2001.

———. *Spain's Centuries of Crisis: 1300–1474.* Malden, MA: Blackwell, 2007.

———. *The City and the Realm of Burgos and Castile, 1080–1492.* Hampshire: Variorum, 1992.

Rumeu de Armas, Antonio. *La Política Indigentista de Isabel la Católica.* Valladolid: Instituto "Isabel la Católica" de História Eclesiastica, 1969.

Russell, Fredrick H. *The Just War in the Middle Ages.* Studies in Medieval Life and Thought Series, 3rd ed. Vol. 8. Cambridge: Cambridge Univ. Press, 1975.

Sáenz de Santa María, Carmelo. *El licenciado don Francisco Marroquín, primer obispo de Guatemala, 1499–1563.* Madrid: Ediciones Cultura Hispánica, 1964.

Saint-Lu, André. *Las Casas indigeniste: Études sur la vie et l'oeuvre du défenseur des Indiens*. Paris: L'Hammattan, 1982.

Sala Balust, Luis. *Constituciones, estatutos y ceremonias de los antiquos colegios seculars de la Universidad de Salamanca*. Vol. 3. Madrid: CSIC, 1974.

Salas, Alberto M. *Tres Cronistas de Indias: Pedro Mártir de Anglería, Gonzalo Fernández de Oviedo, Fray Bartolomé de las Casas*. México, DF: Fondo de Cultura Económica, 1959.

Saranyana, Josep Ignasi, ed. *Teología en América Latina: Desde los orígenes a la Guerra de Sucesión (1493–1715)*. Vol. 1. Madrid: Iberoamericana, 1999.

Schmitt, Charles B., Quentin Skinner, Erkhard Kessler, and Jill Kraye, eds. *The Cambridge History of Renaissance Philosophy*. Cambridge: Cambridge Univ. Press, 1988.

Schneider, Reinhold. *Bartolome de las Casas frente a Carlos V*. Translated by Jorge C. Lehmann. Madrid: Ediciones Encuentro, 1979.

Schroeder, Susan, Stephanie Wood, and Robert Haskett, eds. *Indian Women of Early Mexico*. Norman: Univ. of Oklahoma Press, 1997.

Schwaller, John Fredrick. *The Church and Clergy in Sixteenth-Century Mexico*. Albuquerque: Univ. of New Mexico Press, 1987.

Schwartz, Stuart B. *All Can be Saved: Religious Tolerance and Salvation in the Iberian Atlantic World*. New Haven, CT: Yale Univ. Press, 2008.

Scott, James Brown. *The Spanish Origin of International Law: Francisco de Vitoria and His Law of Nations*. Oxford: Clarendon Press, 1932.

Seed, Patricia. *Ceremonies of Possession in Europe's Conquest of the New World, 1491–1640*. Cambridge: Cambridge Univ. Press, 1995.

Sevilla-Casas, Elias, ed. *Western Expansion and Indigenous Peoples: The Heritage of Las Casas*. Chicago, IL: Mouton Publishers, 1977.

Sherman, William L. *Forced Native Labor in Sixteenth-Century Central America*. Lincoln: Univ. of Nebraska Press, 1979.

Siegel, Jerrold E. *Rhetoric and Philosophy in Renaissance Humanism: The Union of Eloquence and Wisdom, Petrarch to Valla*. Princeton, NJ: Princeton Univ. Press, 1968.

Simpson, Lesley Byrd. *Los Conquistadores y El Indio Americano*. Traducido por Encarnación Rodrírquez Vicente. Berkeley: Univ. of California Press, 1970.

———. *The Encomienda in New Spain: The Beginning of Spanish Mexico*. First published in 1950. Revised edition. Berkeley: Univ. of California Press, 1982.

Skinner, Quentin. *The Foundations of Modern Political Thought: Vol. 1 The Renaissance*; *Vol. 2 The Age of Reformation*. Cambridge: Cambridge Univ. Press, 1978.

Sobaler, María de los Ángeles. *Los colegiales mayores de Santa Cruz (1484–1670): una elite de poder*. Salamanca: Junta de Castilla y León, 1987.

Solórzano y Pereira, Juan de. *Disputationum de Indiarum Jure*. 2 vols. Madrid: 1629–1639.

Sorabji, Richard and David Rodin, eds. *The Ethics of War: Shared Problems in Different Traditions*. Burlington, VT: Ashgate, 2005.

Stein, Peter. *Roman Law in European History*. Cambridge: Cambridge Univ. Press, 1999.

Swales, John M. *Genre Analysis: English in Academic and Research Settings*. Cambridge: Cambridge Univ. Press, 1990.

Taft, Robert. *The Liturgy of the Hours in East and West: The Origins of the Divine Office and Its Meaning for Today.* 2 nd ed. Collegeville, MN: Liturgical Press, 1993.

Talaván, Miquel Luque. *Un Universo de Opiniones: La Literatura Jurídica Indiana.* Madrid: Consejo Superior de Investigaciones Científicas Instituto de Historia, 2003.

The Catholic Encyclopedia: An International Work of Reference on the Constitution, Doctrine, Discipline, and History of the Catholic Church. 18 vols. Edited by Charles George Herbermann, Edward A Pace, Condé Bénoit Pallen, Thomas J Shahan, John J Wynne, et al. New York: Encyclopedia Press, 1913 and 1950.

Thomas, Hugh. *Rivers of Gold: The Rise of Spanish Empire, from Columbus to Magellan.* New York: Random House, 2003.

———. *The Slave Trade: The Story of Atlantic Slave Trade 1440–1870.* New York: Touchstone, 1997.

Tierney, Brian. *The Idea of Natural Rights: Studies on Natural Rights, Natural Law and Church Law 1150–1625.* Emory U. Studies in Law and Religion 5. Atlanta, GA: Scholars Press, 1997.

———. *Rights and Laws and Infallibility in Medieval Thought.* Aldershot: Ashgate Publishing.

Tio, Aurelio. *Dr. Diego Alvarez Chanca (Estudio Biográfico).* San Juan: Instituto de Cultura Puertorriqueña, Universidad Interamericana de Puerto Rico, 1966.

Todorov, Tzvetan. *The Conquest of America: The Question of the Other.* Translated by Richard Howard. New York: Harper Colophon Books, 1995.

Torre Rangel, Jesús Antonio de la. *El uso alternativo del Derecho por Bartolomé de las Casas.* 2nd ed. Mexico, DF: Universidad Autónoma de Aguascalientes, 1996.

Townsend, Camilla. *Malintzin's Choices: An Indian Woman in the Conquest of Mexico.* Albuquerque: Univ. of New Mexico Press, 2006.

Traboulay, David M. *Columbus and Las Casas: The Conquest and Christianization of America, 1492–1566.* New York: Univ. Press of America, 1994.

Trexler, Richard C. *Sex and Conquest: Gendered Violence, Political Order, and the European Conquest of the Americas.* Cambridge: Polity Press, 1955.

Trouillot, Michel-Rolph. *Silencing the Past: Power and the Production of History.* Boston, MA: Beacon Press, 1995.

Tyler, S. Lyman, ed. *Concerning the Indians Lately Discovered: The Indian Cause before the Law of Nations: Colonial Period.* Salt Lake City: American West Center/Univ. of Utah, 1980.

Ureña, Henriquez. *Los corrientes literarias en la América Hispánica.* Mexico, DF: Fondo de Cultural Económica, 1949.

Van De Wiel, Constant. *History of Canon Law.* Louvain: Peeters Press, 1991.

Vega, Pedro de. *Antología de escritores políticos del Siglo de Oro.* Clásico de política, 2. Madrid: Taurus, 1966.

Verástique, Bernardino. *Michoacán and Eden: Vasco de Quiroga adn the Evangelization of Western Mexico.* Austin: Univ. of Texas Press, 2000.

Vicente Pereña, Luciano. *Misión de España en América, 1540–1560.* Madrid: Instituto Francisco de Vitoria, 1954.

Vickery, Paul. S. *Bartolomé de las Casas: Great Prophet of the Americas.* New York: Paulist Press, 2006.

Vilches, Elvira. *New World Gold: Cultural Anxiety and Monetary Disorder in Early Modern Spain.* Chicago, IL: Univ. of Chicago Press, 2010.

Vos, Jan de. *Fray Pedro Lorenzo de la Nada: Misionero de Chiapas y Tabasco.* Mexico, DF: Fondo de Cultura Económica, 2010.

Wachtel, Nathan. *The Vision of the Vanquished. The Spanish Conquest of Peru through Indian Eyes 1530–1570.* Trowbridge: Harvest Press, 1977.

Wagner, Henry Raup and Helen Rand Parish. *The Life and Writings of Bartolomé de Las Casas.* Albuquerque: Univ. of New Mexico Press, 1967.

Weber, David. *The Spanish Frontier in North America.* New Haven, CT: Yale Univ. Press, 1992.

Weckmann, Luis. *The Medieval Heritage of Mexico.* Translated by Frances M. López- Morillas. New York: Fordham Univ. Press, 1992.

Wey Gómez, Nicolás. *The Tropics of Empire: Why Columbus Sailed South to the Indies.* Cambridge: Massachusetts Institute of Technology Press, 2008.

White, Kevin, ed. *Hispanic Philosophy in the Age of Discovery.* Washington, DC: Catholic Univ. of America Press, 1997.

Wilcox, Donald. In Search of God and Self: Renaissance and Reformation Thought. Boston, MA: Houghton Mifflin, 1975.

Wilson, Samuel M. Hispaniola: Caribbean Chiefdoms in the Age of Columbus. Tuscaloosa: Univ. of Alabama Press, 1990.

Winks, Robin W. and Teofilo F. Ruiz, Medieval Europe and the World, From Late Antiquity to Modernity, 400–1500. New York: Oxford Univ. Press, 2005.

Wood, Stephanie G. *Transcending Conquest: Nahua Views of Spanish Colonial Mexico.* Norman: Univ. of Oklahoma Press, 2003.

Wright, A.D. *Catholicism and Spanish Society under the Reign of Philip II, 1555–1598 and Philip III, 1598–1621.* Lewiston, ID: The Edwin Mellen Press, 1991.

Ybot León, Antonio. *La iglesia y los ecclesiásticos Españoles en la empresa de Indias.* Vol. 1. Barcelona: Salvat Editores, 1954.

Zagar, Janko. *Acting on Principles: A Thomistic Perspective in Making Moral Decisions.* Washington, DC: Catholic Univ. of America Press, 1984.

Zavala, Silvio. *Recuerdo de Bartolomé de las Casas.* Guadalajara: Librería Font, 1966.

———. *Sir Thomas More in New Spain: A Utopian Adventure of the Renaissance.* London: Canning House, 1955.

———. *Tributos y servicios personales de indios para Hernán Cortés y su familia. Extractos de documentos del siglo XVI*, AGN. México, DF: 1984.

Zum Felde, Alberto. *Índice crítico de la literatura Hispanoamericana: los ensayistas.* México, DF: Editorial Guarania, 1954.

Audio Recordings

Eakin, Marshall. *Frontiers of Empire: Conquest of the Americas.* Parts 1, 2. Chantilly, VA: The Teaching Company, 2000.

Fix, Andrew C. *The Renaissance, the Reformation, and the Rise of Nations.* Parts 1, 2. Chantilly, VA: The Teaching Company, 2000.

Gregory, Brad S. *The History of Christianity in the Reformation Era.* Parts 1, 2, 3. Chantilly, VA: The Teaching Company, 2000.

Parish, Helen Rand. Interview by David Orique. February 12, 2001. Tape recording. Berkeley, CA.

Pérez Fernández, Isacio. Interview by David Orique. October 15, 1999. Tape recording. Madrid, Spain.

Secondary Sources: Articles, Anthology Chapters

Abellan, José Luis. "Los orígenes españoles del mito del 'buen salvaje,' fray Bartolomé de las Casas y su antropología utópica." *Revista de Indias* 36, nos. 145–146 (Julio-Diciembre, 1976): 157–179.

Addleshaw, G.W. "The Early Parochial System and the Divine Office." *Alcuin Club Prayer Book Revision Pamphlets, XV.* London: A. R. Mowbray, 1957.

Adorno, Rolena. "Discourses on Colonialism: Bernal Díaz, Las Casas, and the Twentieth-Century Reader." *Modern Language Notes* 103 (1988): 239–258.

———. "The Discursive Encounter of Spain in America: The Authority of Eyewitness Testimony in the Writing of History." *The William and Mary Quarterly*, no. 2 (April, 1992): 210–228.

———. "The Intellectual Life of Bartolomé de Las Casas." *The Andrew W. Mellon Lecture*, Tulane Univ., (Fall, 1992).

——— and Patrick Charles Pautz. "Introduction." In Álvar Núñez Cabaza de Vaca, *The Narrative of Cabeza de Vaca.* Edited, translated and introduction by Rolena Adorno, 1–41. Lincoln: Univ. of Nebraska Press, 2003.

———. "La prole de Cabeza de Vaca: El legado multicentenario de una de las primeras Jornadas Europeas en América del Norte." *Revista de Crítica Literaria Latinoamericana* 30, no. 60 (2004): 251–268.

———. "Novedades en el estudio actual de la cronística peruana: Las Casas, Guaman Poma y el Padre Oliva." [article online]. (Accessed March 25, 2006).

———. "The Intellectual Life of Bartolomé de Las Casas: Framing the Literature Classroom." In *Approaches to Teaching the Writings of Bartolomé de Las Casas.* Edited by Santa Arias and Eyda Merediz, 21–32. New York: The Modern Language Association of America, 2008.

Afanasiev, V. "The Literary Heritage of Bartolomé de Las Casas." In Friede and Keen, *Bartolomé de las Casas in History*, 539–578.

Alcina Franch, José. "Introducción." In *Bartolomé de las Casas, Obra indigenista.* Introducción y edición de José Alcina Franch, 7–59. Madrid: Alianza, 1985.

Altez, Rogelio. "Las Casas de la conquista: inglobación, anexión, expropiación de territorios y su legitimación en las estrategias de la conquista española. Breve estudio a través de la capitulación de Bartolomé de las Casas (1520)." *Monalban* 28 (1995): 91–118.

Alvarez, Jesús H. "Fray Bartolomé de las Casas." *Cuadernos Dominicanos* 8 (1984): 5–58.

Álvarez, Salvador. "Conquista y encomienda en la Nueva Galicia durante la primera mitad del siglo XVI: 'bárbaros' y 'civilizados' en las fronteras americanas." *Relaciones* 29, no. 116 (Otoño, 2008): 135–188.

Andújar, Eduardo. Bartolomé de Las Cases and Juan Ginés de Sépulveda: Moral Theology versus Political Philosophy." In *Hispanic Philosophy at the Age of Discovery.* Edited by Kevin White, 69–87. Washington, DC: The Catholic Univ. of America Press, 1997.

Angeles Orts Llopis, María. "Legal genres in English and Spanish: some attempts of analysis." *Ibérica* 18 (2009): 109–130.
Anuario de la Asociación Francisco de Vitoria. Vol. 5 (1932–33). Madrid: Imprenta de la Rafa, 1934.
Áqueda Rodríquez Cruz. "Régimen docente." In *La Universidad de Salamanca.* Directado por Manuel Fernández Álvarez, 2:444–488. Salamanca: Europa Artes Gráficas, S. A., 1990.
Ares Queija, Berta. "La *Apologética historia sumaria* y el debate sobre la naturaleza del indio." In *Bartolomé de las Casas, Obras Completas,* 6:201–214. Madrid: Alianza, 1998.
Arias, Santa. "Bartolomé de las Casas's Sacred Place in History." In *Mapping Colonial Spanish America: Places and Commonplaces of Identity, Culture, and Experience.* Edited by Santa Arias and Mariselle Meléndez, 121–136. Lewisburg, PA: Bucknell Univ., 2002.
———. "Las Casas as Genealogical Keystone for Discourse on Political Independence." In *Approaches to Teaching the Writings of Bartolomé de Las Casas.* Edited by Santa Arias and Eyda Merediz, 168–176. New York: The Modern Language Association of America, 2008.
——— and Mariselle Meléndez. "Empowerment through the Writing of History: Bartolome de Las Casas's Representation of the Other(s)." In *Early Images of the Americas: Transfer and Invention.* Edited by J.M. Williams and R.E. Lewis, 163–179. Tucson: Univ. of Arizona Press, 1993.
———. "Space and the Rhetorics of Power in Colonial Spanish America: An Introduction." In *Mapping Colonial Spanish America: Places and Commonplaces of Identity, Culture, and Experience.* Edited by Santa Arias and Mariselle Meléndez, 13–23. Lewisburg, PA: Bucknell Univ., 2002.
Ariza S., Alberto E. "Acotaciones sobre Fr. Bartolomé de Las Casas." *Boletín de Historia y Antigüedades* 44, no. 718 (Julio-Setiembre, 1977): 509–511.
Arrom, José Juan. "Estudio preliminar, notas y appendices." In Fray Ramón Pané, *Relación acerca de las antigüedade de los indios,* nueva versión con estudio preliminar, notas y apendices por José Juan Arrom. Decimotecera edición. México, DF: Siglo XXI Editores S.A. de C.V., 2004.
Azpiroz, Carlos A. "A Message for Christmas and the New Year 2010 towards the 8th Centenary of the Confirmation Of the Order: 2010 – How Can People Preach Unless They Are Sent?" [article online]. (Accessed May 13, 2010).
Avalle Arce, Juan Baptist. "Las hipérboles del Padre Las Casas." *Revista de la facultad de humanidades* 2, no. 1 (Enero-Marzo, 1960): 35–55.
Barnadas, Joseph M. "Una contribución a la historia del lascasismo." In *Bartolomé de las Casas (1474—1974) e historia de la iglesia en América Latina,* Chiapas CEHILA conferencia, 91–120. Barcelona: Editorial Nova Terra, 1976.
Barreda, Jesús-Angel. "Bibliografía Lascasiana de la *Apologética Historia.*" In *Bartolomé de las Casas, Obras Completas,* 6: 221–233. Madrid: Alianza, 1998.
———. "El encuentro de dos absolutos: el hombre y el Evangelio." *Studium* 32, no. 1 (1992): 123–161.
Barrenechea Porras, Raúl. "Pedro Gutierrez de Santa Clara: Cronista mexicano de la conquista del Perú (1521–1603)." *Revista de Historia de América* 21 (junio, 1946): 1–17.

Bartosik-Vélez, Elise. "Translatio Imperii: Virgil and Peter Martyr's Columbus." *Comparative Literature Studies* 46, no. 4 (2009): 559–588.

Bataillon, Marcel. "The Clérigo Casas, Colonist and Colonial Reformer." In Friede and Keen, *Bartolomé de Las Casas in History*, 353–440.

Benítez-Rojo, Antonio. "Bartolomé de las Casas: Entre el infierno y la ficción." *Modern Language Notes* 103, no. 2 *Hispanic issue* (1988): 259–288.

Beuchot, Mauricio. "Filosofos Humanistas Novohispanos." In *Filosofía iberoamericana en la época del Encuentro*. Edited by Laureano Robles, 281–307. Madrid: Editorial Trotta, S.A., 1992.

———. "The Philosophical Discusión of the Legitimacy of the Conquest of Mexico in the Sixteenth Century." In *Hispanic Philosophy in the Age of Discovery*. Edited by Kevin White, 31–44. Washington, DC: Catholic Univ. of America Press, 1997.

Bilynskyj, Stephen S. "Grace and Freewill: Three Sixteeth Century Debates." [article online]. (Accessed August 31, 2020).

Black, Robert. "The Philosopher and Renaissance Culture." In *The Cambridge Companion to Renaissance Philosophy*. Edited by James Hankins, 13–29. Cambridge: Cambridge Univ. Press, 2007.

Blair, Ann M. "Organizations of Knowledge." In *The Cambridge Companion to Renaissance Philosophy*. Edited by James Hankins, 287–303. Cambridge: Cambridge Univ. Press, 2007.

Boase, Rodger. "The Muslim Expulsion from Spain." *History Today* (April, 2002): 21–27.

Brading, David. "Prophet and Apostle: Bartolomé de Las Casas and the Spiritual Conquest of America." In *Christianity and Missions, 1450–1800*. Edited by J.S. Cummins, 118–138. An Expanding World Series 28. Brookfield, VT: Ashgate Publishing, 1997.

Brion Davis, David. "Constructing Race: A Reflection." *The William and Mary Quarterly* 54, no. 1 (January, 1997): 7–18.

Brundage, James A. "The Teaching and Study of Canon Law in the Law Schools." In *The History of Medieval Canon Law in the Classical Period, 1140–1234: From Gratian to the Decretals of Pope Gregory IX*. Edited by Wilfried Hartmann and Kenneth Pennington, 98–120. Washington, DC: Catholic Univ. of America, 2008.

Burns, Robert I. "Christian-Islamic Confrontation in the West: The Thirteenth-Century Dream of Conversion." *The American Historical Review* 76, no. 5 (December, 1971): 1386–1434.

Burns, Kathryn. "Notaries, Truth and Consequences." *The American Historical Review* 110, no. 2 (April, 2005): 350–379.

Caballero, Julián. "Los Reyes Católicos y los procuradores." *Procuradores* (Octubre, 2004): 57–62.

Cachey Jr., Theodore J. "Italy and the Invention of America." *The New Centennial Review* 2, no. 1 (Spring, 2002): 17–32.

Camacho, Jorge Luis. "Meta-Historia y ficción en la *Brevísima Relación de la destrucción de las Indias*, de Fray Bartolomé de las Casas." *Hispanófila* 134 (2002): 37–47.

Canning, J.P. "Law, Sovereignty and Corporation Theory, 1300–1450." In *The Cambridge History of Medieval Political Thought, c. 350-c. 1450*. Edited by J.H. Burns, 454–476. Cambridge: Cambridge Univ. Press, 1988.

Cano, Reyes. "Introducción." In Bartolomé de las Casas. *Brevisima relación de la destrucción de las Indias*. Editado e introducción por J.M. Reyes Cano, xl-lxi. Barcelona: Planeta, 1994.
Cantor, Norman F. "The Idea of a Christian Commonwealth." *Commonweal* (November 6, 1992): 11–17.
Cantú, Francesca, "Documentos lascasianos." *Historiografía y Bibliografía Americanista* 19, no. 20 (1975–1976): 127–155.
Cardano, Girolamo. "De Sapientia." In *Opera Omni*, 10 vols. Edited by C. Spohn, 1:493–580. New York and London: Johnson, 1967.
Carman, Glen. "On the Pope's Original Intent: Las Casas Reads the Papal Bulls of 1493." *Colonial Latin American Review* 7, no. 2 (1998): 193–204.
Carozzo, Paolo. "From Conquest to Constitutions: The Latin American Tradition of the Idea of Human Rights." *Human Rights Quarterly* 25, no. 2 (May, 2003): 281–313.
Carreño, Antonio. "Una guerra 'sine dolo et fraude': el P. Las Casas y la lucha por la dignidad del Indio en el siglo XVI." *Cuadernos Americanos* 193, no. 2 (Marzo-Abril, 1974): 119–139.
Carro, Venancio D. "The Spanish Theological-Juridical Renaissance and the Ideology of Bartolomé de Las Casas." In Friede and Keen, *Bartolomé de las Casas in History*, 237–278.
Casado, A. Lobato "El obispo Garcés O.P. y la bula Sublimis Deus." In *Los Dominicos y el nuevo mundo*, Actas del Congreso Internacional (Madrid, 1988): 739–795.
Casassa, Charles, "Magister Vacarius 'Hic en Oxo nefordia Legem Docuit': An Analysis of the Dissemination of Roman Law in the Middle Ages," Department of History, University of Kansas, November 26, 1991. [article online]. (Accessed August 30, 2020).
Castañeda Delgado, Paulino. "Las Doctrinas Sobre la Coacción y el 'Ideari-um'de Las Casas." In *Bartolomé de las Casas, Obras Completas*. Editado por Paulino Castañeda y Antonio García del Moral Carlos. 2:xvii-xxxv. Madrid: Alianza Editorial S.A., 1995.
———. "Los métodos misionales en America: ¿evangelización pura coacción?" In *Estudios sobre Fray Bartolomé de las Casas*, 123–189. Filosofía y Letras 24. Sevilla: Universidad de Sevilla, 1974.
Castelló, Vidal Abril. "Estudio preliminar." In *Bartolomé de las Casas, Obras Completas*, 6:15–184.
Chacón y Calvo, J.M. "La experiencia del indio ¿Un antecedente a las doctrinas de Vitoria?" *Anuario de la Asociación Francisco de Vitoria* (Madrid) 5 (1933): 203–225.
Chamberlain, Robert S. "Castillian Backgrounds of the Repartimiento-Encomienda." In *Contributions to American Anthropology and History* 5, no. 25 (June, 1939): 21–64.
Chandler, Daniel. "An Introduction to Genre Theory." (1997). [article online]. (Accessed February 3, 2011).
Checa, Jorge. "Cortes y el espacio de la Conquista: la Segunda carta de relación." *MLN* 111, no. 2 (March, 1996): 187–217.
Christensen, Katherine. "Introduction." In *Gratian, The Treatise on Laws (Decretum DD. 1–20) with the Ordinary Gloss*. Studies in Medieval and Early Modern Canon Law, vol. 2. Translated by Augustine Thompson and James Gordley. 2:ix-xxvii. Washington, DC: Catholic Univ. Press, 1993.

Clayton, Larry. "Teaching Las Casas through the Lens of a Historian." In *Approaches to Teaching the Writings of Bartolomé de Las Casas*. Edited by Santa Arias and Eyda Merediz, 33–41. New York: The Modern Language Association of America, 2008.

Cline, Sarah. "The Spiritual Conquest Reexamined: Baptism and Christian Marriage in Early Sixteenth-Century Mexico." *Hispanic American Historical Review* 73, no. 3 (1993): 453–480.

Coleman, David. "Moral Formation and Social Control in the Catholic Reformation: The Case of San Juan de Avila." *Sixteenth Century Journal* 26, no. 1 (Spring, 1995): 17–30.

Codoñer, Carmen. "Tres croństas reales: Alfonso de Palencia, Antonio de Nebrija y Lucio Marineo Sículo." *Cronica* 37, no. 1 (Otoño, 2008): 111–143.

Comas, Juan. "Fray Bartolomé, La esclavitud y el racismo." *Cuadernos Americanos* 195, no. 2 (Marzo-Abril, 1976): 145–152.

———. "Historical Reality and the Detractors of Father Las Casas." In Friede and Keen, *Bartolomé de Las Casas in History*, 487–537.

Concha Malo, Miquel. "El uso alternativo del derecho en Bartolomé de las Casas." In *Dominicos en Mesoamérica: 500 Años*, 57–75. México, DF: Analogía Revista de Filosofía, 1992.

Cook, Noble David. "Disease and the Depopulation of Hispaniola, 1492–1518." *Colonial Latin American Review* 2, nos. 1–2 (1993): 213–245.

Cortese, Paul. "Introduction to the First Books of the 'Sentences'." In *Renaissance Philosophy*. Edited by Leonard A. Kennedy, 29–40. The Hague: Mouton, 1973.

Costigan, Lúcia Helena. "Bartolomé de Las Casas and His Counterparts in the Luso- Brazilian World." In *Approaches to Teaching the Writings of Bartolomé de Las Casas*. Edited by Santa Arias and Eyda Merediz, 235–242. New York: The Modern Language Association of America, 2008.

Cuart Moner, Baltasar. "Un grupo singular y privilegiado: los colegios mayores." In *Historia de la Universidad de Salamanca: Trayectoria histórica e instituciones vinculadas*. Coordinated by Luis E. Rodríquez-San Pedro Bezares. 1:503–536. Salamanca: Ediciones Universidad de Salamanca, 2002.

Cruz Parcero, Juan Antonio and Roberto Lara Chagoyán. "Argumentación Jurídica." In *Enciclopedia Jurídica Latinoamericana*. 1:481–490. México: Editorial Porrúa, SA de CV, 2006.

D'Amico, John F. "Manuscripts." In *The Cambridge History of Renaissance Philosophy*. Edited by Schmitt, Charles B., Quentin Skinner, Erkhard Kessler, and Jill Kraye, 11–24. Cambridge: Cambridge Univ. Press, 1988.

Danet, Brenda. "Language in the Legal Process." *Law and Society Review* 14, no. 3 (Spring, 1980): 445–564.

Davidson, J.S. "The Rights of Indigenous Peoples in Early International Law." *The Canterbury Law Review* 5 (1994): 391–423.

Deeds, Susan. "Rural Work in Nueva Vizcaya: Forms of Labor Coercion on the Periphery." *The Hispanic American Historical Review* 69, no. 3 (August, 1989): 425–449.

De Lima Urdaneta, Blanca. "Alemanes en la provincia de Venezuela durante el siglo XVI." Conference paper, 53rd International Congress of Americanists: "The People of the Americas: Continuity and Change," Mexico City, July 19–24, 2009.

Derrida, Jacques and Avital Ronell. "The Law of Genre." *Critical Inquiry* 7, no. 1 (Autumn, 1980): 55–81.

Díaz Noci, Javier. "Los raices de los géneros periodisticos interpretativos." [article online]. (Accessed January 20, 2011).

Dille, Glen F. "El descubrimiento y la conquista de América en la comedia del Siglo de Oro." *Hispania* 71, no. 3 (September, 1988): 492–502.

Disalvo, Angelo J. "Spanish Dominicans, the Laws of the Indies, and the Establishment of Human Rights." *Romance Quarterly* 40, no. 2 (1993): 89–96.

Doyle John P. "Hispanic Scholastic Philosophy." In *The Cambridge Companion to Renaissance Philosophy*. Edited by Hankins, James, 250–269. Cambridge: Cambridge Univ. Press, 2007.

Duve, Thomas. "Los que escriven, poco aventuran en elegir opinions; pero es muy peligrosa la elección en el juez que las ha de practicar: algunas observaciones acerca del modus operandi y la prudencia del juez en el Derecho Canónico Indiano." [article online]. (Accessed August 31, 2020).

Duviols, Jean-Paul. "Introducción." In *Brevísima relación de La Destruyción De Las Indias*. Editado por y introducción de Jean-Paul Duviols. Barcelona: Linkqua Ed. S.L., 2009.

Earle, Rebecca. "'If You Eat Their Food…': Diets and Bodies in Early Colonial Spanish America." *The American Historical Review* 115, no. 3 (June, 2010): 688–713.

Estudios Sobre Politica Indigenisa Española en América: Iniciación, Pugna de Ocupación, Demografía, Lingüística, Sedentarización Condición Juridica del Indio. Vol. 1. Seminario de História de América: Valladolid: Universidad de Valladolid, 1975.

Félix Bolaños, Álvaro. "A Place to Live, a Place to Think, and a Place to Die: Sixteenth Century Frontier Cities, Plazas, and 'Relaciones' in Spanish America." In *Mapping Colonial Spanish America: Places and Commonplaces of Identity, Culture, and Experience*. Edited by Santa Arias and Mariselle Meléndez, 275–293. Lewisburg, PA: Bucknell Univ. Press, 2002.

Fernández, A. "Los dominicos en América. Documentos inéditos." *Santísimo Rosario* 18 (1903).

Fernández Álvarez, Manuel. "Etapa renacentista." Vol. 1: 59–101 of *La Universidad de Salamanca:Trayectorio histórico y proyecciones*. Salamanca: Europa Artes Gráficas, 1989.

———. "Etapa Renacentista 1475–1555." Vol. 1: 63–95 of *Historia de la Universidad de Salamanca: Trayectoria histórica e instituciones vinculadas*. Coordinated by Luis E. Rodríquez-San Pedro Bezares. Salamanca: Ediciones Universidad de Salamanca, 2002.

Fernández de Ybarra, A.M. "The Letter of Dr. Diego Alvarez Chanca, Dated 1494, Relating the Second Voyage of Columbus to America (Being the First Written Document on the Natural History, Ethnograpy, and Ethnology of America)." *Smithsonia Miscellaneous Collections* 48 (Quarterly Issue, 1907): 3:428–457.

Fernándo, Gil and Ricardo Corleto. "Fr. Bernardino de Minaya y la Sublimis Deus." (2003). [article online]. (Accessed August, 31, 2020).

Folger, Robert. "Alonso Borregán Writes Himself: The Colonial Subject and the Writing of History in *Relaciones de méritos y servicios*." In *Talleres de la memoria— Reivindicaciones y autoridad en la historigrafía de los siglos XVI y XVII*. Edited by Robert Folger and Wulf Oesterreicher, 267–293. Münster: LIT, Druck, 2005.

Fowler, Alastair. "Genre." In *International Encyclopedia of Communications*. Edited by Erik Barnouw, 2:215–217. New York: Oxford Univ. Press, 1989.

Flynn, Dennis O. "Fiscal Crisis and the Decline of Spain (Castile)." *Economic History* 42, no. 1 (March, 1982): 139–147.

Florescano, Enrique. "Concepciones de la Historia." In *Filosofía iberoamericana en la época del Encuentro*. Edited by Laureano Robles, 309–329. Madrid: Ed. Trotta, S.A., 1992.

Flórez Miguel, Cirilio. "La Ciencia Europea Antes de 1492." In *Filosofía iberoamericana en la época del Encuentro*. Edited by Laureano Robles, 51–78. Madrid: Ed. Trotta, S.A., 1992.

Franco, Jean. "La cultura hispanoamericana en la época colonial." In *Historia de la literatura hispanoamericana, epoca colonial*. Coordinated by Luis Iñigo Madrigal, 1:35–53. Madrid: Catedra, 1982.

Freedman, Paul. "The German and Catalan Peasant Revolts." *American Historical Review* 98, no. 1 (February, 1993): 39–54.

Friede, Juan. "Las Casas and Indigenism of the Sixteenth Century." In Friede and Keen, *Bartolomé de Las Casas in History*, 127–234.

Frost, Elsa Cecilia. "El visión providencialista de la historia." In *Filosofía iberoameriana en la época del encuentro*. Editado por Laureano Robles, 331–346. Madrid: Trotta, 1992.

———. "Fray Bartolomé de las Casas: Conciencia de España." In *Symposium Fray Bartolomé de las Casas: Trascendencia de su obra y doctrina*, 169–177. México, DF: UNAM, 1985.

García-Gallo, Alfonso de Diego. "El desarrollo de la historiografía juridical Indiana." *Revista de estudios políticos* 70 (1953): 163–185.

———. "El encomendero indiano." *Revista de estudios politicos* 55 (1951): 141–162.

García, Jorge J.E. "Hispanic Philosophy: Its Beginning and Golden Age." In *Hispanic Philosophy in the Age of Discovery*. Edited by Kevin White, 3–27. Washington, DC: Catholic Univ. of America Press, 1997.

García y Garcia, Antonio. "Consolidaciones del Siglo XV." In *Historia de la Universidad de Salamanca: Trayectoria histórica e instituciones vinculadas*. Coordinado por Luis E. Rodríquez-San Pedro Bezares, 1:39–64. Salamanca: Ediciones Universidad de Salamanca, 2002.

———. "Consolidaciones del Siglo XV." In *La Universidad de Salamanca*. Directado por Manuel Fernández Álvarez, 1:35–58. Salamanca: Europa Artes Gráficas, S. A., 1989.

———. "El mundo del derecho en el siglo de oro de Salamanca." In *El Siglo de Frai Luis de León: Salamanca y el Renacimiento*. Coordinado por Mercedes Aznar López and Luz de Gaztelu y Quijano, 69–76. Madrid: Junta de Castilla y León, 1991.

———. "Génesis de la universidad, Siglos XIII-XIV." In *Historia de la Universidad de Salamanca: Trayectoria histórica e instituciones vinculadas*. Coordinado por Luis E. Rodríquez-San Pedro Bezares, 1:21–38. Salamanca: Ediciones Universidad Salamanca, 2002.

———. "Miscelanea: la penetración del derecho clásico medieval en España." *Anuario de historia del derecho Español* 36 (1966): 575–592.

Garza, Mercedes de la. "El Pensamiento Maya." In *Filosofía iberoamericana en la época del Encuentro*. Edited by Laureano Robles, 99–125. Madrid: Editorial Trotta, S.A., 1992.

Giménez Fernández, Manuel. "Actualidad de las tésis Lascasianas." In *Estudios Lascasianos*, 445–475. Sevilla: Estudios Hispano-Americanos, 1966.

———. "Bartolomé de las Casas en su IV centenario de su muerte." *Arbor* 62, no. 252 (Diciembre, 1968): 269–329.

———. "Fray Bartolomé de Las Casas: A Biographical Sketch." In Friede and Keen, *Bartolomé de Las Casas in History*, 66–125.

———. "La juventud en Sevilla de Bartolomé de las Casas." *Miscelánea de Estudios dedicados al Doctor Ortiz*, 2:670–717. Havana: 1956.

Gledhill, Christine. "Genre." In *The Cinema Book*. Edited by Pam Cook, 58–64 London: British Film Institute, 1985.

Glendon, Mary Ann. "The Forgotten Crucible: The Latin American Influence on the Universal Human Rights Idea." *Harvard Human Rights Journal* 16 (Spring, 2003): 27–42.

Goizueta, Roberto S. "Bartolomé de Las Casas, Modern Critic of Modernity: An Analysis of a Conversion." *Journal of Hispanic/Latino Theology* 4, no. 4 (1996): 6–19.

González de León, Fernando. "'Doctors of the Military Discipline': Technical Expertise and the Paradigm of the Spanish Soldier in the Early Modern Period." *Sixteenth Century Journal* 27, no. 1 (Spring, 1996): 61–85.

González-Echevarría, Roberto. "The Law of the Letter: Garcilaso's Commentaries and the Origins of the Latin American Narrative." *The Yale Journal of Criticism* 1, no. 1 (1987): 107–132.

Gossman, Lionel. "History and Literature: Reproduction or Signification." In *Writing of History*. Edited by Robert H. Canary and Henry Kozicki, 3–39. Madison: Univ. of Wisconsin Press, 1978.

Granada, Miguel A. "New Visions of the Cosmos." In *The Cambridge Companion to Renaissance Philosophy*. Edited by James Hankins, 270–286. Cambridge: Cambridge Univ. Press, 2007.

Grendler, Paul F. "Printing and Censorship." In *The Cambridge History of Renaissance Philosophy*. Edited by Schmitt, Charles B., Quentin Skinner, Erkhard Kessler, and Jill Kraye, 25–53. Cambridge: Cambridge Univ. Press, 1988.

Guijarro González, Susana. "Las escuelas y la formación del clero de las catedrales en las diócesis castellanos-leonesas (siglos XI al XV)." In *La eseñanza en la edad media: X Semana de Estudios Medievales, Nájera 1999*. Coordinador José Ignacio de la Iglesia Duarte, 61–96. España: Instituto de Estudios Riojanos, 2000.

Guitar, Lynne. "No More Negotiation: Slavery and the Destabilization of Colonial Hispaniola's Encomienda System." [artilce online]. (Accessed August 31, 2020).

Gurría Lacroix, Jorge. "Estudio Preliminar." In *Fray Francisco de Aguilar, Relación breve de la conquista de la Nueva España*. Edición, estudio preliminar, notas y apéndices por Jorge Gurría Lacroix, 37–48. México, DF: UNAM, 1980.

Gutiérrez Cuadrado, Juan, "Christian Universities." In *Medieval Iberia: an Encyclopedia*. Edited by E. Michael Gerli, Samuel G. Armiested, et al., 817–822. New York: Routledge, 2003.

Gy, Pierre-Marie. "On the Consecratory Nature of the Very Act of Solemn Vows in the Theology of Saint Thomas Aquinas." *Analecta O.P.* 106 (1998): 408–410.

G.Y. Pease, Franklin. "Las primeras versiones españoles sobre el Perú." *Colonial Latin America Review* 1, nos. 1–2 (1992): 65–76.

Hamdani, Abbas. "Columbus and the Recovery of Jerusalem." *Journal of the American Oriental Society* 99, no. 1 (January-March, 1979): 39–48.

Hamilton, Alastair. "Humanism and the Bible." In *The Cambridge Companion to Renaissance Humanism*. Edited by Jill Kray, 100–117. Cambridge: Cambridge Univ. Press, 1996.

Hanke, Lewis. "A Modest Proposal for a Moratorium on Grand Generalizations: Some Thoughts on the Black Legend." *Hispanic American Historical Review* 51, no. 1 (1971): 112–127.

———. "Estudio Preliminar." In *Bartolomé de Las Casas, Historia de las Indias*. Edited by Augustín Millares Carlo, 1:lxxv. México, DF: Fondo de Cultura Económica, 1951.

———. "More Heat and Some Light on the Spanish Struggle for Justice in the Conquest of America." *The Hispanic American Historical Review* 44, no. 3 (August, 1964): 293–340.

———. "Notes and Comments: Bartolome de Las Casas, an Essay in Hagiography and Historiography." *Hispanic American Historical Review* 33 (1953): 136–151.

———. "Pope Paul III and the American Indians." *The Harvard Theological Review* 30, no. 2 (April, 1937): 65–102.

———."The Great Debate at Valladolid, 1550–1551." In *The Roman Catholic Church in Colonial America*. Edited Richard E. Greenleaf, 47–52. New York: Alfred E. Knopf, 1971.

———. "The Significance of Renaissance Philosophy." In *Cambridge Companion to Renaissance Philosophy*. Edited by James Hankins, 338–345. Cambridge: Cambridge Univ. Press, 2007.

———. "The Theological Significance of the Discovery of America." In *First Images of America: The Impact of the New World on the Old*. Edited by Fredi Chiappelli, 1:363–374. Berkeley: Univ. of California Press, 1976.

Hankins, James. "Humanism, Scholasticism, and Renaissance Philosophy." In *The Cambridge Companion to Renaissance Philosophy*. Edited by James Hankins, 30–48. Cambridge: Cambridge Univ. Press, 2007.

———. "Introduction." In *The Cambridge Companion to Renaissance Philosophy*. Edited by James Hankins, 1–9. Cambridge: Cambridge Univ. Press, 2007.

Haro, María Paz. "Religious Orders, the Indian, and the Conquest: Fifty Years of Dispute and Contradiction." Translated by James Dunlap. *Encounters* 9. [journal online]. (Accessed August 31, 2020).

Harrison, Regina. "Teaching Restitution: Las Casas, the *Rules for Confessors*, and the Politics of Repayment." In *Approaches to Teaching the Writings of Bartolomé de Las Casas*. Edited by Santa Arias and Eyda Merediz, 132–140. New York: The Modern Language Association of America, 2008.

Haskett, Robert S. "'Our Suffering with the Taxco Tribute': Involuntary Mine Labor and Indigenous Society in Central New Spain." *Hispanic American Historical Review* 71, no. 3 (1991): 447–475.

Henige, David. "On the Contact Population of Hispaniola: History as Higher Mathematics." *Hispanic American Historical Review* 58, no. 2 (1978): 217–237.

Hernandez, Francisco J. Review of *Église et pouvoir dans la Péninsule Ibérique. Les orders militaries dans le royaume de Castille (1252–1369)* by Philipp Josserand. *The Catholic Historical Review* 93, no. 2 (April, 2007): 389–390.

Hernández Martín, Ramón. "El convento y estudio de San Esteban." In *Historia de la Universidad de Salamanca: Trayectoria histórica e instituciones vinculadas*. Coordinado por Luis E. Rodríquez-San Pedro Bezares, 1:589–612. Salamanca: Ediciones Universidad de Salamanca, 2002.

Hernández, Ramón. "El convento y estudio de San Esteban." In *La Universidad de Salamanca:Trayectorio histórico y proyecciones*. Directado por Manuel Fernández Álvarez, 1:368–381. Salamanca: Europa Artes Gráficas, S. A., 1989/1990.

Higginson, Stephen A. "A Short History of the Right to Petition." *Yale Law Journal* 96, no. 1 (November, 1986): 142–166.

Hope, Charles and Elizabeth McGrath, "Artists and Humanists." In *The Cambridge Companion to Renaissance Humanism*. Edited by Jill Kraye, 161–188. Cambridge: Cambridge Univ. Press, 1988.

Huerga, Álvaro. *Bartolomé de las Casas, Obras completas*, Vol. 1: *Vida y Obras*. Madrid: Alianza Editorial, 1998.

———."Los Dominicos y la evangelización de Cuba." In *Cuadernos del Aula: Fray Bartolomé de las Casas*. Havana: 1998, 83–107.

Izbicki, Thomas M. "An Argument from Authority in the Indies Debate." *The Americas* 34, no. 3 (January, 1978): 400–406.

———. "Cajetan on the Acquisition of Stolen Goods in the Old and New Worlds." *Revista di Storia del Cristianesimo* 4, no. 2 (2007): 499–509.

Iannuzzi, Isabella. "La condena a Pedro Martínez de Osma: 'ensayo general' del control ideológico inquisitorial." [article online]. (Accessed August 9, 2010).

Jacobs, James Q. "The Cannibalism Paradigm: Assessing Contact Period Ethnohistorical Discourse." [article online]. (Accessed April 20, 2010).

Jaffé, Janice A. "Apocalypse Then and Now: Las Casas's *Brevísima relación* and Cortázar's 'Apocalipsis de Solentinam'." *Chasqui – Revista de Literatura Latinoamericana* 23, no. 1 (May, 1994): 18–28.

Jiménez, Alfonso Martín. "La retórica clásica al servicio de la predicación: los seis libros de la Retórica eclesiática de Fray Luis de Granada." In *Retóricas y poéticas españolas (siglos XVI-XIX): L. de Granada, Rengifo, Artiga, Hermosilla, R. de Miguel, Milá y Fontanals*. Coordinada por Isabel Paraíso, 11–46. Valladolid: Grafícas Andres Martín, S.L., 2000.

Johnson, Carina L. "Idolatrous Cultures and the Practice of Religion." *Journal of the History of Ideas* 67, no. 4 (October, 2006): 597–621.

Kagan, Richard L. "Pleitos y poder real: La chancillería de Valladolid, 1500–1700." In *Cuadernos de Investigación Histórica* 2 (1978): 291–316.

———. "Universities in Castile 1500–1700." *Past & Present* 49 (November, 1970): 44–71.

Kallendorf, Hilaire. "A Myth Rejected: The Noble Savage in Dominican Dystopia." *Journal of Latin American Studies* 27, no. 2 (May, 1995): 449–470.

Kamen, Henry. "Toleration and Dissent in Sixteenth-Century Spain: The Alternative Tradition." *Sixteenth Century Journal* 19, no. 1 (Spring, 1988): 3–23.

Keen, Benjamin. "Introduction: Approaches to Las Casas, 1537–1970." In Friede and Keen, *Bartolomé de Las Casas in History*, 3–63.

———. "The Black Legend Revisited: Assumptions and Realities." *Hispanic American Historical Review* 49, no. 4 (1969): 703–719.

———."The Legacy of Bartolomé de Las Casas." *Ibero-Americana Pragensia* (Prague) 11 (1977): 57–67.

Kelley, Donald R. "Jurisconsultus Perfecctus: The Lawyer as Renaissance Man." *Journal of the Warburg and Courtauld Institutes* 51 (1988): 84–102.

———. "The Theory of History." In *The Cambridge History of Renaissance Philosophy*. Edited by Charles B. Schmitt, Quentin Skinner, Erkhard Kessler, and Jill Kraye, 746–765. Cambridge: Cambridge Univ. Press, 1988.

Kelly, Henry Ansgar. "Inquisition and the Prosecution of Heresy: Misconceptions and Abuses." *Church History* 58, no. 4 (December, 1989): 439–451.

King, Margaret L. "The Religious Retreat of Isotta Nogarola (1418–1466): Sexism and Its Consequences in the Fifteenth Century," *Signs* 3, no. 4 (Summer, 1978), 807–822. [journal online]. (Accessed August, 31, 2010).

Knighton, Tess and Carmen Morte García. "Ferdinand of Aragon's Entry into Valladolid in 1513: Triumph of a Christian King." *Early Music History* 18 (1999): 119–163.

Knox, Robert B. "Notes on the Identity of Pedro Gutierrez de Santa Clara and Some Members of His Family." *Revista de História de América* 45 (June, 1958): 93–105.

Kohut, Karl. "Crónicas y teoría historiográfica." In *Talleres de la memoria—Reivindicaciones y autoridad en la historigrafía de los siglos XVI y XVII.* Editado por Robert Folger and Wulf Oesterreicher, 125–160. Münster: LIT, Druck, 2005.

Lackey, Michael. "Frantz Fanon on the Theology of Colonization." *Journal of Colonialization and Colonial History* 3, no. 2 (2002): 1–24. [journal online]. (Accessed August 31, 2020).

Landau, Peter. "Aequitas in the Corpus iuris canonici." *Syracuse Journal of International Law and Commerce* 20 (1994): 94–108. [journal online]. (Accessed August 31, 2020).

Leal Salinas, Leonel. "Resumen Historia del Derecho Profesor Óscar Dávila." [article online]. (Accessed August 31, 2020).

León-Portilla, Miguel. "El Pensamiento Nahuatl." In *Filosofía iberoamericana en la época del Encuentro.* Edited by Laureano Robles, 79–98. Madrid: Editorial Trotta, S.A., 1992.

Levene, Ricardo. "Bartolomé de las Casas y la doctrina de la libertad." *Boletín de la Academia Nacional de la Historia* 1 (1924): 111–124.

Livi-Bacci, Massimo. "Return to Hispaniola: Reassessing a Demographic Collapse." *Hispanic American Historical Review* 83, no. 1 (February, 2003): 3–52.

Lockhart, James. "Encomienda and Hacienda: The Evolution of the Great Estate in Spanish Indies." *The Hispanic American Historical Review* 49, no. 3 (1969): 411–429.

Lohr, Charles H. "Renaissance Latin Translators of the Greek Commentators on Aristotle." In *Humanism and Early Modern Philosophy.* Edited by Jill Kraye and M.W.F. Stone, 24–40. London: Routledge, 2000.

López, Jorge Fernández. "Rhetorical Theory in Sixteenth-Century Spain: A Critical Survey." *Rhetorica* 20, no. 2 (Spring, 2002): 133–148.

López Ruiz, Jesús Maria. "Las actividades del Seminario de Historia de América de la Universidad de Valladolid." *Revista de Historia de América* 71–72 (Enero–Junio, 1971): 173–177.

"Los Consejeros de Carlos V." In *La Corte de Carlos V, segunda parte: Los Consejos y los consejeros de Carlos V.* Directado por José Martínez Millán, 333–335. Madrid: Sociedad Estatal para la Comemoración de los Centenarios de Felipe II y Carlos V, 2000.

Losada, Angel. "The Controversy between Sepúlveda and Las Casas in the Junta of Valladolid." In Friede and Keen, *Bartolomé de Las Casas in History*, 282–288.

MacCormack, Sabine. "Gods, Demons, and Idols in the Andes." *Journal of the History of Ideas* 67, no. 4 (October, 2006): 623–647.

MacLeod, Murdo J. "Las Casas, Guatemala, and the Sad but Inevitable Case of Antonio de Remesal." In *Latin American Studies Occasional Papers*. Pittsburgh: Univ. of Pittsburgh Center for Latin American Studies, 1970.

Madureira, Luis. "The Accident of America: Marginal Notes on the European Conquest of the World." *The New Centennial Review* 2, no. 1 (2002): 117–181.

Mandonnet, P. "Order of Preachers." In *The Catholic Encyclopedia: An International Work of Reference on the Constitution, Doctrine, Discipline, and History of the Catholic Church*. Edited by Charles George Herbermann, Edward A. Pace, Condé Bénoist Pallen, Thomas J. Shahan, John J. Wynne et al., 12:354–370. New York: Encyclopedia Press, 1913 and 1950.

Maravall, Jose M. "La utopia politico-religiosa de los franciscanos en Nueva Espana." *Estudios Americanos* 1, no. 2 (1949): 199–227.

Marcus, Raymond. "El primer decenio de Las Casas en el Nuevo Mundo." *Ibero-Amerikanisches Archiv* 3, no. 2 (1977): 87–133.

———. "La Conquête de Cholula: Conflit D'interprétations." *Iberomerikanishches Archiv* 3, no. 2 (1977): 193–213.

———. "Las Casas in Literature." In Friede and Keen, *Bartolomé de Las Casas in History*, 581–600.

Mariscal, George. "Bartolomé de las Casas on Imperial Ethics and the Use of Force." In *Reason and Its Others: Italy, Spain, and the New World*. Edited by David Castillo and Massimo Lollini, 259–278. Nashville, TN: Vanderbilt Univ. Press, 2006.

Martí, Antonio M. "La retórica sacra en el siglo de oro." *Hispanic Review* 38, no. 3 (July, 1970): 264–298.

Martín Hernández, Francisco. "Los colegios menores." In *La Universidad de Salamanca:Trayectorio histórico y proyecciones*. Directado por Manuel Fernández Álvarez, 1:357–368. Salamanca: Europa Artes Gráficas, S. A., 1989/1990.

Martínez, Manuel María. "El obispo Marroquín y el franciscano Motolinía, enemigos de Las Casas. Examen de los motivos de su enemistad." *Boletín de la Real Academia de la Historia* 132 (Abril-Junio, 1953): 173–199.

———. "Las Casas on the Conquest of America." In Friede, Juan and Benjamin Keen, eds. *Bartolomé de Las Casas in History: Toward an Understanding of the Man and His Work*, 309–349. DeKalb: Northern Illinois Univ., 1971.

Martínez de Codes, Rosa María. "Evangelizar y Gobernar: El Derecho de Patronato en Indias." [article online]. (Accessed October 1, 2010).

Martínez Torrejón, José Miguel. "Bartolomé de Las Casas's *Brevísima Relación* as Weapon and Victim." In *Literatura e Pluralidade Cultural*, Actas do 3 Congresso Nacional da Associacão Portuguesa de Literatura Comparada, 401–408. Lisboa: Edicões Colibri, 1999.

McDonough, Kelly. "Estrategias discursivas de la Reconquista y la Conquista: La construcción del "otro" en los romances y en las escrituras de Cristóbol Colón." *Confluencia* 23, no. 1 (Fall, 2007): 10–28.

McKenna, Charles H. "Francisco de Vitoria: Father of International Law." *Studies: An Irish Quarterly Review* 21, no. 84 (December, 1932): 635–648.

Medina, Miquel. "Introducción General." In *Doctrina Cristiana para Instrucción de los Indios: Redactada por fr. Pedro de Córdoba, O.P. y otros religiosos doctos de la misma orden. Impresa en México, 1544 y 1548*, 9–133. Salamanca: Editorial San Esteban, 1987.

Melida y González-Monteagudo, Mónico. "El Padre Las Casas y Valladolid." In *Estudios sobre Política Indigenista Española en América: Iniciación, pugna de ocupación, demografía, linguistica, sedentarización, condición juridical del Indio*. 4 vols. Valladolid: Universidad de Valladolid, 1975.

Menéndez Pidal, Ramon. "Introduction." In *Historia General de las Literaturas Hispánicas*. 6 vols. Directado por Guillermo Díaz-Plaja, vol. 3. Barcelona: Editorial Barna, 1953.

Merrim, Stephanie. "The Counter-Discourse of Bartolomé de Las Casas." In *Early Images of the Americas: Transfer and Invention*. Edited by Jerry M. Williams and Robert E. Lewis, 149–162. Tucson: Univ. of Arizona Press, 1993.

———. "The First Fifty Years of Hispanic New World Historiography: The Caribbean, Mexico and Central America." In *The Cambridge History of Latin American Literature*. Edited by Roberto González Echevarría and Enrique Pupo-Walker, 1:58–100. Cambridge: Cambridge Univ. Press, 1996.

Mertz, Elizabeth. "Legal Language: Pragmatics, Poetics, and Social Power." *Annual Review of Anthropology*, 23 (1994): 435–455.

Mignolo, Walter D. "Cartas, crónicas y relaciones del descubrimiento y la conquista." In *Historia de la literatura hispanoamericana, epoca colonial*. Coordinado ppr Luis Iñigo Madrigal, 1:57–125. Madrid: Catedra, 1982.

———. "El metatexto historiográfico y la historiografía indiana." *Modern Language Notes* 96 (1981): 358–402.

———. "Misión, Represión, Paternalismo e Integración para un Balance de un Siglo de Evangelización en Iberoaméricaa (1520–1620)." In *Los Conquistadores: 1492 y la población indígena de las Américas*. Editado por Heraclio Bonilla, 263–296. Santa Fé de Bogotá, Columbia: Tercer Mundo Editores, 1992.

———. "Nebrija in the New World: The Questions of the Letter, the Discontinuity of the Classical Tradition, and the Colonization of the Native Languages." *L'Homme* 122, no. 24 (avril –diciembre, 1992): xxxii, 187–209.

———. "On the Colonization of Amerindian Languages and Memories: Renaissance Theories of Writing and the Discontinuity of the Classical Tradition." *Comparative Studies in Society and History* 34, no. 2 (April, 1992): 301–330.

Milhou, Alain. "Apocalyptism in Central and South American Colonialism." In *Continuum History of Apocalypticism*. Edited by Bernard McGinn, John J.Collins and Stephen J. Stein, 417–440. New York: Continuum, 2003.

Miller, Carolyn. "Genre as Social Action." *Quarterly Journal of Speech* 70, no. 2 (1984): 151–176.

Monaghan, Peter. "Yale Scholar, Revisiting the '*Decretum*,' Opens a Window on the 12th Century." *The Chronicle of Higher Education* (August 11, 2000).

Morales, Salvador. "1492 y población Indígena del caribe." In *Los Conquistadores: 1492 y la población indígena de las Américas*. Edited by Bonilla, Heraclio, 147–164. Santa Fé de Bogotá, Columbia: Tercer Mundo Editores, 1992.

Moraña, Mabel. "Formacion del pensamiento critico-literario en Hispanoamérica: época colonial. *Revista de crítica Latinoamericana* 16, nos. 31–32 (1990): 155–165.

Morales Valerio, Francisco. "México: La evangelización fundante (Siglo XVI)." In *Historia de la Iglesia en Hispanoamérica y Filipinas (Siglos XV-XIX)*, Vol. 2: Aspectos regionales. Editado por Pedro Borges, 2:125–143. Madrid: Biblioteca de Autores Cristianos, 1992.

Moreiras, Alberto. "Ten Notes on Primitive Imperial Accumulation: Ginés de Sepúlveda, Las Casas, Fernández de Oviedo," *Interventions* 2, no. 3, 343–363.

Muldoon, James. "John Wyclif and the Rights of Infidels: The Requerimiento Re-Examined." *The Americas*, 36, no. 3 (January, 1980): 301–316.

Muller, Wolfgang P. "Medieval Church Law as a Field of Historical Inquiry." In *Medieval Church Law and the Origins of the Western Legal Tradition*. Edited by Wolfgang P. Muller and Mary E. Sommar, 3–26. Washington, DC: Catholic Univ. of America, 2006.

Muñoz Delgado, Vicente. "El pensamiento lógico." In *Filosofía iberoamericana en la época del Encuentro*. Editado por Laureano Robles, 347–404. Madrid: Trotta, 1992.

Muro Orejón, Antonio. "Régimen Legal de los Indios de la Nueva España según el Cedulario del Doctor Vasco de Puga (1563)." [text online]. (Accessed March 1, 2011).

Myers, Kathleen A. "The Representation of New World Phenomena." In *Early Images of the Americas: Transfer and Invention*. Edited by J.M. Williams and R.E. Lewis, 183–213. Tucson: Univ. of Arizona Press, 1993.

Nalle, Sara T. "Literacy and Culture in Early Modern Castile." *Past and Present* 125 (November, 1989): 65–96.

Nauta, Lodi. "Lorenzo Valla and the Rise of Humanist Dialectic." In *The Cambridge Companion to Renaissance Philosophy*. Edited by James Hankins, 193–210. Cambridge: Cambridge Univ. Press, 2007.

Nelson, Eric. "The Problem of the Prince." In *The Cambridge Companion to Renaissance Philosophy*. Edited by James Hankins, 319–337. Cambridge: Cambridge Univ. Press, 2007.

Niermann, Ernst. "Providence." In *Encyclopedia of Theology*. Edited by Karl Rahner, 1313–1315. New York: Crossroads, 1986.

O'Meara, Thomas F. "The Dominican School of Salamanca and the Spanish Conquest of America: Some Bibliographical Notes." *The Thomist* 56 (1992): 555–582.

Orique, David Thomas. "Bartolomé de Las Casas (1484–1566)." *The Literary Encyclopedia*. October 7, 2008.

———. Catalog Entries on Bartolomé de Las Casas: *The Jay I. Kislak Collection of the Library of Congress*, Fall, 2007. [online]; (See Las Casas *Parecer* 1542).

———. "*Confesionario: Avisos y Reglas para Confesores* by Bartolomé de las Casas: A Translation and Introduction to Its Historical Context and Legal Teaching." M.A. thesis, Dominican School of Philosophy and Theology, Graduate Theological Union, Berkeley, CA, 2001.

———. "Journey to the Headwaters: Bartolomé de Las Casas in a Comparative Context." *The Catholic Historical Review* 95, no. 1 (2009): 1–24.

———. "New Discoveries about an Old Manuscript: The Date, Place of Origin, and Role of the *Parcer de fray Bartolomé de las Casas* in the Making of the New Laws of the Indies." *Colonial Latin American Historical Review* 15, no. 4 (Fall, 2006—published in 2010): 419–441.

———. *"Parecer de Fray Bartolomé de las Casas."* Transcription and Translation. The Jay I. Kislak Collection, Library of Congress, Fall, 2008.

Otte, Enrique. "Un episodio desconocido de la vida de los cronistas de Indias, Bartolomé de las Casas y Gonzalo Fernández de Oviedo." *Ibero-Amerikanisches Archiv*, año 3 (1977): 123–133.

Parise, Agustín. "Slave Labor and Labor Activities during the Spanish Colonial Period: A Study of the South American Region of Río de la Plata." *Rutgers Law Record* 32, no. 1 (Spring, 2008): 2–30.

Parish, Helen Rand and Harold Weidman, "The Correct Birthdate of Bartolomé de las Casas." *Hispanic American Historical Review* 56, no. 3 (1976): 385–403.

Patron, Rizzo. "El Pensamiento Juridico de la Escuela de Salamanca, Concrecío de la Ley Natural en la Configuración de la Cultura." [text online]. (Accessed June 16, 2010).

Pagden, Anthony. "Introduction." In *Bartolomé de Las Casas. An Account, Much Abbreviated, of the Destruction of the Indies.* Edited and translated by Nigel Griffin. Introduction by Anthony Pagden. London: Penguin Books, 1992: xiii–xli.

———. "Ius et Factum: Text and Experience in the Writings of Bartolomé de Las Casas." In *New World Encounters.* Edited by Stephen Greenblatt, 85–100. Berkeley: Univ. of California Press, 1993.

Paz Marín García, María. "Propuesta de Ramas y Géneros para los Documentos en la Traducción Jurídica." *Jornades de Foment de la Investigació.* Castellón de la Plana: Universitat Jaume, 2001. [article online]. (Accessed February 2, 2011).

Pennington, Kenneth. "Bartolomé de Las Casas and the Tradition of Medieval Law." In *Popes, Canonists and Texts, 1150–1550.* Edited by Kenneth Pennington, XIII:1–17. Aldershot: Ashgate Publishing, 1993.

———. "Decretal Collections 1190–1234." In *The History of Medieval Canon Law in the Classical Period, 1140–1234: From Gratian to the Decretals of Pope Gregory IX.* Edited by Wilfried Hartmann and Kenneth Pennington, 293–317. Washington, DC: Catholic Univ. of America Press, 2008.

———. "Law, Legislative Authority and Theories of Government, 1150–1300." In *The Cambridge History of Medieval Political Thought, ca. 350-ca. 1450.* Edited by J.H. Burns, 424–453. Cambridge: Cambridge Univ. Press, 1988.

——— and Wolfgang P. Müller. "A Short History of Canon Law from Apostolic Times to 1917." [article online]. (Accessed December 1, 2009).

———. "The Decretists: The Italian School." In *The History of Medieval Canon Law in the Classical Period, 1140–1234: From Gratian to the Decretals of Pope Gregory IX.* Edited by Wilfried Hartmann and Kenneth Pennington, 121–173. Washington, DC: Catholic Univ. of America Press, 2008.

———. "The History of Natural Law." [article online]. (Accessed November 1, 2009).

Pérez Camacho, Juan José and Ignacio Solis Lucía. "Domingo de Soto en el origen de la ciencia moderna." *Revista de Filosofía* 7, no. 12 (1994): 27–49.

Pérez Fernández, Isacio. "Bartolomé de las Casas." In *Filosofía iberoamericana en la época del encuentro.* Editado por Laureano Robles, 243–259. Madrid: Trotta, 1992.

———. "Fray Bartolomé de las Casas en torno a las leyes nuevas de Indias: su promotor, inspirador y perfeccionador." *Ciencia Tomista* 102 (1975): 379–457.

———. "La doctrina de Santo Tomás en la mente y en la acción del Padre las Casas." *Communio* 18 (1985): 269–293.
———. "Las conquistas de Indias fueron, en sí mismas, injustas y antisignos de la evangelización." *Studium* 32, no. 1 (1992): 3–76.
———. "San Augustín y Fray Bartolomé de las Casas, la regula apostólica y la reforma del clero secular en Hispano-América." *Augustinus* 26 (1981): 57–95.
Peset, Mariano and Enrique González González. "Las facultades de leyes y cánones." In *La Universidad de Salamanca.* Directado por Manuel Fernández Álvarez, 2: 9–61. Salamanca: Europa Artes Gráficas, S. A., 1990.
Peset, Mariano and Pilar García Trobat. "Poderes y modelos universitarios, siglos XV-XVI." In *Historia de la Universidad de Salamanca: Estructuras y flujos.* Coordinado por Luis E. Rodríquez-San Pedro Bezares, 2:37–91. Salamanca: Ediciones Universidad de Salamanca, 2002.
Peterson, Vivan A. "The Development of the Canon Law since 1500 A.D." *Church History* 9, no. 3 (September, 1940): 235–252.
Phelan, John Leddy. "El imperio Cristiano de las Casas." *Revista de Occidente* 141 (1974): 292–310.
———. "The Apologetic History of Fray Bartolome de Las Casas." *Hispanic American Historical Review* 49, no. 1 (February, 1969): 94–99.
Pietschmann, Horst. "El desarrollo de la práctica del gobierno Indiano durante el Siglo XVI: novedades, relaciones personales, narrativa, simbolismo, normas y burocracia." In *Talleres de la memoria—Reivindicaciones y autoridad en la historigrafía de los siglos XVI y XVII.* Edited by Robert Folger and Wulf Oesterreicher, 3–21. Münster: LIT, Druck, 2005.
Pinto de Oliveira, Carlos Josaphat. "El interés de las Casas por los Indígenas y la evangelización en el Brasil: Actitude creciente de Las Casas en la cultura y la Iglesia Brasileña hoy." [article online]. (Accessed November 17, 2006).
———. "Las Casas: Prophet of Full Rights for All." In *Justice, Peace and Dominicans 1216–2001.* Edited by John Orme Mills, 96–117. Dublin: Dominican Publications, 2001.
Pons, Bénedicte. "Fiestas y protocolo, los siglos XVI y XVII." In *La Universidad de Salamanca.* Directado por Manuel Fernández Álvarez, 2:531–548. Salamanca: Europa Artes Gráficas, S. A., 1990.
Porter, Jean. "From Natural Law to Human Rights: Or, Why Rights Talk Matters." *The Journal of Law and Religion* 14, no. 1 (1999–2000): 77–96.
Powers, Karen Vieira. "Andeans and Spaniards in the Contact Zone." *American Indian Quarterly* 24, no. 4 (Fall, 2000): 521–537.
Rabasa, José. "The Noble Savage as Utopian Figure?" In *Approaches to Teaching the Writings of Bartolomé de Las Casas.* Edited by Santa Arias and Eyda Merediz, 117–123. New York: Modern Language Association of America, 2008.
Rapp, Christof. "Aristotle's Rhetoric." [text online]. First published May 2, 2002; substantive revision February 1, 2010. (Accessed April 15, 2010).
Rayan, Samuel. "Decolonization of Theology." [text online]. (Accessed July 15, 2010).
Reboiras, Fernando Domínguez. "'Y hasta agora no es poderoso el rey'. Sobre monarquia y élites de poder en los orígenes de la *Brevísima.*'" In *Talleres de la memoria—Reivindicaciones y autoridad en la historigrafía de los siglos XVI y XVII.* Edited by Robert Folger and Wulf Oesterreicher, 45–75. Münster: LIT, Druck, 2005.

Rhan Philips, Carla. "Time and Duration: A Model for the Economy of Early Modern Spain." *The American Historical Review* 92, no. 3 (June, 1987): 531–562.

Ripodas Ardanaz, Daisy. "Los Indios y la Figura Jurídica del Rey durante los Quinientos." In *Justicia, Sociedad, Economía en la América Española (Siglos XVI, XVII, XVIII)*, 275–322. Valladolid: Seminario Americanista de la Universidad de Valladolid, 1983.

Rivara de Tuesta, María Luisa. "El Pensamiento Incaico." In *Filosofía iberoamericana en la época del Encuentro*. Edited by Laureano Robles, 127–153. Madrid: Editorial Trotta, S.A., 1992.

Robles, Laureano. "El Pensamiento filosófico de España." In *Filosofía iberoamericana en la época del Encuentro*. Edited by Laureano Robles, 15–49. Madrid: Ed. Trotta, S.A., 1992.

Rodríquez-San Pedro Bezares, Luis Enrique. "La universidad Hispana del Renacimiento: Salamanca." In *El Siglo de Frai Luis de León: Salamanca y el Renacimiento*. Coordinated by Mercedes Aznar López and Luz de Gaztelu y Quijano, 45–58. Salamanca: Junta de Castilla y León, 1991.

———. "Vida estudiantil en la Salamanca del Quinientos." In *El Siglo de Frai Luis de León: Salamanca y el Renacimiento*. Coordinada por Mercedes Aznar López and Luz de Gaztelu y Quijano, 59–68. Salamanca: Junta de Castilla y León, 1991.

———. Juan Luis Polo Rodríguez, and Francisco Javier Alejo Montes. "Matrículas y grados, siglos XVI-XVII." In *Historia de la Universidad de Salamanca: Estructuras y flujos*. Coordinated by Luis E. Rodríquez-San Pedro Bezares, 2:607–664. Salamanca: Ediciones Universidad de Salamanca, 2002.

Rogers, Rhianna C. "The Resilience of Aztec Women: A Case Study of Modern Aztec Myths." *Journal of Humanities and Social Sciences* 1, no. 2 (2007): 1–18.

Ross, Kathleen. "History of the Conquest and Colonization of the New World: 1550–1620)." In *Cambridge History of Latin American Literature*. Edited by Robert González-Echevarría and Enrique Pupo Walker, 101–142. Cambridge: Cambridge Univ. Press, 1996.

Ruby, Jane E. "The Ambivalence of St. Thomas Aquinas' view of the Relationship of Divine Law to Human Law." *Harvard Theological Review* 48, no. 2 (April, 1955): 101–128.

Ruíz Maldonado, Enrique. "El cardenal Cisneros, Bartolomé de las Casas y la reforma de Indias." In *Dominicos en Mesoamérica: 500 Años*, 321–340. México, DF: Analogía Revista de Filosofía, 1992.

———. "La justicia en la obra de fray Bartolomé de las Casas." In *Bartolomé de las Casas (1474—1974) e historia de la iglesia en América Latina*. Chiapas CEHILA conferencia, 45–65. Barcelona: Editorial Nova Terra, 1976.

———. "La justicia en la obra de fray Bartolomé de las Casas." In *Dominicos en Mesoamérica: 500 Años*, 293–319. México, DF: Analogía Revista de Filosofía, 1992.

———. "Tomás de Aquino, Bartolomé de las Casas y la controversía de Indias." In *Dominicos en Mesoamérica: 500 Años*, 261–292. México, DF: Analogía Revista de Filosofía, 1992.

Ruiz, Teofilo F. "Oligarchy and Royal Power: The Castilian Cortes and the Castilian Crisis 1248–1350." *Parliaments, Estates and Representation* 2, no. 2 (December, 1982): 95–101.

Sacoto, Antonio. "Fray Bartolomé de las Casas: paladin de la justicia social." *Cuadernos Americanos* 193, no. 6 (Noviembre-Diciembre, 1975): 136–148.

Sahagún, Fray Bernardino de, Florentine Codex in chapter one, "Knowledge and Reason in Pre-Columbian Cultures". In *Latin American Philosophy: An Introduction with Readings.* Edited by Susana Nuccetelli and Gary Seay, 24–33. Upper Saddle River, NJ: Pearson Education Inc., 2004.

Saint-Lu, Andre. "Bartolomé de Las Casas en sus escritos." In *España y América en una perspectiva humanista: Homenaje a marcel Bataillon.* Actas reunidas y preparadas por Joseph Pérez, 107–121. Madrid: Casa de Velázquez, 1998.

———. "Fray Bartolomé de Las Casas." In *Historia de la literatura hispanoamericana, epoca colonial.* Coordinated by Luis Iñigo Madrigal, I:117–125. Madrid: Ediciónes Cátedra S.A, 1982.

———. "Introducción." Bartolomé de las Casas, *Brevísima relación de la destruición de las Indias.* Editado por André Saint-Lu, 10–57. Madrid: Ediciónes Cátedra S.A., 1991.

Sainty, Guy Stair. "The Spanish Military Orders." [text online]. (Accessed August 31, 2020).

Salmoral, Manuel Lucena. "Hispanoamérica en la época colonial." In *Historia de la literatura hispanoamericana, época colonial.* Coordinated by Luis Iñigo Madrigal, 1:11–33. Madrid: Catedra, 1982.

Salvadorini, Vittorio. "Las 'Relaciones' de Hernán Cortés." [text online]. (Accessed August 31, 2020).

———. "Las 'relaciones' de Hernán Cortés." *Thesaurus* 18, no. 1 (1963): 77–97.

Sánchez Herrero, José. "El estudio de San Miguel de Sevilla durante el siglo XV." *Historia, Instituciones y Documentos* 10 (1983): 297–333.

Sánchez Sánchez, Daniel. "Catedral y universidad en sus origins." In *La Universidad de Salamanca: Trayectoria história y proyecciones.* Directado por Manuel Fernández Álvarez, 1:323–338. Salamanca: Europa Artes Gráficas, S. A., 1989.

Sauer, Elizabeth. "Las Casas and Early Modern Spanish and English Colonialist Discourses." In *Approaches to Teaching the Writings of Bartolomé de Las Casas.* Edited by Santa Arias and Eyda Merediz, 210–217. New York: The Modern Language Association of America, 2008.

Schmitt, Charles B. "Philosophy of Science in Sixteenth-Century Universities: Some Preliminary Comments." In *Studies in Renaissance Philosophy and Science*, 485–530. London: Variorum Reprints, 1981.

Seed, Patricia. "Taking Possession and Reading Texts: Establishing the Authority of Overseas Empires." In *Early Images of the Americas.* Edited by Jerry M. Williams and Robert E. Lewis, 111–147. Tucson: Univ. of Arizona Press, 1993.

———. "'Are These Not Also Men?': The Indians' Humanity and Capacity for Spanish Civilisation." *Journal of Latin American Studies* 25, no. 3 (October, 1993): 629–652.

———. "Early Modernity: The History of a Word." *The New Centennial Review* 2, no. 1 (Spring, 2002): 1–16.

Sempat Assadourian, Carlos. "Fray Bartolomé de Las Casas obispo: la naturaleza miserable de las naciones indianas y el derecho de la Igelsia: un escrito de 1545." *Historia mexicana* 40, no. 3 (Enero-Marzo, 1991): 387–451.

Schwaller, John F. "Introduction." In *The Church in Colonial Latin America.* Edited by John F. Schwaller, xi-xxiii. Wilmington, DE: Scholarly Resources Books, 2000.

———. "The Cathedral Chapter of Mexico in the Sixteenth Century." *Hispanic American Historical Review* 61, no. 4 (1981): 651–764.

Sorabji, Richard. "Just War: Antiquity, Islam and the Spanish Conquistadors." [text online]. (Accessed August 31, 2020).

Sosnowski, Saúl. "Critica literaria Hispanoamericana en Los Estados Unidos: visions desde la periferia." *Revista de critica literaria Latinoamericana* 31–32 (1990): 267–289.

Spanbauer, Julie M. "The First Amendment Right to Petition Government for a Redress of Grievances: Cut from a Different Clothe." *Hastings Constitutional Law Quarterly* 15 (Fall, 1993): 16–69.

Stein, P.G. "Roman Law." In *The Cambridge History of Medieval Political Thought ca.350-ca.1450*. Edited by J. H. Burns, 37–50. New York: Cambridge Univ. Press, 1988.

Stern, Steve J. "New Approaches to the Study of Peasant Rebellion." In *Resistance, Rebellion, and Consciousness in the Andean Peasant World, 18th to 20th Centuries*. Edited by Steve Stern, 3–28. Madison: Univ. of Wisconsin Pres, 1987.

———. "Paradigms of Conquest: History, Historiography, and Politics." *Journal of Latin American Studies* 24 Quincentenary Supplement: The Colonial and Post Colonial Experience. Five Centuries of Spanish and Portuguese America (1992): 1–34.

Stone, Cynthia L. "Confronting Stereotypes: The *Brevísima relación* as Homily, not History." In *Approaches to Teaching the Writings of Bartolomé de Las Casas*. Edited by Santa Arias and Eyda Merediz, 65–72. New York: Modern Language Association of America, 2008.

Sweet, Leonard I. "Christopher Columbus and the Millennial Vision of the New World." *The Catholic Historical Review* 72, no. 3 (July, 1986): 369–382.

Szásdi Nagy, Ádam. "Los justos títulos y la guerra justa a la luz del Tratado de las Alcázovas." In *Iglesia y Sociedad: 500 Años en Puerto Rico y el Caribe, Siglo XVI*. Editado por Manuel Alvarado Morales y Marie Minette Díaz Burley, 123–146. San Juan de Puerto Rico: Nomos Impresores, S.A., 2008.

Tierney, Brian. "Aristotle and the American Indians–Again: Two Critical Discussions." In *Rights and Laws and Infallability in Medieval Thought*. Variorum Collected Studies Series 578. Aldershot: Ashgate Publishing Limited, 1997.

———. "'Only the Truth Has Authority': The Problem of 'Reception' in the Decretists and in Johannes de Turrecremata.'" In *Law, Church and Society: Essays in Honor of Stephan Kuttner*. Edited by Kenneth Pennington and Robert Somerville, 69–96. Philadelphia: Univ. of Pennsylvania Press, 1977.

———. "The Canonists and the Medieval State." *The Review of Politics* 15, no. 3 (July, 1953): 378–388.

———. "The Idea of Natural Rights-Origins and Persistence." *Northwestern Journal of International Human Rights* 2 (April, 2004): 1–13.

———. "The Origins of Natural Rights Language." In *Rights, Laws and Infallibility in Medieval Thought*. Variorum Collected Studies Series 578. Aldershot: Ashgate Publishing Limited, 1997.

Timmer, David E. "Providence and Perdition: Fray Diego de Landa Justifies His Inquisition against the Yucatecan Maya." *Church History* 66, no. 3 (September, 1997): 477–488.

Tinkler, John F. "Praise and Advice: Rhetorical Approaches in More's *Utopia* and Machiavelli's *The Prince*." *The Sixteenth-Century Journal* 19, no. 2 (Summer, 1988): 187–207.

Tudela y Bueso, Juan Pérez de. "Letra y espiritu de la ley en el padre Las Casas." In *España y América en una perspectiva humanista: Homenaje a marcel Bataillon*. Actas preparadas por Joseph Pérez, 93–105. Madrid: Casa de Velázquez, 1998.

University of Califorina, Santa Barbara, class notes, Linguistics 124, January 17, 2001, "Narrative and Genre." [text online]. (Accessed October 1, 2010).

Valverde, Calixto. "Introducción." In *Historia de la Universidad de Valladolid*. Translado del Libro de Bezerro (1757) por Vicente Velázquez de Figueroa, 1:x-xvi. Valladolid: Imprenta Castellana, 1918.

Van Liere, Katherine Elliot. "After Nebrija: Academic Reformers and the Teaching of Latin in Sixteenth- Century Salamanca." *The Sixteenth Century Journal* 34, no. 4 (2003): 1065–1105.

———. "Humanism and Scholasticism in Sixteenth-Century Academe: Five Student Orations from the University of Salamanca." *Renaissance Quarterly* 53, no. 1 (Spring, 2000): 57–107.

Varela, Consuelo. "Introducción." In *Brevísima relación de la destruición de las Indias*. Introducción por Consuelo Varela. Madrid: Castalia, 1999.

Vasoli, Cesare, "The Renaissance Concept of Philosophy." In *The Cambridge History of Renaissance Philosophy*. Edited by Charles B. Schmitt, Quentin Skinner, Erkhard Kessler, and Jill Kraye, 57–74. Cambridge: Cambridge Univ. Press, 1988.

Vásquez Janeiro, Isaac. "El convento y estudio de San Francisco." In *Historia de la Universidad de Salamanca: Trayectoria histórica e instituciones vinculadas*. Coordinado por Luis E. Rodríquez-San Pedro Bezares, 1:611–633. Salamanca: Ediciones Universidad de Salamanca, 2002.

Vegara Fabregat, Laura. "Los géneros jurídicos y su traducción al castellano: una perspectiva diferente." *Revista electrónica de estudios filológicos* 12 (2006).

Veres, Luis. "El marco de la ficción en la 'Brevísima relación de la destrucción de las Indias' de Fray Bartolomé de las Casas." *Especulo: Revista de Estudios Literarios* 9 (1998).

Villanueva, Francisco Márquez. "Letrados, consejeros y justicias." *Hispanic Review* 53, no. 2 (Spring, 1985): 201–227.

Villegas, SJ, Juan. "Providencialism y denuncia en la 'Historia de las Indias' de fray Bartolomé de las Casas." In *Bartolomé de las Casas (1474—1974) e historia de la iglesia en América Latina*. Chiapas CEHILA Conferencia, 19–43. Barcelona: Editorial Nova Terra, 1976.

Waldegaray, Marta Inés. "Discours et relations de sociabilité dans La Brevísima Relación de las Indias de Bartolomé de Las Casas." *Caravelle: Cahiers du Monde Hispanique et Luso-Bresilen* 82 (2004): 17–39.

Wallace, William A. "Domingo de Soto and the Iberian Roots of Galileo's Science." In *Hispanic Philosophy in the Age of Discovery*. Edited by Kevin White, 113–129. Washington, DC: Catholic Univ. of America Press, 1997.

———. "Traditional Natural Philosophy." In *The Cambridge History of Renaissance Philosophy*. Edited by Charles B. Schmitt, Quentin Skinner, Erkhard Kessler, and Jill Kraye, 201–235. Cambridge: Cambridge Univ. Press, 1988.

Watts, Pauline Moffitt. "The Donation of Constantine, Cartography, and Papal *Plenitudo Potestatis* in the Sixteenth Century: A Paper for Salvatore Camporeale." *Modern Language Notes* 119 Supplement (2004): S88–S107.

Weisheipl, James A. "The Place of Study in the Ideal of St. Dominic." [text online]. (Accessed December 17, 2010).

Wells, Allen. "Forgotten Chapters of Yucatán's Past." *Estudios Mexicanos* 12, no. 2 (1996): 195–229.

Widow, Juan Antonio. "The Economic Teachings of Spanish Scholastics." In *Hispanic Philosophy in the Age of Discovery*. Edited by Kevin White, 130–144. Washington, DC: Catholic Univ. of America Press, 1997.

Wolfgang P. Muller. "Medieval Church Law as a Field of Historical Inquiry." In *Medieval Church Law and the Origins of the Western Legal Tradition*. Edited by Wolfgang P. Muller and Mary E. Sommar, 1–14. Washington, DC: Catholic Univ. of America Press, 2006.

Yeager, Timothy J. "Encomienda or Slavery? The Spanish Crown's Choice of Labor Organization in Sixteenth-Century Spanish America." *The Journal of Economic History* 55, no. 4 (December, 1995): 842–859.

Zamora, Margarita. "Christopher Columbus's 'Letter to the Sovereigns': Announcing the Discovery." In *World Encounters*. Edited by Stephen Greenblatt, 1–11. Berkeley: Univ. of California Press, 1993.

Index

Note: *Italic* page numbers refer to figures and page number followed by "n" refer to end notes.

For Product Safety Concerns and Information please contact our EU representative GPSR@taylorandfrancis.com
Taylor & Francis Verlag GmbH, Kaufingerstraße 24, 80331 München, Germany

www.ingramcontent.com/pod-product-compliance
Ingram Content Group UK Ltd.
Pitfield, Milton Keynes, MK11 3LW, UK
UKHW022347190926
475702UK00015B/2145

9780367744496